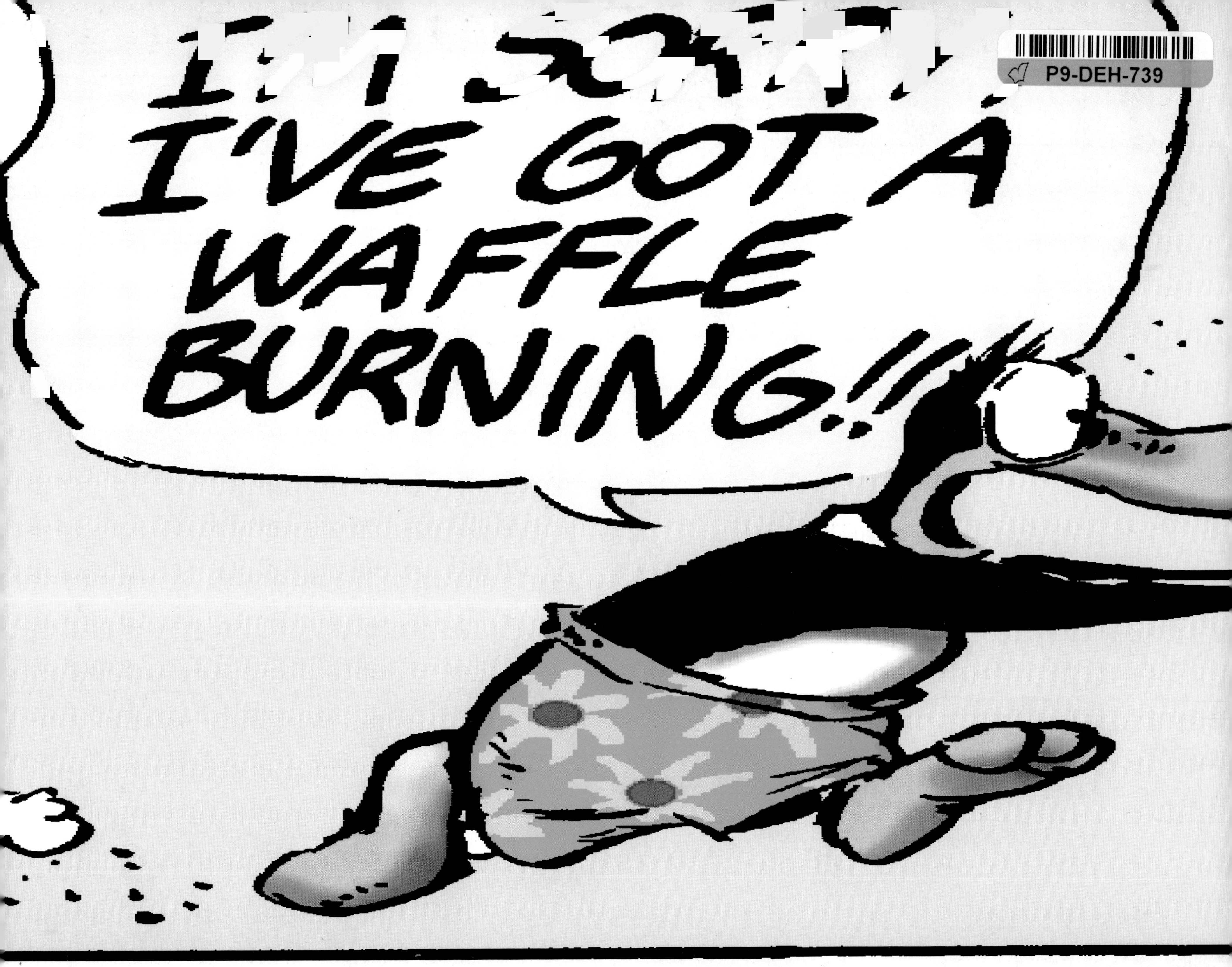
I'VE GOT A WAFFLE BURNING!!

OPUS

25 YEARS OF HIS SUNDAY BEST

Berkeley Breathed

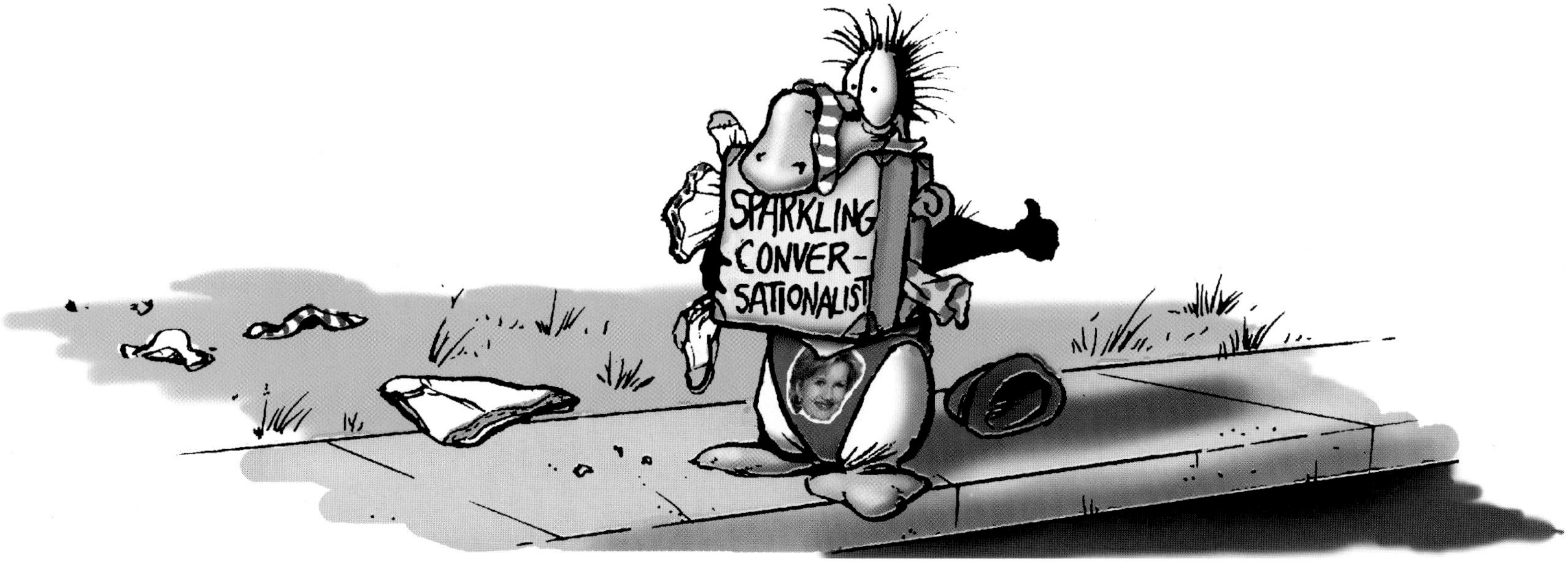
SPARKLING
CONVER-
SATIONALIST

Little, Brown and Company
New York Boston

To Jody, Sophie, and Milo

Also by Berkeley Breathed
Flawed Dogs
Edwurd Fudwupper Fibbed Big
The Last Basselope
Red Ranger Came Calling
Goodnight Opus
A Wish for Wings That Work

Copyright © 2004 Berkeley Breathed

Little, Brown and Company
Time Warner Book Group
1271 Avenue of the Americas, New York, NY 10020
Visit our Web site at www.twbookmark.com

First Edition

Bloom County, Outland, and *Opus* are syndicated by the Washington Post Writers Group.
Secondhand Lions art © 2003 New Line Cinema, images used with permission.

ISBN 0-316-15994-8
Library of Congress Control Number 2004103826

10 9 8 7 6 5 4 3 2 1

LB

Printed in the United States of America

IN THE BEGINNING

I submit this primordial 1981 *Bloom County* Sunday panel as a candidate for my Big Twilight Zone Destiny-Messing Moment.

You'll note that it features a little blond-haired boy with an over-tweaked imagination working out his real-life anxieties and passions via space hero fantasies. Now *that's* a ripping Good Idea to build a classic comic strip around!

So naturally I only drew this one panel.

Most new comic strips don't survive such epic blunders. And *Bloom County* may well have headed for oblivion if in the following week I hadn't also drawn a mumbling penguin sitting on an ottoman watching TV. Mister Rogers asked his viewing tykes if they could say the word "tuba player" and Opus replied, "tuphlem grdlphump," and Mister Rogers said, "Good!" In 1981, this somehow was very funny. (And Michael Jackson was *not* — yet. A savage, backward era.)

So there it is: *a bird* was my Other Good Idea. More odd than good, really. This one almost slipped by too, but the fans — infinitely wise if not patient — let me know immediately. Opus stayed on his ottoman.

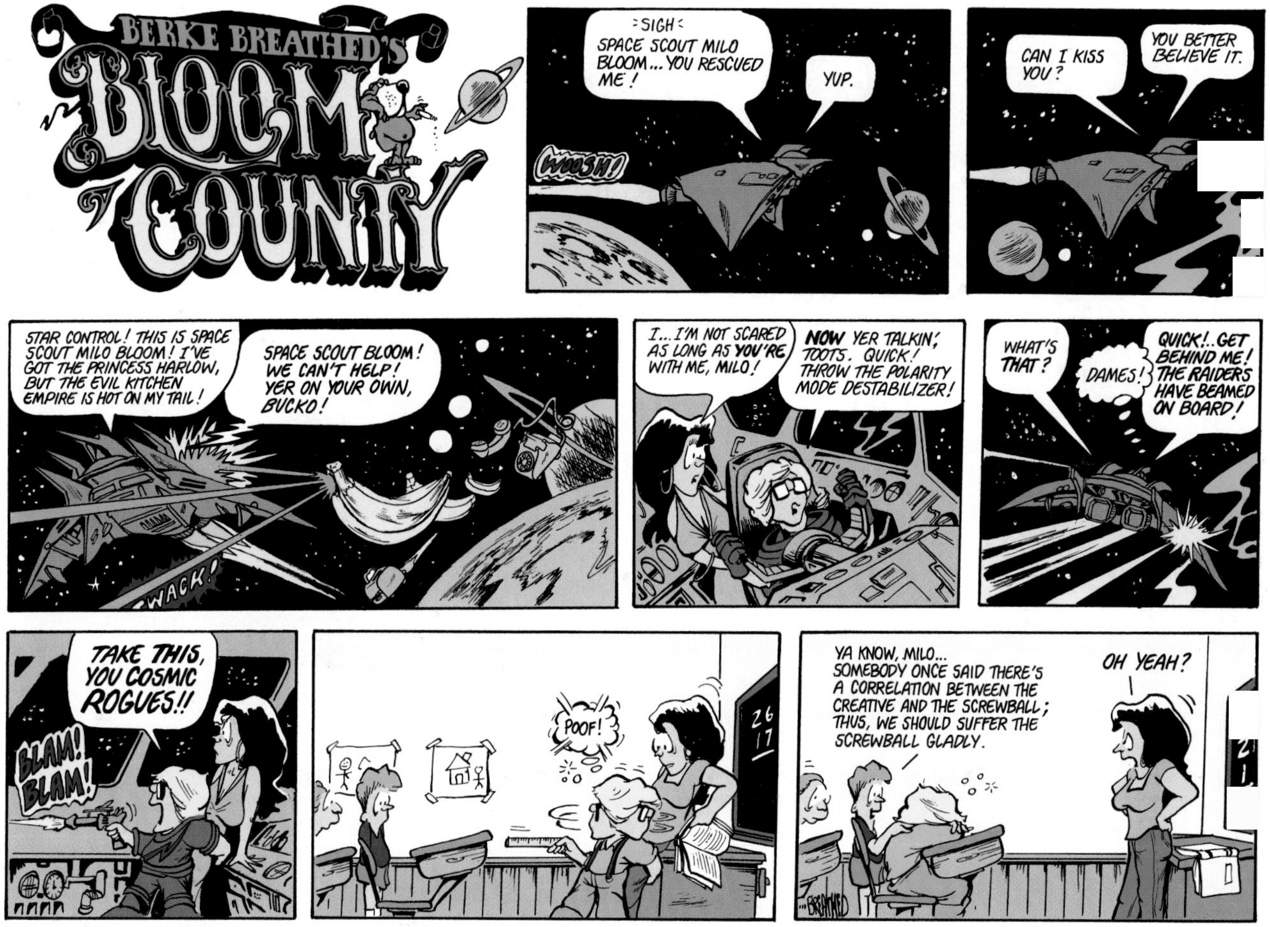
BERKE BREATHED'S
BLOOM COUNTY
SIGH
SPACE SCOUT MILO BLOOM... YOU RESCUED ME!
YUP.
WOOSH!
CAN I KISS YOU?
YOU BETTER BELIEVE IT.
STAR CONTROL! THIS IS SPACE SCOUT MILO BLOOM! I'VE GOT THE PRINCESS HARLOW, BUT THE EVIL KITCHEN EMPIRE IS HOT ON MY TAIL!
SPACE SCOUT BLOOM! WE CAN'T HELP! YER ON YOUR OWN, BUCKO!
WACK!
I... I'M NOT SCARED AS LONG AS YOU'RE WITH ME, MILO!
NOW YER TALKIN', TOOTS. QUICK! THROW THE POLARITY MODE DESTABILIZER!
WHAT'S THAT?
DAMES!
QUICK!.. GET BEHIND ME! THE RAIDERS HAVE BEAMED ON BOARD!
TAKE THIS, YOU COSMIC ROGUES!!
BLAM! BLAM!
POOF!
YA KNOW, MILO... SOMEBODY ONCE SAID THERE'S A CORRELATION BETWEEN THE CREATIVE AND THE SCREWBALL; THUS, WE SHOULD SUFFER THE SCREWBALL GLADLY.
OH YEAH?

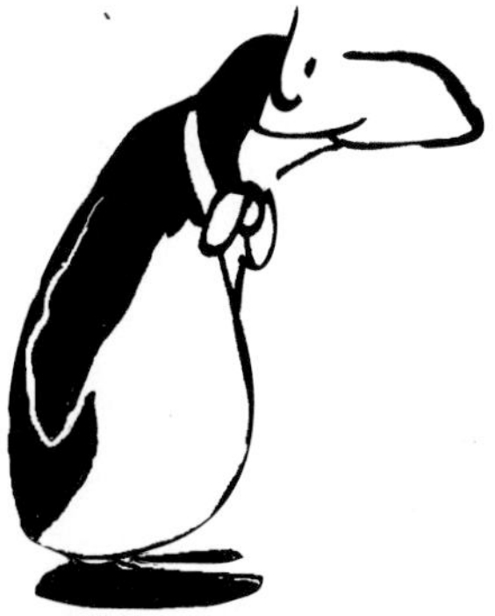

Five years later Bill Watterson's Calvin, aka Spaceman Biff, rocketed gloriously into America's Funny Papers, which was just how the comic universe was meant to be. Yet I came close to preempting Watterson with what surely would have become dreary space adventures of Milo battling Dukakis and Donald Trump aliens.

Like a toddler who imagines bouncing his ball into a freeway, I secretly love contemplating this pop culture pileup.

Two decades and 784 Sunday panels later, Opus still waddles among us. I built this retrospective collection around my favorite Sunday panels simply because they're the most fun. It's an immense pleasure to see them reproduced clear and sizable for once.

It's been a long, strange trip for this complicated penguin. Thanks for being along for the continuing ride.

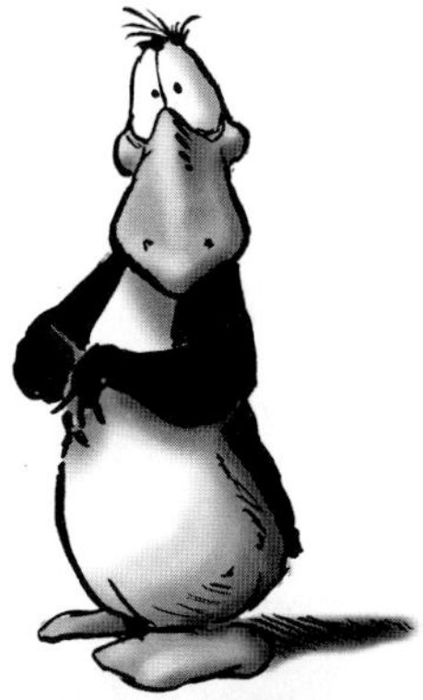

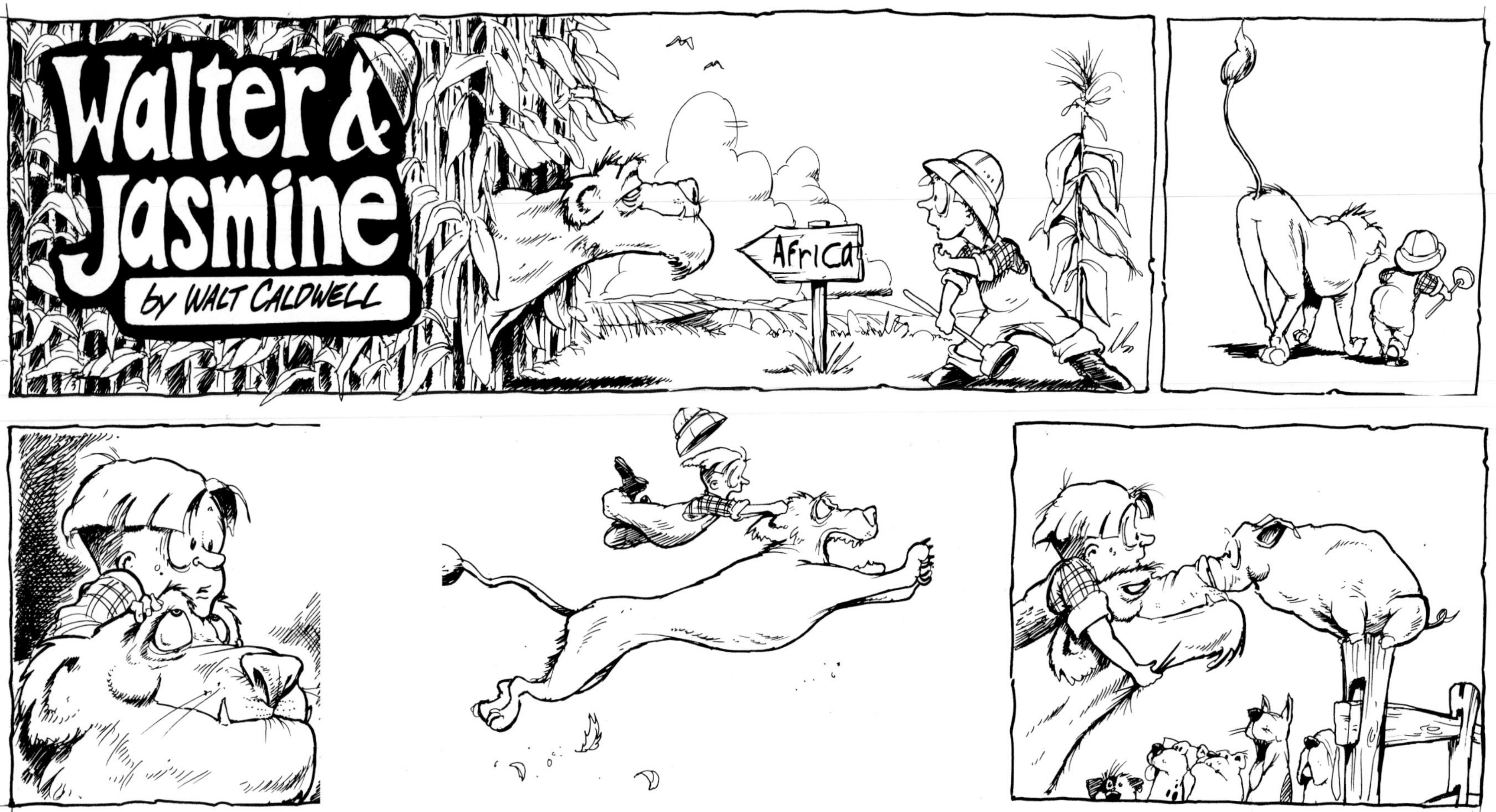
Walter & Jasmine
by WALT CALDWELL
Africa

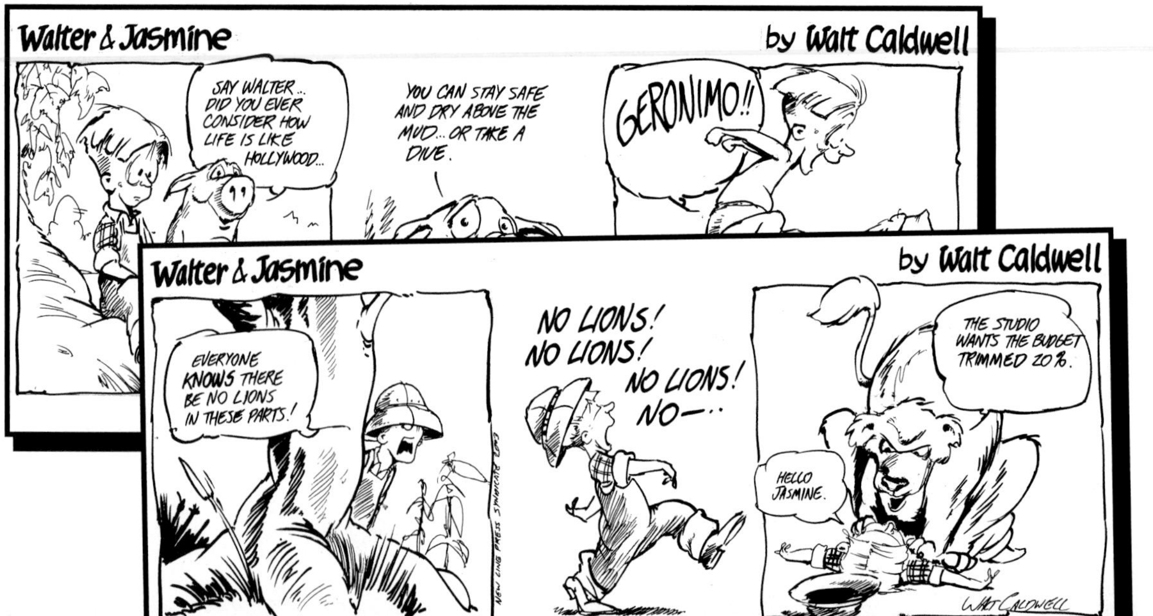
Walter & Jasmine
by Walt Caldwell
SAY WALTER... DID YOU EVER CONSIDER HOW LIFE IS LIKE HOLLYWOOD...
YOU CAN STAY SAFE AND DRY ABOVE THE MUD... OR TAKE A DIVE.
GERONIMO!!
Walter & Jasmine
by Walt Caldwell
EVERYONE KNOWS THERE BE NO LIONS IN THESE PARTS!
NO LIONS! NO LIONS!
NO LIONS! NO—..
THE STUDIO WANTS THE BUDGET TRIMMED 20%.
HELLO JASMINE.
WALT CALDWELL

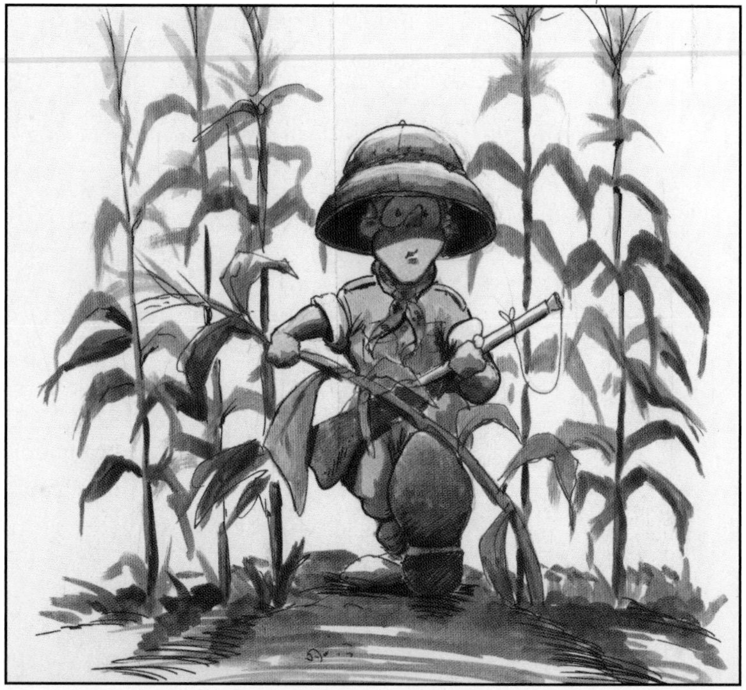

THE STRIP THAT NEVER WAS

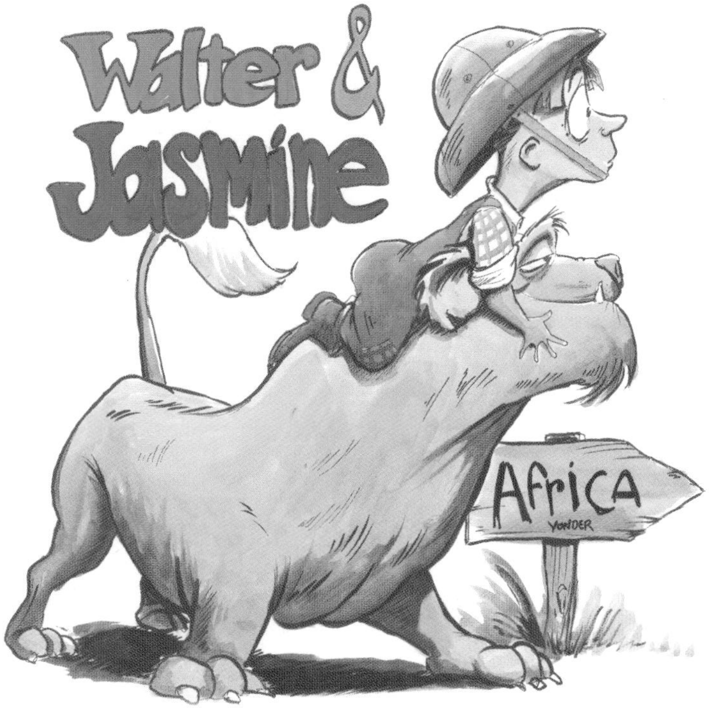
Walter & Jasmine
Africa
YONDER

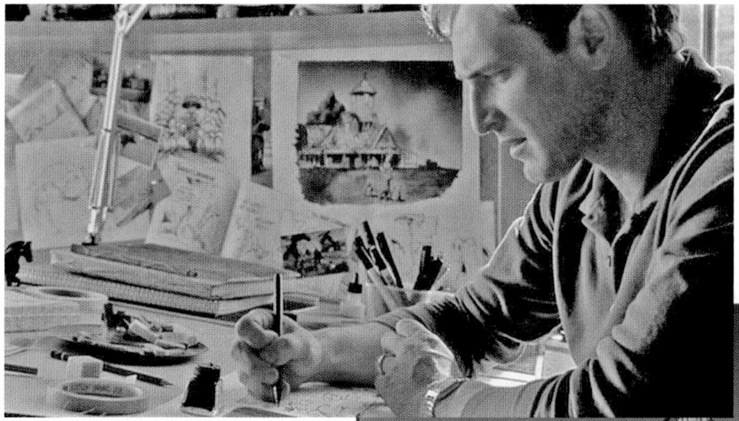

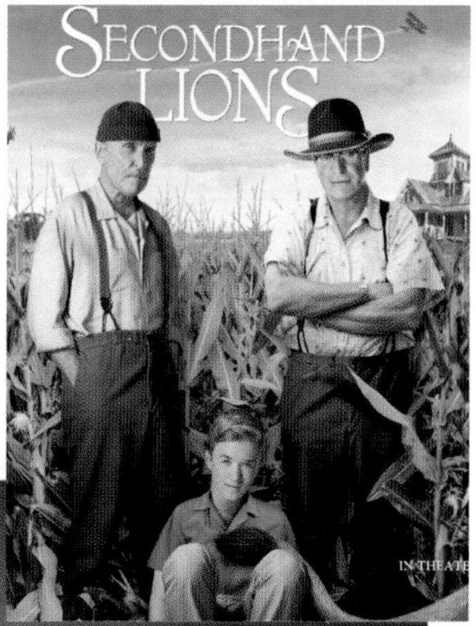
SECONDHAND LIONS

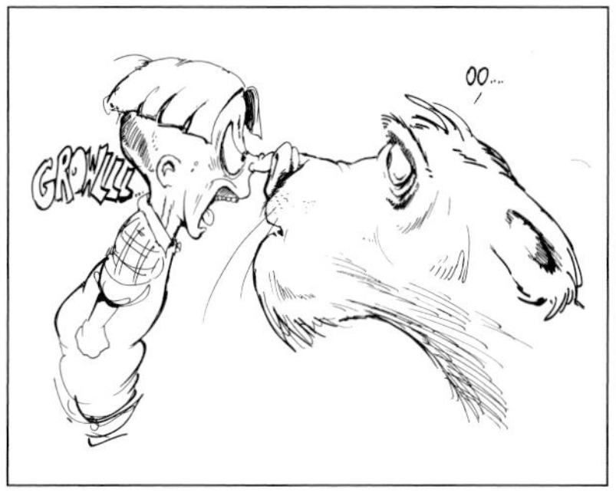

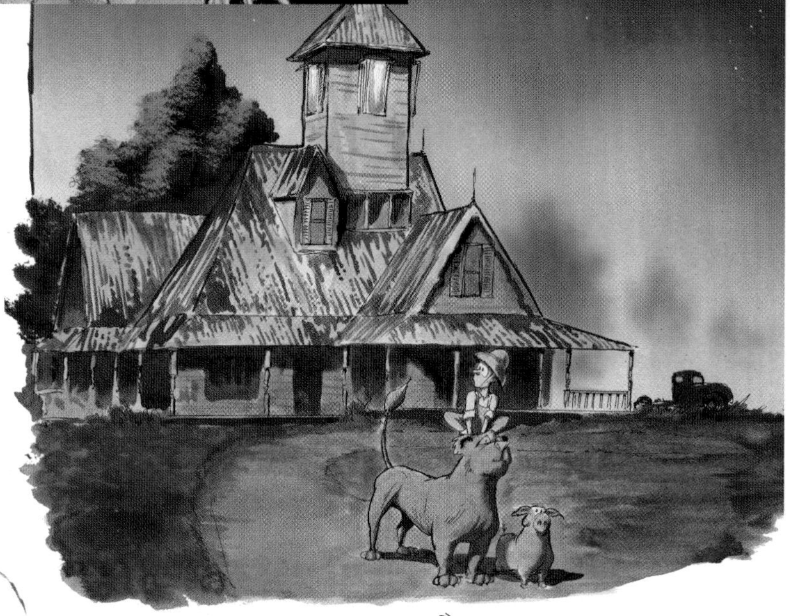

Director Tim McCanlies called me in 2003 and described a movie called *Secondhand Lions* that he'd written and was presently filming in Texas about an adolescent boy — played by Haley Joel Osment — going to live with two crazy uncles, played by Michael Caine and Robert Duvall. At the end, the boy has become a cartoonist (where all coming-of-age movies should go), and his comic strip, *Walter and Jasmine,* stars the characters from his past.

Tim asked if I would draw the cartoon art that was to be hanging around the walls of the set. It'd been years since I'd sat at my cartooning table, so I thought it might be fun to invent a wholly fraudulent comic strip.

The film was terrific and I heard from a surprising number of people who recognized my hand in the art. Why is it here? Because if I hadn't had so much fun drawing these fake comics, it would never have occurred to me soon afterward that I should be drawing the real thing again. Life imitating art, as it should be.

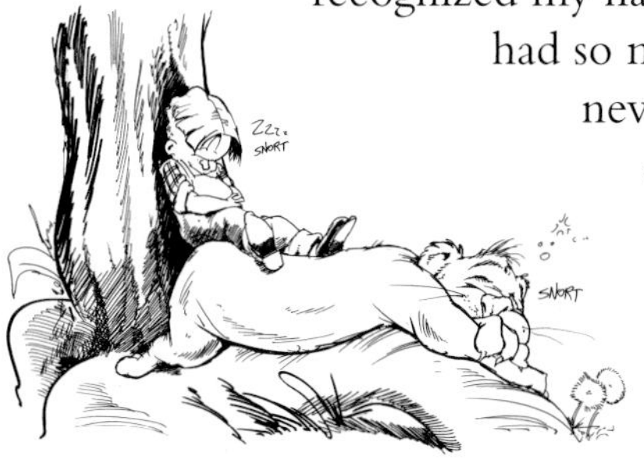
SNORT
SNORT

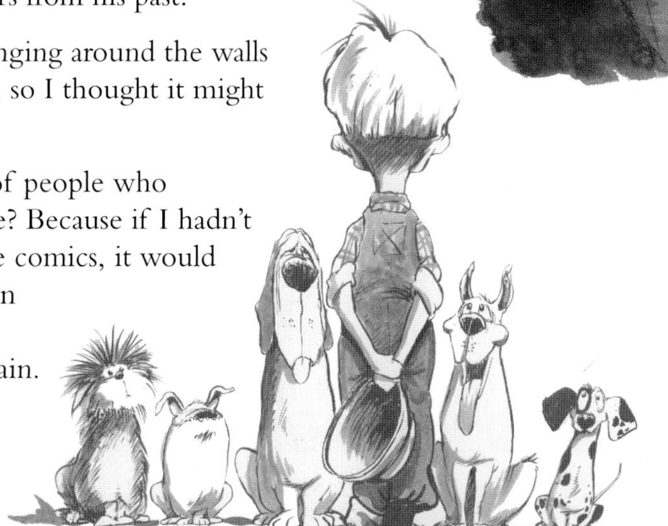

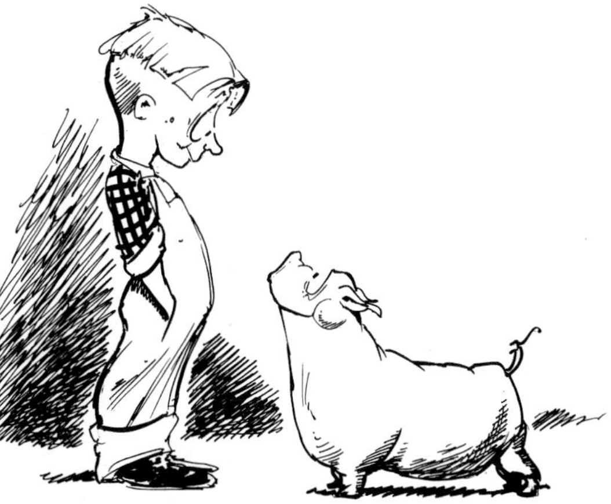

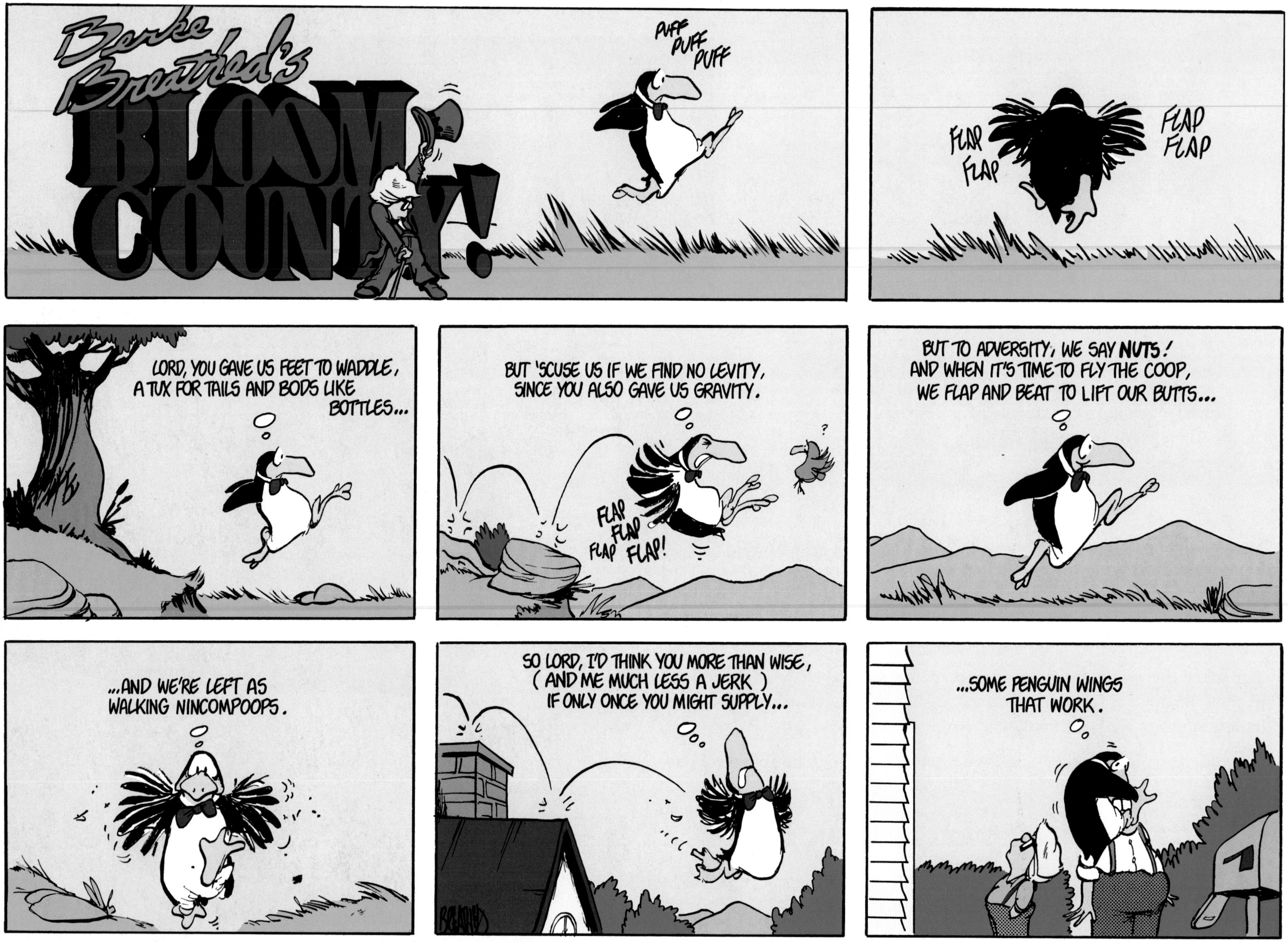

Berke Breathed's
BLOOM COUNTY!
PUFF PUFF PUFF
FLAP FLAP
FLAP FLAP
LORD, YOU GAVE US FEET TO WADDLE, A TUX FOR TAILS AND BODS LIKE BOTTLES...
BUT 'SCUSE US IF WE FIND NO LEVITY, SINCE YOU ALSO GAVE US GRAVITY.
FLAP FLAP FLAP FLAP!
?
BUT TO ADVERSITY, WE SAY NUTS! AND WHEN IT'S TIME TO FLY THE COOP, WE FLAP AND BEAT TO LIFT OUR BUTTS...
...AND WE'RE LEFT AS WALKING NINCOMPOOPS.
SO LORD, I'D THINK YOU MORE THAN WISE, (AND ME MUCH LESS A JERK) IF ONLY ONCE YOU MIGHT SUPPLY...
...SOME PENGUIN WINGS THAT WORK.

BLOOM COUNTY

It's teeth-clenchingly obvious, but I'd like to point out the dramatic evolution of Opus from his first appearance to his present-day incarnation. Both in physical form and personality, he's been relentlessly evolving. I'm not sure that the Opus of today would recognize his scrawny 1981 version there on the left. Inversely, I suspect the early Opus would have an hysterical fit if he were to see where his nose ends up.

I've had nothing to do with this. At least not my conscious self.

This relentless march of Darwinian adaptation isn't necessarily a virtue for a comic strip. Readers seem to view changes in their favorite strips as they would changes in their plumbing: discomforting. But in my case, swinging wildly for the next creative hill is as natural (and irresistible) as breakdancing with my four-year-old in a Denny's. People around me squirm but I'm helpless to do anything about it.

As I'm intensely private, I resent that the only way I seem to be able to do this job is to make the writing personal. I'm scattered transparently throughout these characters. On a certain level, I'd be less embarrassed if I did a strip like *Marmaduke,* where people could only make conjectures about my dog's personal life rather than mine.

But alas, since life isn't standing still for me, I fear it won't for a small penguin.

All of which is to say that as in life, things change in my cartoons.

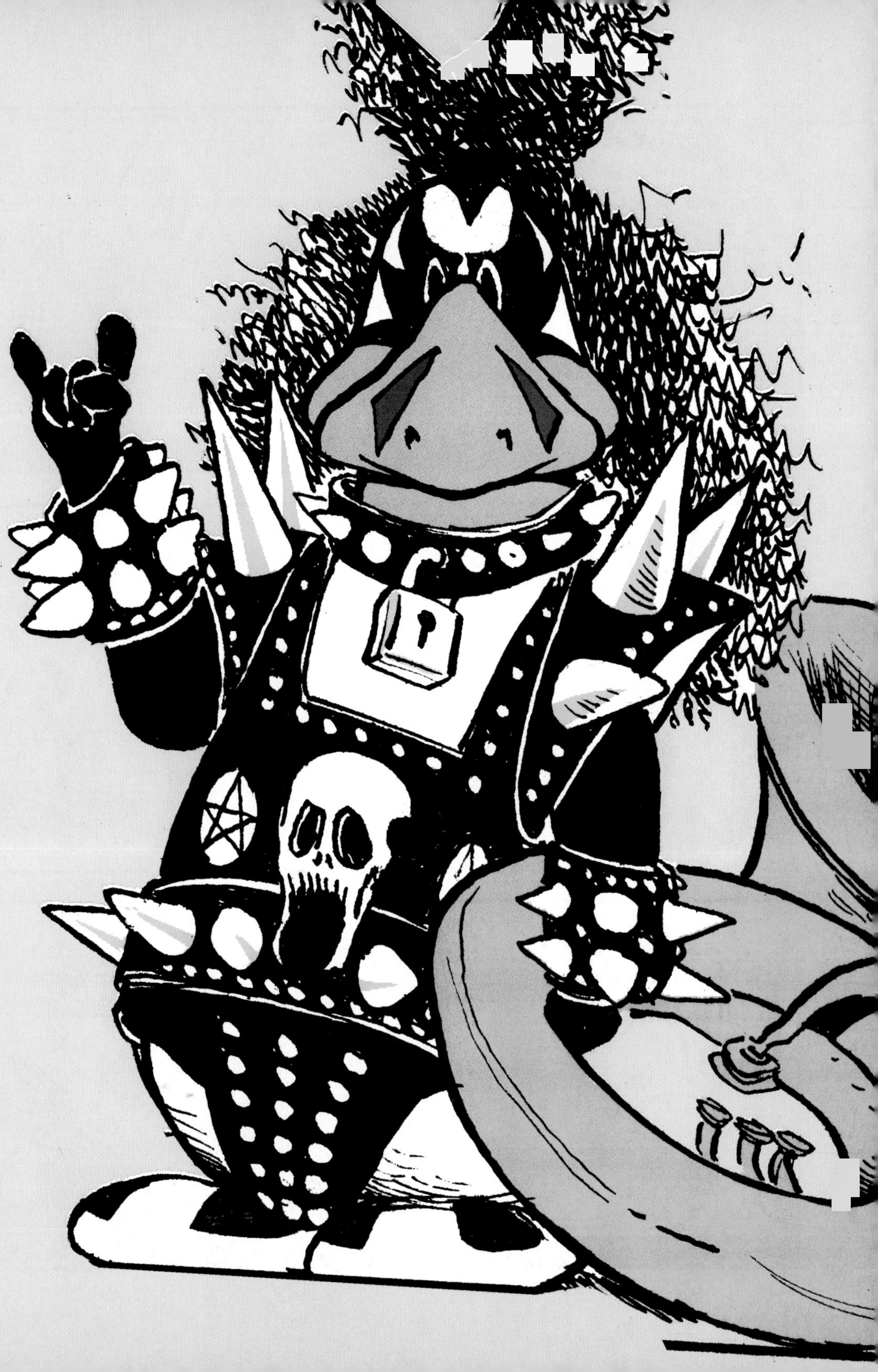

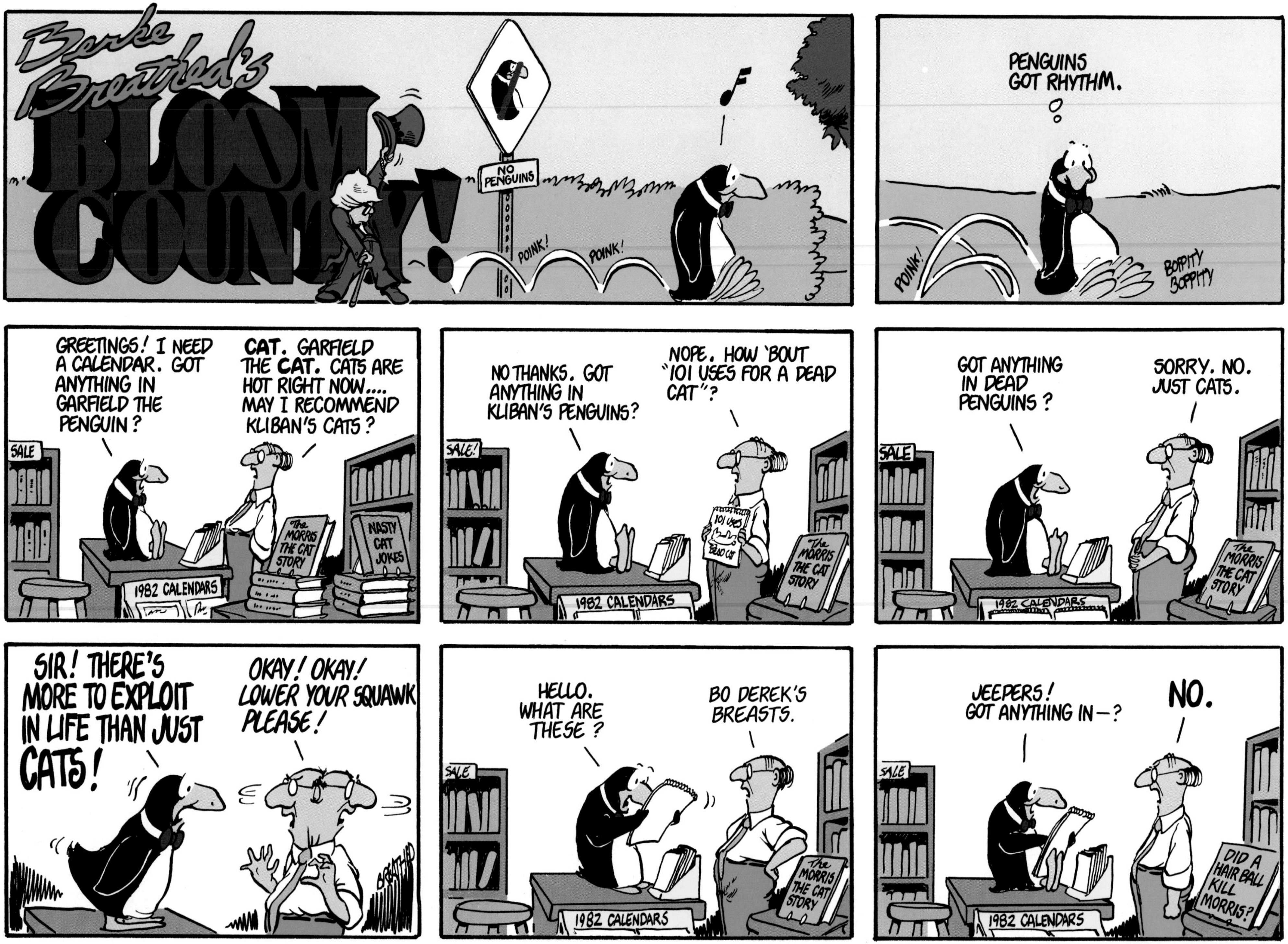
Berke Breathed's
BLOOM COUNTY!
NO PENGUINS
POINK!
POINK!
PENGUINS GOT RHYTHM.
POINK!
BOPPITY BOPPITY
GREETINGS! I NEED A CALENDAR. GOT ANYTHING IN GARFIELD THE PENGUIN?
CAT. GARFIELD THE CAT. CATS ARE HOT RIGHT NOW.... MAY I RECOMMEND KLIBAN'S CATS?
SALE
The MORRIS THE CAT STORY
NASTY CAT JOKES
1982 CALENDARS
NO THANKS. GOT ANYTHING IN KLIBAN'S PENGUINS?
NOPE. HOW 'BOUT "101 USES FOR A DEAD CAT"?
SALE!
101 USES
DEAD CAT
The MORRIS THE CAT STORY
1982 CALENDARS
GOT ANYTHING IN DEAD PENGUINS?
SORRY. NO. JUST CATS.
SALE
The MORRIS THE CAT STORY
1982 CALENDARS
SIR! THERE'S MORE TO EXPLOIT IN LIFE THAN JUST CATS!
OKAY! OKAY! LOWER YOUR SQUAWK PLEASE!
BREATHED
HELLO. WHAT ARE THESE?
BO DEREK'S BREASTS.
SALE
The MORRIS THE CAT STORY
1982 CALENDARS
JEEPERS! GOT ANYTHING IN—?
NO.
SALE
DID A HAIR BALL KILL MORRIS?
1982 CALENDARS

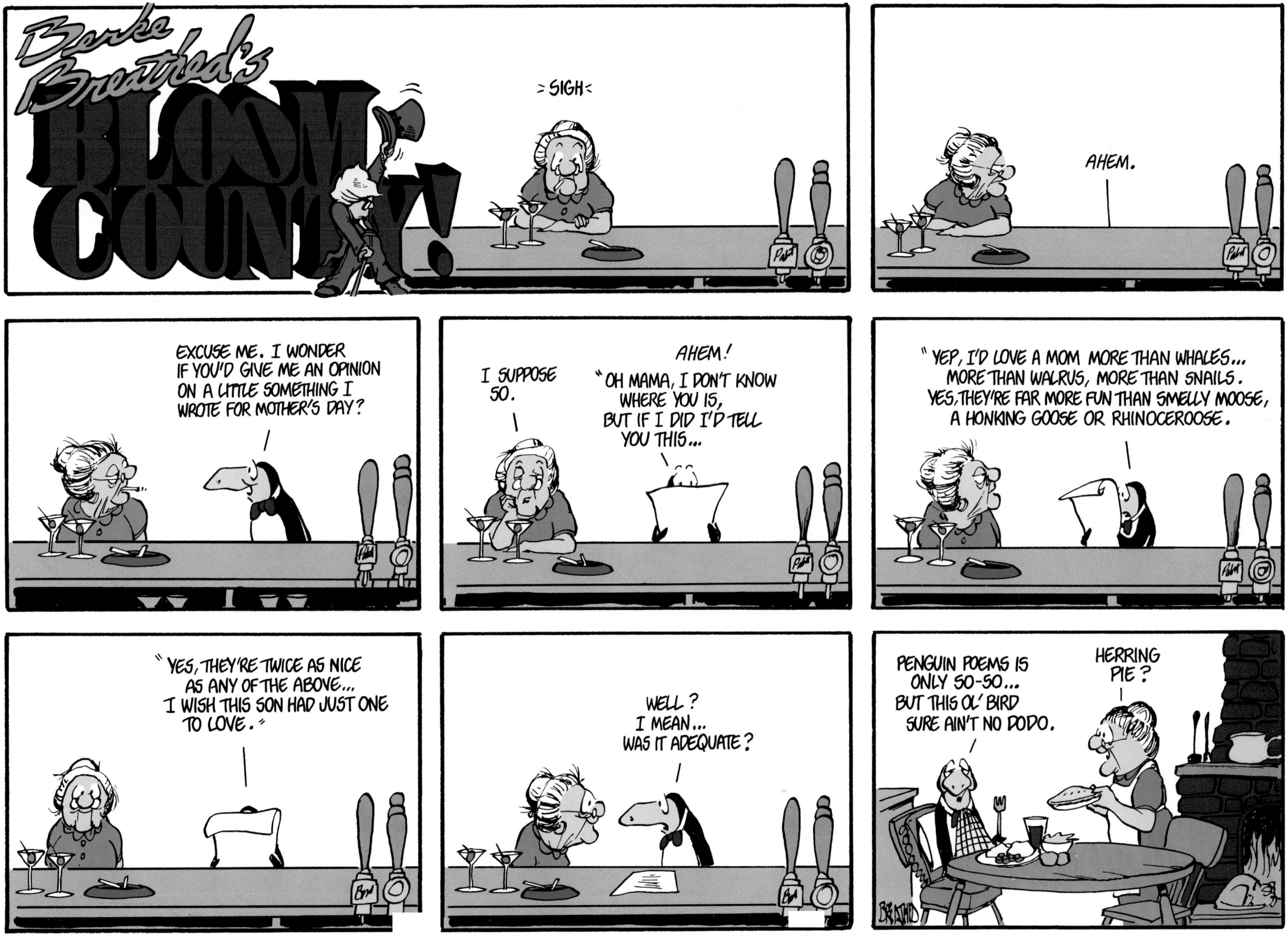
Berke Breathed's
BLOOM COUNTY!
>SIGH<
AHEM.
EXCUSE ME. I WONDER IF YOU'D GIVE ME AN OPINION ON A LITTLE SOMETHING I WROTE FOR MOTHER'S DAY?
I SUPPOSE SO.
AHEM!
"OH MAMA, I DON'T KNOW WHERE YOU IS, BUT IF I DID I'D TELL YOU THIS...
"YEP, I'D LOVE A MOM MORE THAN WHALES... MORE THAN WALRUS, MORE THAN SNAILS. YES, THEY'RE FAR MORE FUN THAN SMELLY MOOSE, A HONKING GOOSE OR RHINOCEROOSE.
"YES, THEY'RE TWICE AS NICE AS ANY OF THE ABOVE... I WISH THIS SON HAD JUST ONE TO LOVE."
WELL? I MEAN... WAS IT ADEQUATE?
PENGUIN POEMS IS ONLY SO-SO... BUT THIS OL' BIRD SURE AIN'T NO DODO.
HERRING PIE?
BREATHED

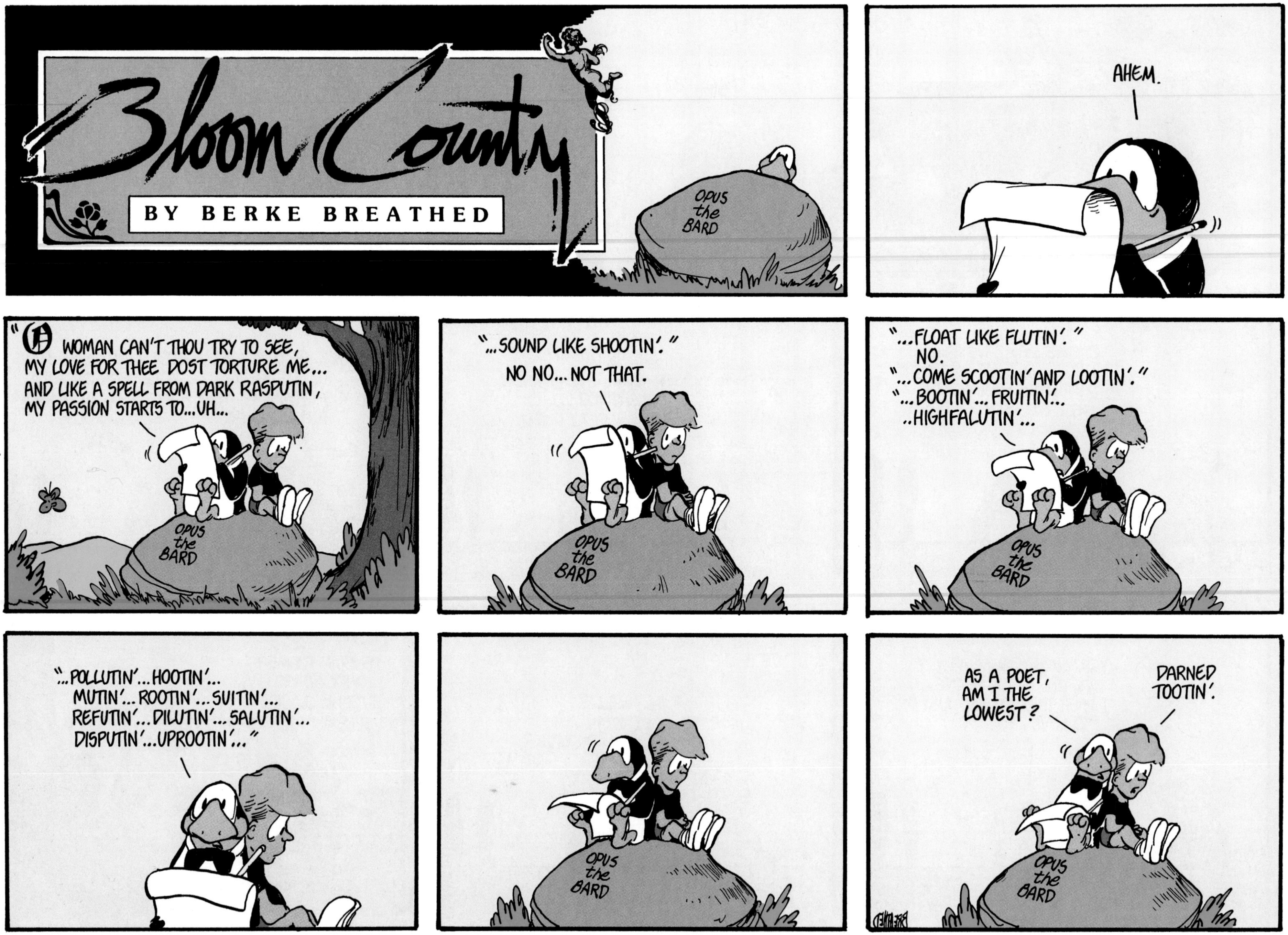
Bloom County
BY BERKE BREATHED
OPUS the BARD
AHEM.
"O WOMAN CAN'T THOU TRY TO SEE, MY LOVE FOR THEE DOST TORTURE ME... AND LIKE A SPELL FROM DARK RASPUTIN, MY PASSION STARTS TO...UH...
"...SOUND LIKE SHOOTIN'."
NO NO... NOT THAT.
"...FLOAT LIKE FLUTIN'."
NO.
"...COME SCOOTIN' AND LOOTIN'."
"...BOOTIN'... FRUITIN'... ..HIGHFALUTIN'...
"...POLLUTIN'...HOOTIN'... MUTIN'... ROOTIN'... SUITIN'... REFUTIN'... DILUTIN'... SALUTIN'... DISPUTIN'...UPROOTIN'..."
AS A POET, AM I THE LOWEST?
DARNED TOOTIN'.

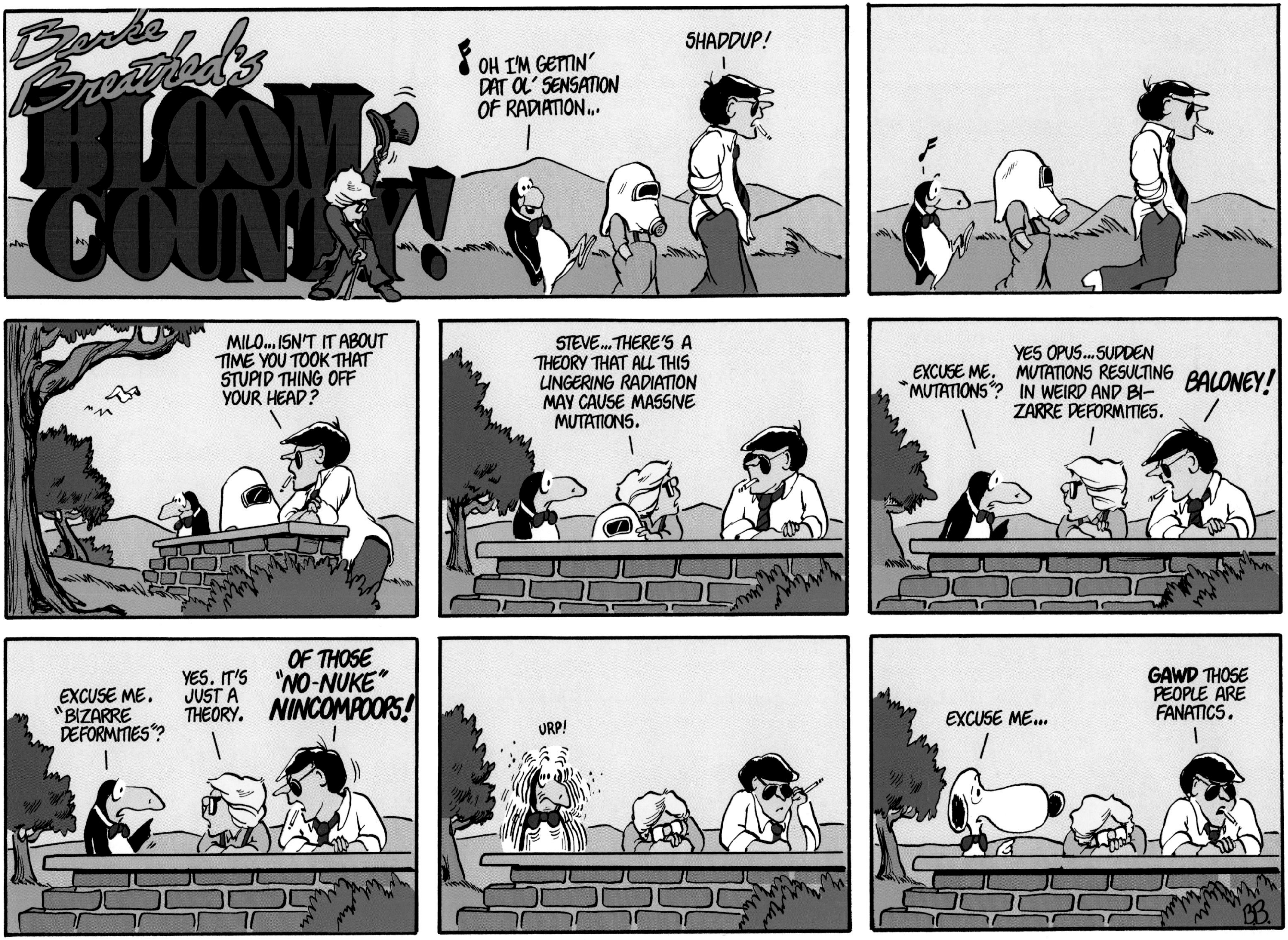
Berke Breathed's
BLOOM COUNTY!
OH I'M GETTIN' DAT OL' SENSATION OF RADIATION...
SHADDUP!
MILO... ISN'T IT ABOUT TIME YOU TOOK THAT STUPID THING OFF YOUR HEAD?
STEVE... THERE'S A THEORY THAT ALL THIS LINGERING RADIATION MAY CAUSE MASSIVE MUTATIONS.
EXCUSE ME. "MUTATIONS"?
YES OPUS... SUDDEN MUTATIONS RESULTING IN WEIRD AND BIZARRE DEFORMITIES.
BALONEY!
EXCUSE ME. "BIZARRE DEFORMITIES"?
YES. IT'S JUST A THEORY.
OF THOSE "NO-NUKE" NINCOMPOOPS!
URP!
EXCUSE ME...
GAWD THOSE PEOPLE ARE FANATICS.
B.B.

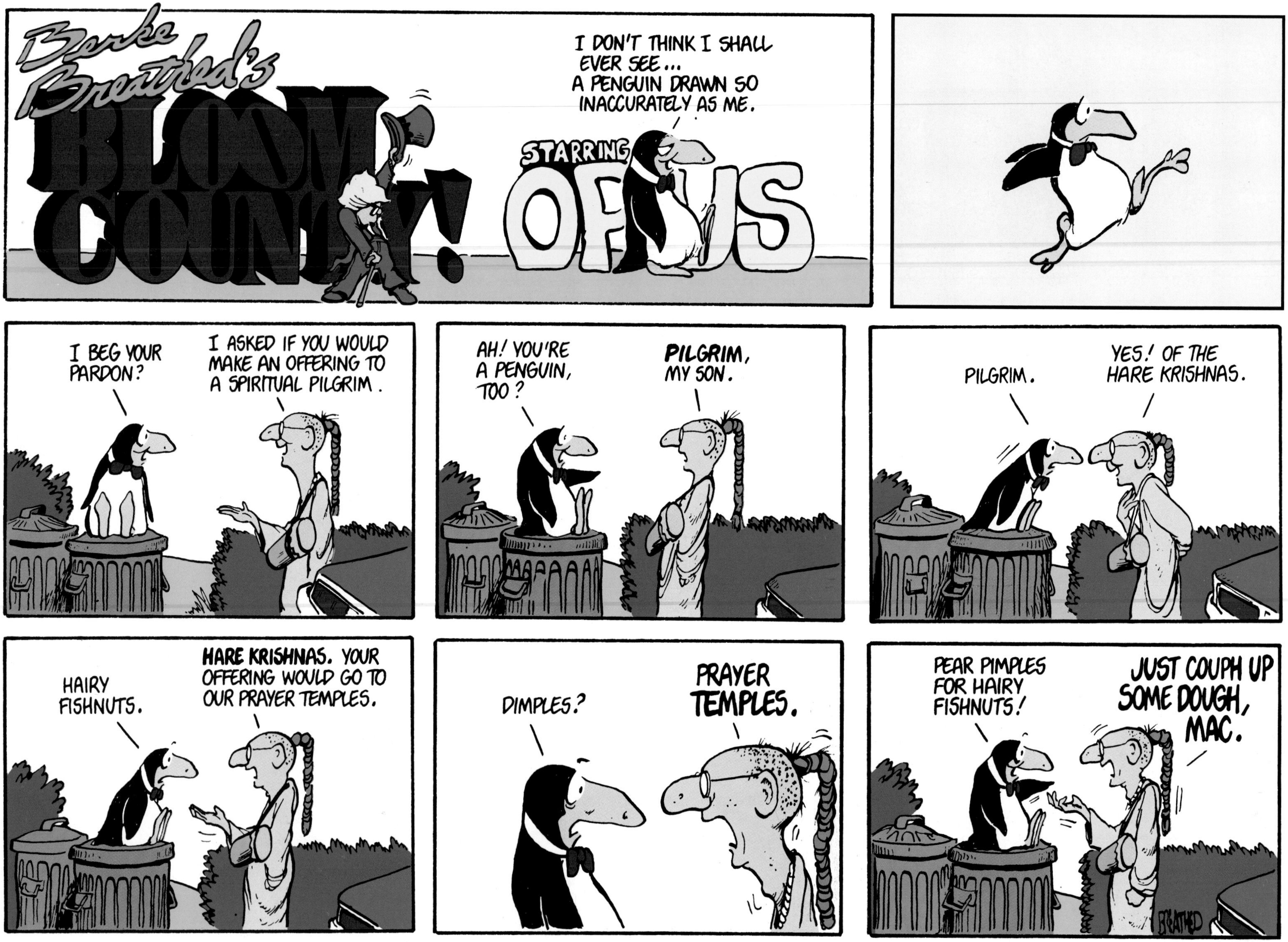

Berke Breathed's
BLOOM COUNTY!
STARRING OPUS
I DON'T THINK I SHALL EVER SEE... A PENGUIN DRAWN SO INACCURATELY AS ME.
I BEG YOUR PARDON?
I ASKED IF YOU WOULD MAKE AN OFFERING TO A SPIRITUAL PILGRIM.
AH! YOU'RE A PENGUIN, TOO?
PILGRIM, MY SON.
PILGRIM.
YES! OF THE HARE KRISHNAS.
HAIRY FISHNUTS.
HARE KRISHNAS. YOUR OFFERING WOULD GO TO OUR PRAYER TEMPLES.
DIMPLES?
PRAYER TEMPLES.
PEAR PIMPLES FOR HAIRY FISHNUTS!
JUST COUGH UP SOME DOUGH, MAC.
BREATHED

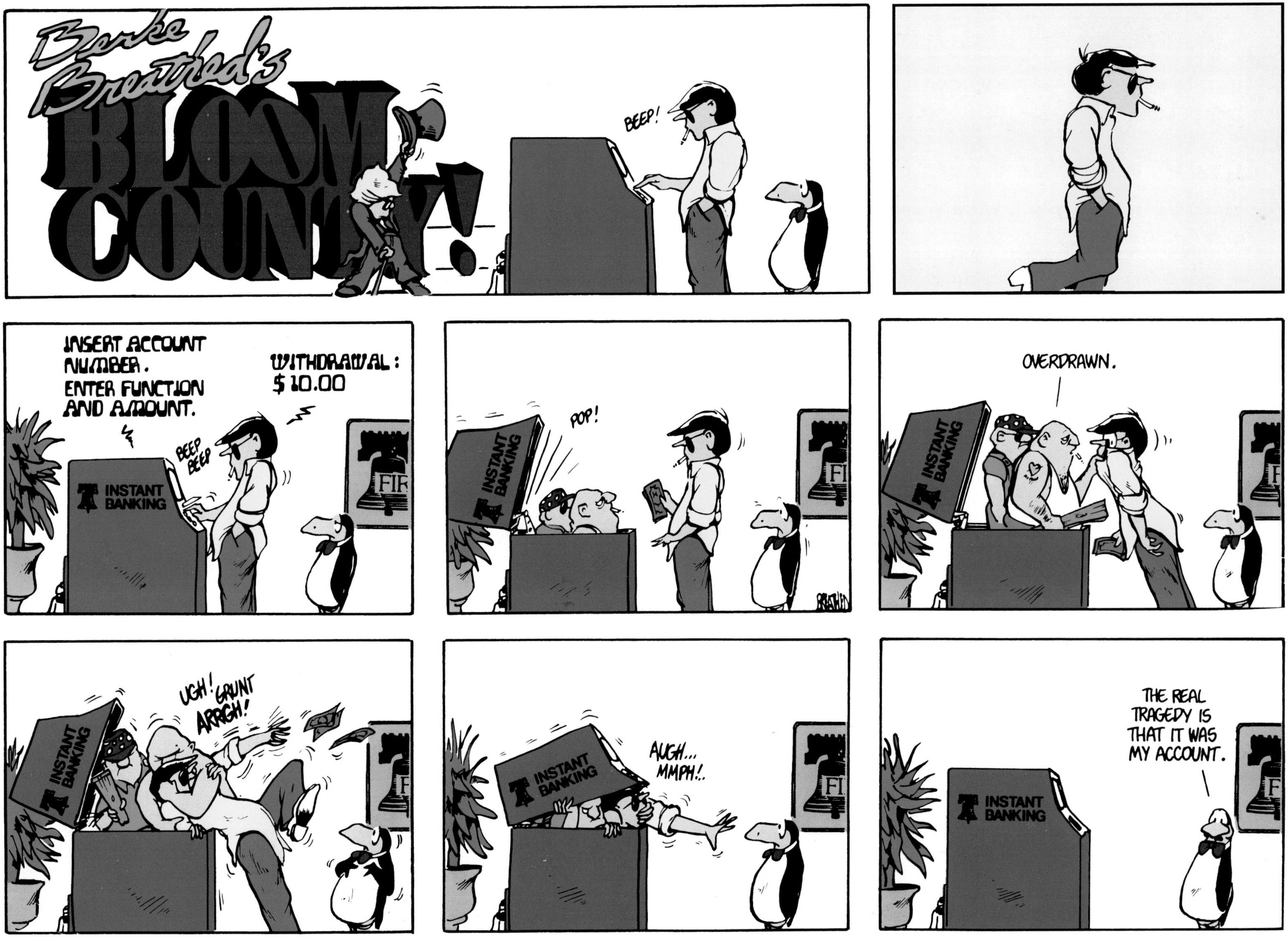

Berke Breathed's
BLOOM COUNTY!
BEEP!
INSERT ACCOUNT NUMBER. ENTER FUNCTION AND AMOUNT.
BEEP BEEP
WITHDRAWAL: $10.00
POP!
OVERDRAWN.
UGH! GRUNT ARRGH!
AUGH... MMPH!.
THE REAL TRAGEDY IS THAT IT WAS MY ACCOUNT.

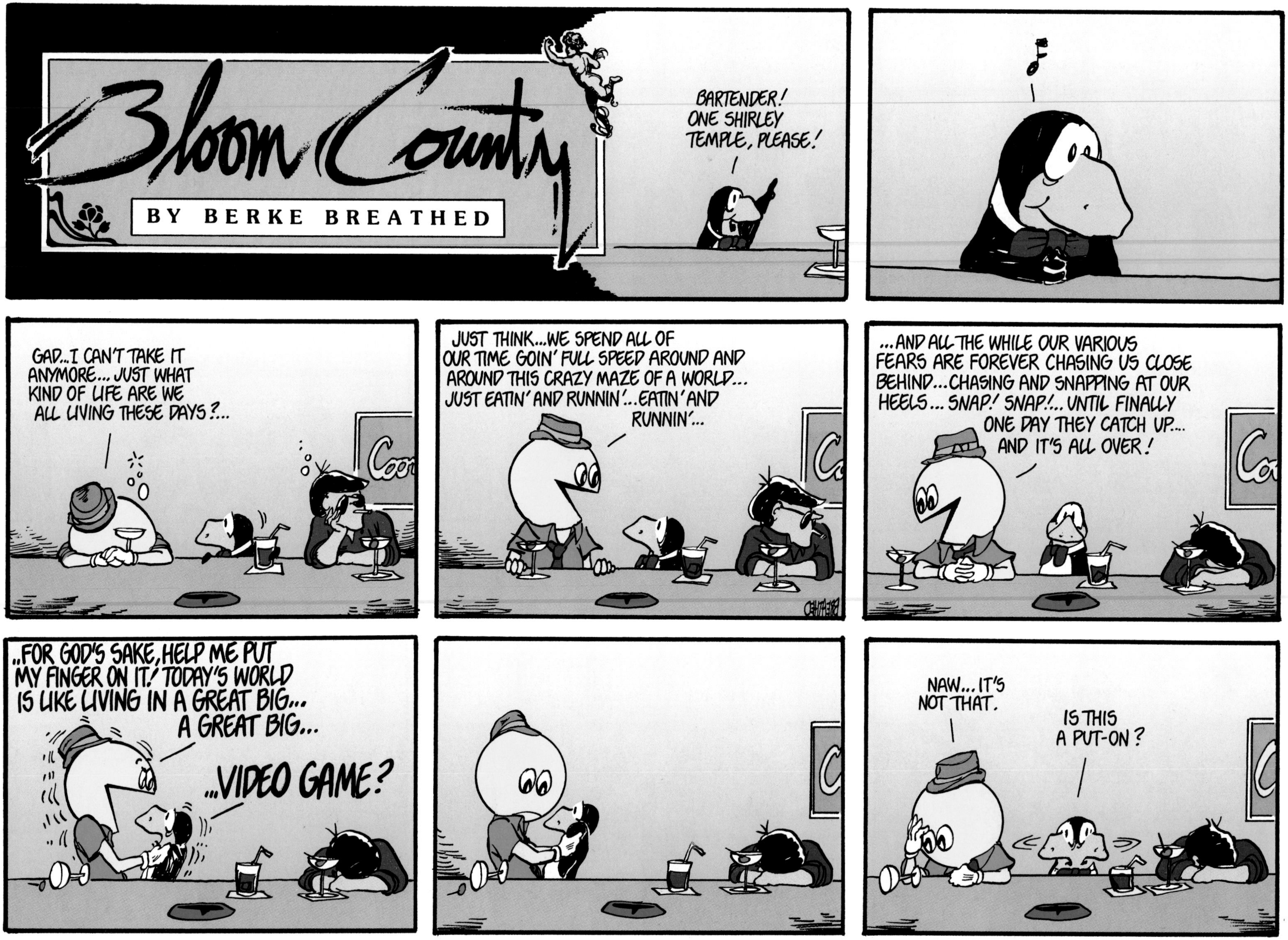
Bloom County
BY BERKE BREATHED
BARTENDER! ONE SHIRLEY TEMPLE, PLEASE!
GAD..I CAN'T TAKE IT ANYMORE... JUST WHAT KIND OF LIFE ARE WE ALL LIVING THESE DAYS?...
JUST THINK...WE SPEND ALL OF OUR TIME GOIN' FULL SPEED AROUND AND AROUND THIS CRAZY MAZE OF A WORLD... JUST EATIN' AND RUNNIN'...EATIN' AND RUNNIN'...
...AND ALL THE WHILE OUR VARIOUS FEARS ARE FOREVER CHASING US CLOSE BEHIND...CHASING AND SNAPPING AT OUR HEELS... SNAP! SNAP!... UNTIL FINALLY ONE DAY THEY CATCH UP... AND IT'S ALL OVER!
..FOR GOD'S SAKE, HELP ME PUT MY FINGER ON IT! TODAY'S WORLD IS LIKE LIVING IN A GREAT BIG... A GREAT BIG...
...VIDEO GAME?
NAW... IT'S NOT THAT.
IS THIS A PUT-ON?

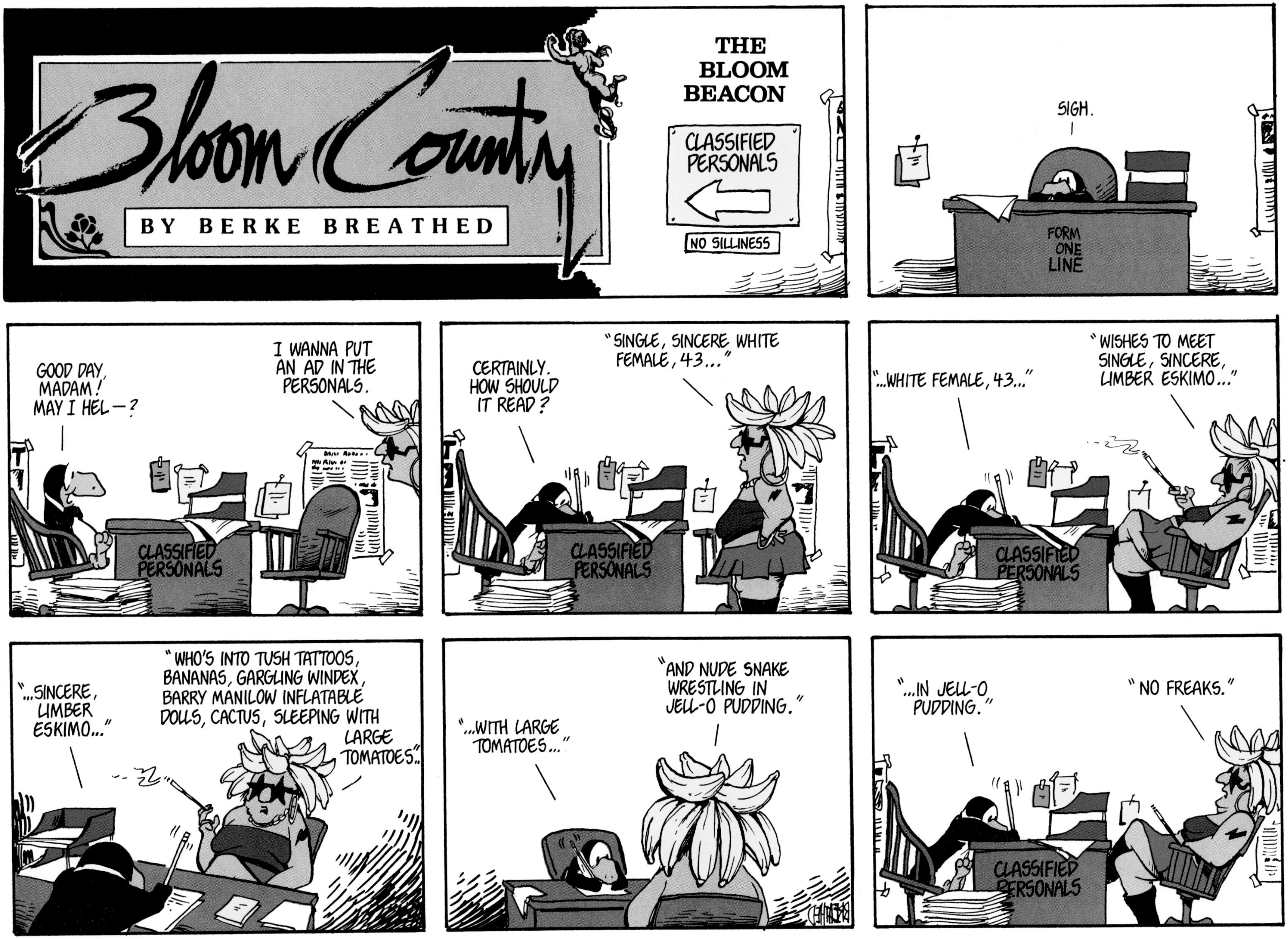
Bloom County
BY BERKE BREATHED
THE BLOOM BEACON
CLASSIFIED PERSONALS
NO SILLINESS
SIGH.
FORM ONE LINE
GOOD DAY, MADAM! MAY I HEL—?
I WANNA PUT AN AD IN THE PERSONALS.
CLASSIFIED PERSONALS
CERTAINLY. HOW SHOULD IT READ?
"SINGLE, SINCERE WHITE FEMALE, 43..."
CLASSIFIED PERSONALS
"...WHITE FEMALE, 43..."
"WISHES TO MEET SINGLE, SINCERE, LIMBER ESKIMO..."
CLASSIFIED PERSONALS
"...SINCERE, LIMBER ESKIMO..."
"WHO'S INTO TUSH TATTOOS, BANANAS, GARGLING WINDEX, BARRY MANILOW INFLATABLE DOLLS, CACTUS, SLEEPING WITH LARGE TOMATOES..."
"...WITH LARGE TOMATOES..."
"AND NUDE SNAKE WRESTLING IN JELL-O PUDDING."
"...IN JELL-O PUDDING."
"NO FREAKS."
CLASSIFIED PERSONALS

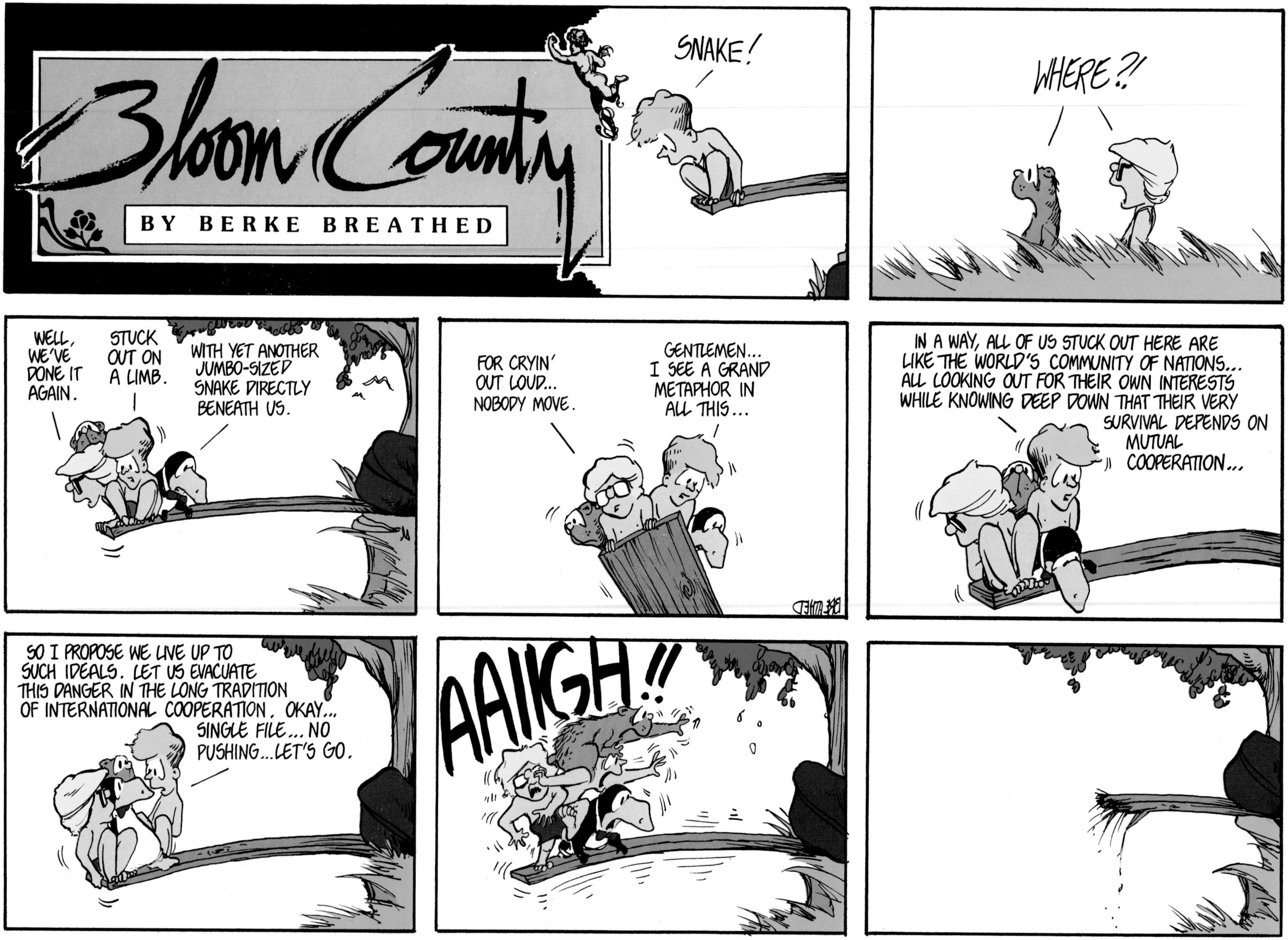
Bloom County
BY BERKE BREATHED
SNAKE!
WHERE?!
WELL, WE'VE DONE IT AGAIN.
STUCK OUT ON A LIMB.
WITH YET ANOTHER JUMBO-SIZED SNAKE DIRECTLY BENEATH US.
FOR CRYIN' OUT LOUD... NOBODY MOVE.
GENTLEMEN... I SEE A GRAND METAPHOR IN ALL THIS...
IN A WAY, ALL OF US STUCK OUT HERE ARE LIKE THE WORLD'S COMMUNITY OF NATIONS... ALL LOOKING OUT FOR THEIR OWN INTERESTS WHILE KNOWING DEEP DOWN THAT THEIR VERY SURVIVAL DEPENDS ON MUTUAL COOPERATION...
SO I PROPOSE WE LIVE UP TO SUCH IDEALS. LET US EVACUATE THIS DANGER IN THE LONG TRADITION OF INTERNATIONAL COOPERATION. OKAY...
SINGLE FILE... NO PUSHING... LET'S GO.
AAIIGH!!

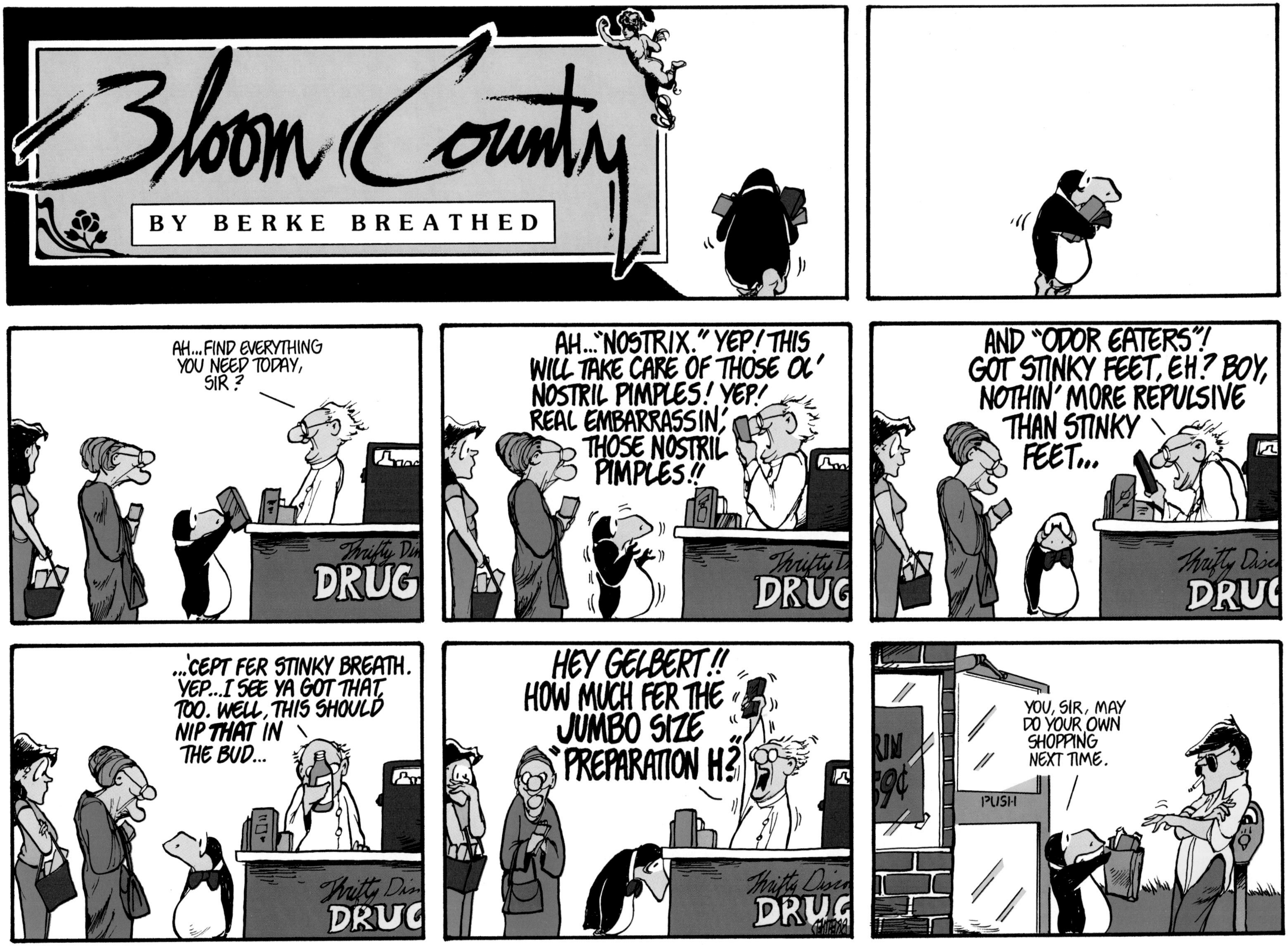
Bloom County
BY BERKE BREATHED
AH...FIND EVERYTHING YOU NEED TODAY, SIR?
AH..."NOSTRIX." YEP! THIS WILL TAKE CARE OF THOSE OL' NOSTRIL PIMPLES! YEP! REAL EMBARRASSIN', THOSE NOSTRIL PIMPLES!!
AND "ODOR EATERS"! GOT STINKY FEET, EH? BOY, NOTHIN' MORE REPULSIVE THAN STINKY FEET...
...'CEPT FER STINKY BREATH. YEP...I SEE YA GOT THAT, TOO. WELL, THIS SHOULD NIP THAT IN THE BUD...
HEY GELBERT!! HOW MUCH FER THE JUMBO SIZE "PREPARATION H?"
YOU, SIR, MAY DO YOUR OWN SHOPPING NEXT TIME.
Thrifty Discount
DRUG
PUSH

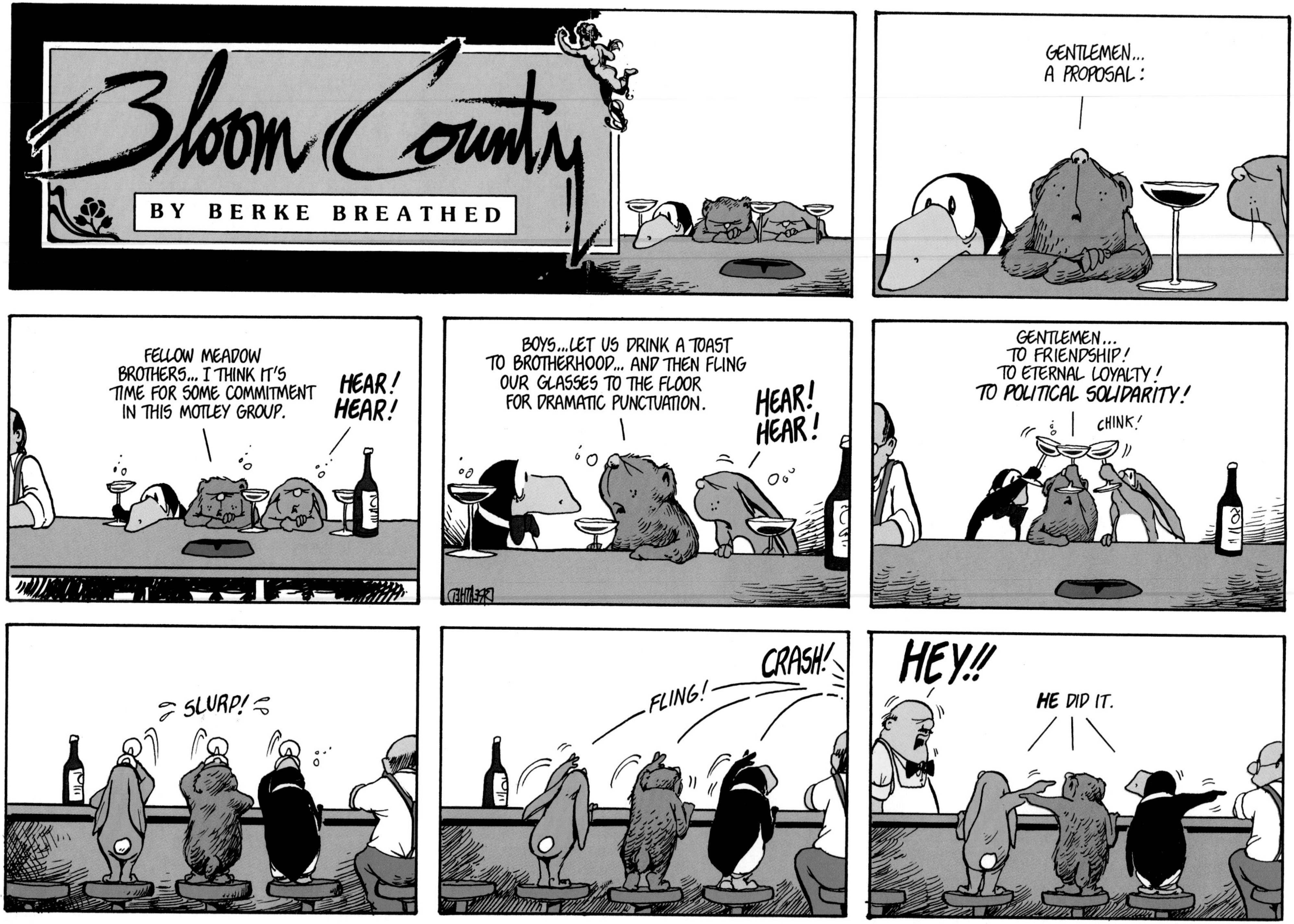
Bloom County
BY BERKE BREATHED
GENTLEMEN... A PROPOSAL:
FELLOW MEADOW BROTHERS... I THINK IT'S TIME FOR SOME COMMITMENT IN THIS MOTLEY GROUP.
HEAR! HEAR!
BOYS...LET US DRINK A TOAST TO BROTHERHOOD... AND THEN FLING OUR GLASSES TO THE FLOOR FOR DRAMATIC PUNCTUATION.
HEAR! HEAR!
GENTLEMEN... TO FRIENDSHIP! TO ETERNAL LOYALTY! TO POLITICAL SOLIDARITY!
CHINK!
SLURP!
FLING!
CRASH!
HEY!!
HE DID IT.

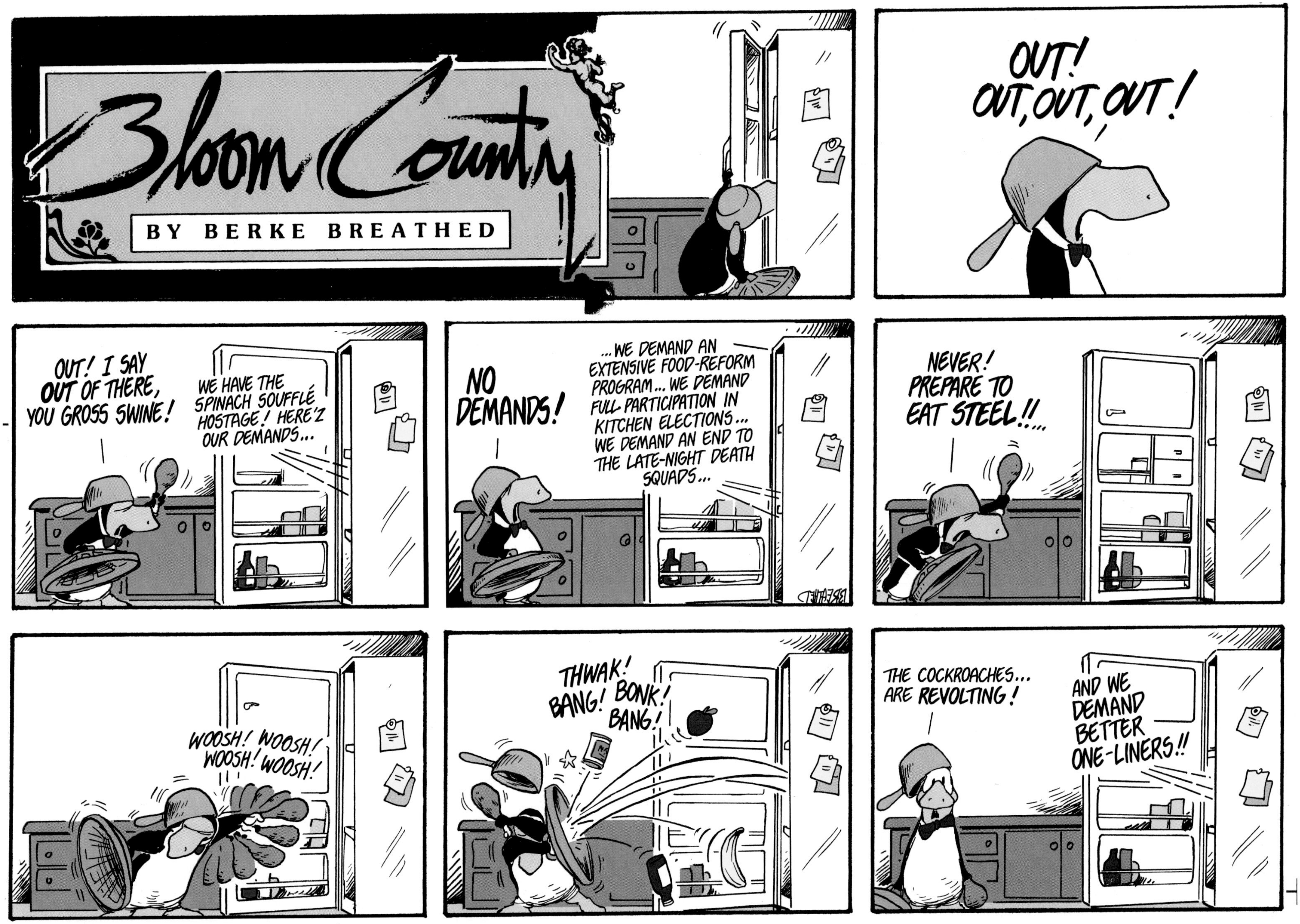
Bloom County
BY BERKE BREATHED
OUT! OUT, OUT, OUT!
OUT! I SAY OUT OF THERE, YOU GROSS SWINE!
WE HAVE THE SPINACH SOUFFLÉ HOSTAGE! HERE'Z OUR DEMANDS...
NO DEMANDS!
...WE DEMAND AN EXTENSIVE FOOD-REFORM PROGRAM... WE DEMAND FULL PARTICIPATION IN KITCHEN ELECTIONS... WE DEMAND AN END TO THE LATE-NIGHT DEATH SQUADS...
NEVER! PREPARE TO EAT STEEL!!...
WOOSH! WOOSH! WOOSH! WOOSH!
THWAK! BANG! BONK! BANG!
THE COCKROACHES... ARE REVOLTING!
AND WE DEMAND BETTER ONE-LINERS!!

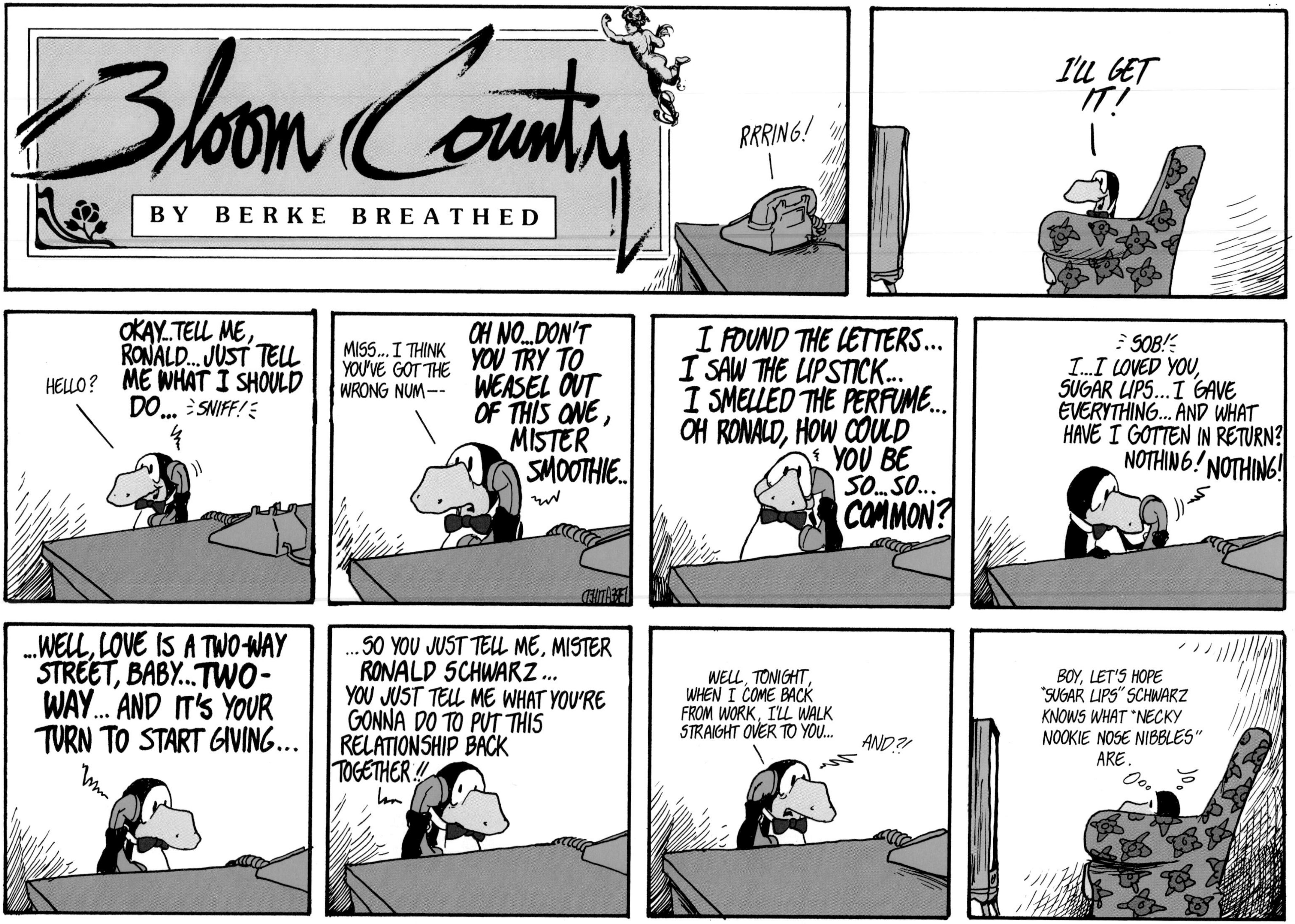
Bloom County
BY BERKE BREATHED
RRRING!
I'LL GET IT!
HELLO?
OKAY...TELL ME, RONALD...JUST TELL ME WHAT I SHOULD DO... SNIFF!
MISS... I THINK YOU'VE GOT THE WRONG NUM--
OH NO...DON'T YOU TRY TO WEASEL OUT OF THIS ONE, MISTER SMOOTHIE..
I FOUND THE LETTERS... I SAW THE LIPSTICK... I SMELLED THE PERFUME... OH RONALD, HOW COULD YOU BE SO...SO... COMMON?
SOB!
I...I LOVED YOU, SUGAR LIPS... I GAVE EVERYTHING... AND WHAT HAVE I GOTTEN IN RETURN? NOTHING! NOTHING!
...WELL, LOVE IS A TWO-WAY STREET, BABY...TWO-WAY... AND IT'S YOUR TURN TO START GIVING...
...SO YOU JUST TELL ME, MISTER RONALD SCHWARZ... YOU JUST TELL ME WHAT YOU'RE GONNA DO TO PUT THIS RELATIONSHIP BACK TOGETHER!!
WELL, TONIGHT, WHEN I COME BACK FROM WORK, I'LL WALK STRAIGHT OVER TO YOU...
AND?!
BOY, LET'S HOPE "SUGAR LIPS" SCHWARZ KNOWS WHAT "NECKY NOOKIE NOSE NIBBLES" ARE.

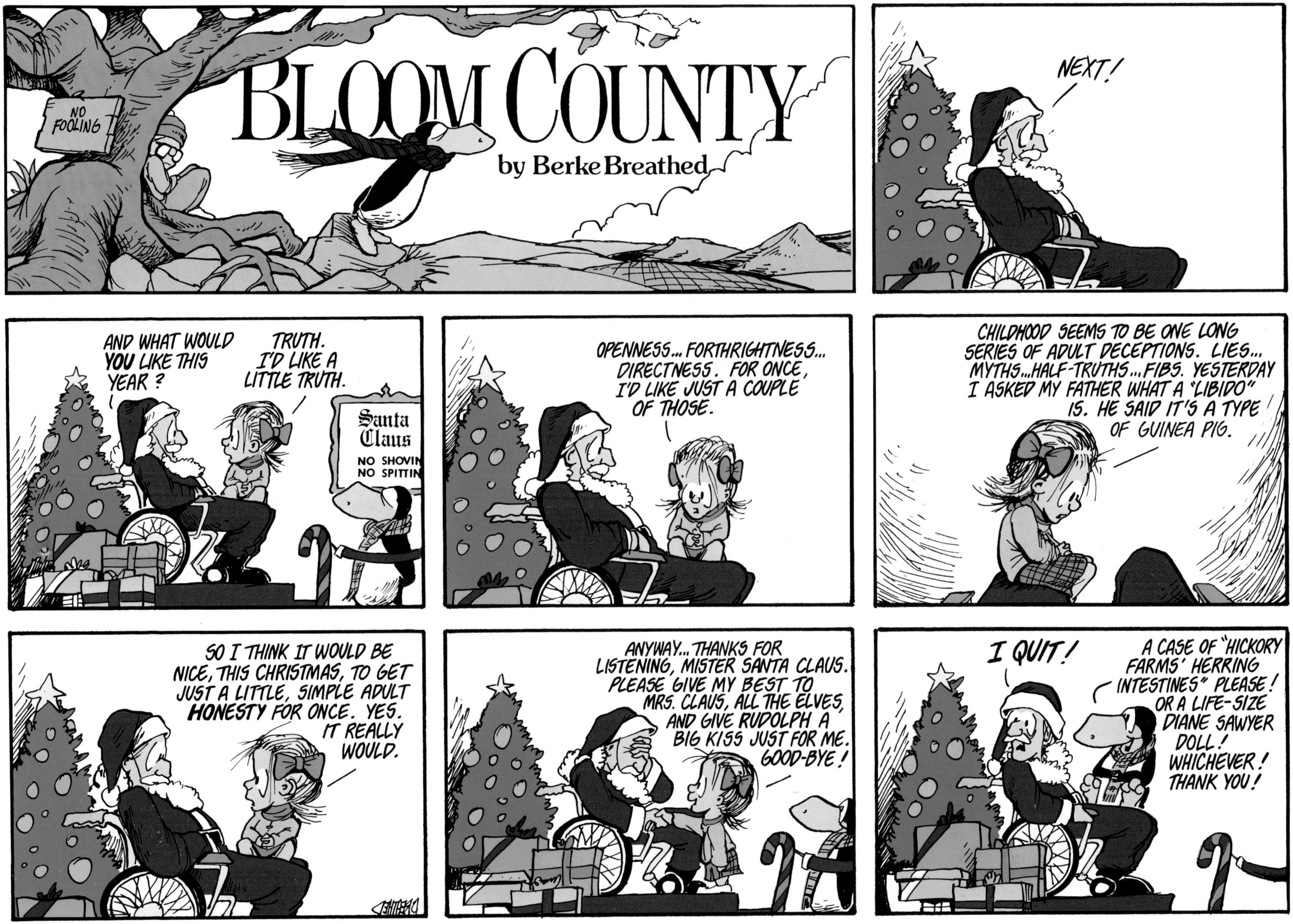

NO FOOLING
BLOOM COUNTY
by Berke Breathed
NEXT!
AND WHAT WOULD YOU LIKE THIS YEAR?
TRUTH. I'D LIKE A LITTLE TRUTH.
Santa Claus
NO SHOVIN
NO SPITTIN
OPENNESS... FORTHRIGHTNESS... DIRECTNESS. FOR ONCE, I'D LIKE JUST A COUPLE OF THOSE.
CHILDHOOD SEEMS TO BE ONE LONG SERIES OF ADULT DECEPTIONS. LIES... MYTHS...HALF-TRUTHS...FIBS. YESTERDAY I ASKED MY FATHER WHAT A "LIBIDO" IS. HE SAID IT'S A TYPE OF GUINEA PIG.
SO I THINK IT WOULD BE NICE, THIS CHRISTMAS, TO GET JUST A LITTLE, SIMPLE ADULT HONESTY FOR ONCE. YES. IT REALLY WOULD.
ANYWAY... THANKS FOR LISTENING, MISTER SANTA CLAUS. PLEASE GIVE MY BEST TO MRS. CLAUS, ALL THE ELVES, AND GIVE RUDOLPH A BIG KISS JUST FOR ME. GOOD-BYE!
I QUIT!
A CASE OF "HICKORY FARMS' HERRING INTESTINES" PLEASE! OR A LIFE-SIZE DIANE SAWYER DOLL! WHICHEVER! THANK YOU!

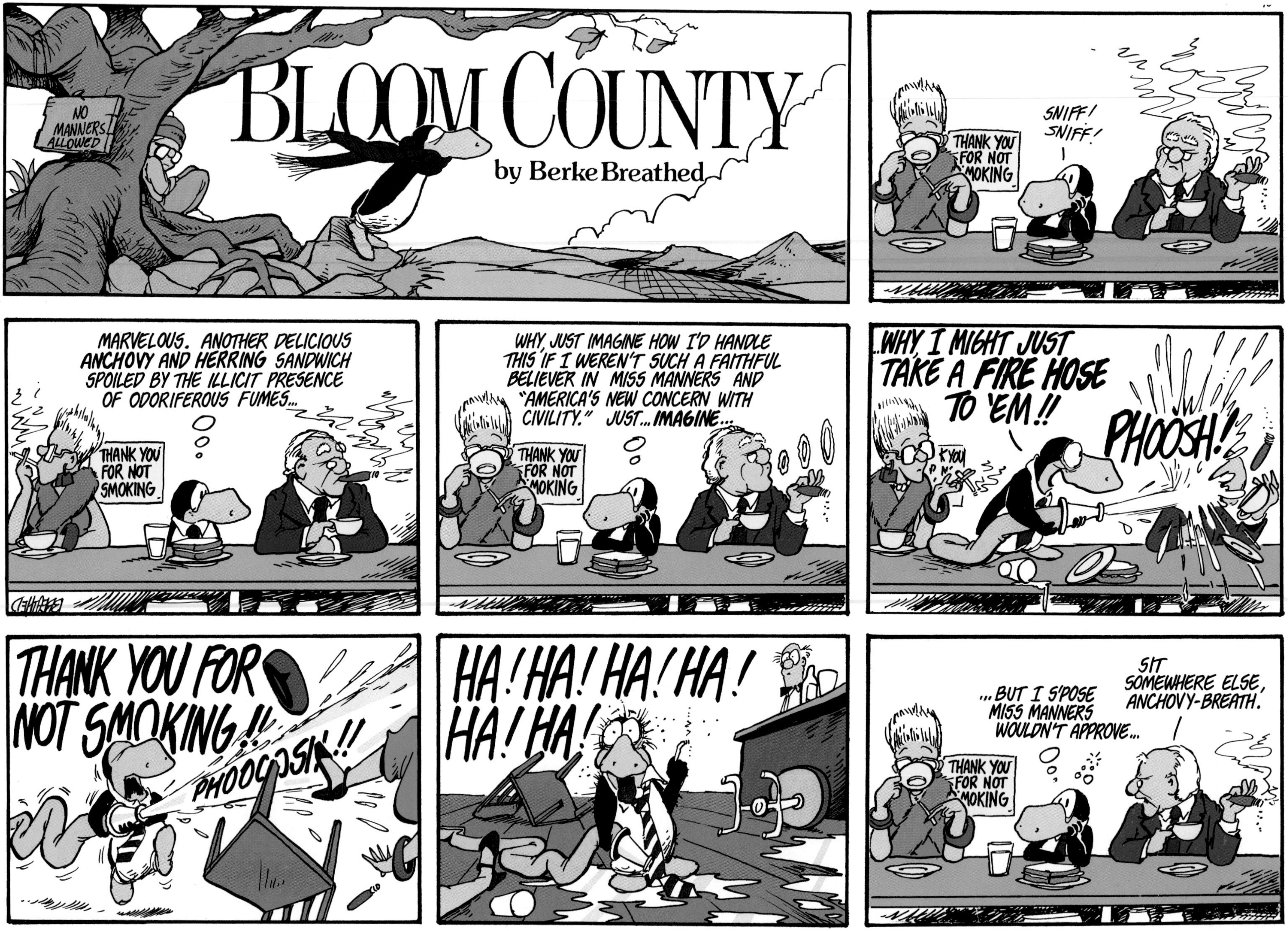
BLOOM COUNTY
by Berke Breathed
NO MANNERS ALLOWED
THANK YOU FOR NOT SMOKING
SNIFF! SNIFF!
MARVELOUS. ANOTHER DELICIOUS ANCHOVY AND HERRING SANDWICH SPOILED BY THE ILLICIT PRESENCE OF ODORIFEROUS FUMES...
THANK YOU FOR NOT SMOKING
WHY, JUST IMAGINE HOW I'D HANDLE THIS IF I WEREN'T SUCH A FAITHFUL BELIEVER IN MISS MANNERS AND "AMERICA'S NEW CONCERN WITH CIVILITY." JUST... IMAGINE...
THANK YOU FOR NOT SMOKING
..WHY, I MIGHT JUST TAKE A FIRE HOSE TO 'EM!!
PHOOSH!
THANK YOU FOR NOT SMOKING!!
PHOOOOSH!!
HA! HA! HA! HA! HA! HA!
...BUT I S'POSE MISS MANNERS WOULDN'T APPROVE...
SIT SOMEWHERE ELSE, ANCHOVY-BREATH.
THANK YOU FOR NOT SMOKING

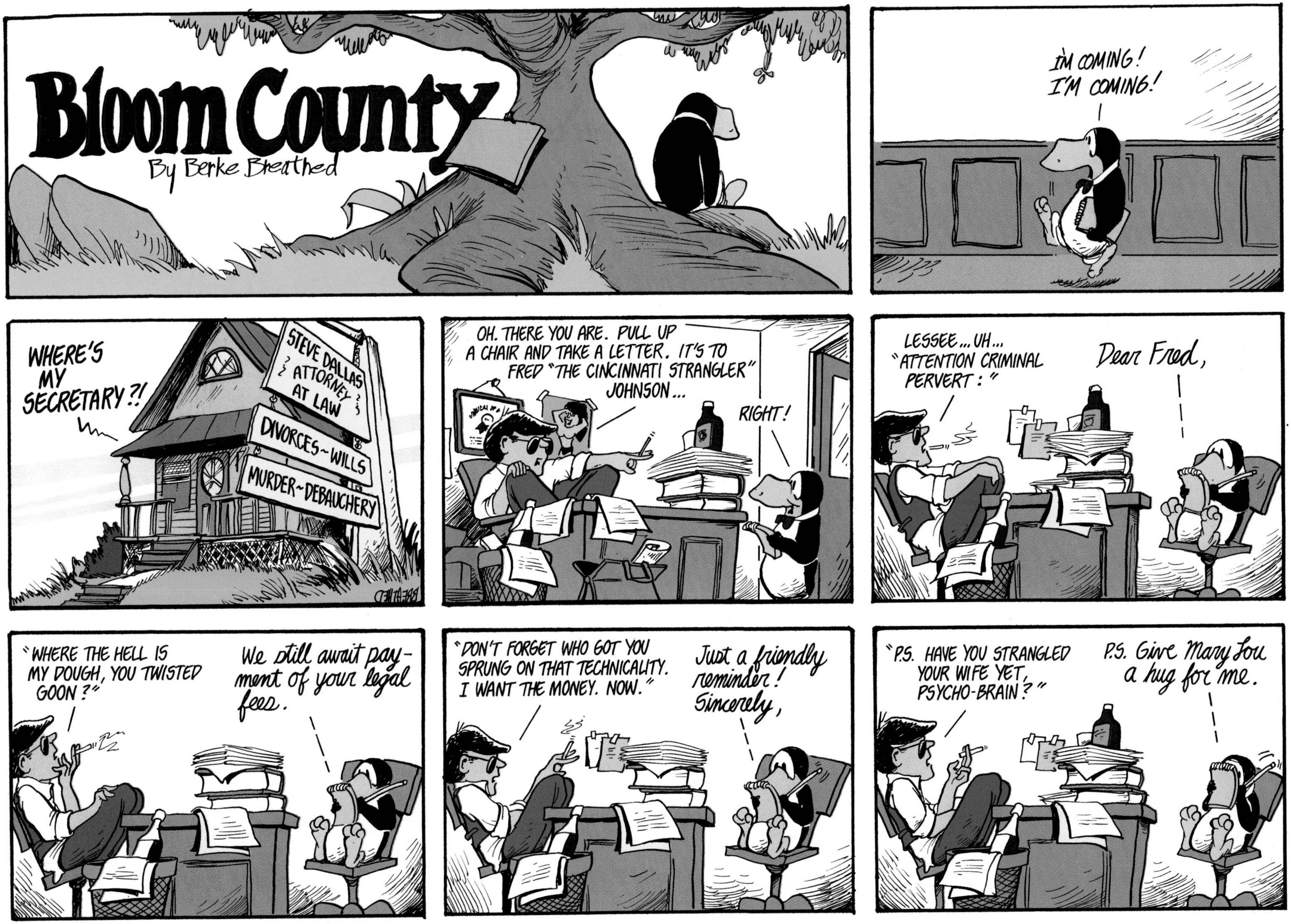
Bloom County
By Berke Breathed
I'M COMING! I'M COMING!
WHERE'S MY SECRETARY?!
STEVE DALLAS ATTORNEY AT LAW
DIVORCES~WILLS
MURDER~DEBAUCHERY
OH. THERE YOU ARE. PULL UP A CHAIR AND TAKE A LETTER. IT'S TO FRED "THE CINCINNATI STRANGLER" JOHNSON...
RIGHT!
LESSEE... UH... "ATTENTION CRIMINAL PERVERT:"
Dear Fred,
"WHERE THE HELL IS MY DOUGH, YOU TWISTED GOON?"
We still await payment of your legal fees.
"DON'T FORGET WHO GOT YOU SPRUNG ON THAT TECHNICALITY. I WANT THE MONEY. NOW."
Just a friendly reminder! Sincerely,
"P.S. HAVE YOU STRANGLED YOUR WIFE YET, PSYCHO-BRAIN?"
P.S. Give Mary Lou a hug for me.

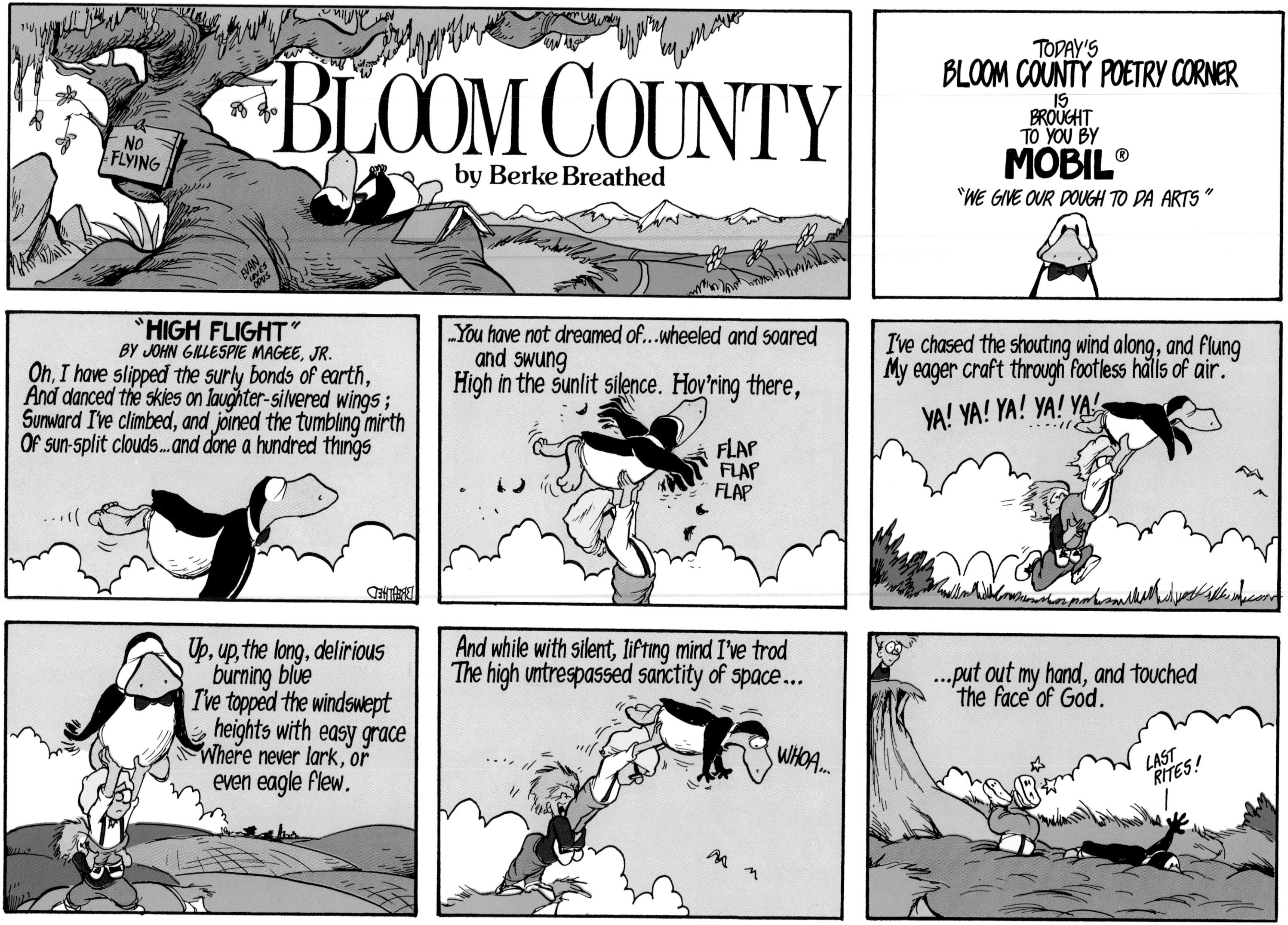

NO FLYING
BLOOM COUNTY
by Berke Breathed
EVAN LOVES OPUS
TODAY'S BLOOM COUNTY POETRY CORNER IS BROUGHT TO YOU BY MOBIL®
"WE GIVE OUR DOUGH TO DA ARTS"
"HIGH FLIGHT"
BY JOHN GILLESPIE MAGEE, JR.
Oh, I have slipped the surly bonds of earth,
And danced the skies on laughter-silvered wings;
Sunward I've climbed, and joined the tumbling mirth
Of sun-split clouds...and done a hundred things
BREATHED
...You have not dreamed of...wheeled and soared and swung
High in the sunlit silence. Hov'ring there,
FLAP FLAP FLAP
I've chased the shouting wind along, and flung
My eager craft through footless halls of air.
YA! YA! YA! YA! YA!
Up, up, the long, delirious burning blue
I've topped the windswept heights with easy grace
Where never lark, or even eagle flew.
And while with silent, lifting mind I've trod
The high untrespassed sanctity of space...
WHOA...
...put out my hand, and touched the face of God.
LAST RITES!

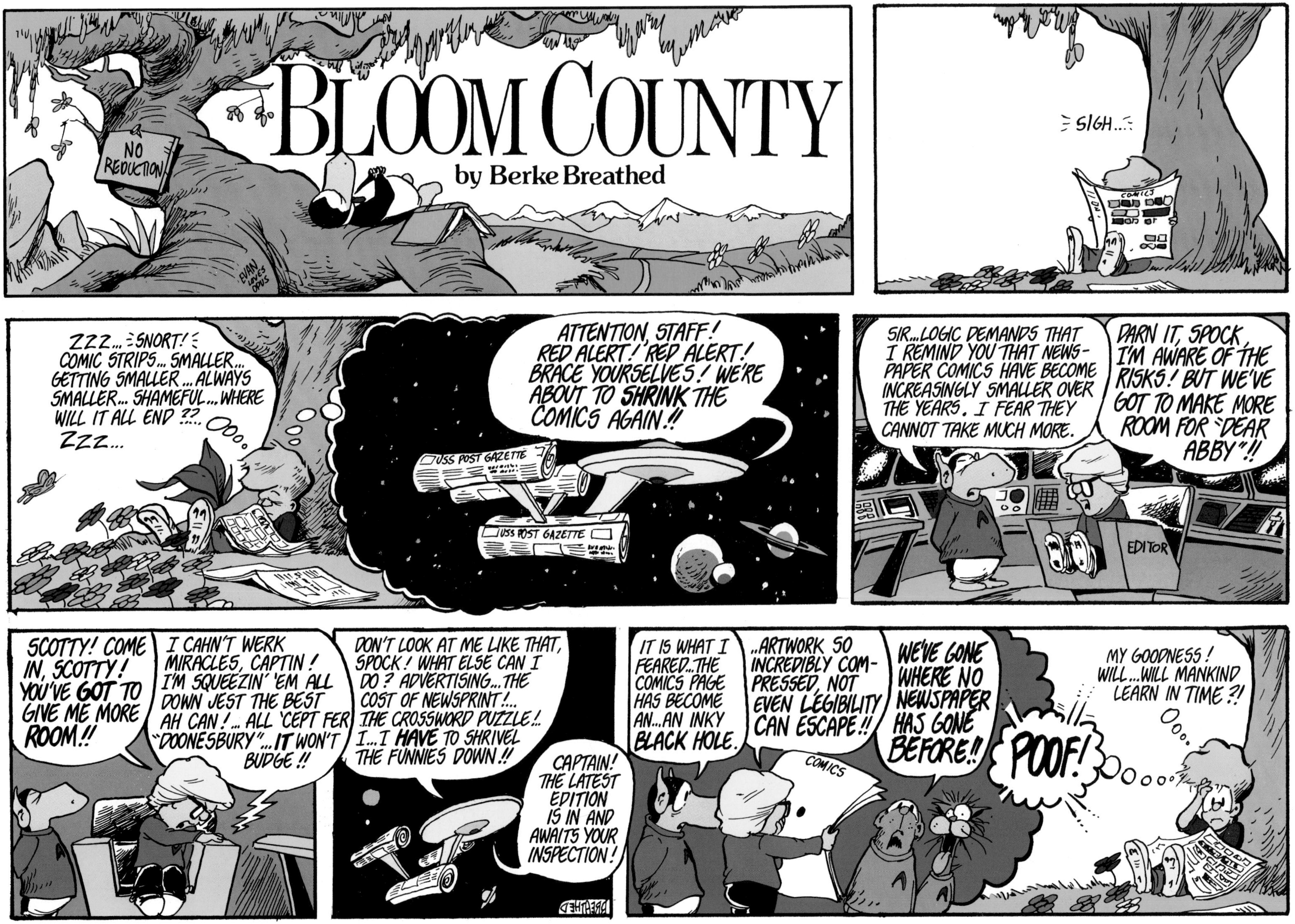
BLOOM COUNTY
by Berke Breathed
NO REDUCTION
EVAN LOVES OPUS
SIGH...
ZZZ... SNORT! COMIC STRIPS... SMALLER... GETTING SMALLER... ALWAYS SMALLER... SHAMEFUL... WHERE WILL IT ALL END ??... ZZZ...
ATTENTION, STAFF! RED ALERT! RED ALERT! BRACE YOURSELVES! WE'RE ABOUT TO SHRINK THE COMICS AGAIN!!
USS POST GAZETTE
USS POST GAZETTE
SIR...LOGIC DEMANDS THAT I REMIND YOU THAT NEWSPAPER COMICS HAVE BECOME INCREASINGLY SMALLER OVER THE YEARS. I FEAR THEY CANNOT TAKE MUCH MORE.
DARN IT, SPOCK, I'M AWARE OF THE RISKS! BUT WE'VE GOT TO MAKE MORE ROOM FOR "DEAR ABBY"!!
EDITOR
SCOTTY! COME IN, SCOTTY! YOU'VE GOT TO GIVE ME MORE ROOM!!
I CAHN'T WERK MIRACLES, CAPTIN! I'M SQUEEZIN' 'EM ALL DOWN JEST THE BEST AH CAN!... ALL 'CEPT FER "DOONESBURY"... IT WON'T BUDGE!!
DON'T LOOK AT ME LIKE THAT, SPOCK! WHAT ELSE CAN I DO? ADVERTISING... THE COST OF NEWSPRINT!... THE CROSSWORD PUZZLE!... I...I HAVE TO SHRIVEL THE FUNNIES DOWN!!
CAPTAIN! THE LATEST EDITION IS IN AND AWAITS YOUR INSPECTION!
BREATHED
IT IS WHAT I FEARED...THE COMICS PAGE HAS BECOME AN...AN INKY BLACK HOLE.
..ARTWORK SO INCREDIBLY COMPRESSED, NOT EVEN LEGIBILITY CAN ESCAPE!!
COMICS
WE'VE GONE WHERE NO NEWSPAPER HAS GONE BEFORE!!
POOF!
MY GOODNESS! WILL...WILL MANKIND LEARN IN TIME ?!

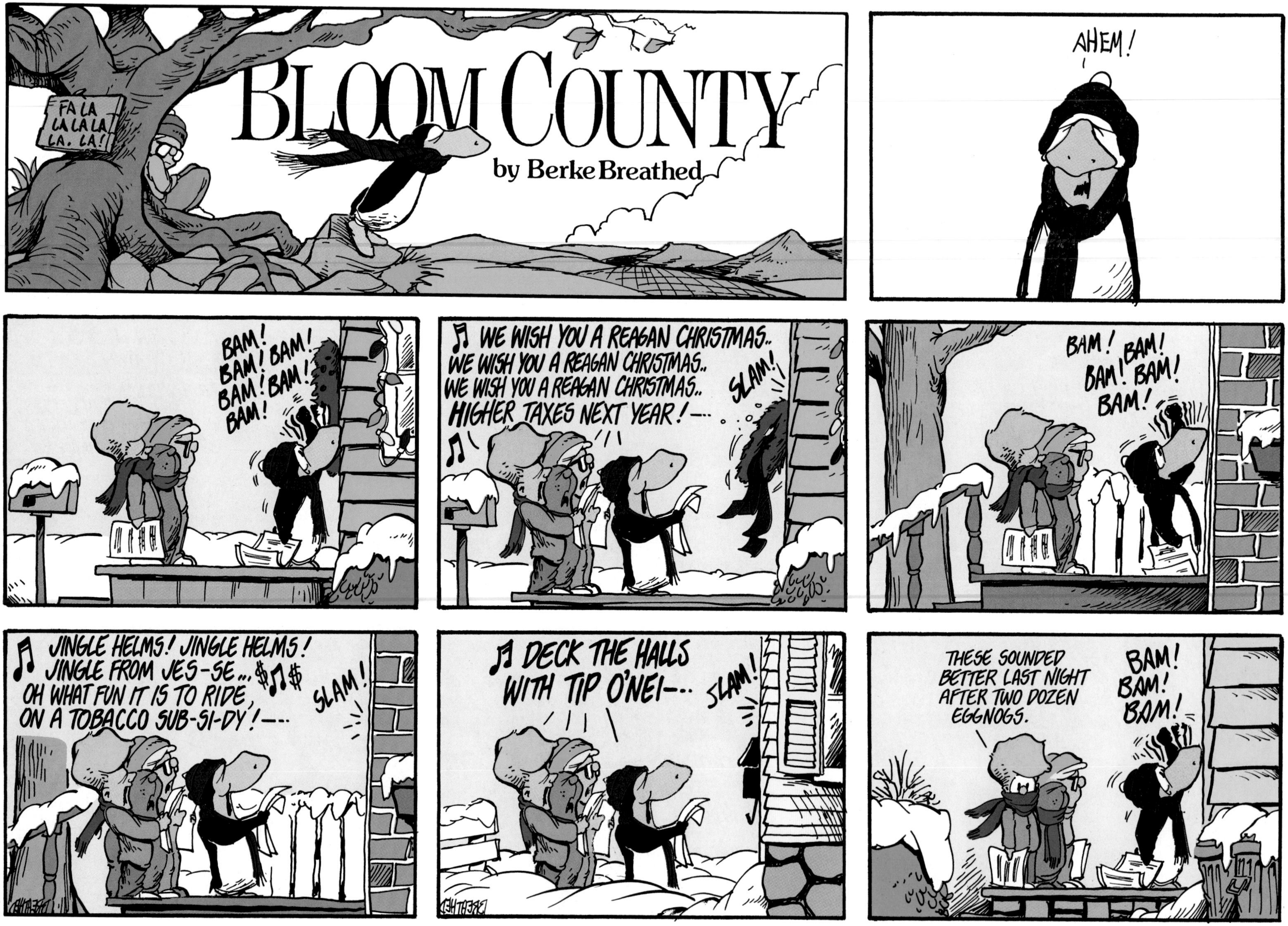

FA LA LA LA LA. LA. LA!
BLOOM COUNTY
by Berke Breathed
AHEM!
BAM! BAM! BAM! BAM! BAM! BAM!
♫ WE WISH YOU A REAGAN CHRISTMAS.. WE WISH YOU A REAGAN CHRISTMAS.. WE WISH YOU A REAGAN CHRISTMAS.. HIGHER TAXES NEXT YEAR! —..
SLAM!
BAM! BAM! BAM! BAM! BAM!
♫ JINGLE HELMS! JINGLE HELMS! JINGLE FROM JES-SE... $♫$ OH WHAT FUN IT IS TO RIDE, ON A TOBACCO SUB-SI-DY! —..
SLAM!
♫ DECK THE HALLS WITH TIP O'NEI—..
SLAM!
THESE SOUNDED BETTER LAST NIGHT AFTER TWO DOZEN EGGNOGS.
BAM! BAM! BAM!

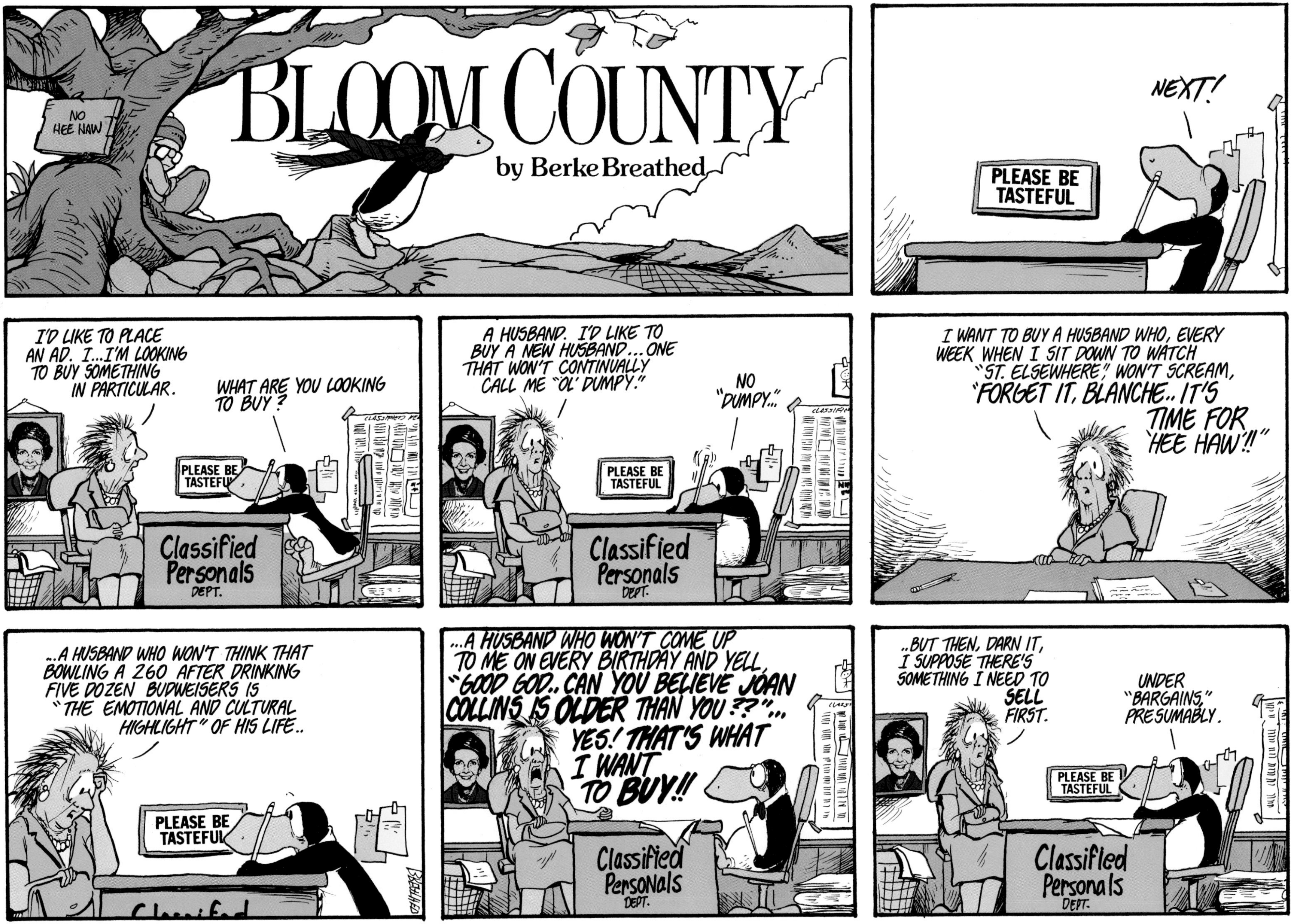

BLOOM COUNTY
by Berke Breathed
NO HEE HAW
PLEASE BE TASTEFUL
NEXT!
I'D LIKE TO PLACE AN AD. I...I'M LOOKING TO BUY SOMETHING IN PARTICULAR.
WHAT ARE YOU LOOKING TO BUY?
Classified Personals DEPT.
A HUSBAND. I'D LIKE TO BUY A NEW HUSBAND... ONE THAT WON'T CONTINUALLY CALL ME "OL' DUMPY."
NO "DUMPY."
I WANT TO BUY A HUSBAND WHO, EVERY WEEK WHEN I SIT DOWN TO WATCH "ST. ELSEWHERE," WON'T SCREAM, "FORGET IT, BLANCHE.. IT'S TIME FOR 'HEE HAW'!!"
...A HUSBAND WHO WON'T THINK THAT BOWLING A 260 AFTER DRINKING FIVE DOZEN BUDWEISERS IS "THE EMOTIONAL AND CULTURAL HIGHLIGHT" OF HIS LIFE..
...A HUSBAND WHO WON'T COME UP TO ME ON EVERY BIRTHDAY AND YELL, "GOOD GOD.. CAN YOU BELIEVE JOAN COLLINS IS OLDER THAN YOU??"...
YES! THAT'S WHAT I WANT TO BUY!!
..BUT THEN, DARN IT, I SUPPOSE THERE'S SOMETHING I NEED TO SELL FIRST.
UNDER "BARGAINS," PRESUMABLY.

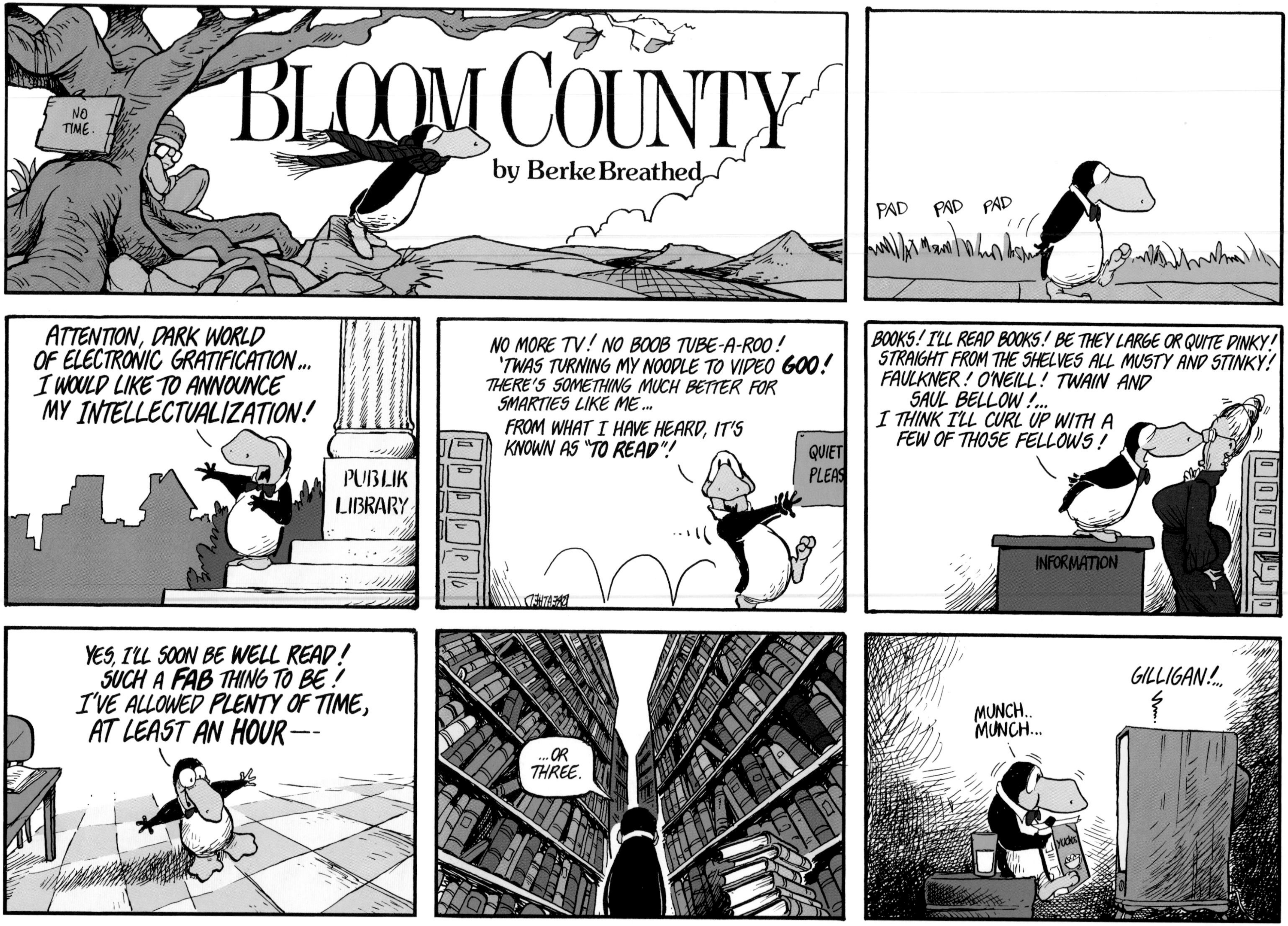
BLOOM COUNTY
by Berke Breathed
NO TIME.
PAD PAD PAD
ATTENTION, DARK WORLD OF ELECTRONIC GRATIFICATION... I WOULD LIKE TO ANNOUNCE MY INTELLECTUALIZATION!
PUBLIK LIBRARY
NO MORE TV! NO BOOB TUBE-A-ROO! 'TWAS TURNING MY NOODLE TO VIDEO GOO! THERE'S SOMETHING MUCH BETTER FOR SMARTIES LIKE ME...
FROM WHAT I HAVE HEARD, IT'S KNOWN AS "TO READ"!
QUIET PLEAS
BOOKS! I'LL READ BOOKS! BE THEY LARGE OR QUITE DINKY! STRAIGHT FROM THE SHELVES ALL MUSTY AND STINKY! FAULKNER! O'NEILL! TWAIN AND SAUL BELLOW!... I THINK I'LL CURL UP WITH A FEW OF THOSE FELLOWS!
INFORMATION
YES, I'LL SOON BE WELL READ! SUCH A FAB THING TO BE! I'VE ALLOWED PLENTY OF TIME, AT LEAST AN HOUR---
...OR THREE.
MUNCH.. MUNCH...
GILLIGAN!...

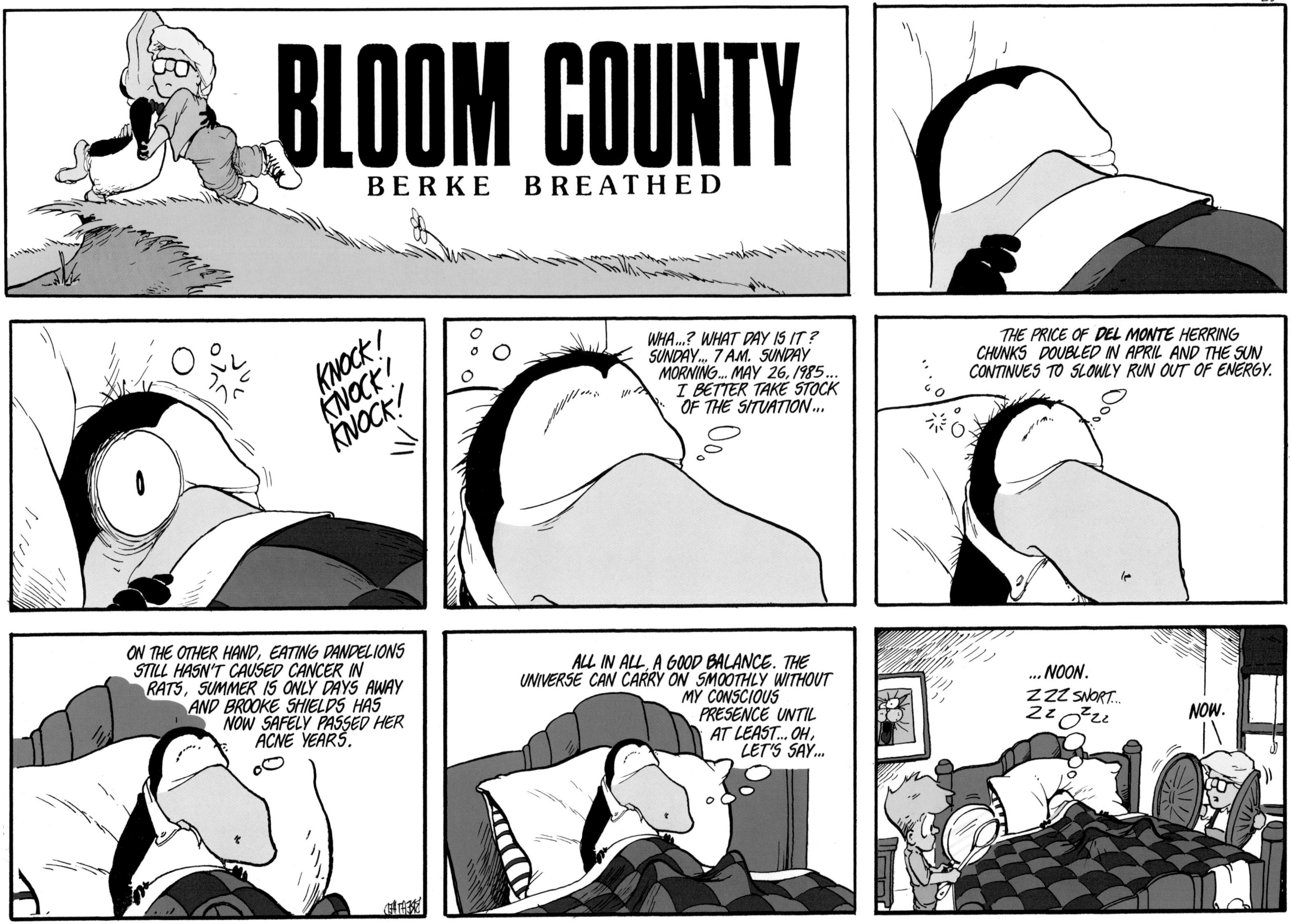

BLOOM COUNTY
BERKE BREATHED
KNOCK! KNOCK! KNOCK!
WHA...? WHAT DAY IS IT? SUNDAY... 7 A.M. SUNDAY MORNING... MAY 26, 1985... I BETTER TAKE STOCK OF THE SITUATION...
THE PRICE OF DEL MONTE HERRING CHUNKS DOUBLED IN APRIL AND THE SUN CONTINUES TO SLOWLY RUN OUT OF ENERGY.
ON THE OTHER HAND, EATING DANDELIONS STILL HASN'T CAUSED CANCER IN RATS, SUMMER IS ONLY DAYS AWAY AND BROOKE SHIELDS HAS NOW SAFELY PASSED HER ACNE YEARS.
ALL IN ALL, A GOOD BALANCE. THE UNIVERSE CAN CARRY ON SMOOTHLY WITHOUT MY CONSCIOUS PRESENCE UNTIL AT LEAST... OH, LET'S SAY...
...NOON.
Z ZZ SNORT... Z z z z z
NOW.

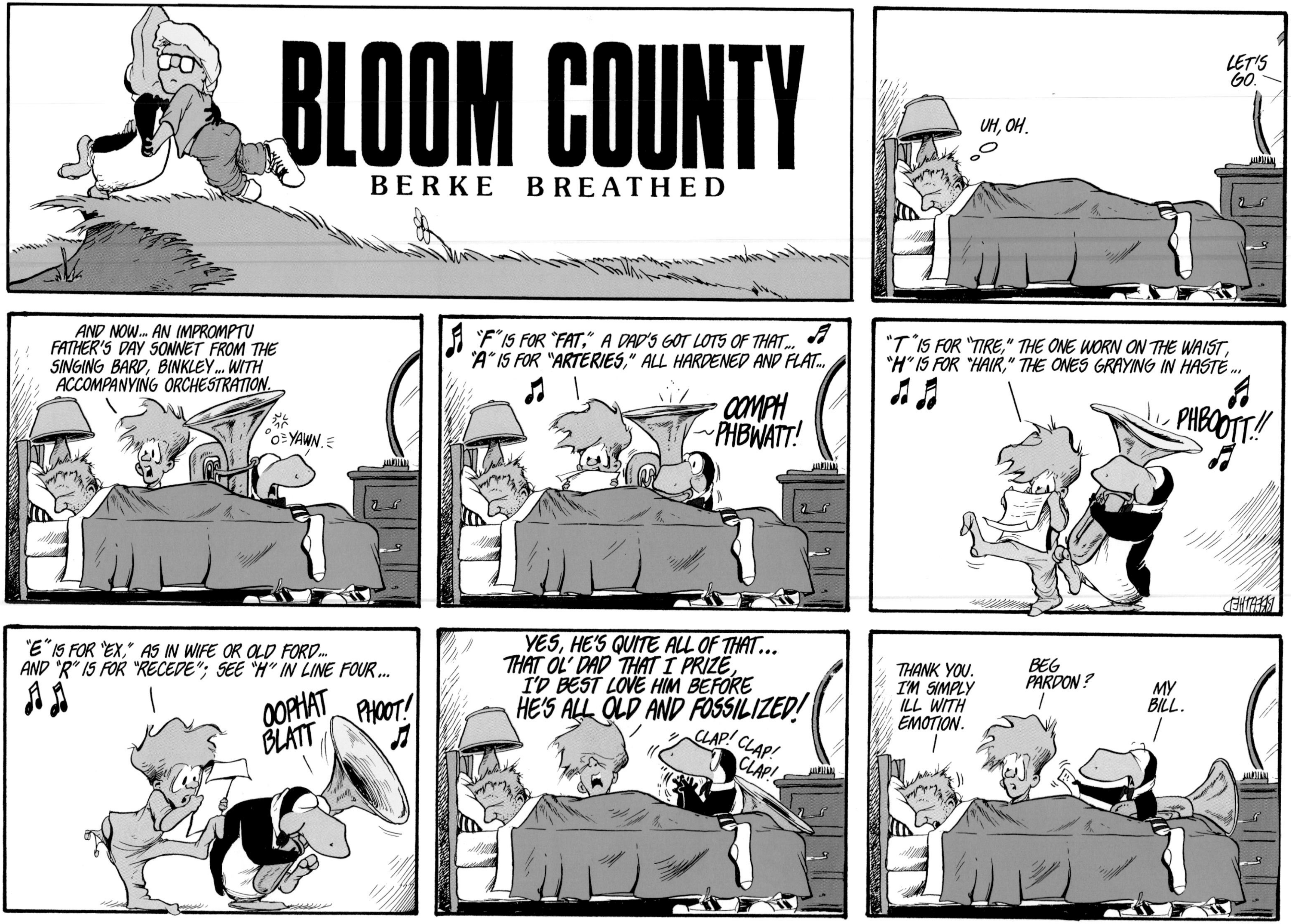
BLOOM COUNTY
BERKE BREATHED
LET'S GO.
UH, OH.
AND NOW... AN IMPROMPTU FATHER'S DAY SONNET FROM THE SINGING BARD, BINKLEY... WITH ACCOMPANYING ORCHESTRATION.
YAWN.
"F" IS FOR "FAT," A DAD'S GOT LOTS OF THAT... "A" IS FOR "ARTERIES," ALL HARDENED AND FLAT...
OOMPH PHBWATT!
"T" IS FOR "TIRE," THE ONE WORN ON THE WAIST, "H" IS FOR "HAIR," THE ONES GRAYING IN HASTE...
PHBOOTT!!
"E" IS FOR "EX," AS IN WIFE OR OLD FORD... AND "R" IS FOR "RECEDE"; SEE "H" IN LINE FOUR...
OOPHAT BLATT
PHOOT!
YES, HE'S QUITE ALL OF THAT... THAT OL' DAD THAT I PRIZE, I'D BEST LOVE HIM BEFORE HE'S ALL OLD AND FOSSILIZED!
CLAP! CLAP! CLAP!
THANK YOU. I'M SIMPLY ILL WITH EMOTION.
BEG PARDON?
MY BILL.

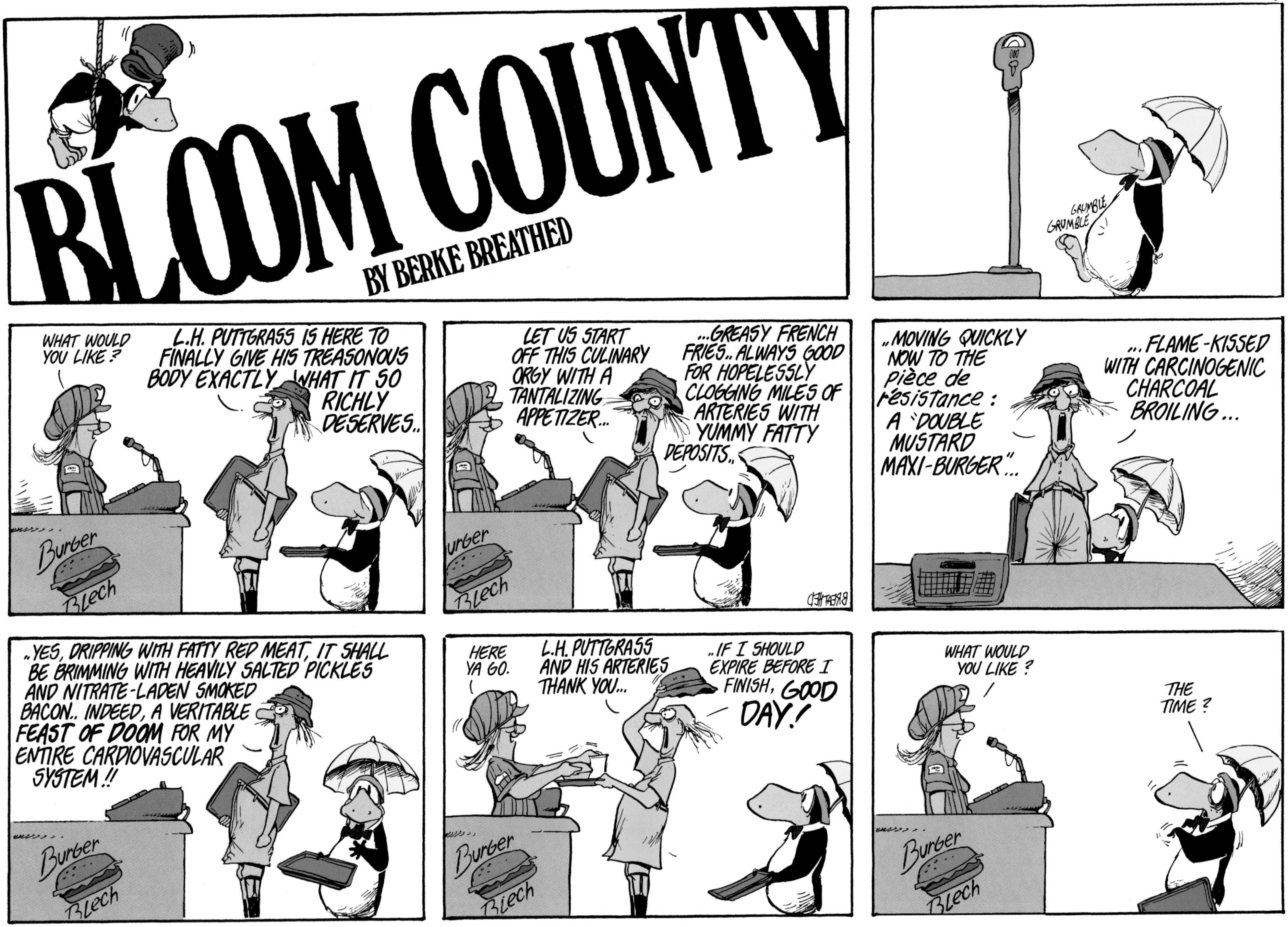
BLOOM COUNTY
BY BERKE BREATHED
GRUMBLE GRUMBLE
WHAT WOULD YOU LIKE?
L.H. PUTTGRASS IS HERE TO FINALLY GIVE HIS TREASONOUS BODY EXACTLY WHAT IT SO RICHLY DESERVES..
Burger Blech
LET US START OFF THIS CULINARY ORGY WITH A TANTALIZING APPETIZER...
...GREASY FRENCH FRIES.. ALWAYS GOOD FOR HOPELESSLY CLOGGING MILES OF ARTERIES WITH YUMMY FATTY DEPOSITS..
..MOVING QUICKLY NOW TO THE pièce de résistance: A "DOUBLE MUSTARD MAXI-BURGER"...
...FLAME-KISSED WITH CARCINOGENIC CHARCOAL BROILING...
..YES, DRIPPING WITH FATTY RED MEAT, IT SHALL BE BRIMMING WITH HEAVILY SALTED PICKLES AND NITRATE-LADEN SMOKED BACON.. INDEED, A VERITABLE **FEAST OF DOOM** FOR MY ENTIRE CARDIOVASCULAR SYSTEM!!
HERE YA GO.
L.H. PUTTGRASS AND HIS ARTERIES THANK YOU...
..IF I SHOULD EXPIRE BEFORE I FINISH, **GOOD DAY!**
WHAT WOULD YOU LIKE?
THE TIME?

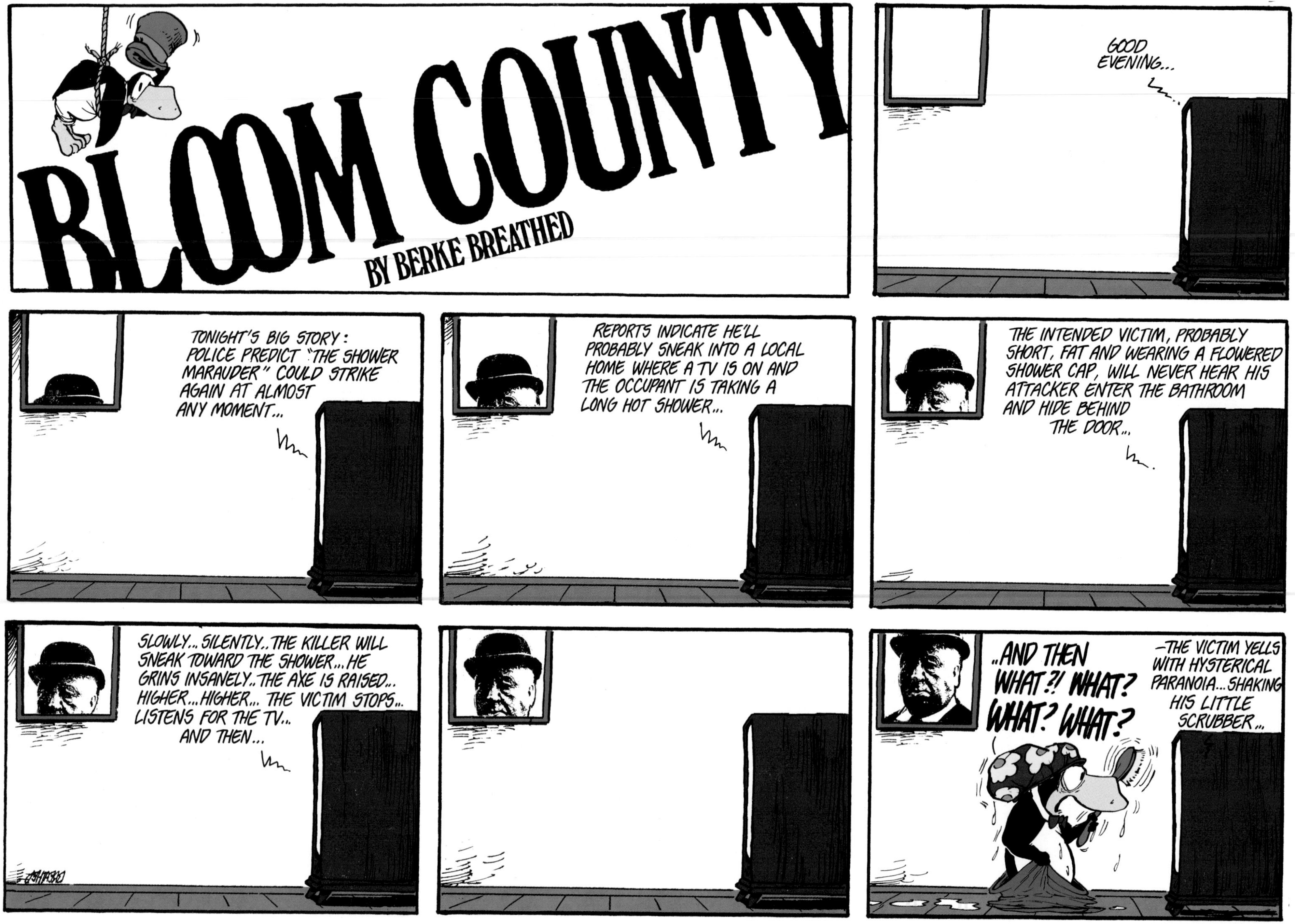
BLOOM COUNTY
BY BERKE BREATHED
GOOD EVENING...
TONIGHT'S BIG STORY: POLICE PREDICT "THE SHOWER MARAUDER" COULD STRIKE AGAIN AT ALMOST ANY MOMENT...
REPORTS INDICATE HE'LL PROBABLY SNEAK INTO A LOCAL HOME WHERE A TV IS ON AND THE OCCUPANT IS TAKING A LONG HOT SHOWER...
THE INTENDED VICTIM, PROBABLY SHORT, FAT AND WEARING A FLOWERED SHOWER CAP, WILL NEVER HEAR HIS ATTACKER ENTER THE BATHROOM AND HIDE BEHIND THE DOOR...
SLOWLY... SILENTLY.. THE KILLER WILL SNEAK TOWARD THE SHOWER... HE GRINS INSANELY.. THE AXE IS RAISED... HIGHER... HIGHER... THE VICTIM STOPS... LISTENS FOR THE TV... AND THEN...
..AND THEN WHAT?! WHAT? WHAT? WHAT?
–THE VICTIM YELLS WITH HYSTERICAL PARANOIA... SHAKING HIS LITTLE SCRUBBER...

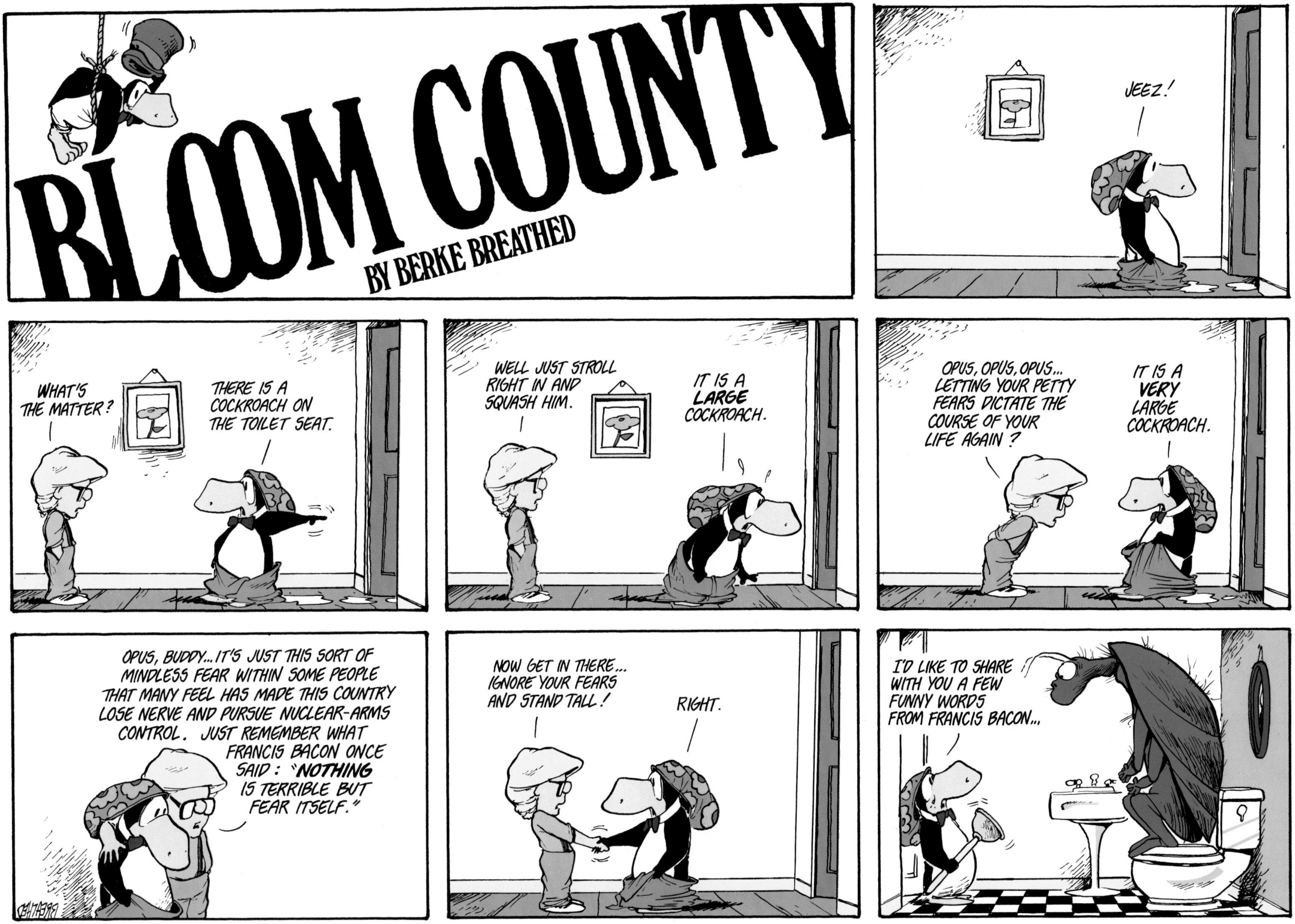
BLOOM COUNTY
BY BERKE BREATHED
JEEZ!
WHAT'S THE MATTER?
THERE IS A COCKROACH ON THE TOILET SEAT.
WELL JUST STROLL RIGHT IN AND SQUASH HIM.
IT IS A LARGE COCKROACH.
OPUS, OPUS, OPUS... LETTING YOUR PETTY FEARS DICTATE THE COURSE OF YOUR LIFE AGAIN?
IT IS A VERY LARGE COCKROACH.
OPUS, BUDDY... IT'S JUST THIS SORT OF MINDLESS FEAR WITHIN SOME PEOPLE THAT MANY FEEL HAS MADE THIS COUNTRY LOSE NERVE AND PURSUE NUCLEAR-ARMS CONTROL. JUST REMEMBER WHAT FRANCIS BACON ONCE SAID: "NOTHING IS TERRIBLE BUT FEAR ITSELF."
BREATHED
NOW GET IN THERE... IGNORE YOUR FEARS AND STAND TALL!
RIGHT.
I'D LIKE TO SHARE WITH YOU A FEW FUNNY WORDS FROM FRANCIS BACON...

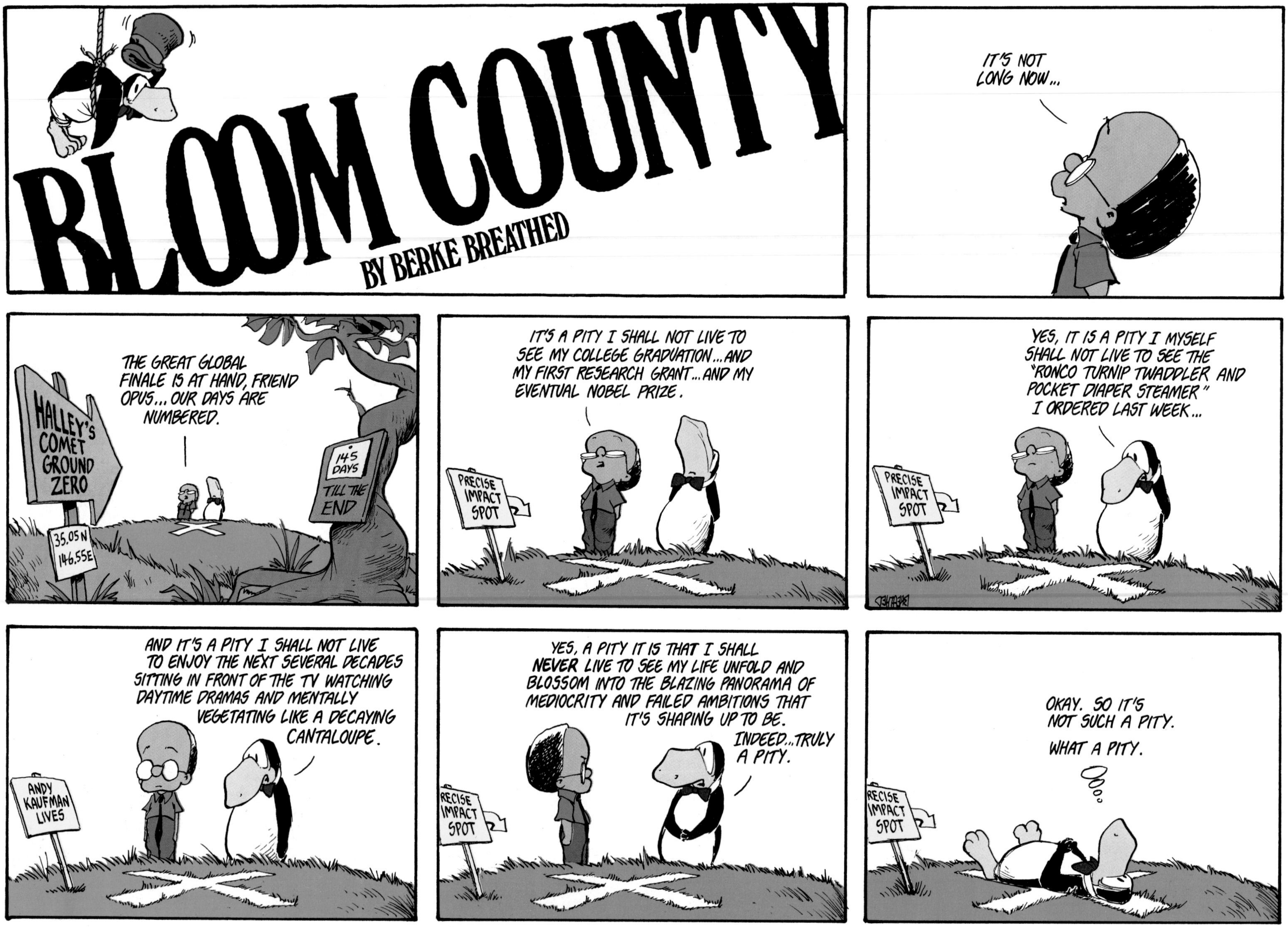
BLOOM COUNTY
BY BERKE BREATHED
IT'S NOT LONG NOW...
HALLEY'S COMET GROUND ZERO
35.05 N 146.55E
145 DAYS TILL THE END
THE GREAT GLOBAL FINALE IS AT HAND, FRIEND OPUS... OUR DAYS ARE NUMBERED.
PRECISE IMPACT SPOT
IT'S A PITY I SHALL NOT LIVE TO SEE MY COLLEGE GRADUATION... AND MY FIRST RESEARCH GRANT... AND MY EVENTUAL NOBEL PRIZE.
YES, IT IS A PITY I MYSELF SHALL NOT LIVE TO SEE THE "RONCO TURNIP TWADDLER AND POCKET DIAPER STEAMER" I ORDERED LAST WEEK...
ANDY KAUFMAN LIVES
AND IT'S A PITY I SHALL NOT LIVE TO ENJOY THE NEXT SEVERAL DECADES SITTING IN FRONT OF THE TV WATCHING DAYTIME DRAMAS AND MENTALLY VEGETATING LIKE A DECAYING CANTALOUPE.
YES, A PITY IT IS THAT I SHALL **NEVER** LIVE TO SEE MY LIFE UNFOLD AND BLOSSOM INTO THE BLAZING PANORAMA OF MEDIOCRITY AND FAILED AMBITIONS THAT IT'S SHAPING UP TO BE.
INDEED...TRULY A PITY.
OKAY. SO IT'S NOT SUCH A PITY.
WHAT A PITY.

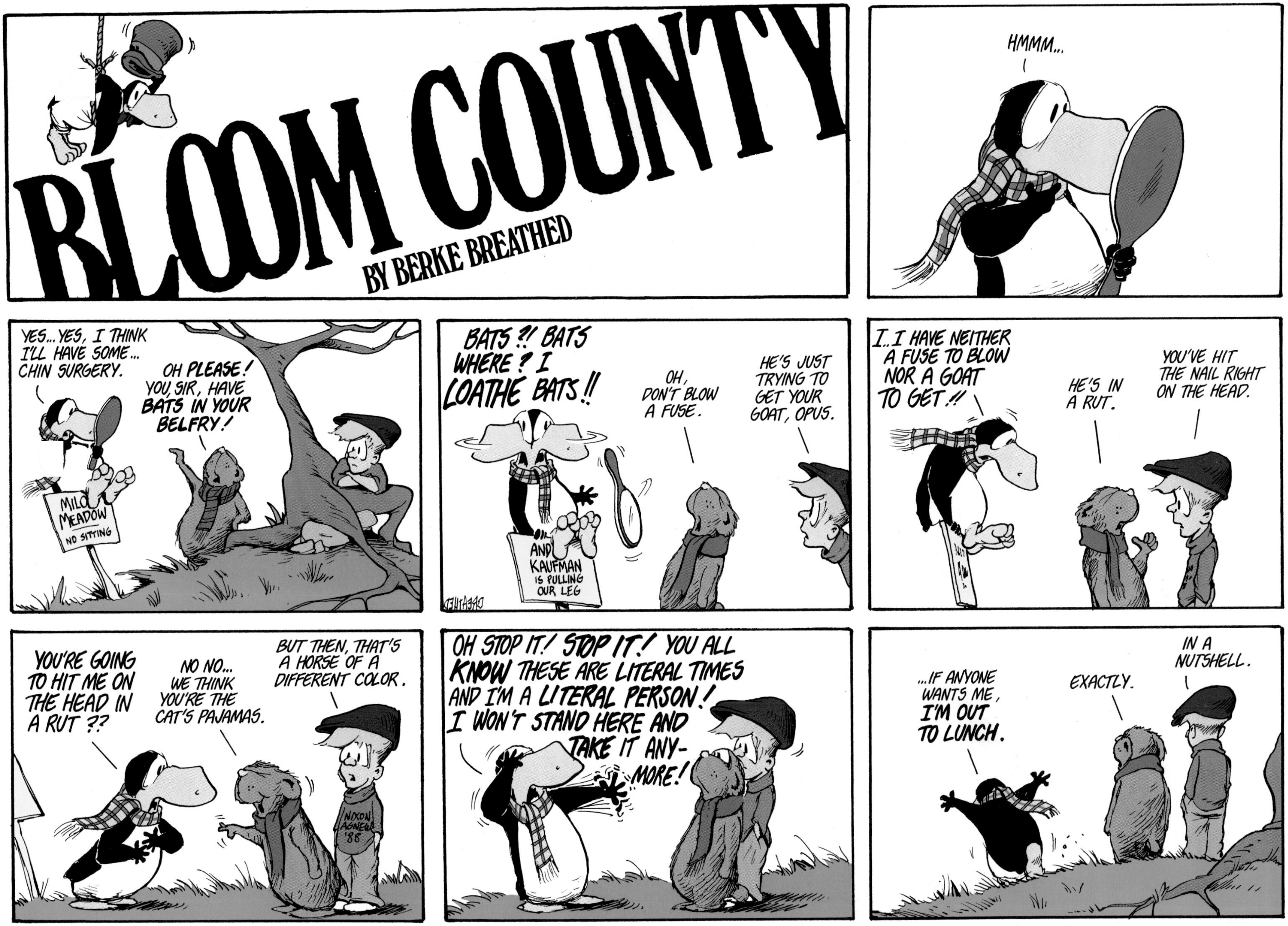
BLOOM COUNTY
BY BERKE BREATHED
HMMM...
YES... YES, I THINK I'LL HAVE SOME... CHIN SURGERY.
OH PLEASE! YOU, SIR, HAVE BATS IN YOUR BELFRY!
MILO MEADOW
NO SITTING
BATS?! BATS WHERE? I LOATHE BATS!!
OH, DON'T BLOW A FUSE.
HE'S JUST TRYING TO GET YOUR GOAT, OPUS.
AND KAUFMAN IS PULLING OUR LEG
I.. I HAVE NEITHER A FUSE TO BLOW NOR A GOAT TO GET!!
HE'S IN A RUT.
YOU'VE HIT THE NAIL RIGHT ON THE HEAD.
YOU'RE GOING TO HIT ME ON THE HEAD IN A RUT??
NO NO... WE THINK YOU'RE THE CAT'S PAJAMAS.
BUT THEN, THAT'S A HORSE OF A DIFFERENT COLOR.
NIXON AGNEW '88
OH STOP IT! STOP IT! YOU ALL KNOW THESE ARE LITERAL TIMES AND I'M A LITERAL PERSON! I WON'T STAND HERE AND TAKE IT ANY-MORE!
...IF ANYONE WANTS ME, I'M OUT TO LUNCH.
EXACTLY.
IN A NUTSHELL.

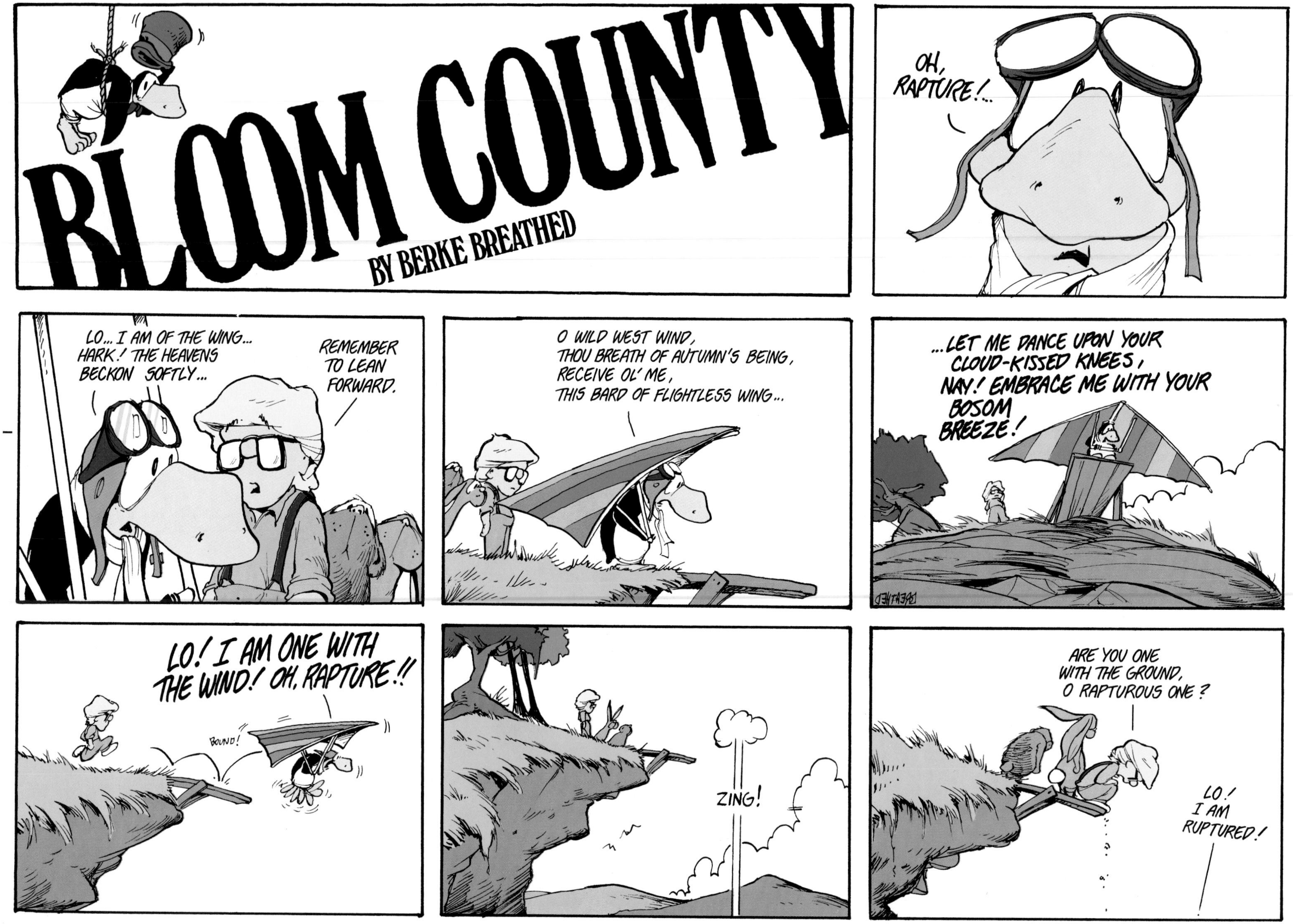
BLOOM COUNTY
BY BERKE BREATHED
OH, RAPTURE!...
LO... I AM OF THE WING... HARK! THE HEAVENS BECKON SOFTLY...
REMEMBER TO LEAN FORWARD.
O WILD WEST WIND, THOU BREATH OF AUTUMN'S BEING, RECEIVE OL' ME, THIS BARD OF FLIGHTLESS WING...
...LET ME DANCE UPON YOUR CLOUD-KISSED KNEES, NAY! EMBRACE ME WITH YOUR BOSOM BREEZE!
LO! I AM ONE WITH THE WIND! OH, RAPTURE!!
BOUND!
ZING!
ARE YOU ONE WITH THE GROUND, O RAPTUROUS ONE?
LO! I AM RUPTURED!

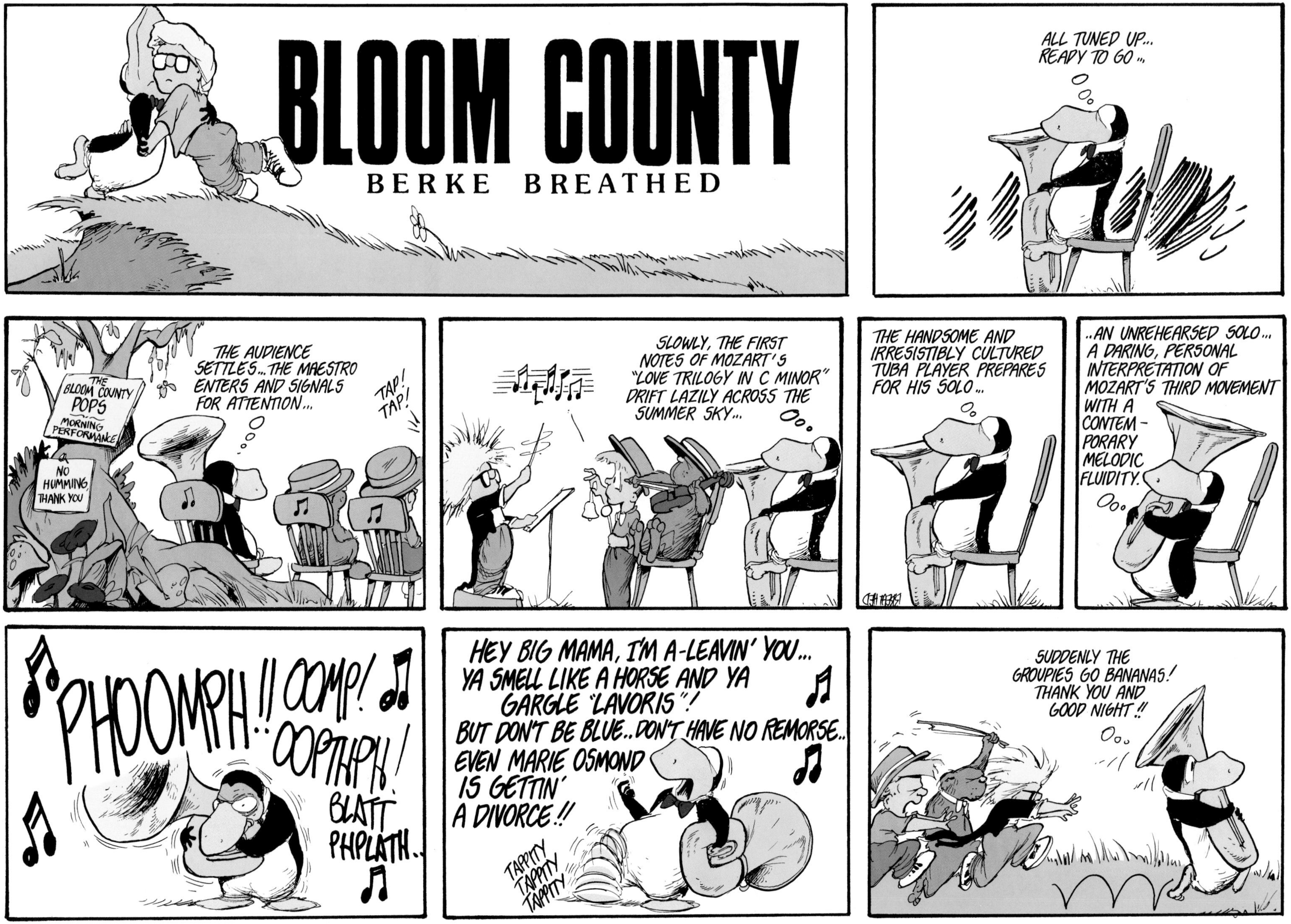
BLOOM COUNTY
BERKE BREATHED
ALL TUNED UP... READY TO GO...
THE AUDIENCE SETTLES... THE MAESTRO ENTERS AND SIGNALS FOR ATTENTION...
THE BLOOM COUNTY POPS
MORNING PERFORMANCE
NO HUMMING THANK YOU
TAP! TAP!
SLOWLY, THE FIRST NOTES OF MOZART'S "LOVE TRILOGY IN C MINOR" DRIFT LAZILY ACROSS THE SUMMER SKY...
THE HANDSOME AND IRRESISTIBLY CULTURED TUBA PLAYER PREPARES FOR HIS SOLO...
..AN UNREHEARSED SOLO... A DARING, PERSONAL INTERPRETATION OF MOZART'S THIRD MOVEMENT WITH A CONTEM-PORARY MELODIC FLUIDITY.
PHOOMPH!! OOMP! OOPTHPH!
BLATT PHPLATH..
HEY BIG MAMA, I'M A-LEAVIN' YOU... YA SMELL LIKE A HORSE AND YA GARGLE "LAVORIS"!
BUT DON'T BE BLUE.. DON'T HAVE NO REMORSE..
EVEN MARIE OSMOND IS GETTIN' A DIVORCE!!
TAPPITY TAPPITY TAPPITY
SUDDENLY THE GROUPIES GO BANANAS! THANK YOU AND GOOD NIGHT!!

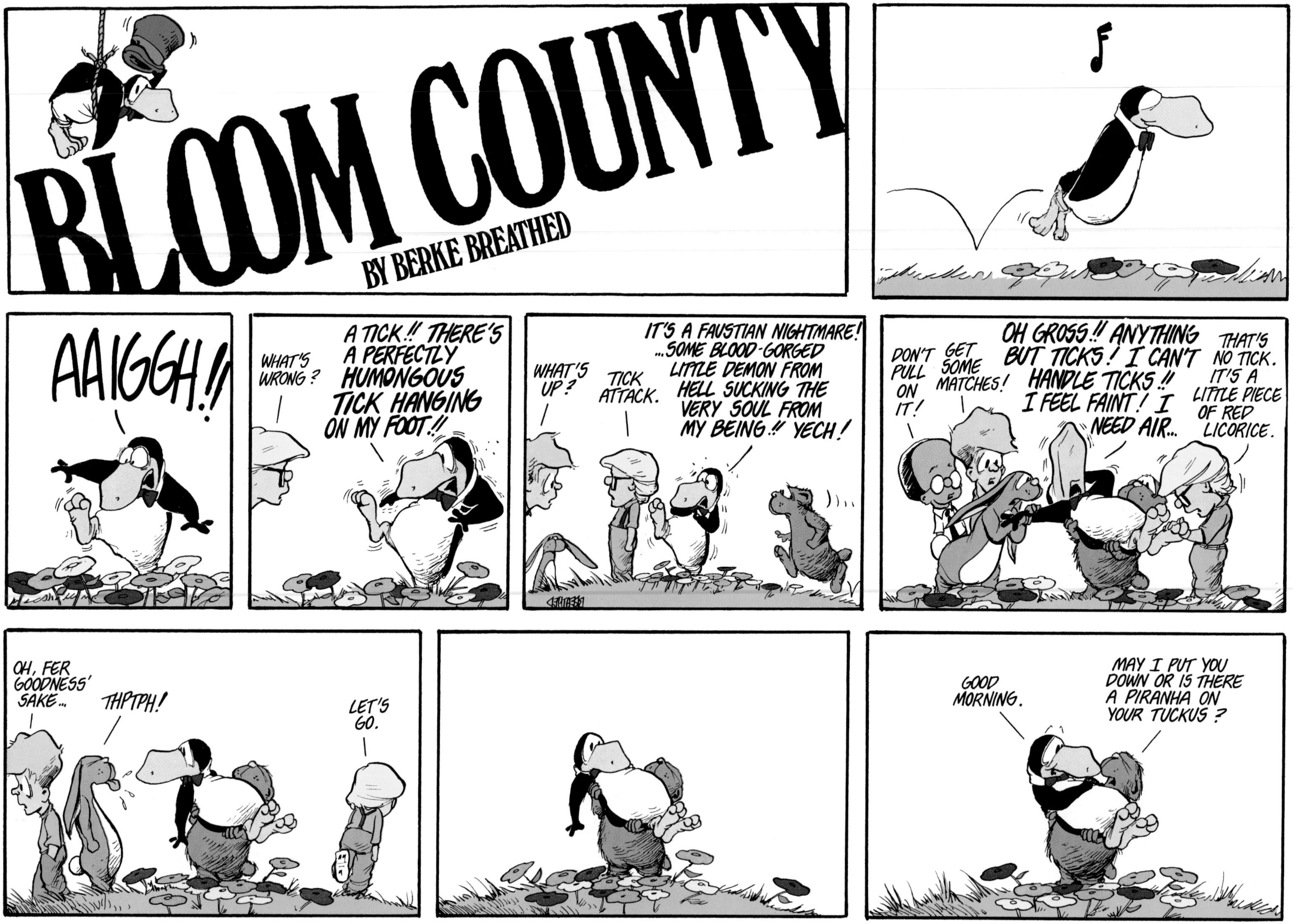
BLOOM COUNTY
BY BERKE BREATHED
AAIGGH!!
WHAT'S WRONG?
A TICK!! THERE'S A PERFECTLY HUMONGOUS TICK HANGING ON MY FOOT!!
WHAT'S UP?
TICK ATTACK.
IT'S A FAUSTIAN NIGHTMARE! ...SOME BLOOD-GORGED LITTLE DEMON FROM HELL SUCKING THE VERY SOUL FROM MY BEING!! YECH!
DON'T PULL ON IT!
GET SOME MATCHES!
OH GROSS!! ANYTHING BUT TICKS! I CAN'T HANDLE TICKS!! I FEEL FAINT! I NEED AIR...
THAT'S NO TICK. IT'S A LITTLE PIECE OF RED LICORICE.
OH, FER GOODNESS' SAKE...
THPTPH!
LET'S GO.
GOOD MORNING.
MAY I PUT YOU DOWN OR IS THERE A PIRANHA ON YOUR TUCKUS?

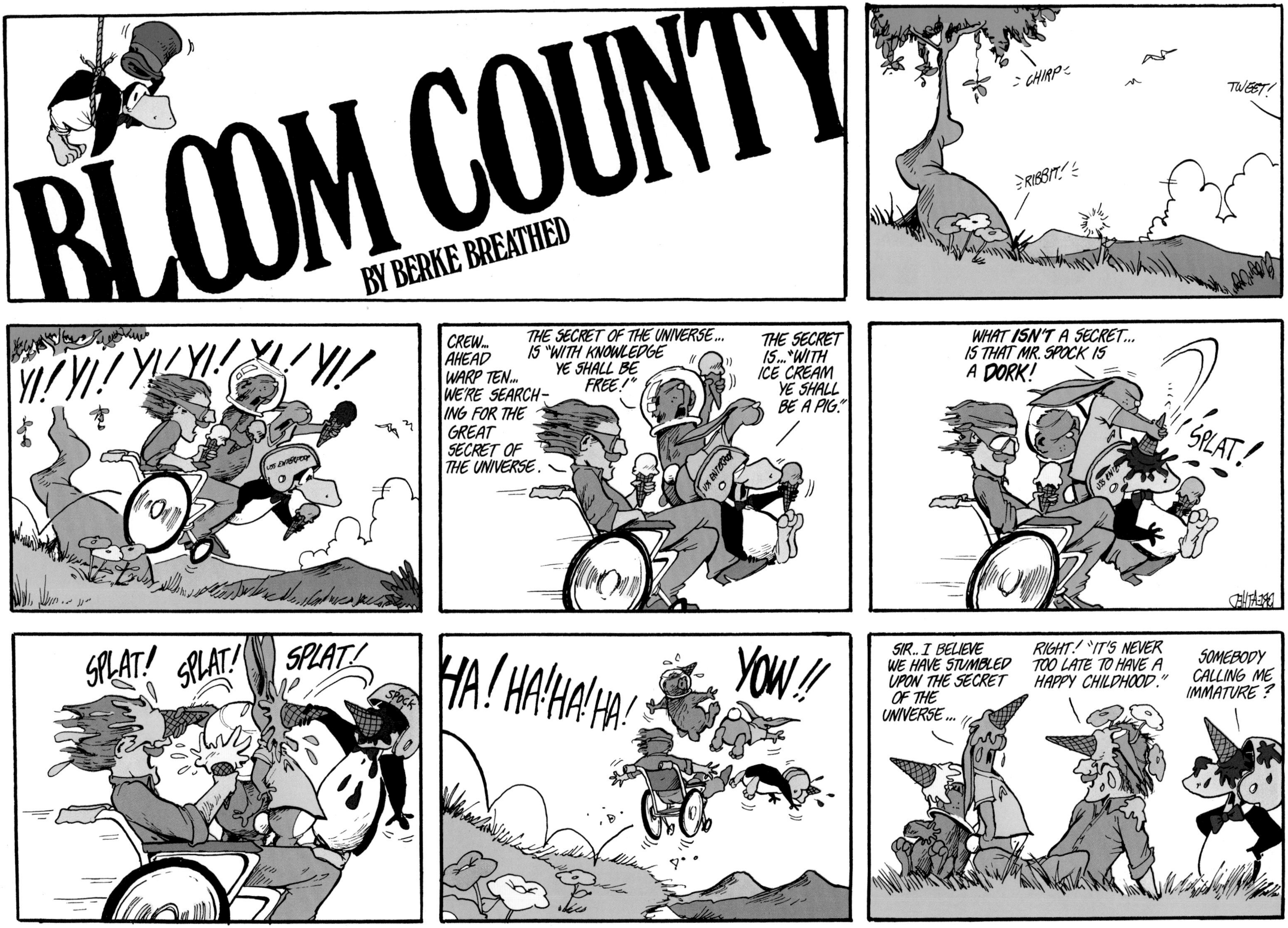
BLOOM COUNTY
BY BERKE BREATHED
CHIRP
TWEET!
RIBBIT!
YI! YI! YI! YI! YI! YI!
USS ENTERPRISE
CREW... AHEAD WARP TEN... WE'RE SEARCHING FOR THE GREAT SECRET OF THE UNIVERSE.
THE SECRET OF THE UNIVERSE... IS "WITH KNOWLEDGE YE SHALL BE FREE!"
THE SECRET IS... "WITH ICE CREAM YE SHALL BE A PIG."
WHAT ISN'T A SECRET... IS THAT MR. SPOCK IS A DORK!
SPLAT!
SPLAT!
SPLAT!
SPLAT!
SPOCK
HA! HA! HA! HA!
YOW!!
SIR.. I BELIEVE WE HAVE STUMBLED UPON THE SECRET OF THE UNIVERSE...
RIGHT! "IT'S NEVER TOO LATE TO HAVE A HAPPY CHILDHOOD."
SOMEBODY CALLING ME IMMATURE?

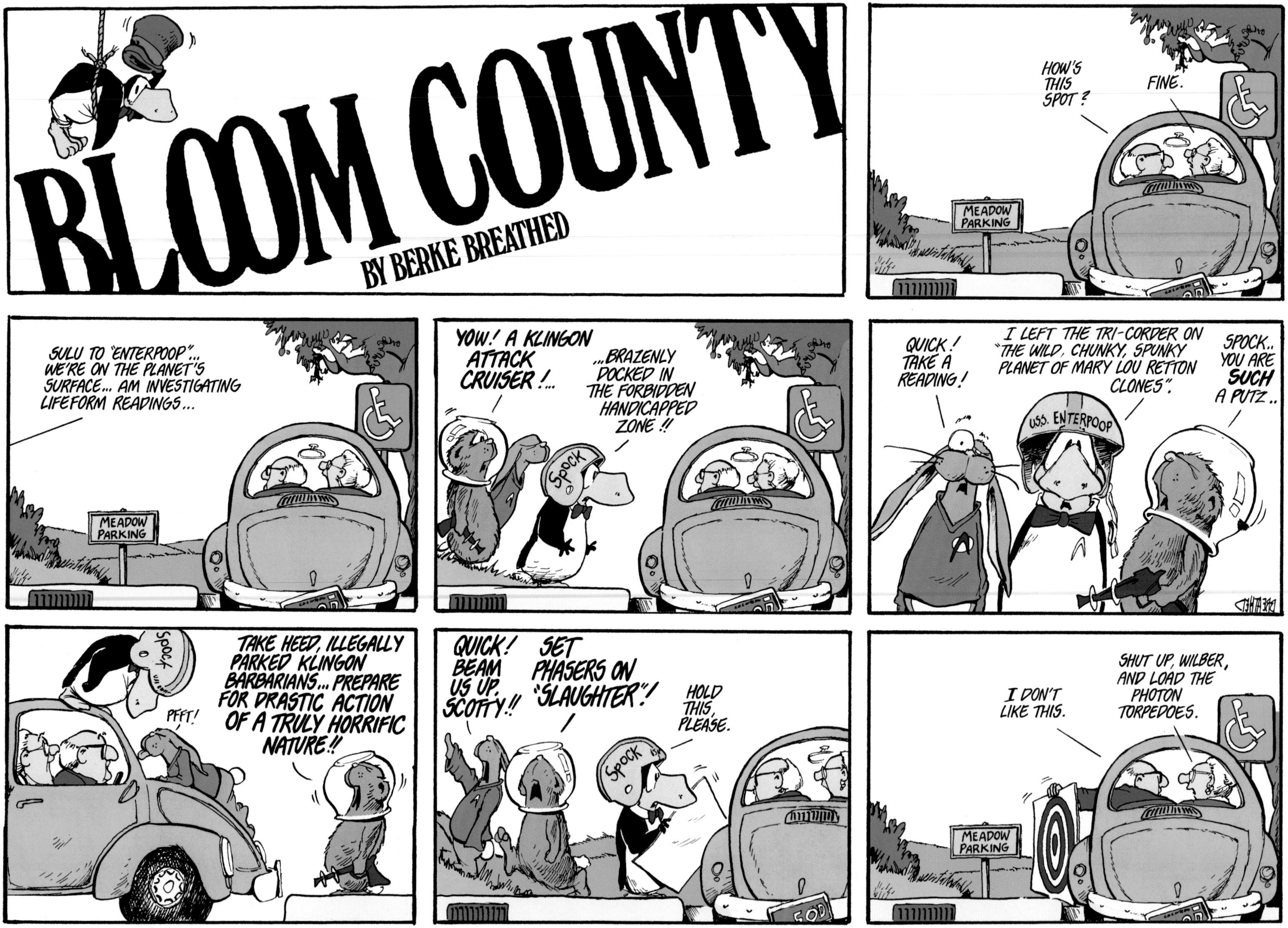
BLOOM COUNTY
BY BERKE BREATHED
HOW'S THIS SPOT?
FINE.
MEADOW PARKING
SULU TO "ENTERPOOP"... WE'RE ON THE PLANET'S SURFACE... AM INVESTIGATING LIFEFORM READINGS...
MEADOW PARKING
YOW! A KLINGON ATTACK CRUISER!...
...BRAZENLY DOCKED IN THE FORBIDDEN HANDICAPPED ZONE!!
Spock
QUICK! TAKE A READING!
I LEFT THE TRI-CORDER ON "THE WILD, CHUNKY, SPUNKY PLANET OF MARY LOU RETTON CLONES".
SPOCK.. YOU ARE SUCH A PUTZ..
U.S.S. ENTERPOOP
SPOCK
PFFT!
TAKE HEED, ILLEGALLY PARKED KLINGON BARBARIANS... PREPARE FOR DRASTIC ACTION OF A TRULY HORRIFIC NATURE!!
QUICK! BEAM US UP, SCOTTY!!
SET PHASERS ON "SLAUGHTER"!
HOLD THIS, PLEASE.
Spock
I DON'T LIKE THIS.
SHUT UP, WILBER, AND LOAD THE PHOTON TORPEDOES.
MEADOW PARKING

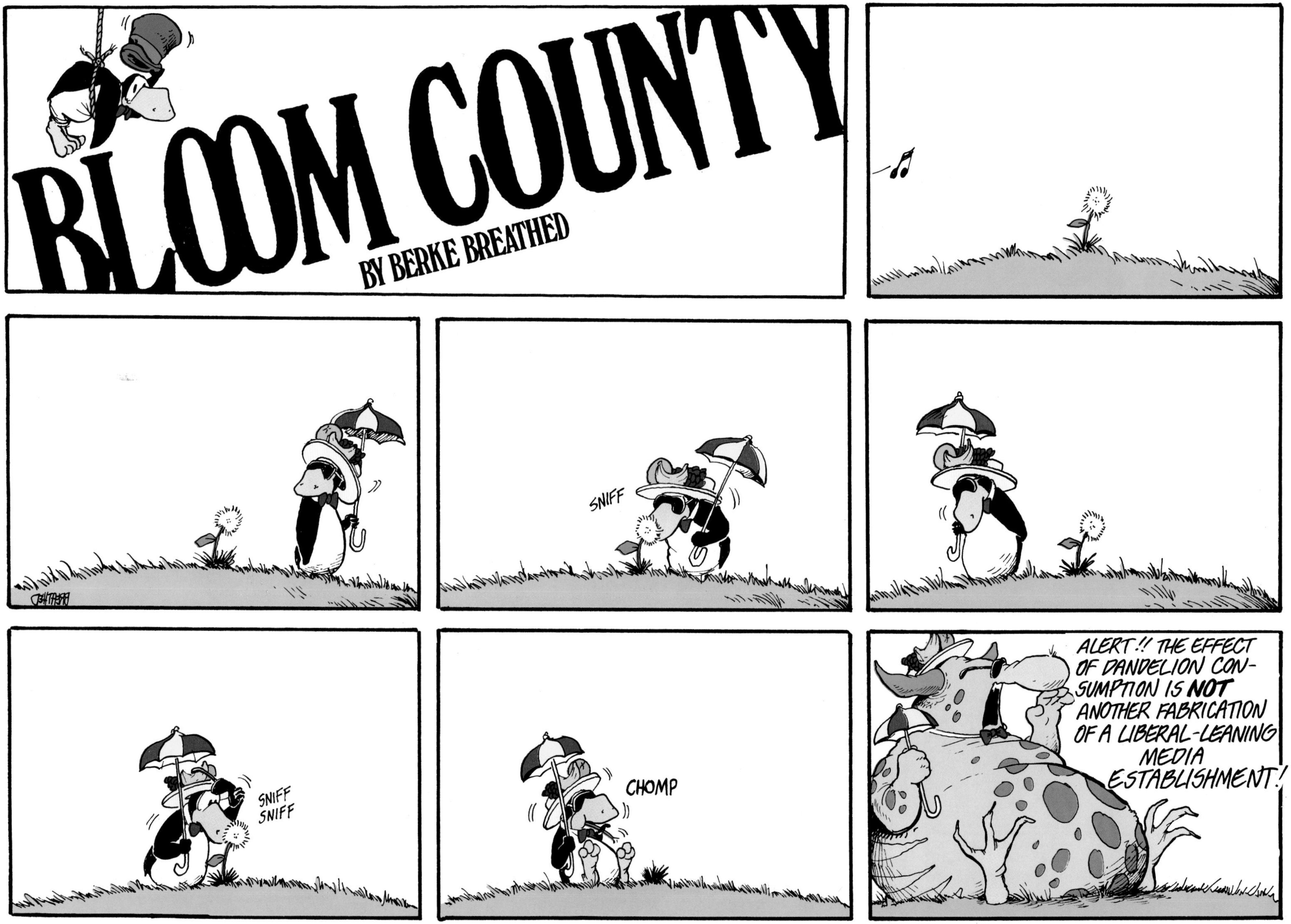

BLOOM COUNTY
BY BERKE BREATHED
SNIFF
SNIFF
SNIFF
CHOMP
ALERT !! THE EFFECT OF DANDELION CON-SUMPTION IS **NOT** ANOTHER FABRICATION OF A LIBERAL-LEANING MEDIA ESTABLISHMENT !

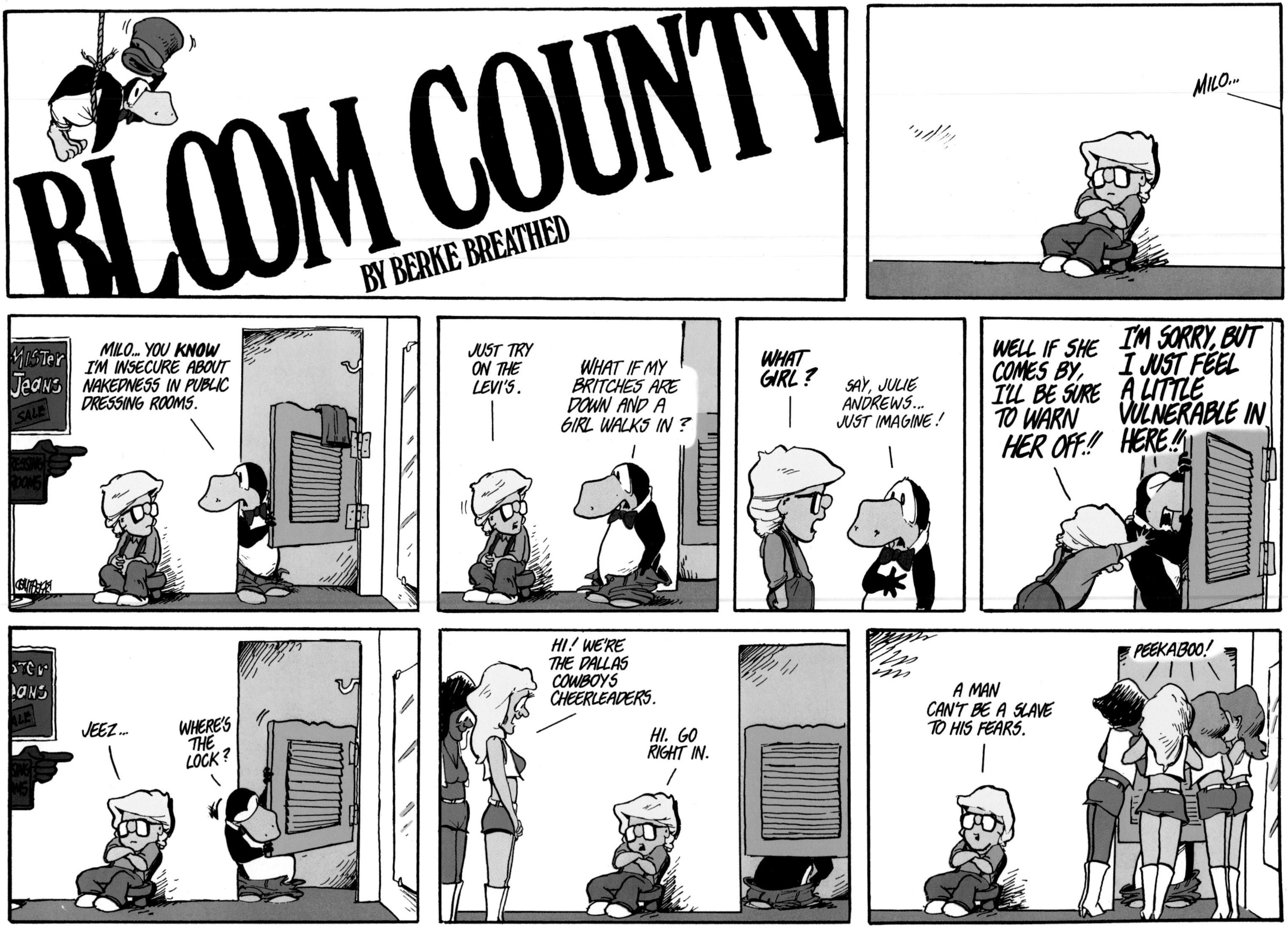
BLOOM COUNTY
BY BERKE BREATHED
MILO...
Mister Jeans
SALE
DRESSING ROOMS
MILO... YOU KNOW I'M INSECURE ABOUT NAKEDNESS IN PUBLIC DRESSING ROOMS.
JUST TRY ON THE LEVI'S.
WHAT IF MY BRITCHES ARE DOWN AND A GIRL WALKS IN ?
WHAT GIRL ?
SAY, JULIE ANDREWS... JUST IMAGINE !
WELL IF SHE COMES BY, I'LL BE SURE TO WARN HER OFF!!
I'M SORRY, BUT I JUST FEEL A LITTLE VULNERABLE IN HERE!!
JEEZ...
WHERE'S THE LOCK ?
HI! WE'RE THE DALLAS COWBOYS CHEERLEADERS.
HI. GO RIGHT IN.
A MAN CAN'T BE A SLAVE TO HIS FEARS.
PEEKABOO!

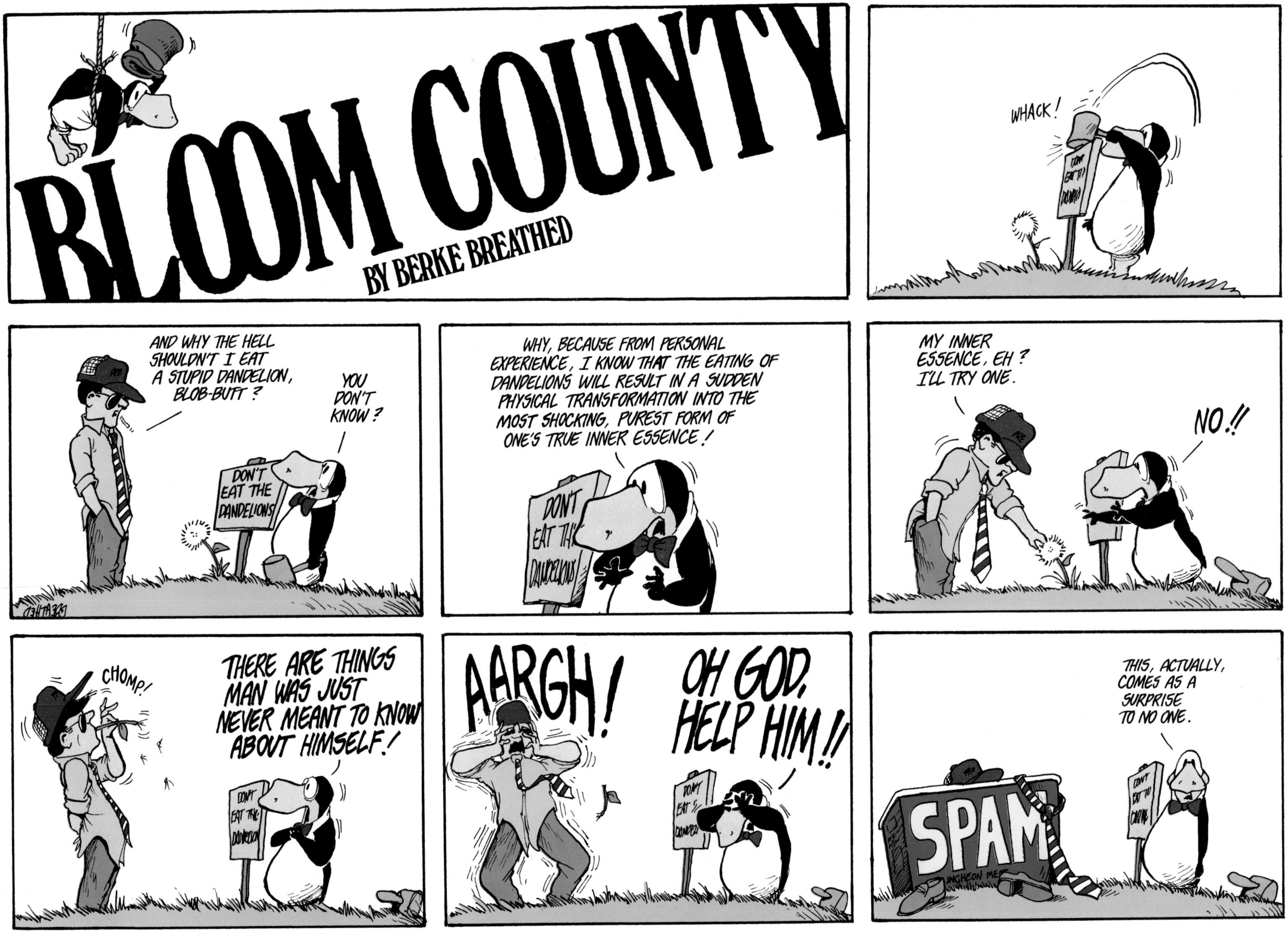
BLOOM COUNTY
BY BERKE BREATHED
WHACK!
AND WHY THE HELL SHOULDN'T I EAT A STUPID DANDELION, BLOB-BUTT?
YOU DON'T KNOW?
DON'T EAT THE DANDELIONS
WHY, BECAUSE FROM PERSONAL EXPERIENCE, I KNOW THAT THE EATING OF DANDELIONS WILL RESULT IN A SUDDEN PHYSICAL TRANSFORMATION INTO THE MOST SHOCKING, PUREST FORM OF ONE'S TRUE INNER ESSENCE!
MY INNER ESSENCE, EH? I'LL TRY ONE.
NO!!
CHOMP!
THERE ARE THINGS MAN WAS JUST NEVER MEANT TO KNOW ABOUT HIMSELF!
AARGH!
OH GOD, HELP HIM!!
THIS, ACTUALLY, COMES AS A SURPRISE TO NO ONE.
SPAM

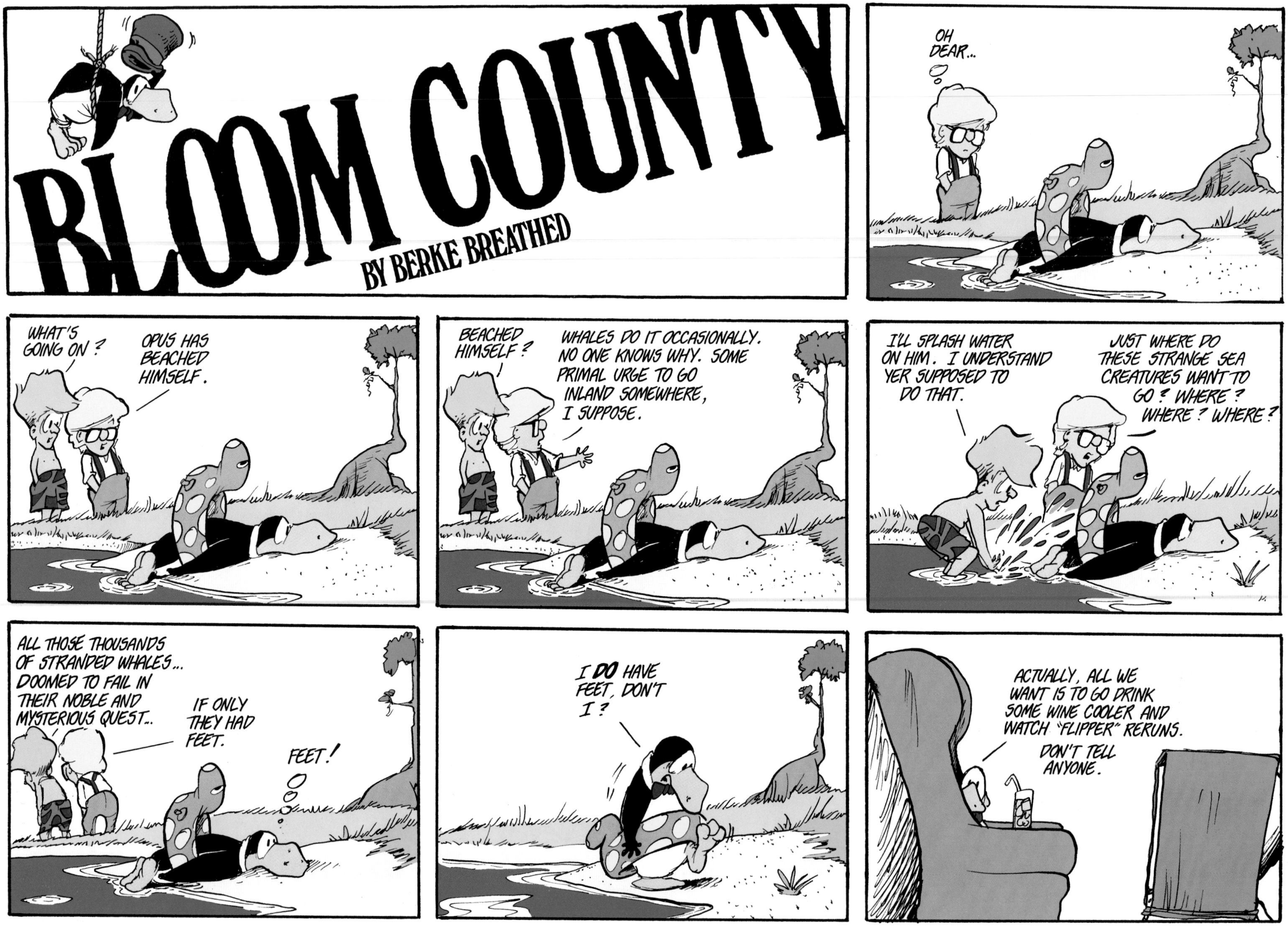
BLOOM COUNTY
BY BERKE BREATHED
OH DEAR...
WHAT'S GOING ON ?
OPUS HAS BEACHED HIMSELF.
BEACHED HIMSELF ?
WHALES DO IT OCCASIONALLY. NO ONE KNOWS WHY. SOME PRIMAL URGE TO GO INLAND SOMEWHERE, I SUPPOSE.
I'LL SPLASH WATER ON HIM. I UNDERSTAND YER SUPPOSED TO DO THAT.
JUST WHERE DO THESE STRANGE SEA CREATURES WANT TO GO ? WHERE ? WHERE ? WHERE ?
ALL THOSE THOUSANDS OF STRANDED WHALES... DOOMED TO FAIL IN THEIR NOBLE AND MYSTERIOUS QUEST...
IF ONLY THEY HAD FEET.
FEET !
I DO HAVE FEET, DON'T I ?
ACTUALLY, ALL WE WANT IS TO GO DRINK SOME WINE COOLER AND WATCH "FLIPPER" RERUNS.
DON'T TELL ANYONE.

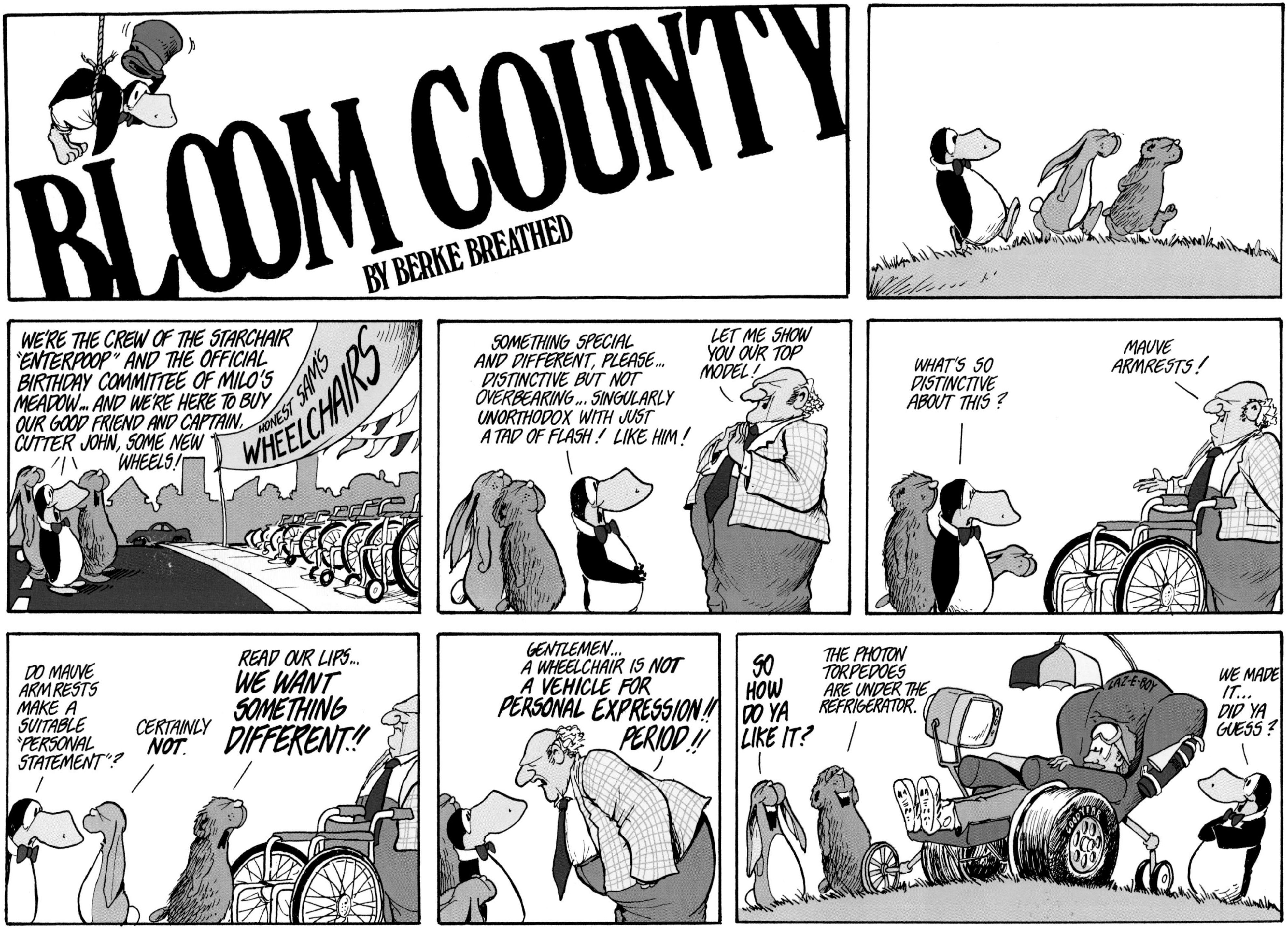
BLOOM COUNTY
BY BERKE BREATHED
WE'RE THE CREW OF THE STARCHAIR "ENTERPOOP" AND THE OFFICIAL BIRTHDAY COMMITTEE OF MILO'S MEADOW... AND WE'RE HERE TO BUY OUR GOOD FRIEND AND CAPTAIN, CUTTER JOHN, SOME NEW WHEELS!
HONEST SAM'S WHEELCHAIRS
SOMETHING SPECIAL AND DIFFERENT, PLEASE... DISTINCTIVE BUT NOT OVERBEARING... SINGULARLY UNORTHODOX WITH JUST A TAD OF FLASH! LIKE HIM!
LET ME SHOW YOU OUR TOP MODEL!
WHAT'S SO DISTINCTIVE ABOUT THIS?
MAUVE ARMRESTS!
DO MAUVE ARMRESTS MAKE A SUITABLE "PERSONAL STATEMENT"?
CERTAINLY NOT.
READ OUR LIPS... WE WANT SOMETHING DIFFERENT!!
GENTLEMEN... A WHEELCHAIR IS NOT A VEHICLE FOR PERSONAL EXPRESSION!! PERIOD!!
SO HOW DO YA LIKE IT?
THE PHOTON TORPEDOES ARE UNDER THE REFRIGERATOR.
WE MADE IT... DID YA GUESS?
LAZ-E-BOY
GOODYEAR

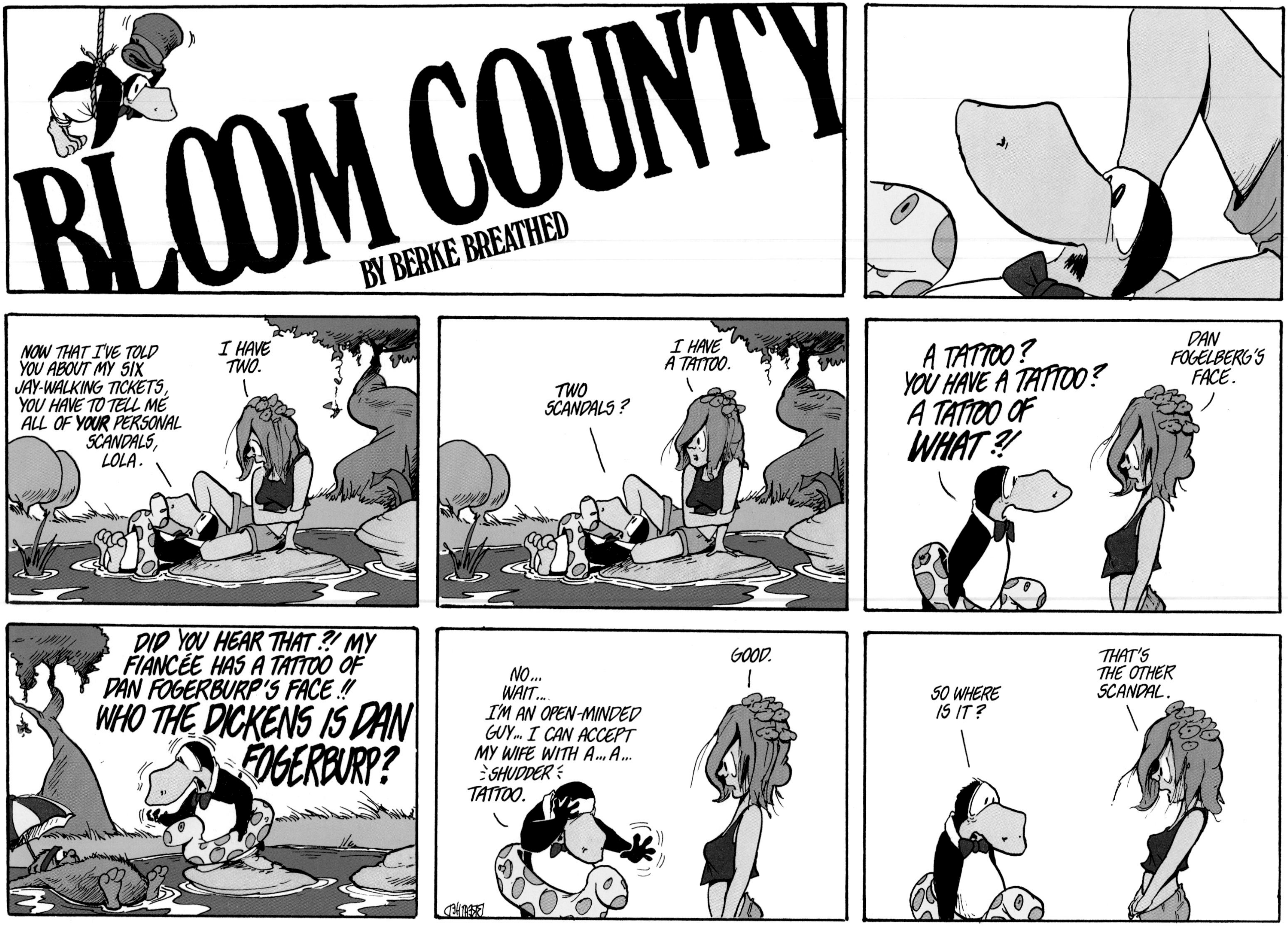
BLOOM COUNTY
BY BERKE BREATHED
NOW THAT I'VE TOLD YOU ABOUT MY SIX JAY-WALKING TICKETS, YOU HAVE TO TELL ME ALL OF YOUR PERSONAL SCANDALS, LOLA.
I HAVE TWO.
TWO SCANDALS?
I HAVE A TATTOO.
A TATTOO? YOU HAVE A TATTOO? A TATTOO OF WHAT?!
DAN FOGELBERG'S FACE.
DID YOU HEAR THAT?! MY FIANCÉE HAS A TATTOO OF DAN FOGERBURP'S FACE!!
WHO THE DICKENS IS DAN FOGERBURP?
NO... WAIT... I'M AN OPEN-MINDED GUY... I CAN ACCEPT MY WIFE WITH A... A... SHUDDER TATTOO.
GOOD.
SO WHERE IS IT?
THAT'S THE OTHER SCANDAL.

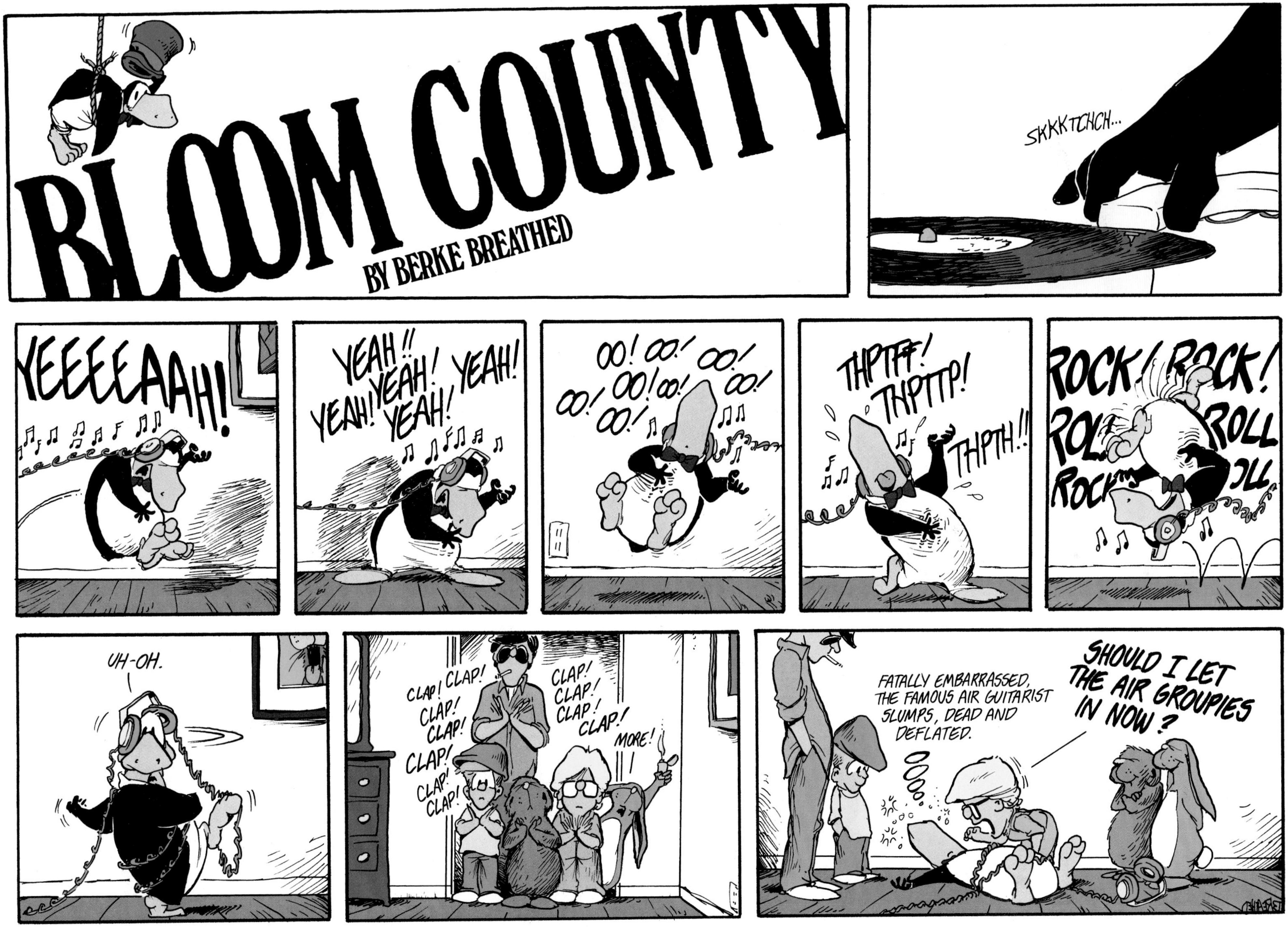
BLOOM COUNTY
BY BERKE BREATHED
SKKKTCHCH...
YEEEEAAH!
YEAH!! YEAH! YEAH! YEAH! YEAH! YEAH!
OO! OO! OO! OO! OO! OO! OO! OO! OO!
THPTFF! THPTTP! THPTH!!
ROCK! ROCK! ROLL ROLL ROCK ROLL
UH-OH.
CLAP! CLAP! CLAP! CLAP! CLAP! CLAP! CLAP!
CLAP! CLAP! CLAP! CLAP!
MORE!
FATALLY EMBARRASSED, THE FAMOUS AIR GUITARIST SLUMPS, DEAD AND DEFLATED.
SHOULD I LET THE AIR GROUPIES IN NOW?

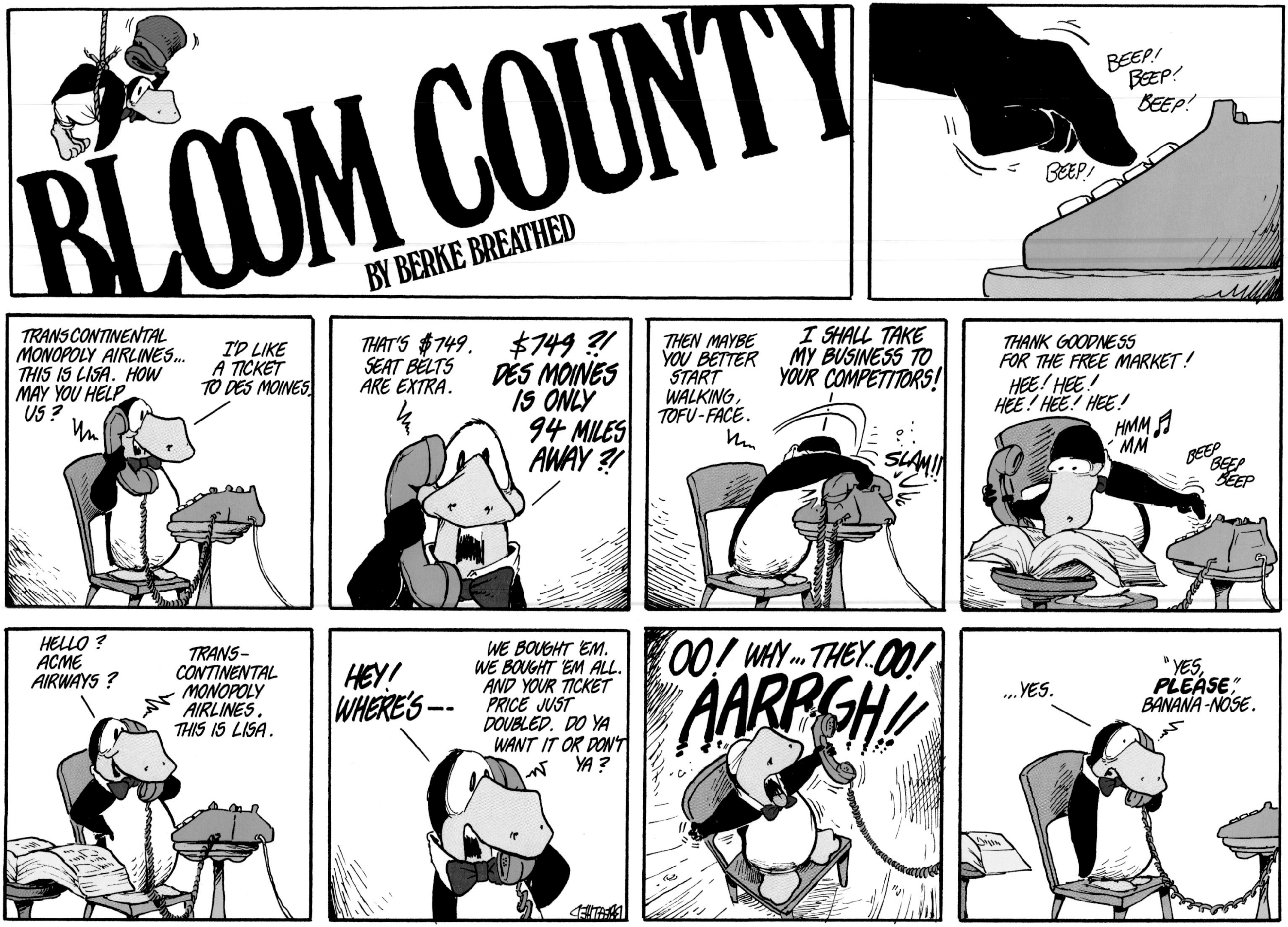
BLOOM COUNTY
BY BERKE BREATHED
BEEP! BEEP! BEEP!
BEEP!
TRANSCONTINENTAL MONOPOLY AIRLINES... THIS IS LISA. HOW MAY YOU HELP US?
I'D LIKE A TICKET TO DES MOINES.
THAT'S $749. SEAT BELTS ARE EXTRA.
$749 ?! DES MOINES IS ONLY 94 MILES AWAY ?!
THEN MAYBE YOU BETTER START WALKING, TOFU-FACE.
I SHALL TAKE MY BUSINESS TO YOUR COMPETITORS!
SLAM!!
THANK GOODNESS FOR THE FREE MARKET!
HEE! HEE! HEE! HEE! HEE!
HMM MM
BEEP BEEP BEEP
HELLO? ACME AIRWAYS?
TRANS-CONTINENTAL MONOPOLY AIRLINES. THIS IS LISA.
HEY! WHERE'S --
WE BOUGHT 'EM. WE BOUGHT 'EM ALL. AND YOUR TICKET PRICE JUST DOUBLED. DO YA WANT IT OR DON'T YA?
OO! WHY... THEY.. OO! AARRGH!!
...YES.
"YES, PLEASE," BANANA-NOSE.

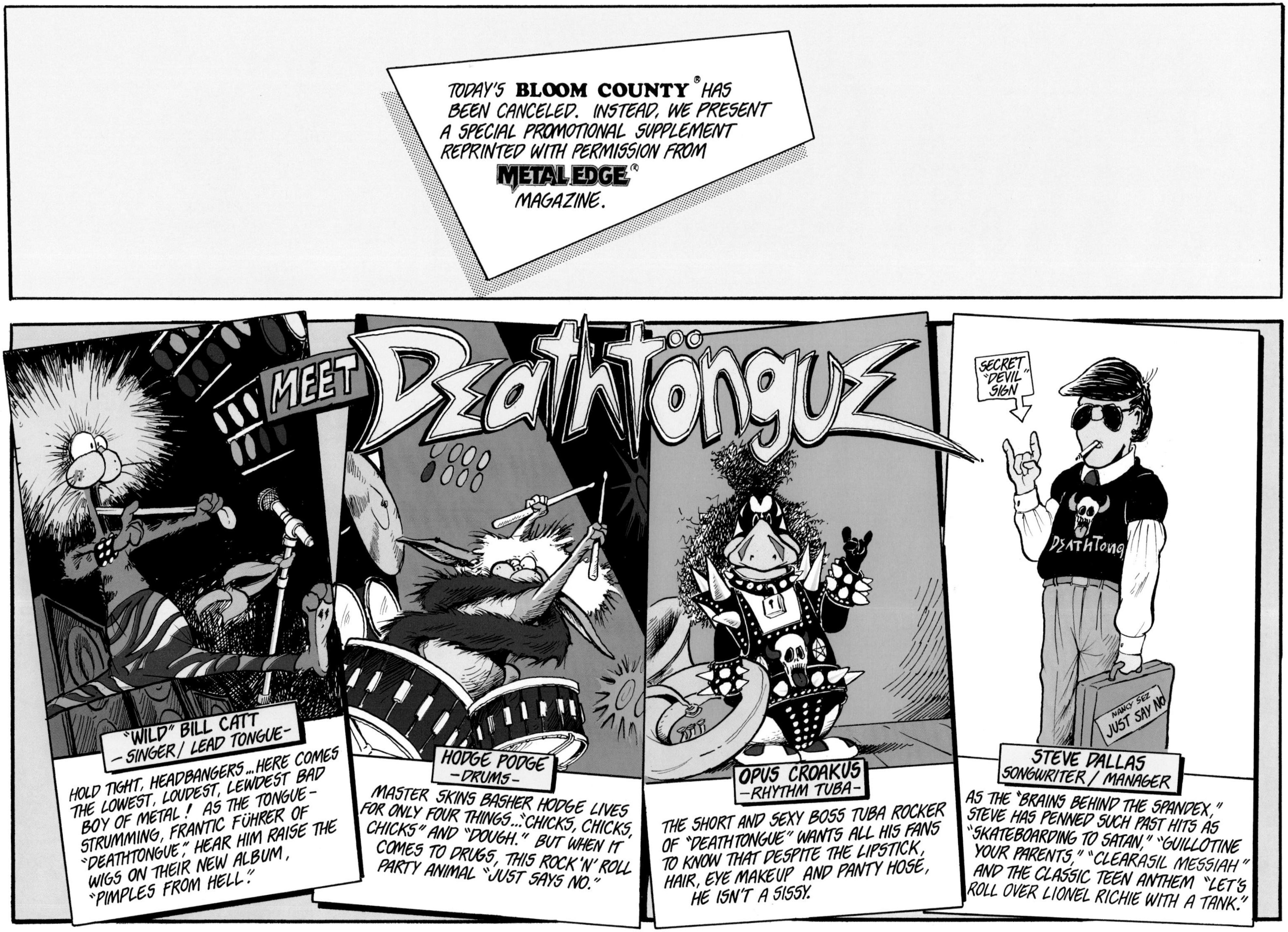
TODAY'S BLOOM COUNTY® HAS BEEN CANCELED. INSTEAD, WE PRESENT A SPECIAL PROMOTIONAL SUPPLEMENT REPRINTED WITH PERMISSION FROM METAL EDGE® MAGAZINE.
MEET DEATHTÖNGUE
"WILD" BILL CATT
-SINGER/ LEAD TONGUE-
HOLD TIGHT, HEADBANGERS...HERE COMES THE LOWEST, LOUDEST, LEWDEST BAD BOY OF METAL! AS THE TONGUE-STRUMMING, FRANTIC FÜHRER OF "DEATHTONGUE," HEAR HIM RAISE THE WIGS ON THEIR NEW ALBUM, "PIMPLES FROM HELL."
HODGE PODGE
-DRUMS-
MASTER SKINS BASHER HODGE LIVES FOR ONLY FOUR THINGS..."CHICKS, CHICKS, CHICKS" AND "DOUGH." BUT WHEN IT COMES TO DRUGS, THIS ROCK'N' ROLL PARTY ANIMAL "JUST SAYS NO."
OPUS CROAKUS
-RHYTHM TUBA-
THE SHORT AND SEXY BOSS TUBA ROCKER OF "DEATHTONGUE" WANTS ALL HIS FANS TO KNOW THAT DESPITE THE LIPSTICK, HAIR, EYE MAKEUP AND PANTY HOSE, HE ISN'T A SISSY.
SECRET "DEVIL" SIGN
DEATHTONG
NANCY SEZ JUST SAY NO
STEVE DALLAS
SONGWRITER / MANAGER
AS THE "BRAINS BEHIND THE SPANDEX," STEVE HAS PENNED SUCH PAST HITS AS "SKATEBOARDING TO SATAN," "GUILLOTINE YOUR PARENTS," "CLEARASIL MESSIAH" AND THE CLASSIC TEEN ANTHEM "LET'S ROLL OVER LIONEL RICHIE WITH A TANK."

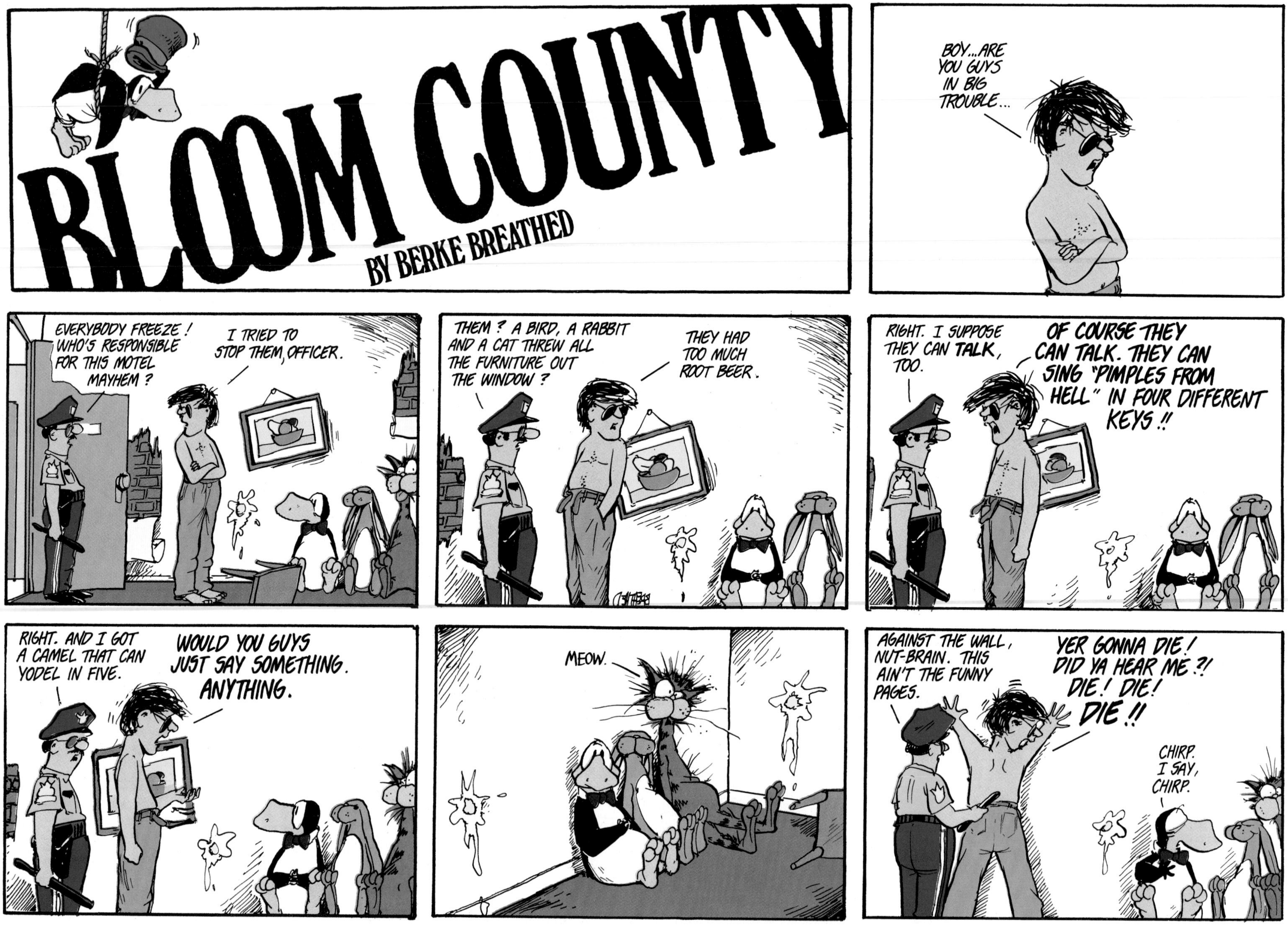
BLOOM COUNTY
BY BERKE BREATHED
BOY...ARE YOU GUYS IN BIG TROUBLE...
EVERYBODY FREEZE! WHO'S RESPONSIBLE FOR THIS MOTEL MAYHEM?
I TRIED TO STOP THEM, OFFICER.
THEM? A BIRD, A RABBIT AND A CAT THREW ALL THE FURNITURE OUT THE WINDOW?
THEY HAD TOO MUCH ROOT BEER.
RIGHT. I SUPPOSE THEY CAN TALK, TOO.
OF COURSE THEY CAN TALK. THEY CAN SING "PIMPLES FROM HELL" IN FOUR DIFFERENT KEYS!!
RIGHT. AND I GOT A CAMEL THAT CAN YODEL IN FIVE.
WOULD YOU GUYS JUST SAY SOMETHING. ANYTHING.
MEOW.
AGAINST THE WALL, NUT-BRAIN. THIS AIN'T THE FUNNY PAGES.
YER GONNA DIE! DID YA HEAR ME?! DIE! DIE! DIE!!
CHIRP. I SAY, CHIRP.

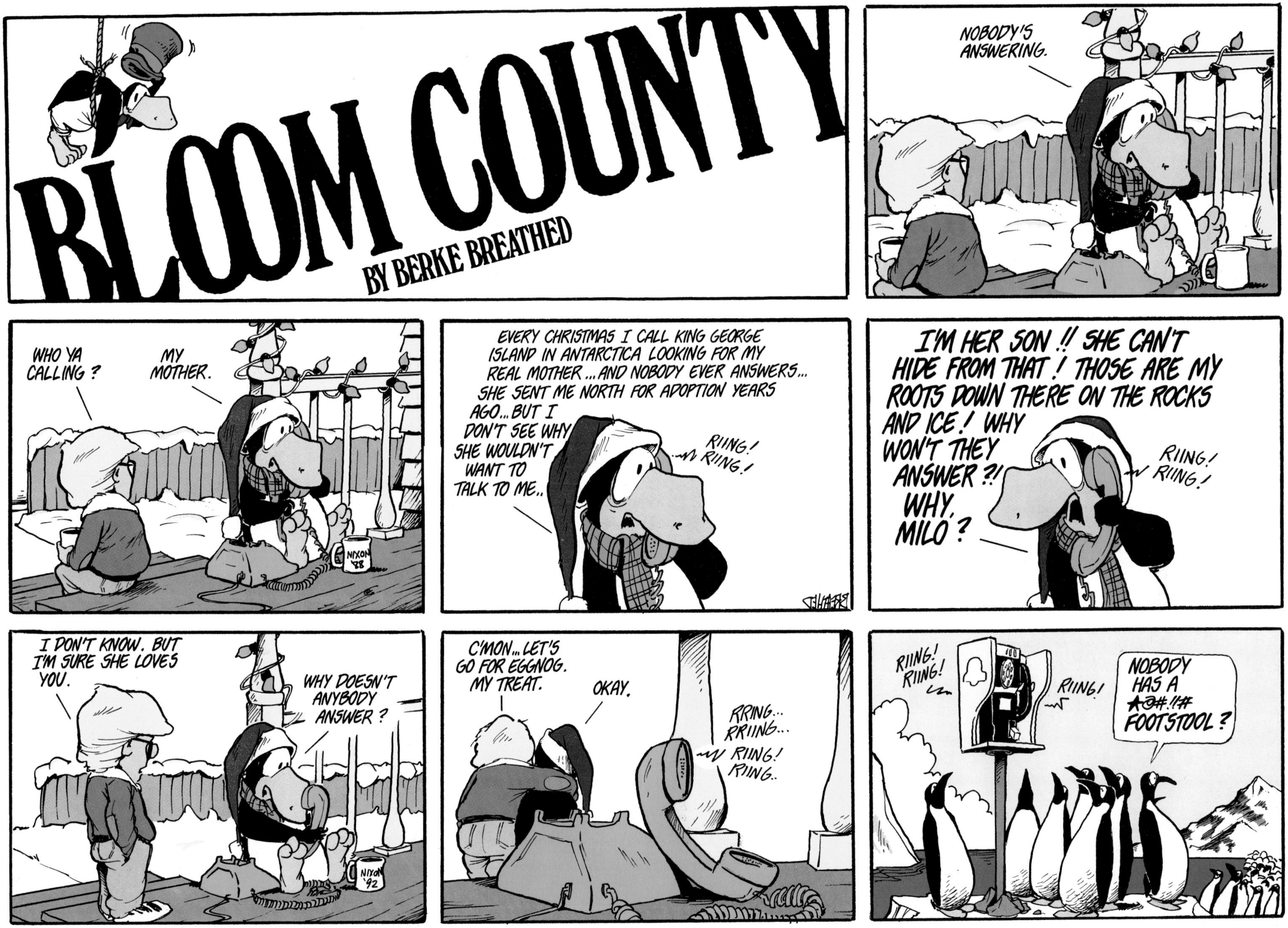
BLOOM COUNTY
BY BERKE BREATHED
NOBODY'S ANSWERING.
WHO YA CALLING ?
MY MOTHER.
NIXON '88
EVERY CHRISTMAS I CALL KING GEORGE ISLAND IN ANTARCTICA LOOKING FOR MY REAL MOTHER ... AND NOBODY EVER ANSWERS... SHE SENT ME NORTH FOR ADOPTION YEARS AGO... BUT I DON'T SEE WHY SHE WOULDN'T WANT TO TALK TO ME..
RIING! RIING!
I'M HER SON !! SHE CAN'T HIDE FROM THAT ! THOSE ARE MY ROOTS DOWN THERE ON THE ROCKS AND ICE ! WHY WON'T THEY ANSWER ?! WHY, MILO ?
RIING! RIING!
I DON'T KNOW. BUT I'M SURE SHE LOVES YOU.
WHY DOESN'T ANYBODY ANSWER ?
NIXON '92
C'MON... LET'S GO FOR EGGNOG. MY TREAT.
OKAY.
RRING... RRIING...
RIING! RIING..
RIING! RIING!
RIING!
NOBODY HAS A ★@#.!!# FOOTSTOOL ?

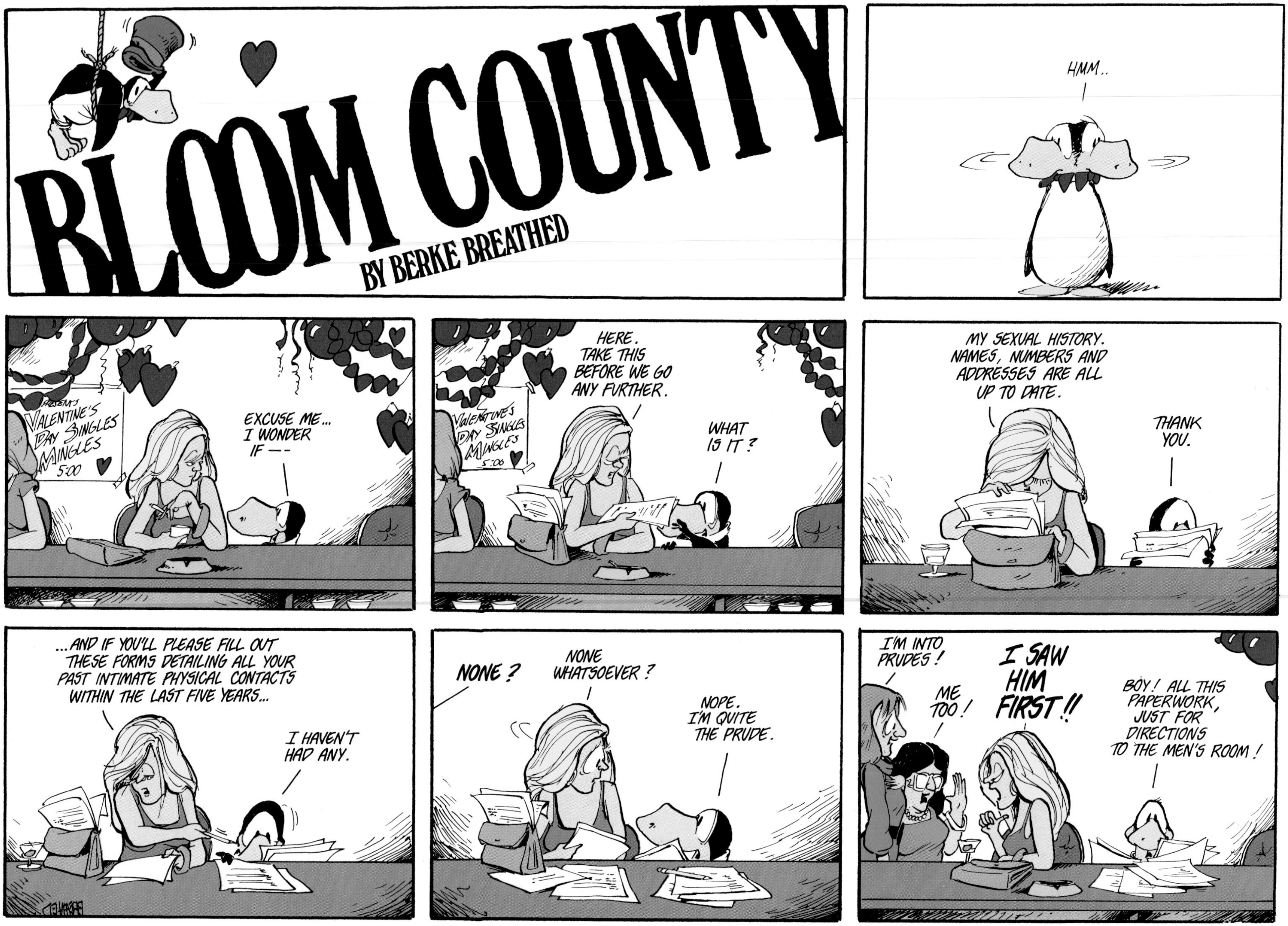
BLOOM COUNTY
BY BERKE BREATHED
HMM..
PRESENTS VALENTINE'S DAY SINGLES MINGLES 5:00
EXCUSE ME... I WONDER IF ——
HERE. TAKE THIS BEFORE WE GO ANY FURTHER.
WHAT IS IT ?
MY SEXUAL HISTORY. NAMES, NUMBERS AND ADDRESSES ARE ALL UP TO DATE.
THANK YOU.
...AND IF YOU'LL PLEASE FILL OUT THESE FORMS DETAILING ALL YOUR PAST INTIMATE PHYSICAL CONTACTS WITHIN THE LAST FIVE YEARS...
I HAVEN'T HAD ANY.
NONE ?
NONE WHATSOEVER ?
NOPE. I'M QUITE THE PRUDE.
I'M INTO PRUDES !
ME TOO !
I SAW HIM FIRST !!
BOY ! ALL THIS PAPERWORK, JUST FOR DIRECTIONS TO THE MEN'S ROOM !

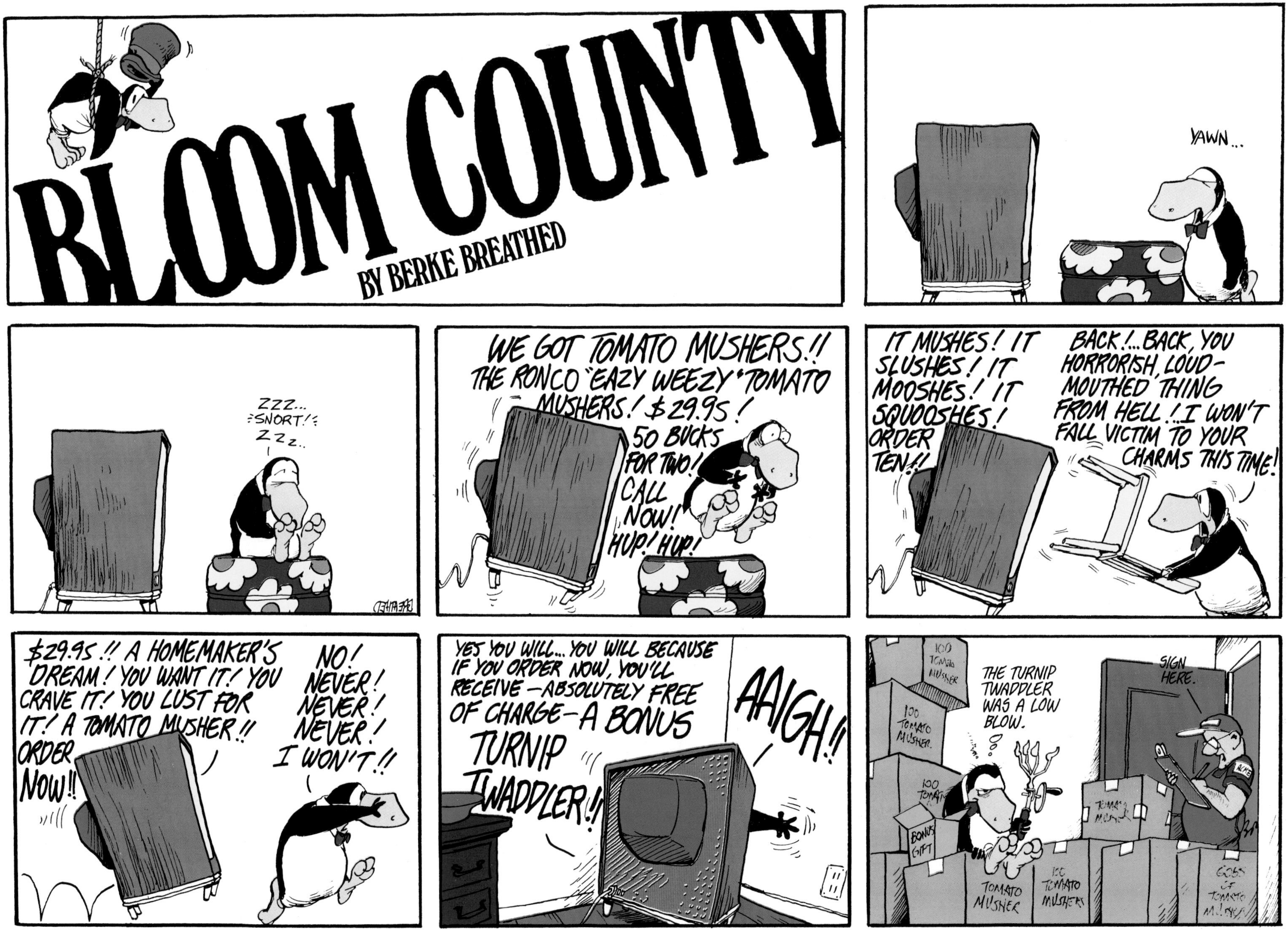
BLOOM COUNTY
BY BERKE BREATHED
YAWN...
ZZZ... SNORT! ZZZ..
WE GOT TOMATO MUSHERS!! THE RONCO "EAZY WEEZY" TOMATO MUSHERS! $29.95!
50 BUCKS FOR TWO! CALL NOW! HUP! HUP!
IT MUSHES! IT SLUSHES! IT MOOSHES! IT SQUOOSHES! ORDER TEN!!
BACK!...BACK, YOU HORRORISH, LOUD-MOUTHED THING FROM HELL!..I WON'T FALL VICTIM TO YOUR CHARMS THIS TIME!
$29.95!! A HOMEMAKER'S DREAM! YOU WANT IT! YOU CRAVE IT! YOU LUST FOR IT! A TOMATO MUSHER!! ORDER NOW!!
NO! NEVER! NEVER! NEVER! I WON'T!!
YES YOU WILL... YOU WILL BECAUSE IF YOU ORDER NOW, YOU'LL RECEIVE—ABSOLUTELY FREE OF CHARGE—A BONUS TURNIP TWADDLER!!
AAIGH!!
100 TOMATO MUSHER
100 TOMATO MUSHER.
BONUS GIFT
THE TURNIP TWADDLER WAS A LOW BLOW.
SIGN HERE.
ACME
TOMATO MUSHER
100 TOMATO MUSHERS

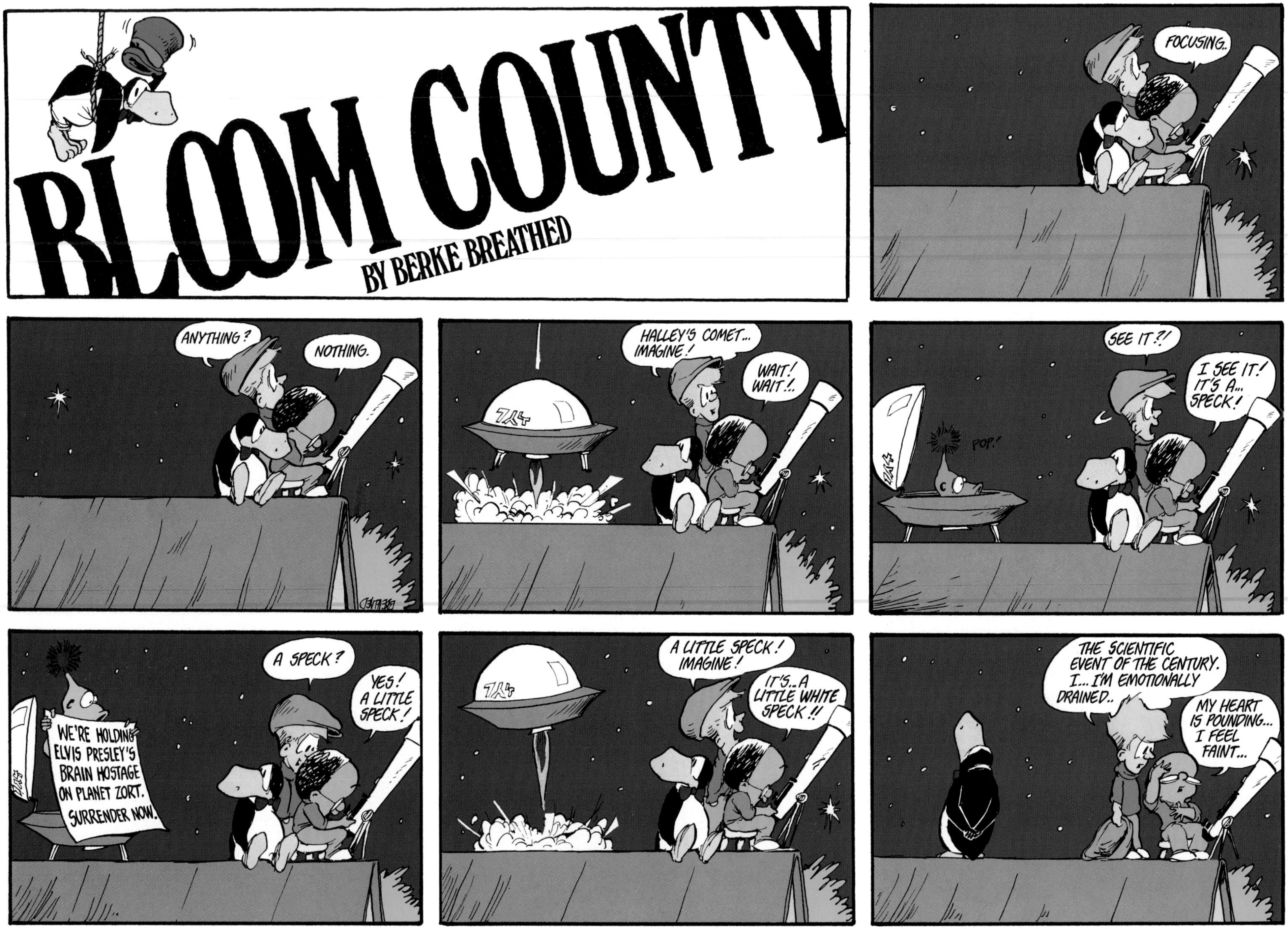
BLOOM COUNTY
BY BERKE BREATHED
FOCUSING..
ANYTHING?
NOTHING.
HALLEY'S COMET... IMAGINE!
WAIT! WAIT!.
SEE IT?!
I SEE IT! IT'S A... SPECK!
POP!
A SPECK?
YES! A LITTLE SPECK!
WE'RE HOLDING ELVIS PRESLEY'S BRAIN HOSTAGE ON PLANET ZORT. SURRENDER NOW.
A LITTLE SPECK! IMAGINE!
IT'S.. A LITTLE WHITE SPECK!!
THE SCIENTIFIC EVENT OF THE CENTURY. I... I'M EMOTIONALLY DRAINED..
MY HEART IS POUNDING... I FEEL FAINT...

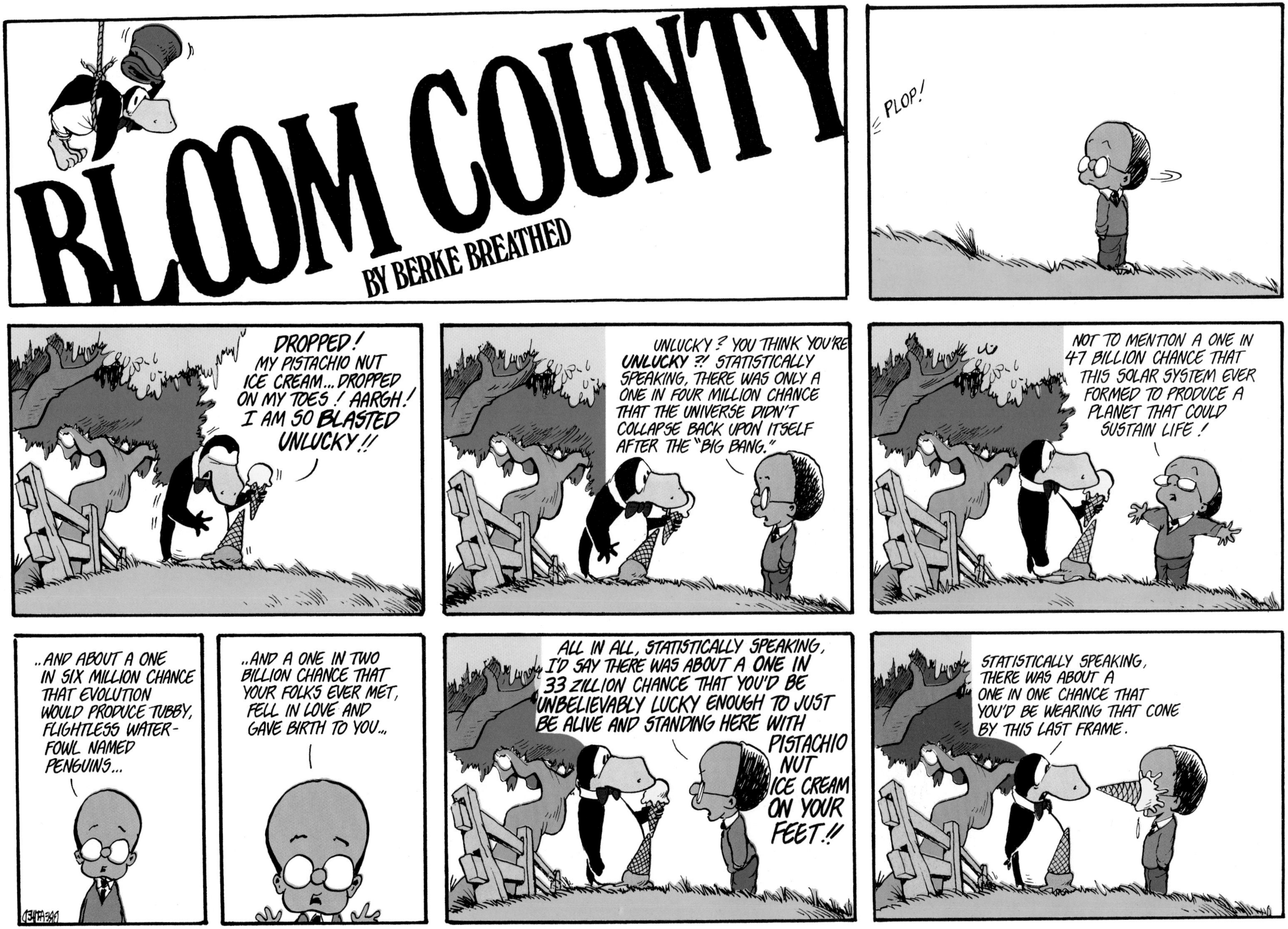
BLOOM COUNTY
BY BERKE BREATHED
PLOP!
DROPPED! MY PISTACHIO NUT ICE CREAM... DROPPED ON MY TOES! AARGH! I AM SO BLASTED UNLUCKY!!
UNLUCKY? YOU THINK YOU'RE UNLUCKY?! STATISTICALLY SPEAKING, THERE WAS ONLY A ONE IN FOUR MILLION CHANCE THAT THE UNIVERSE DIDN'T COLLAPSE BACK UPON ITSELF AFTER THE "BIG BANG."
NOT TO MENTION A ONE IN 47 BILLION CHANCE THAT THIS SOLAR SYSTEM EVER FORMED TO PRODUCE A PLANET THAT COULD SUSTAIN LIFE!
..AND ABOUT A ONE IN SIX MILLION CHANCE THAT EVOLUTION WOULD PRODUCE TUBBY, FLIGHTLESS WATER-FOWL NAMED PENGUINS...
..AND A ONE IN TWO BILLION CHANCE THAT YOUR FOLKS EVER MET, FELL IN LOVE AND GAVE BIRTH TO YOU...
ALL IN ALL, STATISTICALLY SPEAKING, I'D SAY THERE WAS ABOUT A ONE IN 33 ZILLION CHANCE THAT YOU'D BE UNBELIEVABLY LUCKY ENOUGH TO JUST BE ALIVE AND STANDING HERE WITH PISTACHIO NUT ICE CREAM ON YOUR FEET!!
STATISTICALLY SPEAKING, THERE WAS ABOUT A ONE IN ONE CHANCE THAT YOU'D BE WEARING THAT CONE BY THIS LAST FRAME.

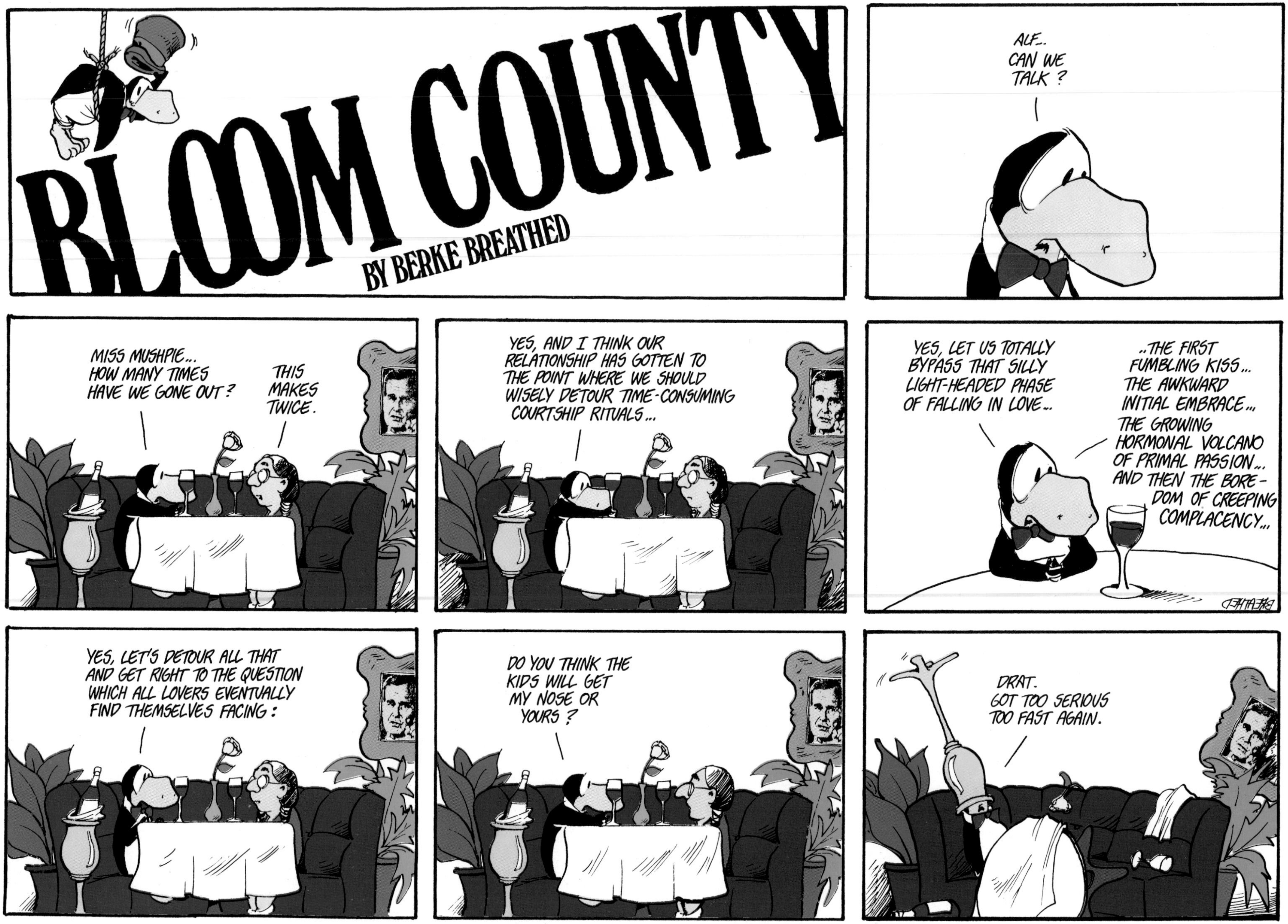
BLOOM COUNTY
BY BERKE BREATHED
ALF.. CAN WE TALK ?
MISS MUSHPIE... HOW MANY TIMES HAVE WE GONE OUT ?
THIS MAKES TWICE.
YES, AND I THINK OUR RELATIONSHIP HAS GOTTEN TO THE POINT WHERE WE SHOULD WISELY DETOUR TIME-CONSUMING COURTSHIP RITUALS...
YES, LET US TOTALLY BYPASS THAT SILLY LIGHT-HEADED PHASE OF FALLING IN LOVE...
..THE FIRST FUMBLING KISS... THE AWKWARD INITIAL EMBRACE... THE GROWING HORMONAL VOLCANO OF PRIMAL PASSION... AND THEN THE BORE-DOM OF CREEPING COMPLACENCY...
YES, LET'S DETOUR ALL THAT AND GET RIGHT TO THE QUESTION WHICH ALL LOVERS EVENTUALLY FIND THEMSELVES FACING :
DO YOU THINK THE KIDS WILL GET MY NOSE OR YOURS ?
DRAT. GOT TOO SERIOUS TOO FAST AGAIN.

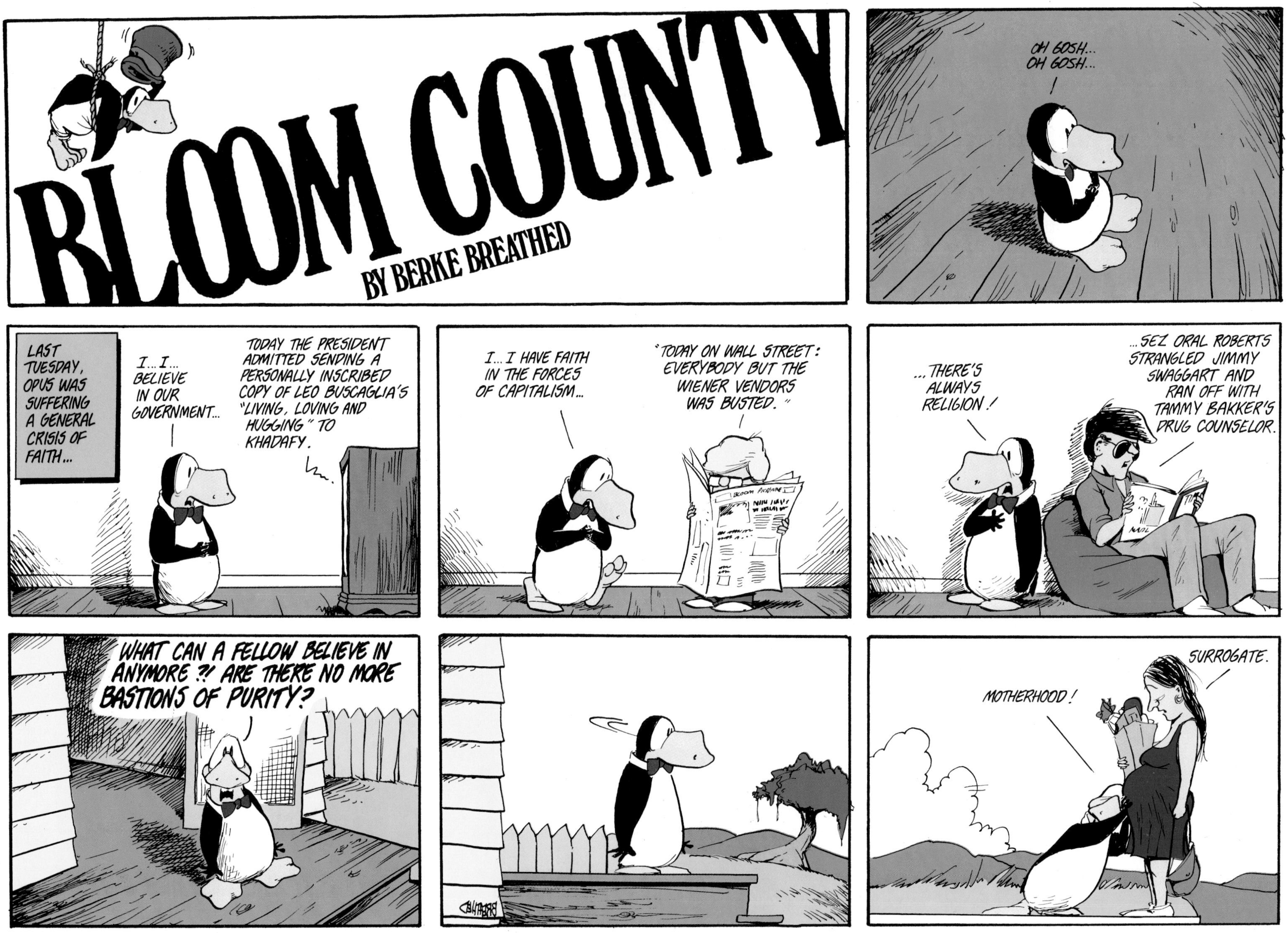

BLOOM COUNTY
BY BERKE BREATHED
OH GOSH...
OH GOSH...
LAST TUESDAY, OPUS WAS SUFFERING A GENERAL CRISIS OF FAITH...
I... I... BELIEVE IN OUR GOVERNMENT...
TODAY THE PRESIDENT ADMITTED SENDING A PERSONALLY INSCRIBED COPY OF LEO BUSCAGLIA'S "LIVING, LOVING AND HUGGING" TO KHADAFY.
I... I HAVE FAITH IN THE FORCES OF CAPITALISM...
"TODAY ON WALL STREET: EVERYBODY BUT THE WIENER VENDORS WAS BUSTED."
BLOOM PICAYUNE
...THERE'S ALWAYS RELIGION!
...SEZ ORAL ROBERTS STRANGLED JIMMY SWAGGART AND RAN OFF WITH TAMMY BAKKER'S DRUG COUNSELOR.
WHAT CAN A FELLOW BELIEVE IN ANYMORE?! ARE THERE NO MORE BASTIONS OF PURITY?
MOTHERHOOD!
SURROGATE.

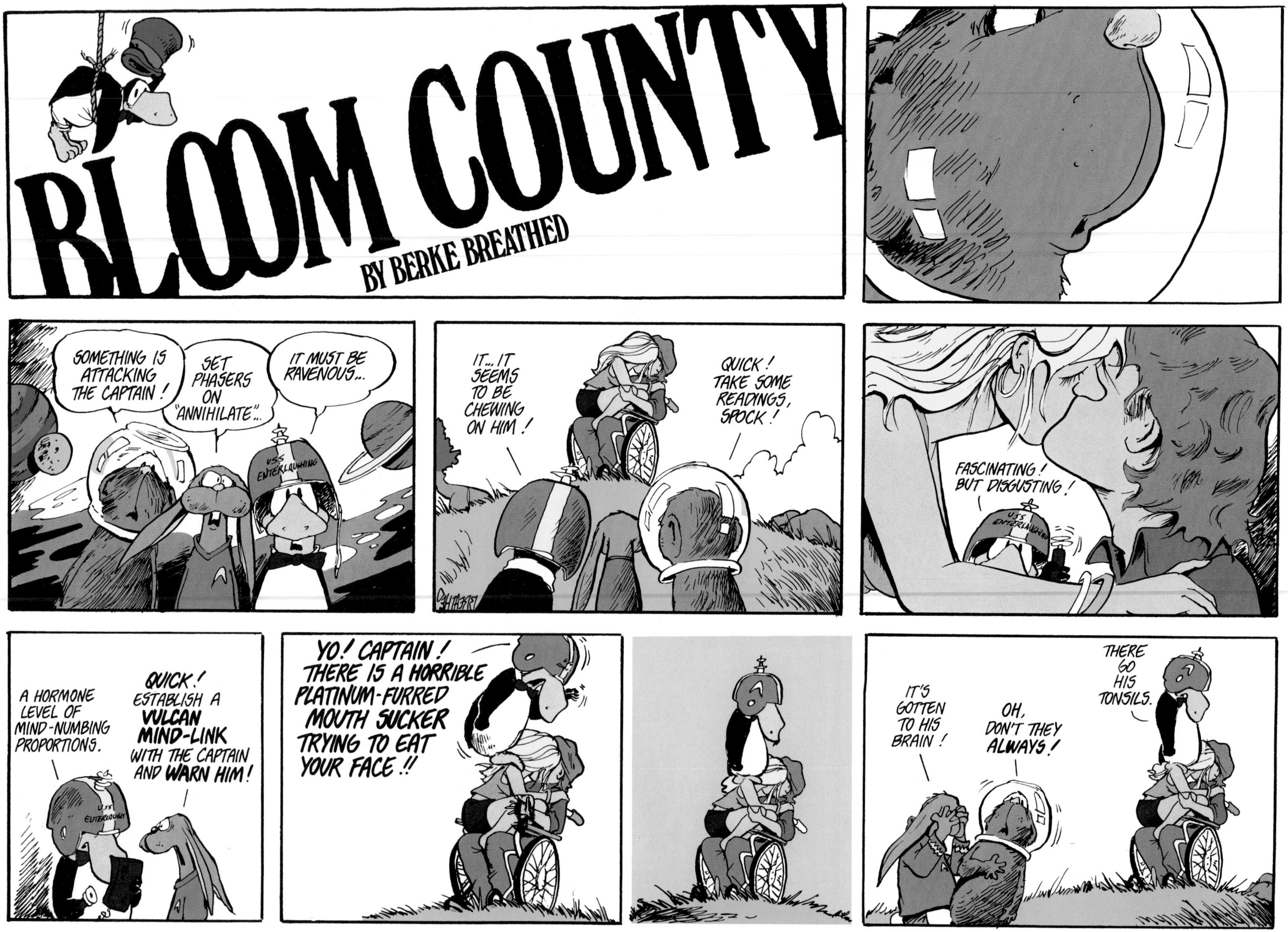

BLOOM COUNTY
BY BERKE BREATHED
SOMETHING IS ATTACKING THE CAPTAIN!
SET PHASERS ON "ANNIHILATE"...
IT MUST BE RAVENOUS...
USS ENTERLAUGHING
IT... IT SEEMS TO BE CHEWING ON HIM!
QUICK! TAKE SOME READINGS, SPOCK!
FASCINATING! BUT DISGUSTING!
A HORMONE LEVEL OF MIND-NUMBING PROPORTIONS.
QUICK! ESTABLISH A VULCAN MIND-LINK WITH THE CAPTAIN AND WARN HIM!
YO! CAPTAIN! THERE IS A HORRIBLE PLATINUM-FURRED MOUTH SUCKER TRYING TO EAT YOUR FACE!!
IT'S GOTTEN TO HIS BRAIN!
OH, DON'T THEY ALWAYS!
THERE GO HIS TONSILS.

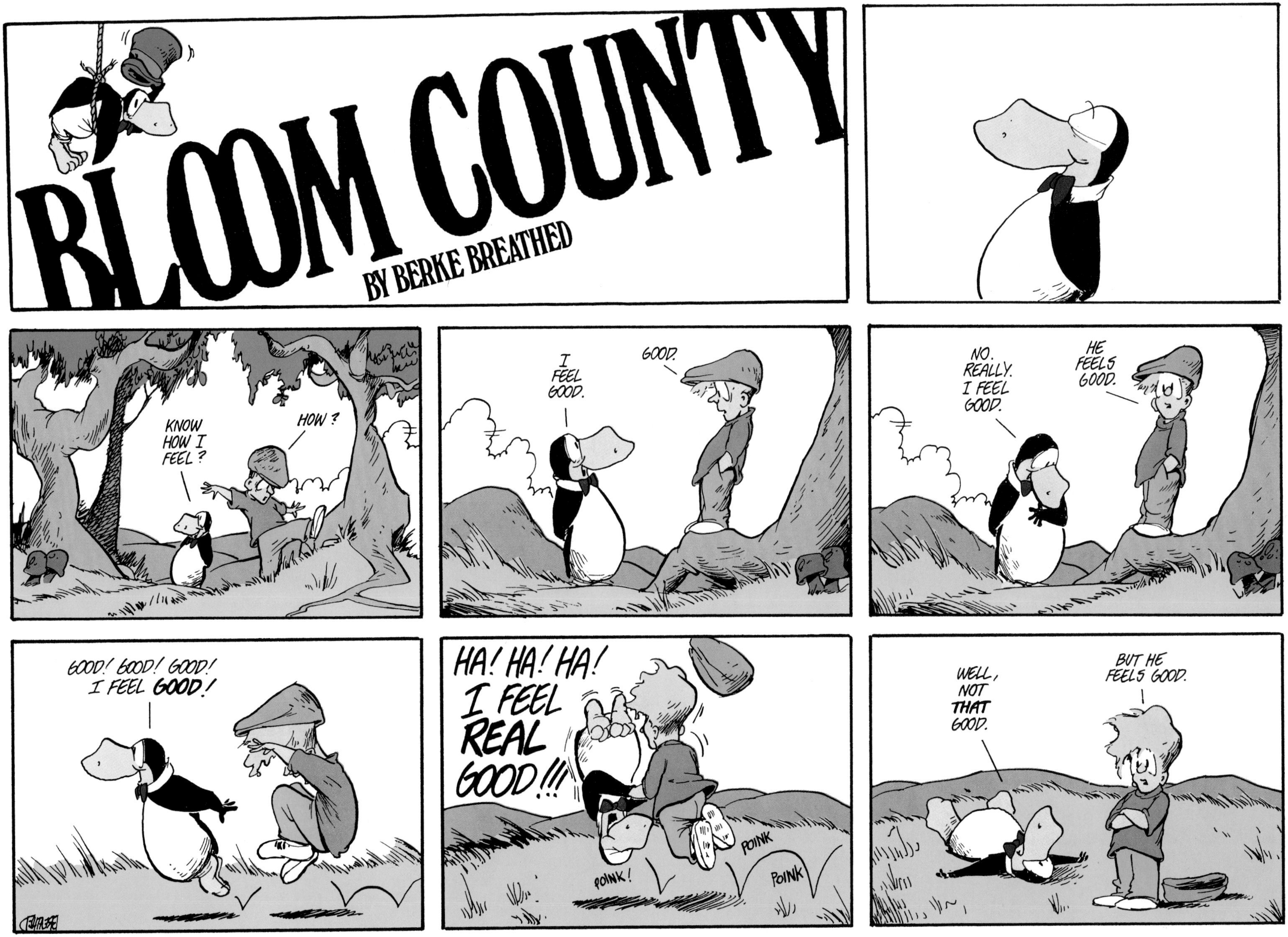
BLOOM COUNTY
BY BERKE BREATHED
KNOW HOW I FEEL?
HOW?
I FEEL GOOD.
GOOD.
NO. REALLY. I FEEL GOOD.
HE FEELS GOOD.
GOOD! GOOD! GOOD! I FEEL **GOOD**!
HA! HA! HA! I FEEL **REAL** GOOD!!!
POINK!
POINK
POINK
WELL, NOT **THAT** GOOD.
BUT HE FEELS GOOD.

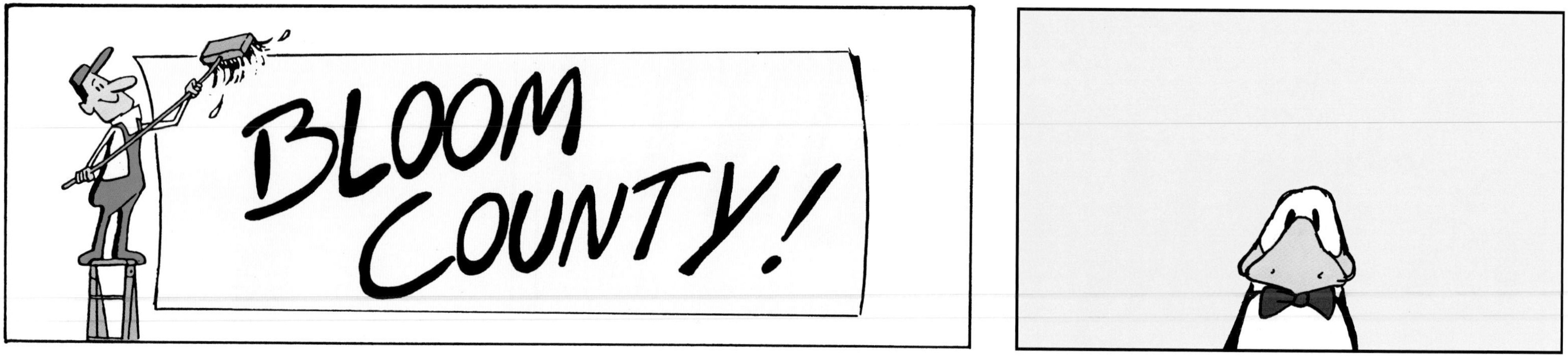
BLOOM COUNTY!

NOTICE
TO CLIENT EDITORS:

The regular artist of this feature is on vacation for 10 days at PTL's "Heritage USA" in South Carolina. Filling in for Mr. Breathed this week is Mr. Mort Svenson, 73, whose cartoons have appeared in "The Saturday Evening Post" and "Parrot World."

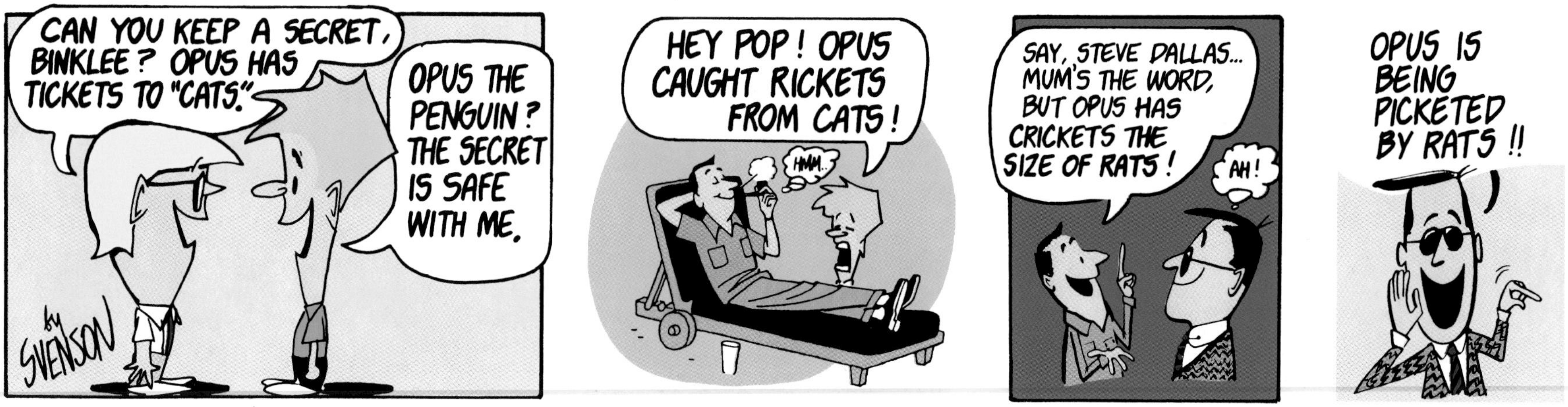
CAN YOU KEEP A SECRET, BINKLEE? OPUS HAS TICKETS TO "CATS."
OPUS THE PENGUIN? THE SECRET IS SAFE WITH ME.
by SVENSON
HEY POP! OPUS CAUGHT RICKETS FROM CATS!
HMM..
SAY, STEVE DALLAS... MUM'S THE WORD, BUT OPUS HAS CRICKETS THE SIZE OF RATS!
AH!
OPUS IS BEING PICKETED BY RATS !!

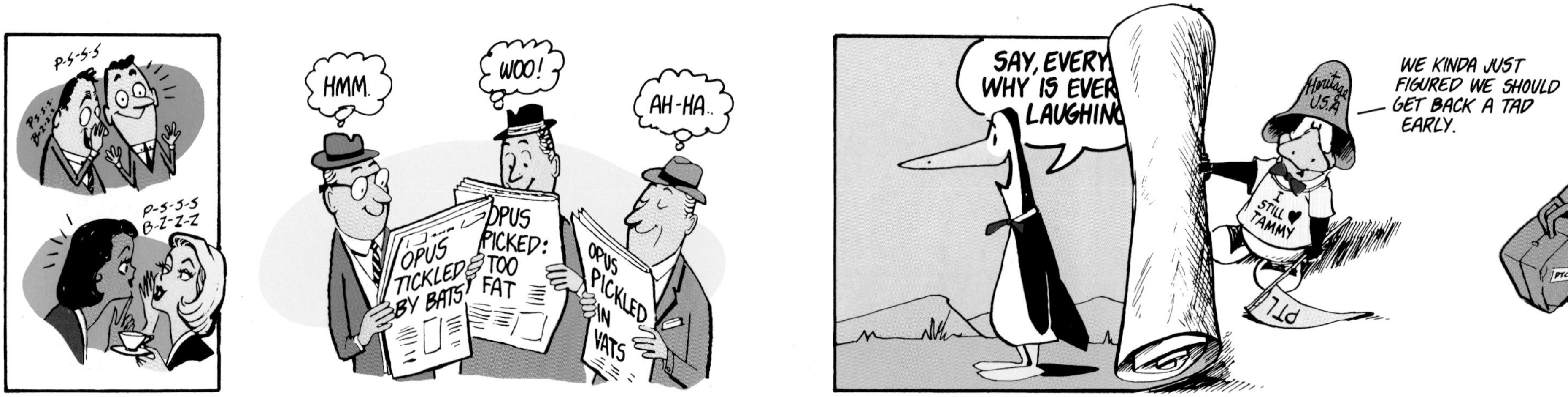
P-S-S-S
P-S-S-S B-Z-Z-Z
HMM.
WOO!
AH-HA..
OPUS TICKLED BY BATS
OPUS PICKED: TOO FAT
OPUS PICKLED IN VATS
SAY, EVERY
WHY IS EVER
LAUGHING
Heritage U.S.A
I STILL ♥ TAMMY
PTL
WE KINDA JUST FIGURED WE SHOULD GET BACK A TAD EARLY.

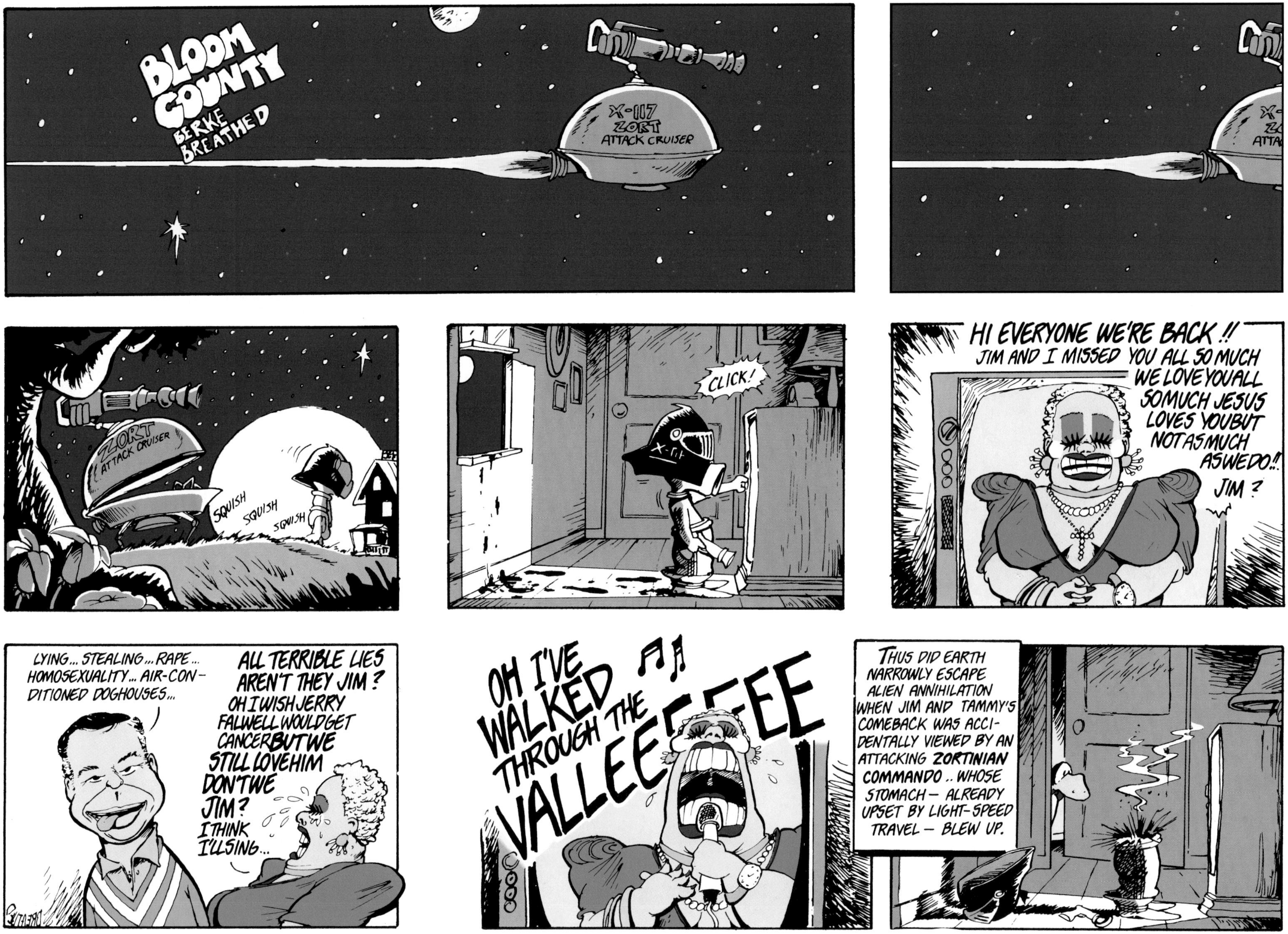
BLOOM COUNTY
BERKE BREATHED
X-117 ZORT ATTACK CRUISER
ZORT ATTACK CRUISER
SQUISH SQUISH SQUISH
CLICK!
X-117
HI EVERYONE WE'RE BACK!! JIM AND I MISSED YOU ALL SO MUCH WE LOVE YOU ALL SO MUCH JESUS LOVES YOU BUT NOT AS MUCH AS WE DO!! JIM?
LYING... STEALING... RAPE... HOMOSEXUALITY... AIR-CONDITIONED DOGHOUSES...
ALL TERRIBLE LIES AREN'T THEY JIM? OH I WISH JERRY FALWELL WOULD GET CANCER BUT WE STILL LOVE HIM DON'T WE JIM? I THINK I'LL SING...
OH I'VE WALKED THROUGH THE VALLEEEEEE
THUS DID EARTH NARROWLY ESCAPE ALIEN ANNIHILATION WHEN JIM AND TAMMY'S COMEBACK WAS ACCIDENTALLY VIEWED BY AN ATTACKING ZORTINIAN COMMANDO.. WHOSE STOMACH — ALREADY UPSET BY LIGHT-SPEED TRAVEL — BLEW UP.

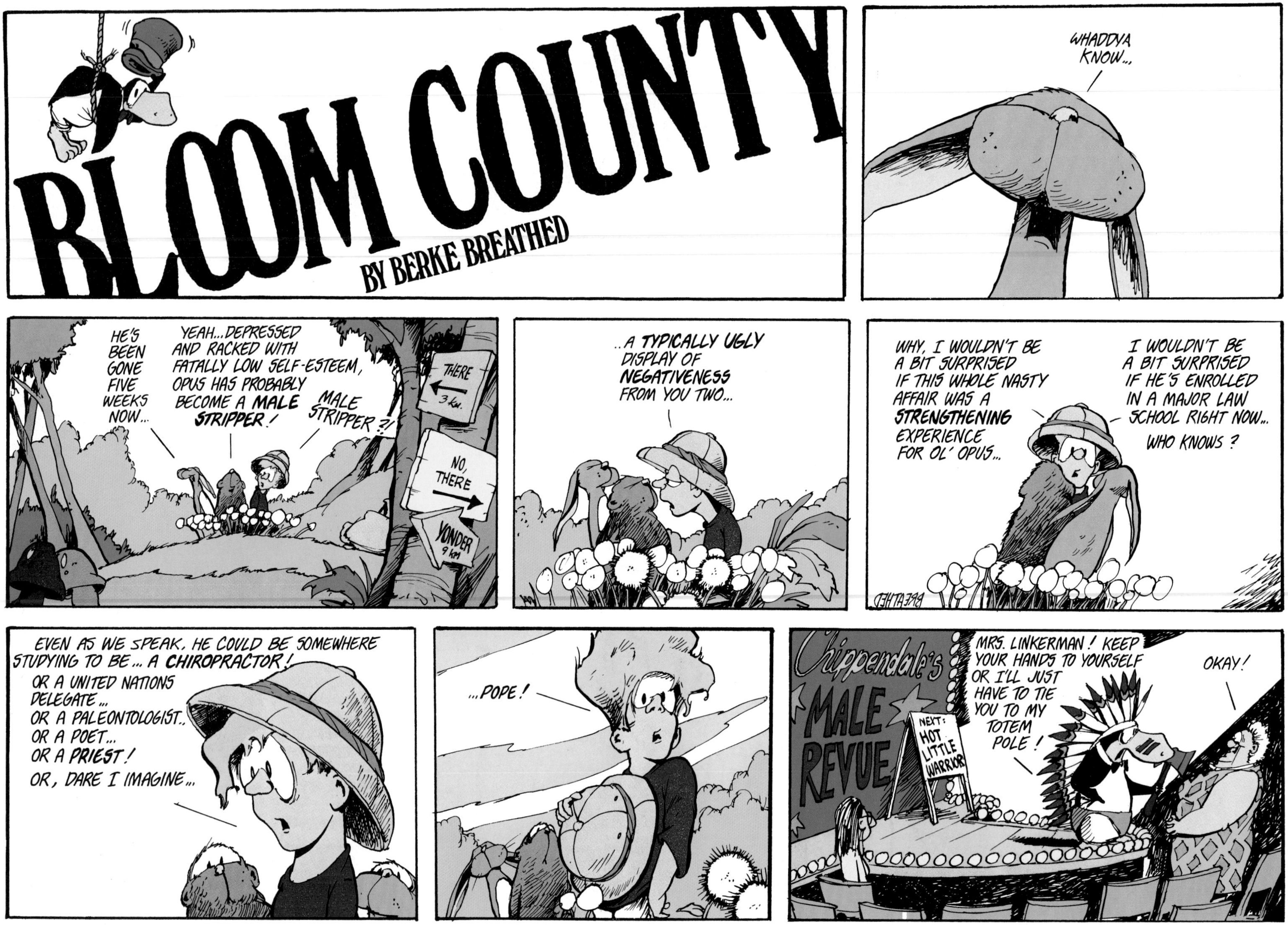
BLOOM COUNTY
BY BERKE BREATHED
WHADDYA KNOW...
HE'S BEEN GONE FIVE WEEKS NOW...
YEAH... DEPRESSED AND RACKED WITH FATALLY LOW SELF-ESTEEM, OPUS HAS PROBABLY BECOME A MALE STRIPPER!
MALE STRIPPER ?!
THERE 3 Km.
NO, THERE
YONDER 9 Km
..A TYPICALLY UGLY DISPLAY OF NEGATIVENESS FROM YOU TWO...
WHY, I WOULDN'T BE A BIT SURPRISED IF THIS WHOLE NASTY AFFAIR WAS A STRENGTHENING EXPERIENCE FOR OL' OPUS...
I WOULDN'T BE A BIT SURPRISED IF HE'S ENROLLED IN A MAJOR LAW SCHOOL RIGHT NOW...
WHO KNOWS ?
EVEN AS WE SPEAK, HE COULD BE SOMEWHERE STUDYING TO BE... A CHIROPRACTOR!
OR A UNITED NATIONS DELEGATE...
OR A PALEONTOLOGIST..
OR A POET...
OR A PRIEST!
OR, DARE I IMAGINE...
...POPE!
Chippendale's MALE REVUE
NEXT: HOT LITTLE WARRIOR
MRS. LINKERMAN! KEEP YOUR HANDS TO YOURSELF OR I'LL JUST HAVE TO TIE YOU TO MY TOTEM POLE!
OKAY!

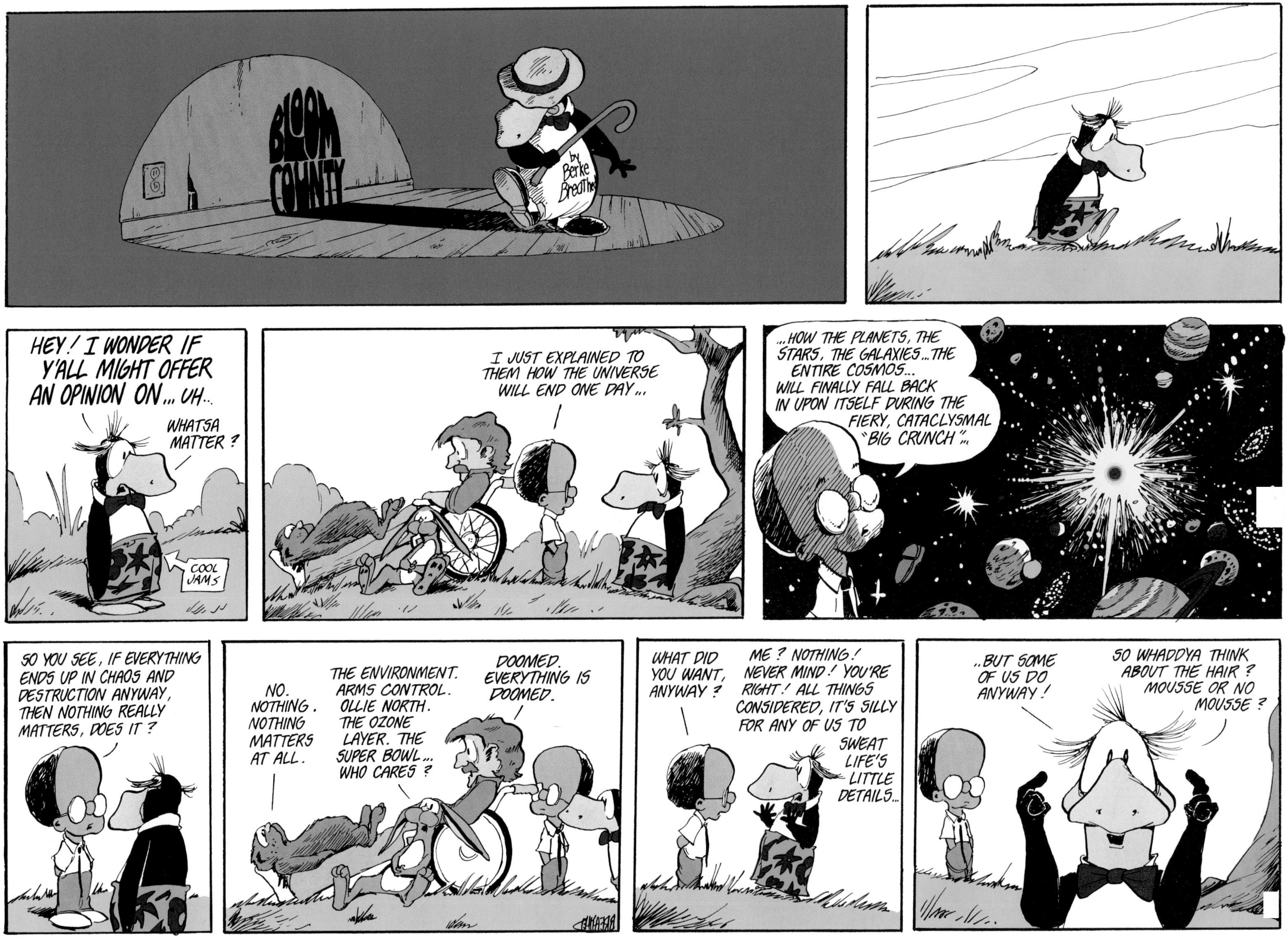
BLOOM COUNTY
by Berke Breathed
HEY! I WONDER IF Y'ALL MIGHT OFFER AN OPINION ON... UH..
WHATSA MATTER ?
COOL JAMS
I JUST EXPLAINED TO THEM HOW THE UNIVERSE WILL END ONE DAY...
...HOW THE PLANETS, THE STARS, THE GALAXIES...THE ENTIRE COSMOS... WILL FINALLY FALL BACK IN UPON ITSELF DURING THE FIERY, CATACLYSMAL "BIG CRUNCH"...
SO YOU SEE, IF EVERYTHING ENDS UP IN CHAOS AND DESTRUCTION ANYWAY, THEN NOTHING REALLY MATTERS, DOES IT ?
NO. NOTHING. NOTHING MATTERS AT ALL.
THE ENVIRONMENT. ARMS CONTROL. OLLIE NORTH. THE OZONE LAYER. THE SUPER BOWL... WHO CARES ?
DOOMED. EVERYTHING IS DOOMED.
WHAT DID YOU WANT, ANYWAY ?
ME ? NOTHING! NEVER MIND! YOU'RE RIGHT! ALL THINGS CONSIDERED, IT'S SILLY FOR ANY OF US TO SWEAT LIFE'S LITTLE DETAILS...
..BUT SOME OF US DO ANYWAY!
SO WHADDYA THINK ABOUT THE HAIR ? MOUSSE OR NO MOUSSE ?

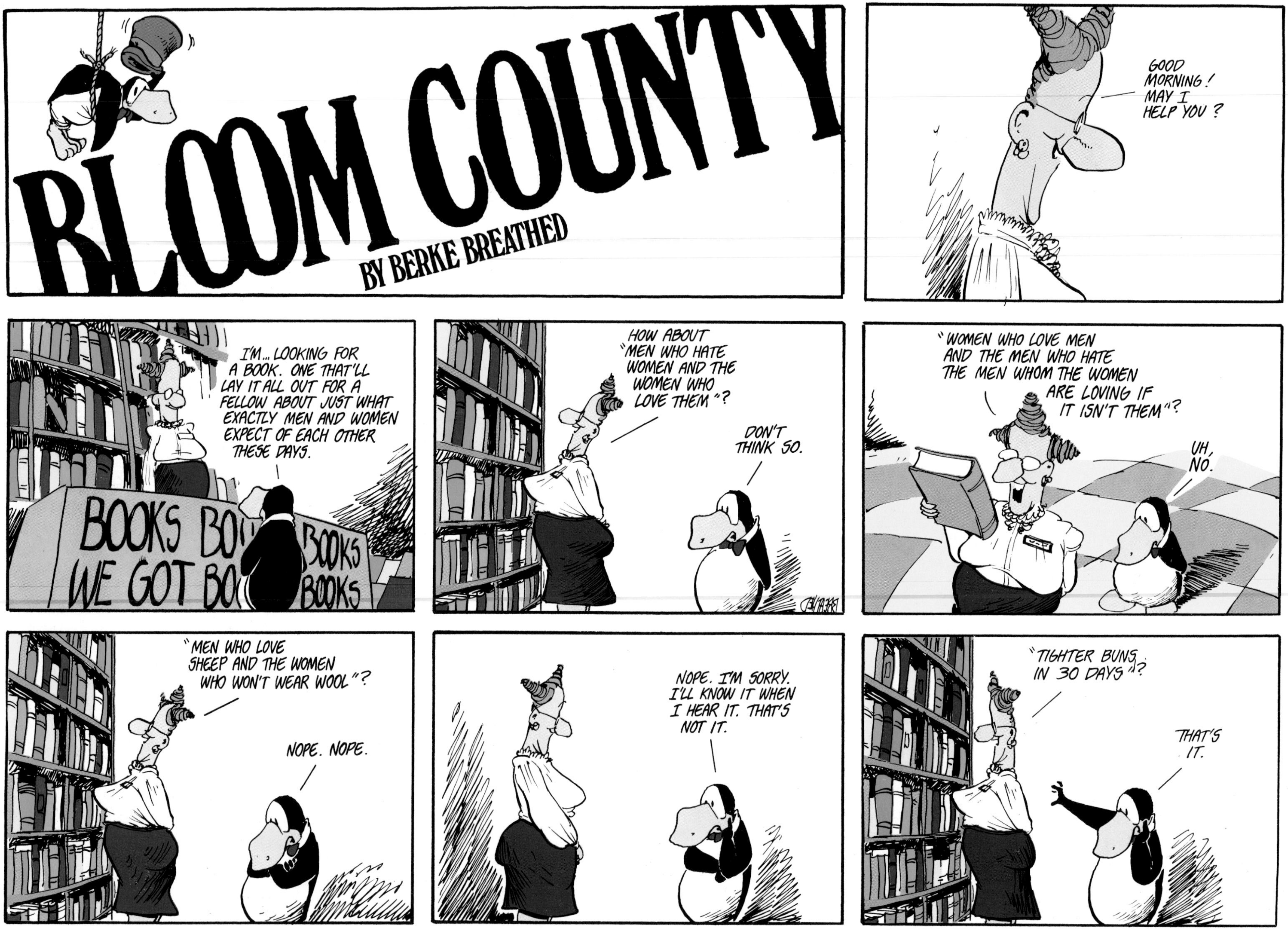
BLOOM COUNTY
BY BERKE BREATHED
GOOD MORNING! MAY I HELP YOU?
I'M... LOOKING FOR A BOOK. ONE THAT'LL LAY IT ALL OUT FOR A FELLOW ABOUT JUST WHAT EXACTLY MEN AND WOMEN EXPECT OF EACH OTHER THESE DAYS.
BOOKS BO
WE GOT BO
BOOKS BOOKS
HOW ABOUT "MEN WHO HATE WOMEN AND THE WOMEN WHO LOVE THEM"?
DON'T THINK SO.
"WOMEN WHO LOVE MEN AND THE MEN WHO HATE THE MEN WHOM THE WOMEN ARE LOVING IF IT ISN'T THEM"?
UH, NO.
"MEN WHO LOVE SHEEP AND THE WOMEN WHO WON'T WEAR WOOL"?
NOPE. NOPE.
NOPE. I'M SORRY. I'LL KNOW IT WHEN I HEAR IT. THAT'S NOT IT.
"TIGHTER BUNS IN 30 DAYS"?
THAT'S IT.

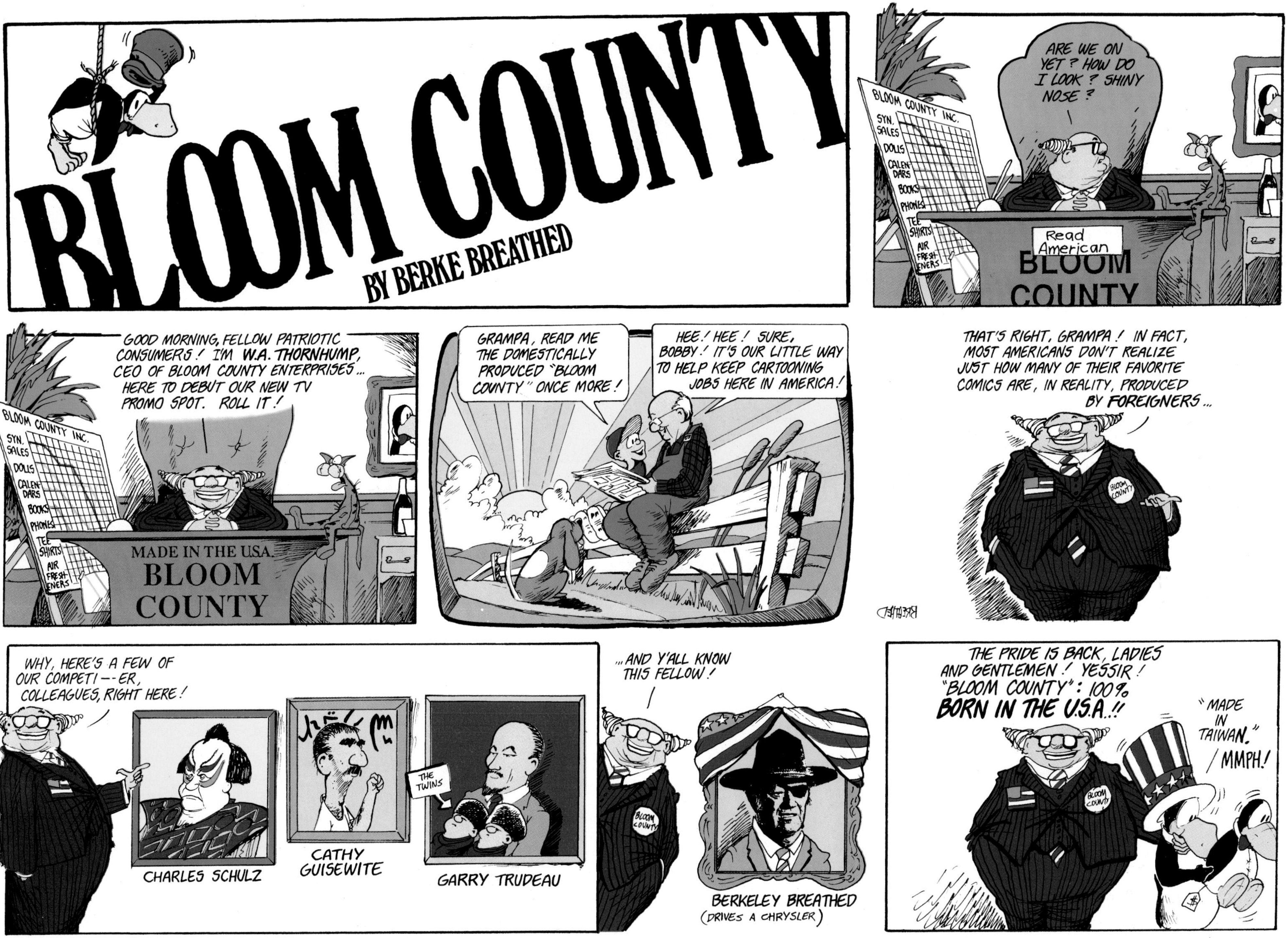
BLOOM COUNTY
BY BERKE BREATHED
ARE WE ON YET? HOW DO I LOOK? SHINY NOSE?
BLOOM COUNTY INC.
SYN. SALES
DOLLS
CALEN-DARS
BOOKS
PHONES
TEE SHIRTS
AIR FRESH-ENERS
Read American
BLOOM COUNTY
GOOD MORNING, FELLOW PATRIOTIC CONSUMERS! I'M W.A. THORNHUMP, CEO OF BLOOM COUNTY ENTERPRISES... HERE TO DEBUT OUR NEW TV PROMO SPOT. ROLL IT!
MADE IN THE U.S.A. BLOOM COUNTY
GRAMPA, READ ME THE DOMESTICALLY PRODUCED "BLOOM COUNTY" ONCE MORE!
HEE! HEE! SURE, BOBBY! IT'S OUR LITTLE WAY TO HELP KEEP CARTOONING JOBS HERE IN AMERICA!
THAT'S RIGHT, GRAMPA! IN FACT, MOST AMERICANS DON'T REALIZE JUST HOW MANY OF THEIR FAVORITE COMICS ARE, IN REALITY, PRODUCED BY FOREIGNERS...
BLOOM COUNTY
WHY, HERE'S A FEW OF OUR COMPETI--ER, COLLEAGUES, RIGHT HERE!
CHARLES SCHULZ
CATHY GUISEWITE
THE TWINS
GARRY TRUDEAU
...AND Y'ALL KNOW THIS FELLOW!
BLOOM COUNTY
BERKELEY BREATHED (DRIVES A CHRYSLER)
THE PRIDE IS BACK, LADIES AND GENTLEMEN! YESSIR! "BLOOM COUNTY": 100% BORN IN THE U.S.A.!!
BLOOM COUNTY
"MADE IN TAIWAN."
MMPH!

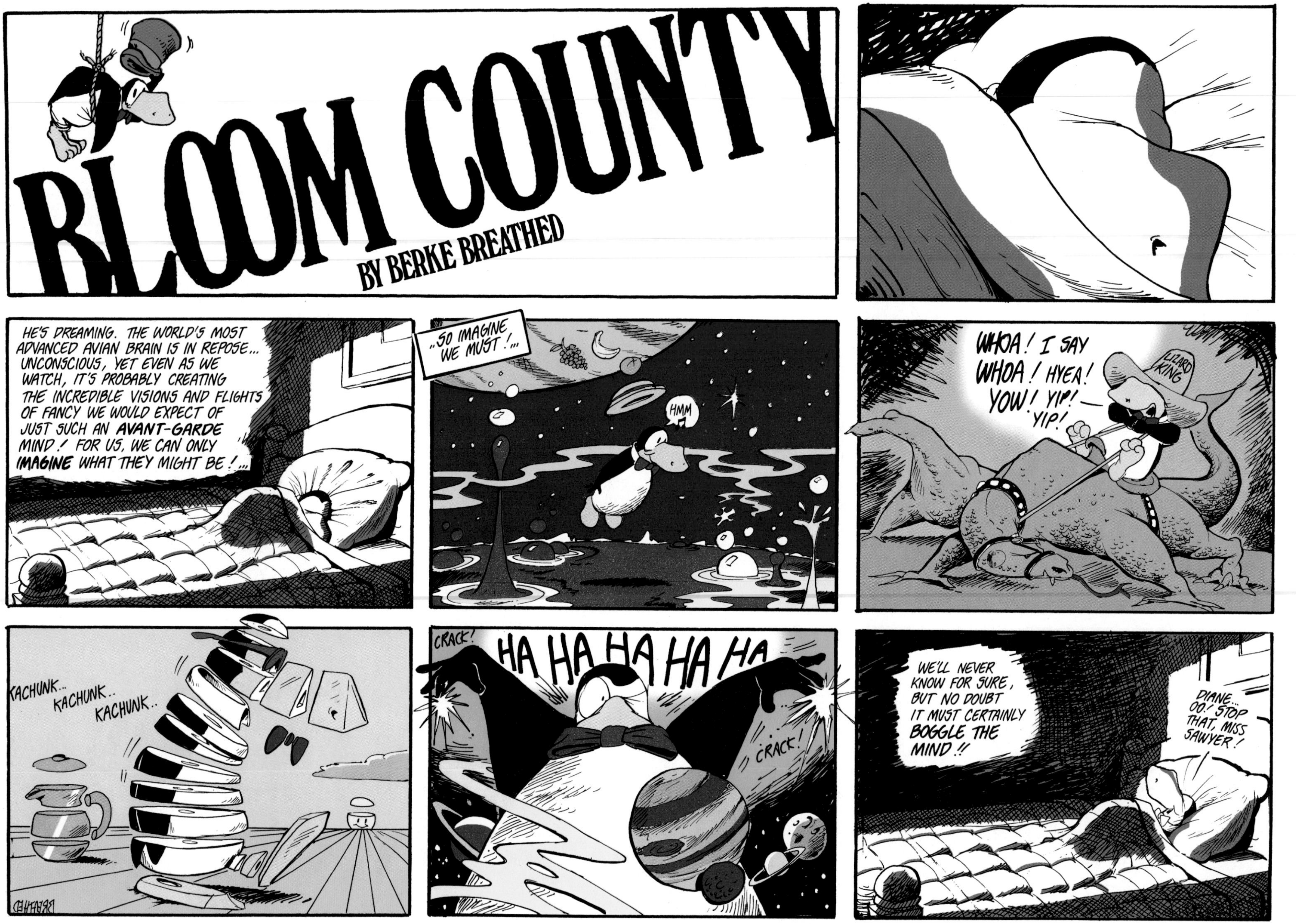
BLOOM COUNTY
BY BERKE BREATHED
HE'S DREAMING. THE WORLD'S MOST ADVANCED AVIAN BRAIN IS IN REPOSE... UNCONSCIOUS, YET EVEN AS WE WATCH, IT'S PROBABLY CREATING THE INCREDIBLE VISIONS AND FLIGHTS OF FANCY WE WOULD EXPECT OF JUST SUCH AN AVANT-GARDE MIND! FOR US, WE CAN ONLY IMAGINE WHAT THEY MIGHT BE!...
..SO IMAGINE WE MUST!...
HMM
WHOA! I SAY WHOA! HYEA! YOW! YIP! YIP!
LIZARD KING
KACHUNK.. KACHUNK.. KACHUNK..
CRACK!
HA HA HA HA HA
CRACK!
WE'LL NEVER KNOW FOR SURE, BUT NO DOUBT IT MUST CERTAINLY BOGGLE THE MIND!!
DIANE... OO! STOP THAT, MISS SAWYER!
BREATHED

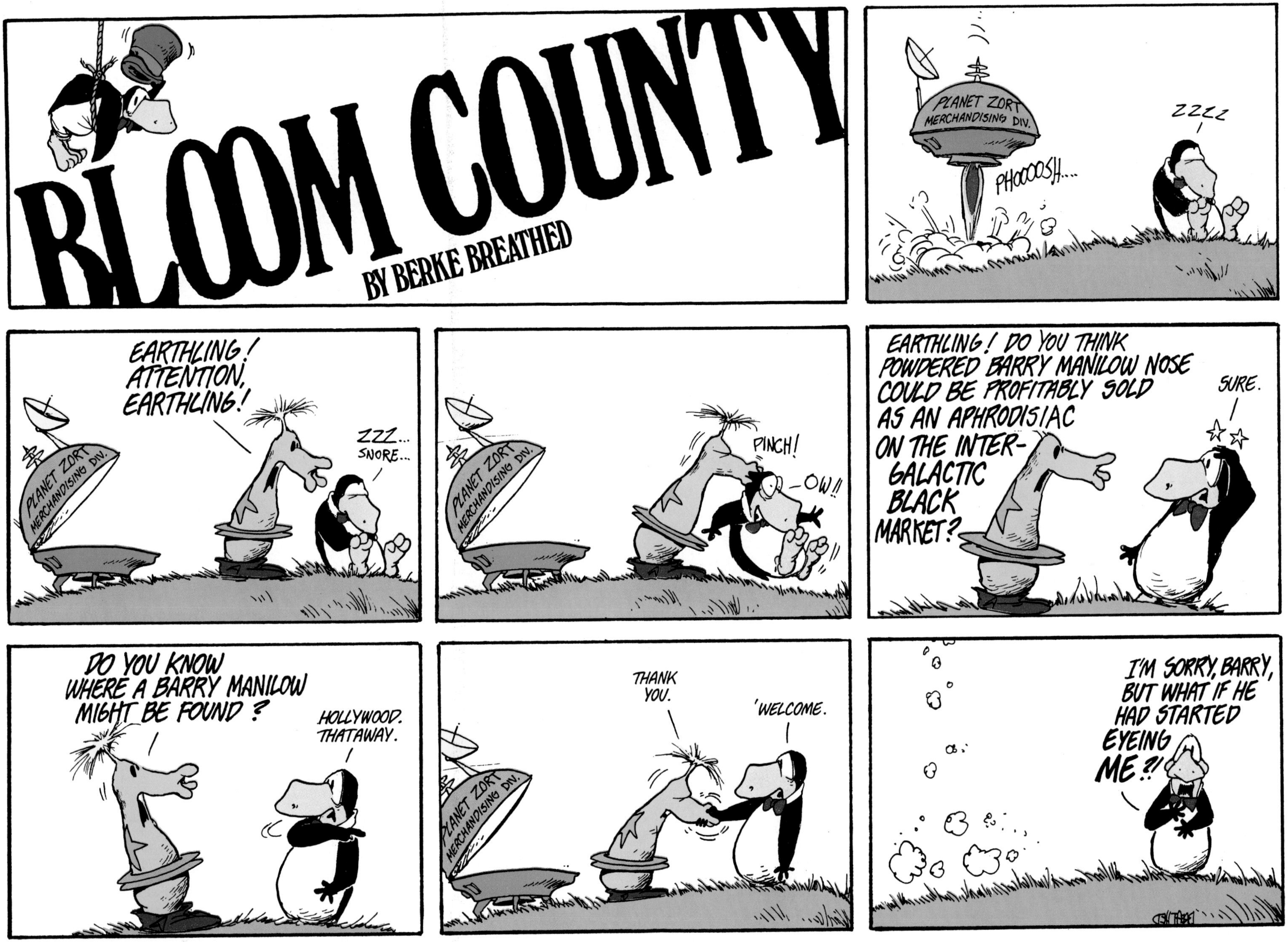
BLOOM COUNTY
BY BERKE BREATHED
PLANET ZORT MERCHANDISING DIV.
PHOOOOSH....
ZZZZ
EARTHLING! ATTENTION, EARTHLING!
ZZZ... SNORE...
PINCH!
OW!!
EARTHLING! DO YOU THINK POWDERED BARRY MANILOW NOSE COULD BE PROFITABLY SOLD AS AN APHRODISIAC ON THE INTER-GALACTIC BLACK MARKET?
SURE.
DO YOU KNOW WHERE A BARRY MANILOW MIGHT BE FOUND?
HOLLYWOOD. THATAWAY.
THANK YOU.
'WELCOME.
I'M SORRY, BARRY, BUT WHAT IF HE HAD STARTED EYEING ME?!

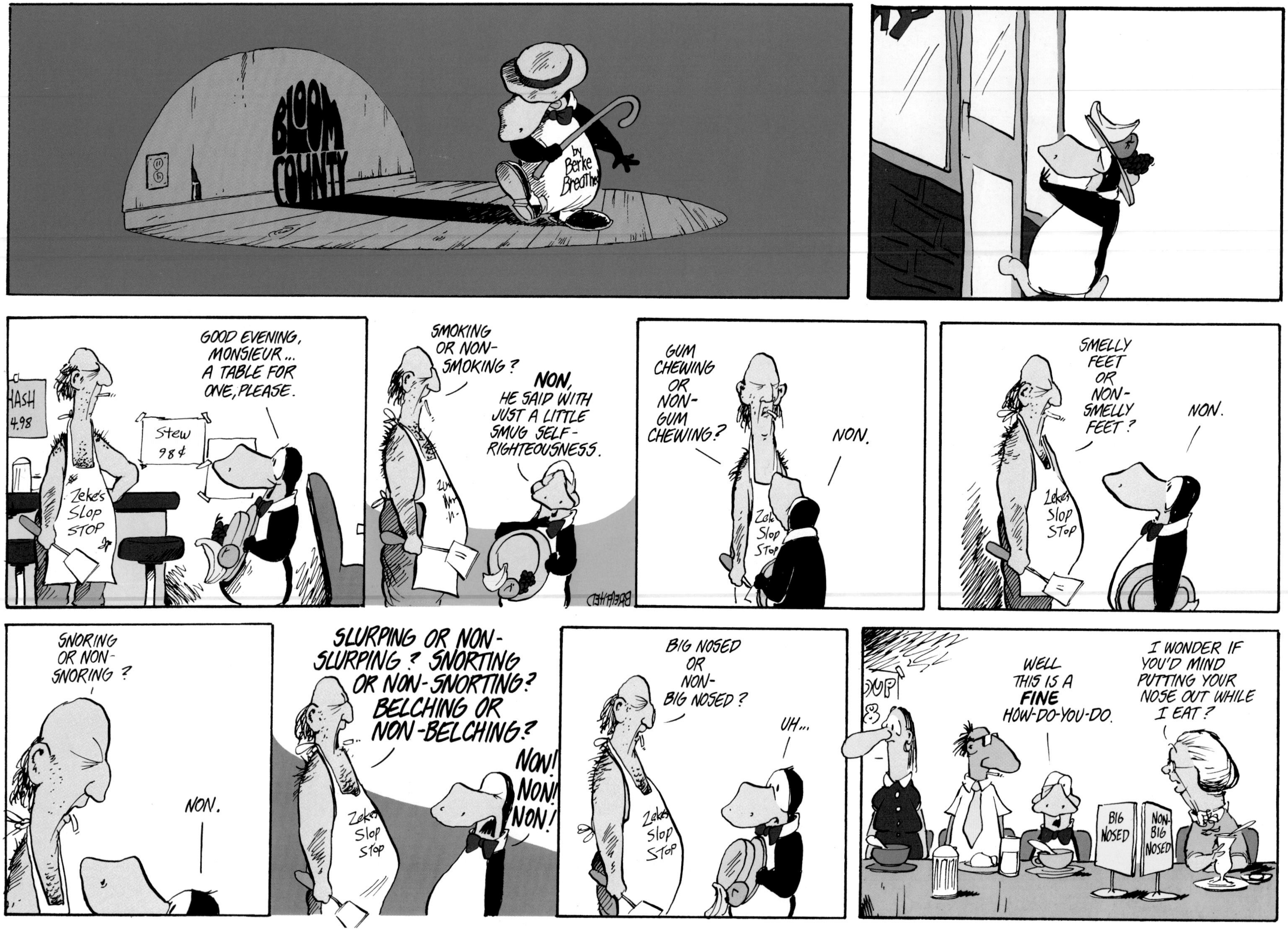

BLOOM COUNTY
by Berke Breathed
HASH 4.98
Stew 98¢
GOOD EVENING, MONSIEUR... A TABLE FOR ONE, PLEASE.
Zeke's Slop Stop
SMOKING OR NON-SMOKING?
NON, HE SAID WITH JUST A LITTLE SMUG SELF-RIGHTEOUSNESS.
BREATHED
GUM CHEWING OR NON-GUM CHEWING?
NON.
SMELLY FEET OR NON-SMELLY FEET?
NON.
SNORING OR NON-SNORING?
NON.
SLURPING OR NON-SLURPING? SNORTING OR NON-SNORTING? BELCHING OR NON-BELCHING?
NON! NON! NON!
BIG NOSED OR NON-BIG NOSED?
UH...
WELL THIS IS A FINE HOW-DO-YOU-DO.
I WONDER IF YOU'D MIND PUTTING YOUR NOSE OUT WHILE I EAT?
BIG NOSED
NON-BIG NOSED

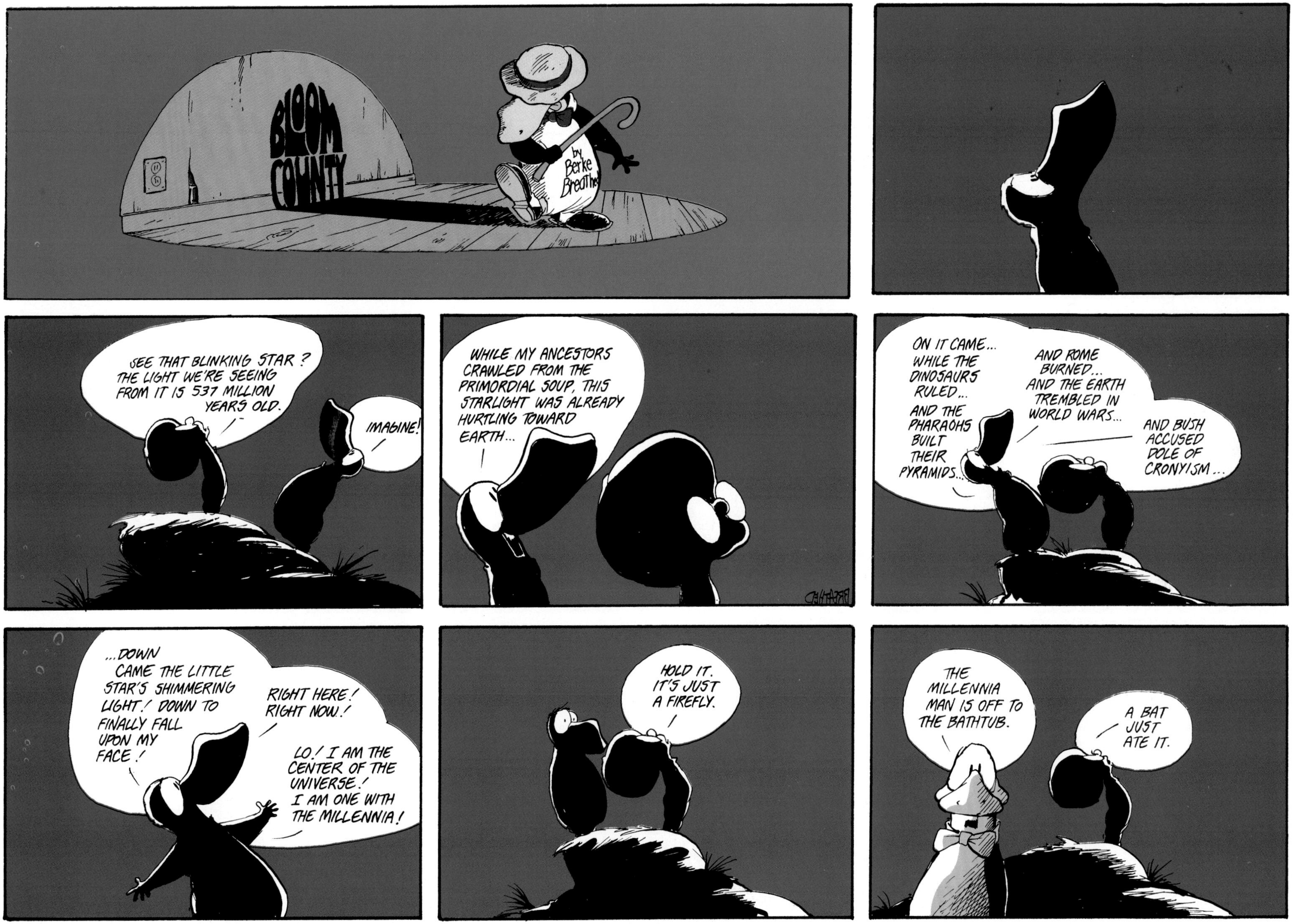
BLOOM COUNTY
by Berke Breathed
SEE THAT BLINKING STAR? THE LIGHT WE'RE SEEING FROM IT IS 537 MILLION YEARS OLD.
IMAGINE!
WHILE MY ANCESTORS CRAWLED FROM THE PRIMORDIAL SOUP, THIS STARLIGHT WAS ALREADY HURTLING TOWARD EARTH...
ON IT CAME... WHILE THE DINOSAURS RULED... AND THE PHARAOHS BUILT THEIR PYRAMIDS...
AND ROME BURNED... AND THE EARTH TREMBLED IN WORLD WARS...
AND BUSH ACCUSED DOLE OF CRONYISM...
...DOWN CAME THE LITTLE STAR'S SHIMMERING LIGHT! DOWN TO FINALLY FALL UPON MY FACE!
RIGHT HERE! RIGHT NOW!
LO! I AM THE CENTER OF THE UNIVERSE! I AM ONE WITH THE MILLENNIA!
HOLD IT. IT'S JUST A FIREFLY.
THE MILLENNIA MAN IS OFF TO THE BATHTUB.
A BAT JUST ATE IT.

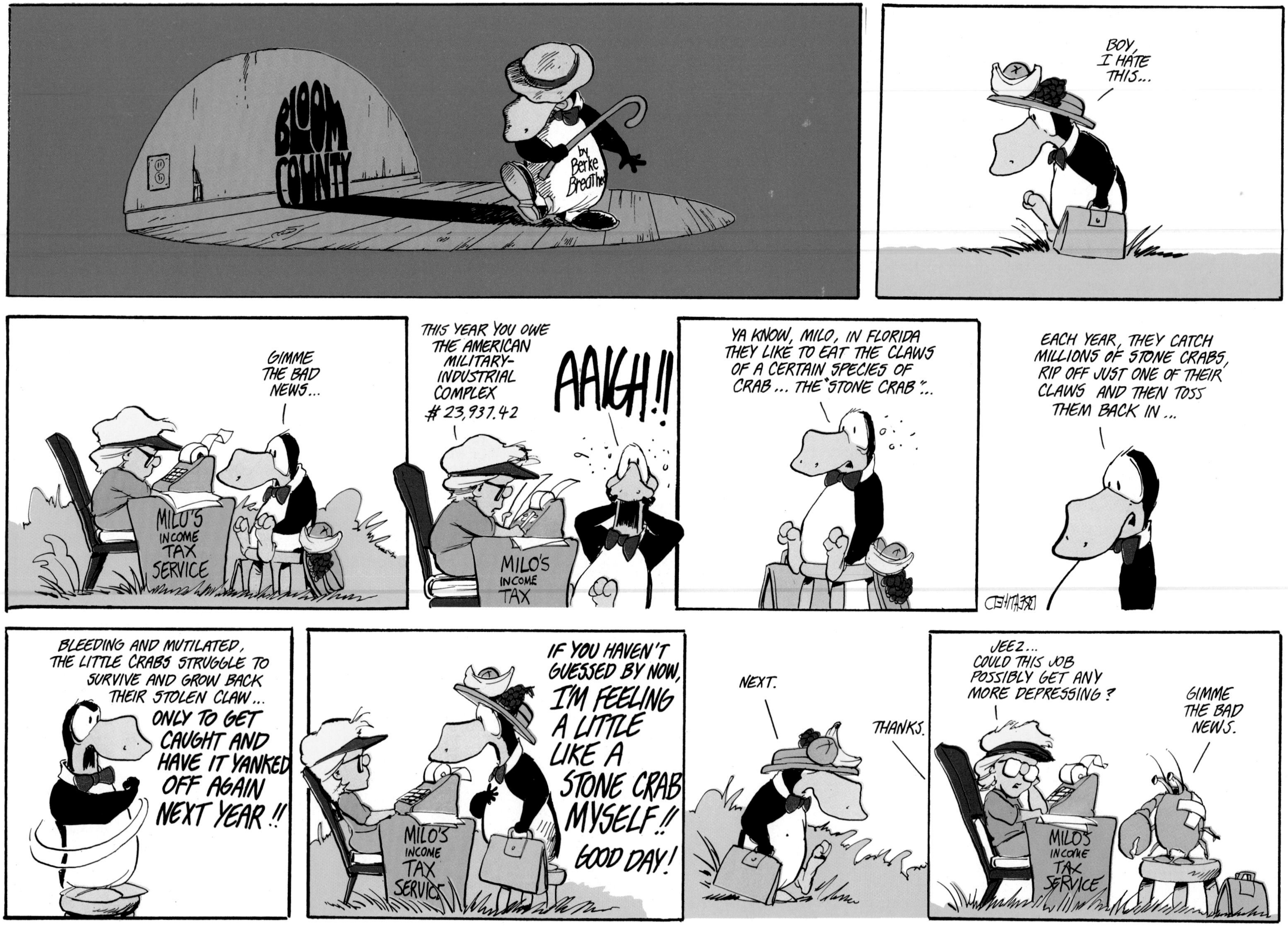
BLOOM COUNTY
by Berke Breathed
BOY, I HATE THIS...
GIMME THE BAD NEWS...
THIS YEAR YOU OWE THE AMERICAN MILITARY-INDUSTRIAL COMPLEX $23,937.42
AAIGH!!
YA KNOW, MILO, IN FLORIDA THEY LIKE TO EAT THE CLAWS OF A CERTAIN SPECIES OF CRAB... THE "STONE CRAB"...
EACH YEAR, THEY CATCH MILLIONS OF STONE CRABS, RIP OFF JUST ONE OF THEIR CLAWS AND THEN TOSS THEM BACK IN...
BLEEDING AND MUTILATED, THE LITTLE CRABS STRUGGLE TO SURVIVE AND GROW BACK THEIR STOLEN CLAW... ONLY TO GET CAUGHT AND HAVE IT YANKED OFF AGAIN NEXT YEAR!!
IF YOU HAVEN'T GUESSED BY NOW, I'M FEELING A LITTLE LIKE A STONE CRAB MYSELF!! GOOD DAY!
NEXT.
THANKS.
JEEZ... COULD THIS JOB POSSIBLY GET ANY MORE DEPRESSING?
GIMME THE BAD NEWS.
MILO'S INCOME TAX SERVICE

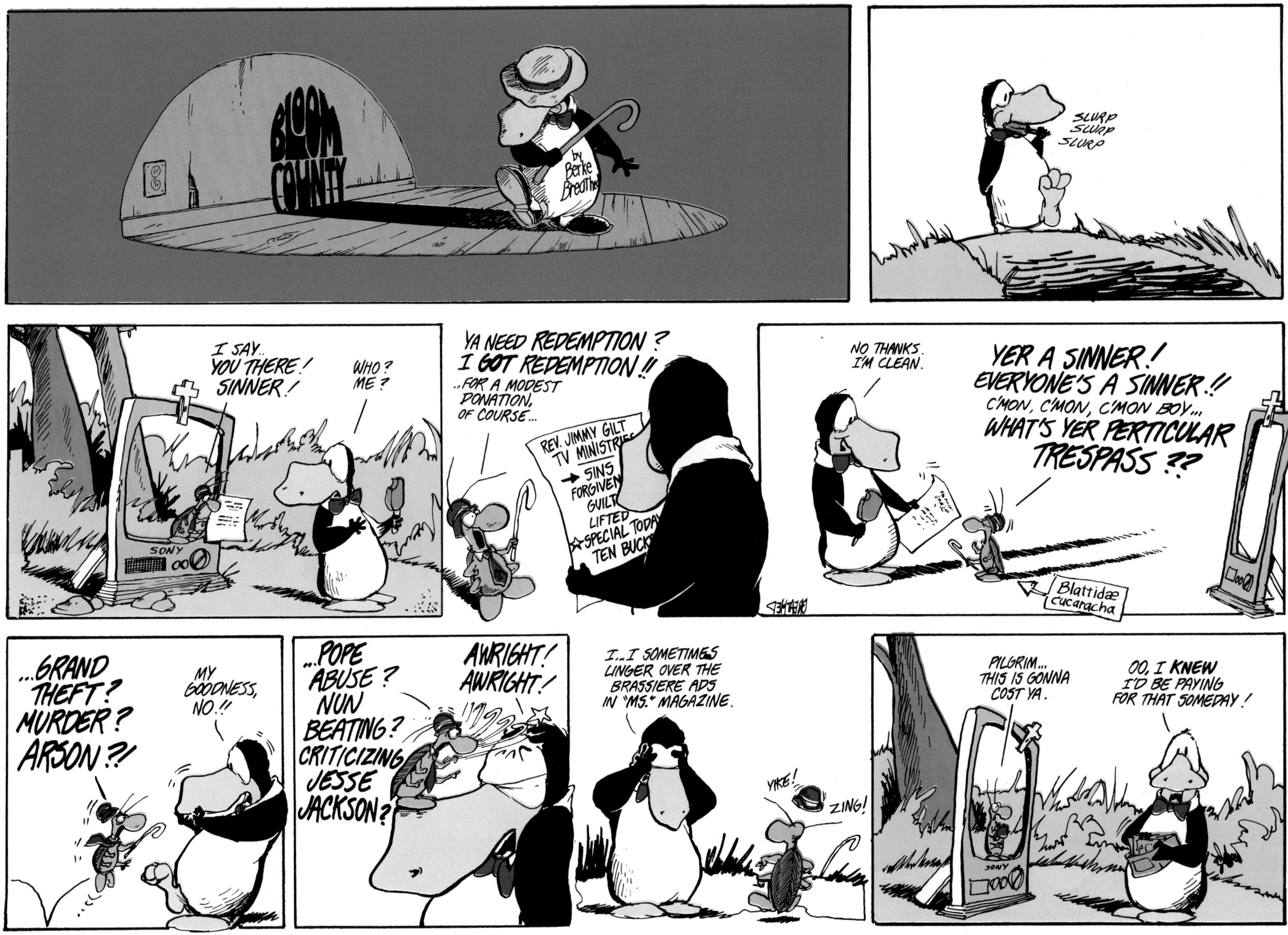
BLOOM COUNTY
by Berke Breathed
SLURP SLURP SLURP
I SAY.. YOU THERE! SINNER!
WHO? ME?
SONY
YA NEED REDEMPTION? I GOT REDEMPTION!!
..FOR A MODEST DONATION, OF COURSE...
REV. JIMMY GILT TV MINISTRIES
SINS FORGIVEN
GUILT LIFTED
SPECIAL TODAY TEN BUCKS
NO THANKS. I'M CLEAN.
YER A SINNER! EVERYONE'S A SINNER!!
C'MON, C'MON, C'MON BOY...
WHAT'S YER PERTICULAR TRESPASS??
Blattidæ cucaracha
...GRAND THEFT? MURDER? ARSON?!
MY GOODNESS, NO.!!
...POPE ABUSE? NUN BEATING? CRITICIZING JESSE JACKSON?
AWRIGHT! AWRIGHT!
I..I SOMETIMES LINGER OVER THE BRASSIERE ADS IN "MS." MAGAZINE.
YIKE!
ZING!
PILGRIM... THIS IS GONNA COST YA.
OO, I KNEW I'D BE PAYING FOR THAT SOMEDAY!
SONY

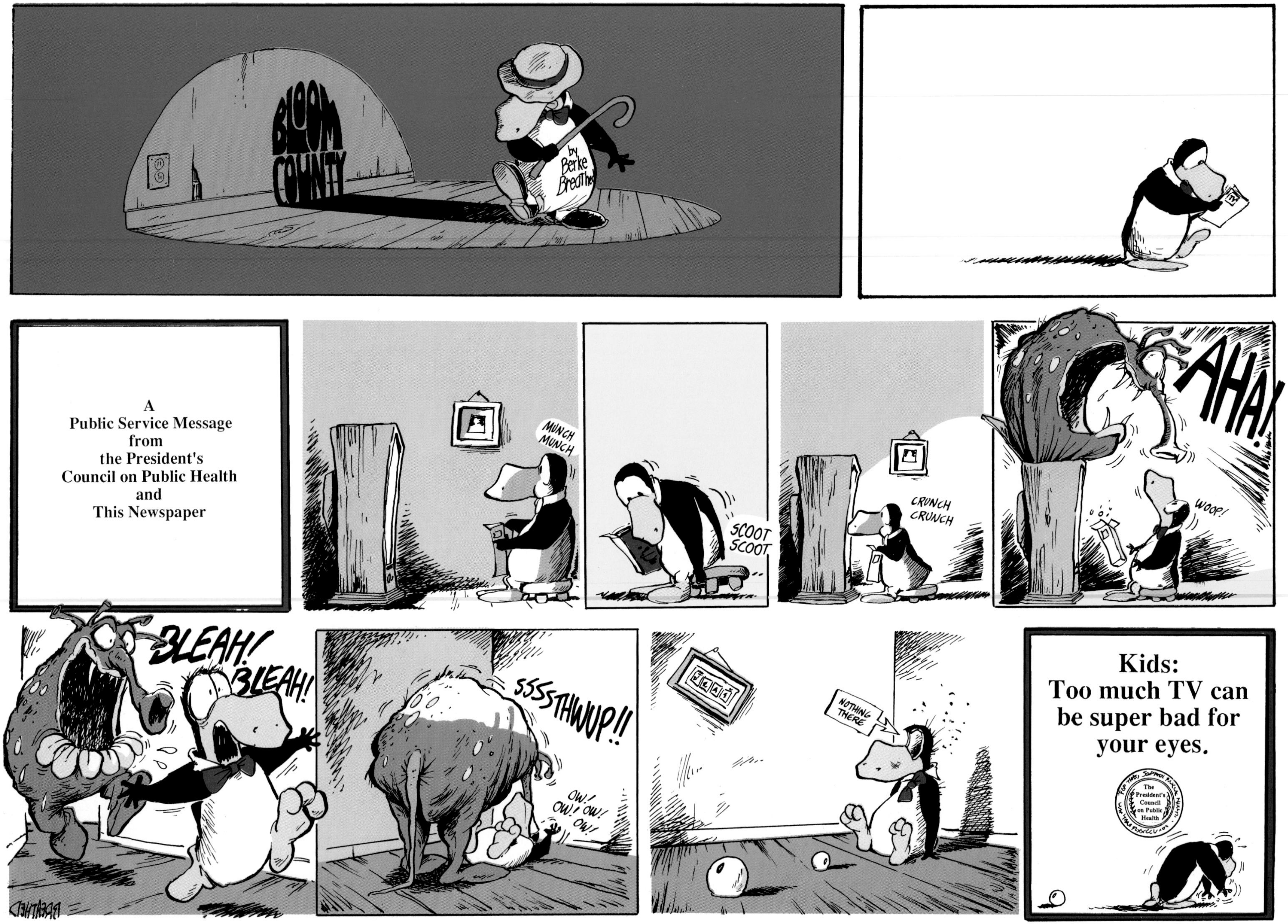
BLOOM COUNTY
by Berke Breathed
A Public Service Message from the President's Council on Public Health and This Newspaper
MUNCH MUNCH
SCOOT SCOOT
CRUNCH CRUNCH
AHA!
WOOP!
BLEAH! BLEAH!
SSSSTHWUP!!
OW! OW! OW! OW!
NOTHING THERE
Kids: Too much TV can be super bad for your eyes.
The President's Council on Public Health
BREATHED

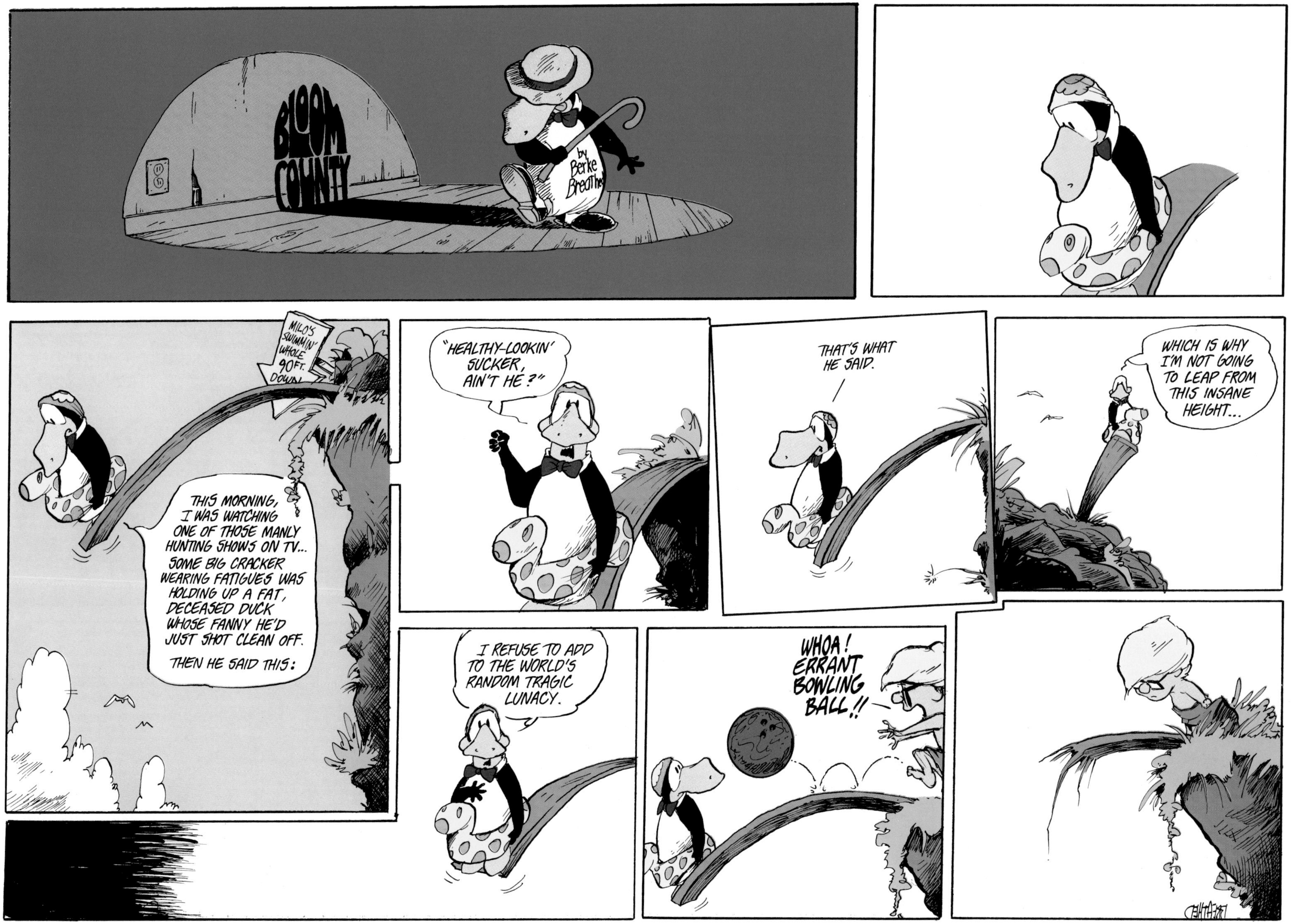
BLOOM COUNTY
by Berke Breathed
MILO'S SWIMMIN' WHOLE 90 FT. DOWN
THIS MORNING, I WAS WATCHING ONE OF THOSE MANLY HUNTING SHOWS ON TV... SOME BIG CRACKER WEARING FATIGUES WAS HOLDING UP A FAT, DECEASED DUCK WHOSE FANNY HE'D JUST SHOT CLEAN OFF.
THEN HE SAID THIS:
"HEALTHY-LOOKIN' SUCKER, AIN'T HE?"
THAT'S WHAT HE SAID.
WHICH IS WHY I'M NOT GOING TO LEAP FROM THIS INSANE HEIGHT...
I REFUSE TO ADD TO THE WORLD'S RANDOM TRAGIC LUNACY.
WHOA! ERRANT BOWLING BALL!!

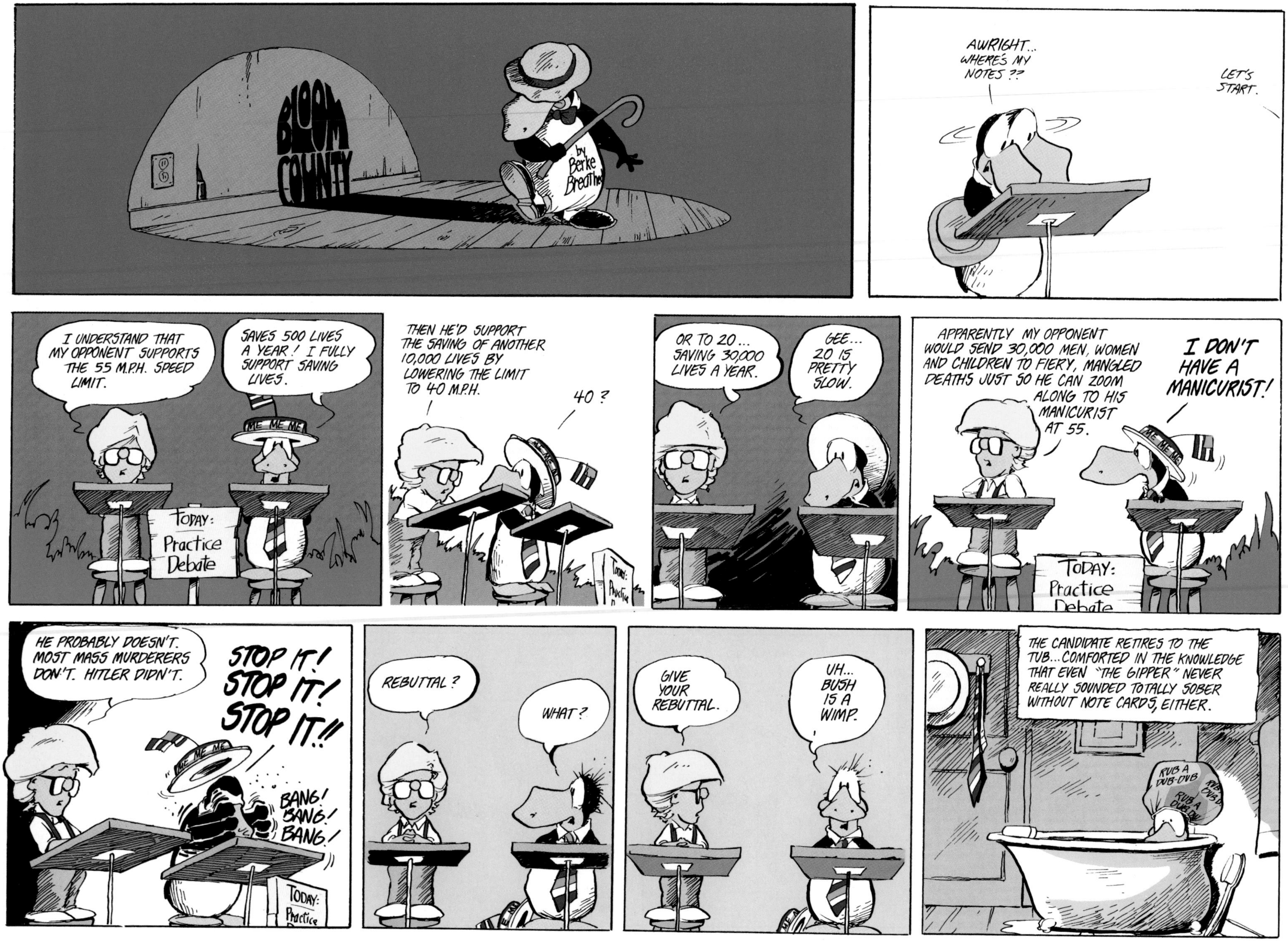
BLOOM COUNTY
by Berke Breathed
AWRIGHT... WHERE'S MY NOTES ??
LET'S START.
I UNDERSTAND THAT MY OPPONENT SUPPORTS THE 55 M.P.H. SPEED LIMIT.
SAVES 500 LIVES A YEAR! I FULLY SUPPORT SAVING LIVES.
ME ME ME
TODAY: Practice Debate
THEN HE'D SUPPORT THE SAVING OF ANOTHER 10,000 LIVES BY LOWERING THE LIMIT TO 40 M.P.H.
40 ?
OR TO 20... SAVING 30,000 LIVES A YEAR.
GEE... 20 IS PRETTY SLOW.
APPARENTLY MY OPPONENT WOULD SEND 30,000 MEN, WOMEN AND CHILDREN TO FIERY, MANGLED DEATHS JUST SO HE CAN ZOOM ALONG TO HIS MANICURIST AT 55.
I DON'T HAVE A MANICURIST!
HE PROBABLY DOESN'T. MOST MASS MURDERERS DON'T. HITLER DIDN'T.
STOP IT! STOP IT! STOP IT!!
BANG! BANG! BANG!
REBUTTAL ?
WHAT ?
GIVE YOUR REBUTTAL.
UH... BUSH IS A WIMP.
THE CANDIDATE RETIRES TO THE TUB... COMFORTED IN THE KNOWLEDGE THAT EVEN "THE GIPPER" NEVER REALLY SOUNDED TOTALLY SOBER WITHOUT NOTE CARDS, EITHER.
RUB A DUB-DUB

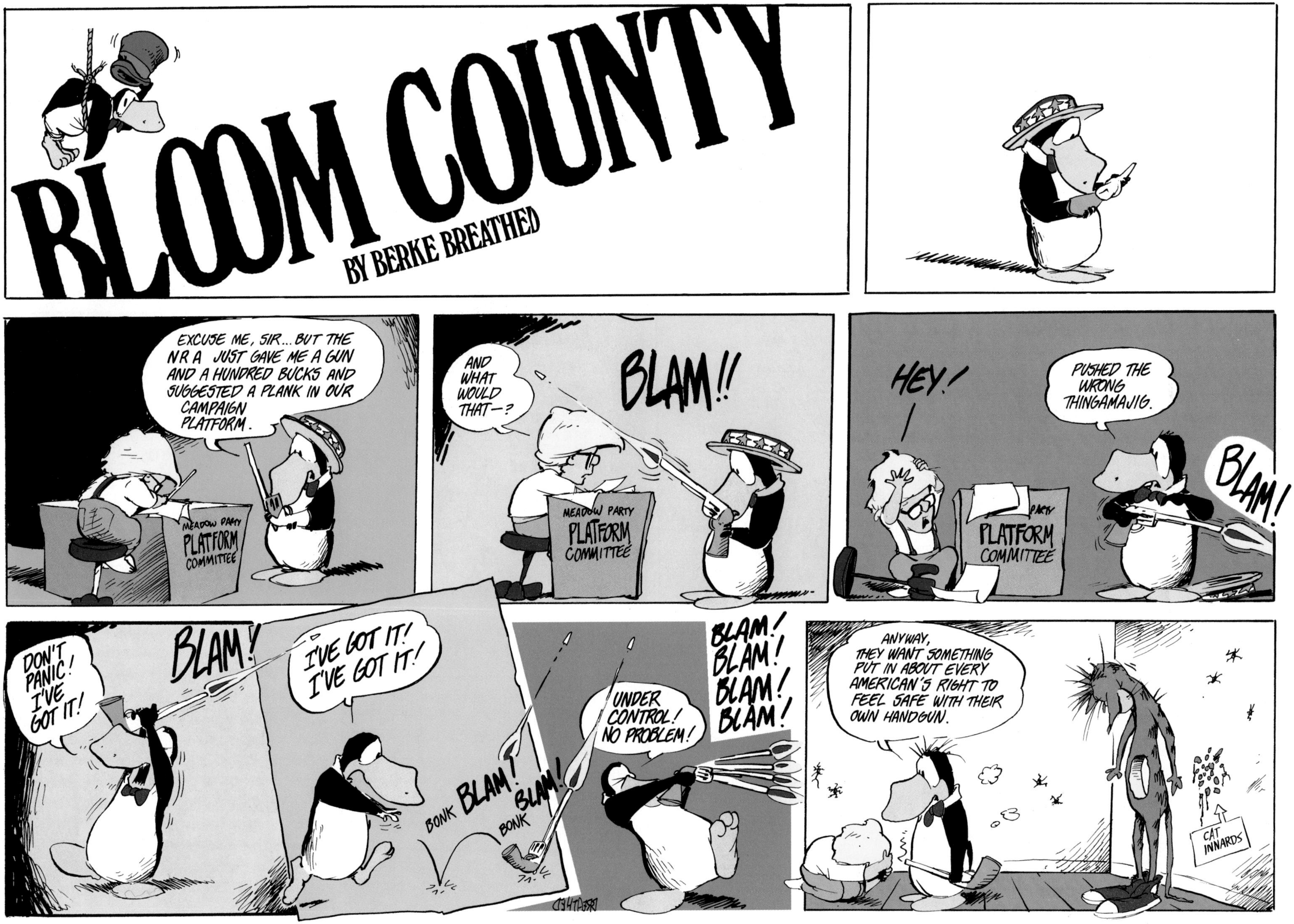
BLOOM COUNTY
BY BERKE BREATHED
EXCUSE ME, SIR... BUT THE NRA JUST GAVE ME A GUN AND A HUNDRED BUCKS AND SUGGESTED A PLANK IN OUR CAMPAIGN PLATFORM.
MEADOW PARTY PLATFORM COMMITTEE
AND WHAT WOULD THAT—?
BLAM!!
MEADOW PARTY PLATFORM COMMITTEE
HEY!
PUSHED THE WRONG THINGAMAJIG.
BLAM!
DON'T PANIC! I'VE GOT IT!
BLAM!
I'VE GOT IT! I'VE GOT IT!
BONK BLAM!
BONK BLAM!
UNDER CONTROL! NO PROBLEM!
BLAM! BLAM! BLAM! BLAM!
ANYWAY, THEY WANT SOMETHING PUT IN ABOUT EVERY AMERICAN'S RIGHT TO FEEL SAFE WITH THEIR OWN HANDGUN.
CAT INNARDS

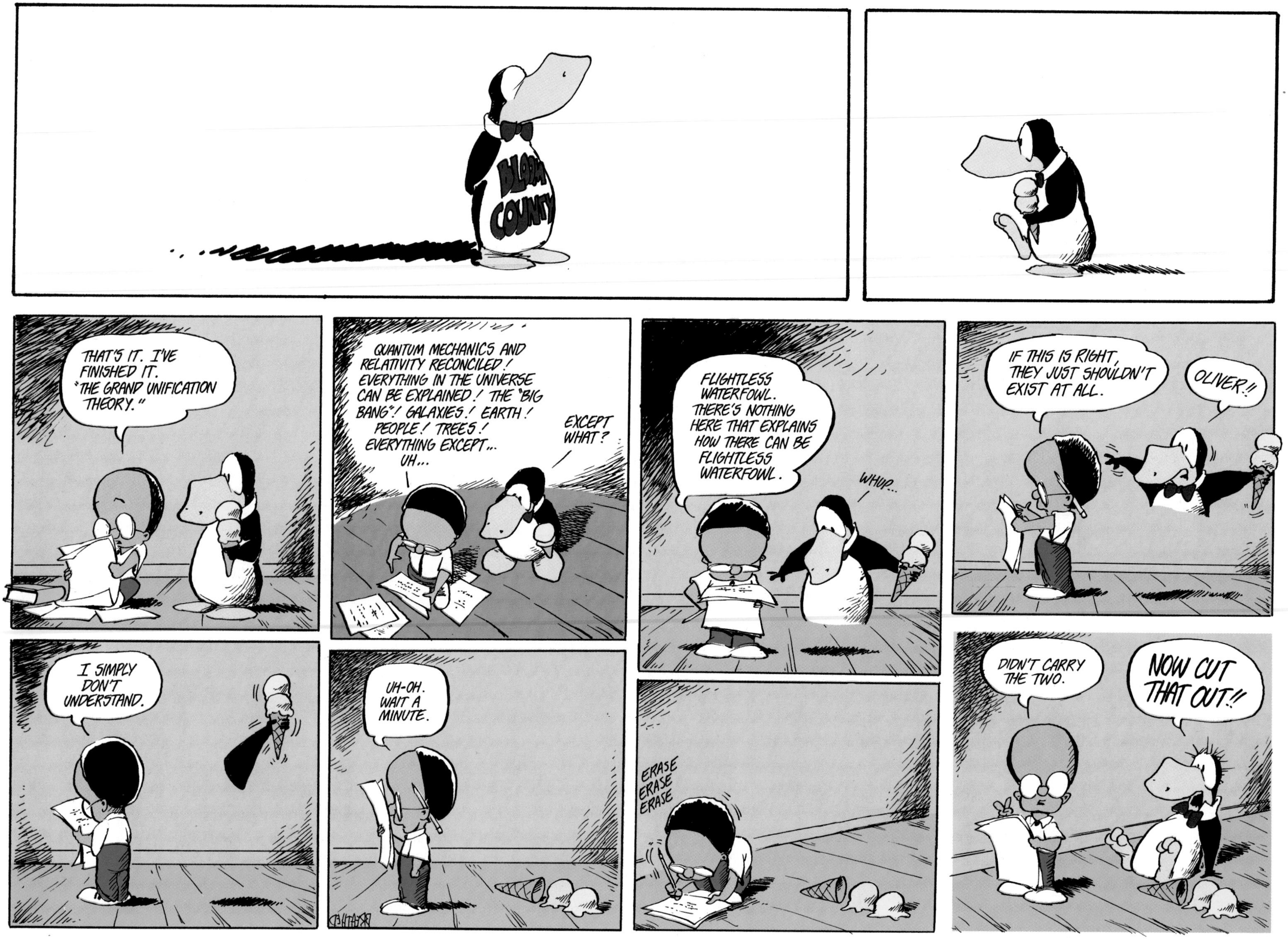

BLOOM COUNTY
THAT'S IT. I'VE FINISHED IT. "THE GRAND UNIFICATION THEORY."
QUANTUM MECHANICS AND RELATIVITY RECONCILED! EVERYTHING IN THE UNIVERSE CAN BE EXPLAINED! THE "BIG BANG"! GALAXIES! EARTH! PEOPLE! TREES! EVERYTHING EXCEPT... UH...
EXCEPT WHAT?
FLIGHTLESS WATERFOWL. THERE'S NOTHING HERE THAT EXPLAINS HOW THERE CAN BE FLIGHTLESS WATERFOWL.
WHUP...
IF THIS IS RIGHT, THEY JUST SHOULDN'T EXIST AT ALL.
OLIVER?!
I SIMPLY DON'T UNDERSTAND.
UH-OH. WAIT A MINUTE.
ERASE
ERASE
ERASE
DIDN'T CARRY THE TWO.
NOW CUT THAT OUT!!

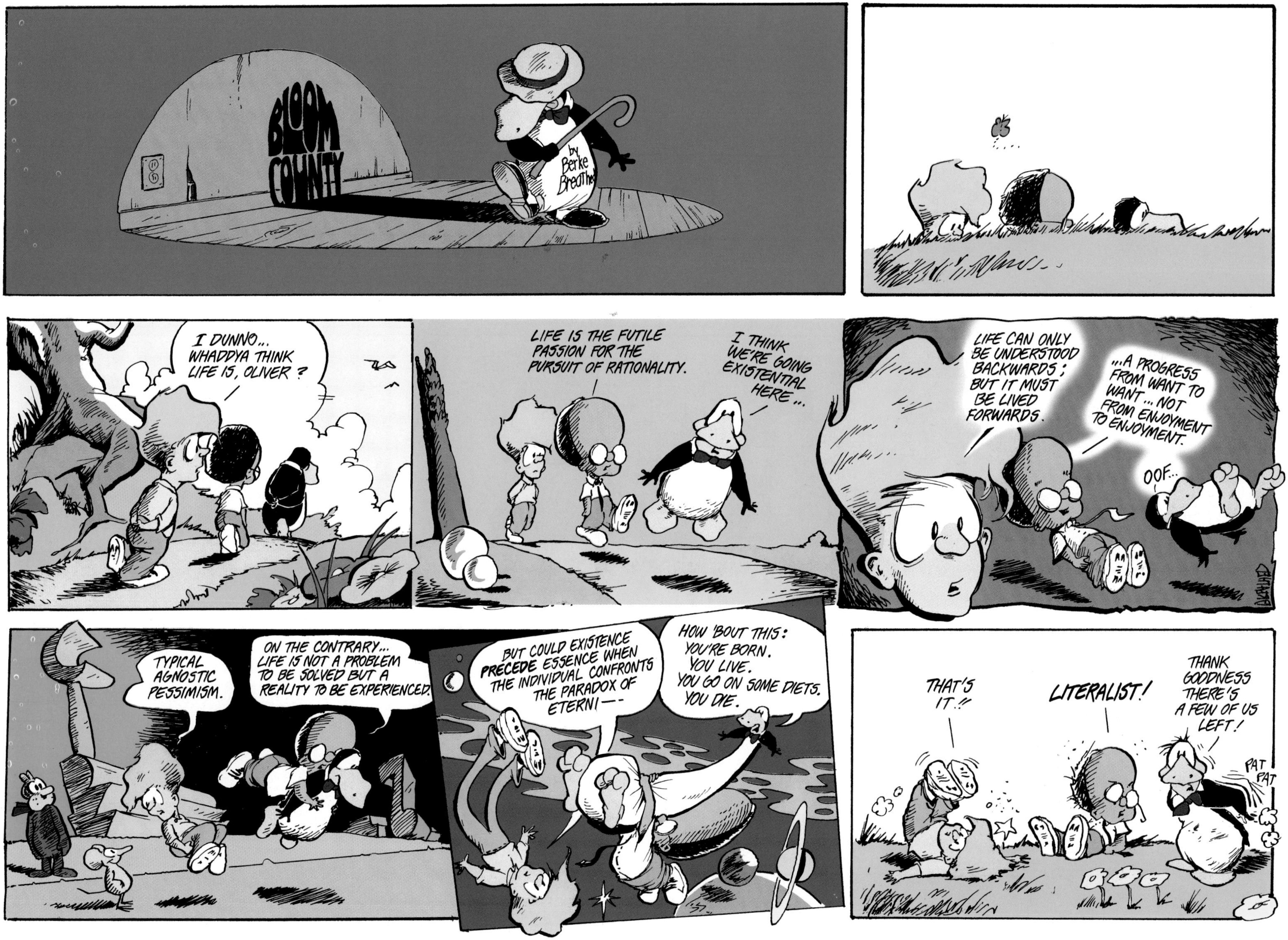
BLOOM COUNTY
by Berke Breathed
I DUNNO... WHADDYA THINK LIFE IS, OLIVER ?
LIFE IS THE FUTILE PASSION FOR THE PURSUIT OF RATIONALITY.
I THINK WE'RE GOING EXISTENTIAL HERE...
LIFE CAN ONLY BE UNDERSTOOD BACKWARDS ; BUT IT MUST BE LIVED FORWARDS.
...A PROGRESS FROM WANT TO WANT... NOT FROM ENJOYMENT TO ENJOYMENT.
OOF...
TYPICAL AGNOSTIC PESSIMISM.
ON THE CONTRARY... LIFE IS NOT A PROBLEM TO BE SOLVED BUT A REALITY TO BE EXPERIENCED.
BUT COULD EXISTENCE PRECEDE ESSENCE WHEN THE INDIVIDUAL CONFRONTS THE PARADOX OF ETERNI—-
HOW 'BOUT THIS : YOU'RE BORN. YOU LIVE. YOU GO ON SOME DIETS. YOU DIE.
THAT'S IT.!!
LITERALIST !
THANK GOODNESS THERE'S A FEW OF US LEFT !
PAT PAT

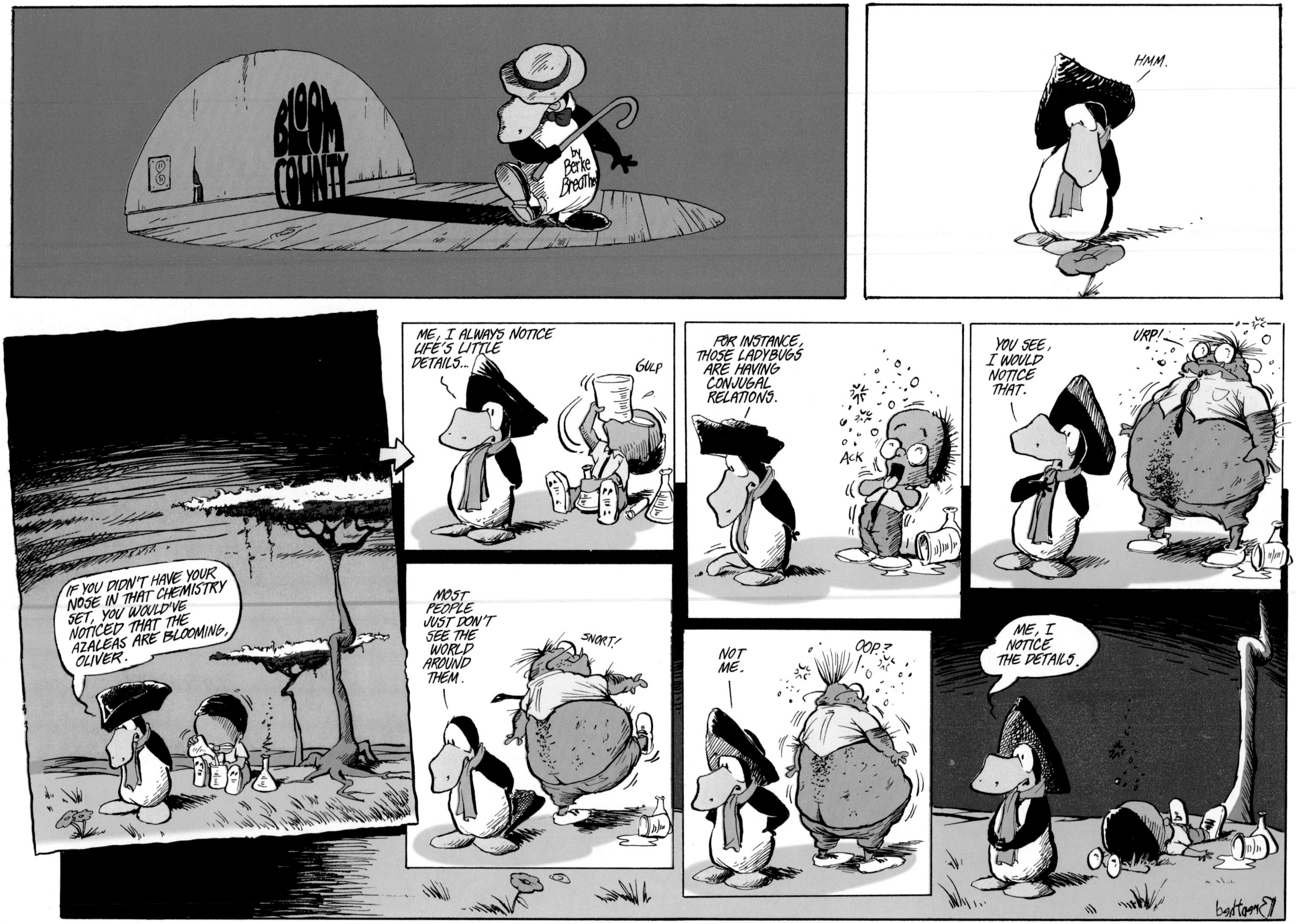
BLOOM COUNTY
by Berke Breathed
HMM.
IF YOU DIDN'T HAVE YOUR NOSE IN THAT CHEMISTRY SET, YOU WOULD'VE NOTICED THAT THE AZALEAS ARE BLOOMING, OLIVER.
ME, I ALWAYS NOTICE LIFE'S LITTLE DETAILS...
GULP
FOR INSTANCE, THOSE LADYBUGS ARE HAVING CONJUGAL RELATIONS.
ACK
YOU SEE, I WOULD NOTICE THAT.
URP!
MOST PEOPLE JUST DON'T SEE THE WORLD AROUND THEM.
SNORT!
NOT ME.
OOP?
ME, I NOTICE THE DETAILS.

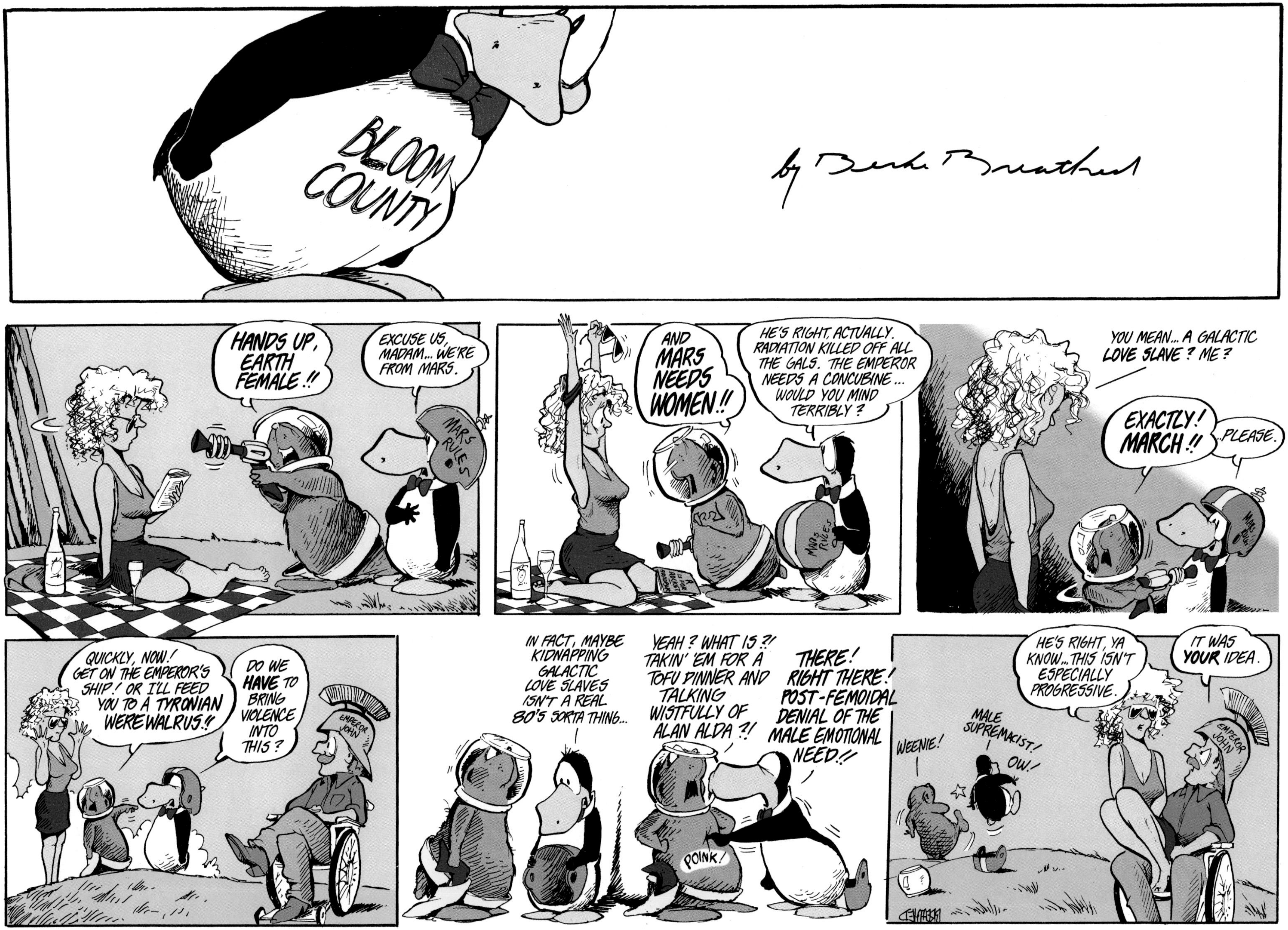
BLOOM COUNTY
by Berke Breathed
HANDS UP, EARTH FEMALE!!
EXCUSE US, MADAM... WE'RE FROM MARS.
MARS RULES
AND MARS NEEDS WOMEN!!
HE'S RIGHT, ACTUALLY. RADIATION KILLED OFF ALL THE GALS. THE EMPEROR NEEDS A CONCUBINE... WOULD YOU MIND TERRIBLY?
YOU MEAN... A GALACTIC LOVE SLAVE? ME?
EXACTLY! MARCH!!
...PLEASE.
QUICKLY, NOW! GET ON THE EMPEROR'S SHIP! OR I'LL FEED YOU TO A TYRONIAN WEREWALRUS!!
DO WE HAVE TO BRING VIOLENCE INTO THIS?
EMPEROR JOHN
IN FACT, MAYBE KIDNAPPING GALACTIC LOVE SLAVES ISN'T A REAL 80'S SORTA THING...
YEAH? WHAT IS?! TAKIN' 'EM FOR A TOFU DINNER AND TALKING WISTFULLY OF ALAN ALDA?!
THERE! RIGHT THERE! POST-FEMOIDAL DENIAL OF THE MALE EMOTIONAL NEED!!
POINK!
HE'S RIGHT, YA KNOW... THIS ISN'T ESPECIALLY PROGRESSIVE.
IT WAS YOUR IDEA.
WEENIE!
MALE SUPREMACIST!
OW!

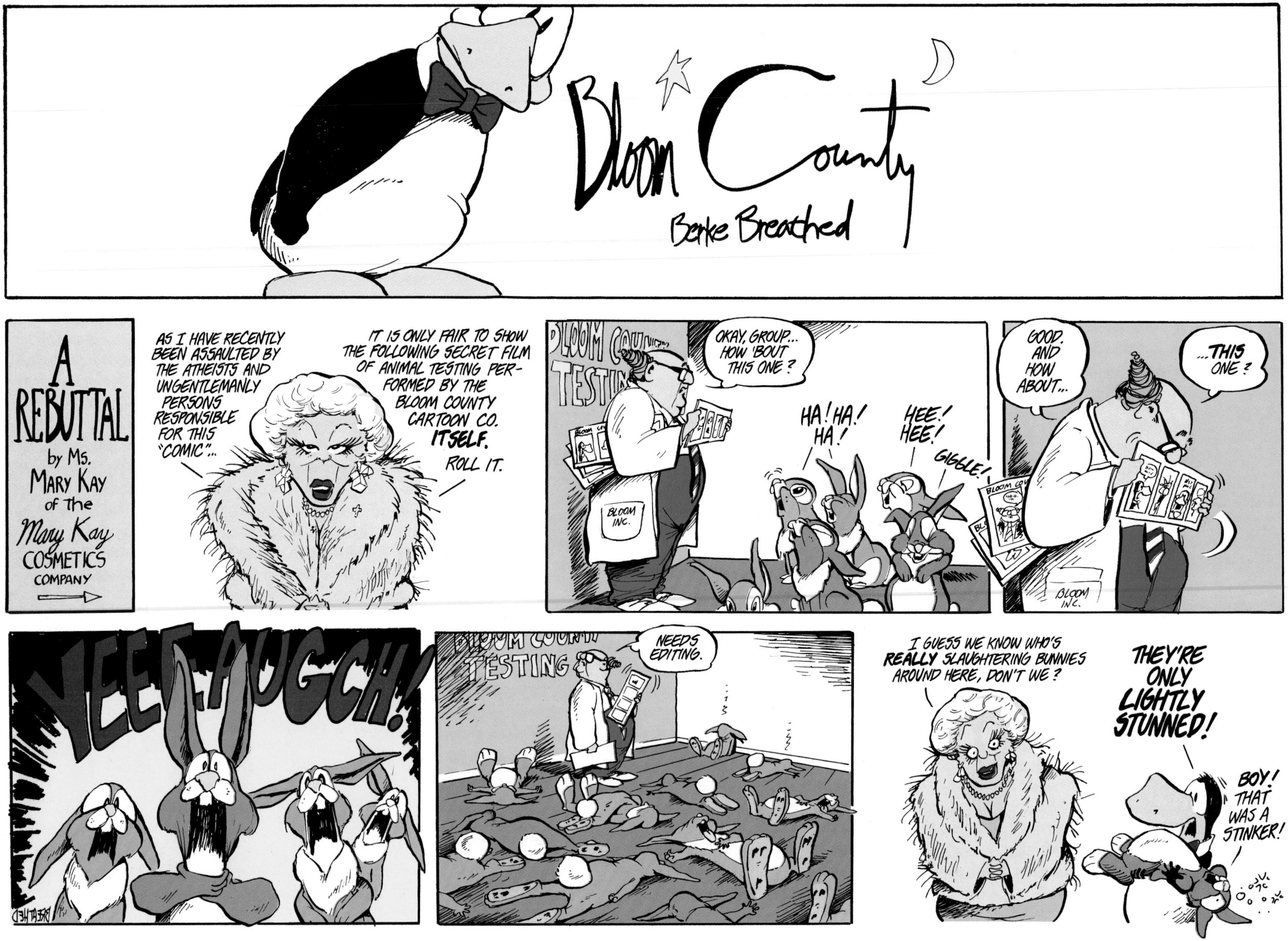
Bloom County
Berke Breathed
A REBUTTAL by Ms. Mary Kay of the Mary Kay COSMETICS COMPANY
AS I HAVE RECENTLY BEEN ASSAULTED BY THE ATHEISTS AND UNGENTLEMANLY PERSONS RESPONSIBLE FOR THIS "COMIC"...
IT IS ONLY FAIR TO SHOW THE FOLLOWING SECRET FILM OF ANIMAL TESTING PERFORMED BY THE BLOOM COUNTY CARTOON CO. ITSELF.
ROLL IT.
BLOOM COUNTY TESTING
OKAY, GROUP... HOW 'BOUT THIS ONE ?
HA! HA! HA!
HEE! HEE!
GIGGLE!
BLOOM INC.
GOOD. AND HOW ABOUT...
...THIS ONE ?
BLOOM INC.
YEEEAUGCH!
BLOOM COUNTY TESTING
NEEDS EDITING.
I GUESS WE KNOW WHO'S REALLY SLAUGHTERING BUNNIES AROUND HERE, DON'T WE ?
THEY'RE ONLY LIGHTLY STUNNED!
BOY! THAT WAS A STINKER!

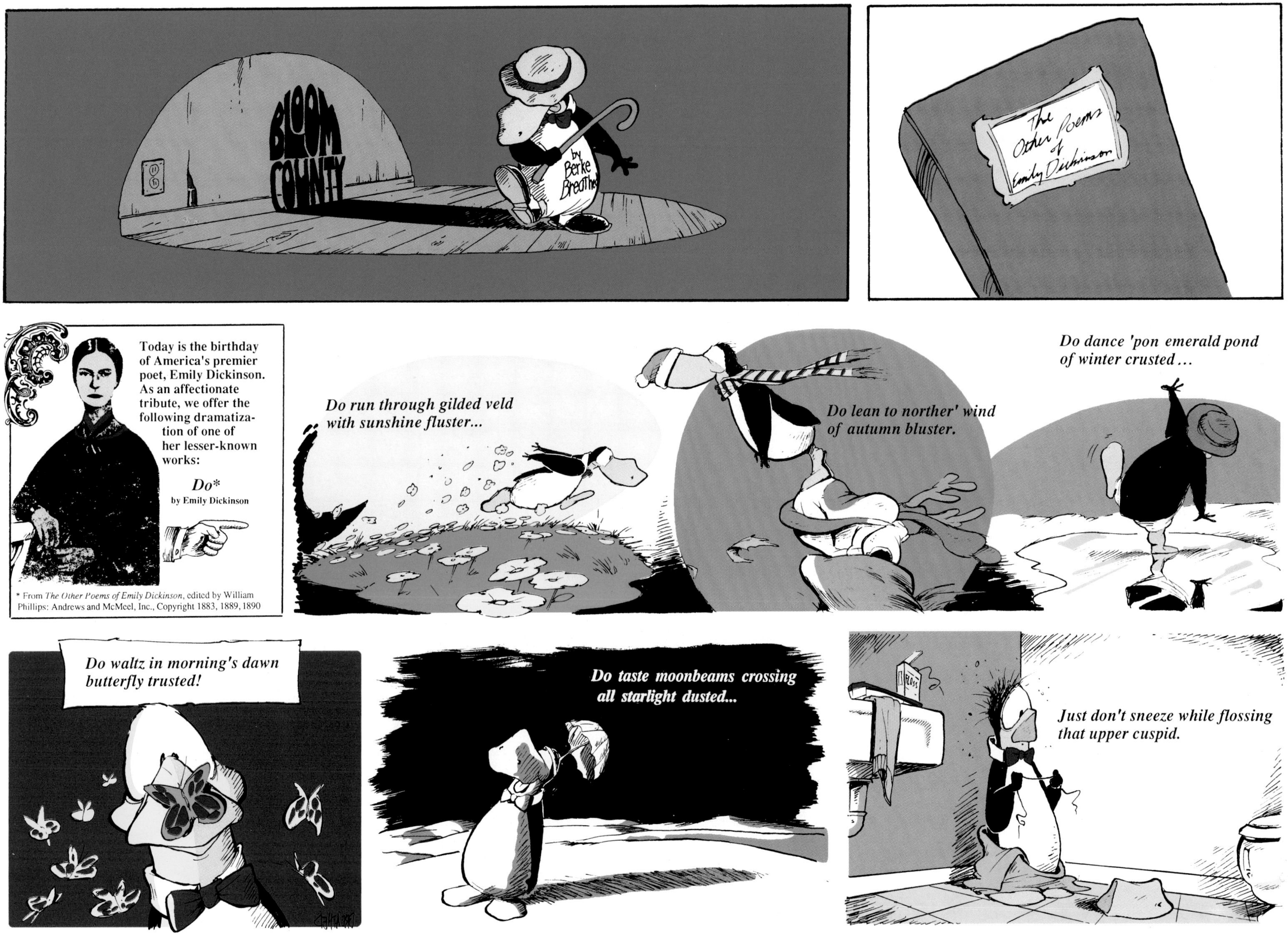
BLOOM COUNTY
by Berke Breathed
The Other Poems of Emily Dickinson
Today is the birthday of America's premier poet, Emily Dickinson. As an affectionate tribute, we offer the following dramatization of one of her lesser-known works:
Do*
by Emily Dickinson
* From The Other Poems of Emily Dickinson, edited by William Phillips: Andrews and McMeel, Inc., Copyright 1883, 1889, 1890
Do run through gilded veld with sunshine fluster...
Do lean to norther' wind of autumn bluster.
Do dance 'pon emerald pond of winter crusted...
Do waltz in morning's dawn butterfly trusted!
Do taste moonbeams crossing all starlight dusted...
FLOSS
Just don't sneeze while flossing that upper cuspid.

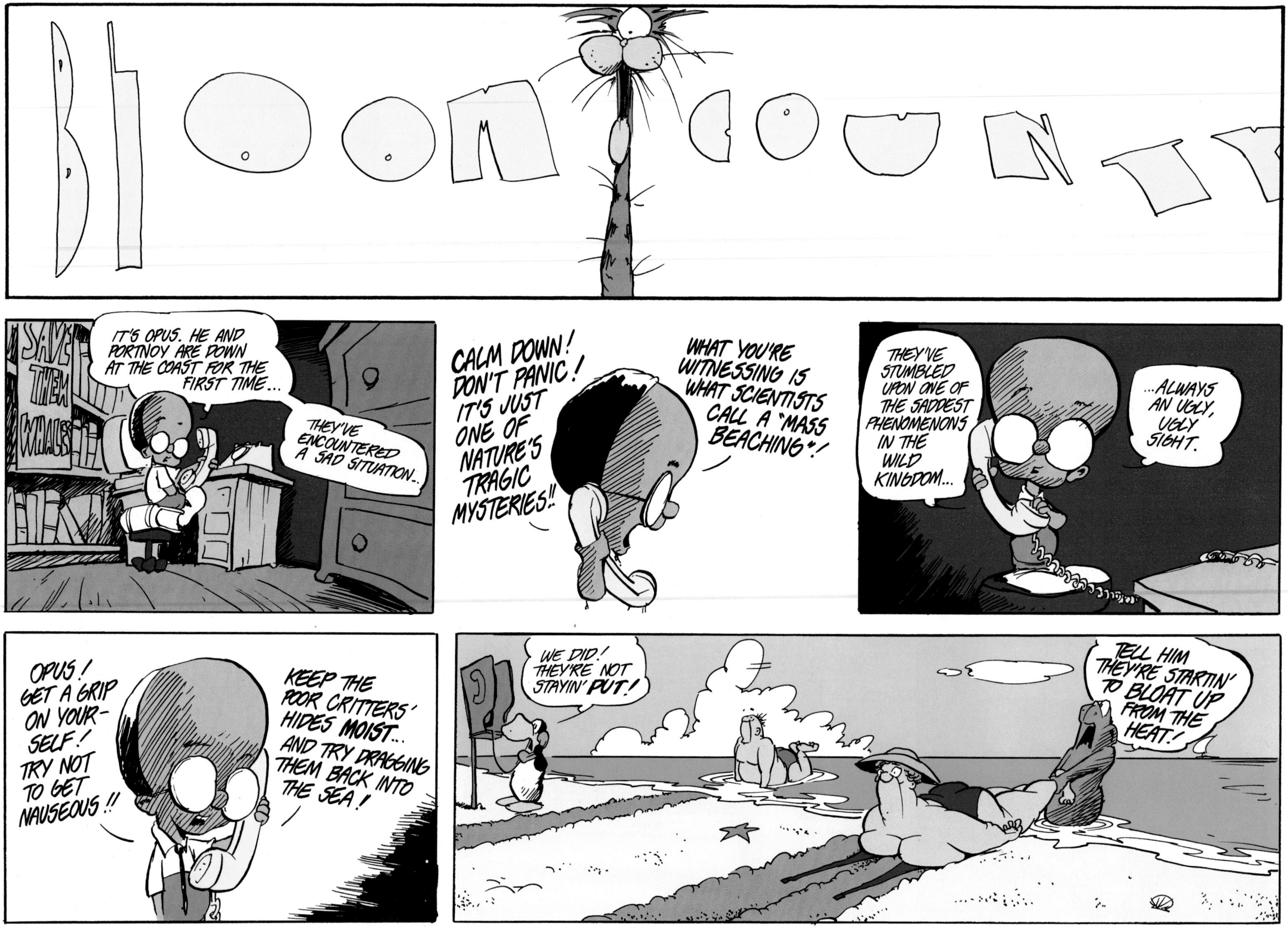
BLOOM COUNTY
IT'S OPUS. HE AND PORTNOY ARE DOWN AT THE COAST FOR THE FIRST TIME...
THEY'VE ENCOUNTERED A SAD SITUATION...
SAVE THEM WHALES
CALM DOWN! DON'T PANIC! IT'S JUST ONE OF NATURE'S TRAGIC MYSTERIES!!
WHAT YOU'RE WITNESSING IS WHAT SCIENTISTS CALL A "MASS BEACHING"!
THEY'VE STUMBLED UPON ONE OF THE SADDEST PHENOMENONS IN THE WILD KINGDOM...
...ALWAYS AN UGLY, UGLY SIGHT.
OPUS! GET A GRIP ON YOURSELF! TRY NOT TO GET NAUSEOUS!!
KEEP THE POOR CRITTERS' HIDES MOIST... AND TRY DRAGGING THEM BACK INTO THE SEA!
WE DID! THEY'RE NOT STAYIN' PUT!
TELL HIM THEY'RE STARTIN' TO BLOAT UP FROM THE HEAT!

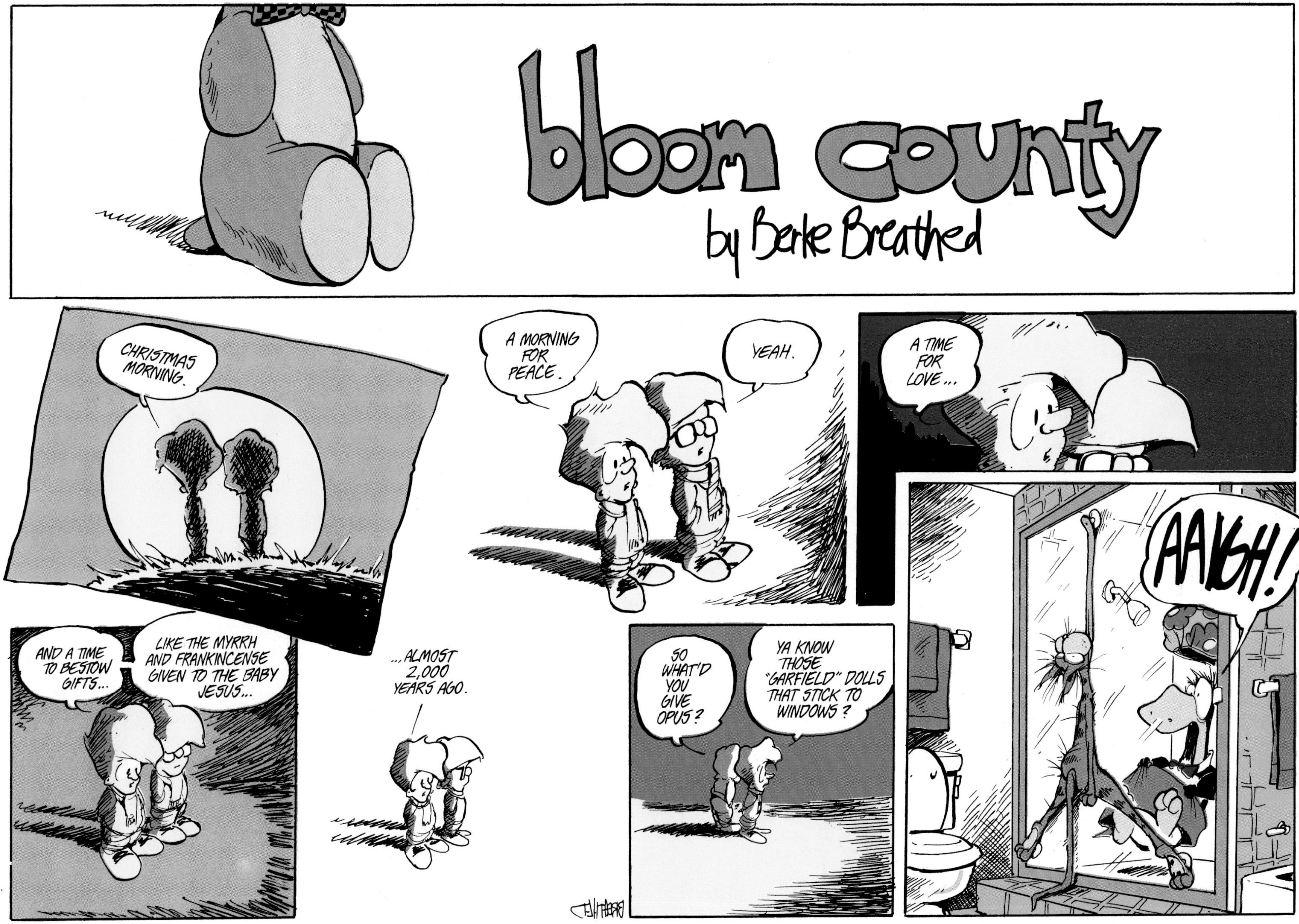
bloom county
by Berke Breathed
CHRISTMAS MORNING.
A MORNING FOR PEACE.
YEAH.
A TIME FOR LOVE...
AND A TIME TO BESTOW GIFTS...
LIKE THE MYRRH AND FRANKINCENSE GIVEN TO THE BABY JESUS...
...ALMOST 2,000 YEARS AGO.
SO WHAT'D YOU GIVE OPUS ?
YA KNOW THOSE "GARFIELD" DOLLS THAT STICK TO WINDOWS ?
AAUGH!

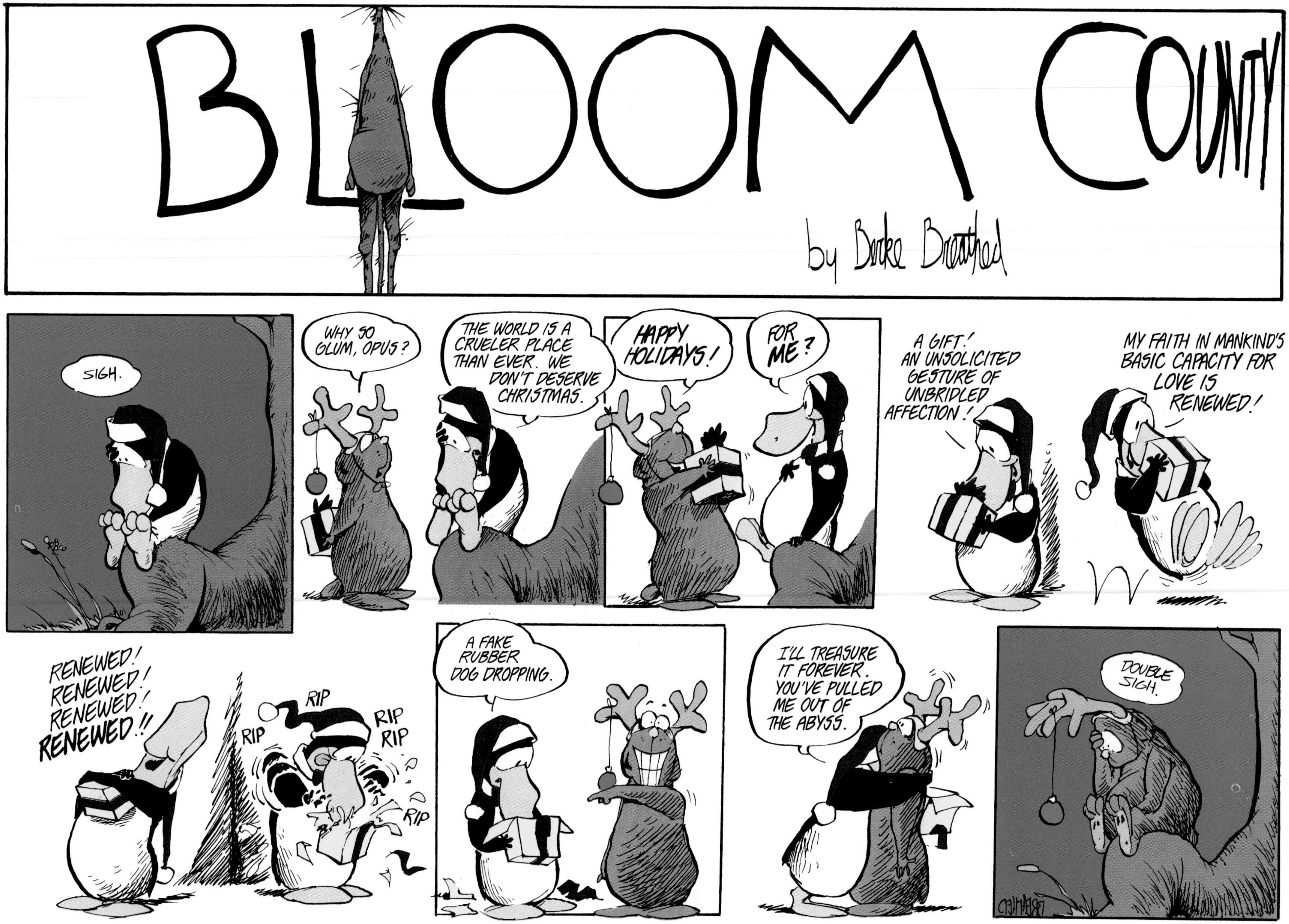
BLOOM COUNTY
by Berke Breathed
SIGH.
WHY SO GLUM, OPUS?
THE WORLD IS A CRUELER PLACE THAN EVER. WE DON'T DESERVE CHRISTMAS.
HAPPY HOLIDAYS!
FOR ME?
A GIFT! AN UNSOLICITED GESTURE OF UNBRIDLED AFFECTION!
MY FAITH IN MANKIND'S BASIC CAPACITY FOR LOVE IS RENEWED!
RENEWED! RENEWED! RENEWED! RENEWED!!
RIP
RIP
RIP RIP
RIP
A FAKE RUBBER DOG DROPPING.
I'LL TREASURE IT FOREVER. YOU'VE PULLED ME OUT OF THE ABYSS.
DOUBLE SIGH.

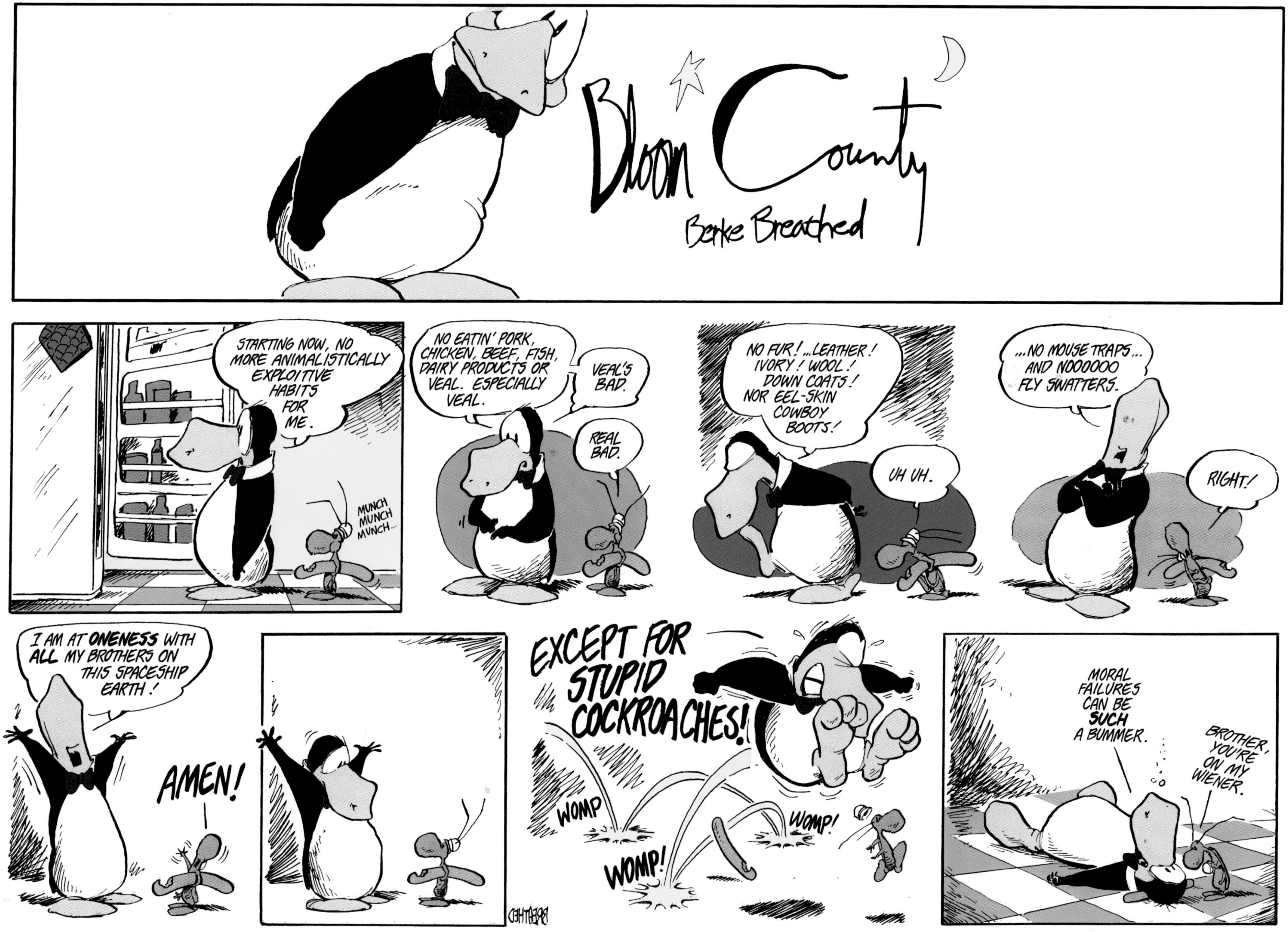

Bloom County
Berke Breathed
STARTING NOW, NO MORE ANIMALISTICALLY EXPLOITIVE HABITS FOR ME.
MUNCH MUNCH MUNCH...
NO EATIN' PORK, CHICKEN, BEEF, FISH, DAIRY PRODUCTS OR VEAL. ESPECIALLY VEAL.
VEAL'S BAD.
REAL BAD.
NO FUR! ...LEATHER! IVORY! WOOL! DOWN COATS! NOR EEL-SKIN COWBOY BOOTS!
UH UH.
...NO MOUSE TRAPS... AND NOOOOOO FLY SWATTERS.
RIGHT!
I AM AT **ONENESS** WITH **ALL** MY BROTHERS ON THIS SPACESHIP EARTH!
AMEN!
EXCEPT FOR STUPID COCKROACHES!
WOMP
WOMP!
WOMP!
MORAL FAILURES CAN BE **SUCH** A BUMMER.
BROTHER, YOU'RE ON MY WIENER.

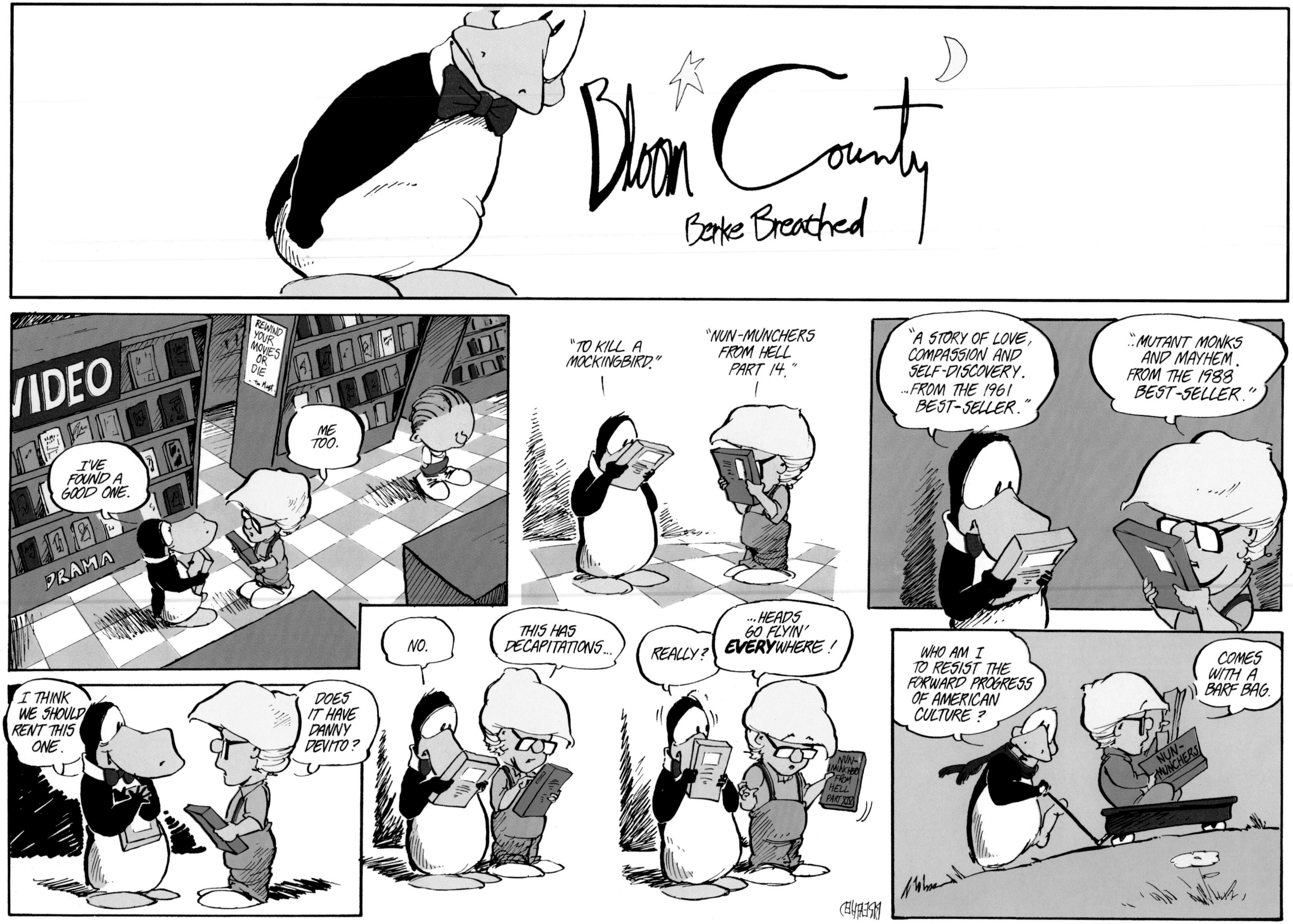
Bloom County
Berke Breathed
VIDEO
REWIND YOUR MOVIES OR DIE
DRAMA
I'VE FOUND A GOOD ONE.
ME TOO.
"TO KILL A MOCKINGBIRD."
"NUN-MUNCHERS FROM HELL PART 14."
"A STORY OF LOVE, COMPASSION AND SELF-DISCOVERY. ...FROM THE 1961 BEST-SELLER."
"...MUTANT MONKS AND MAYHEM. FROM THE 1988 BEST-SELLER."
I THINK WE SHOULD RENT THIS ONE.
DOES IT HAVE DANNY DEVITO?
NO.
THIS HAS DECAPITATIONS...
REALLY?
...HEADS GO FLYIN' EVERYWHERE!
NUN-MUNCHERS FROM HELL PART XIV
WHO AM I TO RESIST THE FORWARD PROGRESS OF AMERICAN CULTURE?
COMES WITH A BARF BAG.
NUN-MUNCHERS

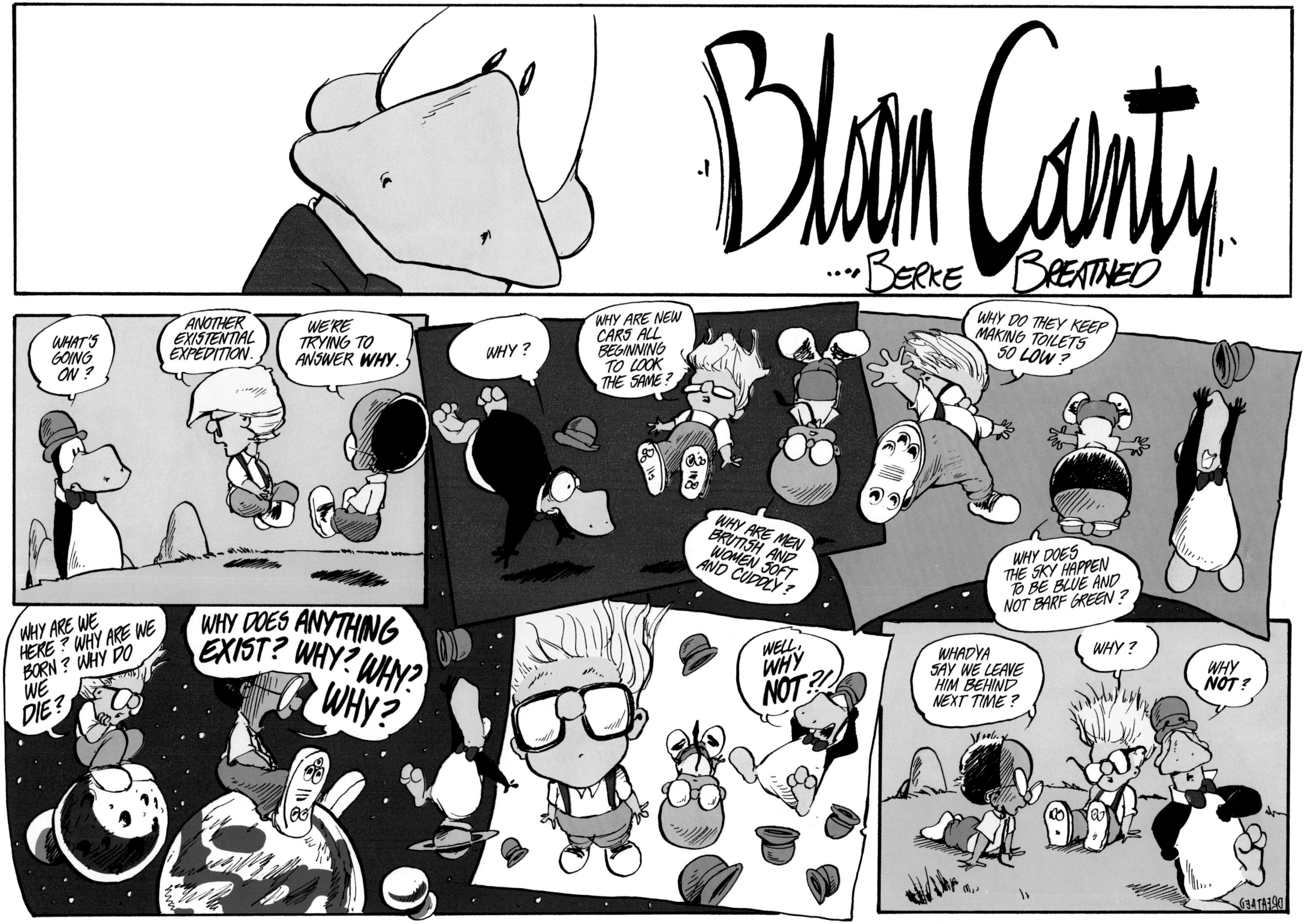
Bloom County
Berke Breathed
WHAT'S GOING ON?
ANOTHER EXISTENTIAL EXPEDITION.
WE'RE TRYING TO ANSWER WHY.
WHY?
WHY ARE NEW CARS ALL BEGINNING TO LOOK THE SAME?
WHY ARE MEN BRUTISH AND WOMEN SOFT AND CUDDLY?
WHY DO THEY KEEP MAKING TOILETS SO LOW?
WHY DOES THE SKY HAPPEN TO BE BLUE AND NOT BARF GREEN?
WHY ARE WE HERE? WHY ARE WE BORN? WHY DO WE DIE?
WHY DOES ANYTHING EXIST? WHY? WHY? WHY?
WELL, WHY NOT?!
WHADYA SAY WE LEAVE HIM BEHIND NEXT TIME?
WHY?
WHY NOT?

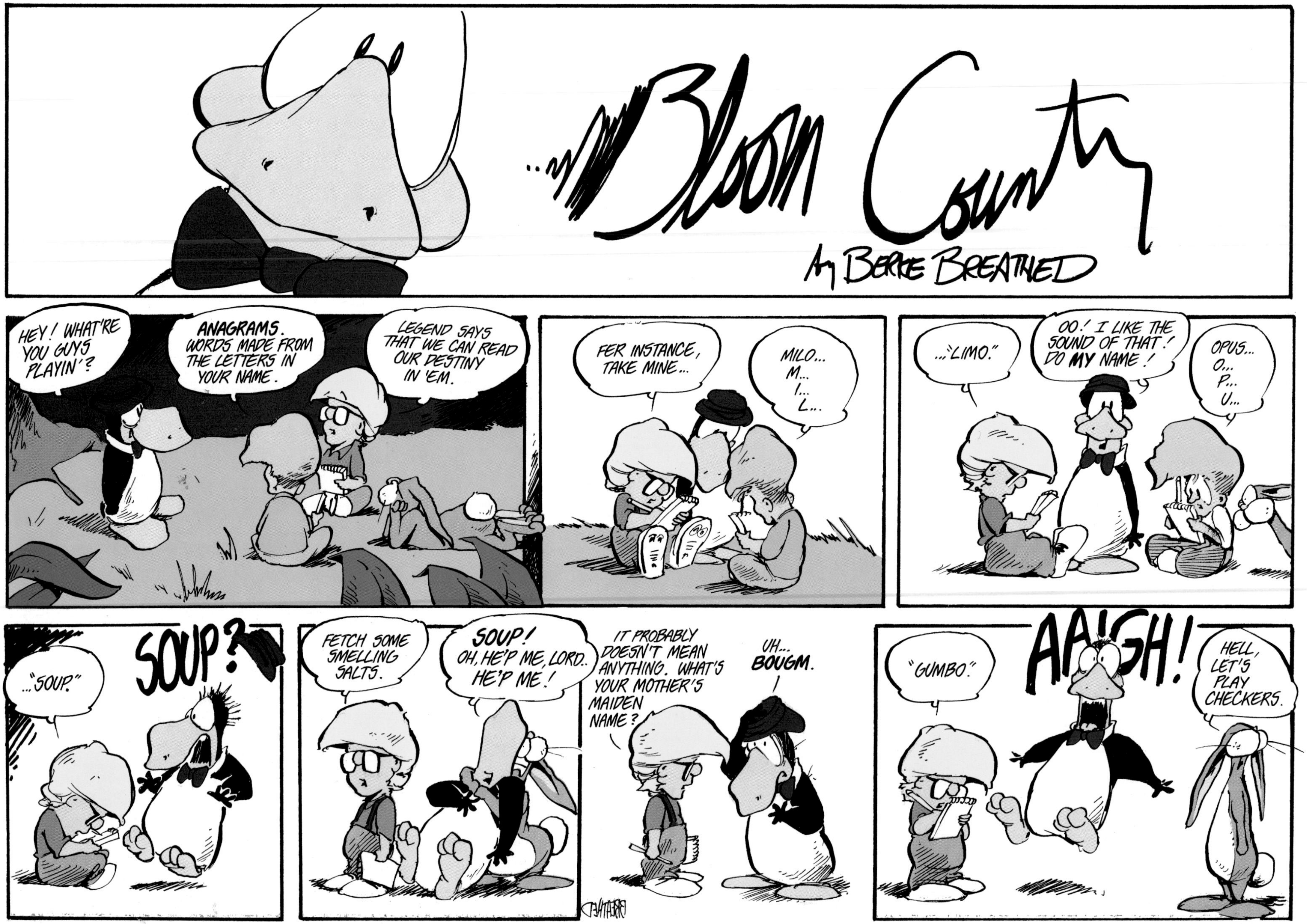

Bloom County
by Berke Breathed
HEY! WHAT'RE YOU GUYS PLAYIN'?
ANAGRAMS. WORDS MADE FROM THE LETTERS IN YOUR NAME.
LEGEND SAYS THAT WE CAN READ OUR DESTINY IN 'EM.
FER INSTANCE, TAKE MINE...
MILO... M... I... L...
..."LIMO."
OO! I LIKE THE SOUND OF THAT! DO MY NAME!
OPUS... O... P... U...
..."SOUP."
SOUP?
FETCH SOME SMELLING SALTS.
SOUP! OH, HE'P ME, LORD.. HE'P ME!
IT PROBABLY DOESN'T MEAN ANYTHING. WHAT'S YOUR MOTHER'S MAIDEN NAME?
UH... BOUGM.
"GUMBO."
AAIGH!
HELL, LET'S PLAY CHECKERS.

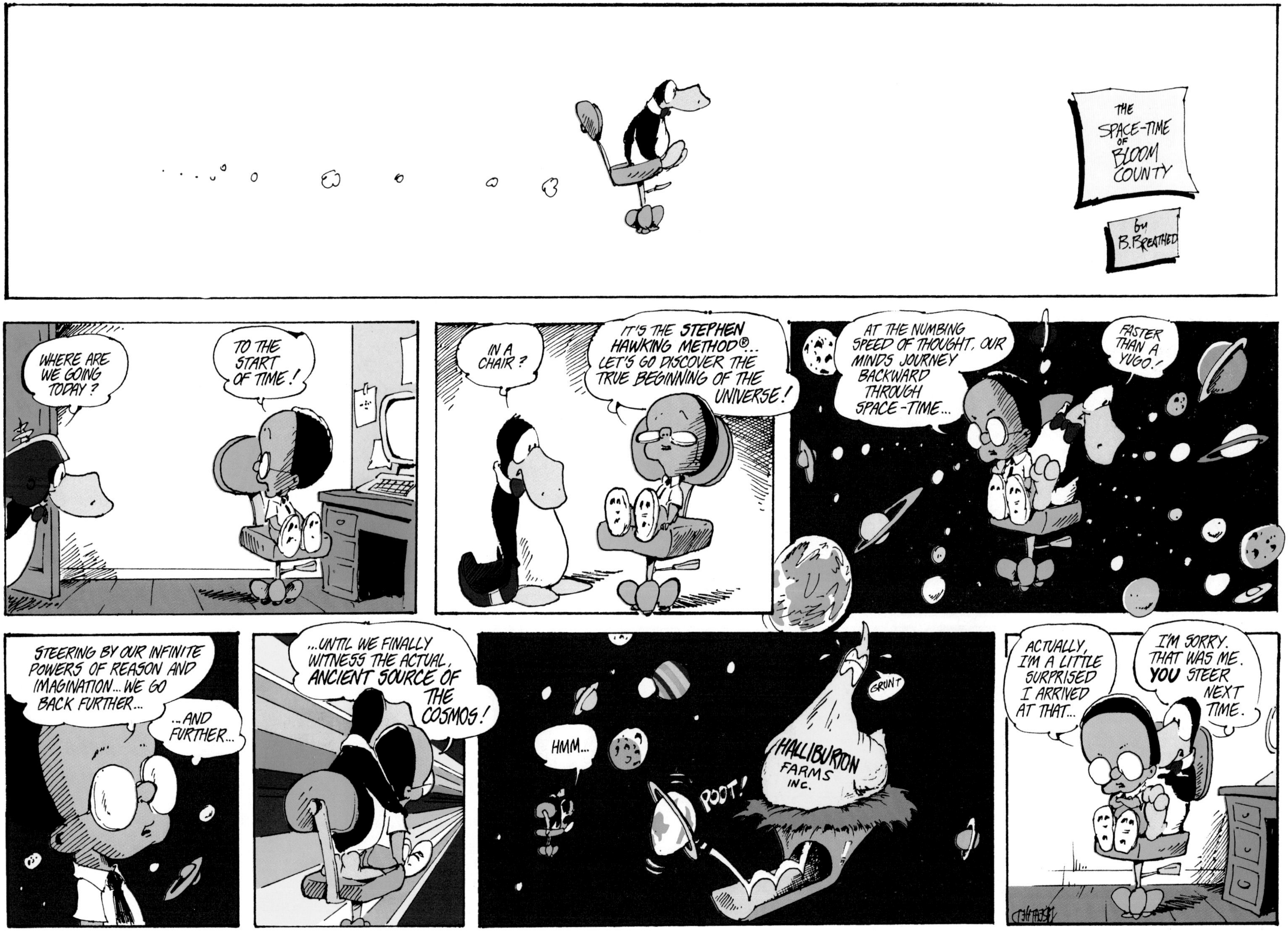
THE SPACE-TIME OF BLOOM COUNTY
by B. BREATHED
WHERE ARE WE GOING TODAY?
TO THE START OF TIME!
IN A CHAIR?
IT'S THE STEPHEN HAWKING METHOD®... LET'S GO DISCOVER THE TRUE BEGINNING OF THE UNIVERSE!
AT THE NUMBING SPEED OF THOUGHT, OUR MINDS JOURNEY BACKWARD THROUGH SPACE-TIME...
FASTER THAN A YUGO!
STEERING BY OUR INFINITE POWERS OF REASON AND IMAGINATION... WE GO BACK FURTHER...
...AND FURTHER...
...UNTIL WE FINALLY WITNESS THE ACTUAL, ANCIENT SOURCE OF THE COSMOS!
GRUNT
HMM...
HALLIBURTON FARMS INC.
POOT!
ACTUALLY, I'M A LITTLE SURPRISED I ARRIVED AT THAT...
I'M SORRY. THAT WAS ME. YOU STEER NEXT TIME.

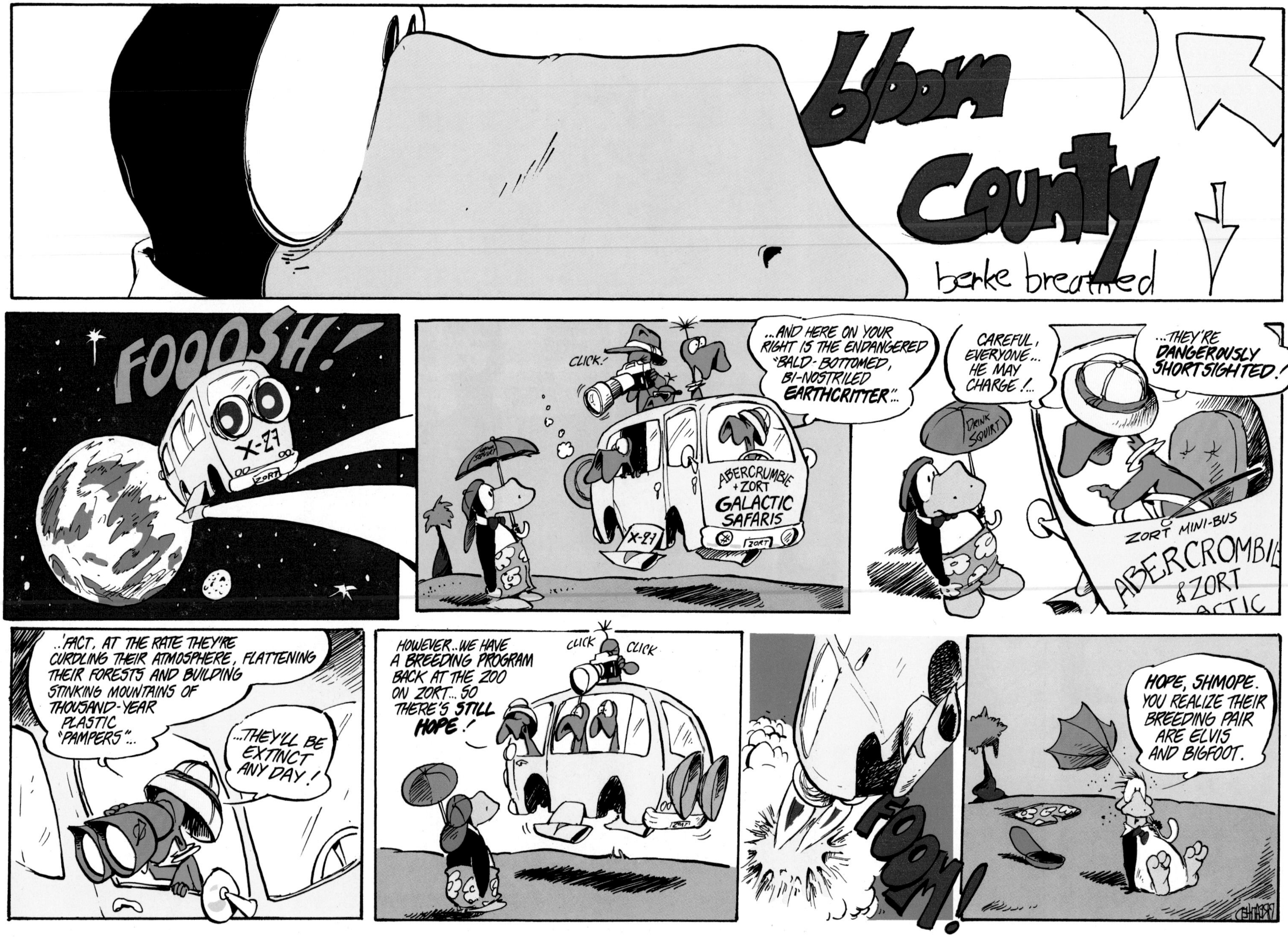
bloom County
berke breathed
FOOOSH!
X-27
ZORT
CLICK!
ABERCRUMBIE + ZORT GALACTIC SAFARIS
...AND HERE ON YOUR RIGHT IS THE ENDANGERED "BALD-BOTTOMED, BI-NOSTRILED EARTHCRITTER"...
DRINK SQUIRT
CAREFUL, EVERYONE... HE MAY CHARGE!...
...THEY'RE DANGEROUSLY SHORTSIGHTED!
ZORT MINI-BUS
ABERCROMBIE & ZORT
..'FACT, AT THE RATE THEY'RE CURDLING THEIR ATMOSPHERE, FLATTENING THEIR FORESTS AND BUILDING STINKING MOUNTAINS OF THOUSAND-YEAR PLASTIC "PAMPERS"...
...THEY'LL BE EXTINCT ANY DAY!
HOWEVER...WE HAVE A BREEDING PROGRAM BACK AT THE ZOO ON ZORT... SO THERE'S STILL HOPE!
CLICK CLICK
FOOOM!
HOPE, SHMOPE. YOU REALIZE THEIR BREEDING PAIR ARE ELVIS AND BIGFOOT.

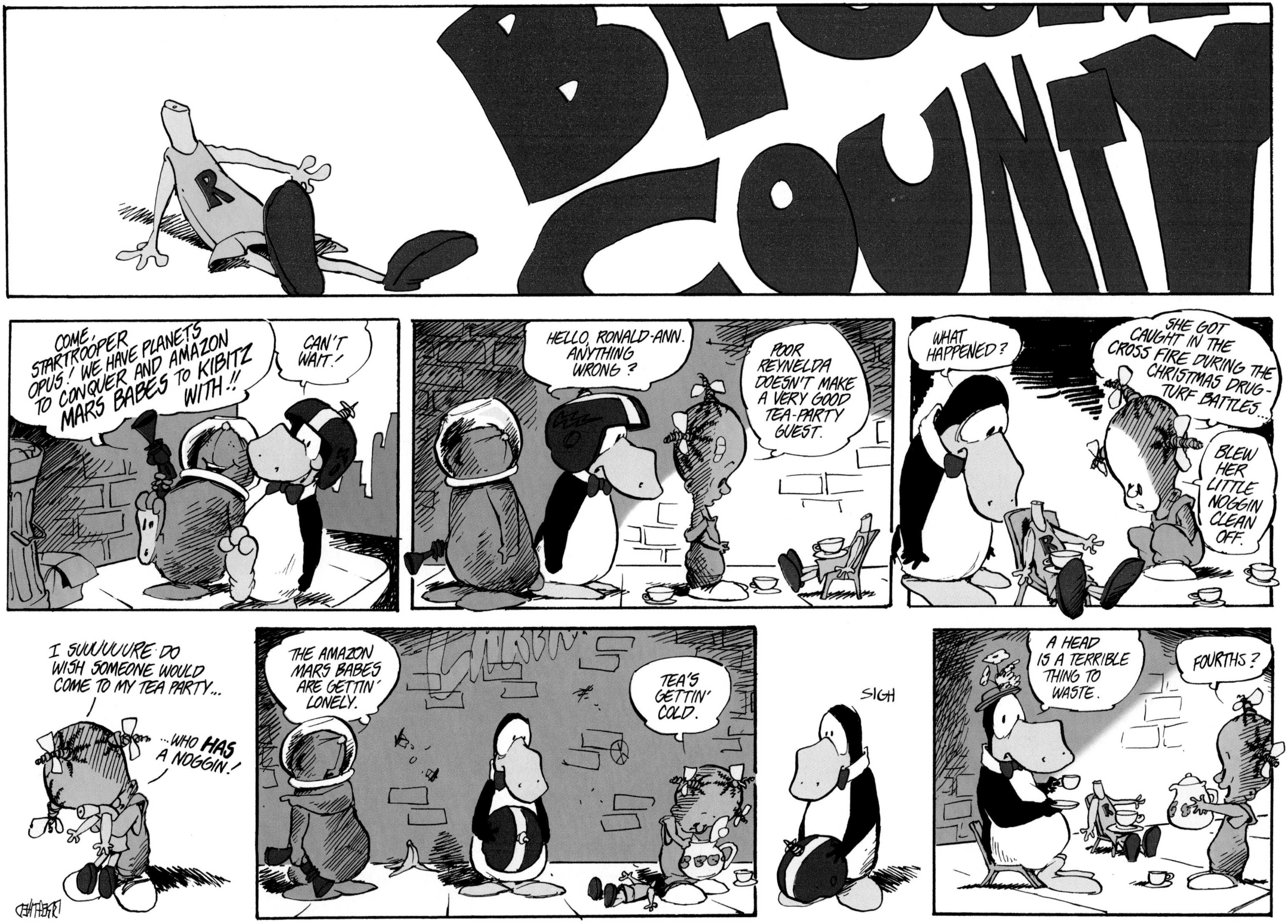

COME, STARTROOPER OPUS! WE HAVE PLANETS TO CONQUER AND AMAZON MARS BABES TO KIBITZ WITH!!
CAN'T WAIT!
HELLO, RONALD-ANN. ANYTHING WRONG?
POOR REYNELDA DOESN'T MAKE A VERY GOOD TEA-PARTY GUEST.
WHAT HAPPENED?
SHE GOT CAUGHT IN THE CROSS FIRE DURING THE CHRISTMAS DRUG-TURF BATTLES...
BLEW HER LITTLE NOGGIN CLEAN OFF.
I SUUUUUURE DO WISH SOMEONE WOULD COME TO MY TEA PARTY...
...WHO HAS A NOGGIN!
THE AMAZON MARS BABES ARE GETTIN' LONELY.
TEA'S GETTIN' COLD.
SIGH
A HEAD IS A TERRIBLE THING TO WASTE.
FOURTHS?

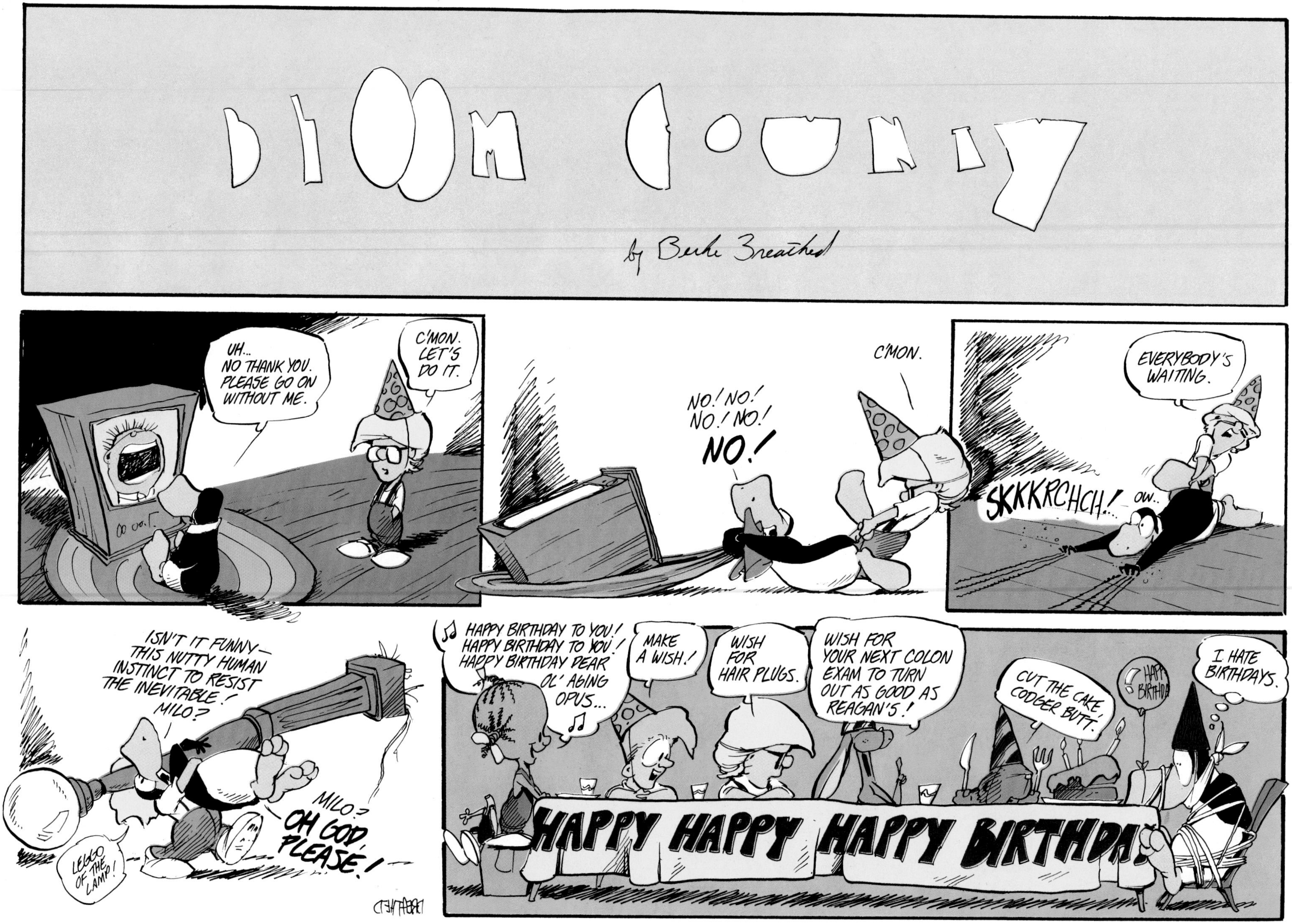
bloom county
by Berke Breathed
UH... NO THANK YOU. PLEASE GO ON WITHOUT ME.
C'MON. LET'S DO IT.
NO! NO! NO! NO! NO!
C'MON.
EVERYBODY'S WAITING.
SKKKRCHCH!...
OW..
ISN'T IT FUNNY— THIS NUTTY HUMAN INSTINCT TO RESIST THE INEVITABLE! MILO?
MILO?
OH GOD. PLEASE!
LEGGO OF THE LAMP!
HAPPY BIRTHDAY TO YOU! HAPPY BIRTHDAY TO YOU! HAPPY BIRTHDAY DEAR OL' AGING OPUS...
MAKE A WISH!
WISH FOR HAIR PLUGS.
WISH FOR YOUR NEXT COLON EXAM TO TURN OUT AS GOOD AS REAGAN'S!
CUT THE CAKE, CODGER BUTT.
I HATE BIRTHDAYS.
HAPPY HAPPY HAPPY BIRTHDA

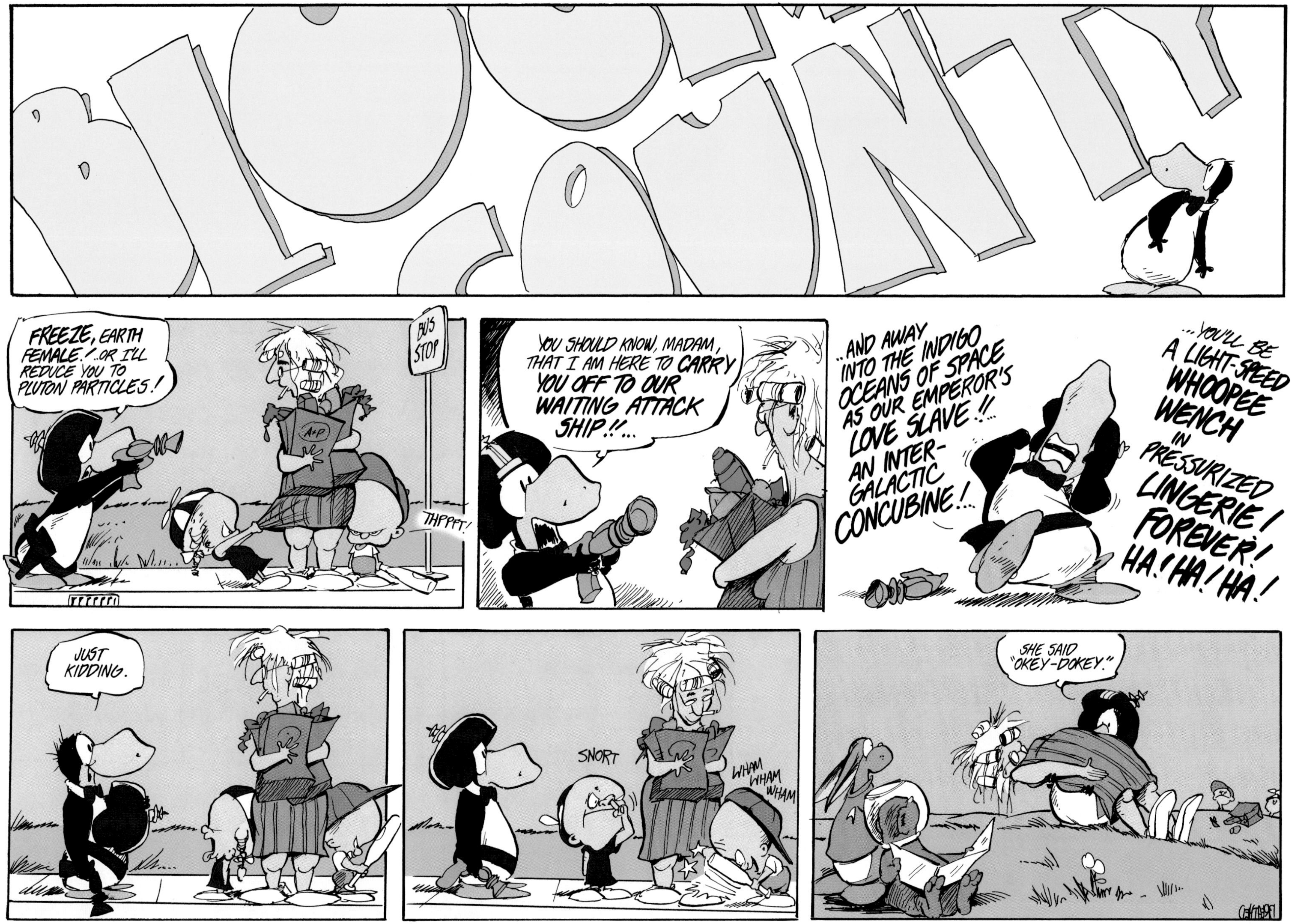
BLOOM COUNTY
FREEZE, EARTH FEMALE! ..OR I'LL REDUCE YOU TO PLUTON PARTICLES!
BUS STOP
A&P
THPPFT!
YOU SHOULD KNOW, MADAM, THAT I AM HERE TO CARRY YOU OFF TO OUR WAITING ATTACK SHIP!!...
..AND AWAY INTO THE INDIGO OCEANS OF SPACE AS OUR EMPEROR'S LOVE SLAVE!!... AN INTER-GALACTIC CONCUBINE!...
...YOU'LL BE A LIGHT-SPEED WHOOPEE WENCH IN PRESSURIZED LINGERIE FOREVER! HA! HA! HA!
JUST KIDDING.
SNORT
WHAM WHAM WHAM
SHE SAID "OKEY-DOKEY."

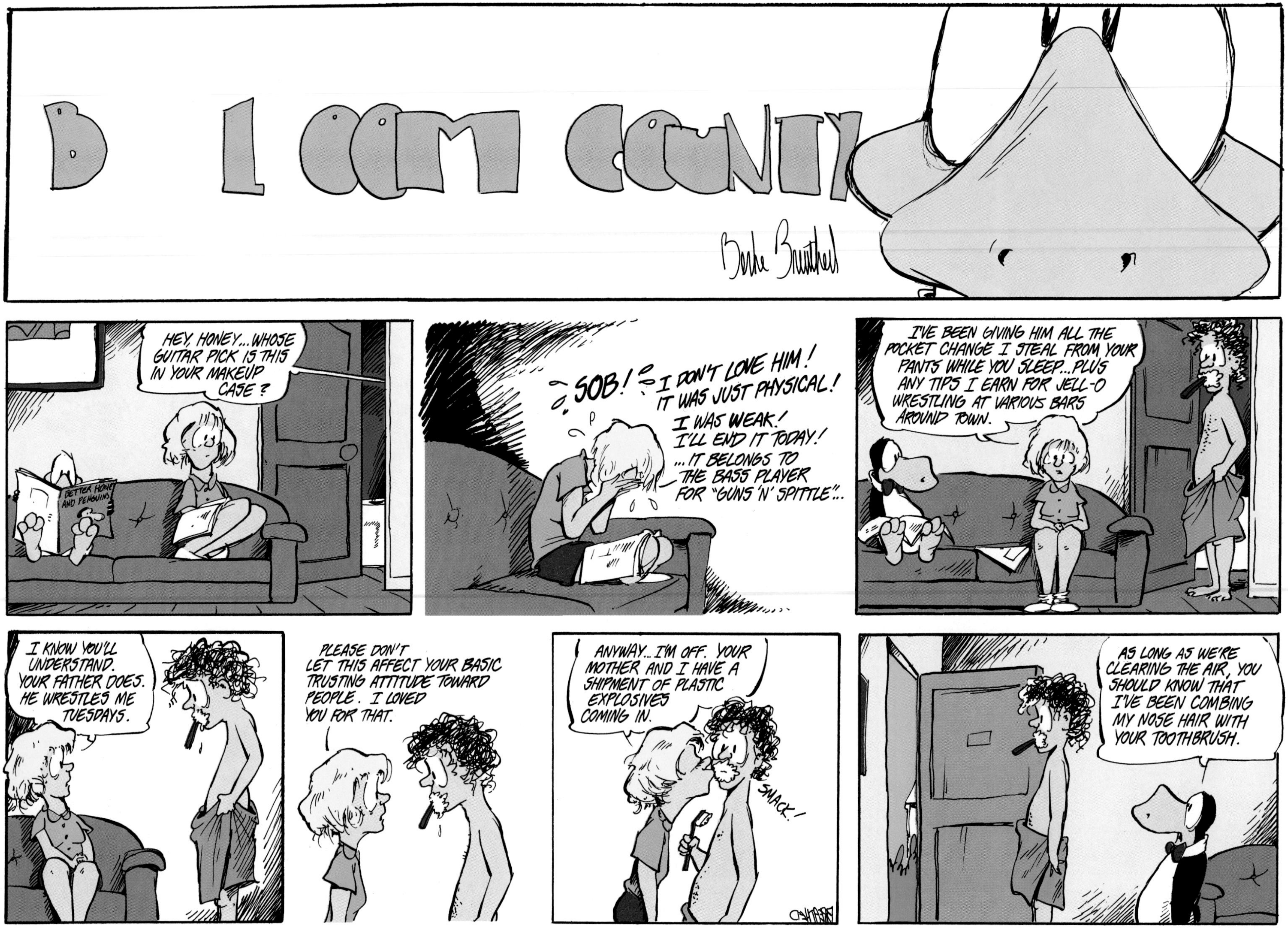
BLOOM COUNTY
Berke Breathed
BETTER HOMES AND PENGUINS
HEY, HONEY... WHOSE GUITAR PICK IS THIS IN YOUR MAKEUP CASE?
SOB! I DON'T LOVE HIM! IT WAS JUST PHYSICAL!
I WAS WEAK! I'LL END IT TODAY!
...IT BELONGS TO THE BASS PLAYER FOR "GUNS 'N' SPITTLE"...
I'VE BEEN GIVING HIM ALL THE POCKET CHANGE I STEAL FROM YOUR PANTS WHILE YOU SLEEP... PLUS ANY TIPS I EARN FOR JELL-O WRESTLING AT VARIOUS BARS AROUND TOWN.
I KNOW YOU'LL UNDERSTAND. YOUR FATHER DOES. HE WRESTLES ME TUESDAYS.
PLEASE DON'T LET THIS AFFECT YOUR BASIC TRUSTING ATTITUDE TOWARD PEOPLE. I LOVED YOU FOR THAT.
ANYWAY... I'M OFF. YOUR MOTHER AND I HAVE A SHIPMENT OF PLASTIC EXPLOSIVES COMING IN.
SMACK!
AS LONG AS WE'RE CLEARING THE AIR, YOU SHOULD KNOW THAT I'VE BEEN COMBING MY NOSE HAIR WITH YOUR TOOTHBRUSH.

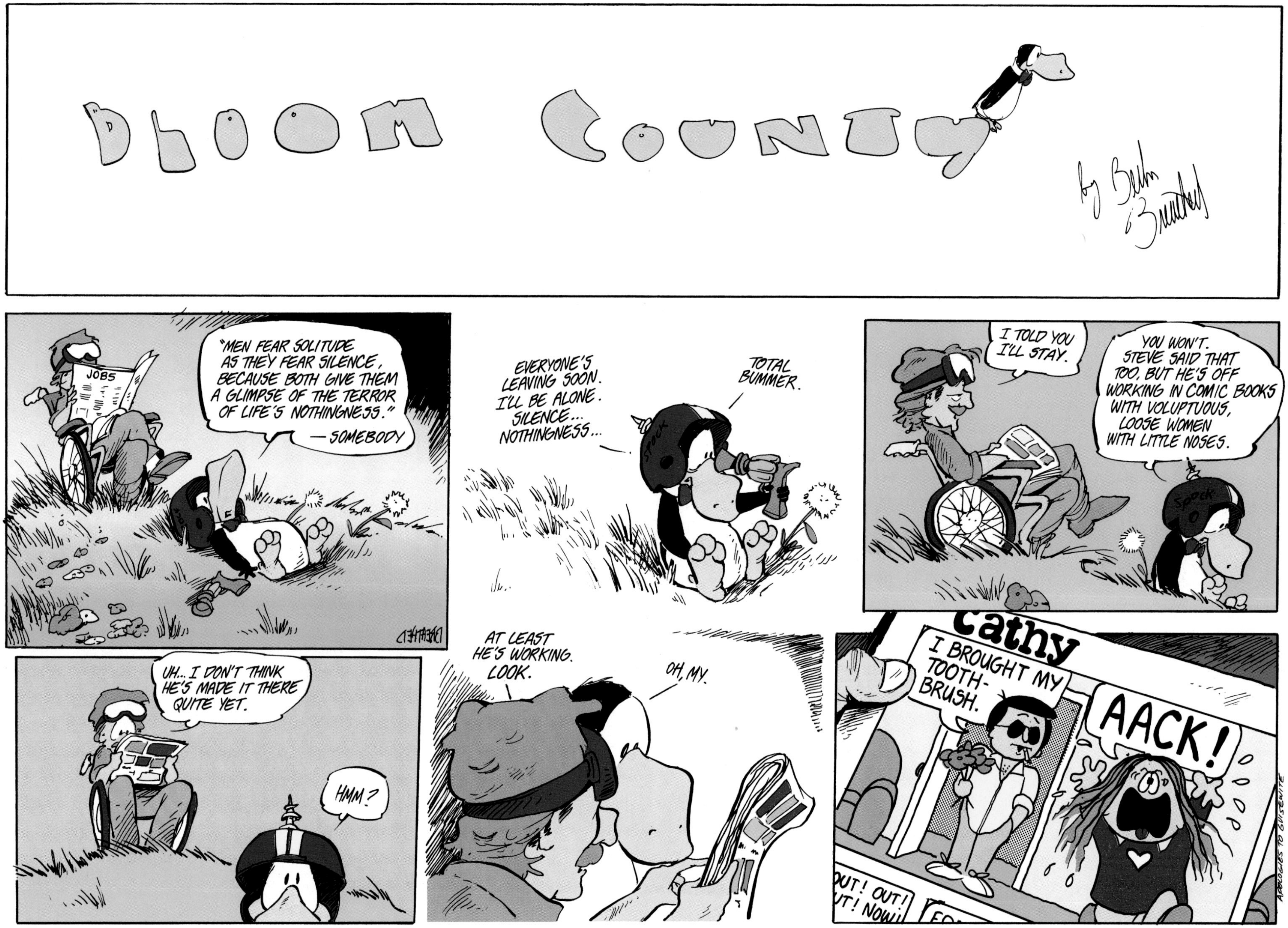
BLOOM COUNTY
by Berke Breathed
JOBS
"MEN FEAR SOLITUDE AS THEY FEAR SILENCE, BECAUSE BOTH GIVE THEM A GLIMPSE OF THE TERROR OF LIFE'S NOTHINGNESS." —SOMEBODY
EVERYONE'S LEAVING SOON. I'LL BE ALONE. SILENCE... NOTHINGNESS...
TOTAL BUMMER.
SPOCK
I TOLD YOU I'LL STAY.
YOU WON'T. STEVE SAID THAT TOO, BUT HE'S OFF WORKING IN COMIC BOOKS WITH VOLUPTUOUS, LOOSE WOMEN WITH LITTLE NOSES.
UH... I DON'T THINK HE'S MADE IT THERE QUITE YET.
HMM?
AT LEAST HE'S WORKING. LOOK.
OH, MY.
cathy
I BROUGHT MY TOOTH-BRUSH.
AACK!
OUT! OUT! OUT! NOW!
APOLOGIES TO GUISEWITE

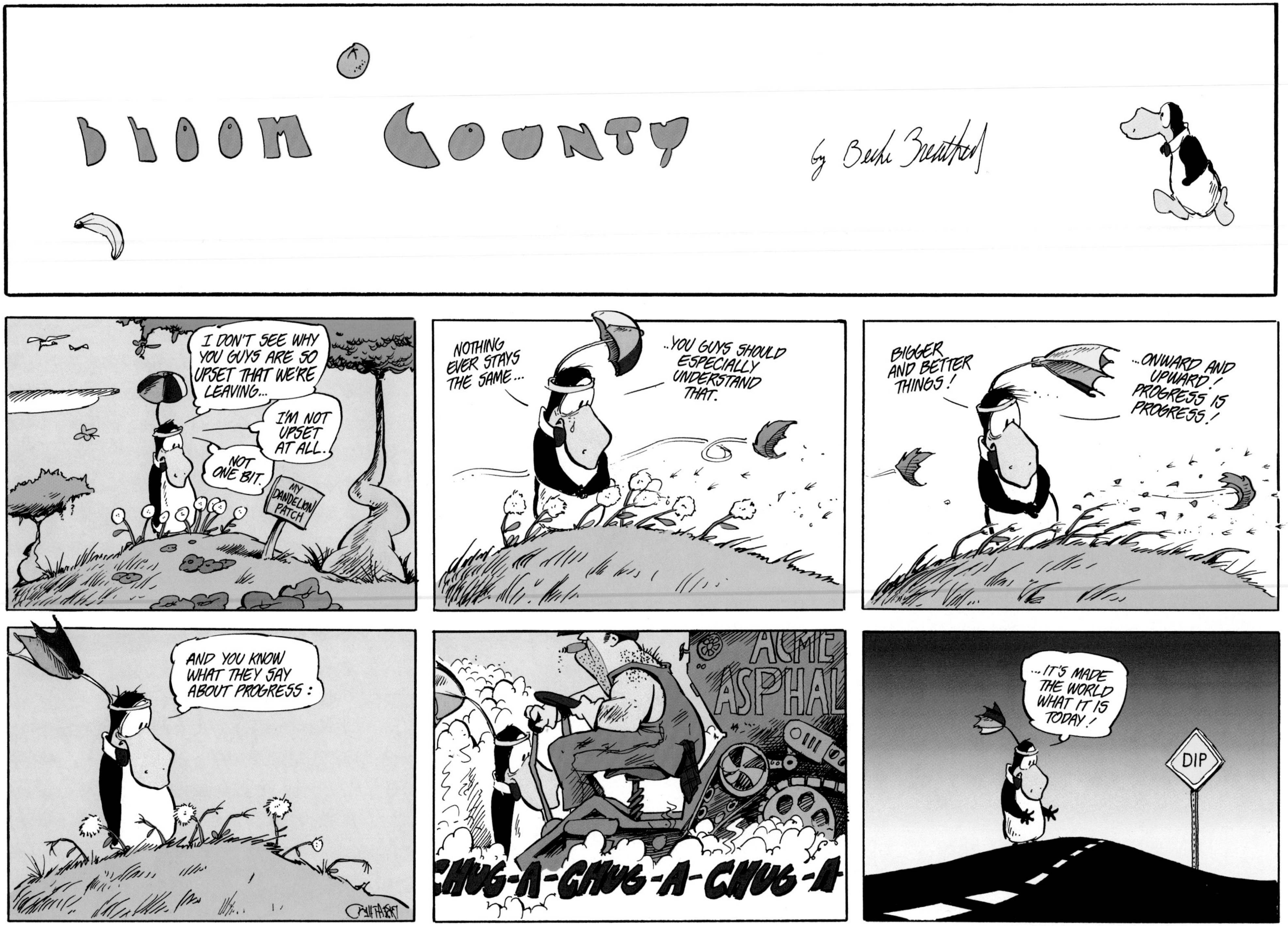
BLOOM COUNTY
by Berke Breathed
I DON'T SEE WHY YOU GUYS ARE SO UPSET THAT WE'RE LEAVING...
I'M NOT UPSET AT ALL.
NOT ONE BIT.
MY DANDELION PATCH
NOTHING EVER STAYS THE SAME...
..YOU GUYS SHOULD ESPECIALLY UNDERSTAND THAT.
BIGGER AND BETTER THINGS!
...ONWARD AND UPWARD! PROGRESS IS PROGRESS!
AND YOU KNOW WHAT THEY SAY ABOUT PROGRESS:
ACME ASPHAL
CHUG-A-CHUG-A-CHUG-A
...IT'S MADE THE WORLD WHAT IT IS TODAY!
DIP

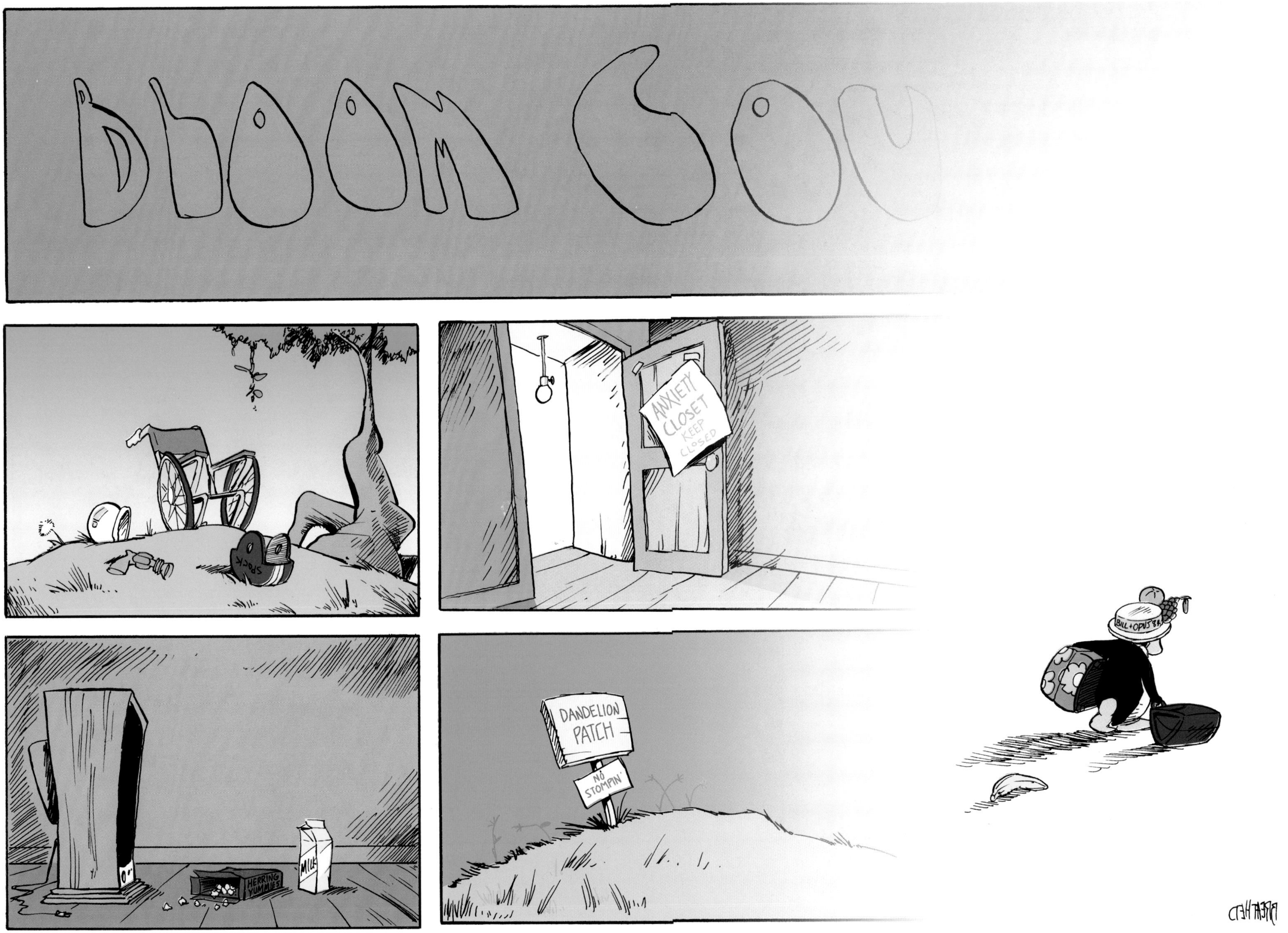
BLOOM COU
SPOCK
ANXIETY CLOSET KEEP CLOSED
HERRING YUMMIES
MILK
DANDELION PATCH
NO STOMPIN'
BILL + OPUS '84
BREATHED

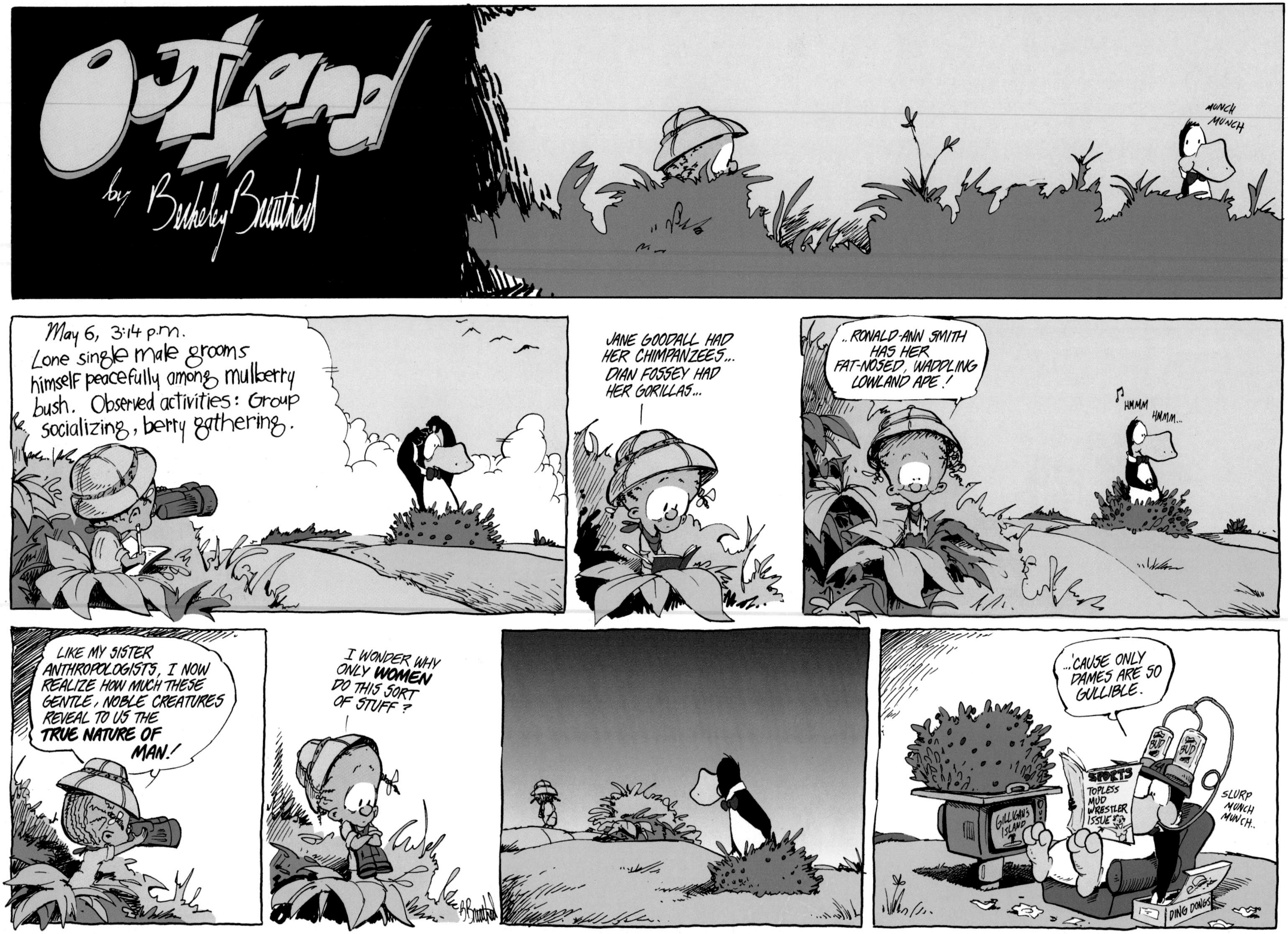
Outland
by Berkeley Breathed
MUNCH MUNCH
May 6, 3:14 p.m. Lone single male grooms himself peacefully among mulberry bush. Observed activities: Group socializing, berry gathering.
JANE GOODALL HAD HER CHIMPANZEES... DIAN FOSSEY HAD HER GORILLAS...
..RONALD-ANN SMITH HAS HER FAT-NOSED, WADDLING LOWLAND APE!
HMMM HMMM...
LIKE MY SISTER ANTHROPOLOGISTS, I NOW REALIZE HOW MUCH THESE GENTLE, NOBLE CREATURES REVEAL TO US THE TRUE NATURE OF MAN!
I WONDER WHY ONLY WOMEN DO THIS SORT OF STUFF?
...'CAUSE ONLY DAMES ARE SO GULLIBLE.
SPORTS
TOPLESS MUD WRESTLER ISSUE
BUD
BUD
GILLIGAN'S ISLAND
SLURP MUNCH MUNCH..
DING DONGS

OUTLAND

I seem to be the author of a series of Ignominious Firsts in cartooning.

I was the first to quit a perfectly good and embarrassingly profitable comic strip. I was also the first to return with another comic after canceling the original, which had nothing wrong with it in the first place. I was also the first to do a strip only once a week. Then retire that one and declare that I was done with stripping once and for all.

Only to return eight years later and start all over again.

Warning to the impressionable young cartoonists watching: Don't try this stunt at home. Study Jim Davis's career instead.

As its inventor, I really don't know what to call a once-a-week cartoon panel. It's not really a comic strip in the traditional sense. It's something else . . . and something less, I fear. Showing up in their homes only on Sundays isn't as ingratiating to the readers as sharing coffee with them seven mornings a week. A Sunday-only strip simply cannot tell the stories nor instill the weirdly intimate familiarity readers can have with cartoon characters in a daily panel.

But what it *can* do is allow its author to keep from burning out and disappearing entirely. You've noticed that this has happened. A writing and drawing staff can forestall such an unfortunate scenario, but there's a creative price to be paid, I think.

So I scale back and take a few more naps. This, if little else, I share with G. W. Bush Jr.

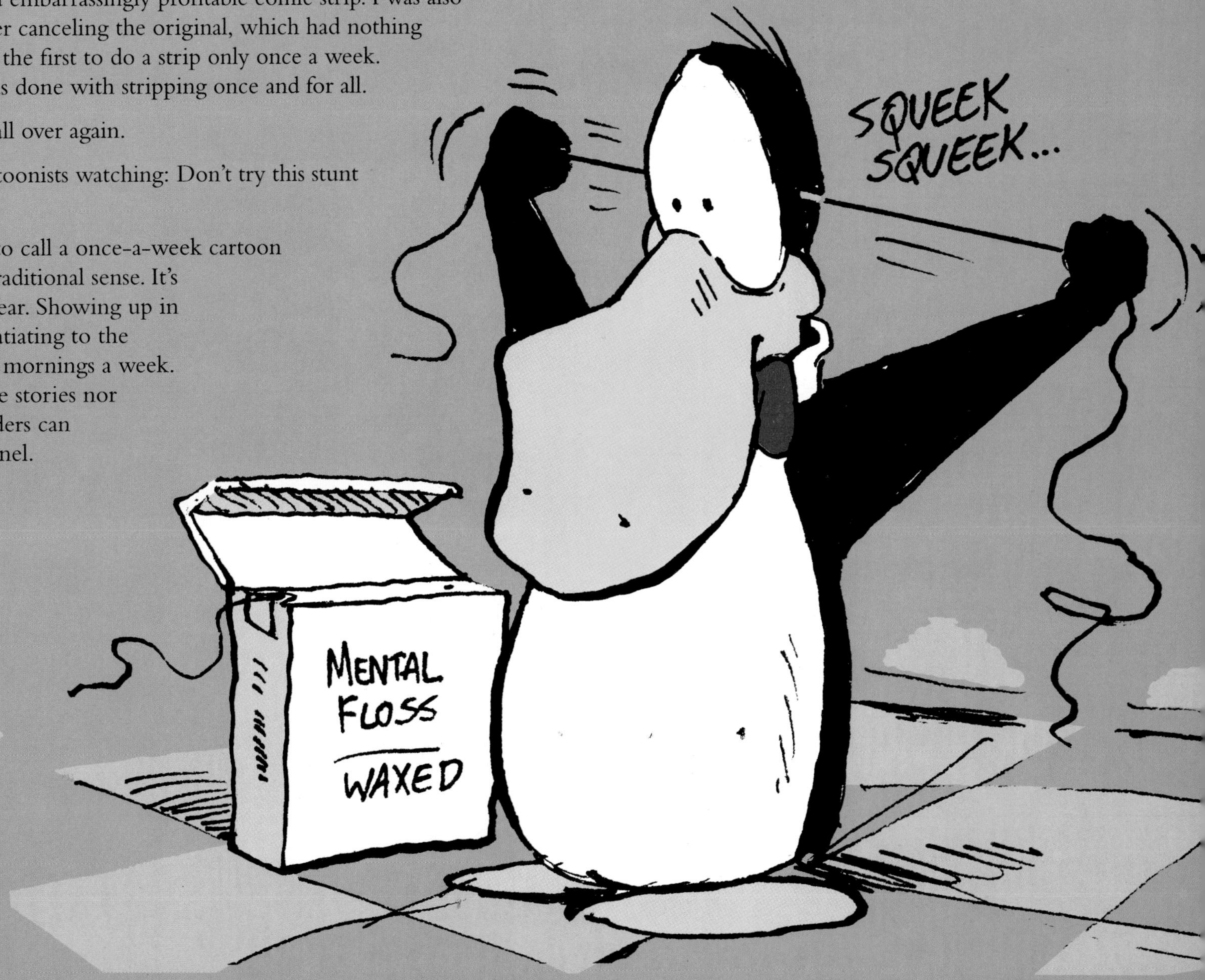
SQUEEK SQUEEK...
MENTAL FLOSS
WAXED

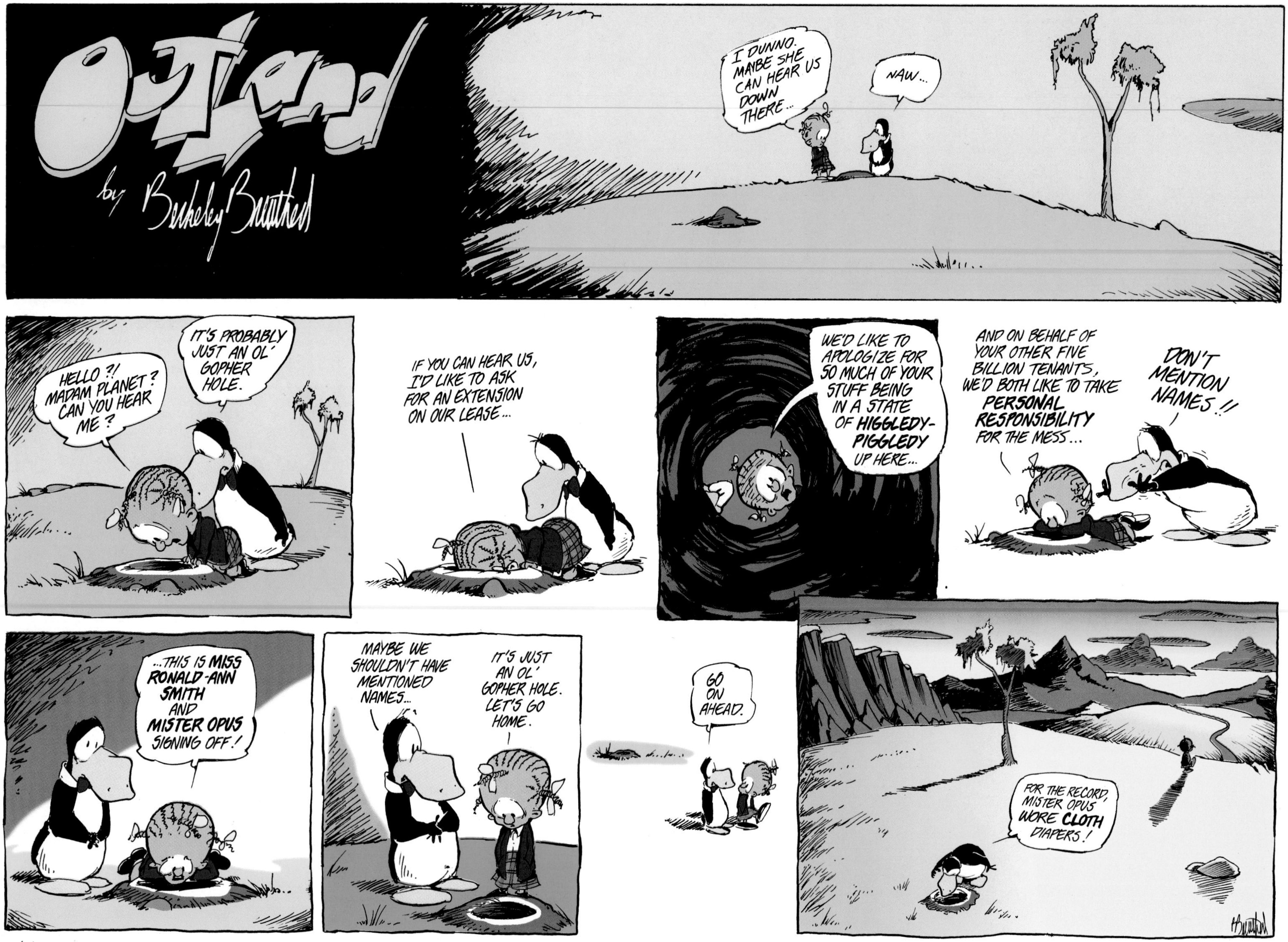
Outland
by Berkeley Breathed
I DUNNO. MAYBE SHE CAN HEAR US DOWN THERE...
NAW...
HELLO ?! MADAM PLANET ? CAN YOU HEAR ME ?
IT'S PROBABLY JUST AN OL' GOPHER HOLE.
IF YOU CAN HEAR US, I'D LIKE TO ASK FOR AN EXTENSION ON OUR LEASE...
WE'D LIKE TO APOLOGIZE FOR SO MUCH OF YOUR STUFF BEING IN A STATE OF HIGGLEDY-PIGGLEDY UP HERE...
AND ON BEHALF OF YOUR OTHER FIVE BILLION TENANTS, WE'D BOTH LIKE TO TAKE PERSONAL RESPONSIBILITY FOR THE MESS...
DON'T MENTION NAMES !!
...THIS IS MISS RONALD-ANN SMITH AND MISTER OPUS SIGNING OFF !
MAYBE WE SHOULDN'T HAVE MENTIONED NAMES...
IT'S JUST AN OL' GOPHER HOLE. LET'S GO HOME.
GO ON AHEAD.
FOR THE RECORD, MISTER OPUS WORE CLOTH DIAPERS !

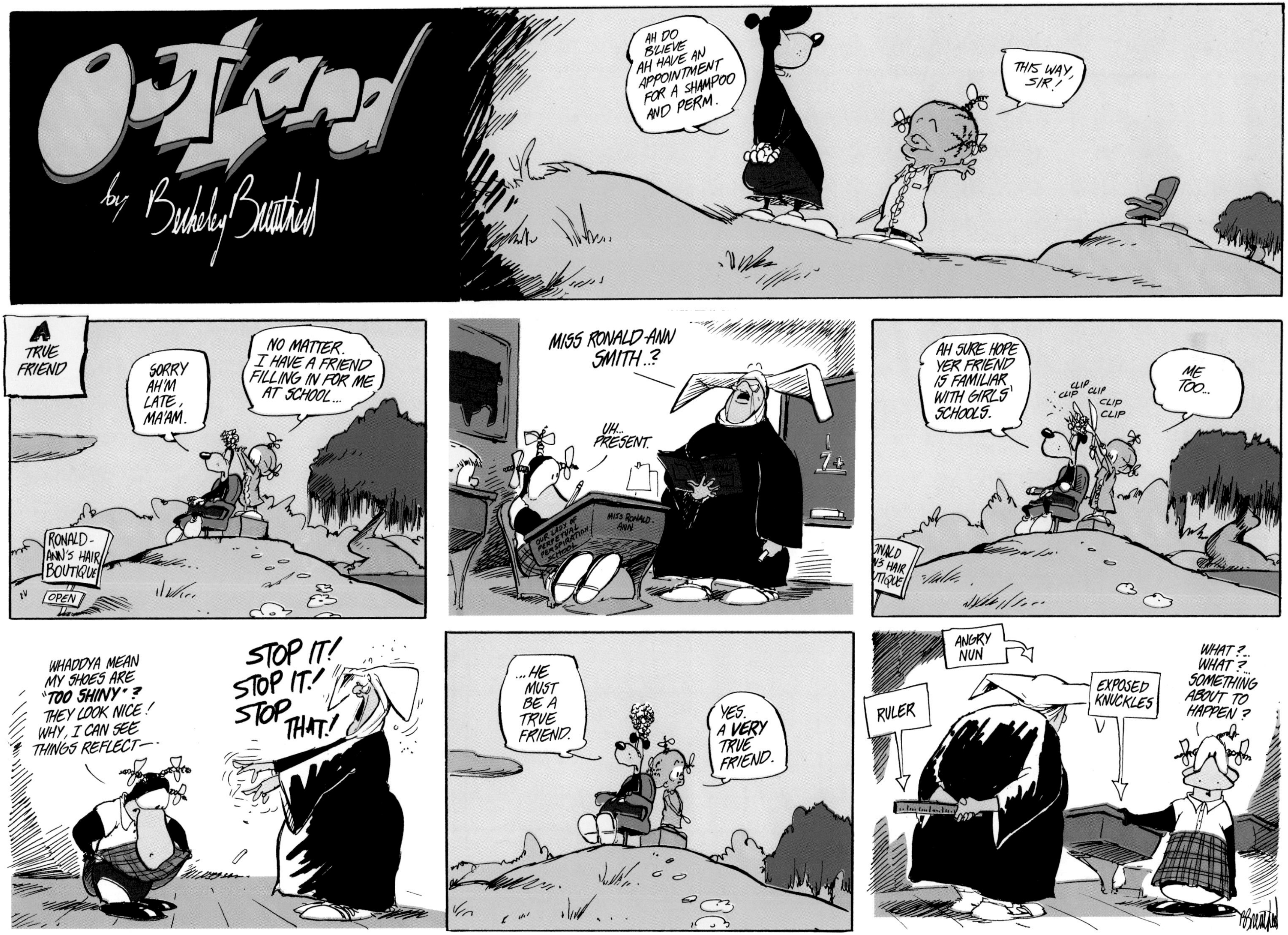
Outland
by Berkeley Breathed
AH DO B'LIEVE AH HAVE AN APPOINTMENT FOR A SHAMPOO AND PERM.
THIS WAY, SIR!
A TRUE FRIEND
SORRY AH'M LATE, MA'AM.
NO MATTER. I HAVE A FRIEND FILLING IN FOR ME AT SCHOOL...
RONALD-ANN'S HAIR BOUTIQUE
OPEN
MISS RONALD-ANN SMITH..?
UH... PRESENT.
OUR LADY OF PERPETUAL PERSPIRATION SCHOOL
MISS RONALD-ANN
AH SURE HOPE YER FRIEND IS FAMILIAR WITH GIRLS' SCHOOLS.
CLIP CLIP CLIP CLIP CLIP
ME TOO...
WHADDYA MEAN MY SHOES ARE "TOO SHINY"? THEY LOOK NICE! WHY, I CAN SEE THINGS REFLECT—
STOP IT! STOP IT! STOP THAT!
...HE MUST BE A TRUE FRIEND.
YES. A VERY TRUE FRIEND.
ANGRY NUN
RULER
EXPOSED KNUCKLES
WHAT?.. WHAT?... SOMETHING ABOUT TO HAPPEN?

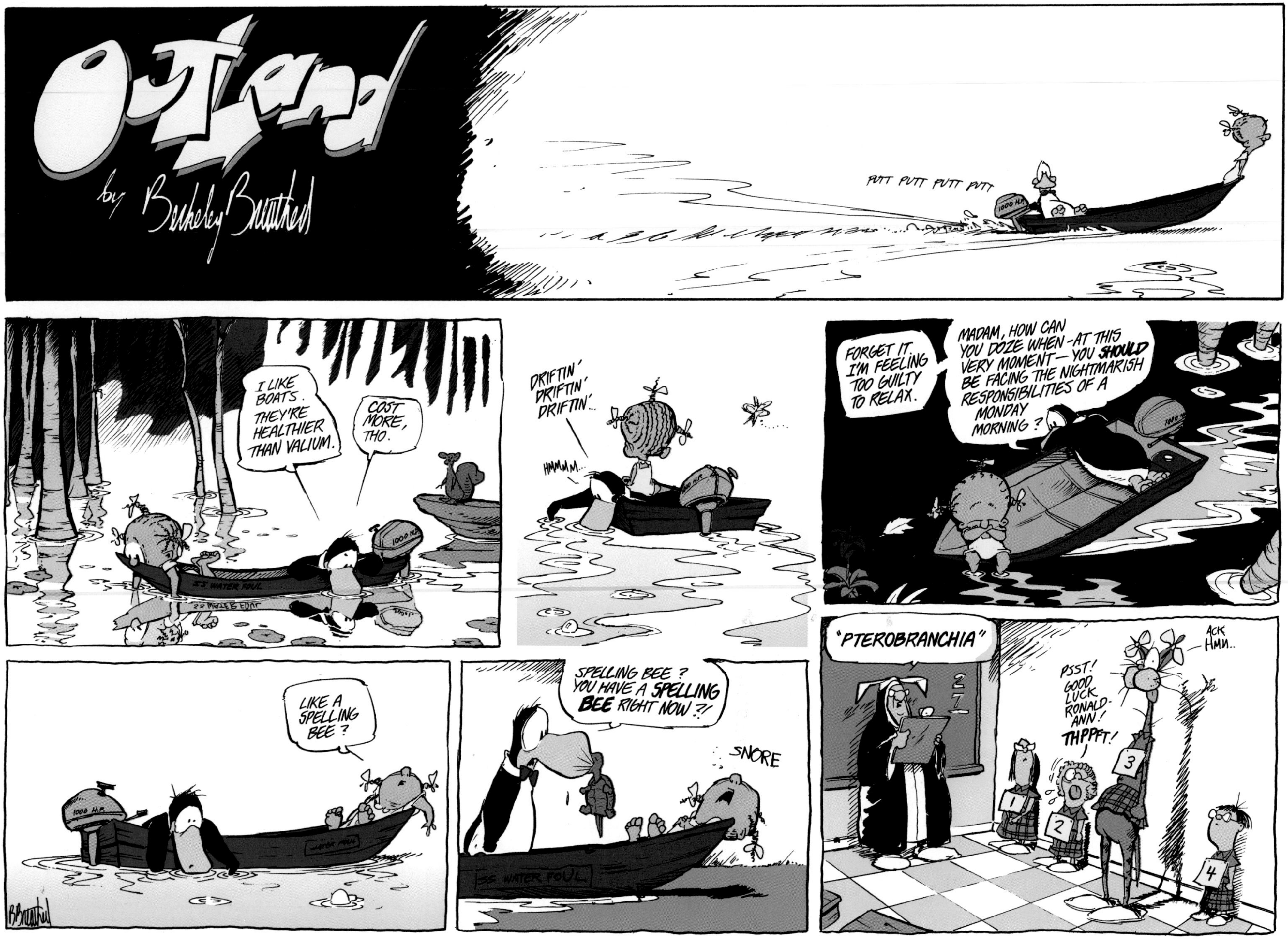
Outland
by Berkeley Breathed
PUTT PUTT PUTT PUTT
1000 H.P.
I LIKE BOATS. THEY'RE HEALTHIER THAN VALIUM.
COST MORE, THO.
1000 H.P.
S.S. WATER FOUL
DRIFTIN' DRIFTIN' DRIFTIN'...
HMMMM...
FORGET IT. I'M FEELING TOO GUILTY TO RELAX.
MADAM, HOW CAN YOU DOZE WHEN—AT THIS VERY MOMENT— YOU SHOULD BE FACING THE NIGHTMARISH RESPONSIBILITIES OF A MONDAY MORNING?
LIKE A SPELLING BEE?
1000 H.P.
SPELLING BEE? YOU HAVE A SPELLING BEE RIGHT NOW?!
SNORE
S.S. WATER FOUL
"PTEROBRANCHIA"
ACK HMM..
PSST! GOOD LUCK RONALD-ANN!
THPPFT!
1
2
3
4
B. Breathed

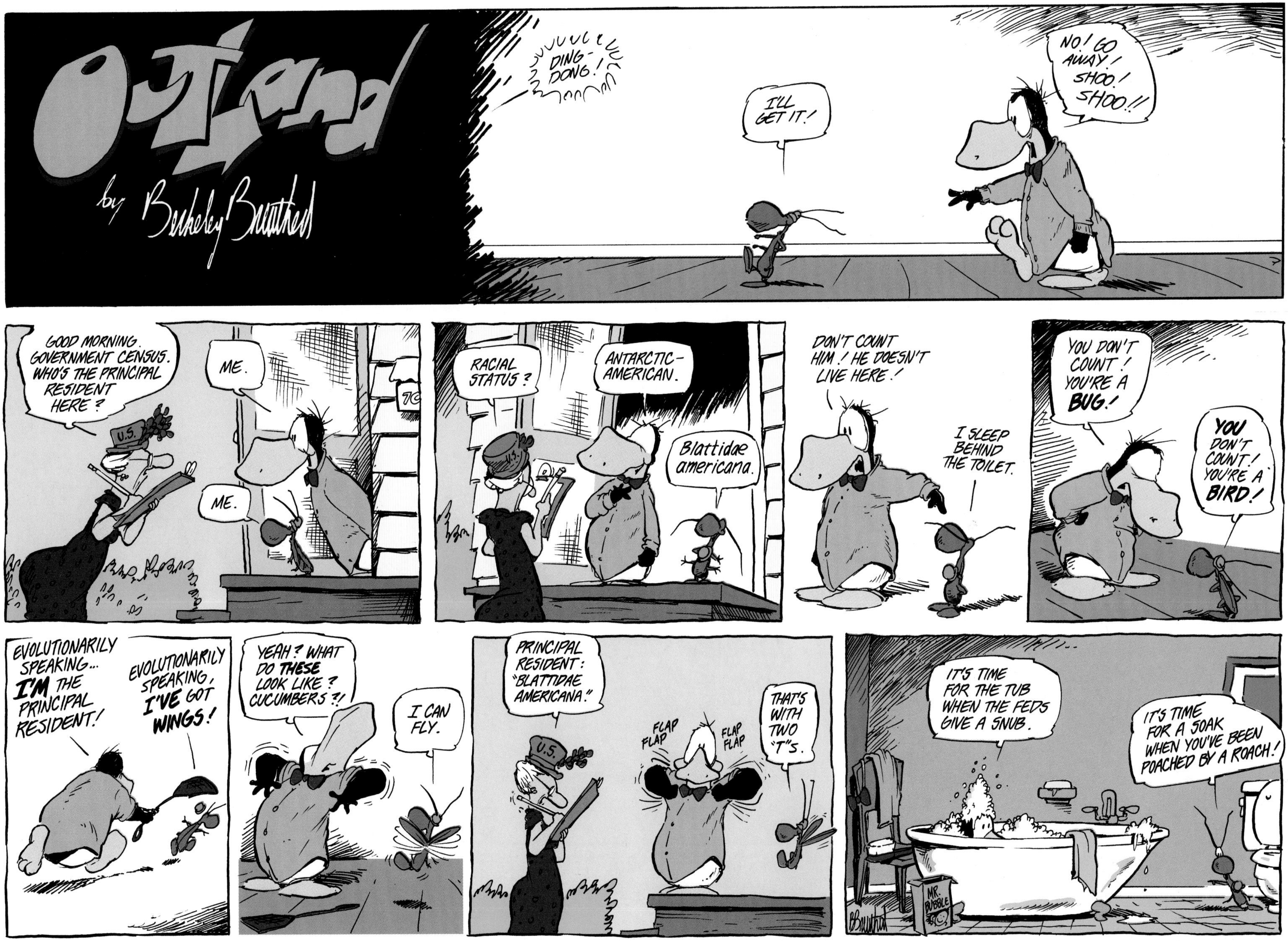

Outland
by Berkeley Breathed
DING-DONG!
I'LL GET IT!
NO! GO AWAY! SHOO! SHOO!!
GOOD MORNING. GOVERNMENT CENSUS. WHO'S THE PRINCIPAL RESIDENT HERE?
U.S.
ME.
ME.
RACIAL STATUS?
ANTARCTIC-AMERICAN.
Blattidae americana.
DON'T COUNT HIM! HE DOESN'T LIVE HERE!
I SLEEP BEHIND THE TOILET.
YOU DON'T COUNT! YOU'RE A BUG!
YOU DON'T COUNT! YOU'RE A BIRD!
EVOLUTIONARILY SPEAKING... I'M THE PRINCIPAL RESIDENT!
EVOLUTIONARILY SPEAKING, I'VE GOT WINGS!
YEAH? WHAT DO THESE LOOK LIKE? CUCUMBERS?!
I CAN FLY.
PRINCIPAL RESIDENT: "BLATTIDAE AMERICANA."
U.S.
FLAP FLAP
FLAP FLAP
THAT'S WITH TWO "T"s.
IT'S TIME FOR THE TUB WHEN THE FEDS GIVE A SNUB.
IT'S TIME FOR A SOAK WHEN YOU'VE BEEN POACHED BY A ROACH!
MR. BUBBLE
BBreathed

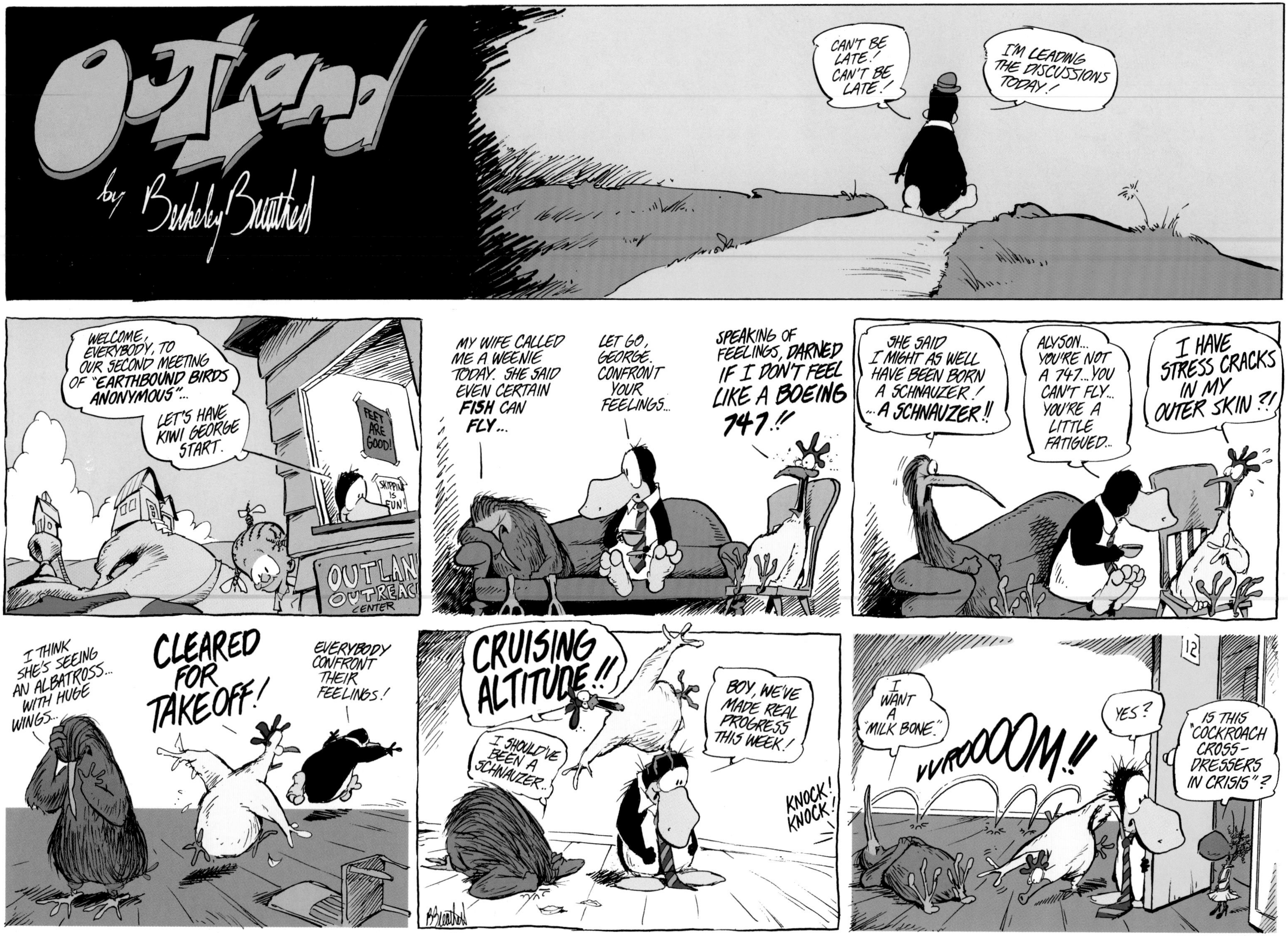
Outland
by Berkeley Breathed
CAN'T BE LATE! CAN'T BE LATE!
I'M LEADING THE DISCUSSIONS TODAY!
WELCOME, EVERYBODY, TO OUR SECOND MEETING OF "EARTHBOUND BIRDS ANONYMOUS"...
LET'S HAVE KIWI GEORGE START.
FEET ARE GOOD!
SKIPPING IS FUN!
OUTLAND OUTREACH CENTER
MY WIFE CALLED ME A WEENIE TODAY. SHE SAID EVEN CERTAIN FISH CAN FLY...
LET GO, GEORGE. CONFRONT YOUR FEELINGS...
SPEAKING OF FEELINGS, DARNED IF I DON'T FEEL LIKE A BOEING 747.!!
SHE SAID I MIGHT AS WELL HAVE BEEN BORN A SCHNAUZER! ...A SCHNAUZER!!
ALYSON... YOU'RE NOT A 747... YOU CAN'T FLY... YOU'RE A LITTLE FATIGUED...
I HAVE STRESS CRACKS IN MY OUTER SKIN?!
I THINK SHE'S SEEING AN ALBATROSS... WITH HUGE WINGS...
CLEARED FOR TAKEOFF!
EVERYBODY CONFRONT THEIR FEELINGS!
CRUISING ALTITUDE!!
I SHOULD'VE BEEN A SCHNAUZER...
BOY, WE'VE MADE REAL PROGRESS THIS WEEK!
KNOCK! KNOCK!
B Breathed
12
I WANT A "MILK BONE."
VVROOOOOM!!
YES?
IS THIS "COCKROACH CROSS-DRESSERS IN CRISIS"?

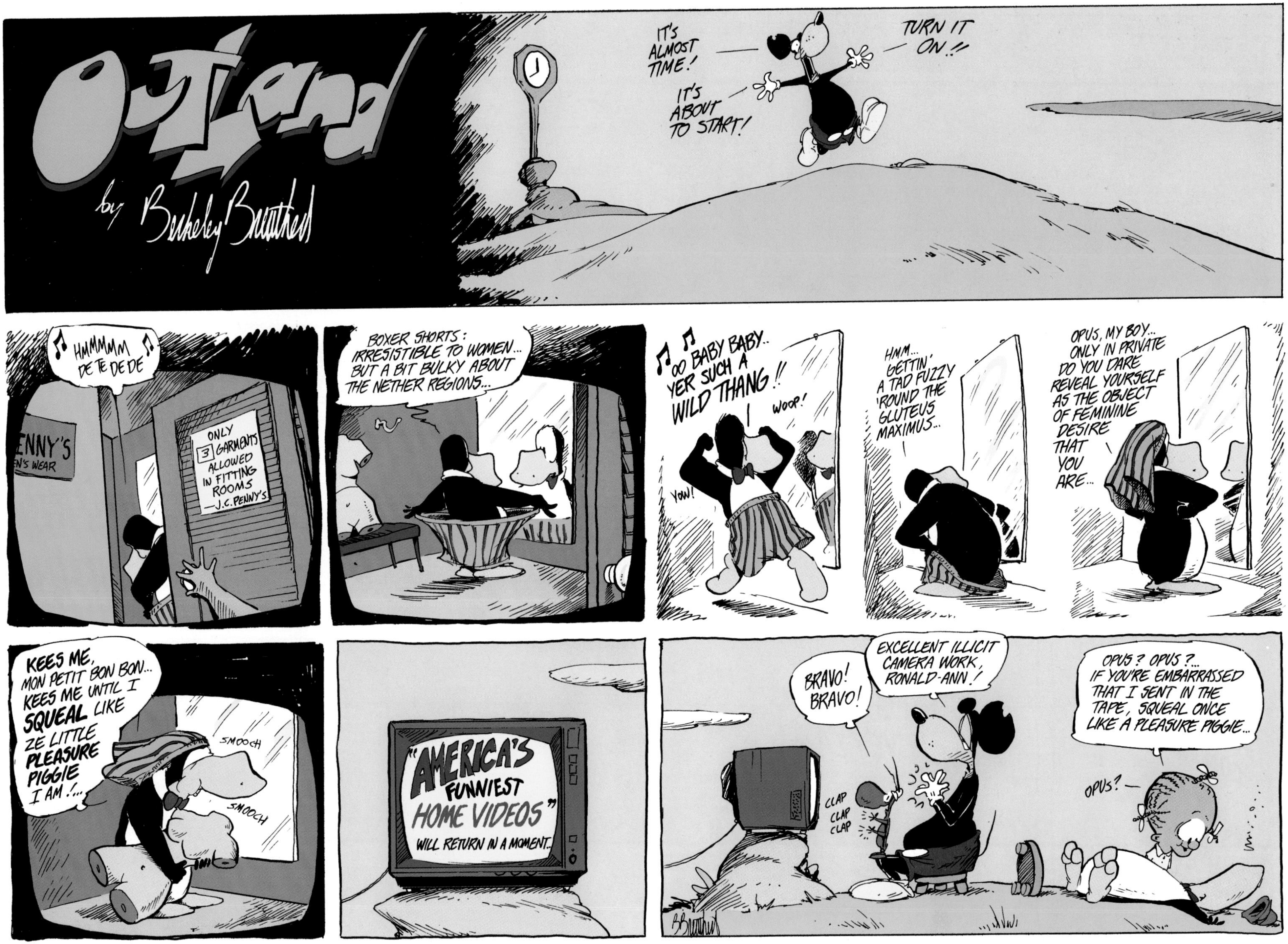

Outland
by Berkeley Breathed
IT'S ALMOST TIME!
IT'S ABOUT TO START!
TURN IT ON!!
HMMMMM DE TE DE DE
ENNY'S EN'S WEAR
ONLY 3 GARMENTS ALLOWED IN FITTING ROOMS —J.C. PENNY'S
BOXER SHORTS: IRRESISTIBLE TO WOMEN... BUT A BIT BULKY ABOUT THE NETHER REGIONS...
OO BABY BABY.. YER SUCH A WILD THANG!!
WOOP!
YOW!
HMM... GETTIN' A TAD FUZZY 'ROUND THE GLUTEUS MAXIMUS...
OPUS, MY BOY... ONLY IN PRIVATE DO YOU DARE REVEAL YOURSELF AS THE OBJECT OF FEMININE DESIRE THAT YOU ARE...
KEES ME, MON PETIT BON BON... KEES ME UNTIL I SQUEAL LIKE ZE LITTLE PLEASURE PIGGIE I AM!...
SMOOCH
SMOOCH
"AMERICA'S FUNNIEST HOME VIDEOS" WILL RETURN IN A MOMENT..
BRAVO! BRAVO!
EXCELLENT ILLICIT CAMERA WORK, RONALD-ANN!
CLAP CLAP CLAP
OPUS? OPUS?... IF YOU'RE EMBARRASSED THAT I SENT IN THE TAPE, SQUEAL ONCE LIKE A PLEASURE PIGGIE...
OPUS?

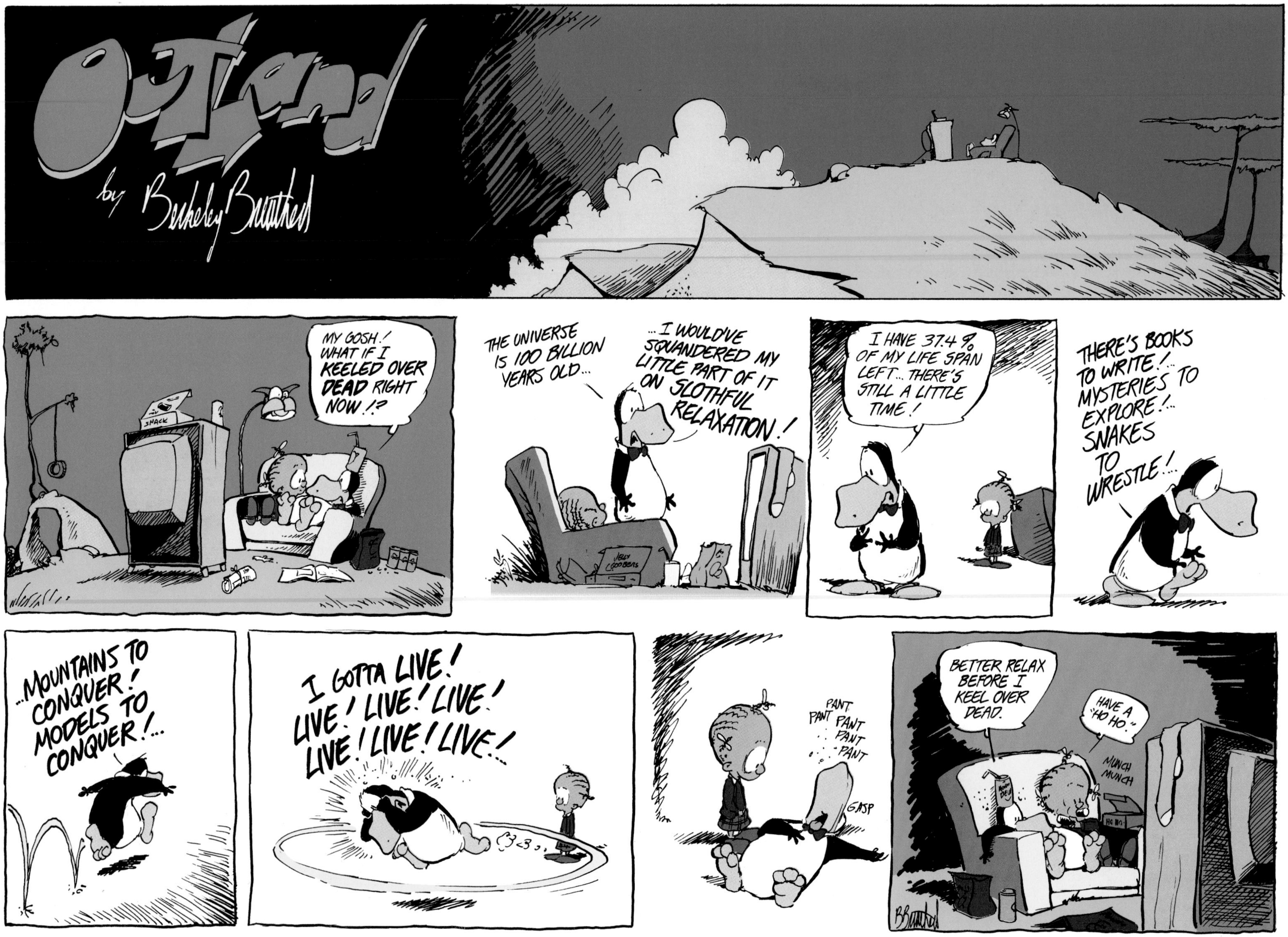
Outland
by Berkeley Breathed
SNACK
MY GOSH! WHAT IF I KEELED OVER DEAD RIGHT NOW!?
THE UNIVERSE IS 100 BILLION YEARS OLD...
...I WOULD'VE SQUANDERED MY LITTLE PART OF IT ON SLOTHFUL RELAXATION!
I HAVE 37.4% OF MY LIFE SPAN LEFT... THERE'S STILL A LITTLE TIME!
THERE'S BOOKS TO WRITE!... MYSTERIES TO EXPLORE!... SNAKES TO WRESTLE!...
...MOUNTAINS TO CONQUER! MODELS TO CONQUER!...
I GOTTA LIVE! LIVE! LIVE! LIVE! LIVE! LIVE! LIVE!...
PANT PANT PANT PANT PANT
GASP
BETTER RELAX BEFORE I KEEL OVER DEAD.
HAVE A "HO HO."
MUNCH MUNCH
BBreathed

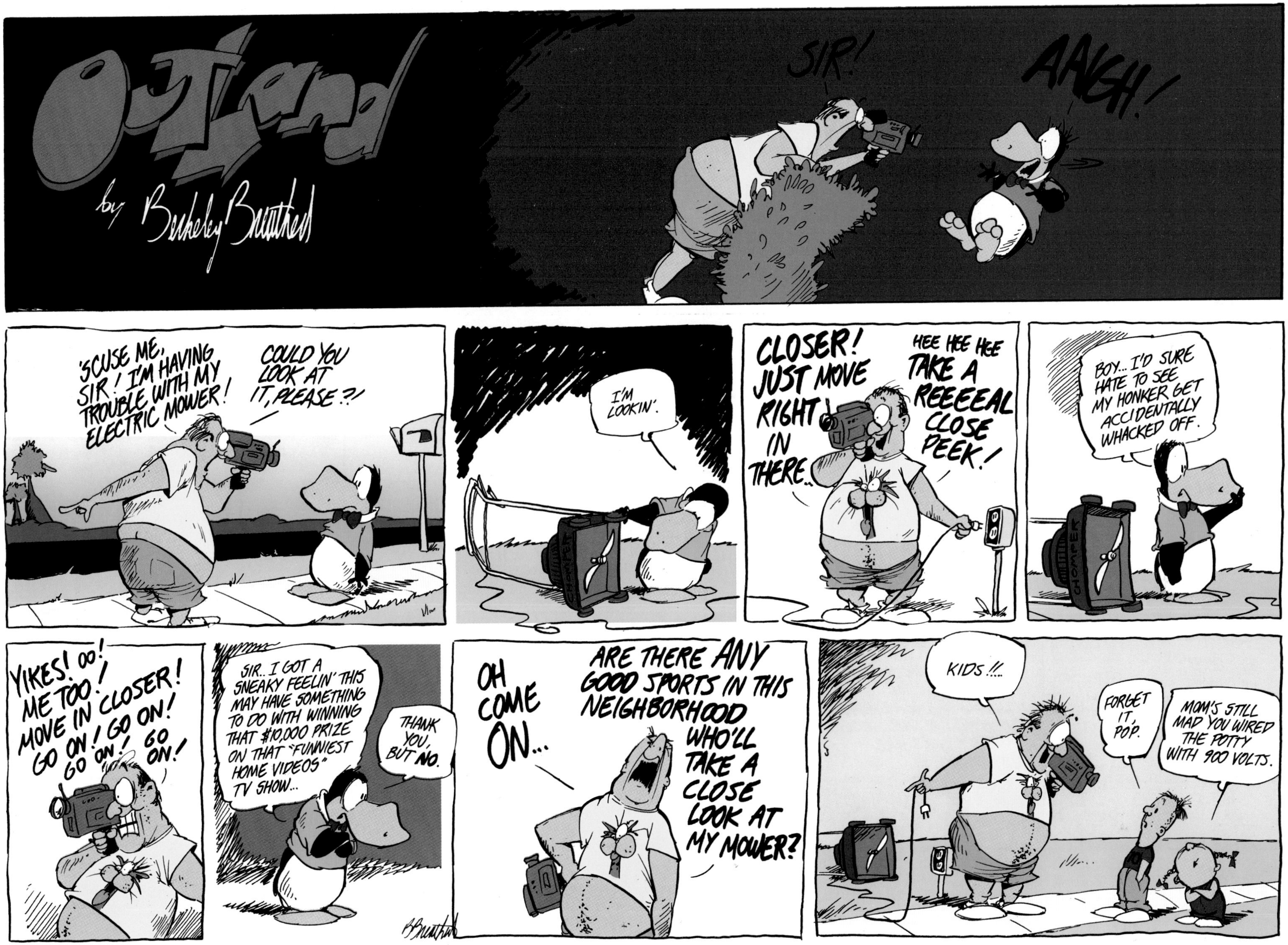
Outland
by Berkeley Breathed
SIR!
AAIGH!
'SCUSE ME, SIR! I'M HAVING TROUBLE WITH MY ELECTRIC MOWER!
COULD YOU LOOK AT IT, PLEASE?!
I'M LOOKIN'.
CLOSER! JUST MOVE RIGHT IN THERE...
HEE HEE HEE TAKE A REEEEAL CLOSE PEEK!
BOY... I'D SURE HATE TO SEE MY HONKER GET ACCIDENTALLY WHACKED OFF.
YIKES! OO! ME TOO! MOVE IN CLOSER! GO ON! GO ON! GO ON! GO ON!
SIR.. I GOT A SNEAKY FEELIN' THIS MAY HAVE SOMETHING TO DO WITH WINNING THAT $10,000 PRIZE ON THAT "FUNNIEST HOME VIDEOS" TV SHOW...
THANK YOU, BUT NO.
OH COME ON...
ARE THERE ANY GOOD SPORTS IN THIS NEIGHBORHOOD WHO'LL TAKE A CLOSE LOOK AT MY MOWER?
KIDS!!!
FORGET IT, POP.
MOM'S STILL MAD YOU WIRED THE POTTY WITH 900 VOLTS.

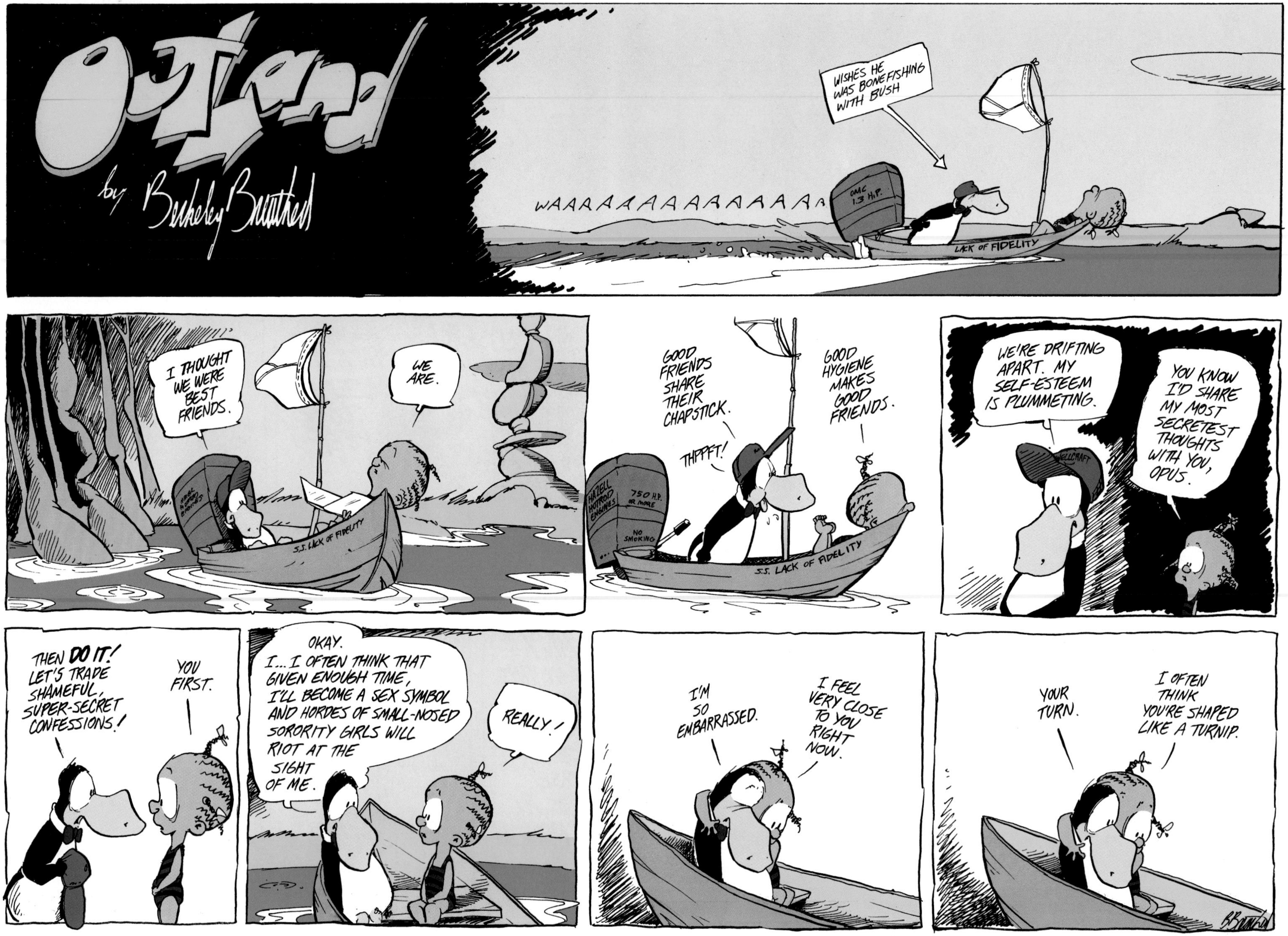
OUTLAND
by Berkeley Breathed
WISHES HE WAS BONEFISHING WITH BUSH
WAAAAAAAAAAAAAA
OMC 1.3 H.P.
LACK OF FIDELITY
I THOUGHT WE WERE BEST FRIENDS.
WE ARE.
S.S. LACK OF FIDELITY
GOOD FRIENDS SHARE THEIR CHAPSTICK.
GOOD HYGIENE MAKES GOOD FRIENDS.
THPPFT!
HAZELL HOTROID ENGINES
750 H.P. OR MORE
NO SMOKING
S.S. LACK OF FIDELITY
WE'RE DRIFTING APART. MY SELF-ESTEEM IS PLUMMETING.
YOU KNOW I'D SHARE MY MOST SECRETEST THOUGHTS WITH YOU, OPUS.
WELLCRAFT
THEN DO IT! LET'S TRADE SHAMEFUL, SUPER-SECRET CONFESSIONS!
YOU FIRST.
OKAY. I... I OFTEN THINK THAT GIVEN ENOUGH TIME, I'LL BECOME A SEX SYMBOL AND HORDES OF SMALL-NOSED SORORITY GIRLS WILL RIOT AT THE SIGHT OF ME.
REALLY!
I'M SO EMBARRASSED.
I FEEL VERY CLOSE TO YOU RIGHT NOW.
YOUR TURN.
I OFTEN THINK YOU'RE SHAPED LIKE A TURNIP.
B Breathed

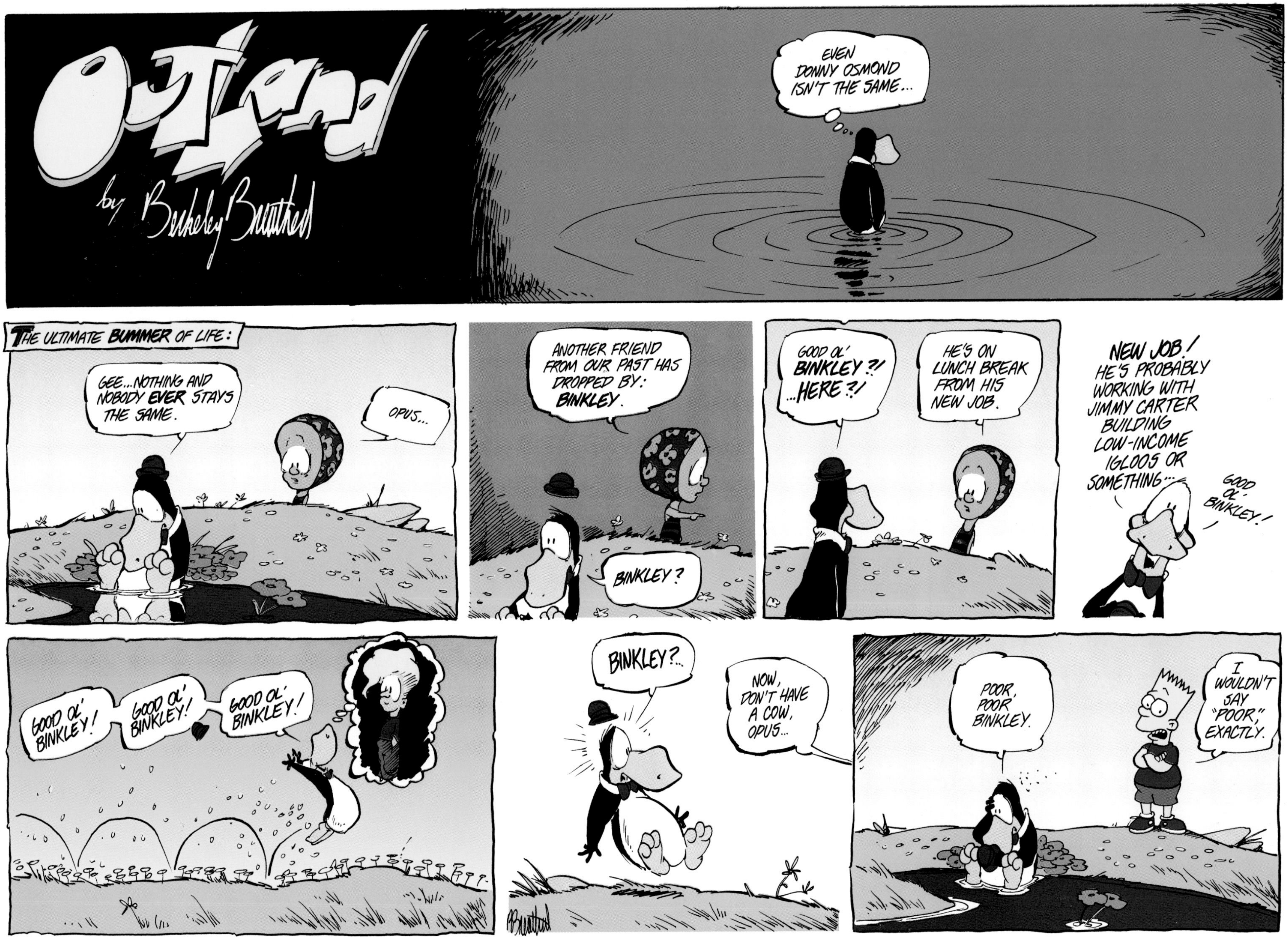

OUTLAND
by Berkeley Breathed
EVEN DONNY OSMOND ISN'T THE SAME...
THE ULTIMATE BUMMER OF LIFE:
GEE...NOTHING AND NOBODY EVER STAYS THE SAME.
OPUS...
ANOTHER FRIEND FROM OUR PAST HAS DROPPED BY: BINKLEY.
BINKLEY?
GOOD OL' BINKLEY?! ...HERE?!
HE'S ON LUNCH BREAK FROM HIS NEW JOB.
NEW JOB! HE'S PROBABLY WORKING WITH JIMMY CARTER BUILDING LOW-INCOME IGLOOS OR SOMETHING...
GOOD OL' BINKLEY!
GOOD OL' BINKLEY!
GOOD OL' BINKLEY!
GOOD OL' BINKLEY!
BINKLEY?...
NOW, DON'T HAVE A COW, OPUS...
POOR, POOR BINKLEY.
I WOULDN'T SAY "POOR," EXACTLY.

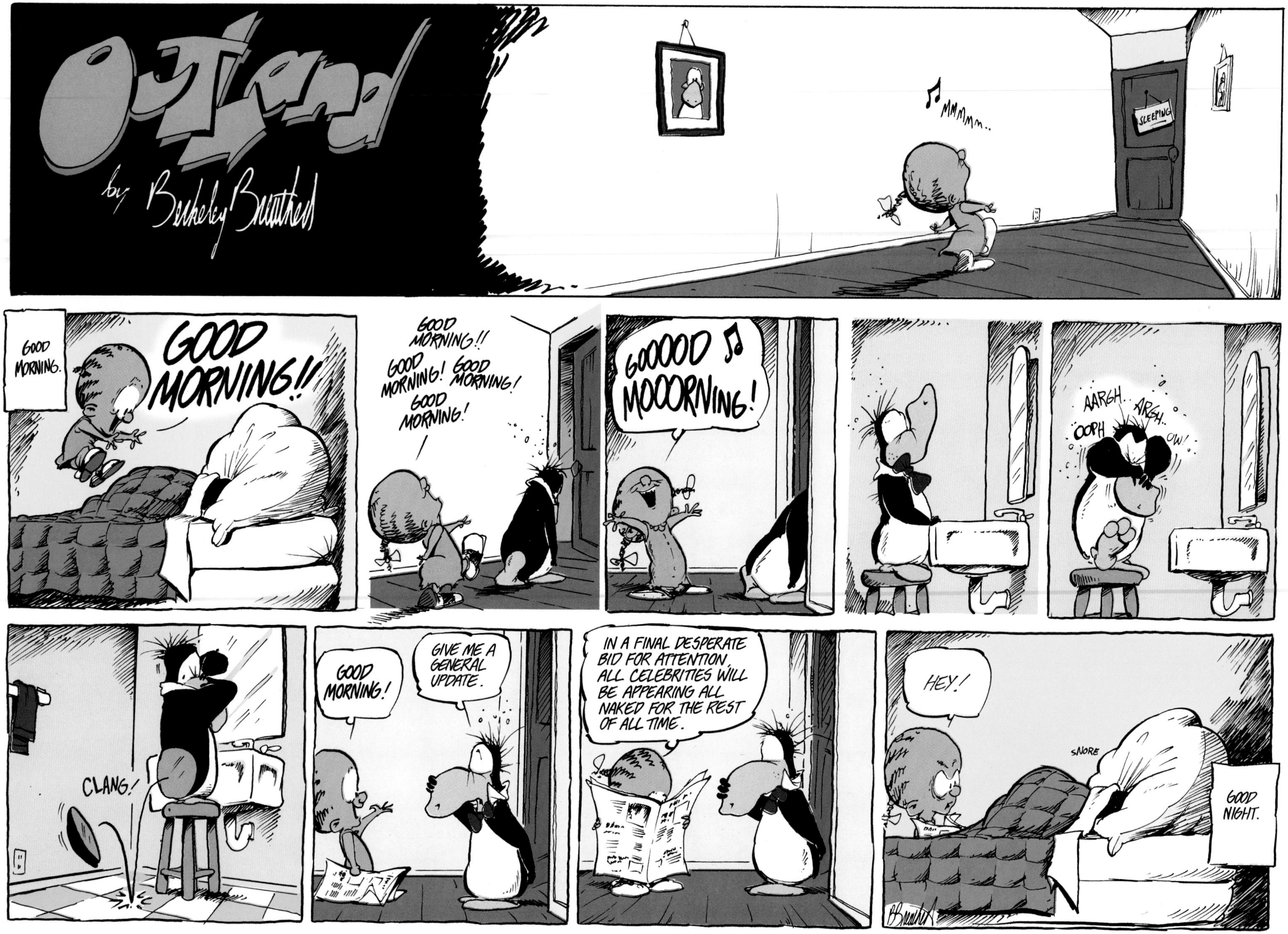
Outland
by Berkeley Breathed
MMMMM..
SLEEPING
GOOD MORNING.
GOOD MORNING!!
GOOD MORNING!!
GOOD MORNING!
GOOD MORNING!
GOOD MORNING!
GOOOOD MOOORNING!
AARGH
ARGH
OOPH
OW!
CLANG!
GOOD MORNING!
GIVE ME A GENERAL UPDATE.
IN A FINAL DESPERATE BID FOR ATTENTION, ALL CELEBRITIES WILL BE APPEARING ALL NAKED FOR THE REST OF ALL TIME.
HEY!
SNORE
GOOD NIGHT.

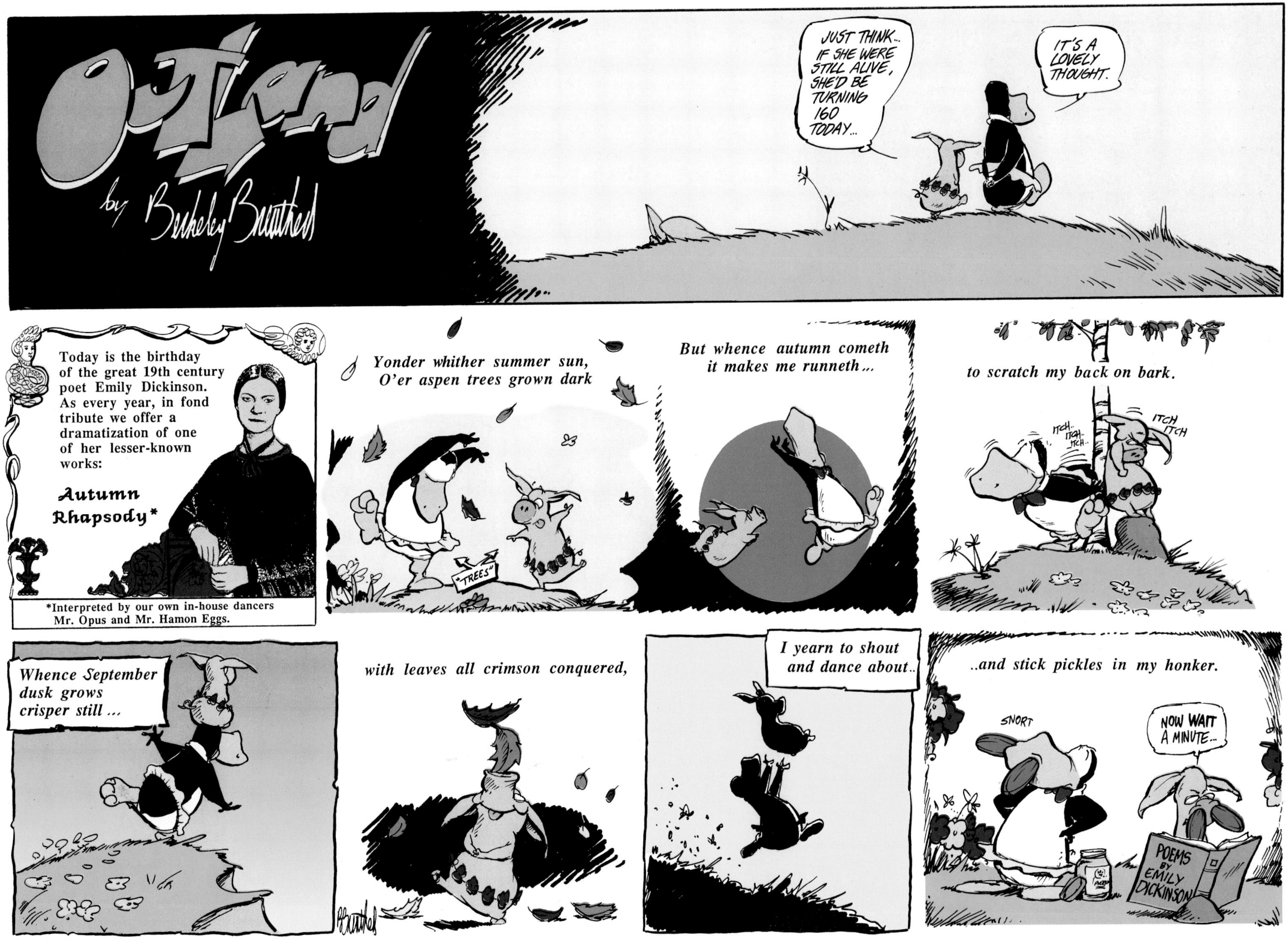

Outland
by Berkeley Breathed
JUST THINK... IF SHE WERE STILL ALIVE, SHE'D BE TURNING 160 TODAY...
IT'S A LOVELY THOUGHT.
Today is the birthday of the great 19th century poet Emily Dickinson. As every year, in fond tribute we offer a dramatization of one of her lesser-known works:
Autumn Rhapsody*
*Interpreted by our own in-house dancers Mr. Opus and Mr. Hamon Eggs.
Yonder whither summer sun, O'er aspen trees grown dark
"TREES"
But whence autumn cometh it makes me runneth...
to scratch my back on bark.
ITCH.. ITCH.. ITCH..
ITCH ITCH
Whence September dusk grows crisper still ...
with leaves all crimson conquered,
I yearn to shout and dance about..
..and stick pickles in my honker.
SNORT
NOW WAIT A MINUTE...
POEMS BY EMILY DICKINSON

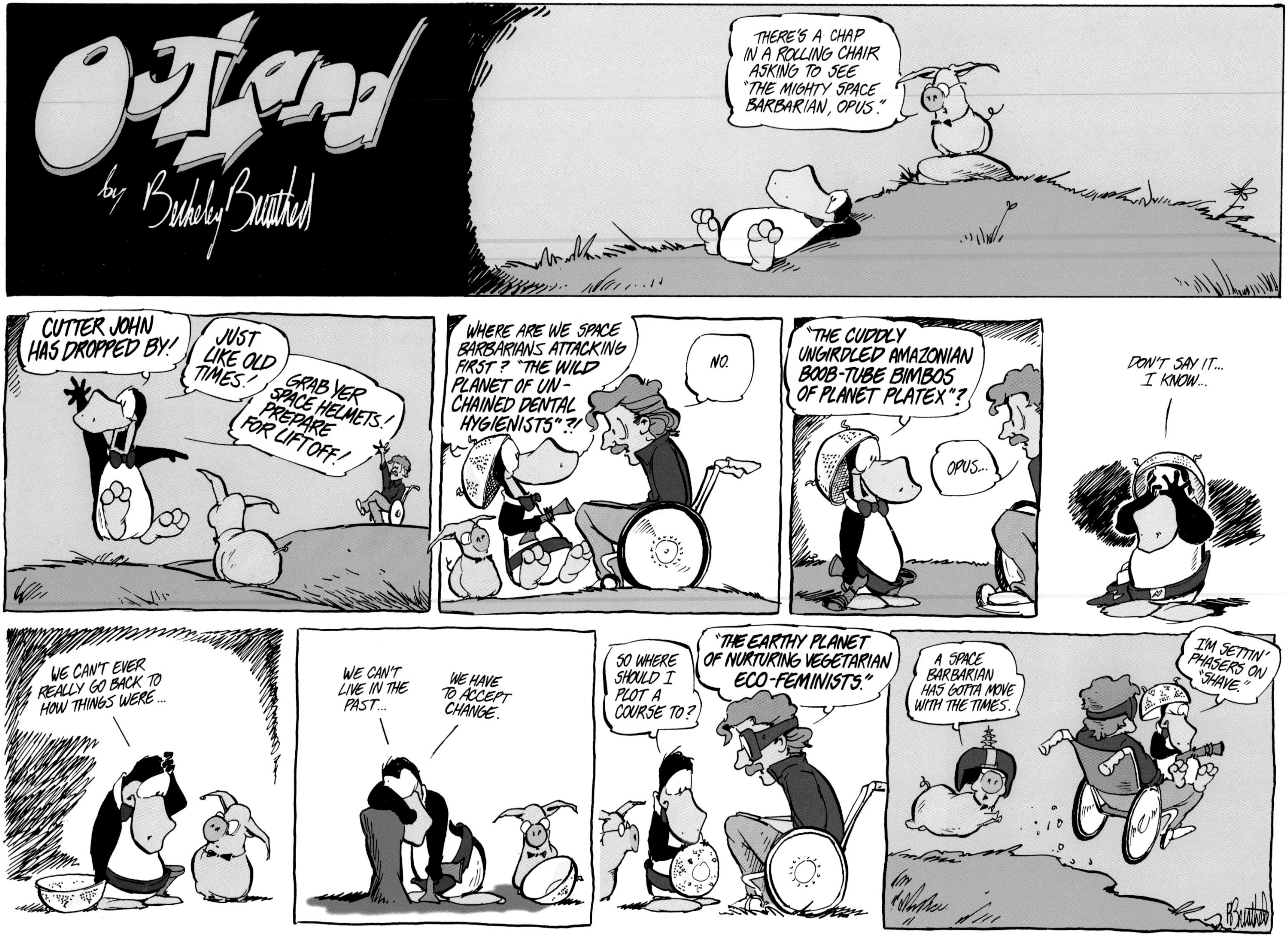
Outland
by Berkeley Breathed
THERE'S A CHAP IN A ROLLING CHAIR ASKING TO SEE "THE MIGHTY SPACE BARBARIAN, OPUS."
CUTTER JOHN HAS DROPPED BY!
JUST LIKE OLD TIMES!
GRAB YER SPACE HELMETS! PREPARE FOR LIFTOFF!
WHERE ARE WE SPACE BARBARIANS ATTACKING FIRST? "THE WILD PLANET OF UN-CHAINED DENTAL HYGIENISTS"?!
NO.
"THE CUDDLY UNGIRDLED AMAZONIAN BOOB-TUBE BIMBOS OF PLANET PLATEX"?
OPUS...
DON'T SAY IT... I KNOW...
WE CAN'T EVER REALLY GO BACK TO HOW THINGS WERE...
WE CAN'T LIVE IN THE PAST...
WE HAVE TO ACCEPT CHANGE.
SO WHERE SHOULD I PLOT A COURSE TO?
"THE EARTHY PLANET OF NURTURING VEGETARIAN ECO-FEMINISTS."
A SPACE BARBARIAN HAS GOTTA MOVE WITH THE TIMES.
I'M SETTIN' PHASERS ON "SHAVE."
B Breathed

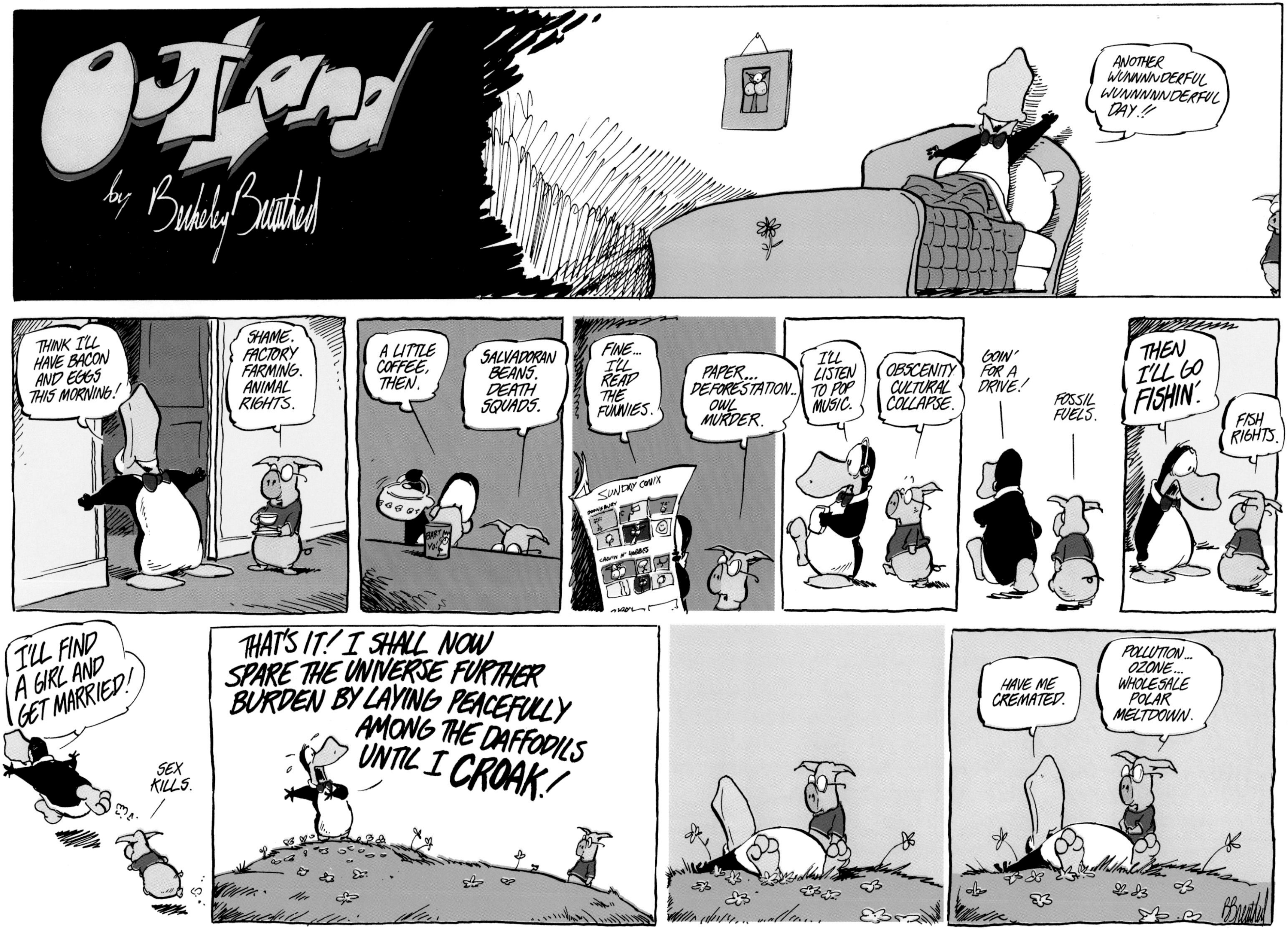
Outland
by Berkeley Breathed
ANOTHER WUNNNNNDERFUL WUNNNNNNDERFUL DAY!!
THINK I'LL HAVE BACON AND EGGS THIS MORNING!
SHAME. FACTORY FARMING. ANIMAL RIGHTS.
A LITTLE COFFEE, THEN.
SALVADORAN BEANS. DEATH SQUADS.
FINE... I'LL READ THE FUNNIES.
SUNDAY COMIX
PAPER... DEFORESTATION.. OWL MURDER.
I'LL LISTEN TO POP MUSIC.
OBSCENITY. CULTURAL COLLAPSE.
GOIN' FOR A DRIVE!
FOSSIL FUELS.
THEN I'LL GO FISHIN'.
FISH RIGHTS.
I'LL FIND A GIRL AND GET MARRIED!
SEX KILLS.
THAT'S IT! I SHALL NOW SPARE THE UNIVERSE FURTHER BURDEN BY LAYING PEACEFULLY AMONG THE DAFFODILS UNTIL I CROAK!
HAVE ME CREMATED.
POLLUTION... OZONE... WHOLESALE POLAR MELTDOWN.

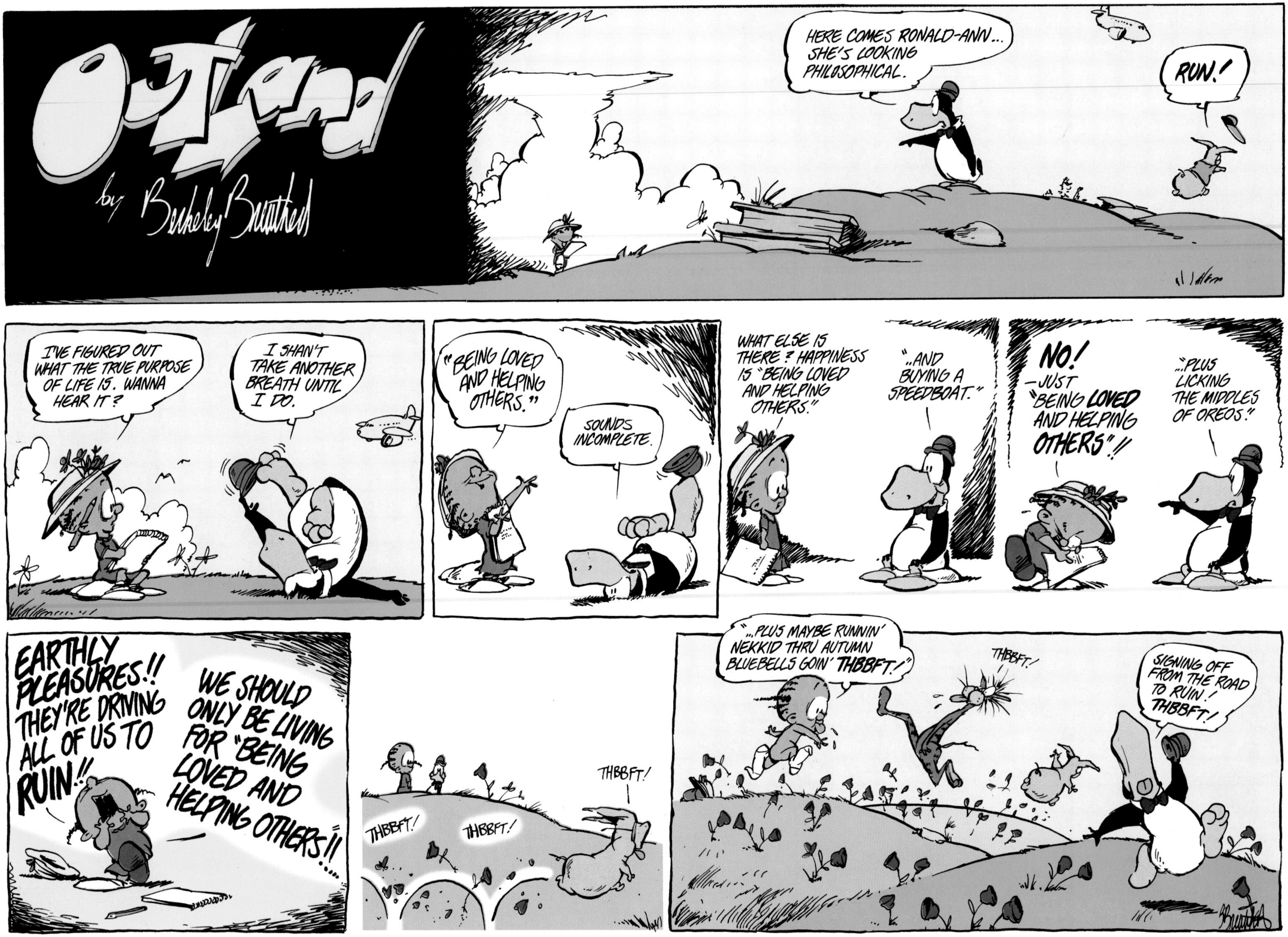

Outland
by Berkeley Breathed
HERE COMES RONALD-ANN... SHE'S LOOKING PHILOSOPHICAL.
RUN!
I'VE FIGURED OUT WHAT THE TRUE PURPOSE OF LIFE IS. WANNA HEAR IT?
I SHAN'T TAKE ANOTHER BREATH UNTIL I DO.
"BEING LOVED AND HELPING OTHERS."
SOUNDS INCOMPLETE.
WHAT ELSE IS THERE? HAPPINESS IS "BEING LOVED AND HELPING OTHERS."
"...AND BUYING A SPEEDBOAT."
NO! –JUST "BEING LOVED AND HELPING OTHERS"!!
"...PLUS LICKING THE MIDDLES OF OREOS."
EARTHLY PLEASURES!! THEY'RE DRIVING ALL OF US TO RUIN!!
WE SHOULD ONLY BE LIVING FOR "BEING LOVED AND HELPING OTHERS!!
THBBFT!
THBBFT!
THBBFT!
"...PLUS MAYBE RUNNIN' NEKKID THRU AUTUMN BLUEBELLS GOIN' THBBFT!"
THBBFT!
SIGNING OFF FROM THE ROAD TO RUIN! THBBFT!

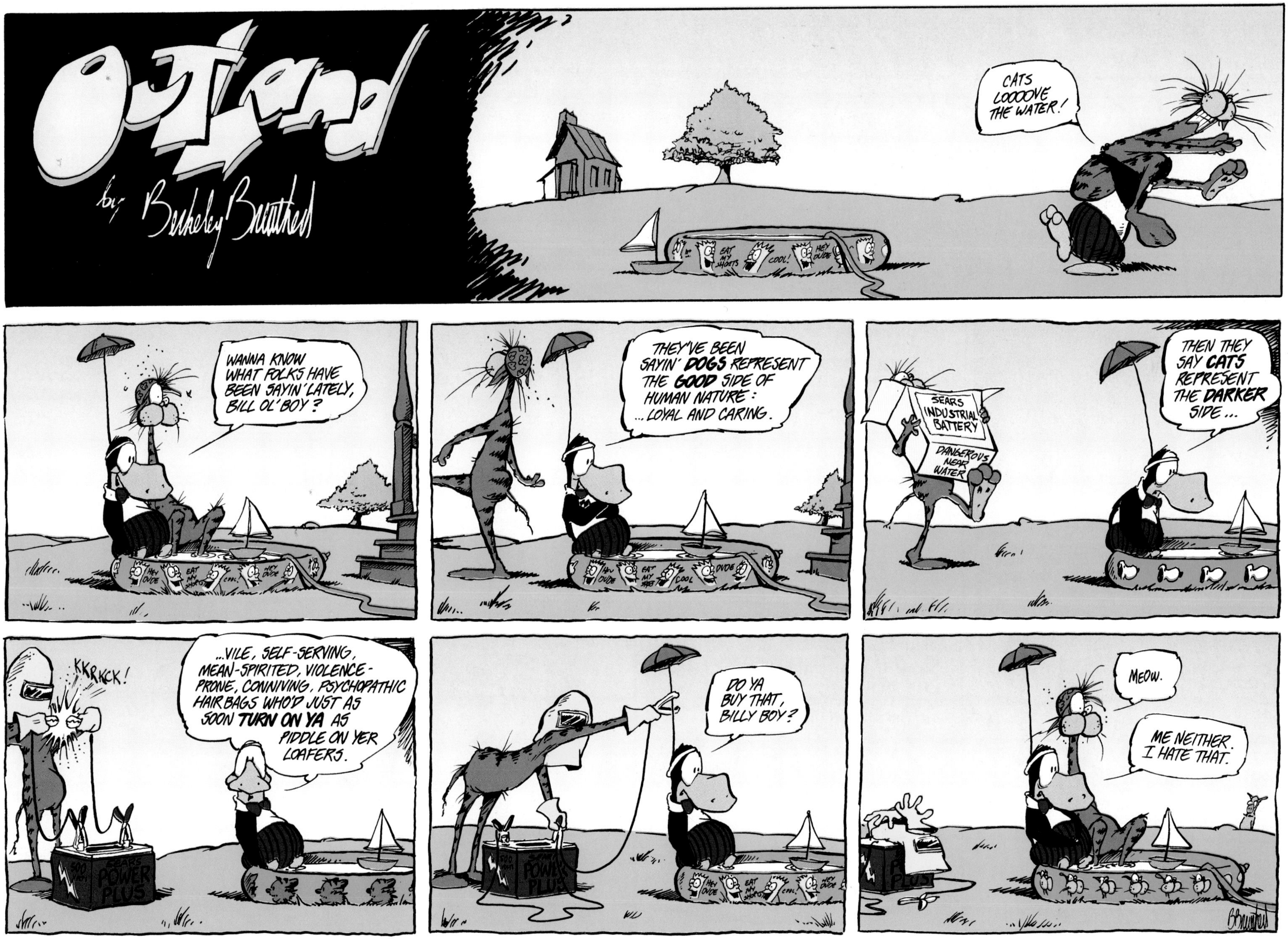
Outland
by Berkeley Breathed
EAT MY SHORTS
COOL!
HEY DUDE
CATS LOOOOVE THE WATER!
WANNA KNOW WHAT FOLKS HAVE BEEN SAYIN' LATELY, BILL OL' BOY?
THEY'VE BEEN SAYIN' DOGS REPRESENT THE GOOD SIDE OF HUMAN NATURE: ...LOYAL AND CARING.
SEARS INDUSTRIAL BATTERY
DANGEROUS NEAR WATER
THEN THEY SAY CATS REPRESENT THE DARKER SIDE...
KKRKCK!
SEARS POWER PLUS
...VILE, SELF-SERVING, MEAN-SPIRITED, VIOLENCE-PRONE, CONNIVING, PSYCHOPATHIC HAIRBAGS WHO'D JUST AS SOON TURN ON YA AS PIDDLE ON YER LOAFERS.
DO YA BUY THAT, BILLY BOY?
MEOW.
ME NEITHER. I HATE THAT.
BBreathed

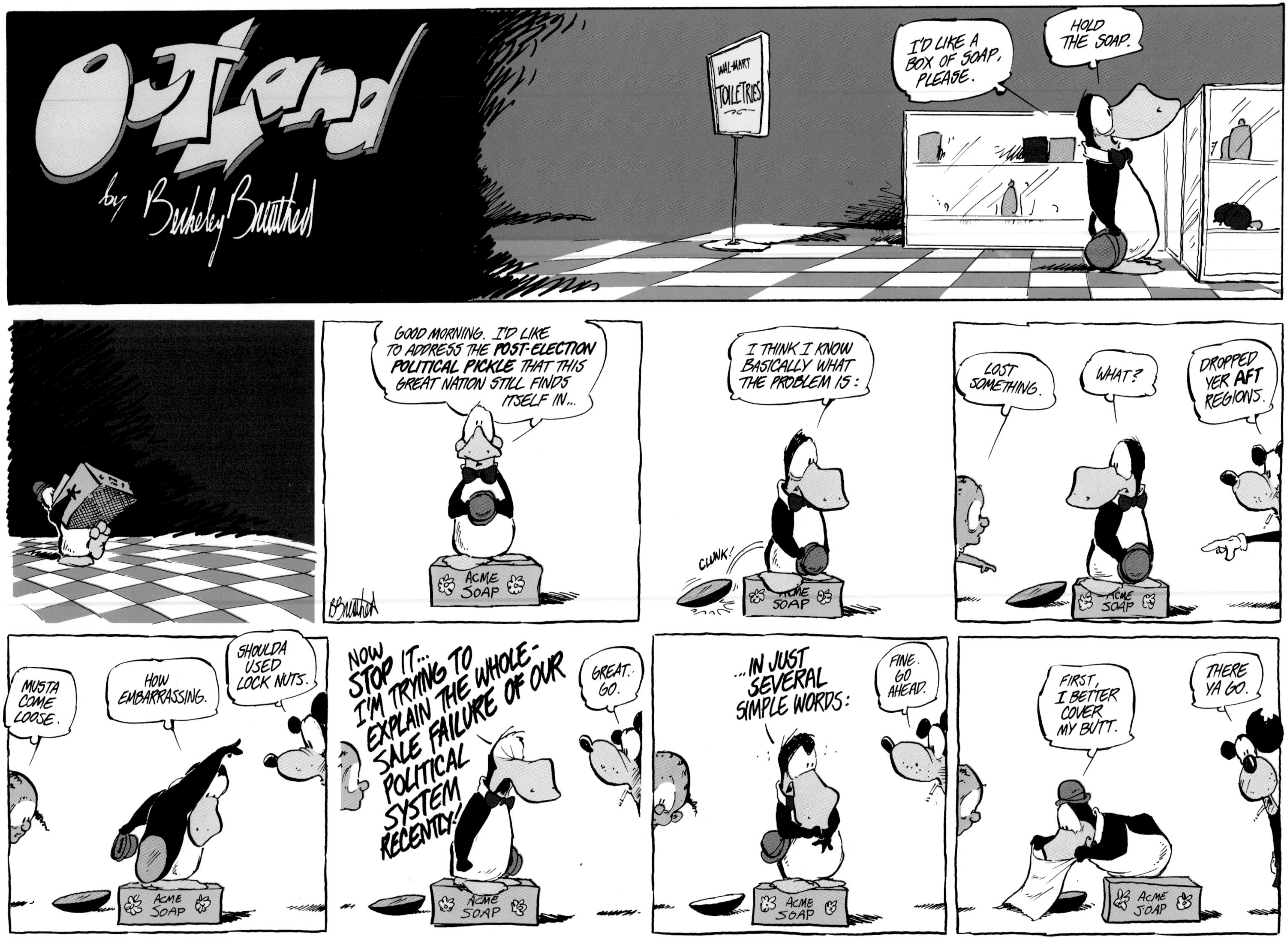
Outland
by Berkeley Breathed
WAL-MART TOILETRIES
I'D LIKE A BOX OF SOAP, PLEASE.
HOLD THE SOAP.
GOOD MORNING. I'D LIKE TO ADDRESS THE POST-ELECTION POLITICAL PICKLE THAT THIS GREAT NATION STILL FINDS ITSELF IN...
ACME SOAP
BBreathed
I THINK I KNOW BASICALLY WHAT THE PROBLEM IS:
CLUNK!
LOST SOMETHING.
WHAT?
DROPPED YER AFT REGIONS.
MUSTA COME LOOSE.
HOW EMBARRASSING.
SHOULDA USED LOCK NUTS.
NOW STOP IT... I'M TRYING TO EXPLAIN THE WHOLESALE FAILURE OF OUR POLITICAL SYSTEM RECENTLY!
GREAT. GO.
...IN JUST SEVERAL SIMPLE WORDS:
FINE. GO AHEAD.
FIRST, I BETTER COVER MY BUTT.
THERE YA GO.

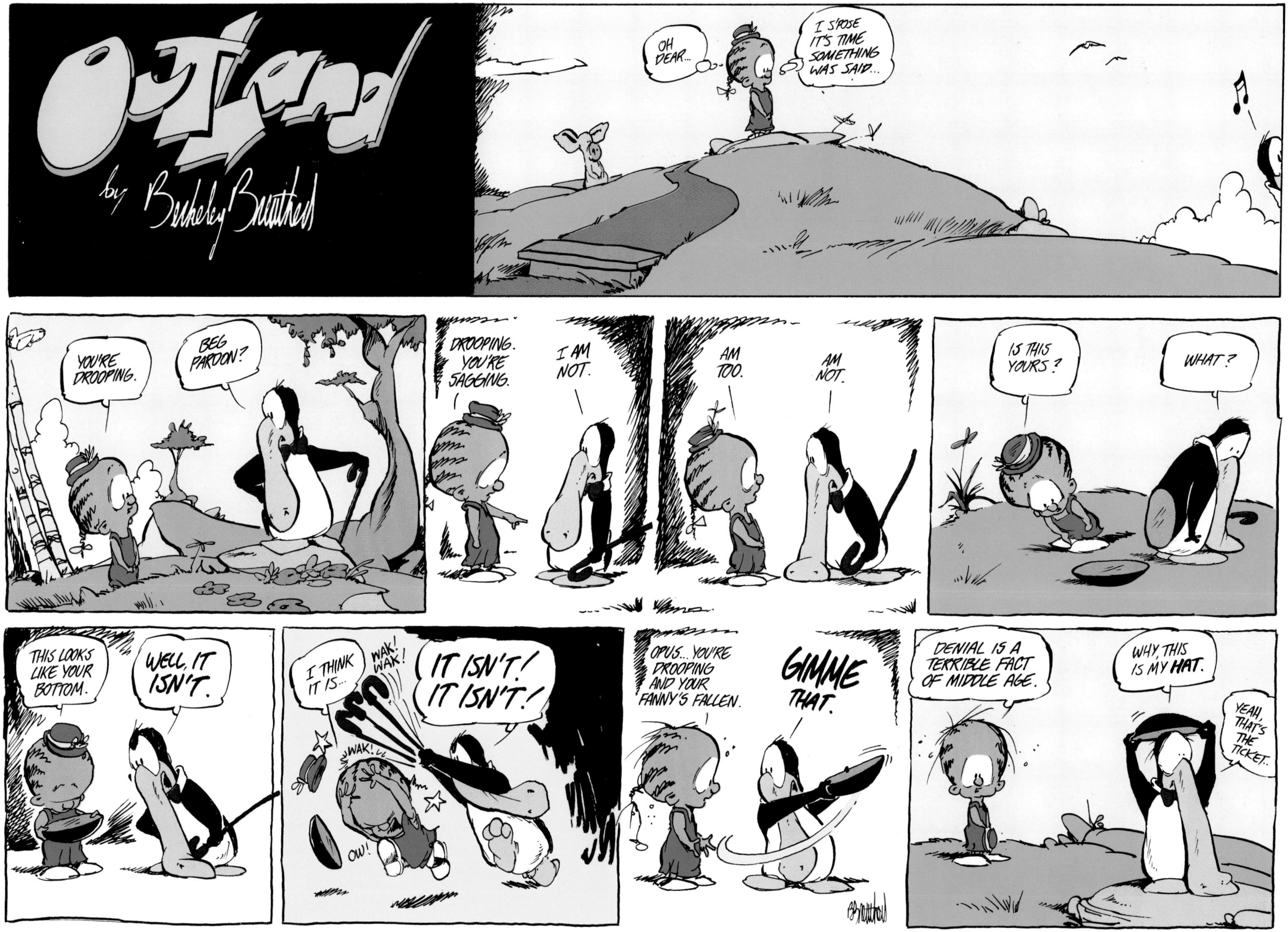
Outland
by Berkeley Breathed
OH DEAR...
I S'POSE IT'S TIME SOMETHING WAS SAID...
YOU'RE DROOPING.
BEG PARDON?
DROOPING. YOU'RE SAGGING.
I AM NOT.
AM TOO.
AM NOT.
IS THIS YOURS?
WHAT?
THIS LOOKS LIKE YOUR BOTTOM.
WELL, IT ISN'T.
I THINK IT IS...
WAK! WAK!
IT ISN'T! IT ISN'T!
WAK!
OW!
OPUS... YOU'RE DROOPING AND YOUR FANNY'S FALLEN.
GIMME THAT.
DENIAL IS A TERRIBLE FACT OF MIDDLE AGE.
WHY, THIS IS MY HAT.
YEAH, THAT'S THE TICKET..
Breathed

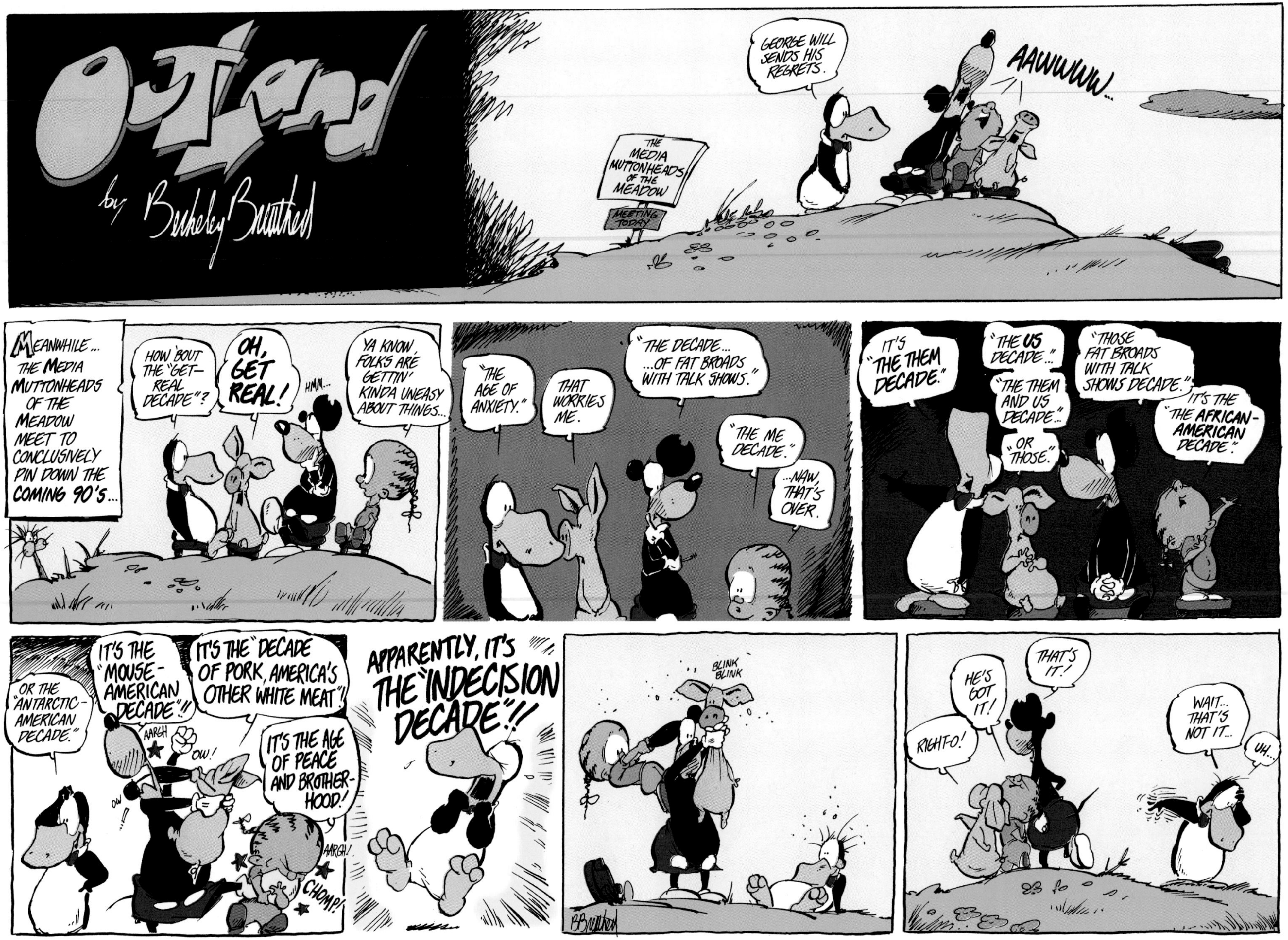
OUTLAND
by Berkeley Breathed
THE MEDIA MUTTONHEADS OF THE MEADOW
MEETING TODAY
GEORGE WILL SENDS HIS REGRETS.
AAWWWW...
MEANWHILE... THE MEDIA MUTTONHEADS OF THE MEADOW MEET TO CONCLUSIVELY PIN DOWN THE COMING 90'S...
HOW 'BOUT THE "GET-REAL DECADE"?
OH, GET REAL!
HMM...
YA KNOW, FOLKS ARE GETTIN' KINDA UNEASY ABOUT THINGS...
"THE AGE OF ANXIETY."
THAT WORRIES ME.
"THE DECADE... ...OF FAT BROADS WITH TALK SHOWS."
"THE ME DECADE."
...NAW, THAT'S OVER.
IT'S "THE THEM DECADE."
"THE US DECADE."
"THE THEM AND US DECADE."
"OR THOSE."
"THOSE FAT BROADS WITH TALK SHOWS DECADE."
IT'S THE "THE AFRICAN-AMERICAN DECADE."
OR THE "ANTARCTIC-AMERICAN DECADE."
IT'S THE "MOUSE-AMERICAN DECADE"!!
IT'S THE "DECADE OF PORK, AMERICA'S OTHER WHITE MEAT"!
AARGH
OW!
OW
IT'S THE AGE OF PEACE AND BROTHER-HOOD!
AARGH!
CHOMP!
APPARENTLY, IT'S THE "INDECISION DECADE"!!
BLINK BLINK
B. Breathed
RIGHT-O!
HE'S GOT IT!
THAT'S IT!
WAIT... THAT'S NOT IT...
UH...

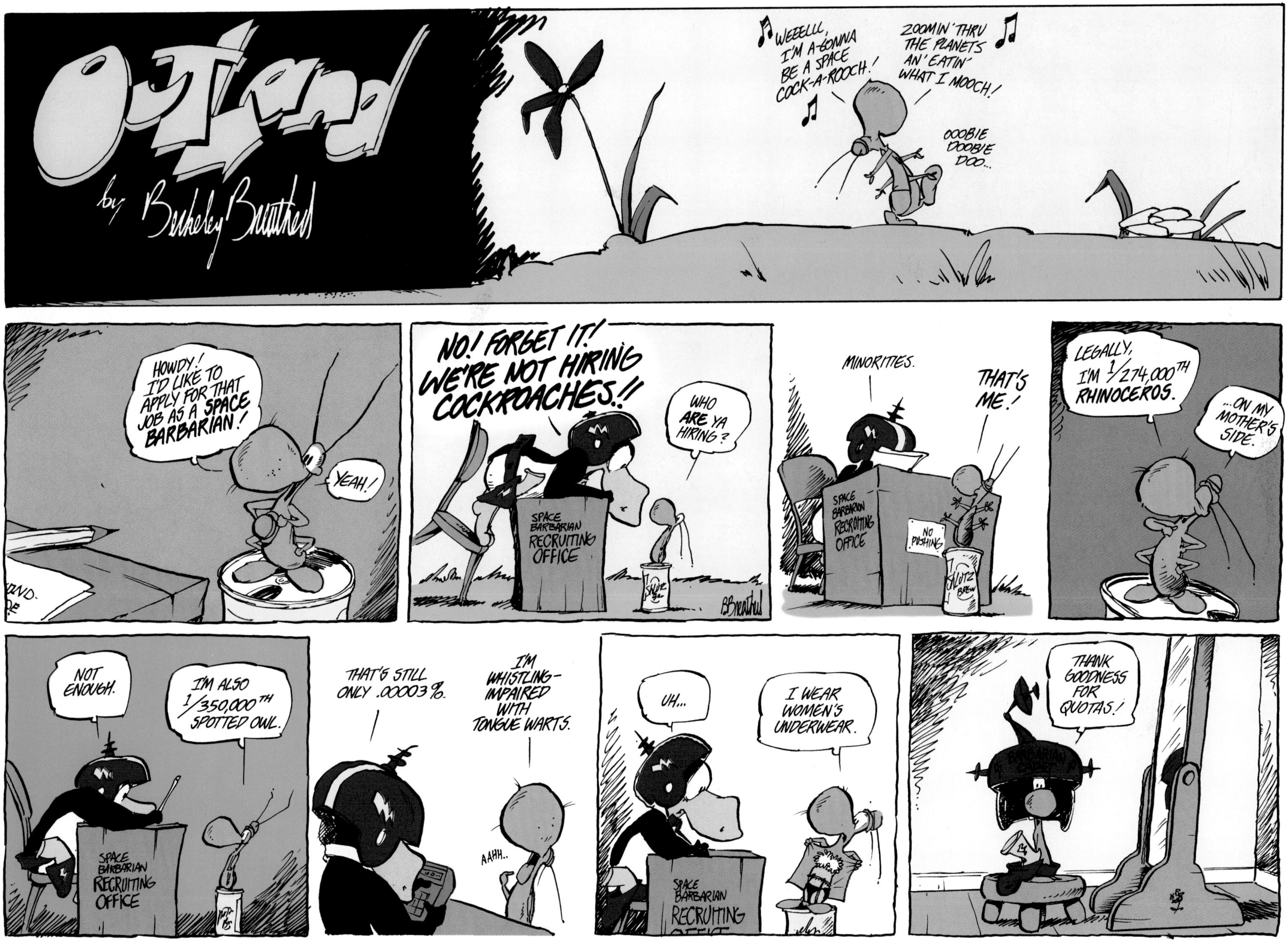
Outland
by Berkeley Breathed
WEEELLL, I'M A-GONNA BE A SPACE COCK-A-ROOCH!
ZOOMIN' THRU THE PLANETS AN' EATIN' WHAT I MOOCH!
OOOBIE DOOBIE DOO...
HOWDY! I'D LIKE TO APPLY FOR THAT JOB AS A SPACE BARBARIAN!
YEAH!
NO! FORGET IT! WE'RE NOT HIRING COCKROACHES!!
WHO ARE YA HIRING?
SPACE BARBARIAN RECRUITING OFFICE
MINORITIES.
THAT'S ME!
NO PUSHING
LEGALLY, I'M 1/274,000TH RHINOCEROS.
...ON MY MOTHER'S SIDE.
NOT ENOUGH.
I'M ALSO 1/350,000TH SPOTTED OWL.
THAT'S STILL ONLY .00003%.
I'M WHISTLING-IMPAIRED WITH TONGUE WARTS.
AAHH..
UH...
I WEAR WOMEN'S UNDERWEAR.
THANK GOODNESS FOR QUOTAS!
BARBARIAN CADET

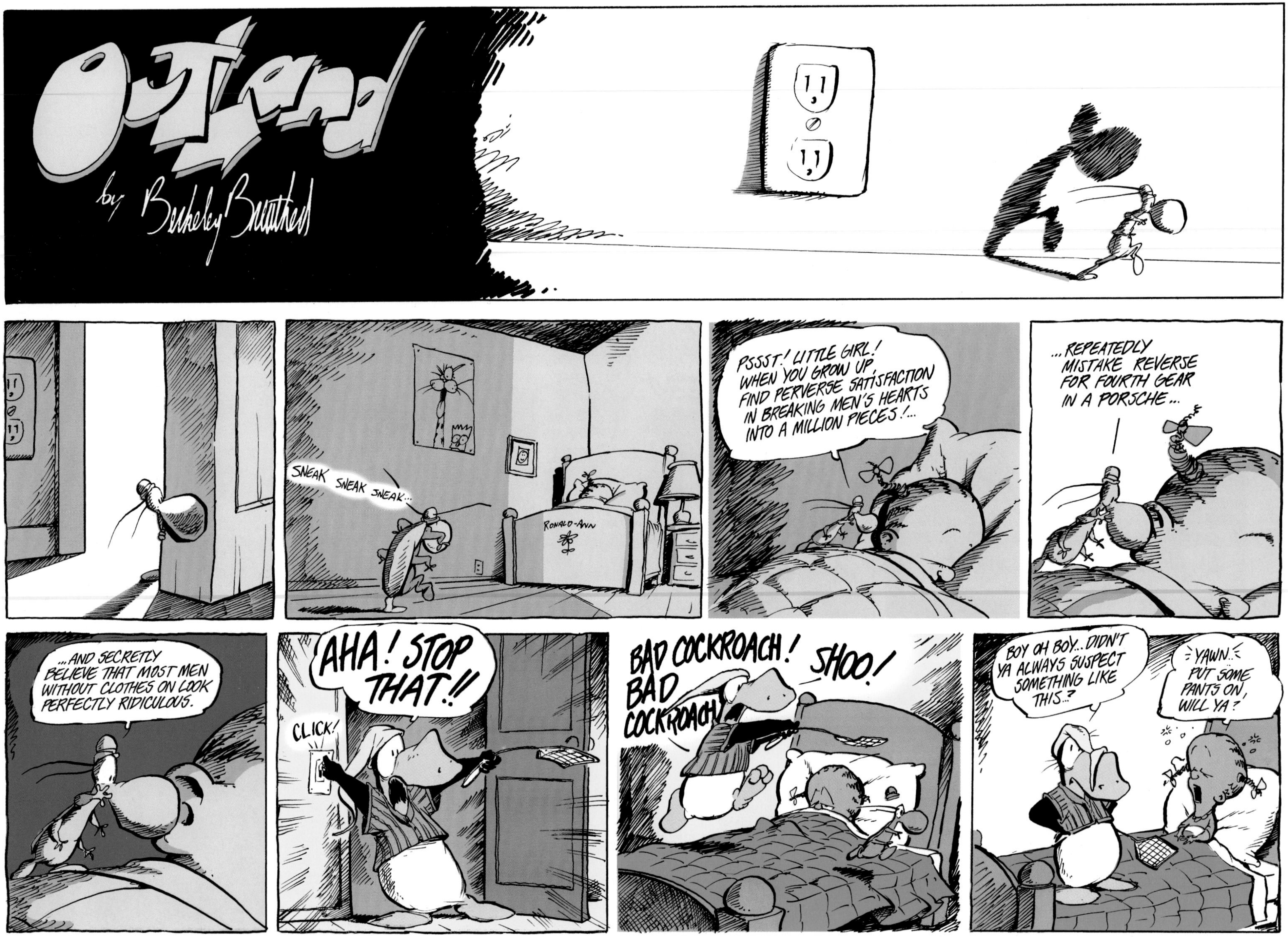

Outland
by Berkeley Breathed
SNEAK SNEAK SNEAK...
RONALD-ANN
PSSST! LITTLE GIRL! WHEN YOU GROW UP, FIND PERVERSE SATISFACTION IN BREAKING MEN'S HEARTS INTO A MILLION PIECES!...
...REPEATEDLY MISTAKE REVERSE FOR FOURTH GEAR IN A PORSCHE...
...AND SECRETLY BELIEVE THAT MOST MEN WITHOUT CLOTHES ON LOOK PERFECTLY RIDICULOUS.
AHA! STOP THAT!!
CLICK!
BAD COCKROACH! BAD BAD COCKROACH
SHOO!
BOY OH BOY... DIDN'T YA ALWAYS SUSPECT SOMETHING LIKE THIS..?
YAWN... PUT SOME PANTS ON, WILL YA?

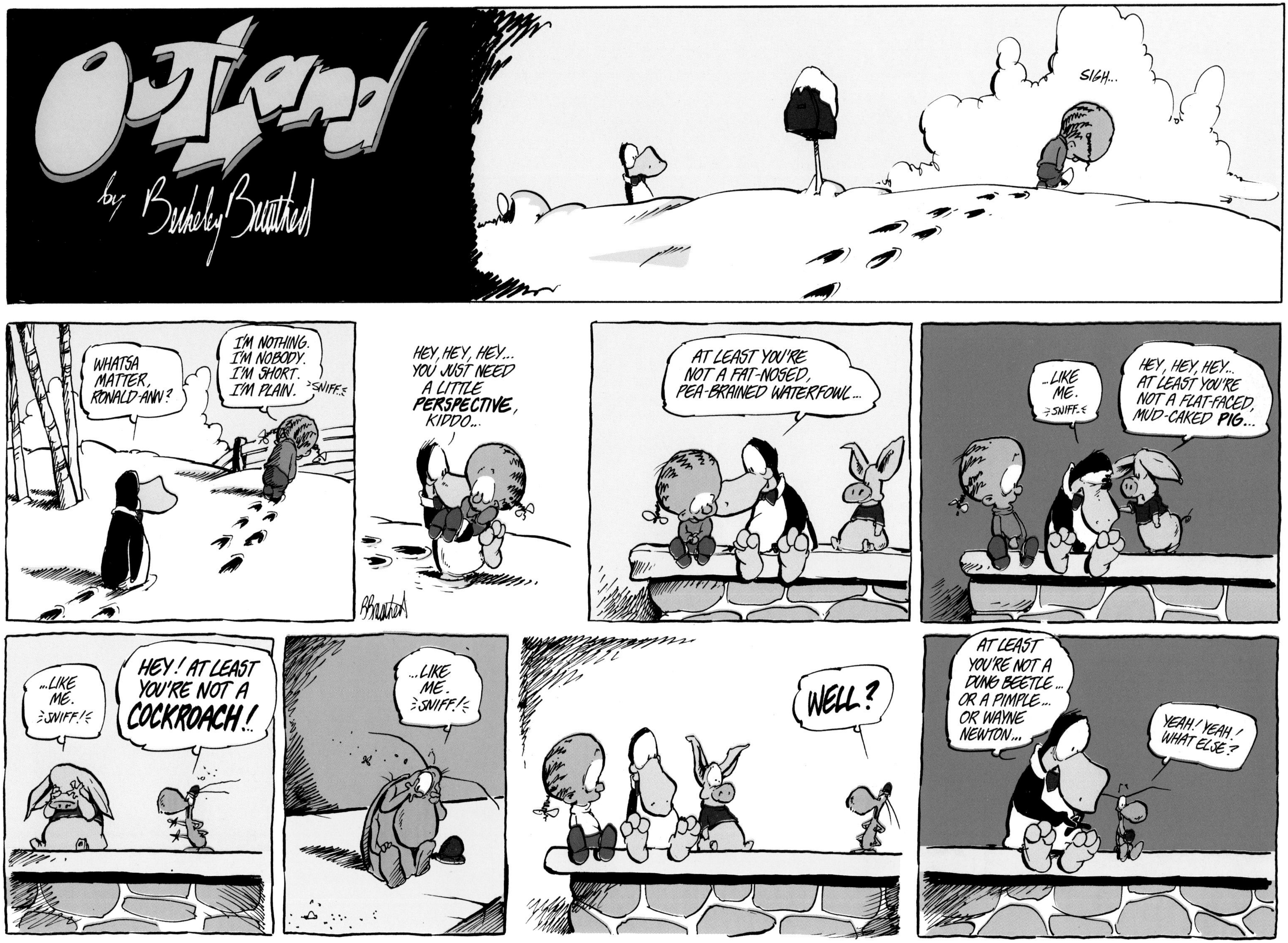
Outland
by Berkeley Breathed
SIGH...
WHATSA MATTER, RONALD-ANN?
I'M NOTHING. I'M NOBODY. I'M SHORT. I'M PLAIN.
SNIFF.
HEY, HEY, HEY... YOU JUST NEED A LITTLE PERSPECTIVE, KIDDO...
AT LEAST YOU'RE NOT A FAT-NOSED, PEA-BRAINED WATERFOWL...
...LIKE ME.
SNIFF.
HEY, HEY, HEY... AT LEAST YOU'RE NOT A FLAT-FACED, MUD-CAKED PIG...
...LIKE ME.
SNIFF!
HEY! AT LEAST YOU'RE NOT A COCKROACH!
...LIKE ME.
SNIFF!
WELL?
AT LEAST YOU'RE NOT A DUNG BEETLE... OR A PIMPLE... OR WAYNE NEWTON...
YEAH! YEAH! WHAT ELSE?

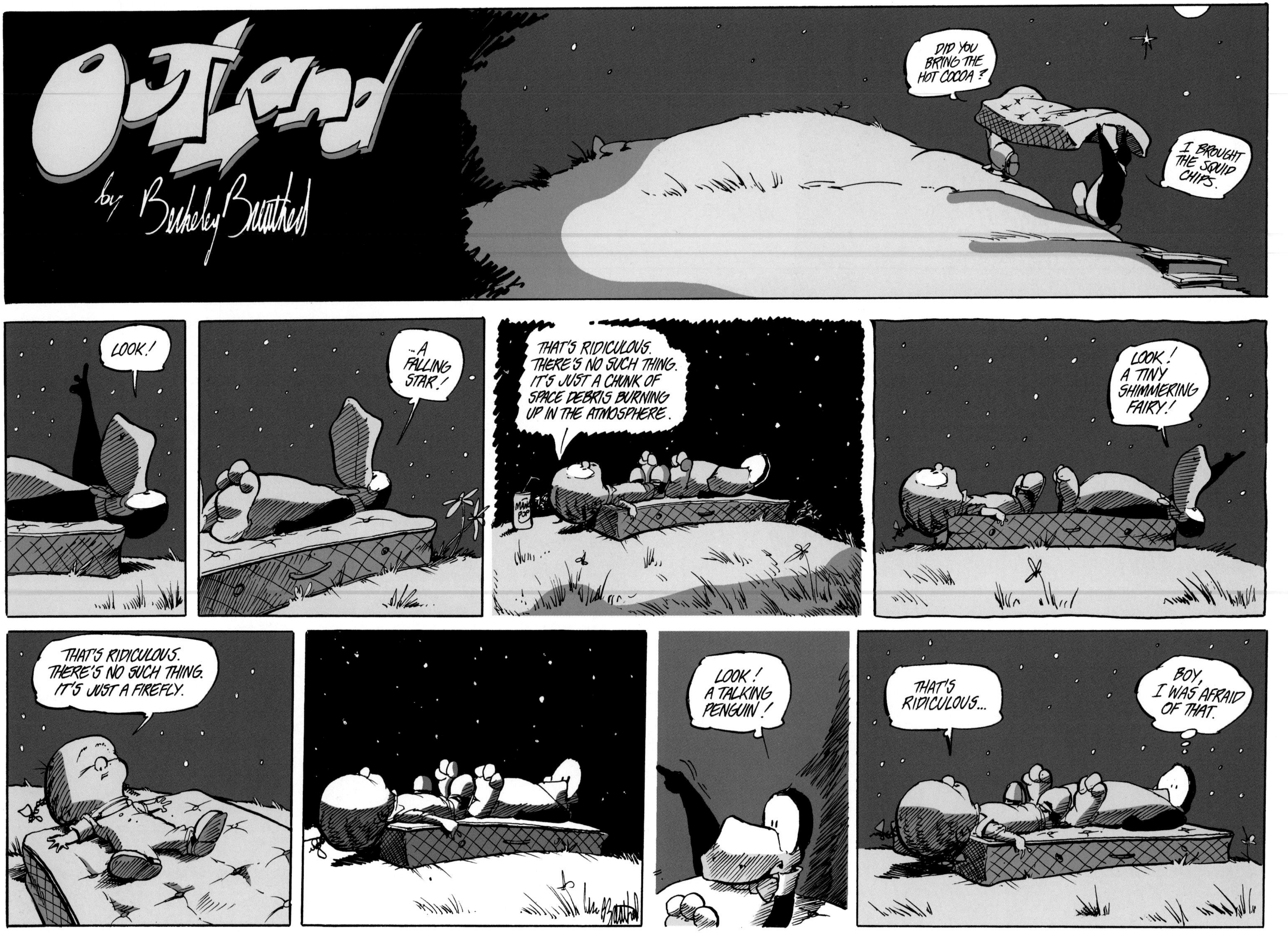
Outland
by Berkeley Breathed
DID YOU BRING THE HOT COCOA ?
I BROUGHT THE SQUID CHIPS.
LOOK !
...A FALLING STAR !
THAT'S RIDICULOUS. THERE'S NO SUCH THING. IT'S JUST A CHUNK OF SPACE DEBRIS BURNING UP IN THE ATMOSPHERE.
LOOK ! A TINY SHIMMERING FAIRY !
THAT'S RIDICULOUS. THERE'S NO SUCH THING. IT'S JUST A FIREFLY.
LOOK ! A TALKING PENGUIN !
THAT'S RIDICULOUS...
BOY, I WAS AFRAID OF THAT.

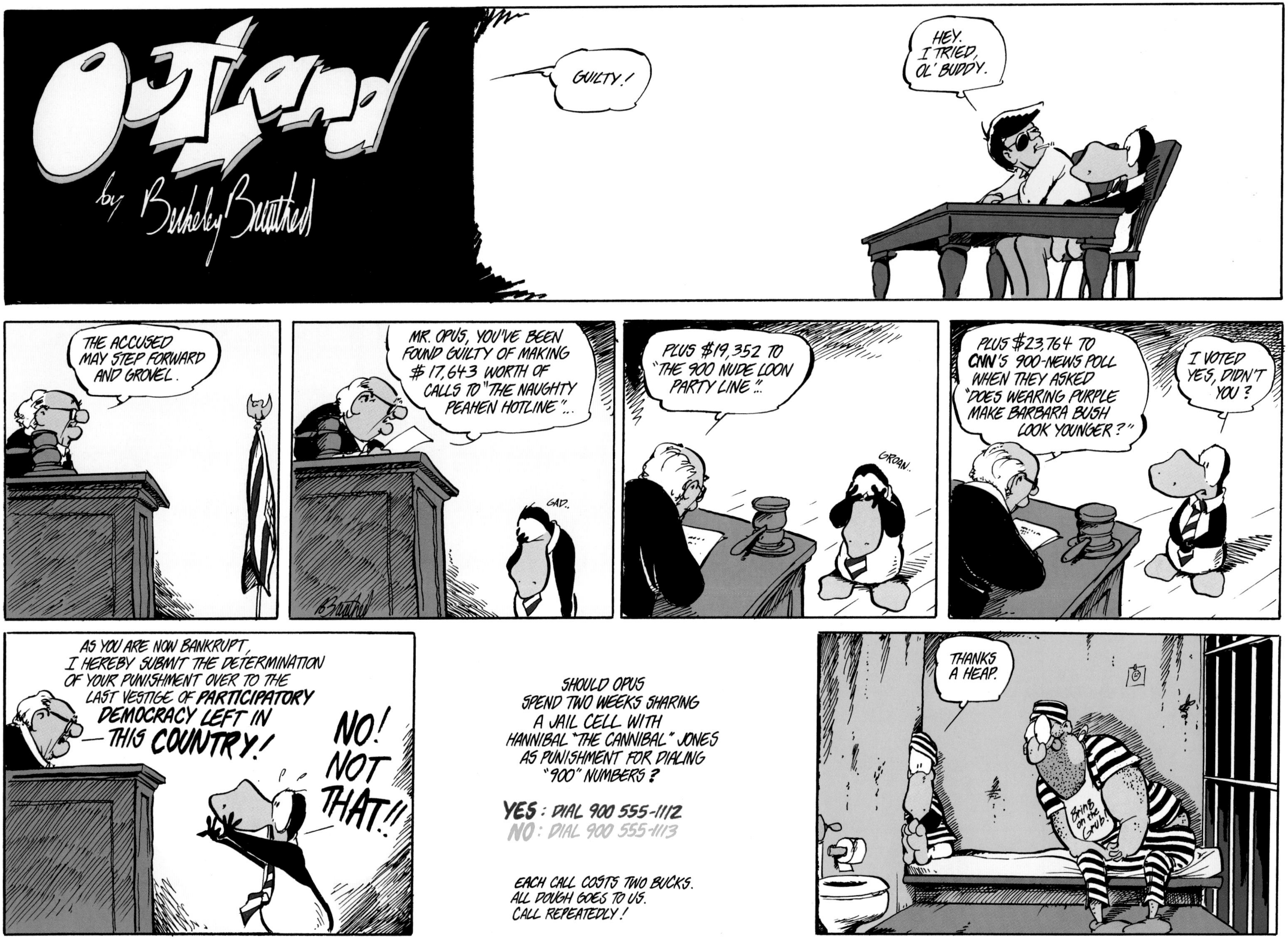
Outland
by Berkeley Breathed
GUILTY!
HEY. I TRIED, OL' BUDDY.
THE ACCUSED MAY STEP FORWARD AND GROVEL.
MR. OPUS, YOU'VE BEEN FOUND GUILTY OF MAKING $17,643 WORTH OF CALLS TO "THE NAUGHTY PEAHEN HOTLINE"...
GAD..
PLUS $19,352 TO "THE 900 NUDE LOON PARTY LINE"...
GROAN..
PLUS $23,764 TO CNN'S 900-NEWS POLL WHEN THEY ASKED "DOES WEARING PURPLE MAKE BARBARA BUSH LOOK YOUNGER?"
I VOTED YES, DIDN'T YOU?
AS YOU ARE NOW BANKRUPT, I HEREBY SUBMIT THE DETERMINATION OF YOUR PUNISHMENT OVER TO THE LAST VESTIGE OF PARTICIPATORY DEMOCRACY LEFT IN THIS COUNTRY!
NO! NOT THAT!!
SHOULD OPUS SPEND TWO WEEKS SHARING A JAIL CELL WITH HANNIBAL "THE CANNIBAL" JONES AS PUNISHMENT FOR DIALING "900" NUMBERS?
YES: DIAL 900 555-1112
NO: DIAL 900 555-1113
EACH CALL COSTS TWO BUCKS. ALL DOUGH GOES TO US. CALL REPEATEDLY!
THANKS A HEAP.
Bring on the Grub!

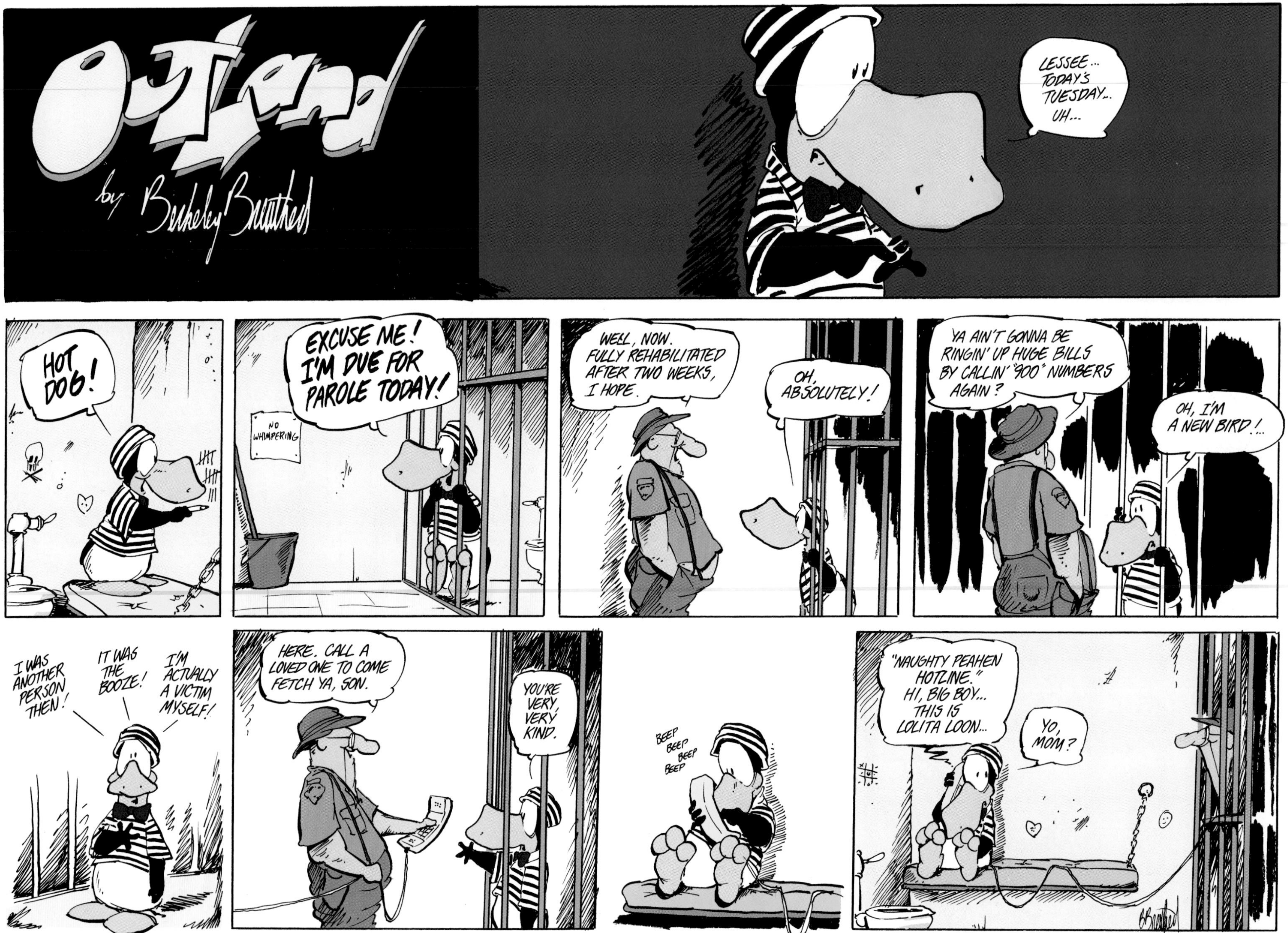
Outland
by Berkeley Breathed
LESSEE... TODAY'S TUESDAY... UH...
HOT DOG!
NO WHIMPERING
EXCUSE ME! I'M DUE FOR PAROLE TODAY!
WELL, NOW. FULLY REHABILITATED AFTER TWO WEEKS, I HOPE.
OH, ABSOLUTELY!
YA AIN'T GONNA BE RINGIN' UP HUGE BILLS BY CALLIN' "900" NUMBERS AGAIN?
OH, I'M A NEW BIRD!...
I WAS ANOTHER PERSON THEN!
IT WAS THE BOOZE!
I'M ACTUALLY A VICTIM MYSELF!
HERE. CALL A LOVED ONE TO COME FETCH YA, SON.
YOU'RE VERY, VERY KIND.
BEEP BEEP BEEP BEEP
"NAUGHTY PEAHEN HOTLINE." HI, BIG BOY... THIS IS LOLITA LOON...
YO, MOM?

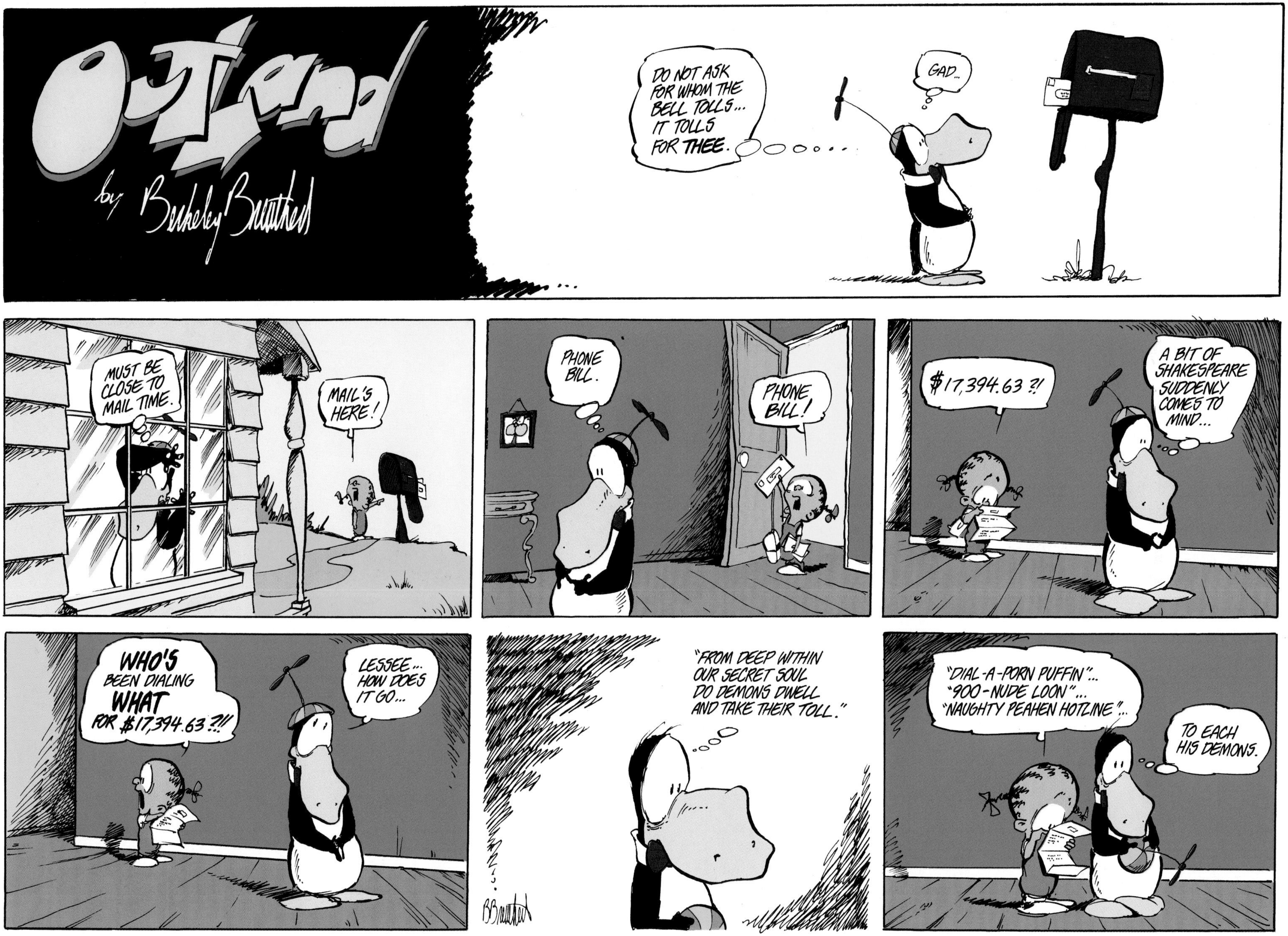
Outland
by Berkeley Breathed
DO NOT ASK FOR WHOM THE BELL TOLLS... IT TOLLS FOR THEE.
GAD...
MUST BE CLOSE TO MAIL TIME.
MAIL'S HERE!
PHONE BILL.
PHONE BILL!
$17,394.63 ?!
A BIT OF SHAKESPEARE SUDDENLY COMES TO MIND...
WHO'S BEEN DIALING WHAT FOR $17,394.63 ?!!
LESSEE... HOW DOES IT GO...
"FROM DEEP WITHIN OUR SECRET SOUL DO DEMONS DWELL AND TAKE THEIR TOLL."
"DIAL-A-PORN PUFFIN"... "900-NUDE LOON"... "NAUGHTY PEAHEN HOTLINE"...
TO EACH HIS DEMONS.
B Breathed

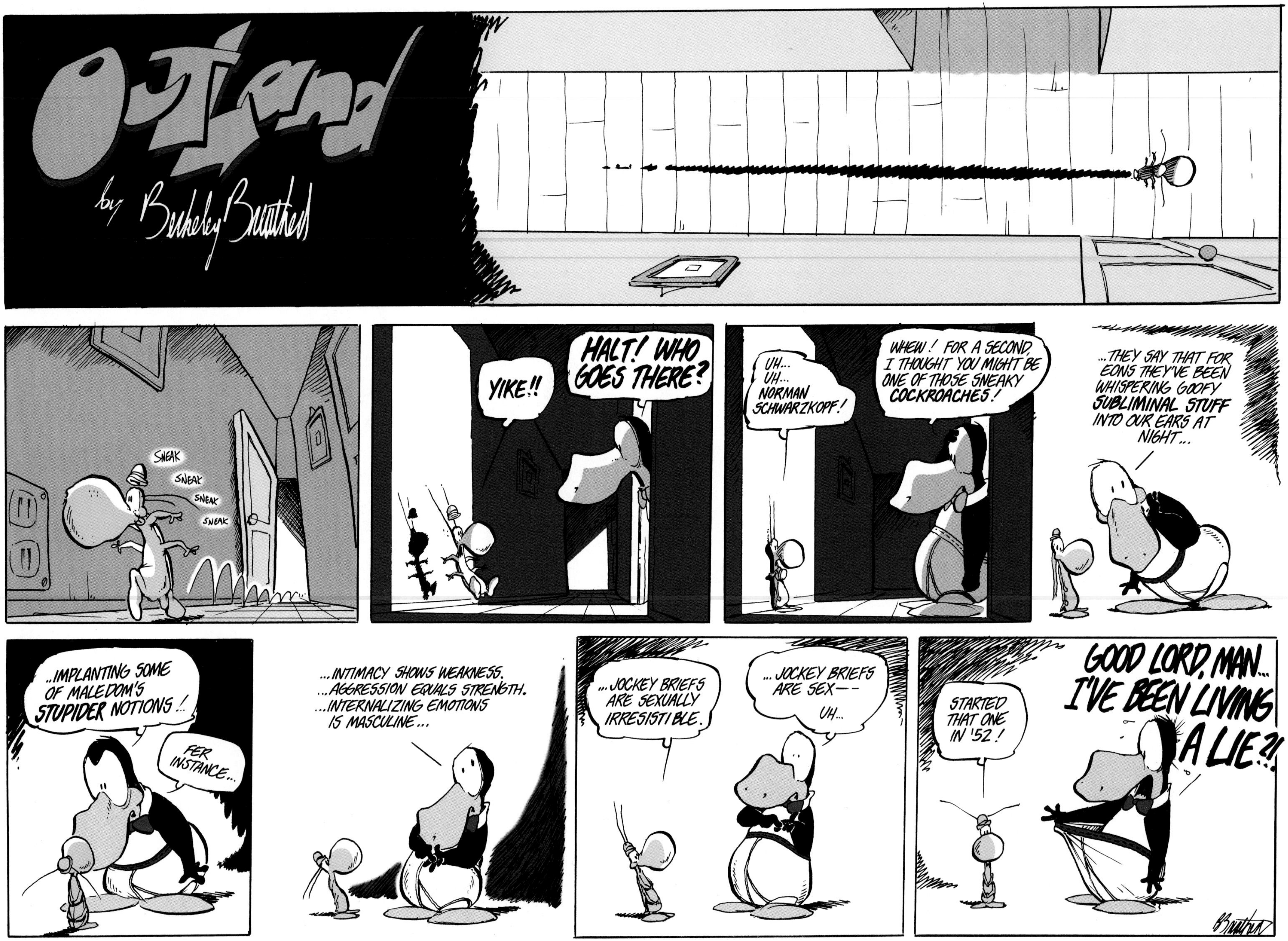
Outland
by Berkeley Breathed
SNEAK
SNEAK
SNEAK
SNEAK
YIKE!!
HALT! WHO GOES THERE?
UH... UH... NORMAN SCHWARZKOPF!
WHEW! FOR A SECOND, I THOUGHT YOU MIGHT BE ONE OF THOSE SNEAKY COCKROACHES!
...THEY SAY THAT FOR EONS THEY'VE BEEN WHISPERING GOOFY SUBLIMINAL STUFF INTO OUR EARS AT NIGHT...
..IMPLANTING SOME OF MALEDOM'S STUPIDER NOTIONS!
FER INSTANCE...
...INTIMACY SHOWS WEAKNESS.
...AGGRESSION EQUALS STRENGTH.
...INTERNALIZING EMOTIONS IS MASCULINE...
...JOCKEY BRIEFS ARE SEXUALLY IRRESISTIBLE.
...JOCKEY BRIEFS ARE SEX--
UH...
STARTED THAT ONE IN '52!
GOOD LORD, MAN... I'VE BEEN LIVING A LIE?!
Breathed

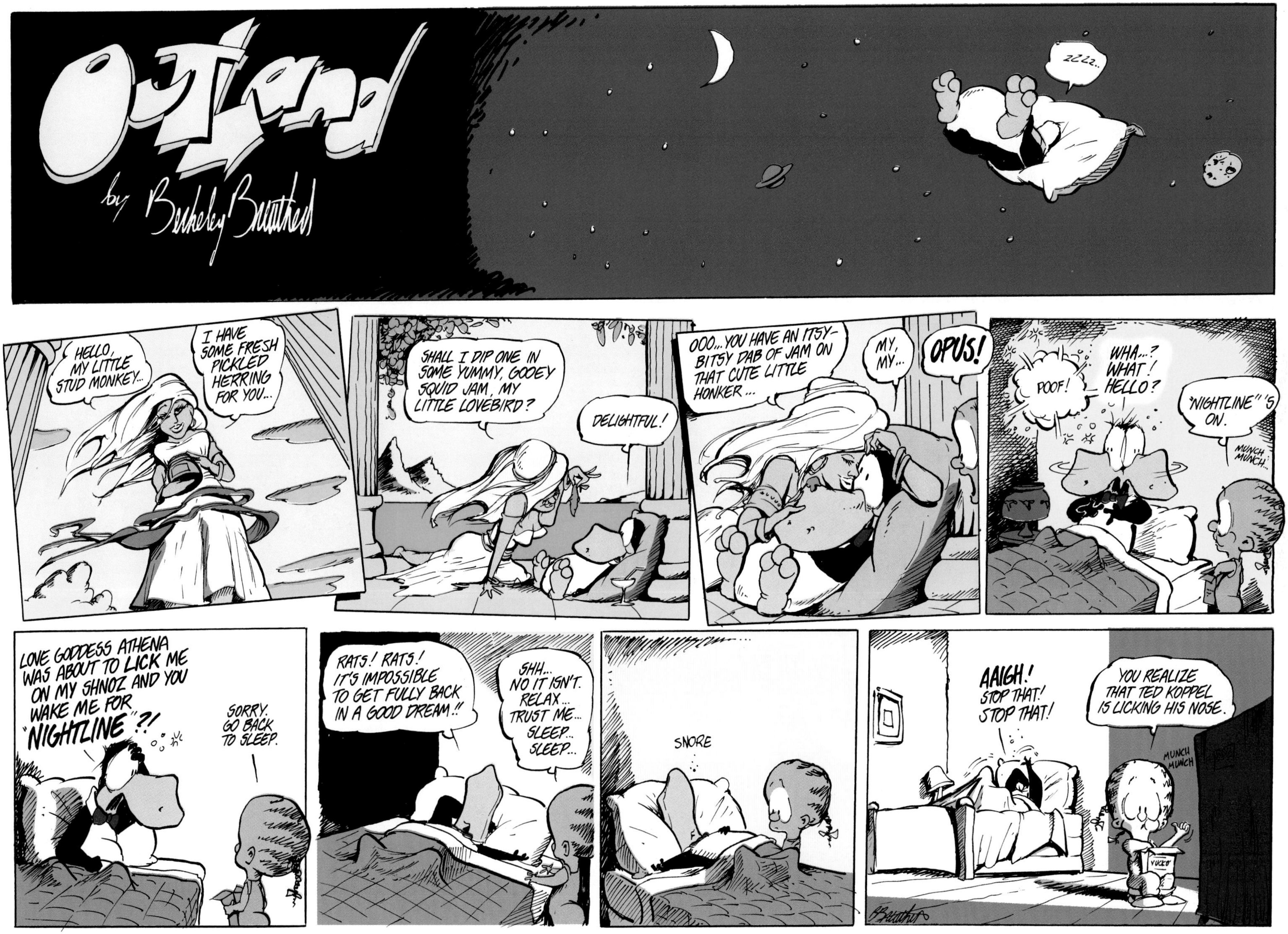

Outland
by Berkeley Breathed
ZZZZ..
HELLO, MY LITTLE STUD MONKEY...
I HAVE SOME FRESH PICKLED HERRING FOR YOU...
SHALL I DIP ONE IN SOME YUMMY, GOOEY SQUID JAM, MY LITTLE LOVEBIRD?
DELIGHTFUL!
OOO... YOU HAVE AN ITSY-BITSY DAB OF JAM ON THAT CUTE LITTLE HONKER...
MY, MY...
OPUS!
POOF!
WHA...? WHAT! HELLO?
"NIGHTLINE" 'S ON.
MUNCH MUNCH...
LOVE GODDESS ATHENA WAS ABOUT TO LICK ME ON MY SHNOZ AND YOU WAKE ME FOR "NIGHTLINE" ?!
SORRY. GO BACK TO SLEEP.
RATS! RATS! IT'S IMPOSSIBLE TO GET FULLY BACK IN A GOOD DREAM!!
SHH... NO IT ISN'T. RELAX... TRUST ME... SLEEP... SLEEP...
SNORE
AAIGH! STOP THAT! STOP THAT!
YOU REALIZE THAT TED KOPPEL IS LICKING HIS NOSE.
MUNCH MUNCH

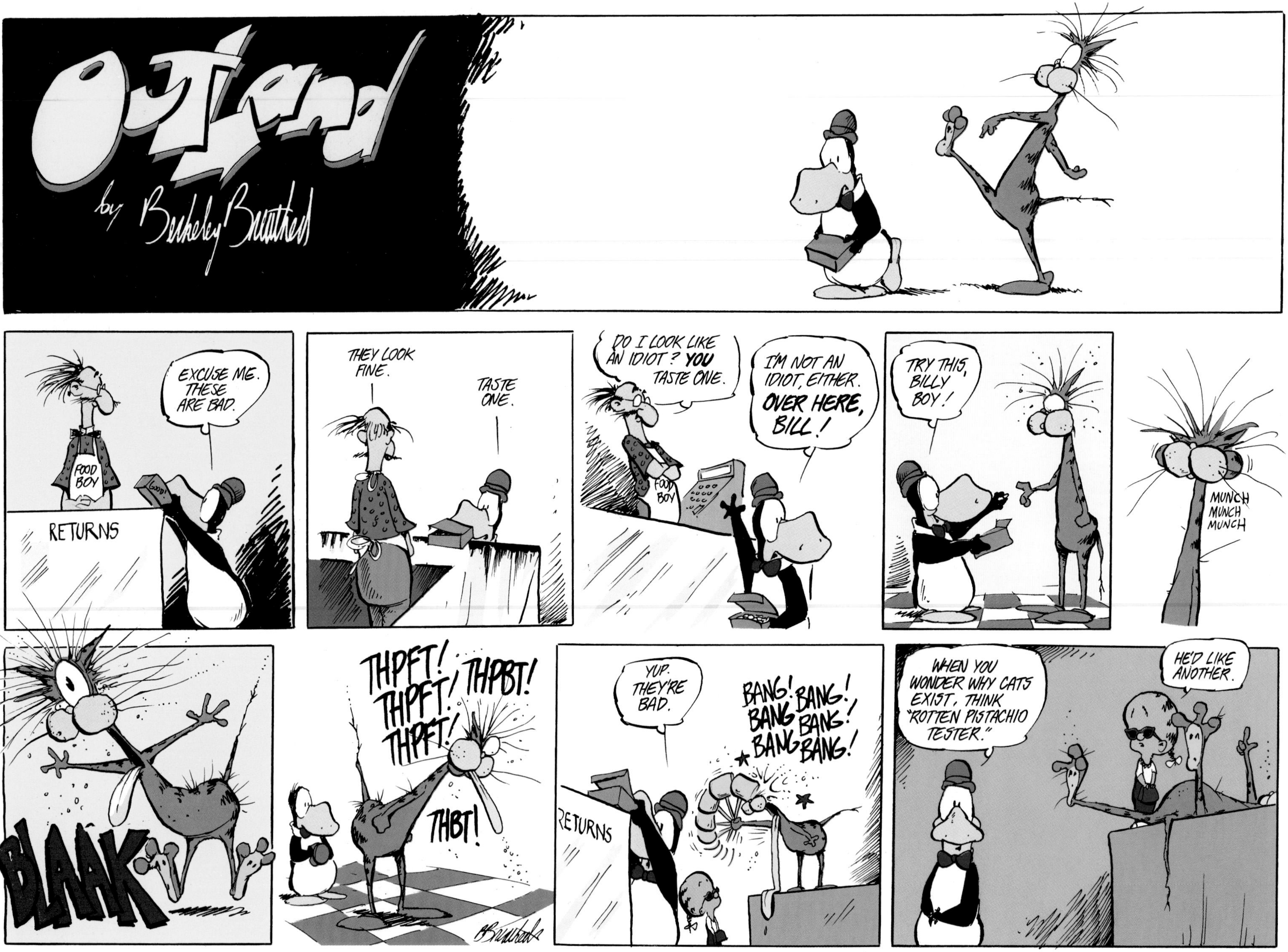
Outland
by Berkeley Breathed
EXCUSE ME. THESE ARE BAD.
FOOD BOY
RETURNS
THEY LOOK FINE.
TASTE ONE.
DO I LOOK LIKE AN IDIOT? **YOU** TASTE ONE.
FOOD BOY
I'M NOT AN IDIOT, EITHER. **OVER HERE, BILL!**
TRY THIS, BILLY BOY!
MUNCH MUNCH MUNCH
BLAAK
THPFT! THPFT! THPFT!
THPBT!
THBT!
YUP. THEY'RE BAD.
BANG! BANG! BANG!
BANG! BANG! BANG!
RETURNS
WHEN YOU WONDER WHY CATS EXIST, THINK "ROTTEN PISTACHIO TESTER."
HE'D LIKE ANOTHER.

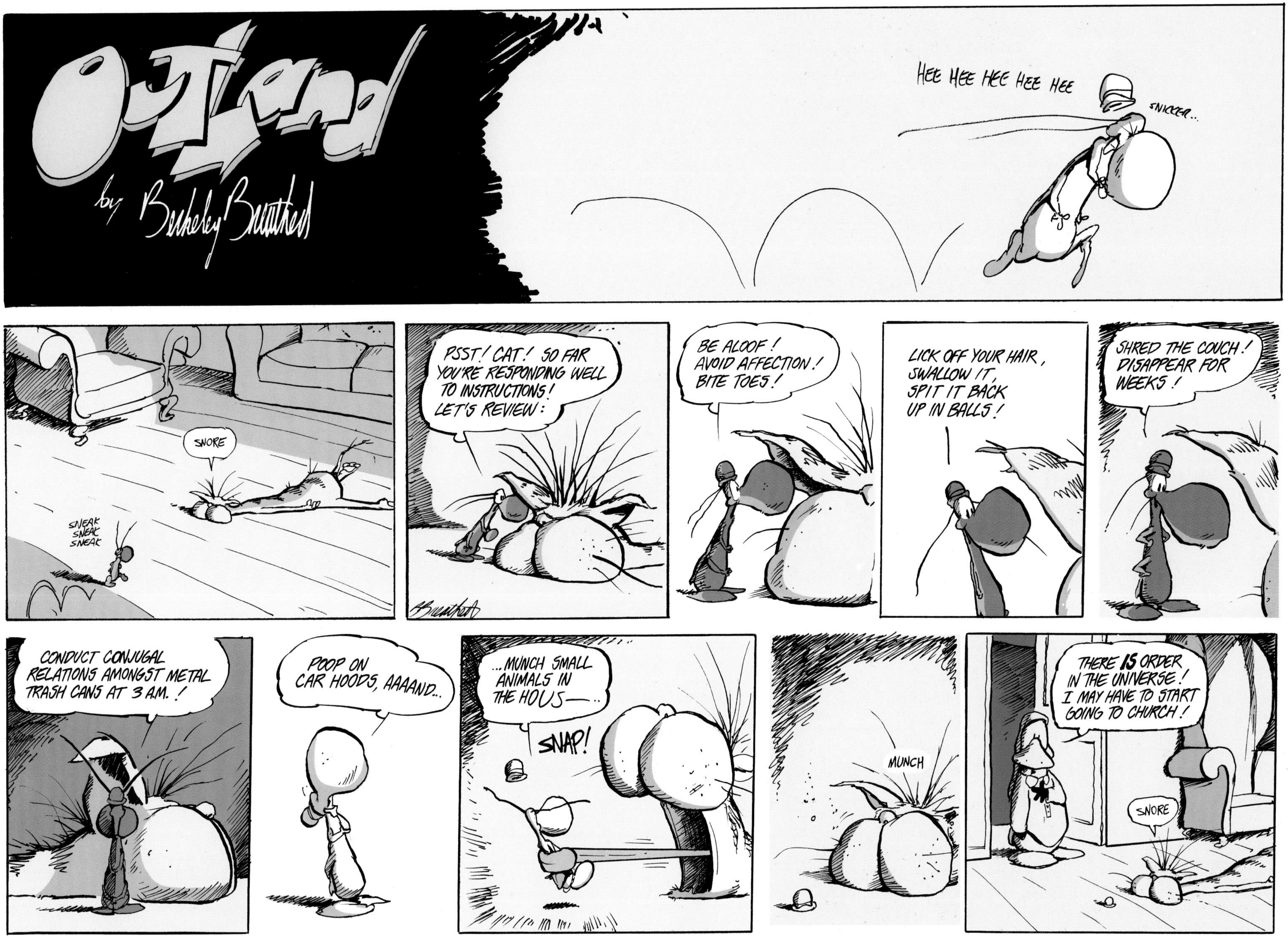

Outland
by Berkeley Breathed
HEE HEE HEE HEE HEE
SNICKER...
SNORE
SNEAK SNEAK SNEAK
PSST! CAT! SO FAR YOU'RE RESPONDING WELL TO INSTRUCTIONS! LET'S REVIEW:
BE ALOOF! AVOID AFFECTION! BITE TOES!
LICK OFF YOUR HAIR, SWALLOW IT, SPIT IT BACK UP IN BALLS!
SHRED THE COUCH! DISAPPEAR FOR WEEKS!
CONDUCT CONJUGAL RELATIONS AMONGST METAL TRASH CANS AT 3 A.M.!
POOP ON CAR HOODS, AAAAND...
...MUNCH SMALL ANIMALS IN THE HOUS—...
SNAP!
MUNCH
THERE IS ORDER IN THE UNIVERSE! I MAY HAVE TO START GOING TO CHURCH!
SNORE

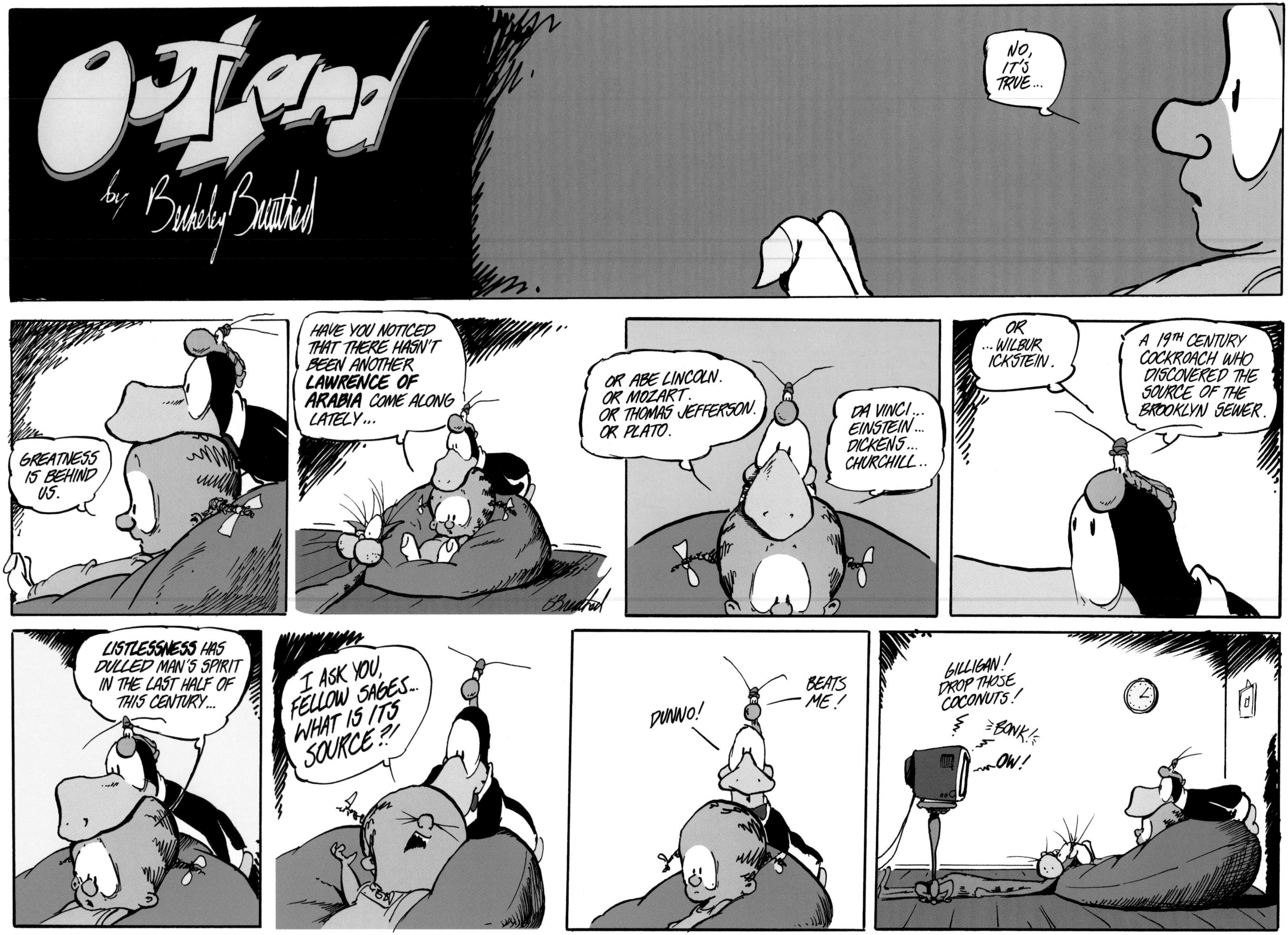
Outland
by Berkeley Breathed
NO, IT'S TRUE...
GREATNESS IS BEHIND US.
HAVE YOU NOTICED THAT THERE HASN'T BEEN ANOTHER **LAWRENCE OF ARABIA** COME ALONG LATELY...
DA VINCI... EINSTEIN... DICKENS... CHURCHILL...
OR ABE LINCOLN. OR MOZART. OR THOMAS JEFFERSON. OR PLATO.
OR ...WILBUR ICKSTEIN.
A 19TH CENTURY COCKROACH WHO DISCOVERED THE SOURCE OF THE BROOKLYN SEWER.
LISTLESSNESS HAS DULLED MAN'S SPIRIT IN THE LAST HALF OF THIS CENTURY...
I ASK YOU, FELLOW SAGES... WHAT IS ITS SOURCE ?!
DUNNO!
BEATS ME!
GILLIGAN! DROP THOSE COCONUTS!
BONK!
OW!

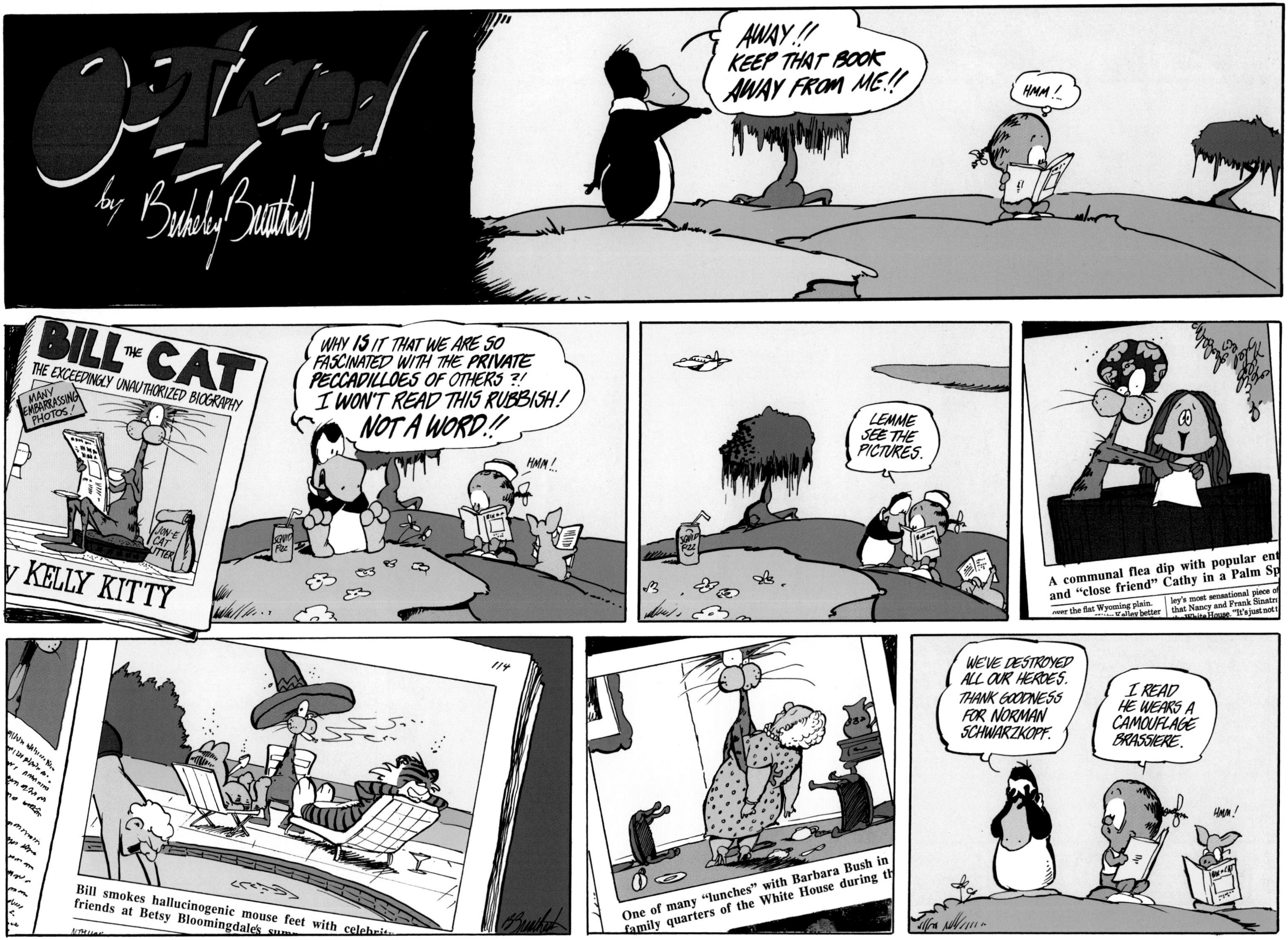

Outland
by Berkeley Breathed
AWAY!! KEEP THAT BOOK AWAY FROM ME!!
HMM!
BILL THE CAT
THE EXCEEDINGLY UNAUTHORIZED BIOGRAPHY
MANY EMBARRASSING PHOTOS!
JON-E CAT LITTER
y KELLY KITTY
WHY IS IT THAT WE ARE SO FASCINATED WITH THE PRIVATE PECCADILLOES OF OTHERS ?! I WON'T READ THIS RUBBISH! NOT A WORD!!
HMM!
SQUID FIZZ
SQUID FIZZ
LEMME SEE THE PICTURES.
A communal flea dip with popular ent
and "close friend" Cathy in a Palm Sp
over the flat Wyoming plain.
ley's most sensational piece of
that Nancy and Frank Sinatra
114
Bill smokes hallucinogenic mouse feet with celebrit
friends at Betsy Bloomingdale's sum
One of many "lunches" with Barbara Bush in
family quarters of the White House during th
WE'VE DESTROYED ALL OUR HEROES. THANK GOODNESS FOR NORMAN SCHWARZKOPF.
I READ HE WEARS A CAMOUFLAGE BRASSIERE.
HMM!

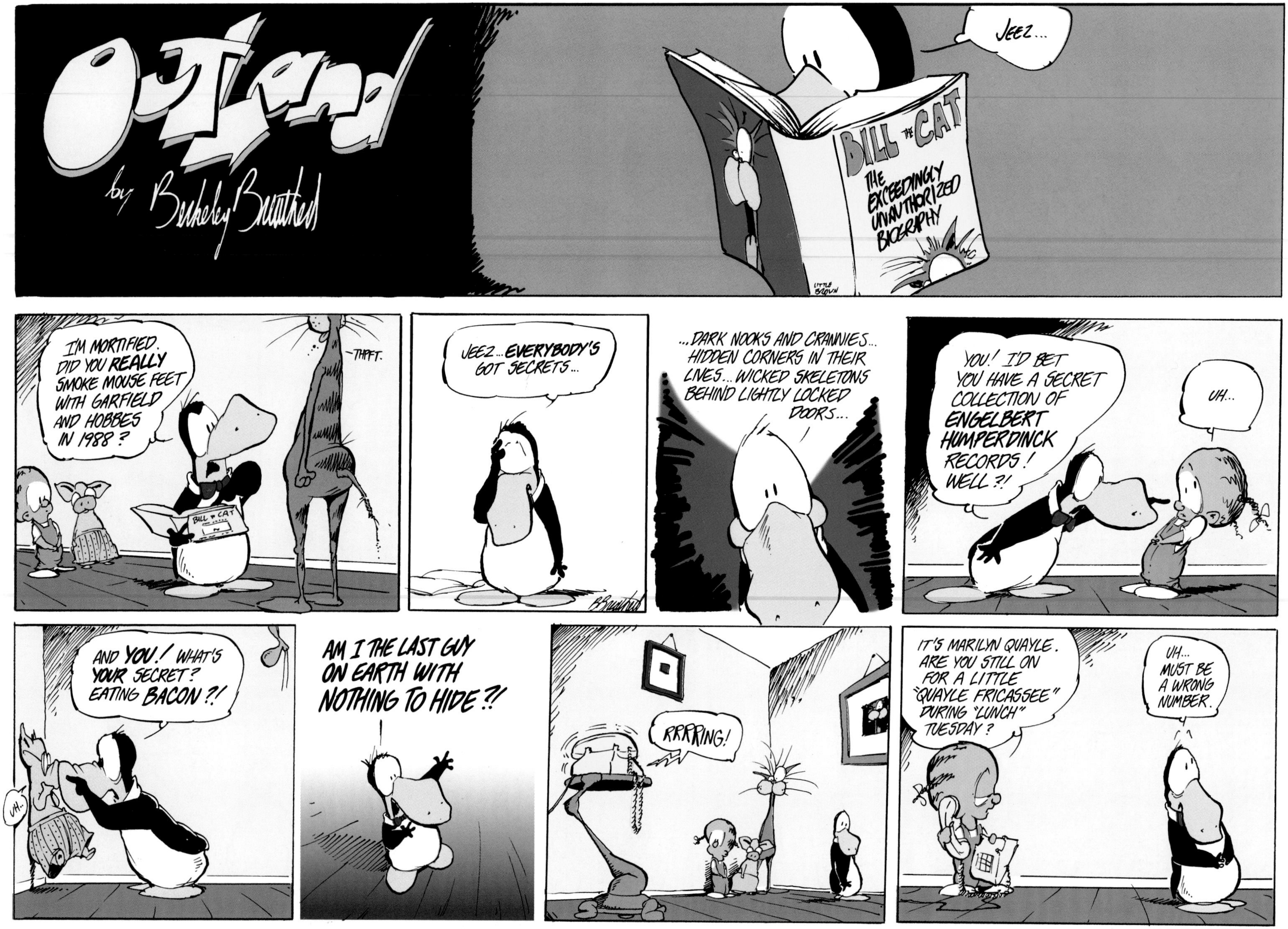
Outland
by Berkeley Breathed
JEEZ...
BILL THE CAT
THE EXCEEDINGLY UNAUTHORIZED BIOGRAPHY
LITTLE BROWN
I'M MORTIFIED. DID YOU REALLY SMOKE MOUSE FEET WITH GARFIELD AND HOBBES IN 1988?
-THPFT.
JEEZ... EVERYBODY'S GOT SECRETS...
...DARK NOOKS AND CRANNIES... HIDDEN CORNERS IN THEIR LIVES... WICKED SKELETONS BEHIND LIGHTLY LOCKED DOORS...
YOU! I'D BET YOU HAVE A SECRET COLLECTION OF ENGELBERT HUMPERDINCK RECORDS! WELL?!
UH...
AND YOU! WHAT'S YOUR SECRET? EATING BACON?!
UH..
AM I THE LAST GUY ON EARTH WITH NOTHING TO HIDE?!
RRRRING!
IT'S MARILYN QUAYLE. ARE YOU STILL ON FOR A LITTLE "QUAYLE FRICASSEE" DURING "LUNCH" TUESDAY?
UH... MUST BE A WRONG NUMBER.

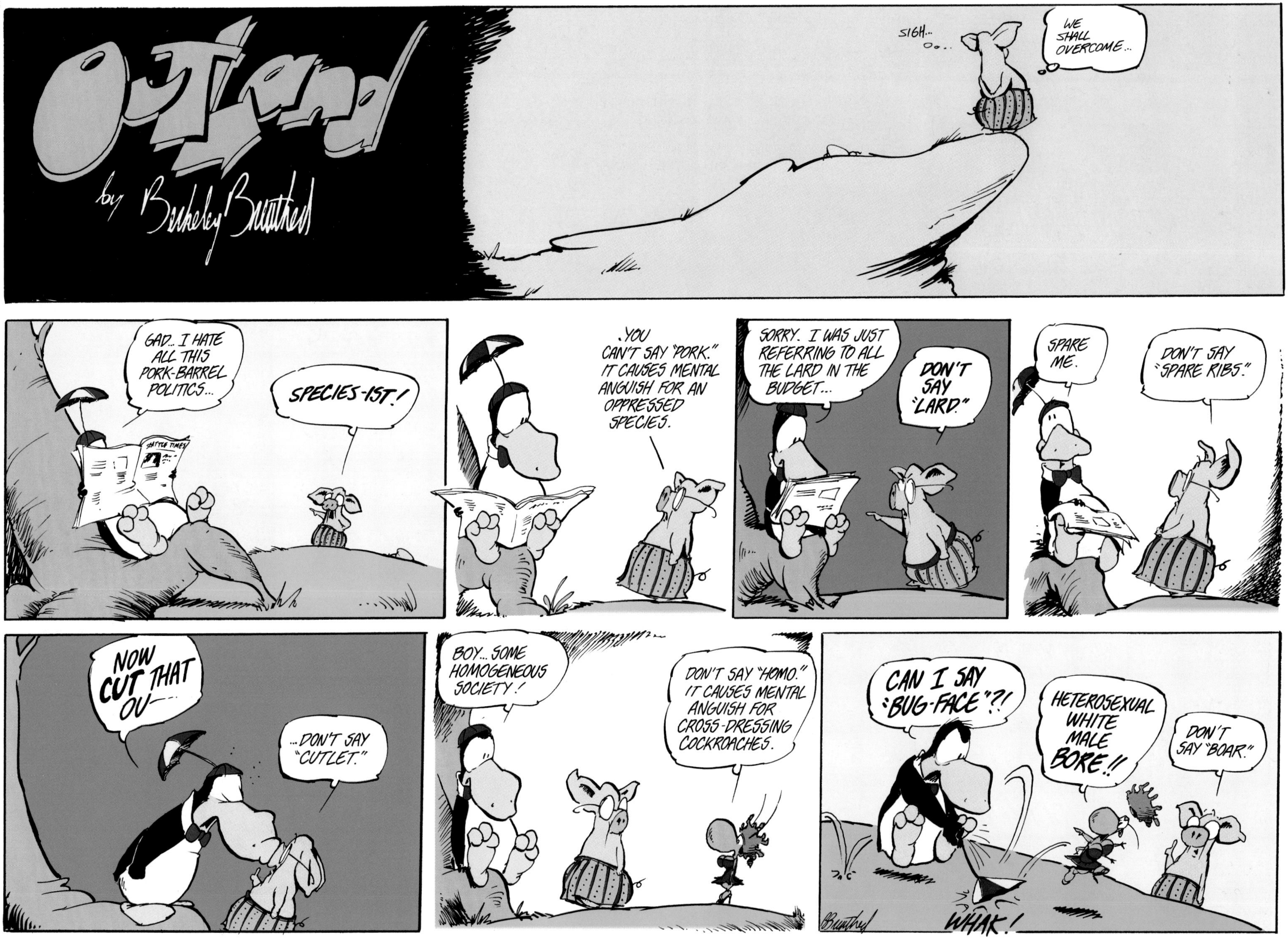
Outland
by Berkeley Breathed
SIGH...
WE SHALL OVERCOME...
GAD... I HATE ALL THIS PORK-BARREL POLITICS...
SPECIES-IST!
SEATTLE TIMES
YOU CAN'T SAY "PORK." IT CAUSES MENTAL ANGUISH FOR AN OPPRESSED SPECIES.
SORRY. I WAS JUST REFERRING TO ALL THE LARD IN THE BUDGET...
DON'T SAY "LARD."
SPARE ME.
DON'T SAY "SPARE RIBS."
NOW CUT THAT OU—
...DON'T SAY "CUTLET."
BOY... SOME HOMOGENEOUS SOCIETY!
DON'T SAY "HOMO." IT CAUSES MENTAL ANGUISH FOR CROSS-DRESSING COCKROACHES.
CAN I SAY "BUG-FACE"?!
HETEROSEXUAL WHITE MALE BORE!!
DON'T SAY "BOAR."
WHAK!
BBreathed

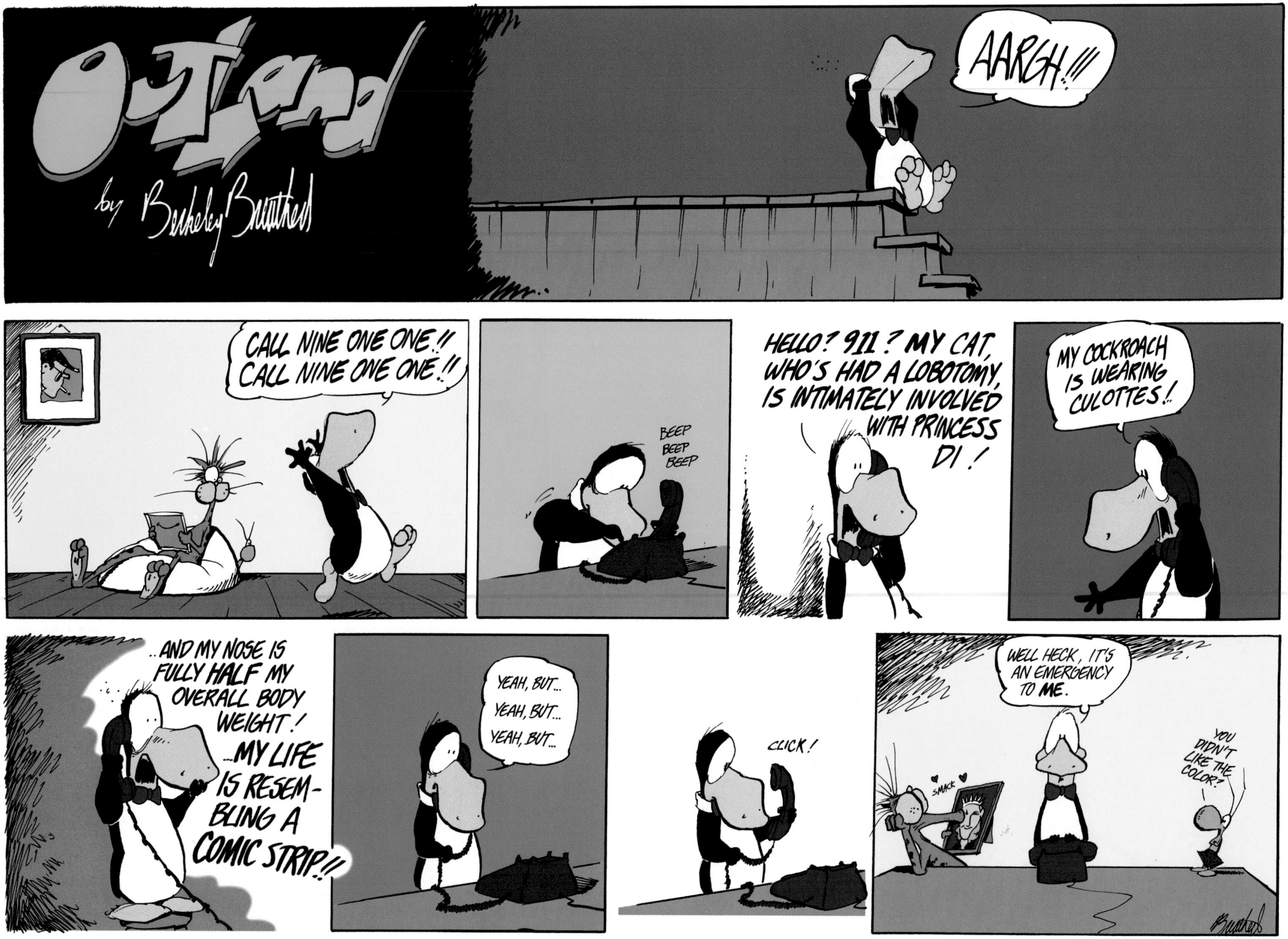
Outland
by Berkeley Breathed
AARGH!!!
CALL NINE ONE ONE!! CALL NINE ONE ONE!!
BEEP BEEP BEEP
HELLO? 911? MY CAT, WHO'S HAD A LOBOTOMY, IS INTIMATELY INVOLVED WITH PRINCESS DI!
MY COCKROACH IS WEARING CULOTTES!
..AND MY NOSE IS FULLY HALF MY OVERALL BODY WEIGHT! ...MY LIFE IS RESEMBLING A COMIC STRIP!!
YEAH, BUT... YEAH, BUT... YEAH, BUT...
CLICK!
WELL HECK, IT'S AN EMERGENCY TO ME.
SMACK
YOU DIDN'T LIKE THE COLOR?
Breathed

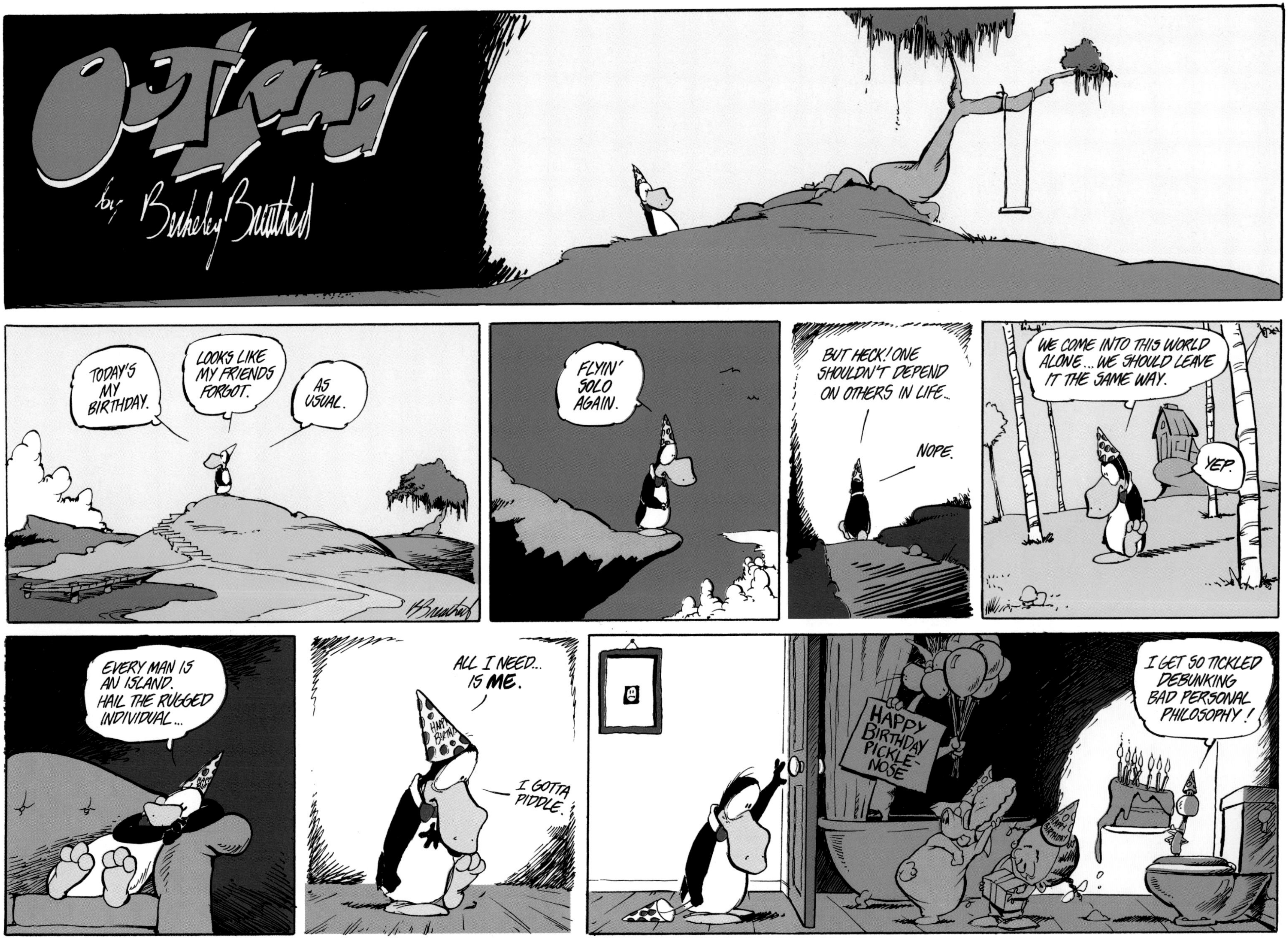
Outland
by Berkeley Breathed
TODAY'S MY BIRTHDAY.
LOOKS LIKE MY FRIENDS FORGOT.
AS USUAL.
FLYIN' SOLO AGAIN.
BUT HECK! ONE SHOULDN'T DEPEND ON OTHERS IN LIFE...
NOPE.
WE COME INTO THIS WORLD ALONE... WE SHOULD LEAVE IT THE SAME WAY.
YEP.
EVERY MAN IS AN ISLAND. HAIL THE RUGGED INDIVIDUAL...
ALL I NEED... IS ME.
I GOTTA PIDDLE.
HAPPY BIRTHDAY PICKLE-NOSE
I GET SO TICKLED DEBUNKING BAD PERSONAL PHILOSOPHY!

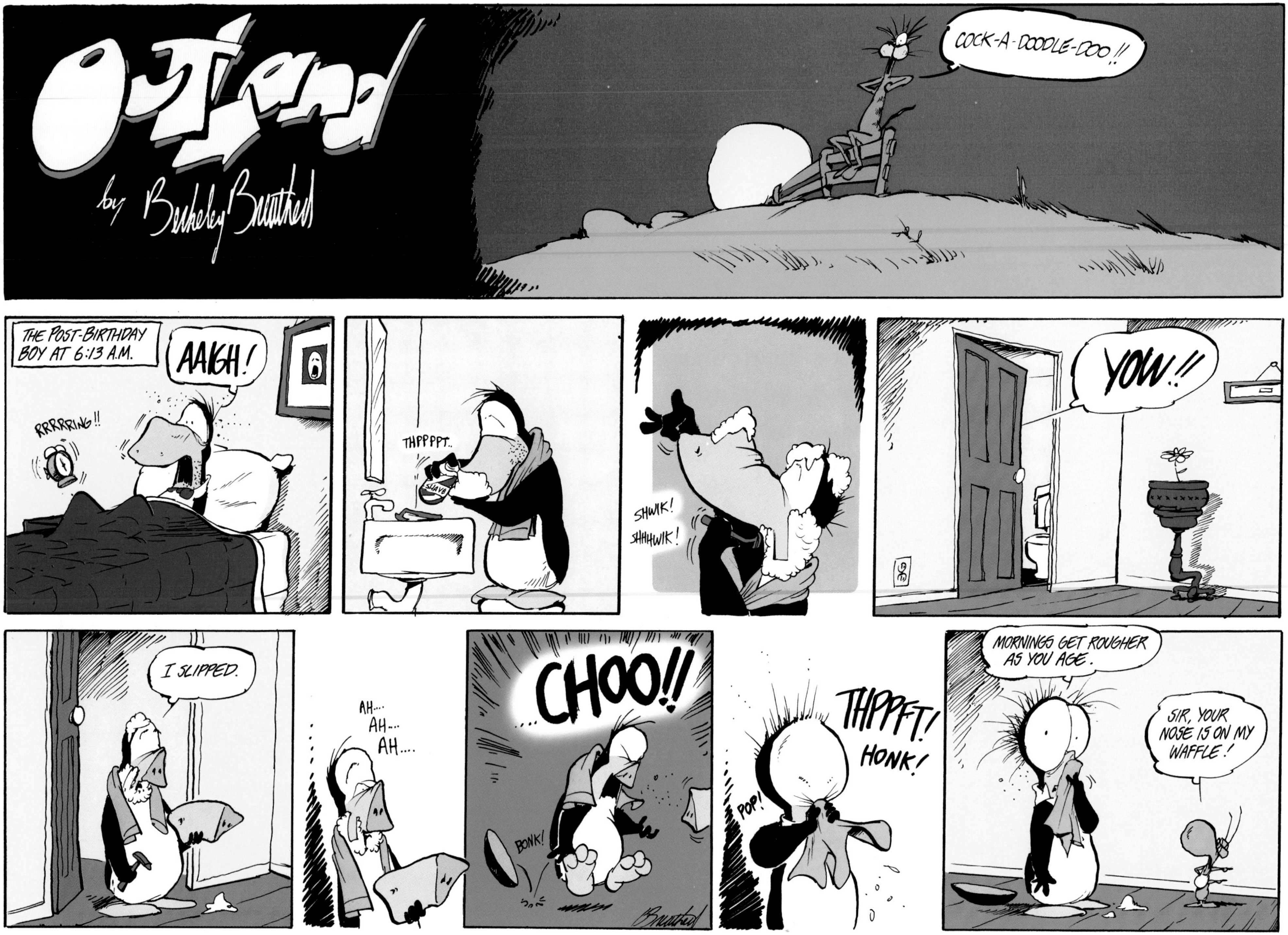
Outland
by Berkeley Breathed
COCK-A-DOODLE-DOO!!
THE POST-BIRTHDAY BOY AT 6:13 A.M.
AAIGH!
RRRRRING!!
THPPPPT..
SHAVE
SHWIK!
SHHHWIK!
YOW!!
I SLIPPED.
AH... AH... AH....
...CHOO!!
BONK!
Breathed
THPPFT!
HONK!
POP!
MORNINGS GET ROUGHER AS YOU AGE.
SIR, YOUR NOSE IS ON MY WAFFLE!

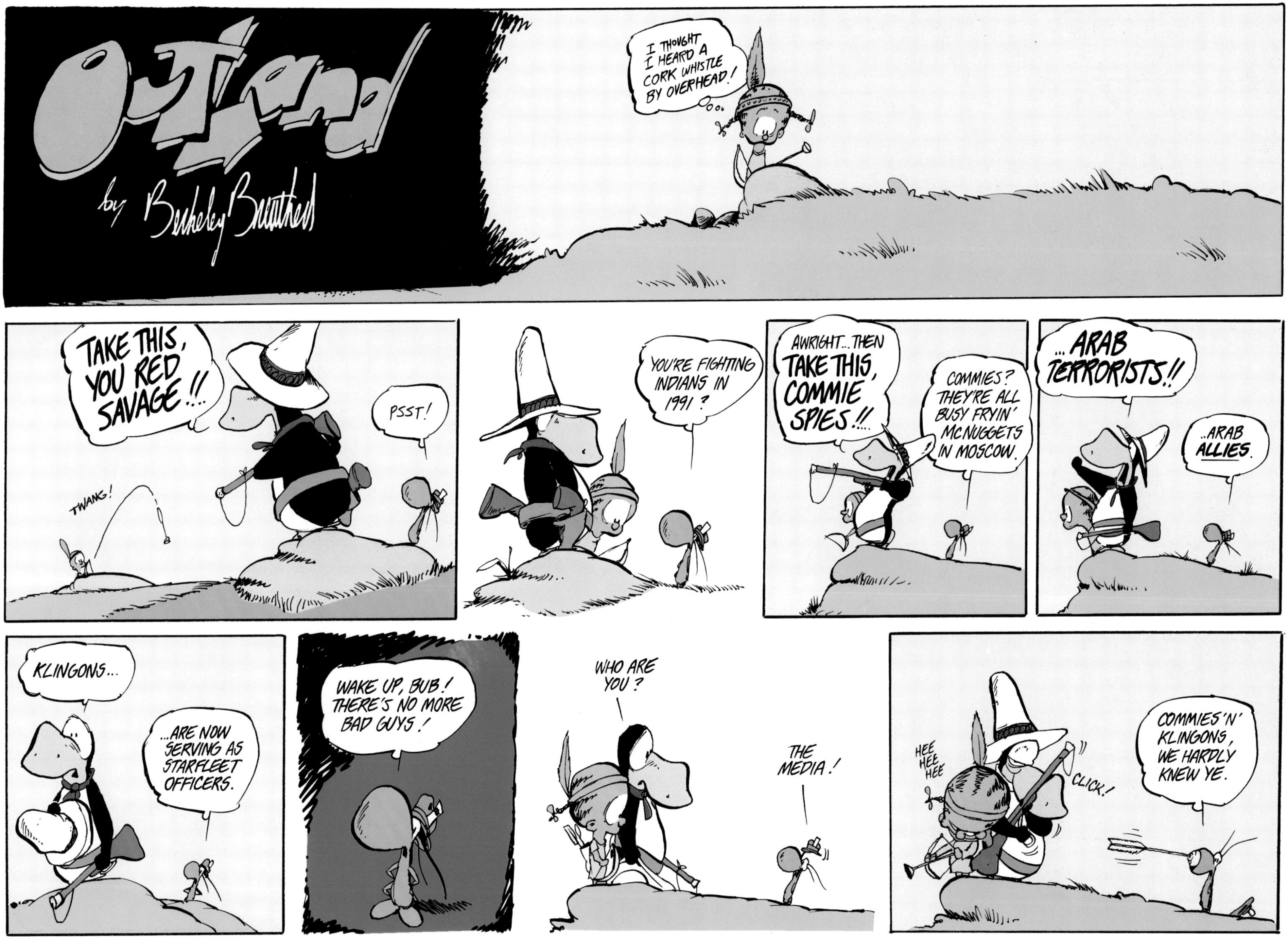
Outland
by Berkeley Breathed
I THOUGHT I HEARD A CORK WHISTLE BY OVERHEAD!
TWANG!
TAKE THIS, YOU RED SAVAGE!!
PSST!
YOU'RE FIGHTING INDIANS IN 1991?
AWRIGHT... THEN TAKE THIS, COMMIE SPIES!!
COMMIES? THEY'RE ALL BUSY FRYIN' McNUGGETS IN MOSCOW.
...ARAB TERRORISTS!!
..ARAB ALLIES.
KLINGONS...
...ARE NOW SERVING AS STARFLEET OFFICERS.
WAKE UP, BUB! THERE'S NO MORE BAD GUYS!
WHO ARE YOU?
THE MEDIA!
HEE HEE HEE
CLICK!
COMMIES 'N' KLINGONS, WE HARDLY KNEW YE.

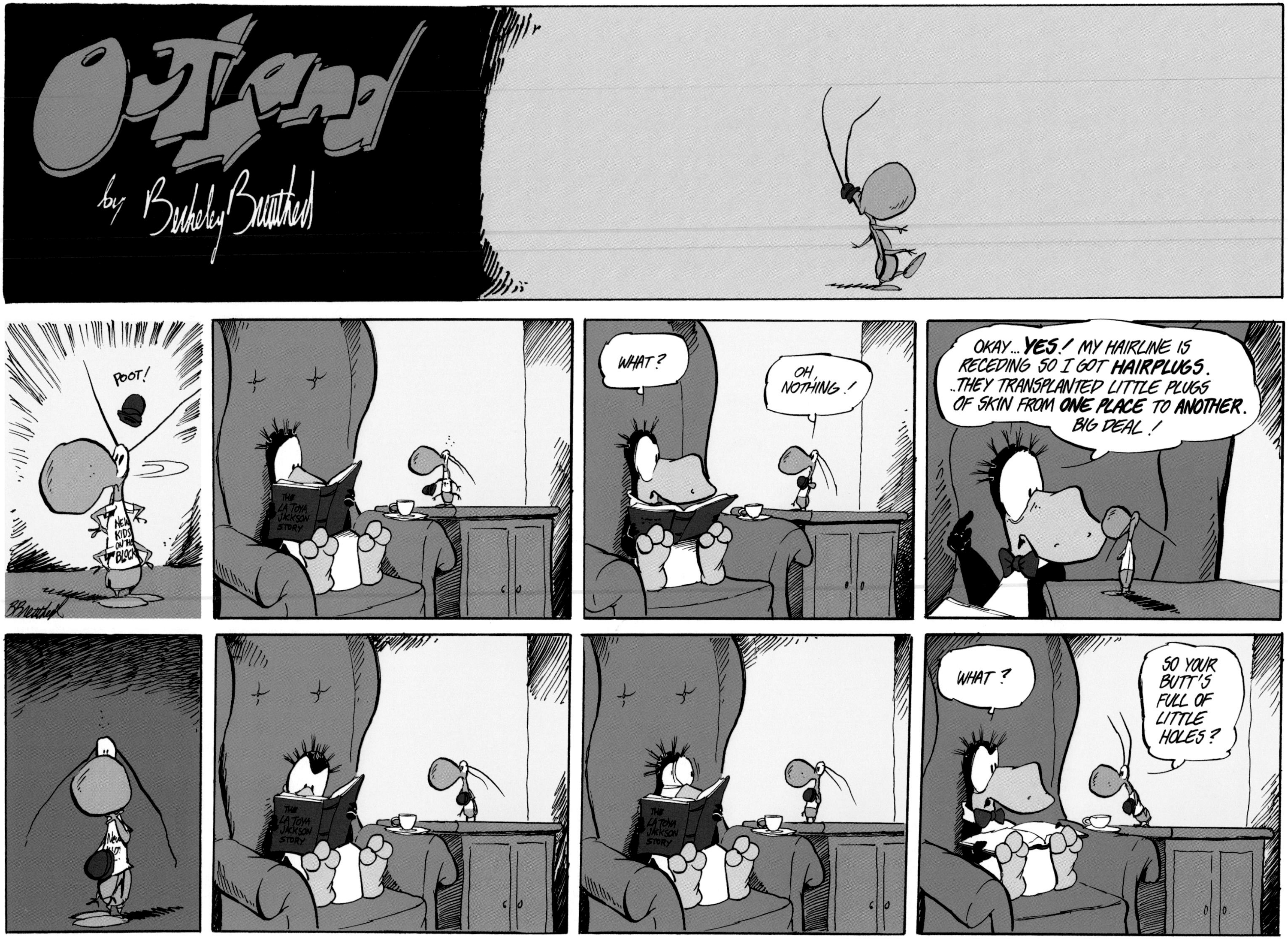
Outland
by Berkeley Breathed
POOT!
NEW KIDS ON THE BLOCK
BBreathed
THE LA TOYA JACKSON STORY
WHAT?
OH, NOTHING!
OKAY... YES! MY HAIRLINE IS RECEDING SO I GOT HAIRPLUGS. ..THEY TRANSPLANTED LITTLE PLUGS OF SKIN FROM ONE PLACE TO ANOTHER. BIG DEAL!
THE LA TOYA JACKSON STORY
THE LA TOYA JACKSON STORY
WHAT?
SO YOUR BUTT'S FULL OF LITTLE HOLES?

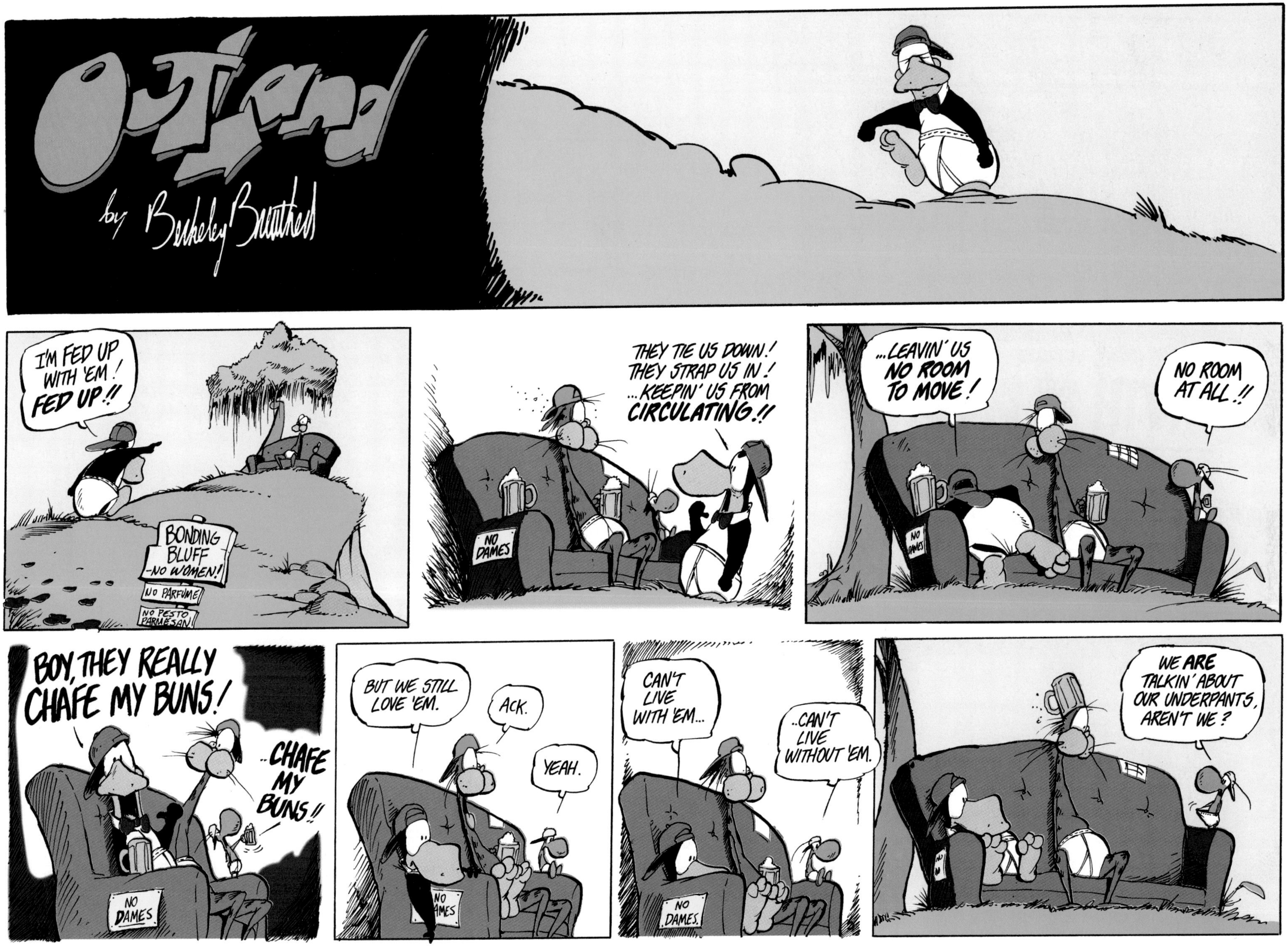
Outland
by Berkeley Breathed
I'M FED UP WITH 'EM! FED UP!!
BONDING BLUFF -NO WOMEN!
NO PARFUME
NO PESTO PARMESAN
THEY TIE US DOWN! THEY STRAP US IN! ...KEEPIN' US FROM CIRCULATING!!
NO DAMES
...LEAVIN' US NO ROOM TO MOVE!
NO ROOM AT ALL!!
NO DAMES
BOY, THEY REALLY CHAFE MY BUNS!
..CHAFE MY BUNS!!
NO DAMES
BUT WE STILL LOVE 'EM.
ACK.
YEAH.
CAN'T LIVE WITH 'EM...
..CAN'T LIVE WITHOUT 'EM.
NO DAMES.
WE ARE TALKIN' ABOUT OUR UNDERPANTS, AREN'T WE?

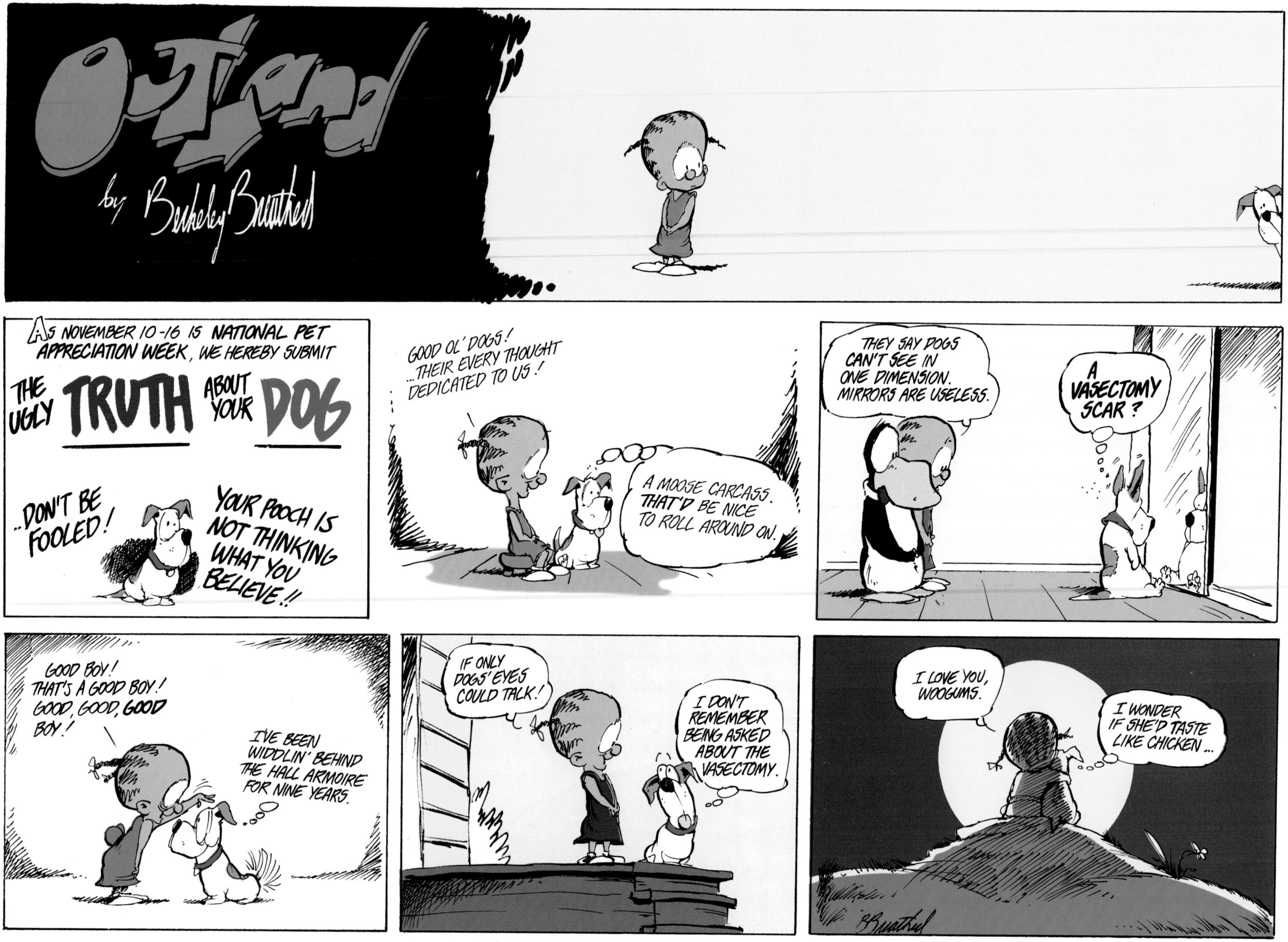
Outland
by Berkeley Breathed
AS NOVEMBER 10-16 IS NATIONAL PET APPRECIATION WEEK, WE HEREBY SUBMIT
THE UGLY TRUTH ABOUT YOUR DOG
..DON'T BE FOOLED!
YOUR POOCH IS NOT THINKING WHAT YOU BELIEVE!!
GOOD OL' DOGS! ...THEIR EVERY THOUGHT DEDICATED TO US!
A MOOSE CARCASS. THAT'D BE NICE TO ROLL AROUND ON.
THEY SAY DOGS CAN'T SEE IN ONE DIMENSION. MIRRORS ARE USELESS.
A VASECTOMY SCAR?
GOOD BOY! THAT'S A GOOD BOY! GOOD, GOOD, GOOD BOY!
I'VE BEEN WIDDLIN' BEHIND THE HALL ARMOIRE FOR NINE YEARS.
IF ONLY DOGS' EYES COULD TALK!
I DON'T REMEMBER BEING ASKED ABOUT THE VASECTOMY.
I LOVE YOU, WOOGUMS.
I WONDER IF SHE'D TASTE LIKE CHICKEN...
B Breathed

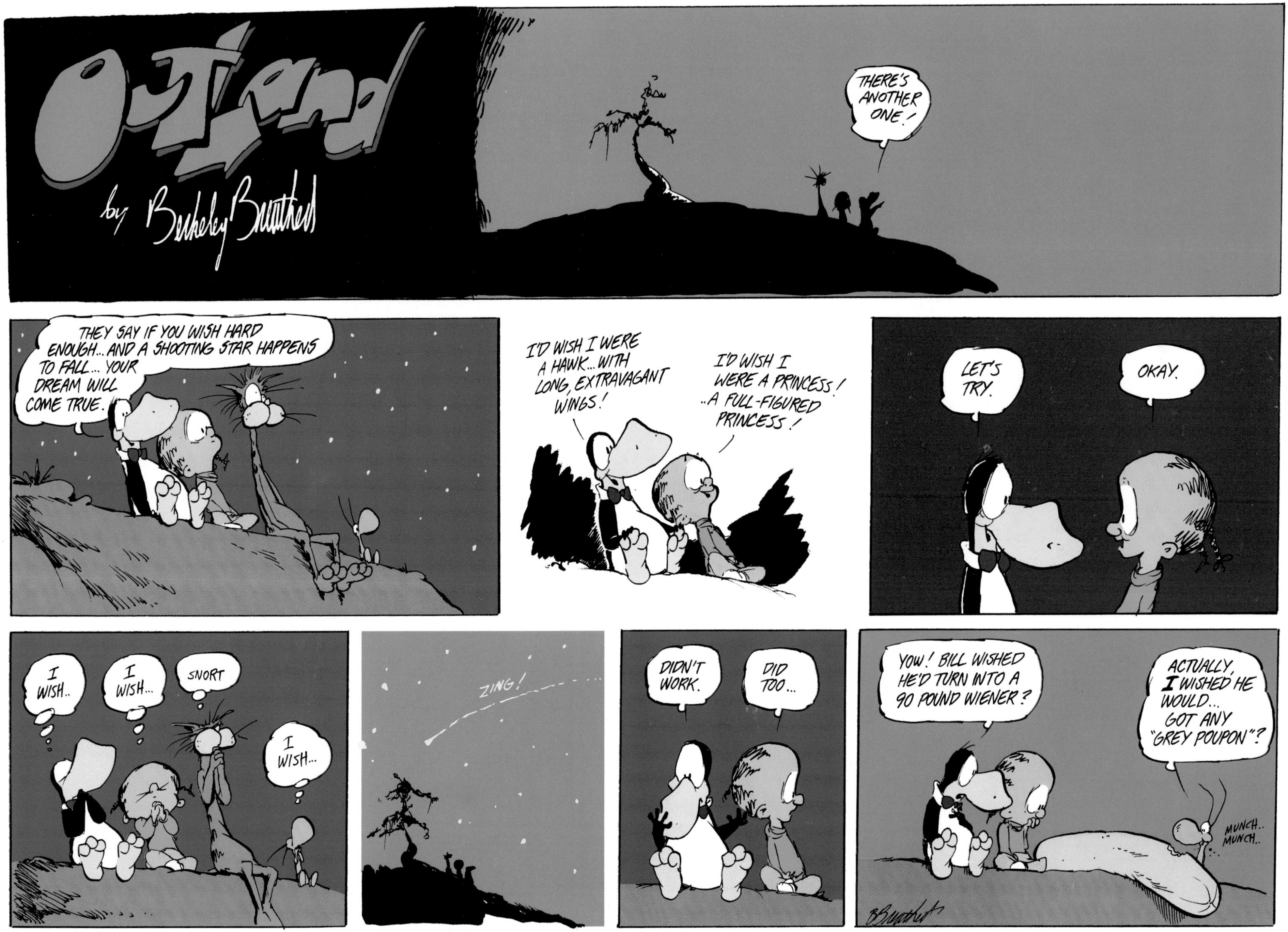

Outland
by Berkeley Breathed
THERE'S ANOTHER ONE!
THEY SAY IF YOU WISH HARD ENOUGH... AND A SHOOTING STAR HAPPENS TO FALL... YOUR DREAM WILL COME TRUE.
I'D WISH I WERE A HAWK... WITH LONG, EXTRAVAGANT WINGS!
I'D WISH I WERE A PRINCESS! ..A FULL-FIGURED PRINCESS!
LET'S TRY.
OKAY.
I WISH..
I WISH...
SNORT
I WISH...
ZING!
DIDN'T WORK.
DID TOO...
YOW! BILL WISHED HE'D TURN INTO A 90 POUND WIENER?
ACTUALLY, I WISHED HE WOULD... GOT ANY "GREY POUPON"?
MUNCH.. MUNCH..
B Breathed

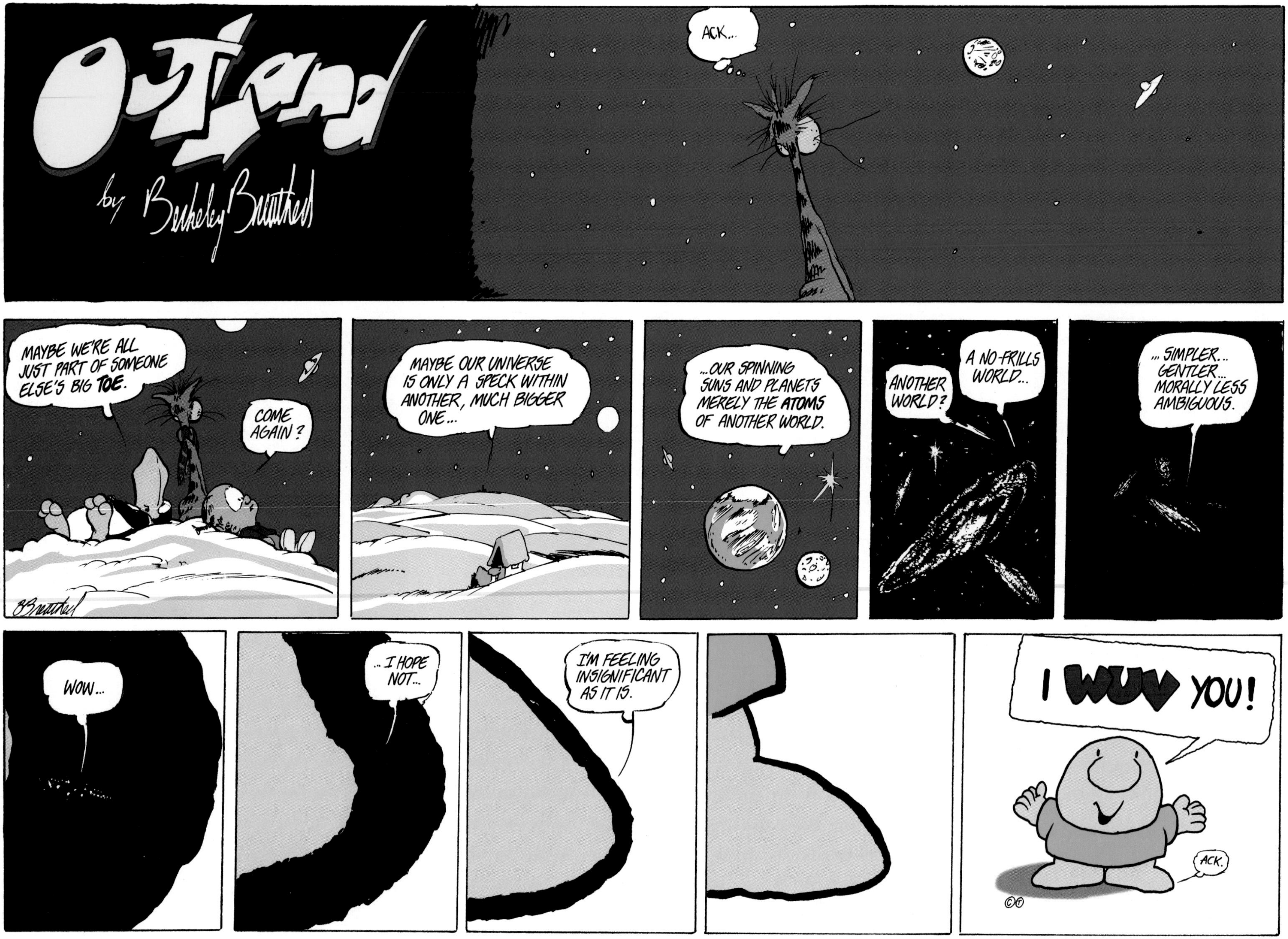
Outland
by Berkeley Breathed
ACK...
MAYBE WE'RE ALL JUST PART OF SOMEONE ELSE'S BIG TOE.
COME AGAIN?
MAYBE OUR UNIVERSE IS ONLY A SPECK WITHIN ANOTHER, MUCH BIGGER ONE...
...OUR SPINNING SUNS AND PLANETS MERELY THE ATOMS OF ANOTHER WORLD.
ANOTHER WORLD?
A NO-FRILLS WORLD...
...SIMPLER... GENTLER... MORALLY LESS AMBIGUOUS.
WOW...
...I HOPE NOT...
I'M FEELING INSIGNIFICANT AS IT IS.
I WUV YOU!
ACK.

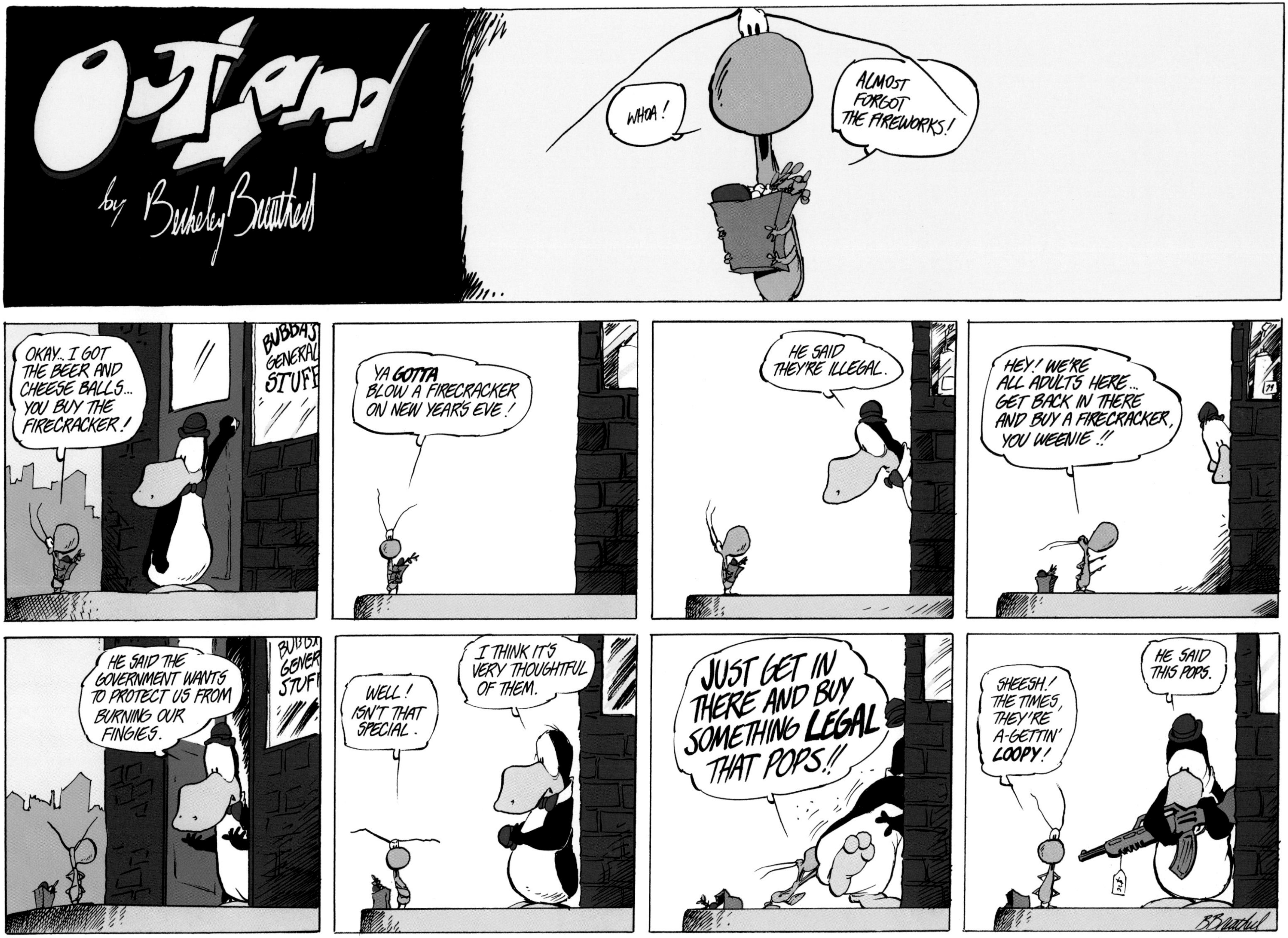
Outland
by Berkeley Breathed
WHOA!
ALMOST FORGOT THE FIREWORKS!
BUBBA'S GENERAL STUFF
OKAY.. I GOT THE BEER AND CHEESE BALLS... YOU BUY THE FIRECRACKER!
YA GOTTA BLOW A FIRECRACKER ON NEW YEAR'S EVE!
HE SAID THEY'RE ILLEGAL.
HEY! WE'RE ALL ADULTS HERE... GET BACK IN THERE AND BUY A FIRECRACKER, YOU WEENIE!!
HE SAID THE GOVERNMENT WANTS TO PROTECT US FROM BURNING OUR FINGIES.
WELL! ISN'T THAT SPECIAL.
I THINK IT'S VERY THOUGHTFUL OF THEM.
JUST GET IN THERE AND BUY SOMETHING LEGAL THAT POPS!!
SHEESH! THE TIMES, THEY'RE A-GETTIN' LOOPY!
HE SAID THIS POPS.
B Breathed

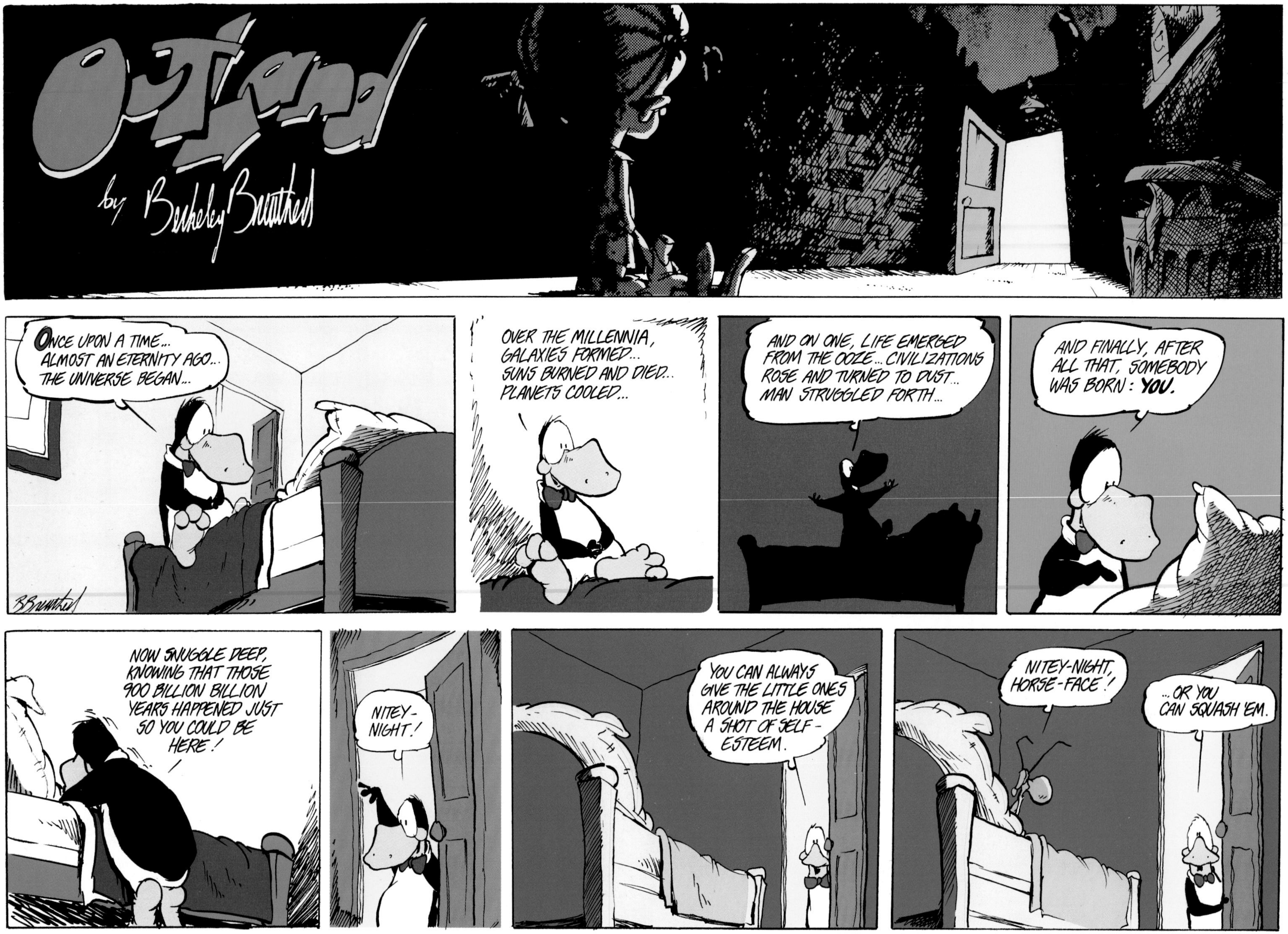
Outland
by Berkeley Breathed
ONCE UPON A TIME... ALMOST AN ETERNITY AGO... THE UNIVERSE BEGAN...
OVER THE MILLENNIA, GALAXIES FORMED... SUNS BURNED AND DIED... PLANETS COOLED...
AND ON ONE, LIFE EMERGED FROM THE OOZE... CIVILIZATIONS ROSE AND TURNED TO DUST... MAN STRUGGLED FORTH...
AND FINALLY, AFTER ALL THAT, SOMEBODY WAS BORN: YOU.
NOW SNUGGLE DEEP, KNOWING THAT THOSE 900 BILLION BILLION YEARS HAPPENED JUST SO YOU COULD BE HERE!
NITEY-NIGHT!
YOU CAN ALWAYS GIVE THE LITTLE ONES AROUND THE HOUSE A SHOT OF SELF-ESTEEM.
NITEY-NIGHT, HORSE-FACE!
...OR YOU CAN SQUASH 'EM.

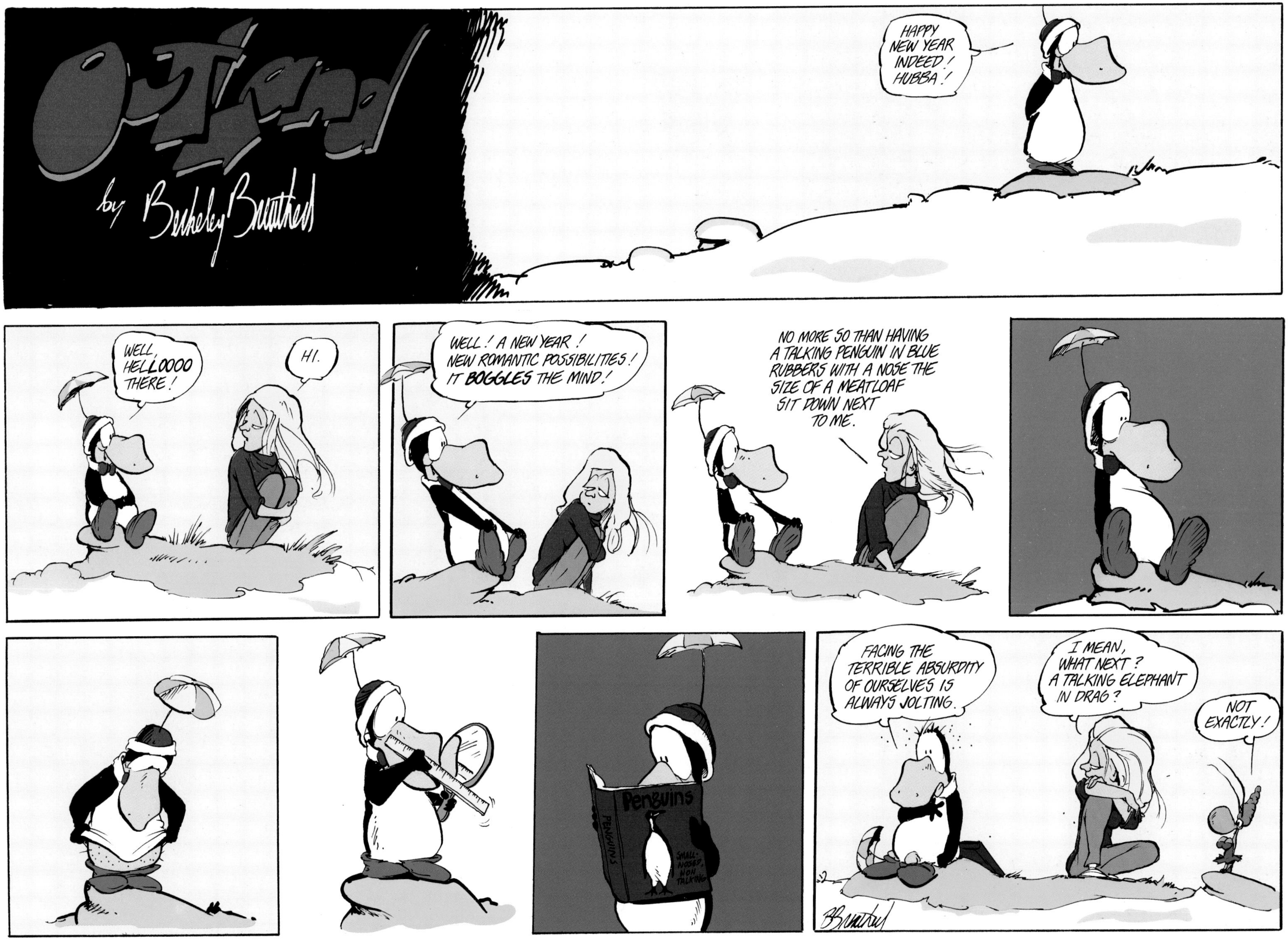
Outland
by Berkeley Breathed
HAPPY NEW YEAR INDEED! HUBBA!
WELL, HELLOOOO THERE!
HI.
WELL! A NEW YEAR! NEW ROMANTIC POSSIBILITIES! IT BOGGLES THE MIND!
NO MORE SO THAN HAVING A TALKING PENGUIN IN BLUE RUBBERS WITH A NOSE THE SIZE OF A MEATLOAF SIT DOWN NEXT TO ME.
PENGUINS
SMALL-NOSED, NON TALKING
FACING THE TERRIBLE ABSURDITY OF OURSELVES IS ALWAYS JOLTING.
I MEAN, WHAT NEXT? A TALKING ELEPHANT IN DRAG?
NOT EXACTLY!
BBreathed

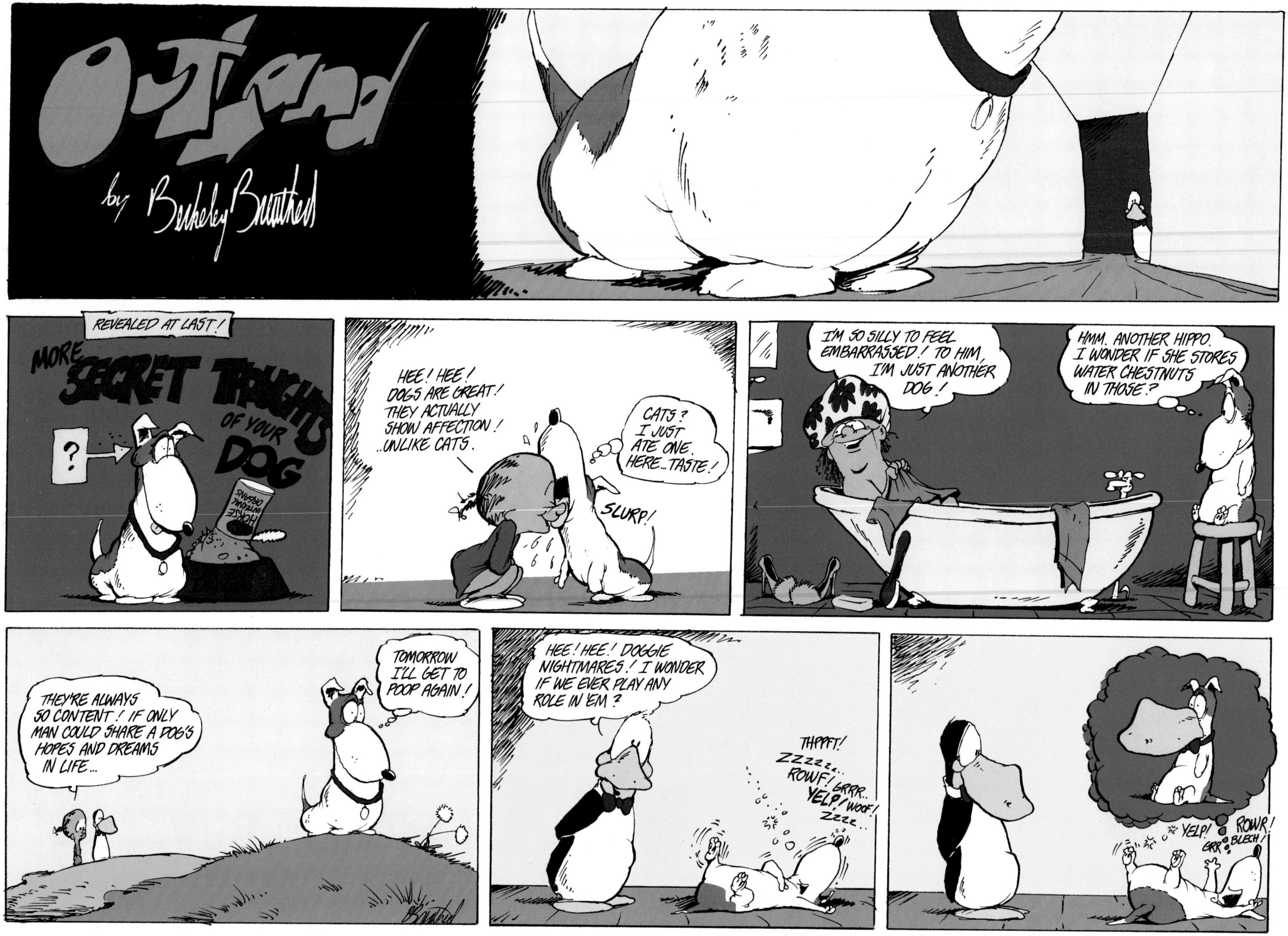
Outland
by Berkeley Breathed
REVEALED AT LAST!
MORE SECRET THOUGHTS OF YOUR DOG
?
HORSE INTERNAL ORGANS
HEE! HEE! DOGS ARE GREAT! THEY ACTUALLY SHOW AFFECTION! ..UNLIKE CATS.
CATS? I JUST ATE ONE. HERE...TASTE!
SLURP!
I'M SO SILLY TO FEEL EMBARRASSED! TO HIM, I'M JUST ANOTHER DOG!
HMM. ANOTHER HIPPO. I WONDER IF SHE STORES WATER CHESTNUTS IN THOSE?
THEY'RE ALWAYS SO CONTENT! IF ONLY MAN COULD SHARE A DOG'S HOPES AND DREAMS IN LIFE...
TOMORROW I'LL GET TO POOP AGAIN!
HEE! HEE! DOGGIE NIGHTMARES! I WONDER IF WE EVER PLAY ANY ROLE IN 'EM?
THPPFT!
ZZZZZ...
ROWF! GRRR..
YELP! WOOF!
ZZZZ...
YELP!
GRR
ROWR!
BLECH!

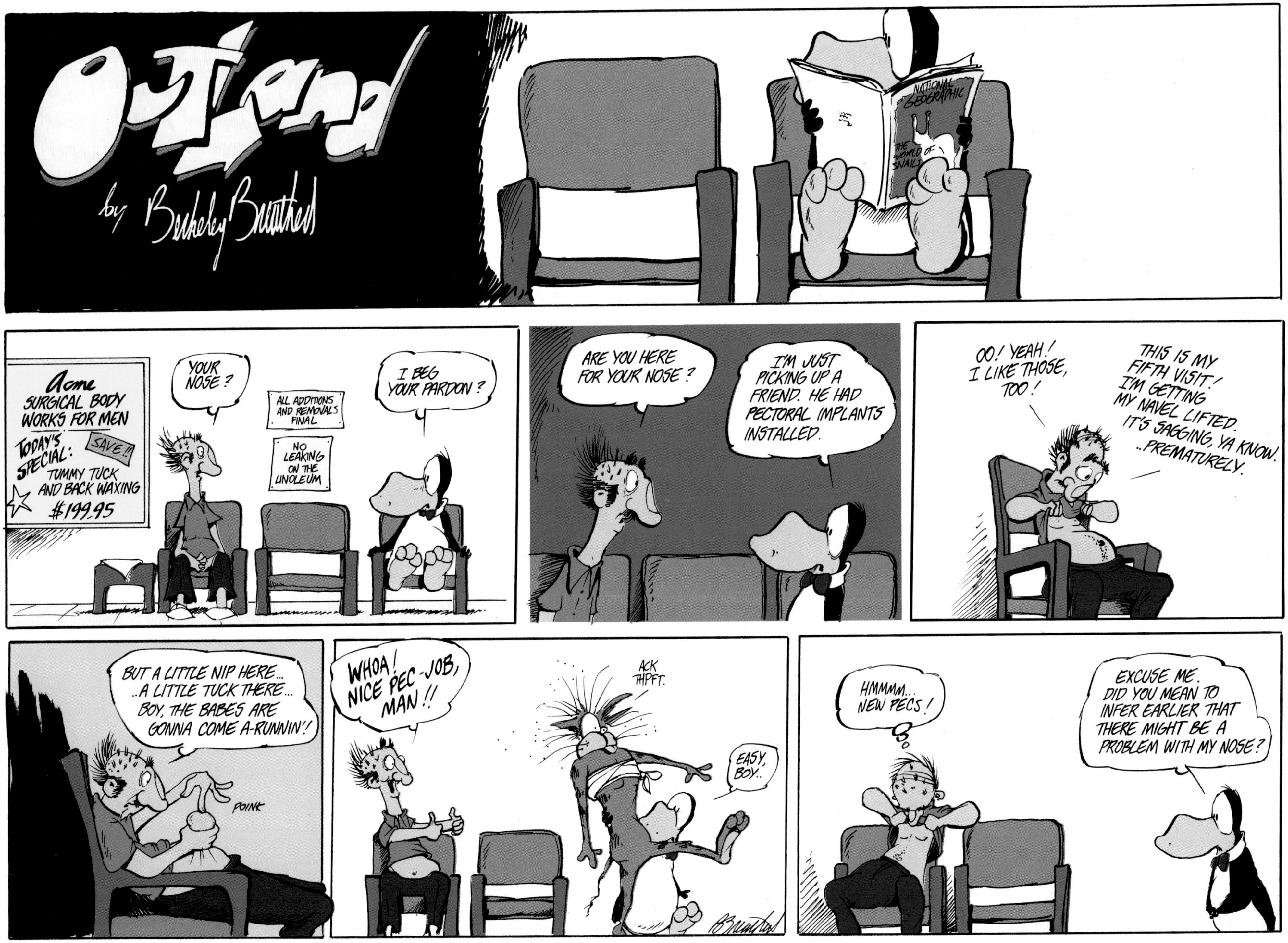
Outland
by Berkeley Breathed
NATIONAL GEOGRAPHIC
THE WORLD OF SNAILS
Acme SURGICAL BODY WORKS FOR MEN
TODAY'S SPECIAL: TUMMY TUCK AND BACK WAXING $199.95
SAVE!!
ALL ADDITIONS AND REMOVALS FINAL
NO LEAKING ON THE LINOLEUM
YOUR NOSE ?
I BEG YOUR PARDON ?
ARE YOU HERE FOR YOUR NOSE ?
I'M JUST PICKING UP A FRIEND. HE HAD PECTORAL IMPLANTS INSTALLED.
OO! YEAH! I LIKE THOSE, TOO!
THIS IS MY FIFTH VISIT! I'M GETTING MY NAVEL LIFTED. IT'S SAGGING, YA KNOW. ..PREMATURELY.
BUT A LITTLE NIP HERE... ..A LITTLE TUCK THERE... BOY, THE BABES ARE GONNA COME A-RUNNIN'!
POINK
WHOA! NICE PEC-JOB, MAN!!
ACK THPFT.
EASY, BOY..
HMMMM... NEW PECS!
EXCUSE ME. DID YOU MEAN TO INFER EARLIER THAT THERE MIGHT BE A PROBLEM WITH MY NOSE?

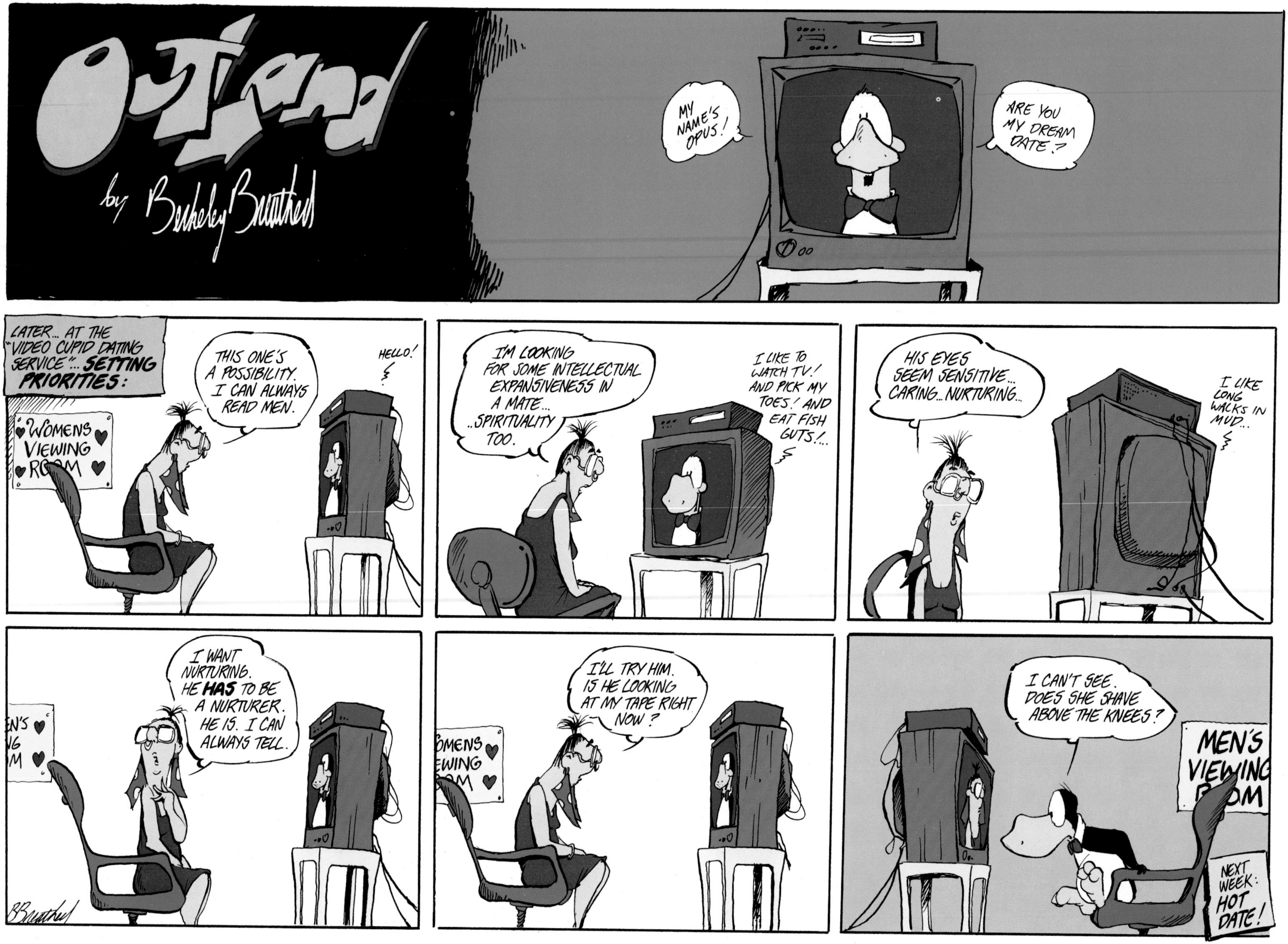
Outland
by Berkeley Breathed
MY NAME'S OPUS!
ARE YOU MY DREAM DATE?
LATER... AT THE "VIDEO CUPID DATING SERVICE"... SETTING PRIORITIES:
WOMENS VIEWING ROOM
THIS ONE'S A POSSIBILITY. I CAN ALWAYS READ MEN.
HELLO!
I'M LOOKING FOR SOME INTELLECTUAL EXPANSIVENESS IN A MATE... ..SPIRITUALITY TOO.
I LIKE TO WATCH TV! AND PICK MY TOES! AND EAT FISH GUTS!...
HIS EYES SEEM SENSITIVE... CARING... NURTURING...
I LIKE LONG WALKS IN MUD...
I WANT NURTURING. HE HAS TO BE A NURTURER. HE IS. I CAN ALWAYS TELL.
I'LL TRY HIM. IS HE LOOKING AT MY TAPE RIGHT NOW?
I CAN'T SEE. DOES SHE SHAVE ABOVE THE KNEES?
MEN'S VIEWING ROOM
NEXT WEEK: HOT DATE!
BBreathed

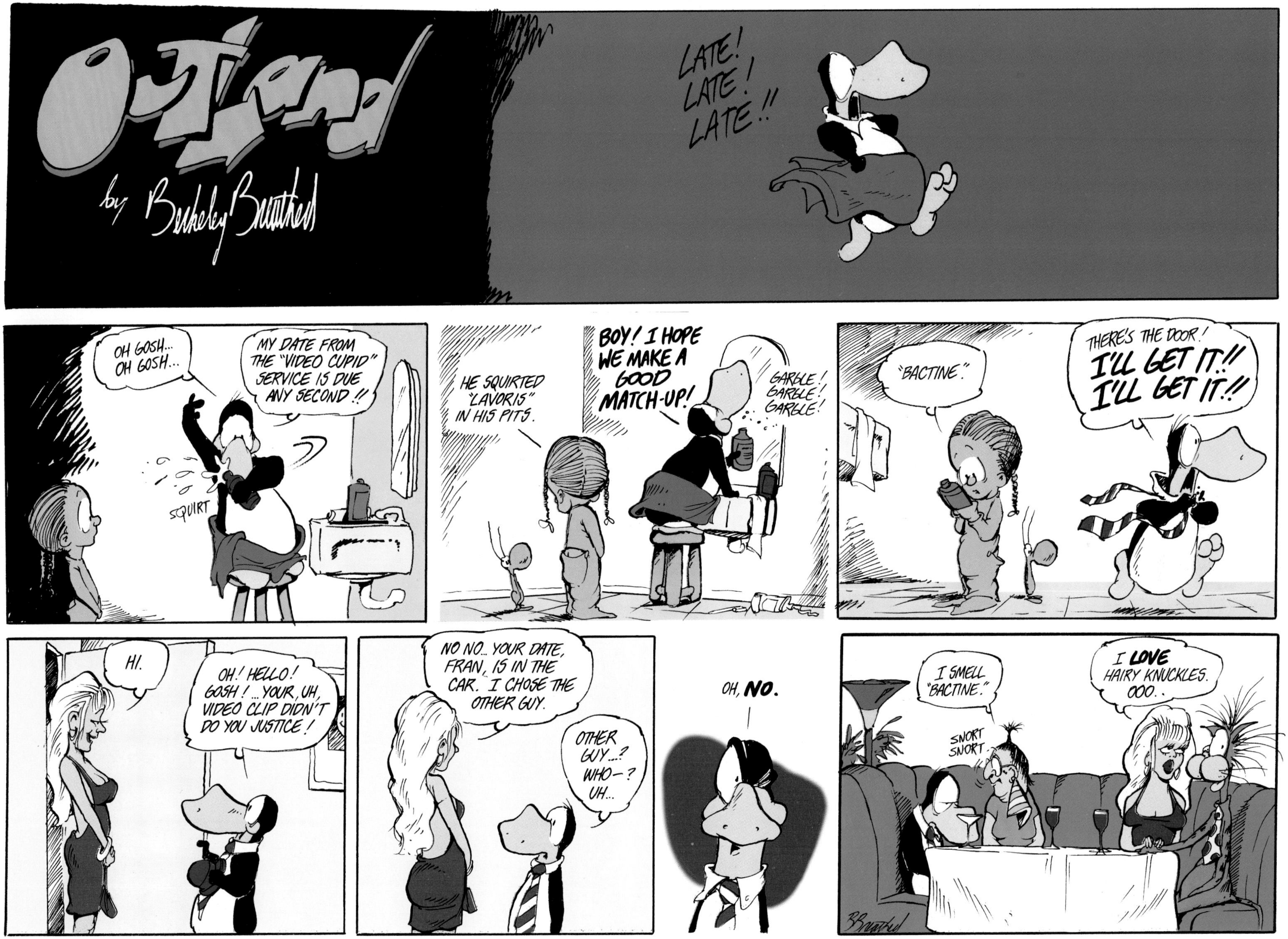
Outland
by Berkeley Breathed
LATE! LATE! LATE!!
OH GOSH... OH GOSH...
MY DATE FROM THE "VIDEO CUPID" SERVICE IS DUE ANY SECOND!!
SQUIRT
HE SQUIRTED "LAVORIS" IN HIS PITS.
BOY! I HOPE WE MAKE A GOOD MATCH-UP!
GARGLE! GARGLE! GARGLE!
"BACTINE."
THERE'S THE DOOR! I'LL GET IT!! I'LL GET IT!!
HI.
OH! HELLO! GOSH! ...YOUR, UH, VIDEO CLIP DIDN'T DO YOU JUSTICE!
NO NO... YOUR DATE, FRAN, IS IN THE CAR. I CHOSE THE OTHER GUY.
OTHER GUY...? WHO-? UH...
OH, NO.
I SMELL "BACTINE."
SNORT SNORT
I LOVE HAIRY KNUCKLES. OOO..
BBreathed

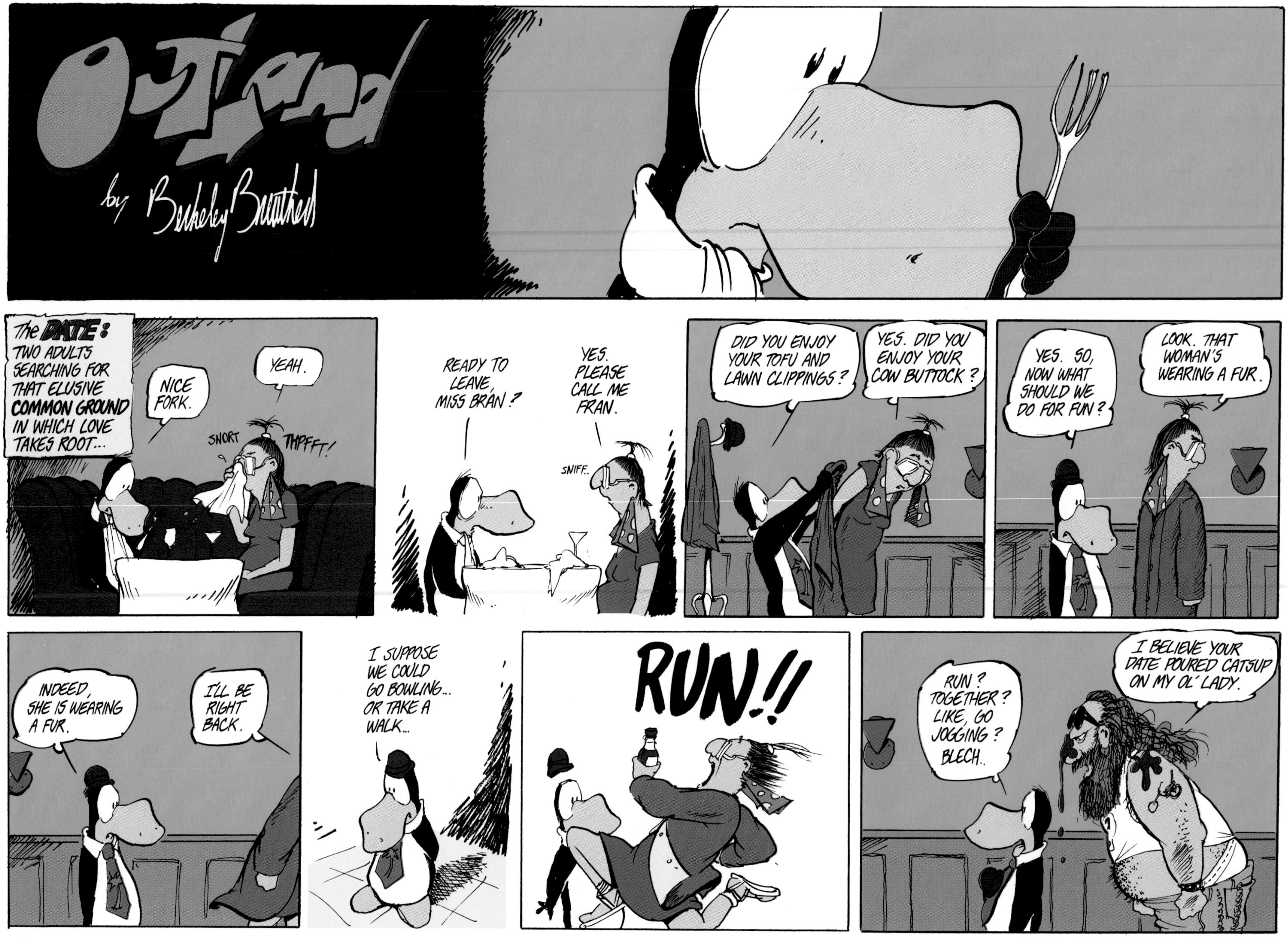
Outland
by Berkeley Breathed
The DATE: TWO ADULTS SEARCHING FOR THAT ELUSIVE COMMON GROUND IN WHICH LOVE TAKES ROOT...
NICE FORK.
YEAH.
SNORT
THPFFT!
READY TO LEAVE, MISS BRAN?
YES. PLEASE CALL ME FRAN.
SNIFF..
DID YOU ENJOY YOUR TOFU AND LAWN CLIPPINGS?
YES. DID YOU ENJOY YOUR COW BUTTOCK?
YES. SO, NOW WHAT SHOULD WE DO FOR FUN?
LOOK. THAT WOMAN'S WEARING A FUR.
INDEED, SHE IS WEARING A FUR.
I'LL BE RIGHT BACK.
I SUPPOSE WE COULD GO BOWLING... OR TAKE A WALK...
RUN!!
RUN? TOGETHER? LIKE, GO JOGGING? BLECH..
I BELIEVE YOUR DATE POURED CATSUP ON MY OL' LADY.

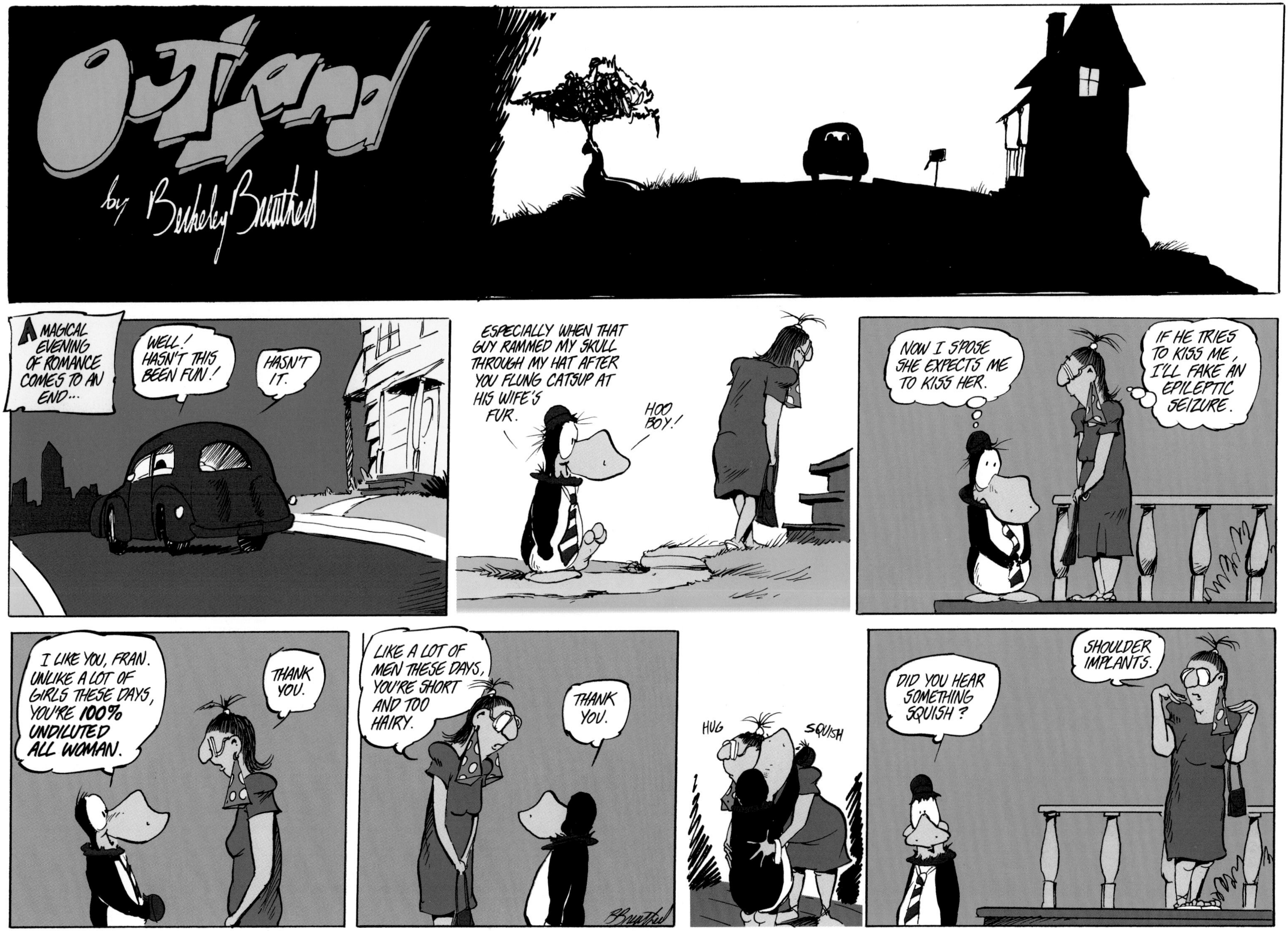

Outland
by Berkeley Breathed
A MAGICAL EVENING OF ROMANCE COMES TO AN END...
WELL! HASN'T THIS BEEN FUN!
HASN'T IT.
ESPECIALLY WHEN THAT GUY RAMMED MY SKULL THROUGH MY HAT AFTER YOU FLUNG CATSUP AT HIS WIFE'S FUR.
HOO BOY!
NOW I S'POSE SHE EXPECTS ME TO KISS HER.
IF HE TRIES TO KISS ME, I'LL FAKE AN EPILEPTIC SEIZURE.
I LIKE YOU, FRAN. UNLIKE A LOT OF GIRLS THESE DAYS, YOU'RE **100% UNDILUTED ALL WOMAN**.
THANK YOU.
LIKE A LOT OF MEN THESE DAYS, YOU'RE SHORT AND TOO HAIRY.
THANK YOU.
HUG
SQUISH
DID YOU HEAR SOMETHING SQUISH?
SHOULDER IMPLANTS.

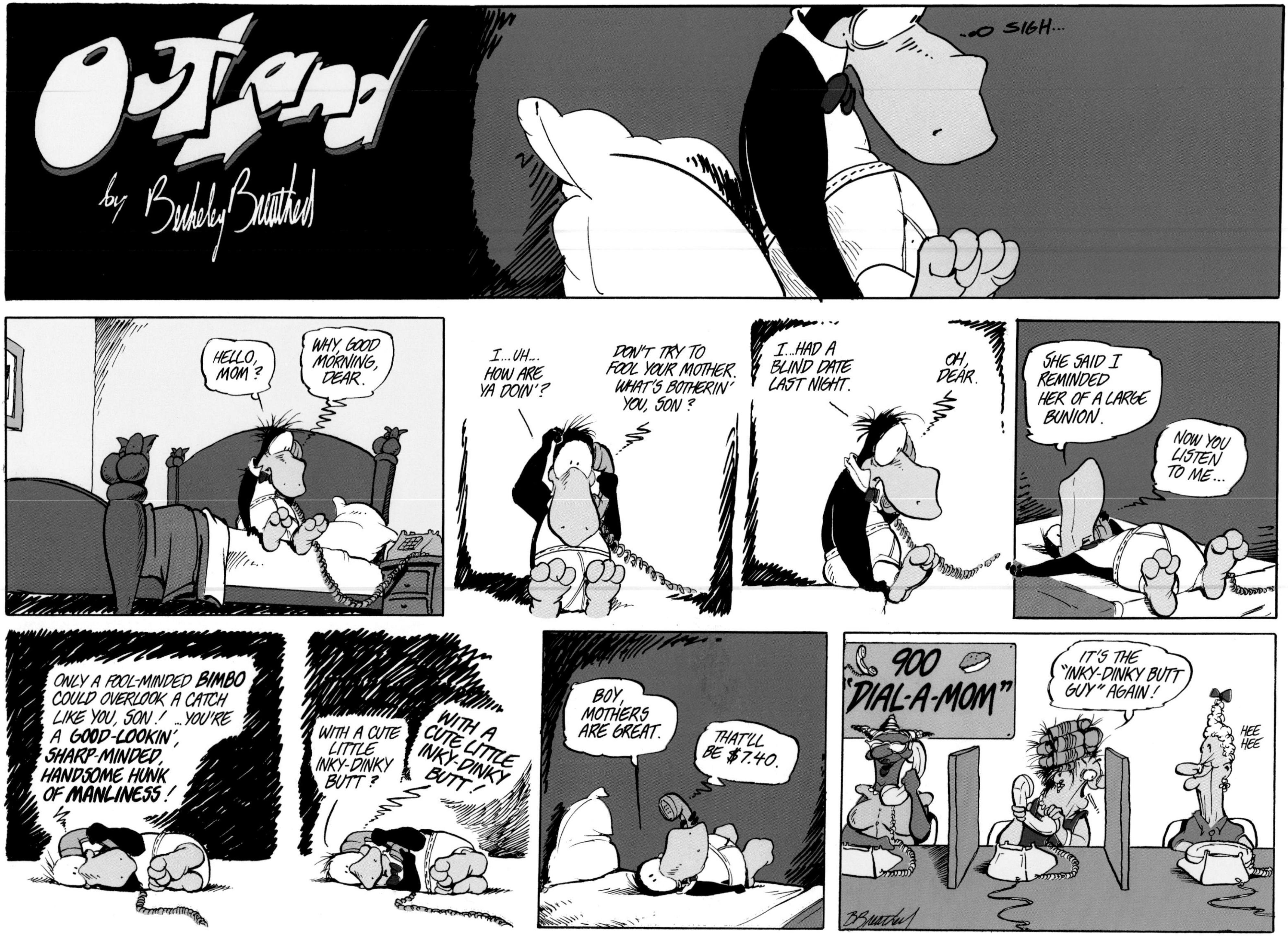
Outland
by Berkeley Breathed
..o SIGH...
HELLO, MOM?
WHY, GOOD MORNING, DEAR.
I...UH... HOW ARE YA DOIN'?
DON'T TRY TO FOOL YOUR MOTHER. WHAT'S BOTHERIN' YOU, SON?
I...HAD A BLIND DATE LAST NIGHT.
OH, DEAR.
SHE SAID I REMINDED HER OF A LARGE BUNION.
NOW YOU LISTEN TO ME...
ONLY A FOOL-MINDED BIMBO COULD OVERLOOK A CATCH LIKE YOU, SON! ...YOU'RE A GOOD-LOOKIN', SHARP-MINDED, HANDSOME HUNK OF MANLINESS!
WITH A CUTE LITTLE INKY-DINKY BUTT?
WITH A CUTE LITTLE INKY-DINKY BUTT!
BOY, MOTHERS ARE GREAT.
THAT'LL BE $7.40.
900 "DIAL-A-MOM"
IT'S THE "INKY-DINKY BUTT GUY" AGAIN!
HEE HEE
B Breathed

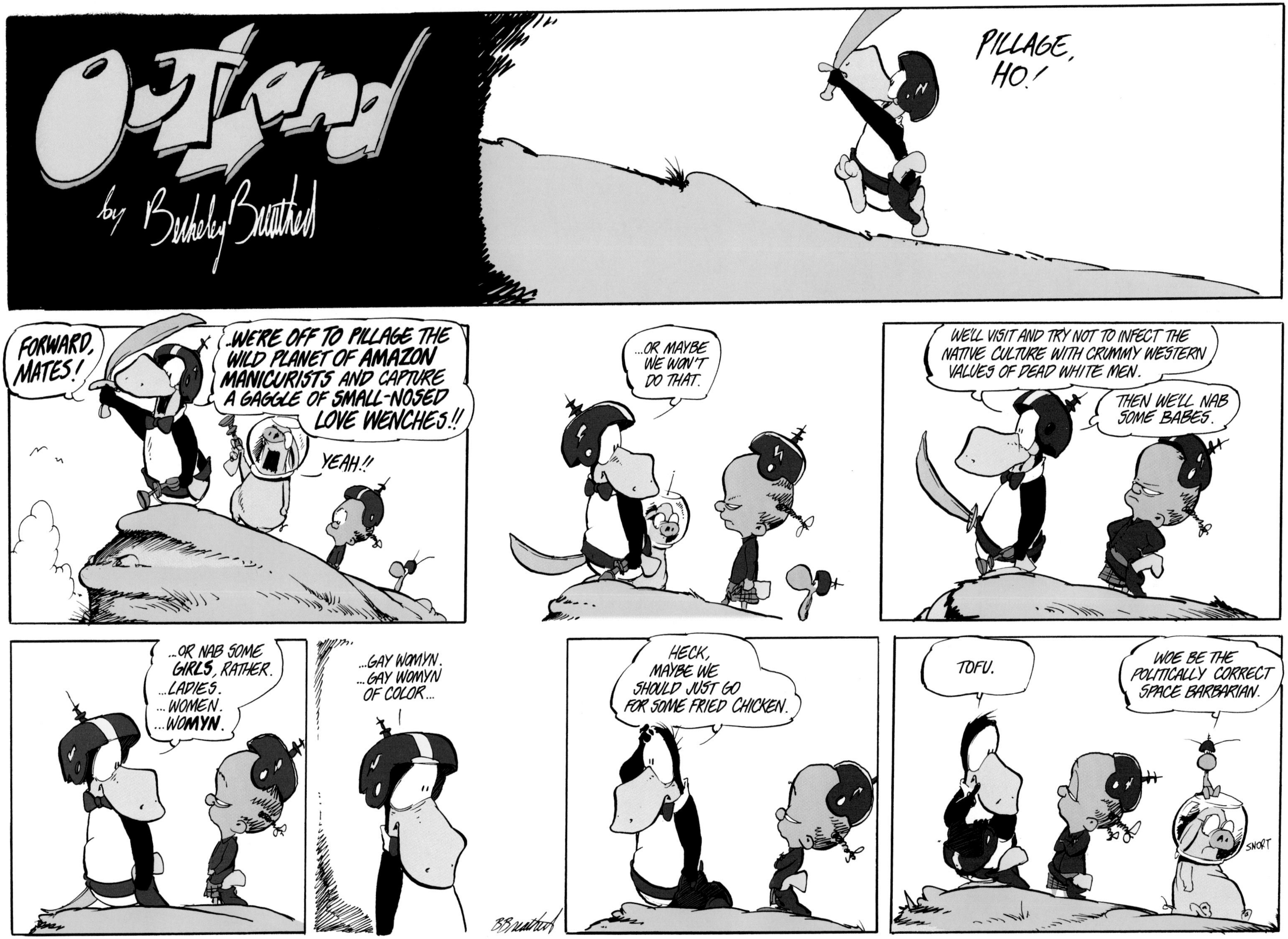
Outland
by Berkeley Breathed
PILLAGE, HO!
FORWARD, MATES!
..WE'RE OFF TO PILLAGE THE WILD PLANET OF AMAZON MANICURISTS AND CAPTURE A GAGGLE OF SMALL-NOSED LOVE WENCHES!!
YEAH!!
...OR MAYBE WE WON'T DO THAT.
WE'LL VISIT AND TRY NOT TO INFECT THE NATIVE CULTURE WITH CRUMMY WESTERN VALUES OF DEAD WHITE MEN.
THEN WE'LL NAB SOME BABES.
...OR NAB SOME GIRLS, RATHER. ...LADIES. ...WOMEN. ...WOMYN.
...GAY WOMYN. ...GAY WOMYN OF COLOR...
HECK, MAYBE WE SHOULD JUST GO FOR SOME FRIED CHICKEN.
TOFU.
WOE BE THE POLITICALLY CORRECT SPACE BARBARIAN.
SNORT
BBreathed

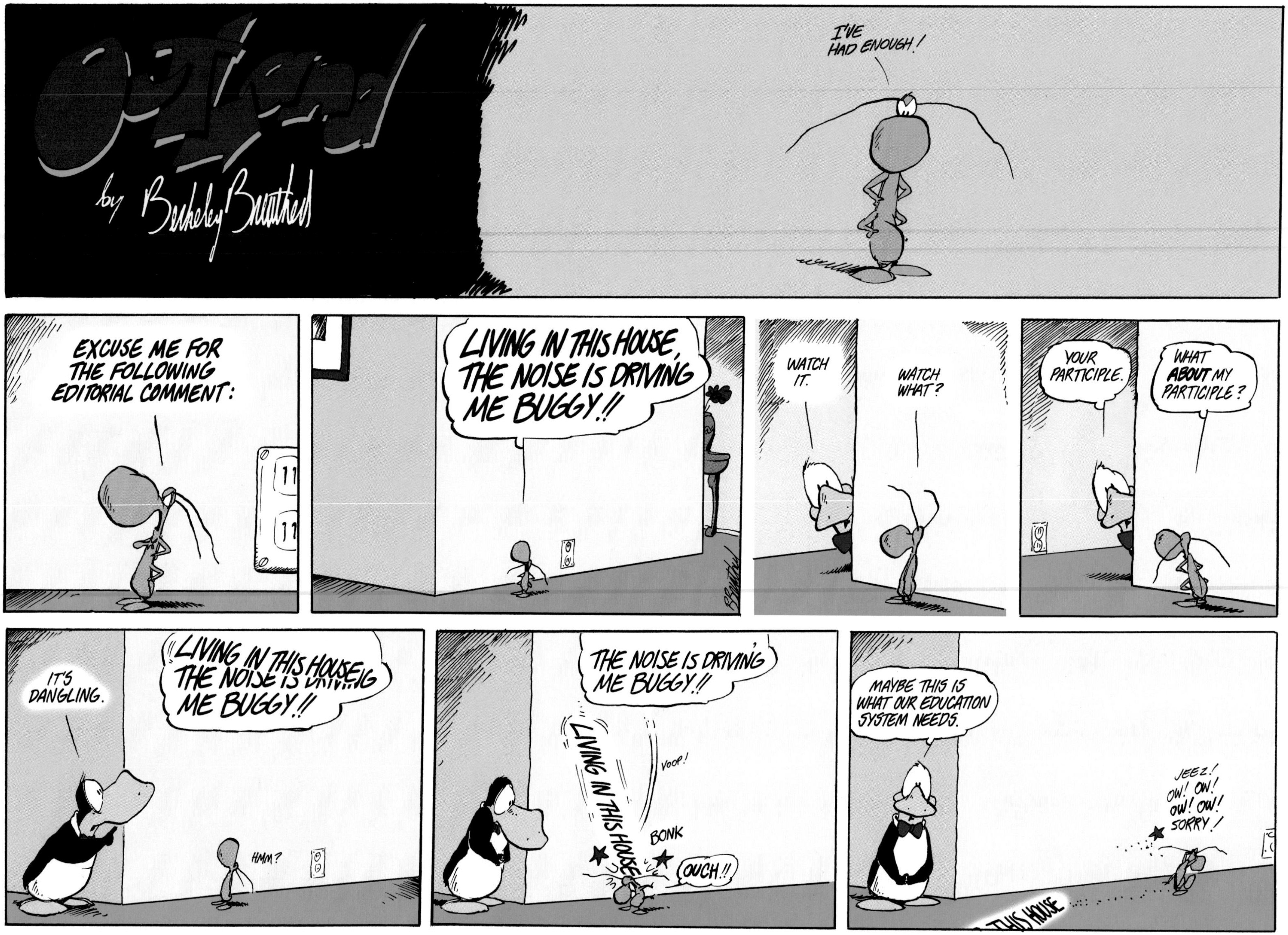
Outland
by Berkeley Breathed
I'VE HAD ENOUGH!
EXCUSE ME FOR THE FOLLOWING EDITORIAL COMMENT:
LIVING IN THIS HOUSE, THE NOISE IS DRIVING ME BUGGY!!
WATCH IT.
WATCH WHAT?
YOUR PARTICIPLE.
WHAT ABOUT MY PARTICIPLE?
IT'S DANGLING.
LIVING IN THIS HOUSE
THE NOISE IS DRIVING ME BUGGY!!
HMM?
THE NOISE IS DRIVING ME BUGGY!!
LIVING IN THIS HOUSE
VOOP!
BONK
OUCH!!
MAYBE THIS IS WHAT OUR EDUCATION SYSTEM NEEDS.
JEEZ! OW! OW! OW! OW! SORRY!
THIS HOUSE

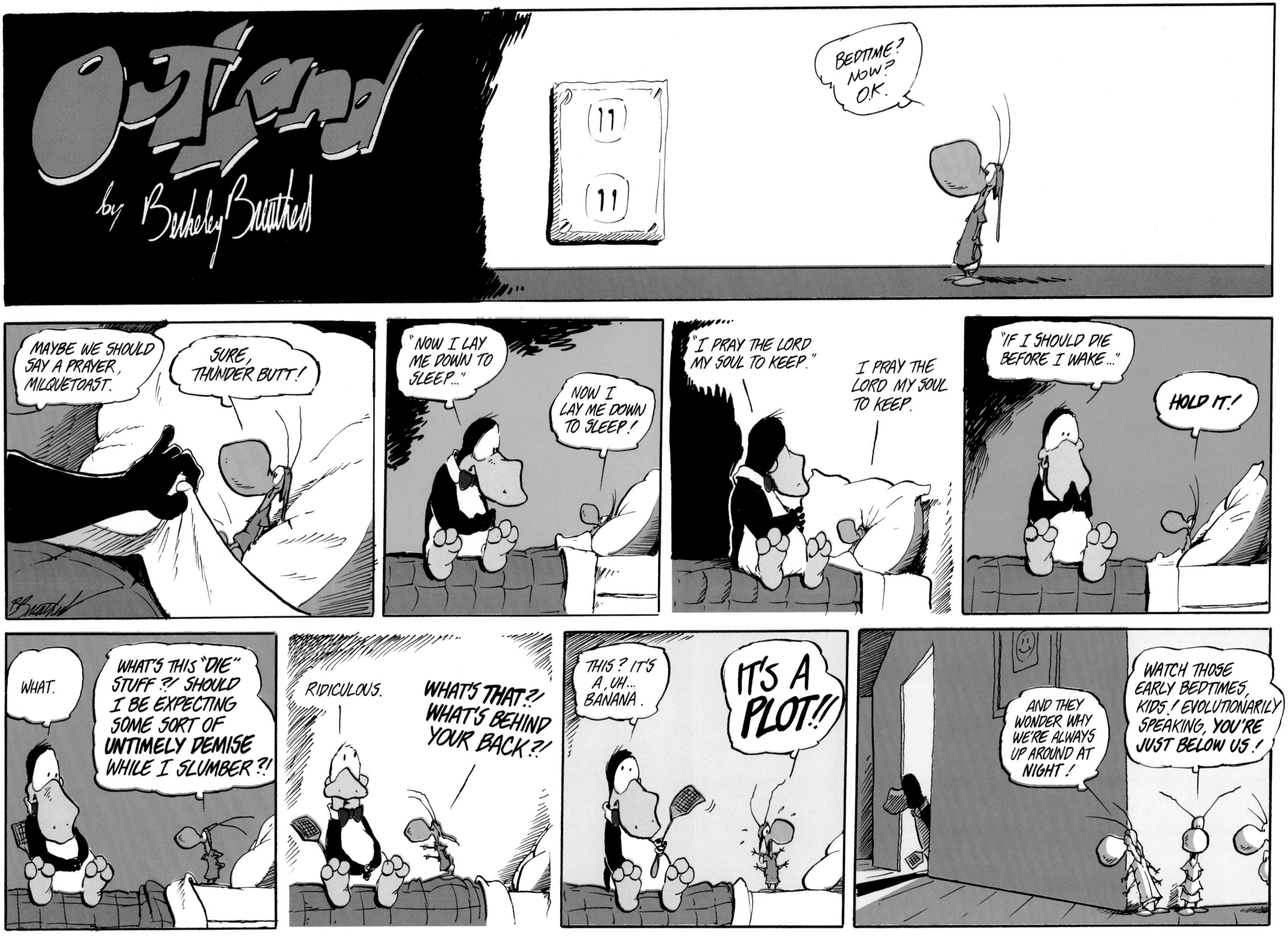

Outland
by Berkeley Breathed
BEDTIME? NOW? O.K.
MAYBE WE SHOULD SAY A PRAYER, MILQUETOAST.
SURE, THUNDER BUTT!
"NOW I LAY ME DOWN TO SLEEP..."
NOW I LAY ME DOWN TO SLEEP!
"I PRAY THE LORD MY SOUL TO KEEP."
I PRAY THE LORD MY SOUL TO KEEP.
"IF I SHOULD DIE BEFORE I WAKE..."
HOLD IT!
WHAT.
WHAT'S THIS "DIE" STUFF?! SHOULD I BE EXPECTING SOME SORT OF UNTIMELY DEMISE WHILE I SLUMBER?!
RIDICULOUS.
WHAT'S THAT?! WHAT'S BEHIND YOUR BACK?!
THIS? IT'S A, UH... BANANA.
IT'S A PLOT!!
AND THEY WONDER WHY WE'RE ALWAYS UP AROUND AT NIGHT!
WATCH THOSE EARLY BEDTIMES, KIDS! EVOLUTIONARILY SPEAKING, YOU'RE JUST BELOW US!

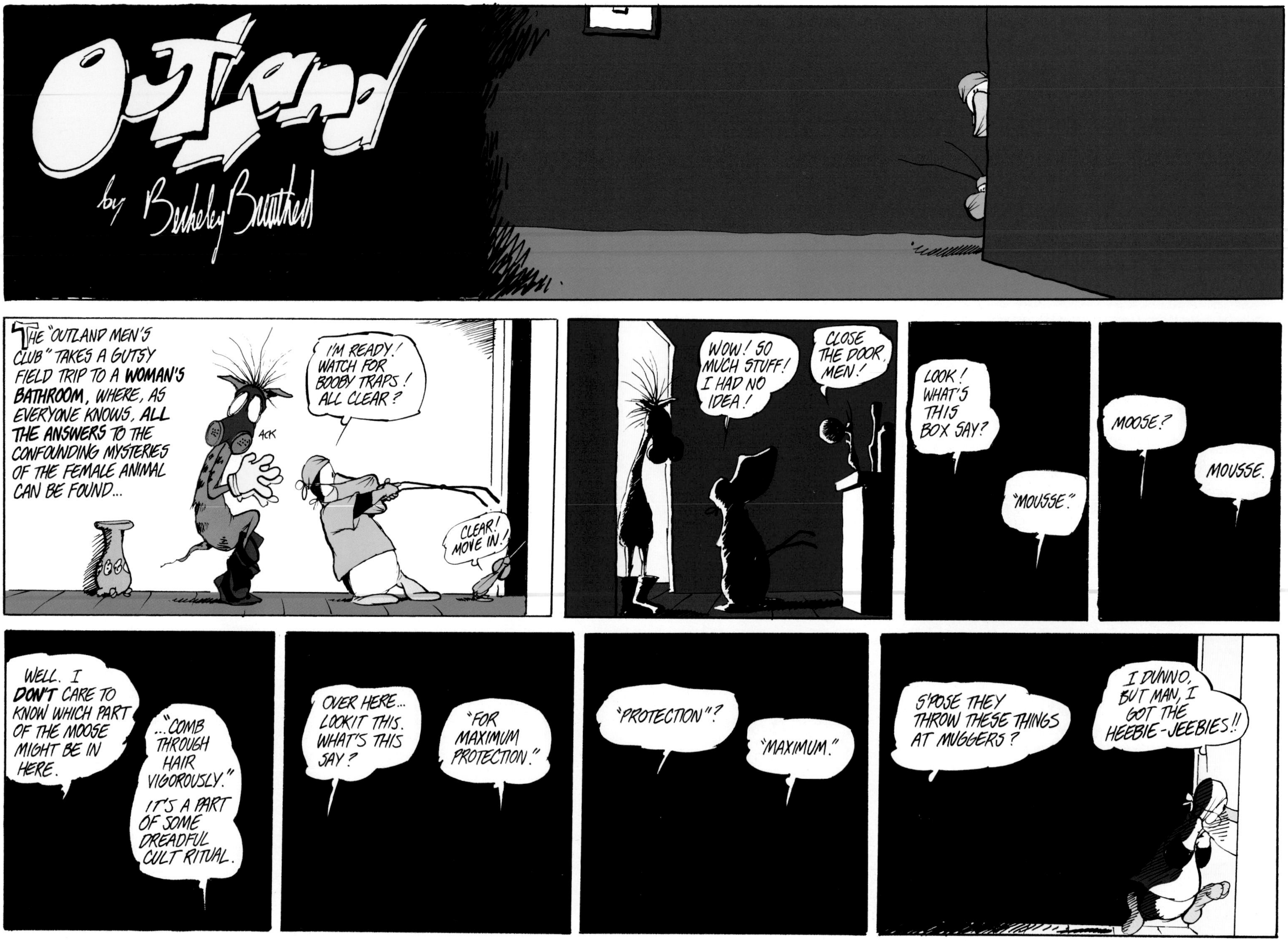
Outland
by Berkeley Breathed
THE "OUTLAND MEN'S CLUB" TAKES A GUTSY FIELD TRIP TO A WOMAN'S BATHROOM, WHERE, AS EVERYONE KNOWS, ALL THE ANSWERS TO THE CONFOUNDING MYSTERIES OF THE FEMALE ANIMAL CAN BE FOUND...
I'M READY! WATCH FOR BOOBY TRAPS! ALL CLEAR?
ACK
CLEAR! MOVE IN!
WOW! SO MUCH STUFF! I HAD NO IDEA!
CLOSE THE DOOR, MEN!
LOOK! WHAT'S THIS BOX SAY?
"MOUSSE."
MOOSE?
MOUSSE.
WELL. I DON'T CARE TO KNOW WHICH PART OF THE MOOSE MIGHT BE IN HERE.
..."COMB THROUGH HAIR VIGOROUSLY." IT'S A PART OF SOME DREADFUL CULT RITUAL.
OVER HERE... LOOKIT THIS. WHAT'S THIS SAY?
"FOR MAXIMUM PROTECTION."
"PROTECTION"?
"MAXIMUM."
S'POSE THEY THROW THESE THINGS AT MUGGERS?
I DUNNO, BUT MAN, I GOT THE HEEBIE-JEEBIES!!

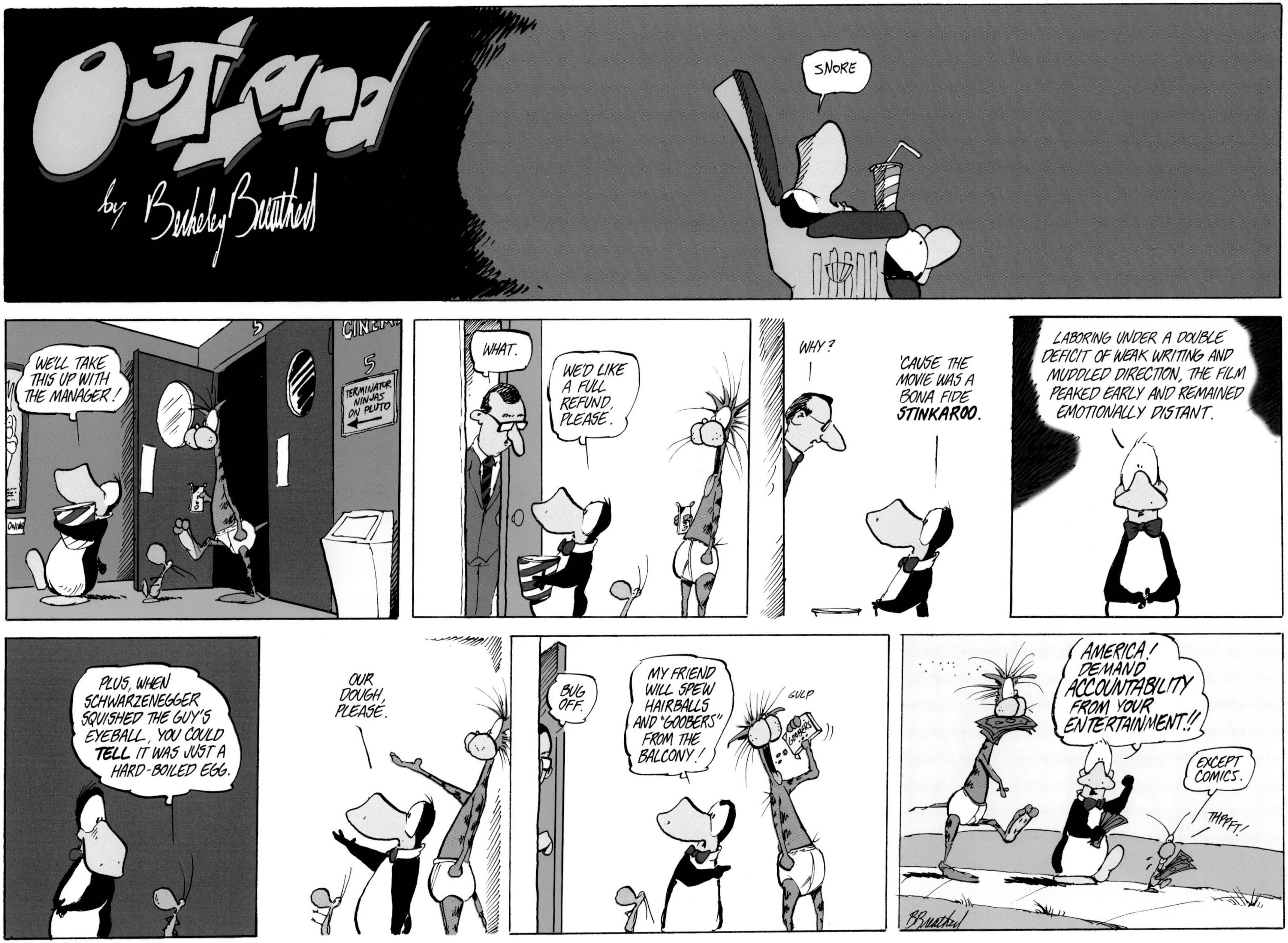
Outland
by Berkeley Breathed
SNORE
WE'LL TAKE THIS UP WITH THE MANAGER!
CINEMA
5
TERMINATOR NINJAS ON PLUTO
WHAT.
WE'D LIKE A FULL REFUND, PLEASE.
WHY?
'CAUSE THE MOVIE WAS A BONA FIDE STINKAROO.
LABORING UNDER A DOUBLE DEFICIT OF WEAK WRITING AND MUDDLED DIRECTION, THE FILM PEAKED EARLY AND REMAINED EMOTIONALLY DISTANT.
PLUS, WHEN SCHWARZENEGGER SQUISHED THE GUY'S EYEBALL, YOU COULD TELL IT WAS JUST A HARD-BOILED EGG.
OUR DOUGH, PLEASE.
BUG OFF.
MY FRIEND WILL SPEW HAIRBALLS AND "GOOBERS" FROM THE BALCONY!
GULP
GOOBERS
AMERICA! DEMAND ACCOUNTABILITY FROM YOUR ENTERTAINMENT!!
EXCEPT COMICS.
THPPFT!
BBreathed

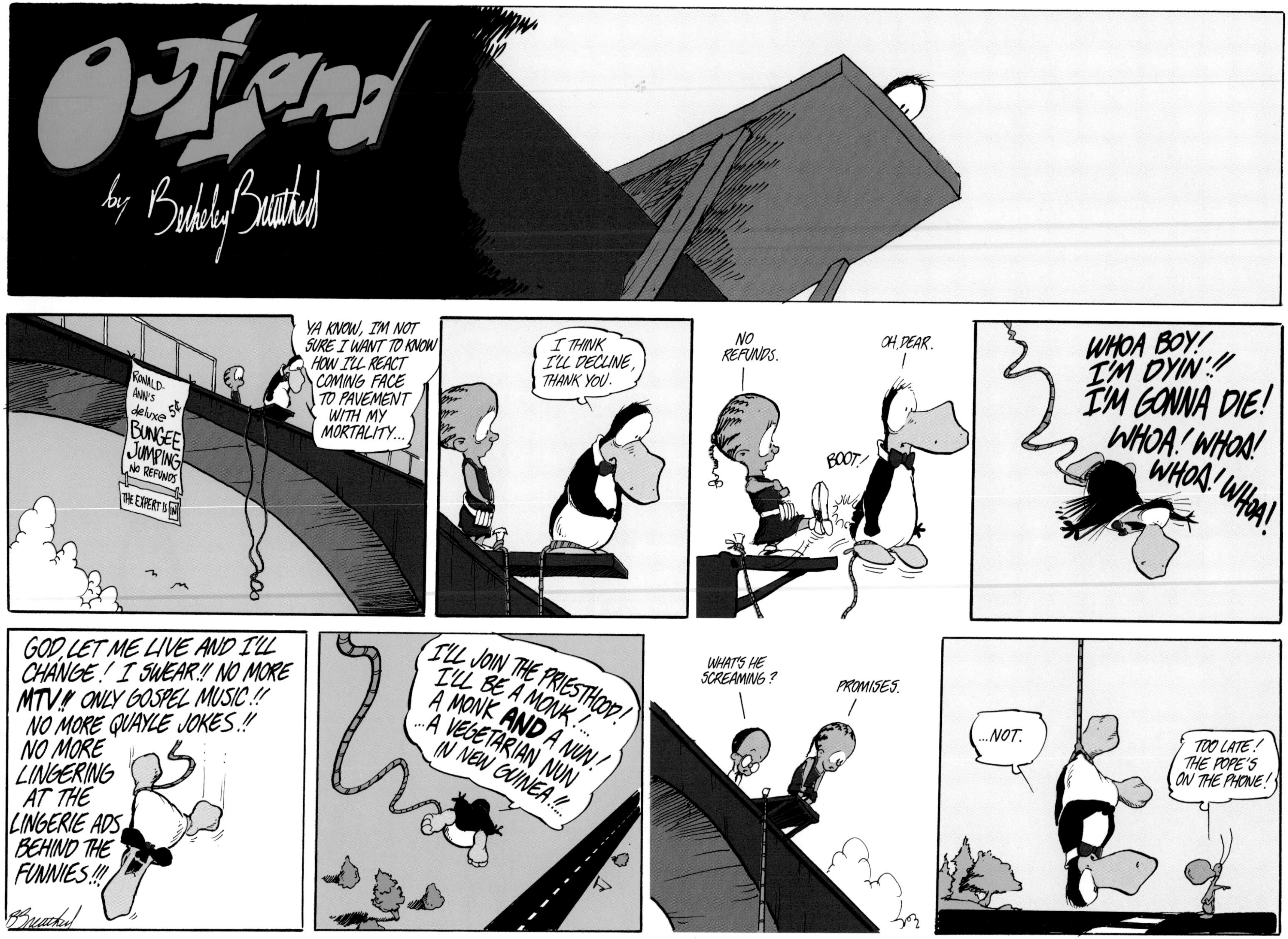

Outland
by Berkeley Breathed
RONALD-ANN'S deluxe 5¢ BUNGEE JUMPING NO REFUNDS
THE EXPERT IS IN
YA KNOW, I'M NOT SURE I WANT TO KNOW HOW I'LL REACT COMING FACE TO PAVEMENT WITH MY MORTALITY...
I THINK I'LL DECLINE, THANK YOU.
NO REFUNDS.
OH, DEAR.
BOOT!
WHOA BOY! I'M DYIN'!! I'M GONNA DIE! WHOA! WHOA! WHOA! WHOA!
GOD, LET ME LIVE AND I'LL CHANGE! I SWEAR!! NO MORE MTV!! ONLY GOSPEL MUSIC!! NO MORE QUAYLE JOKES!! NO MORE LINGERING AT THE LINGERIE ADS BEHIND THE FUNNIES!!!
I'LL JOIN THE PRIESTHOOD! I'LL BE A MONK!... A MONK AND A NUN! ...A VEGETARIAN NUN IN NEW GUINEA!!!
WHAT'S HE SCREAMING?
PROMISES.
...NOT.
TOO LATE! THE POPE'S ON THE PHONE!

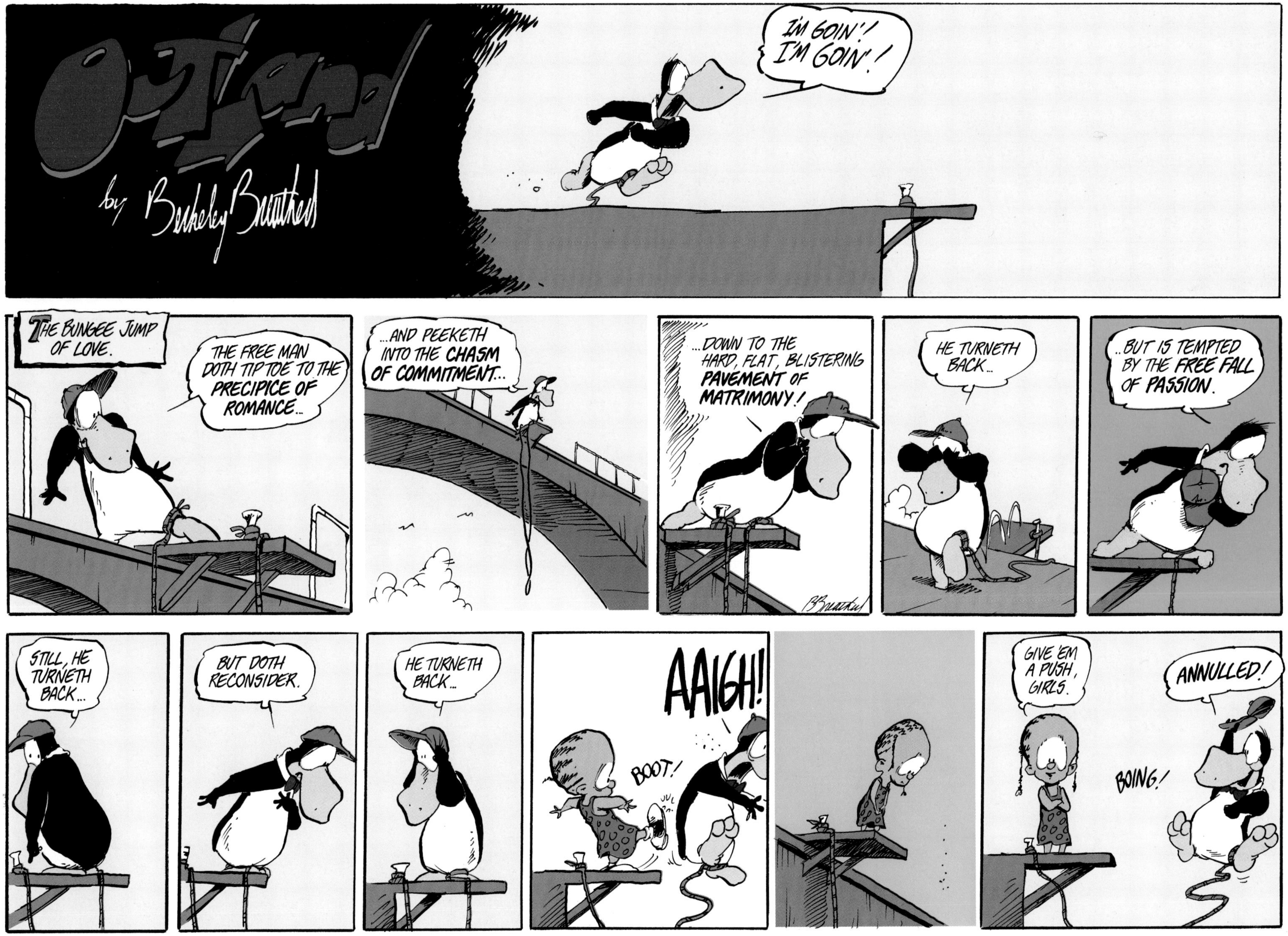
Outland
by Berkeley Breathed
I'M GOIN'! I'M GOIN'!
THE BUNGEE JUMP OF LOVE.
THE FREE MAN DOTH TIPTOE TO THE PRECIPICE OF ROMANCE...
...AND PEEKETH INTO THE CHASM OF COMMITMENT...
...DOWN TO THE HARD, FLAT, BLISTERING PAVEMENT OF MATRIMONY!
HE TURNETH BACK...
..BUT IS TEMPTED BY THE FREE FALL OF PASSION.
STILL, HE TURNETH BACK...
BUT DOTH RECONSIDER.
HE TURNETH BACK...
AAIGH!
BOOT!
GIVE 'EM A PUSH, GIRLS.
BOING!
ANNULLED!

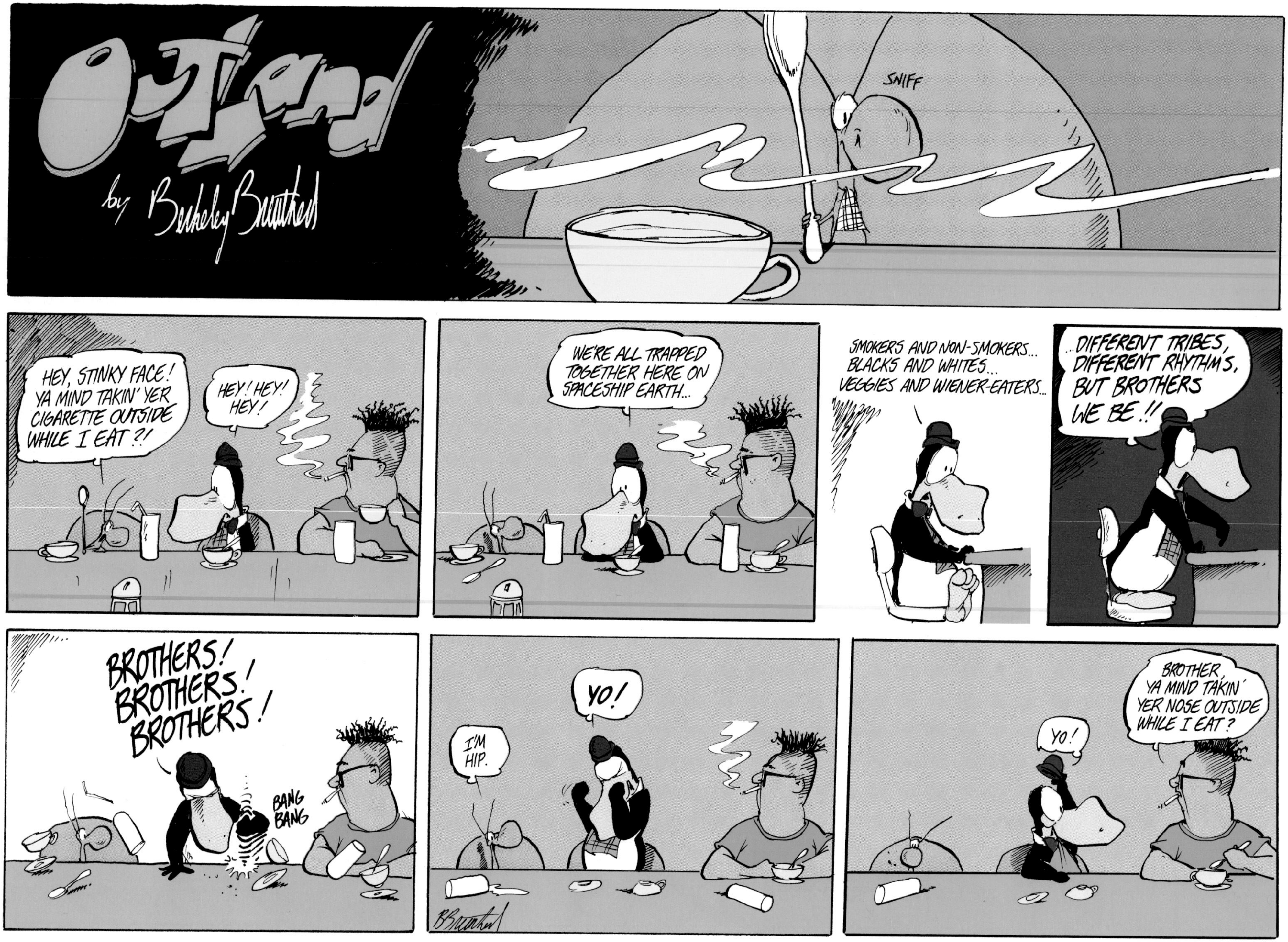
Outland
by Berkeley Breathed
SNIFF
HEY, STINKY FACE! YA MIND TAKIN' YER CIGARETTE OUTSIDE WHILE I EAT ?!
HEY! HEY! HEY!
WE'RE ALL TRAPPED TOGETHER HERE ON SPACESHIP EARTH...
SMOKERS AND NON-SMOKERS... BLACKS AND WHITES... VEGGIES AND WIENER-EATERS...
...DIFFERENT TRIBES, DIFFERENT RHYTHM'S, BUT BROTHERS WE BE!!
BROTHERS! BROTHERS! BROTHERS!
BANG BANG
I'M HIP.
YO!
YO!
BROTHER, YA MIND TAKIN' YER NOSE OUTSIDE WHILE I EAT?

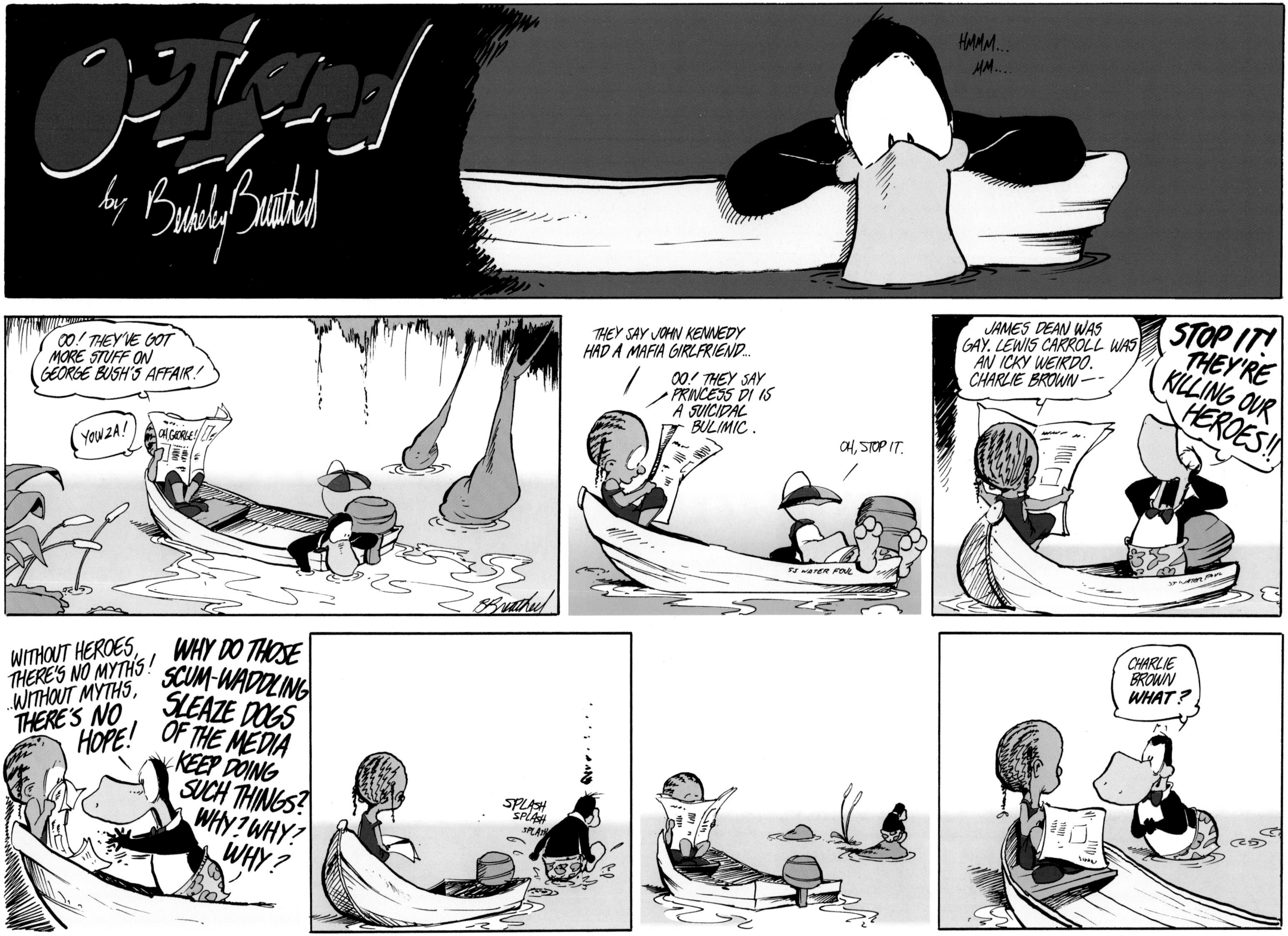
Outland
by Berkeley Breathed
HMMM...
MM...
OO! THEY'VE GOT MORE STUFF ON GEORGE BUSH'S AFFAIR!
YOWZA!
OH, GEORGE!
THEY SAY JOHN KENNEDY HAD A MAFIA GIRLFRIEND...
OO! THEY SAY PRINCESS DI IS A SUICIDAL BULIMIC.
OH, STOP IT.
SS WATER FOWL
JAMES DEAN WAS GAY. LEWIS CARROLL WAS AN ICKY WEIRDO. CHARLIE BROWN—
STOP IT! THEY'RE KILLING OUR HEROES!!
WITHOUT HEROES, THERE'S NO MYTHS! ..WITHOUT MYTHS, THERE'S NO HOPE!
WHY DO THOSE SCUM-WADDLING SLEAZE DOGS OF THE MEDIA KEEP DOING SUCH THINGS? WHY? WHY? WHY?
SPLASH SPLASH SPLASH
CHARLIE BROWN WHAT?

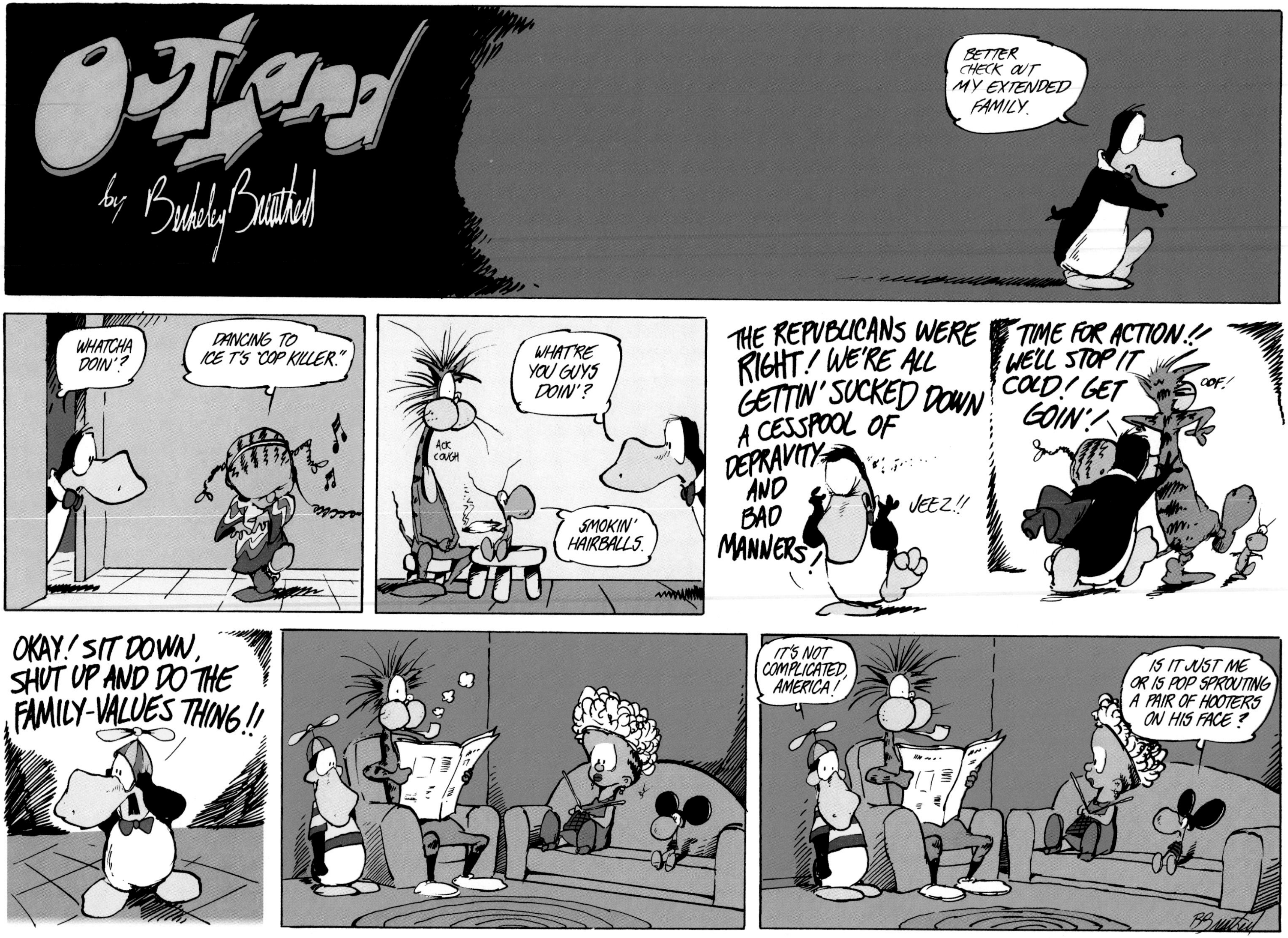
Outland
by Berkeley Breathed
BETTER CHECK OUT MY EXTENDED FAMILY.
WHATCHA DOIN'?
DANCING TO ICE T'S "COP KILLER."
WHAT'RE YOU GUYS DOIN'?
ACK COUGH
SMOKIN' HAIRBALLS.
THE REPUBLICANS WERE RIGHT! WE'RE ALL GETTIN' SUCKED DOWN A CESSPOOL OF DEPRAVITY AND BAD MANNERS!
JEEZ!!
TIME FOR ACTION!! WE'LL STOP IT COLD! GET GOIN'!
OOF!
OKAY! SIT DOWN, SHUT UP AND DO THE FAMILY-VALUES THING!!
IT'S NOT COMPLICATED, AMERICA!
IS IT JUST ME OR IS POP SPROUTING A PAIR OF HOOTERS ON HIS FACE?
B. Breathed

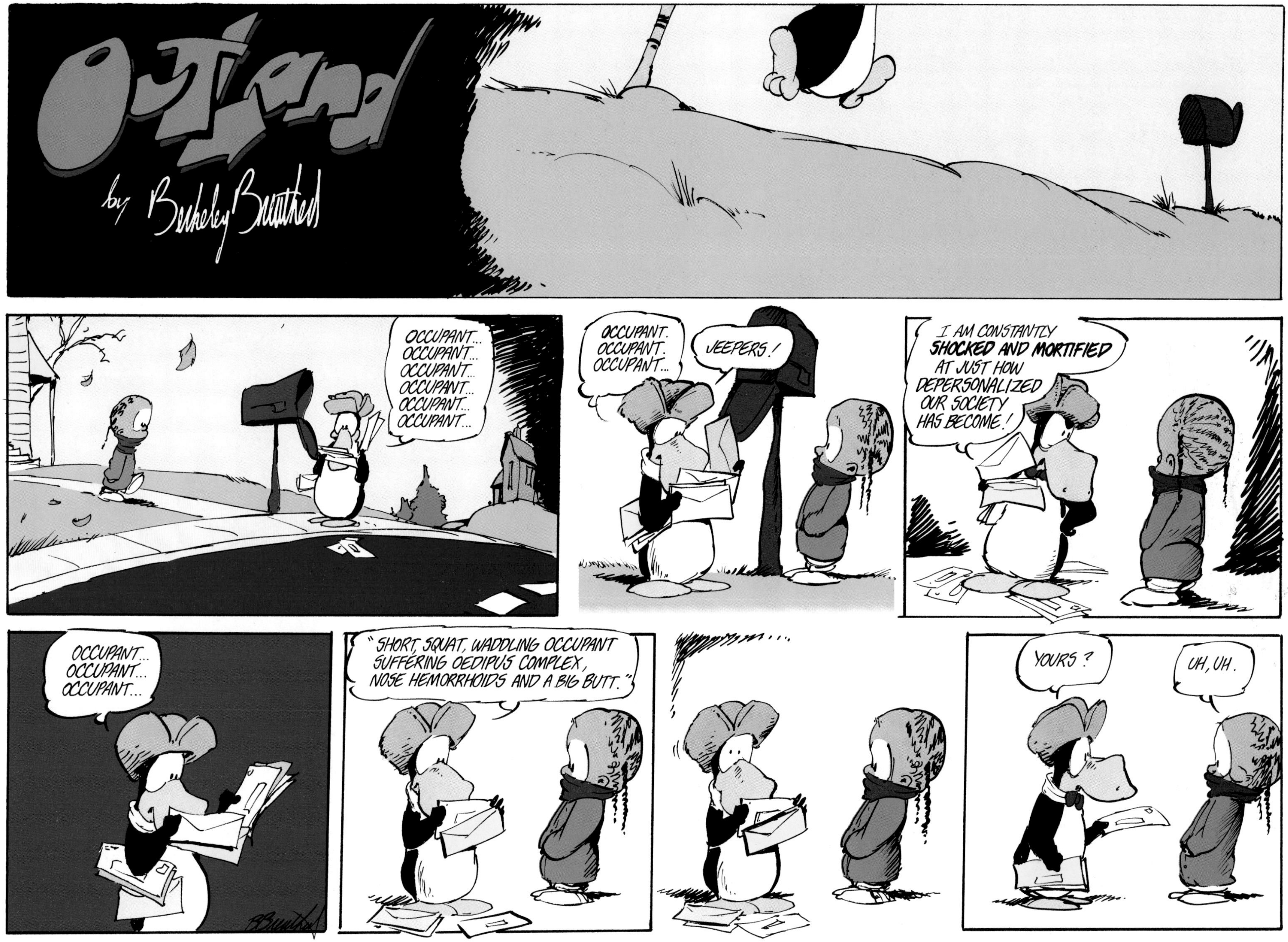
Outland
by Berkeley Breathed
OCCUPANT... OCCUPANT... OCCUPANT... OCCUPANT... OCCUPANT... OCCUPANT...
OCCUPANT. OCCUPANT. OCCUPANT...
JEEPERS!
I AM CONSTANTLY SHOCKED AND MORTIFIED AT JUST HOW DEPERSONALIZED OUR SOCIETY HAS BECOME!
OCCUPANT... OCCUPANT... OCCUPANT...
"SHORT, SQUAT, WADDLING OCCUPANT SUFFERING OEDIPUS COMPLEX, NOSE HEMORRHOIDS AND A BIG BUTT."
YOURS?
UH, UH.

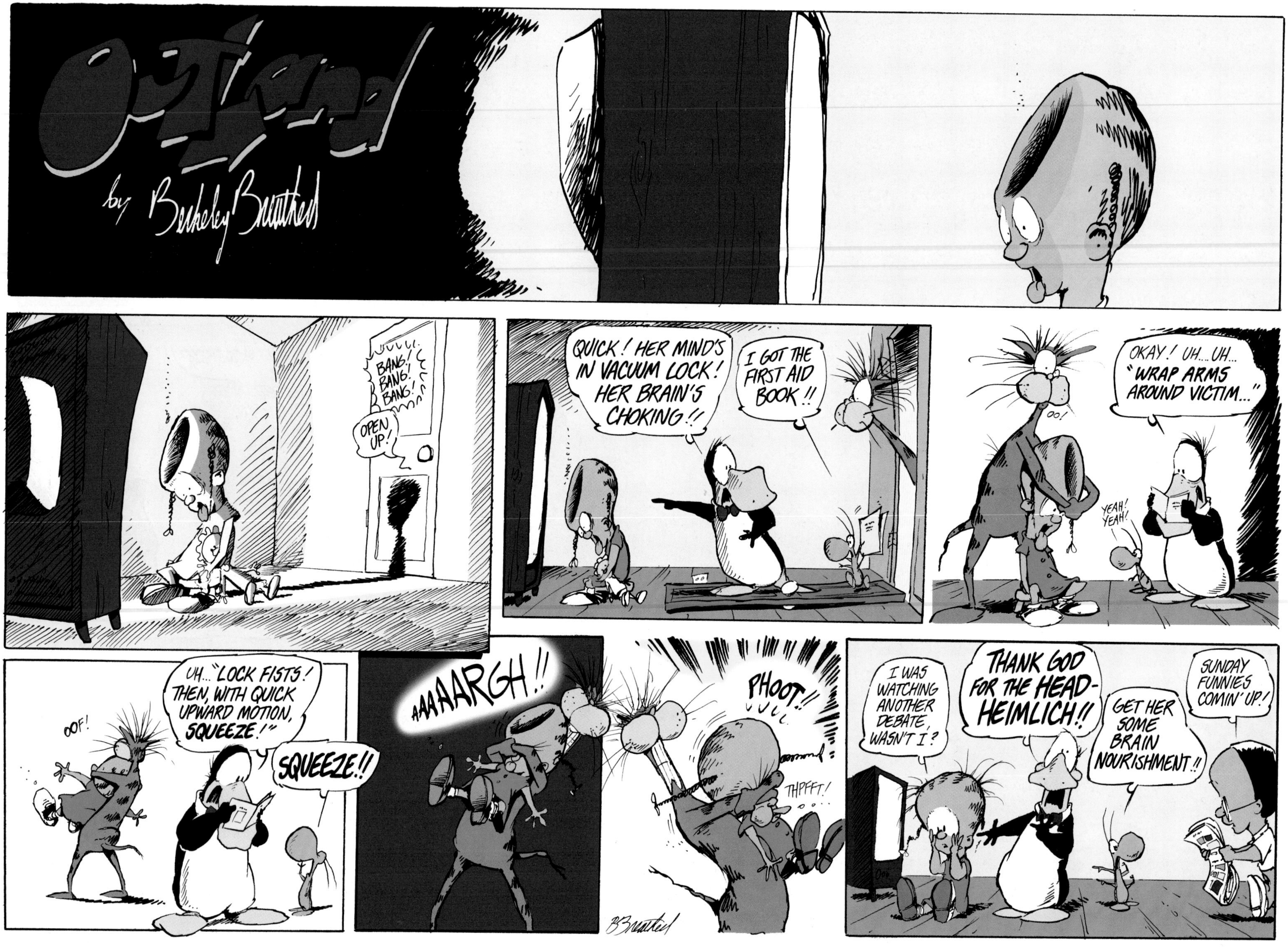
Outland
by Berkeley Breathed
BANG! BANG! BANG!
OPEN UP!
QUICK! HER MIND'S IN VACUUM LOCK! HER BRAIN'S CHOKING!!
I GOT THE FIRST AID BOOK!!
OO!
OKAY! UH...UH... "WRAP ARMS AROUND VICTIM..."
YEAH! YEAH!
OOF!
UH..."LOCK FISTS! THEN, WITH QUICK UPWARD MOTION, SQUEEZE!"
SQUEEZE!!
AAAAARGH!!
PHOOT!!
THPFFT!
I WAS WATCHING ANOTHER DEBATE, WASN'T I?
THANK GOD FOR THE HEAD-HEIMLICH!!
GET HER SOME BRAIN NOURISHMENT!!
SUNDAY FUNNIES COMIN' UP!
B Breathed

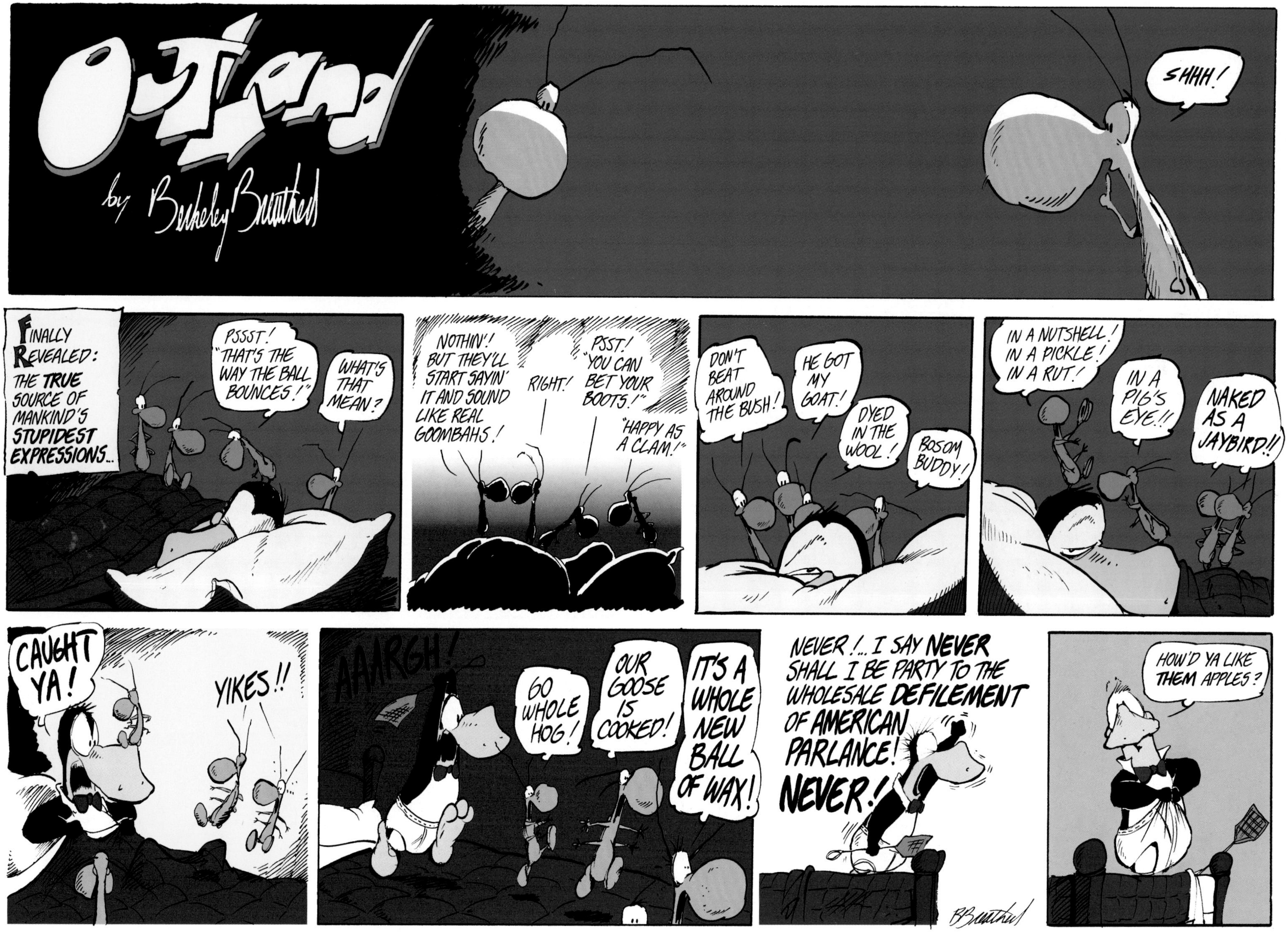
Outland
by Berkeley Breathed
SHHH!
FINALLY REVEALED: THE TRUE SOURCE OF MANKIND'S STUPIDEST EXPRESSIONS...
PSSST! "THAT'S THE WAY THE BALL BOUNCES!"
WHAT'S THAT MEAN?
NOTHIN'! BUT THEY'LL START SAYIN' IT AND SOUND LIKE REAL GOOMBAHS!
RIGHT!
PSST! "YOU CAN BET YOUR BOOTS!"
"HAPPY AS A CLAM!"
DON'T BEAT AROUND THE BUSH!
HE GOT MY GOAT!
DYED IN THE WOOL!
BOSOM BUDDY!
IN A NUTSHELL! IN A PICKLE! IN A RUT!
IN A PIG'S EYE!!
NAKED AS A JAYBIRD!!
CAUGHT YA!
YIKES!!
AAARGH!
GO WHOLE HOG!
OUR GOOSE IS COOKED!
IT'S A WHOLE NEW BALL OF WAX!
NEVER!... I SAY NEVER SHALL I BE PARTY TO THE WHOLESALE DEFILEMENT OF AMERICAN PARLANCE! NEVER!
BBreathed
HOW'D YA LIKE THEM APPLES?

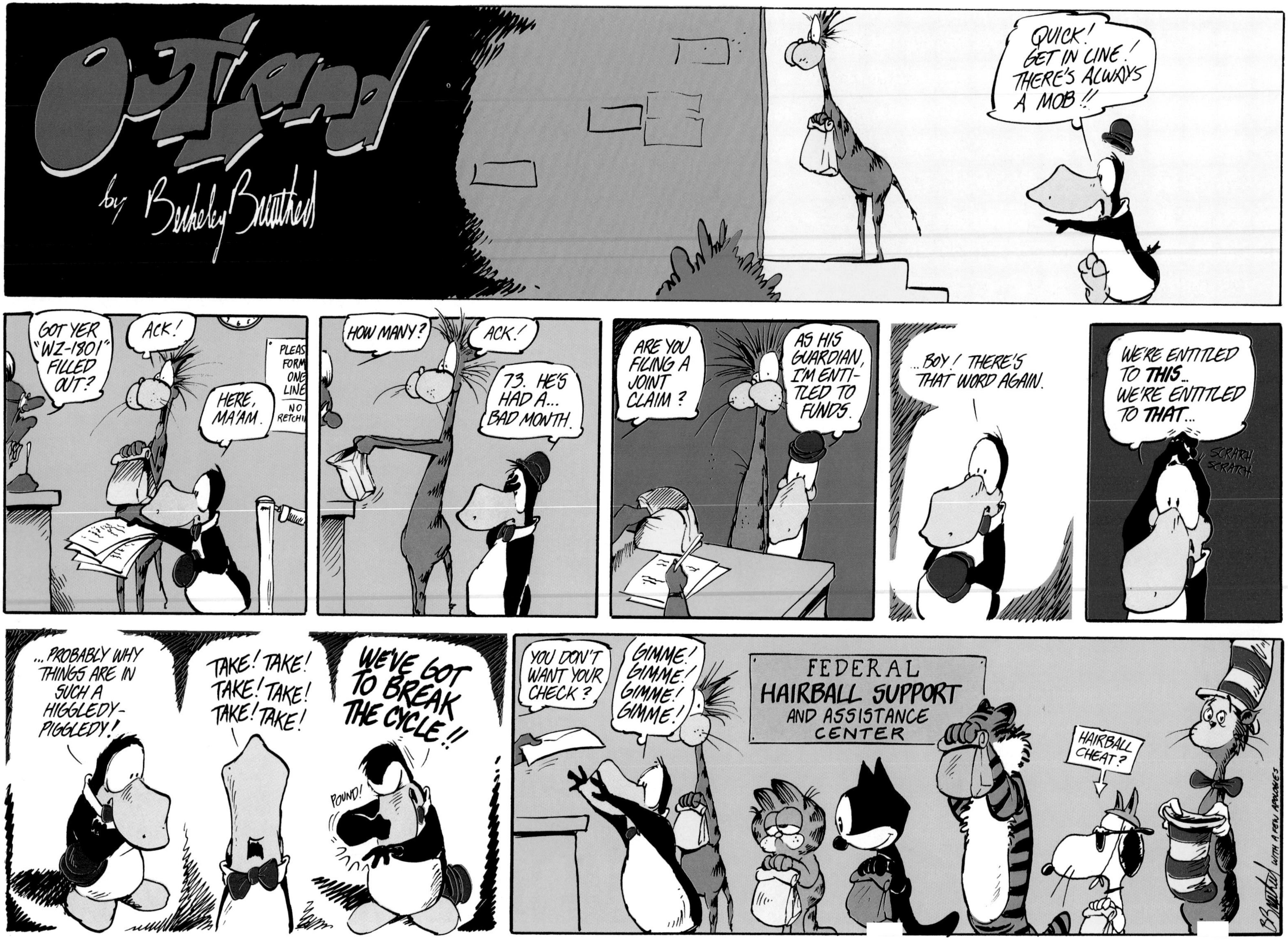
Outland
by Berkeley Breathed
QUICK! GET IN LINE! THERE'S ALWAYS A MOB!!
GOT YER "WZ-1801" FILLED OUT?
ACK!
HERE, MA'AM.
HOW MANY?
ACK!
73. HE'S HAD A... BAD MONTH.
ARE YOU FILING A JOINT CLAIM?
AS HIS GUARDIAN, I'M ENTI-TLED TO FUNDS.
...BOY! THERE'S THAT WORD AGAIN.
WE'RE ENTITLED TO THIS... WE'RE ENTITLED TO THAT...
SCRATCH. SCRATCH.
...PROBABLY WHY THINGS ARE IN SUCH A HIGGLEDY-PIGGLEDY!
TAKE! TAKE! TAKE! TAKE! TAKE! TAKE!
WE'VE GOT TO BREAK THE CYCLE!!
POUND!
YOU DON'T WANT YOUR CHECK?
GIMME! GIMME! GIMME! GIMME!
FEDERAL HAIRBALL SUPPORT AND ASSISTANCE CENTER
HAIRBALL CHEAT?
WITH A FEW APOLOGIES

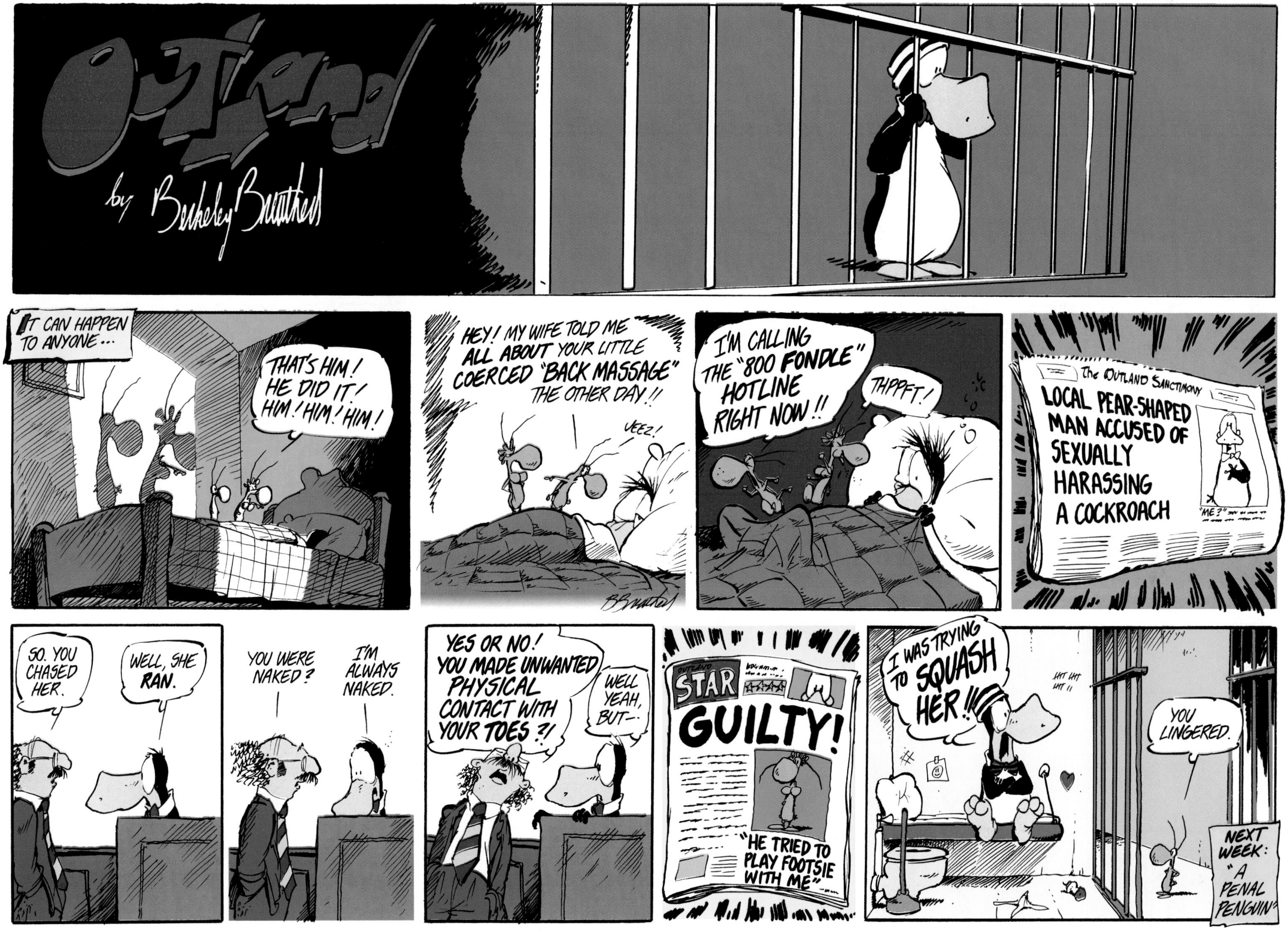
Outland
by Berkeley Breathed
IT CAN HAPPEN TO ANYONE...
THAT'S HIM! HE DID IT! HIM! HIM! HIM!
HEY! MY WIFE TOLD ME ALL ABOUT YOUR LITTLE COERCED "BACK MASSAGE" THE OTHER DAY!!
JEEZ!
I'M CALLING THE "800 FONDLE" HOTLINE RIGHT NOW!!
THPPFT!
The OUTLAND SANCTIMONY
LOCAL PEAR-SHAPED MAN ACCUSED OF SEXUALLY HARASSING A COCKROACH
"ME?"
SO. YOU CHASED HER.
WELL, SHE RAN.
YOU WERE NAKED?
I'M ALWAYS NAKED.
YES OR NO! YOU MADE UNWANTED PHYSICAL CONTACT WITH YOUR TOES?!
WELL YEAH, BUT-
STAR
GUILTY!
"HE TRIED TO PLAY FOOTSIE WITH ME"
I WAS TRYING TO SQUASH HER!!
YOU LINGERED.
NEXT WEEK: "A PENAL PENGUIN"

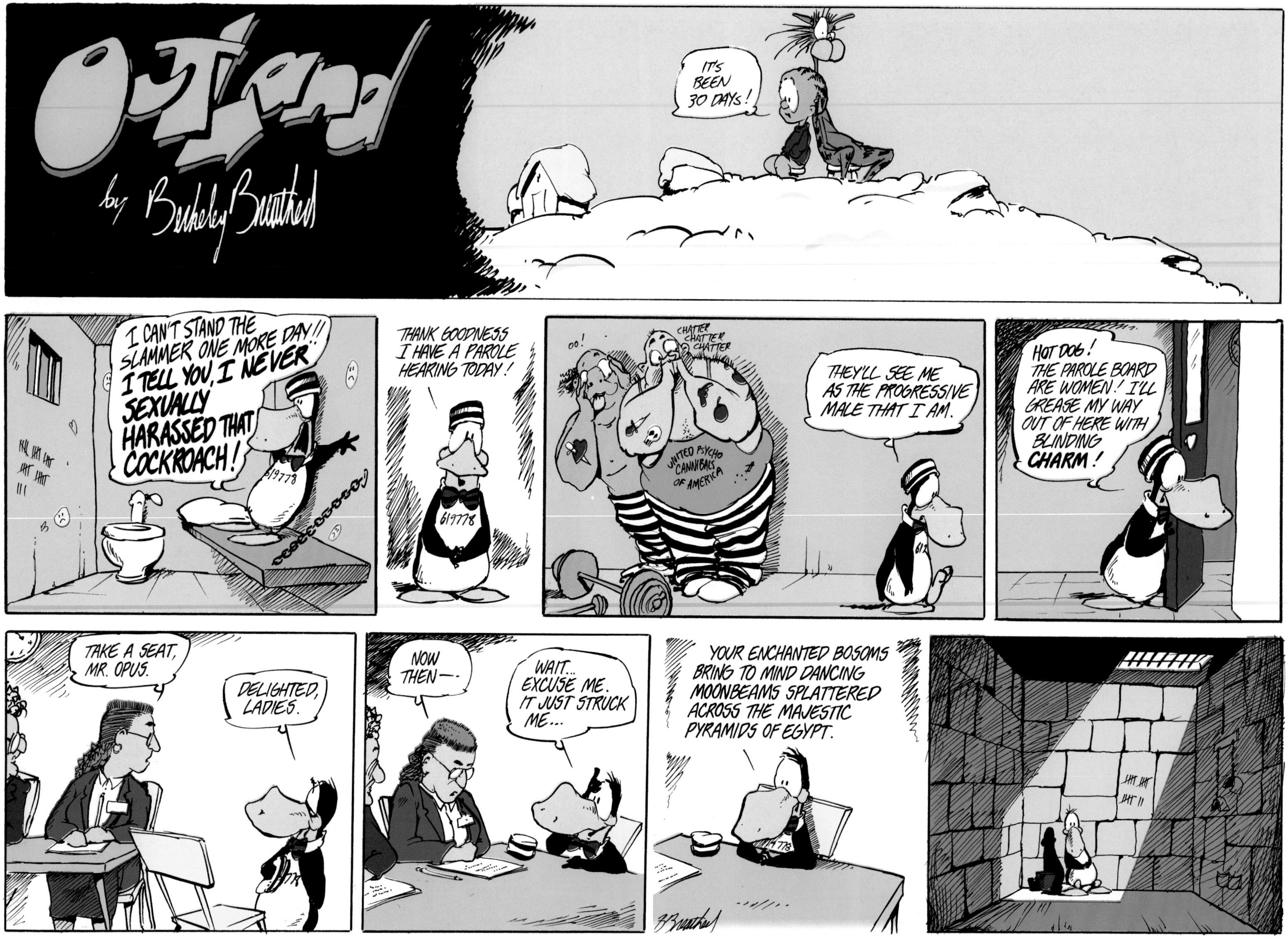
Outland
by Berkeley Breathed
IT'S BEEN 30 DAYS!
I CAN'T STAND THE SLAMMER ONE MORE DAY!! I TELL YOU, I NEVER SEXUALLY HARASSED THAT COCKROACH!
619778
THANK GOODNESS I HAVE A PAROLE HEARING TODAY!
619778
CHATTER CHATTER CHATTER
UNITED PSYCHO CANNIBALS OF AMERICA
THEY'LL SEE ME AS THE PROGRESSIVE MALE THAT I AM.
HOT DOG! THE PAROLE BOARD ARE WOMEN! I'LL GREASE MY WAY OUT OF HERE WITH BLINDING CHARM!
TAKE A SEAT, MR. OPUS.
DELIGHTED, LADIES.
NOW THEN —.
WAIT... EXCUSE ME. IT JUST STRUCK ME...
YOUR ENCHANTED BOSOMS BRING TO MIND DANCING MOONBEAMS SPLATTERED ACROSS THE MAJESTIC PYRAMIDS OF EGYPT.

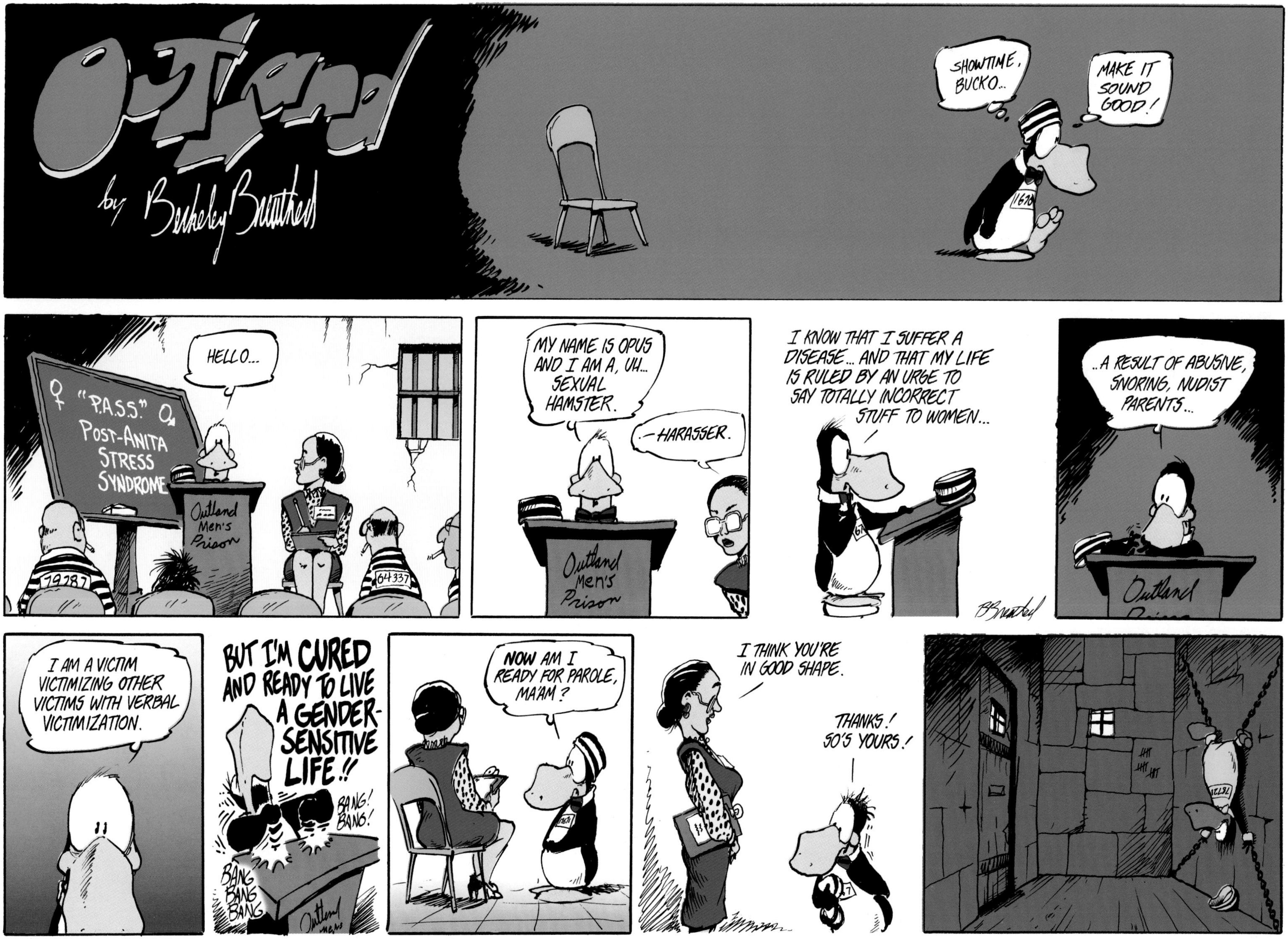
Outland
by Berkeley Breathed
SHOWTIME, BUCKO...
MAKE IT SOUND GOOD!
HELLO...
"P.A.S.S." Post-Anita Stress Syndrome
Outland Men's Prison
79287
64337
MY NAME IS OPUS AND I AM A, UH... SEXUAL HAMSTER.
—HARASSER.
Outland Men's Prison
I KNOW THAT I SUFFER A DISEASE... AND THAT MY LIFE IS RULED BY AN URGE TO SAY TOTALLY INCORRECT STUFF TO WOMEN...
..A RESULT OF ABUSIVE, SNORING, NUDIST PARENTS...
I AM A VICTIM VICTIMIZING OTHER VICTIMS WITH VERBAL VICTIMIZATION.
BUT I'M CURED AND READY TO LIVE A GENDER-SENSITIVE LIFE!!
BANG! BANG!
BANG BANG BANG
NOW AM I READY FOR PAROLE, MA'AM?
I THINK YOU'RE IN GOOD SHAPE.
THANKS! SO'S YOURS!

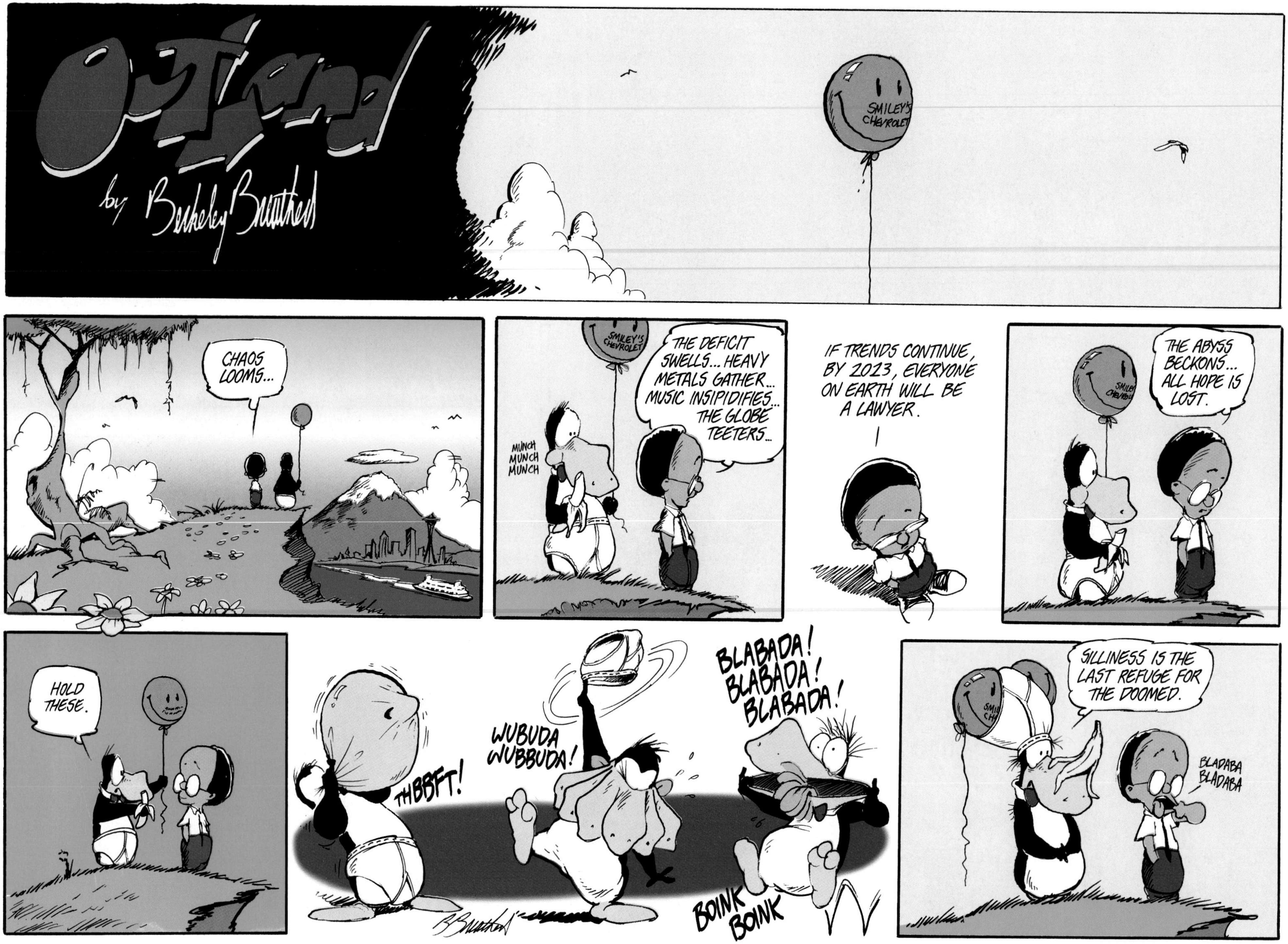

Outland
by Berkeley Breathed
SMILEY'S CHEVROLET
CHAOS LOOMS...
SMILEY'S CHEVROLET
THE DEFICIT SWELLS... HEAVY METALS GATHER... MUSIC INSIPIDIFIES... THE GLOBE TEETERS...
MUNCH MUNCH MUNCH
IF TRENDS CONTINUE, BY 2023, EVERYONE ON EARTH WILL BE A LAWYER.
THE ABYSS BECKONS... ALL HOPE IS LOST.
HOLD THESE.
THBBFT!
WUBUDA WUBBUDA!
BLABADA! BLABADA! BLABADA!
BOINK BOINK
SILLINESS IS THE LAST REFUGE FOR THE DOOMED.
BLADABA BLADABA
B. Breathed

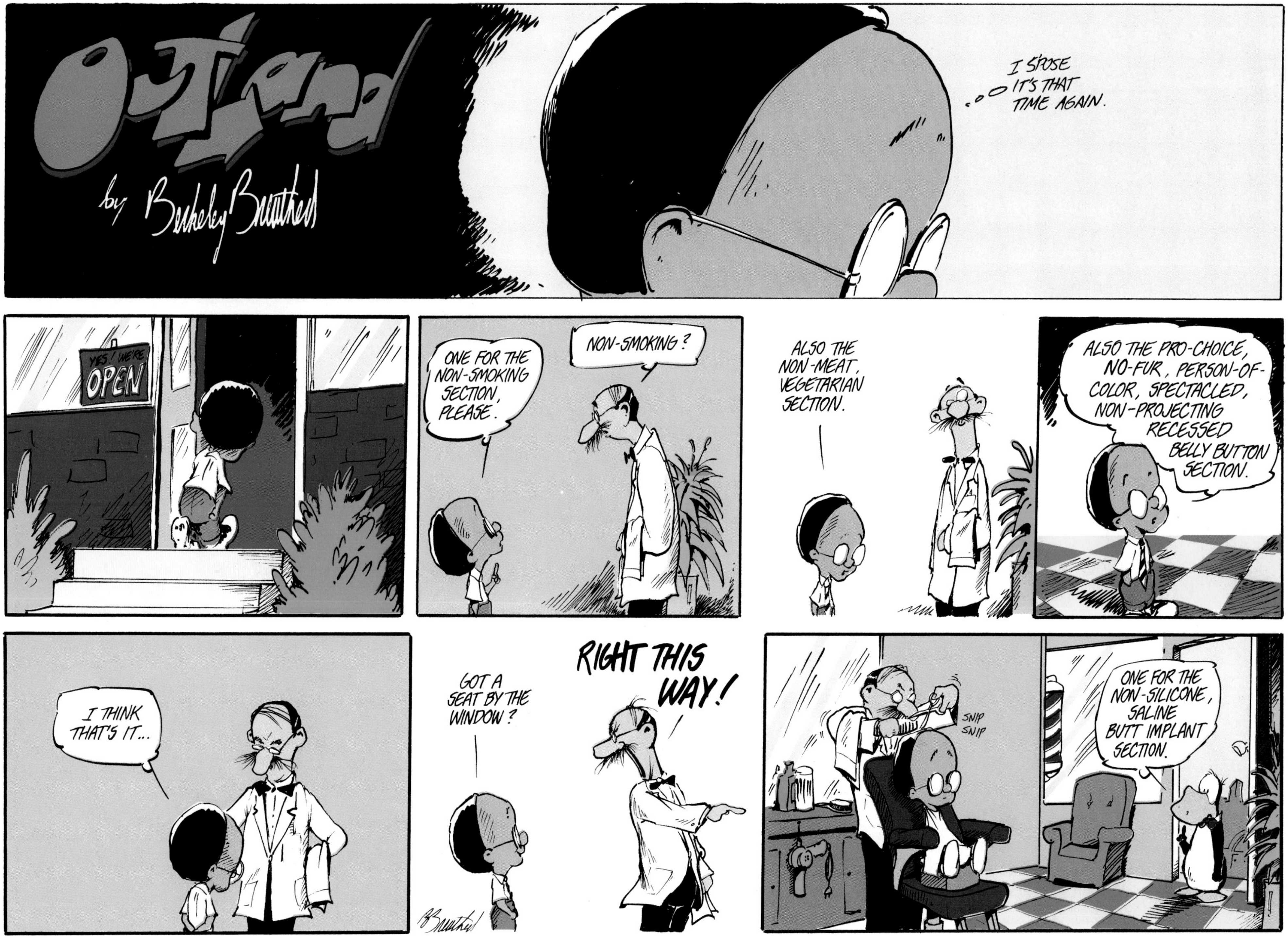

Outland
by Berkeley Breathed
I S'POSE IT'S THAT TIME AGAIN.
YES! WE'RE OPEN
ONE FOR THE NON-SMOKING SECTION, PLEASE.
NON-SMOKING?
ALSO THE NON-MEAT, VEGETARIAN SECTION.
ALSO THE PRO-CHOICE, NO-FUR, PERSON-OF-COLOR, SPECTACLED, NON-PROJECTING RECESSED BELLY BUTTON SECTION.
I THINK THAT'S IT...
GOT A SEAT BY THE WINDOW?
RIGHT THIS WAY!
SNIP SNIP
ONE FOR THE NON-SILICONE, SALINE BUTT IMPLANT SECTION.

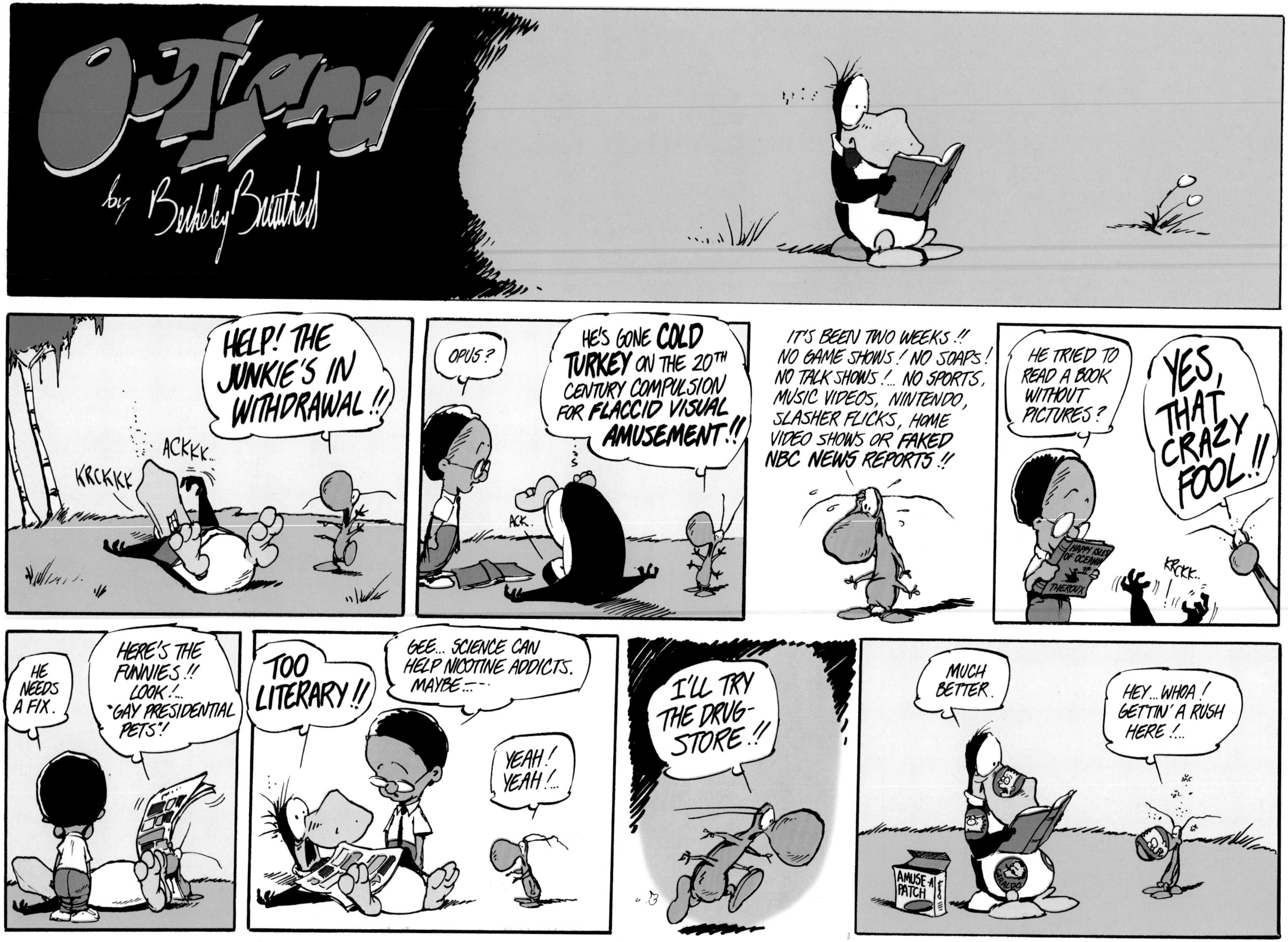

Outland
by Berkeley Breathed
HELP! THE JUNKIE'S IN WITHDRAWAL!!
ACKKK...
KRCKKK
OPUS?
HE'S GONE COLD TURKEY ON THE 20TH CENTURY COMPULSION FOR FLACCID VISUAL AMUSEMENT!!
ACK.
IT'S BEEN TWO WEEKS!! NO GAME SHOWS! NO SOAPS! NO TALK SHOWS!... NO SPORTS, MUSIC VIDEOS, NINTENDO, SLASHER FLICKS, HOME VIDEO SHOWS OR FAKED NBC NEWS REPORTS!!
HE TRIED TO READ A BOOK WITHOUT PICTURES?
YES, THAT CRAZY FOOL!!
HAPPY ISLES OF OCEANIA
THEROUX
KRCKK..
HE NEEDS A FIX.
HERE'S THE FUNNIES!! LOOK!... "GAY PRESIDENTIAL PETS"!
TOO LITERARY!!
GEE... SCIENCE CAN HELP NICOTINE ADDICTS. MAYBE...
YEAH! YEAH!...
I'LL TRY THE DRUG-STORE!!
MUCH BETTER.
HEY... WHOA! GETTIN' A RUSH HERE!...
AMUSE-A PATCH
GERALDO

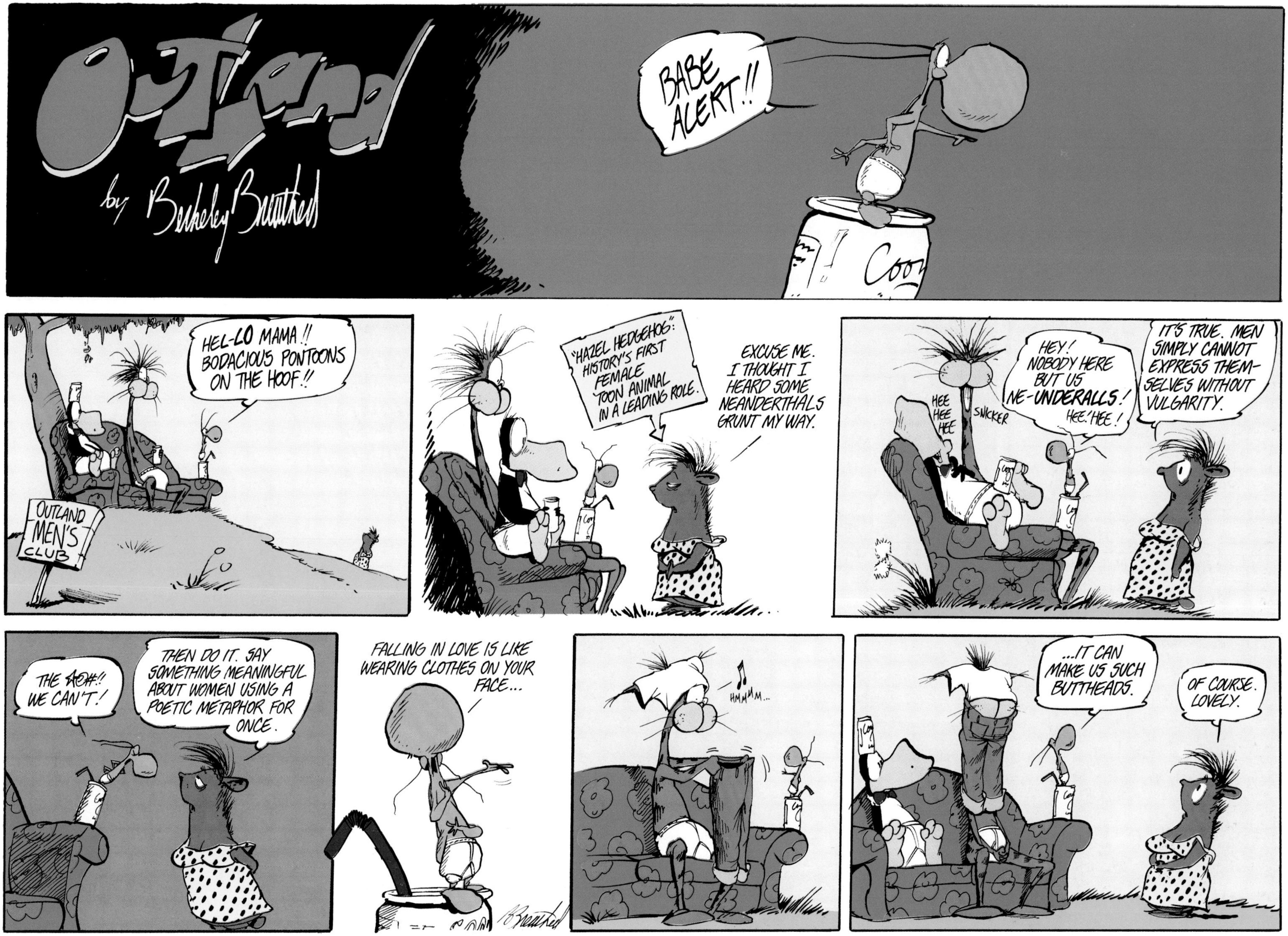

Outland
by Berkeley Breathed
BABE ALERT!!
OUTLAND MEN'S CLUB
HEL-LO MAMA!! BODACIOUS PONTOONS ON THE HOOF!!
"HAZEL HEDGEHOG": HISTORY'S FIRST FEMALE 'TOON ANIMAL IN A LEADING ROLE.
EXCUSE ME. I THOUGHT I HEARD SOME NEANDERTHALS GRUNT MY WAY.
HEE HEE HEE
SNICKER
HEY! NOBODY HERE BUT US NE-**UNDERALLS**! HEE! HEE!
IT'S TRUE. MEN SIMPLY CANNOT EXPRESS THEM-SELVES WITHOUT VULGARITY.
THE *@#!! WE CAN'T!
THEN DO IT. SAY SOMETHING MEANINGFUL ABOUT WOMEN USING A POETIC METAPHOR FOR ONCE.
FALLING IN LOVE IS LIKE WEARING CLOTHES ON YOUR FACE...
HMMMM...
...IT CAN MAKE US SUCH BUTTHEADS.
OF COURSE. LOVELY.
Breathed

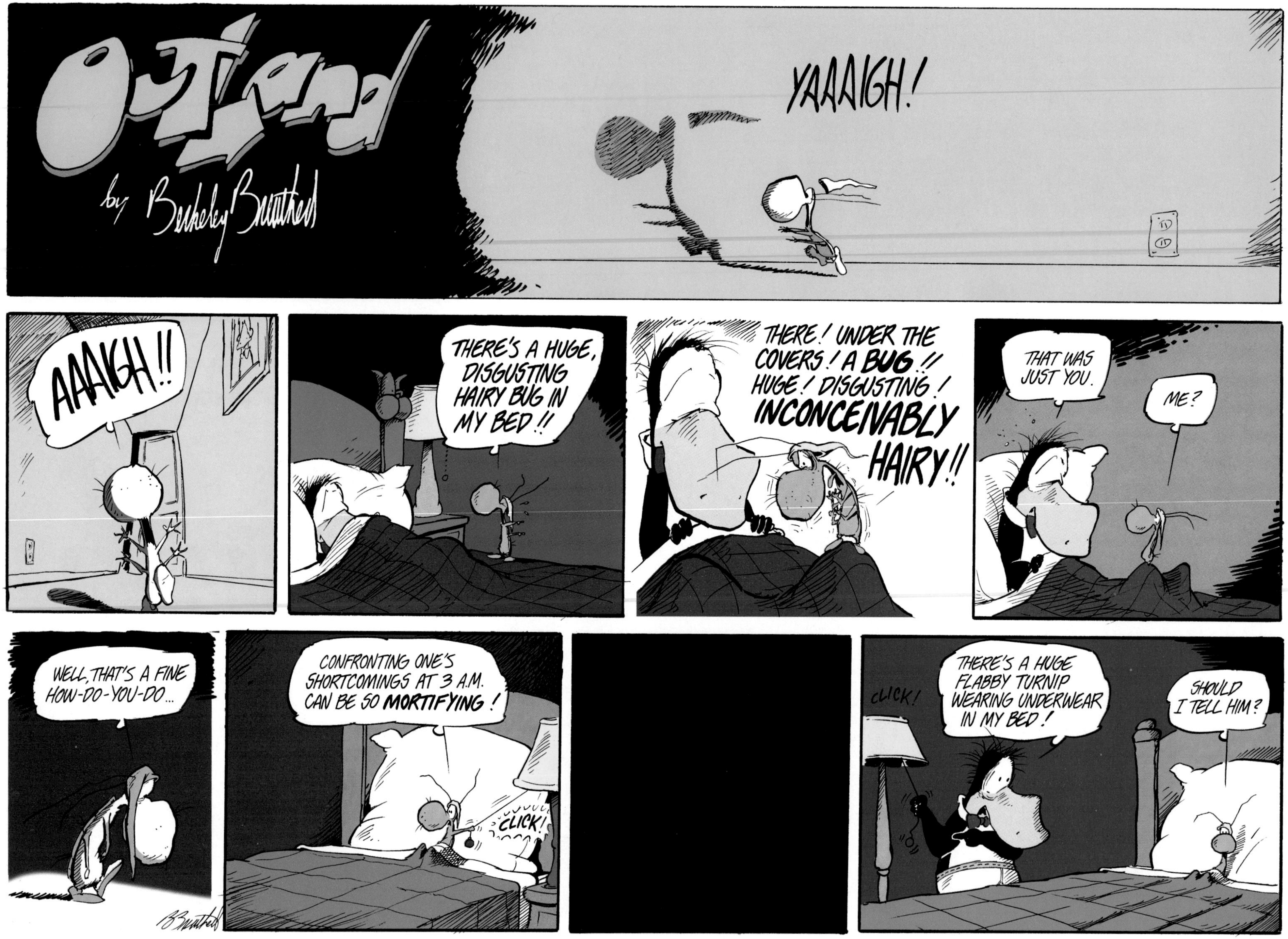
Outland
by Berkeley Breathed
YAAAIGH!
AAAIGH!!
THERE'S A HUGE, DISGUSTING HAIRY BUG IN MY BED!!
THERE! UNDER THE COVERS! A BUG!! HUGE! DISGUSTING! INCONCEIVABLY HAIRY!!
THAT WAS JUST YOU.
ME?
WELL, THAT'S A FINE HOW-DO-YOU-DO...
CONFRONTING ONE'S SHORTCOMINGS AT 3 A.M. CAN BE SO MORTIFYING!
CLICK!
CLICK!
THERE'S A HUGE FLABBY TURNIP WEARING UNDERWEAR IN MY BED!
SHOULD I TELL HIM?
B Breathed

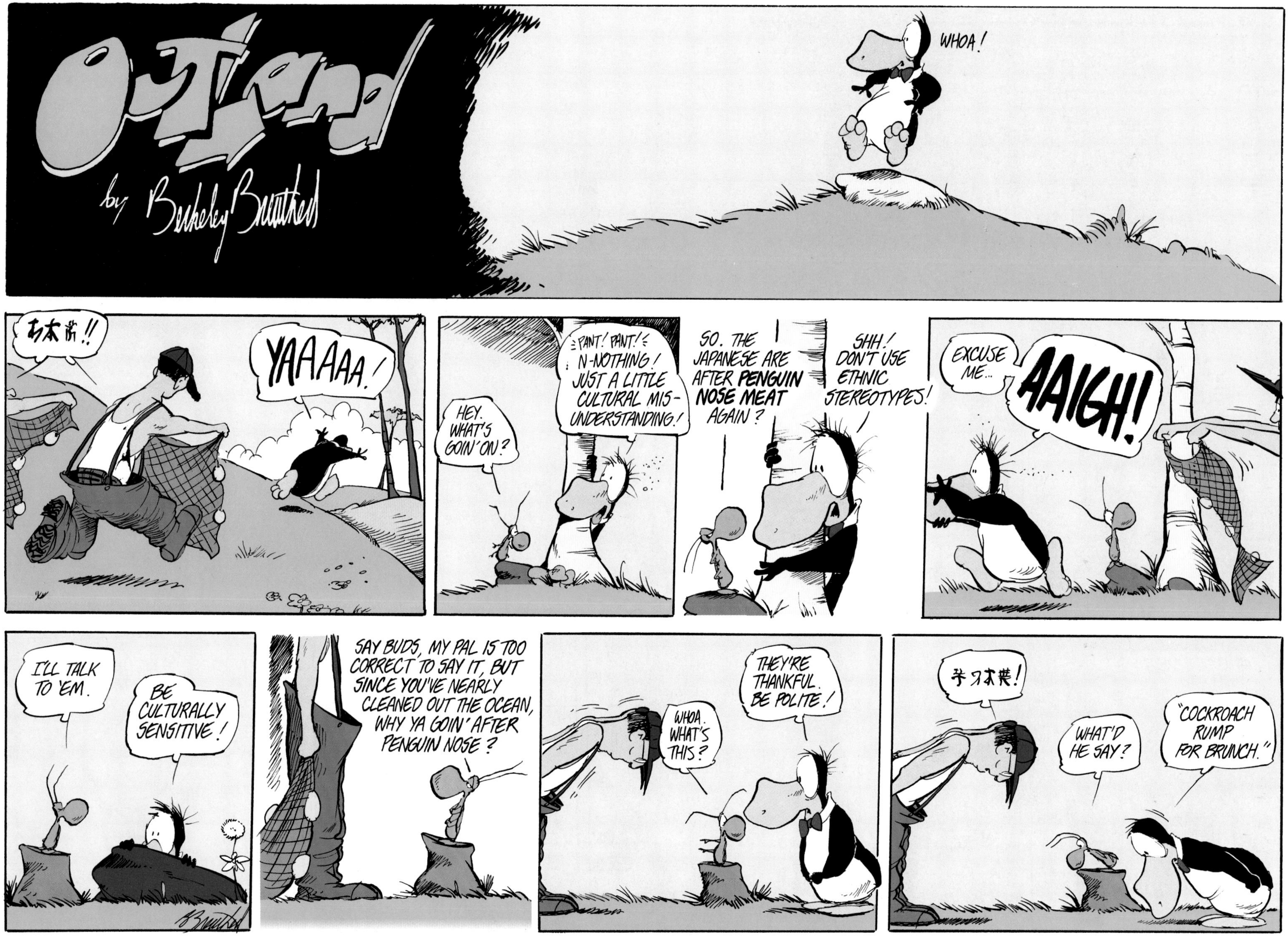
Outland
by Berkeley Breathed
WHOA!
YAAAAA!
HEY. WHAT'S GOIN' ON?
PANT! PANT! N-NOTHING! JUST A LITTLE CULTURAL MIS-UNDERSTANDING!
SO. THE JAPANESE ARE AFTER **PENGUIN NOSE MEAT** AGAIN?
SHH! DON'T USE ETHNIC STEREOTYPES!
EXCUSE ME...
AAIGH!
I'LL TALK TO 'EM.
BE CULTURALLY SENSITIVE!
SAY BUDS, MY PAL IS TOO CORRECT TO SAY IT, BUT SINCE YOU'VE NEARLY CLEANED OUT THE OCEAN, WHY YA GOIN' AFTER PENGUIN NOSE?
WHOA. WHAT'S THIS?
THEY'RE THANKFUL. BE POLITE!
WHAT'D HE SAY?
"COCKROACH RUMP FOR BRUNCH."

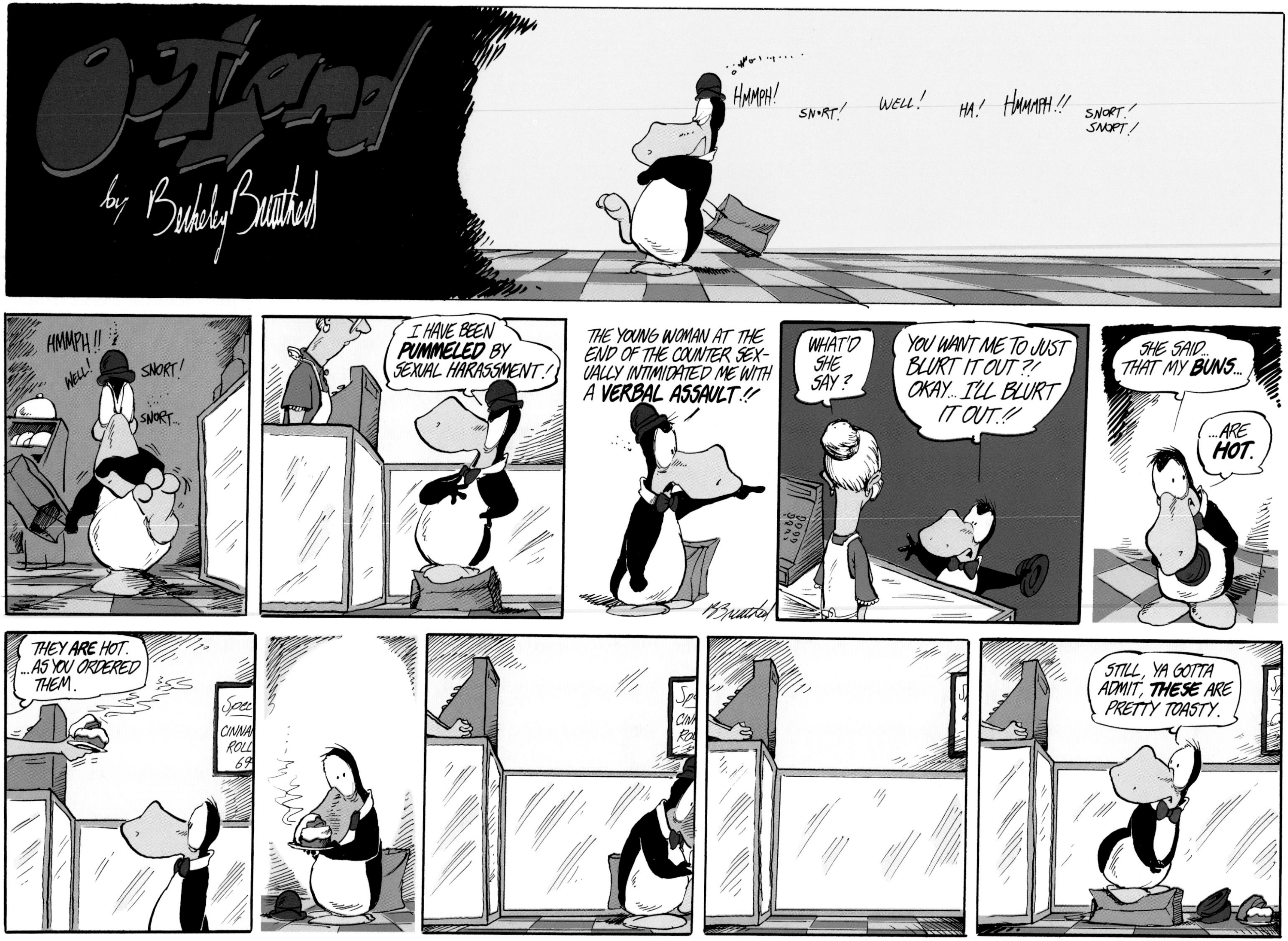
Outland
by Berkeley Breathed
HMMPH!
SNORT!
WELL!
HA!
HMMPH!!
SNORT! SNORT!
HMMPH!!
WELL!
SNORT!
SNORT...
I HAVE BEEN **PUMMELED** BY SEXUAL HARASSMENT!
THE YOUNG WOMAN AT THE END OF THE COUNTER SEXUALLY INTIMIDATED ME WITH A **VERBAL ASSAULT**!!
WHAT'D SHE SAY?
YOU WANT ME TO JUST BLURT IT OUT?! OKAY... I'LL BLURT IT OUT!!
SHE SAID... THAT MY **BUNS**...
...ARE **HOT**.
THEY **ARE** HOT. ...AS YOU ORDERED THEM.
STILL, YA GOTTA ADMIT, **THESE** ARE PRETTY TOASTY.

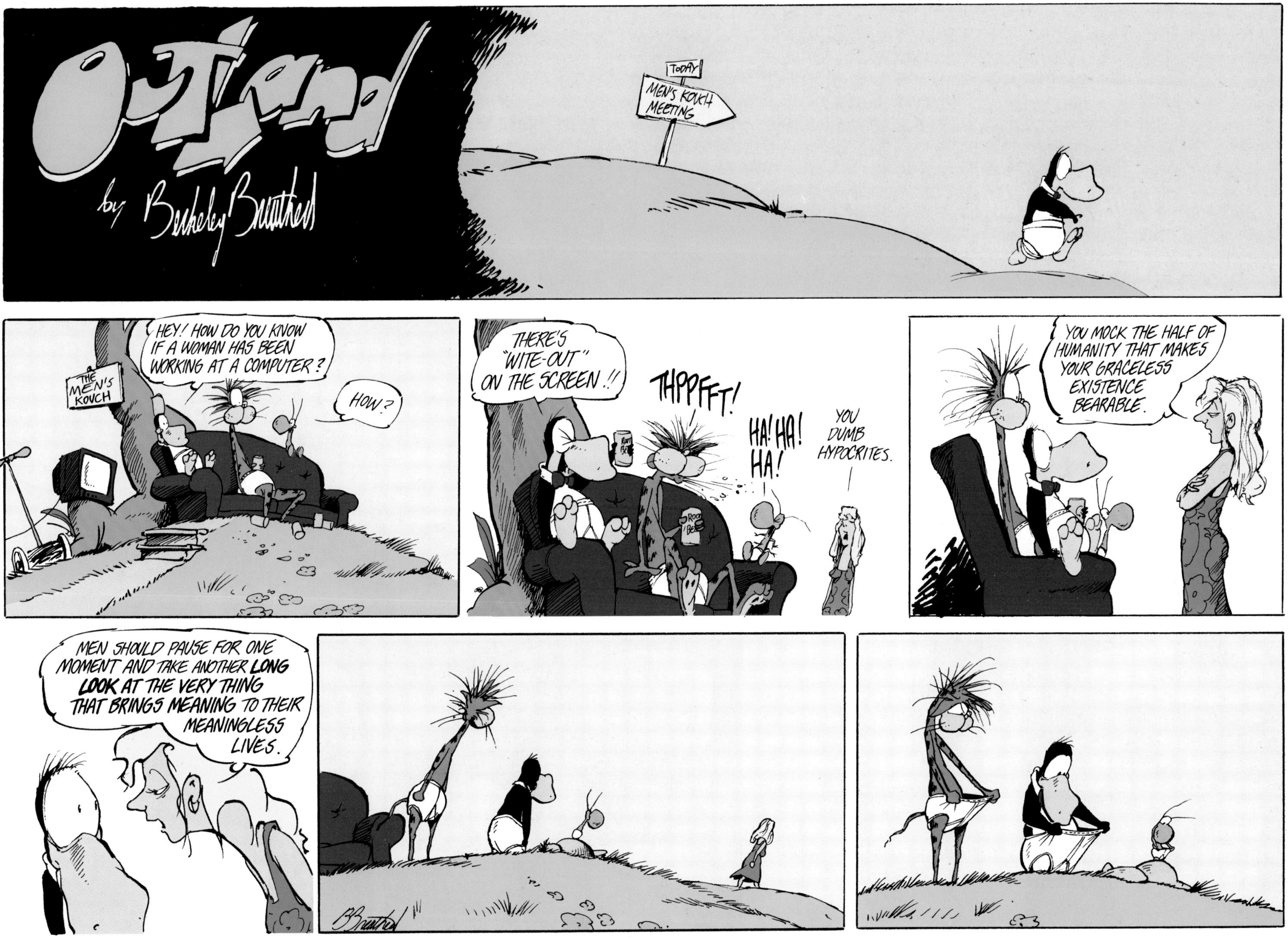
Outland
by Berkeley Breathed
TODAY
MEN'S KOUCH MEETING
THE MEN'S KOUCH
HEY! HOW DO YOU KNOW IF A WOMAN HAS BEEN WORKING AT A COMPUTER?
HOW?
THERE'S "WITE-OUT" ON THE SCREEN!!
THPPFFT!
HA! HA! HA!
YOU DUMB HYPOCRITES.
YOU MOCK THE HALF OF HUMANITY THAT MAKES YOUR GRACELESS EXISTENCE BEARABLE.
MEN SHOULD PAUSE FOR ONE MOMENT AND TAKE ANOTHER **LONG LOOK** AT THE VERY THING THAT BRINGS **MEANING** TO THEIR MEANINGLESS LIVES.
B Breathed

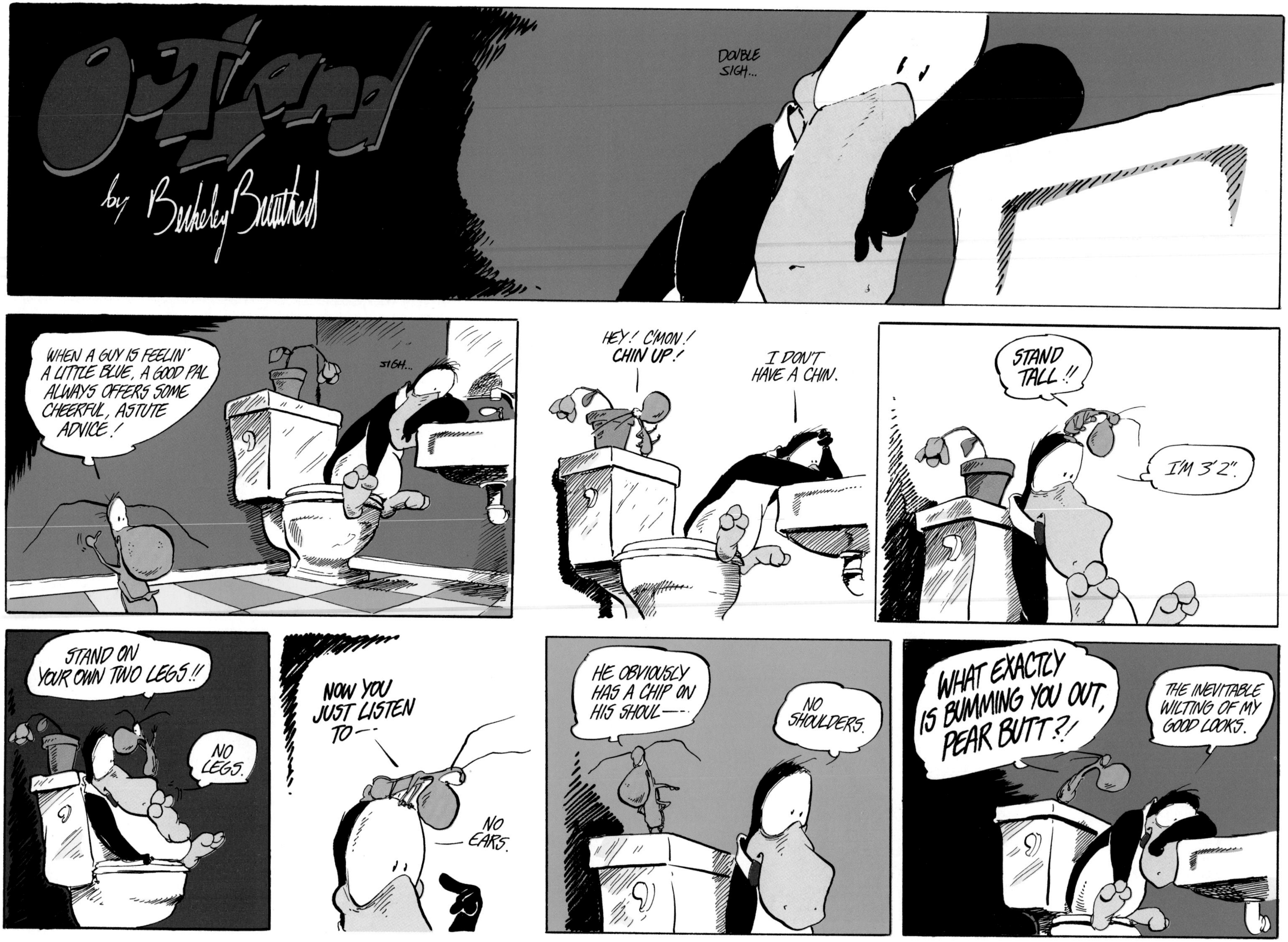
Outland
by Berkeley Breathed
DOUBLE SIGH...
WHEN A GUY IS FEELIN' A LITTLE BLUE, A GOOD PAL ALWAYS OFFERS SOME CHEERFUL, ASTUTE ADVICE!
SIGH...
HEY! C'MON! CHIN UP!
I DON'T HAVE A CHIN.
STAND TALL!!
I'M 3'2".
STAND ON YOUR OWN TWO LEGS!!
NO LEGS.
NOW YOU JUST LISTEN TO--
NO EARS.
HE OBVIOUSLY HAS A CHIP ON HIS SHOUL--
NO SHOULDERS.
WHAT EXACTLY IS BUMMING YOU OUT, PEAR BUTT?!
THE INEVITABLE WILTING OF MY GOOD LOOKS.

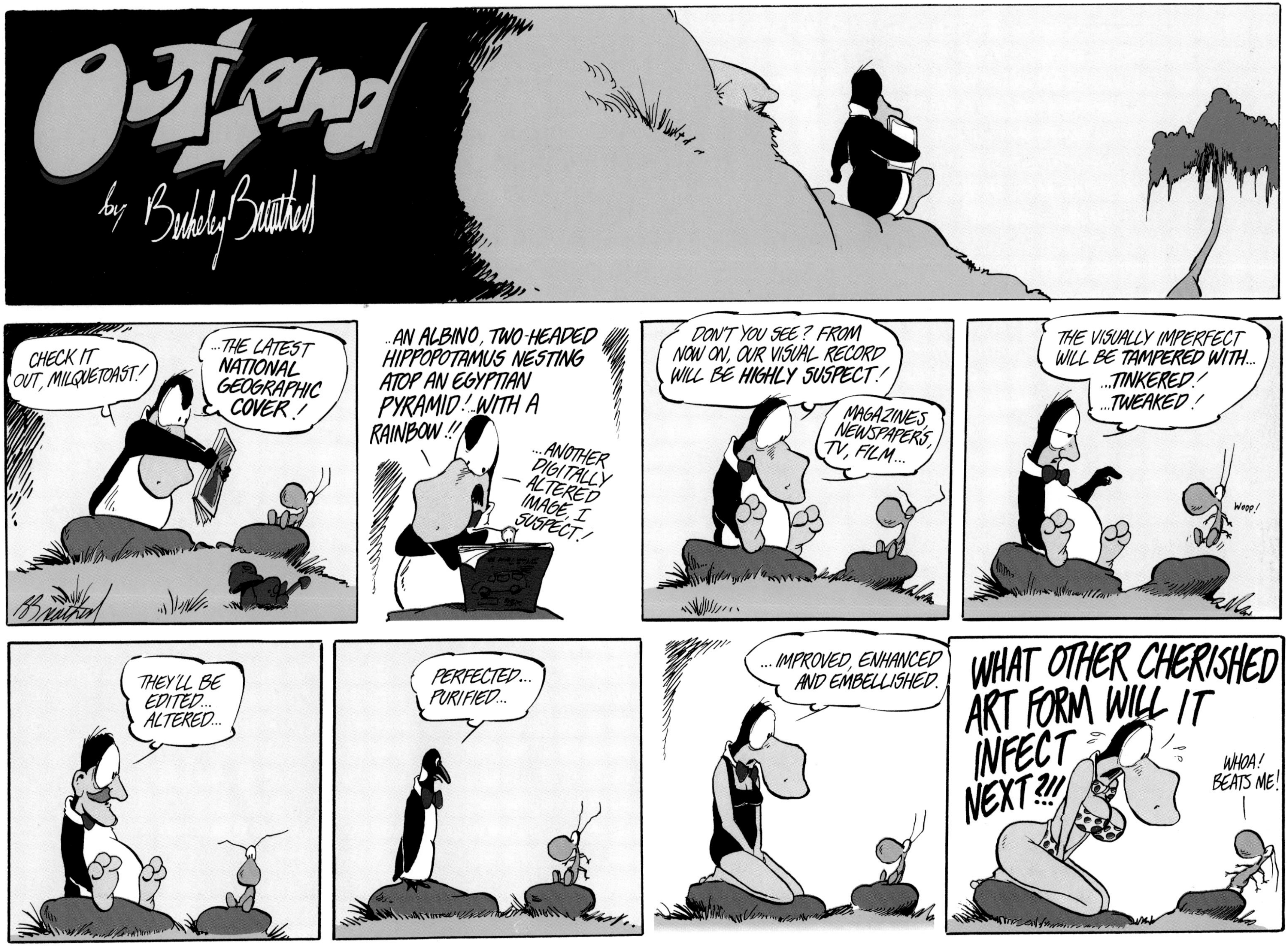

Outland
by Berkeley Breathed
CHECK IT OUT, MILQUETOAST!
...THE LATEST NATIONAL GEOGRAPHIC COVER!
...AN ALBINO, TWO-HEADED HIPPOPOTAMUS NESTING ATOP AN EGYPTIAN PYRAMID!...WITH A RAINBOW!!
...ANOTHER DIGITALLY ALTERED IMAGE, I SUSPECT!
DON'T YOU SEE? FROM NOW ON, OUR VISUAL RECORD WILL BE HIGHLY SUSPECT!
MAGAZINES, NEWSPAPERS, TV, FILM...
THE VISUALLY IMPERFECT WILL BE TAMPERED WITH... ...TINKERED! ...TWEAKED!
WOOP!
THEY'LL BE EDITED... ALTERED...
PERFECTED... PURIFIED...
...IMPROVED, ENHANCED AND EMBELLISHED.
WHAT OTHER CHERISHED ART FORM WILL IT INFECT NEXT?!!
WHOA! BEATS ME!

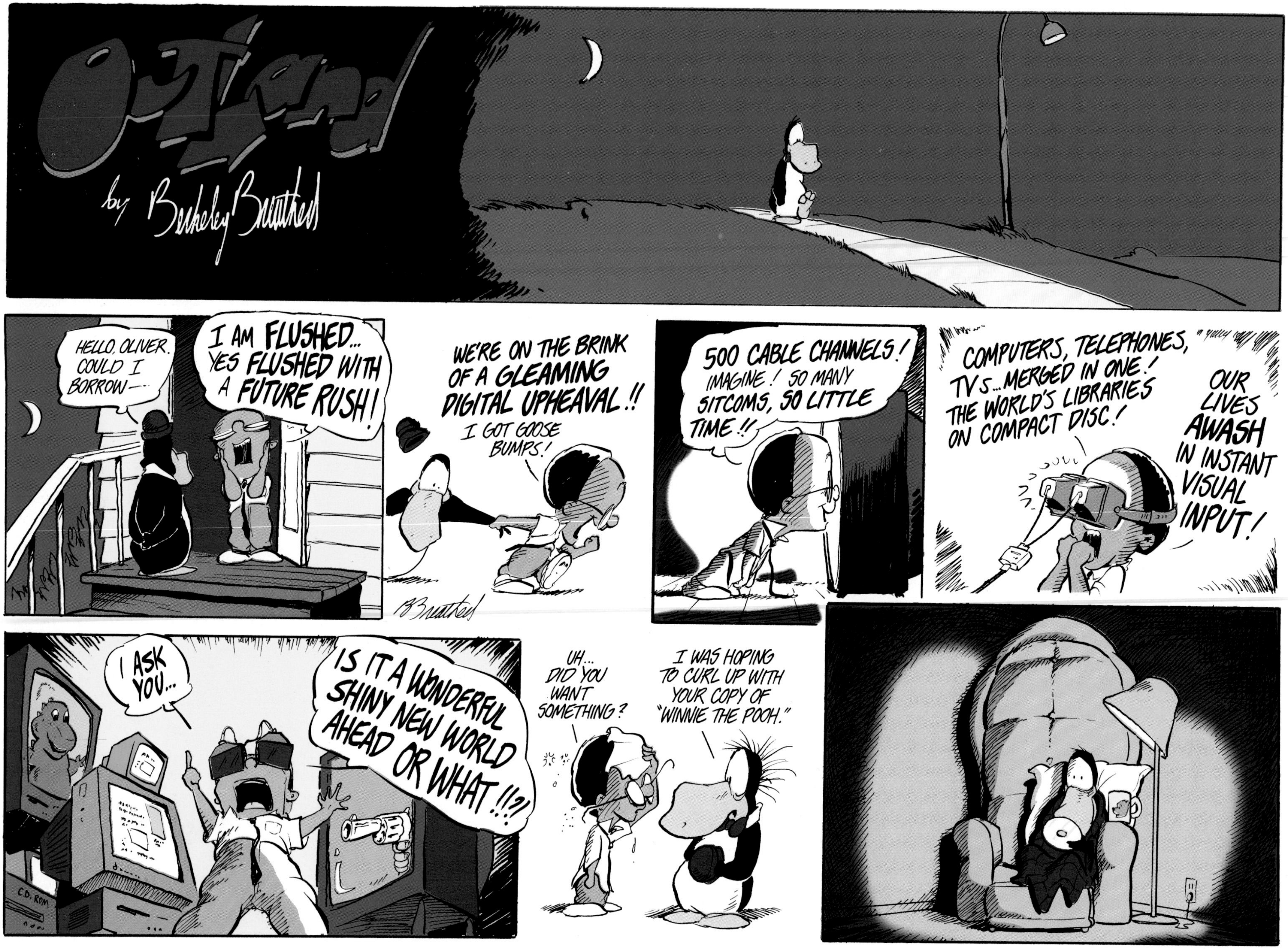
Outland
by Berkeley Breathed
HELLO, OLIVER. COULD I BORROW—
I AM FLUSHED... YES FLUSHED WITH A FUTURE RUSH!
WE'RE ON THE BRINK OF A GLEAMING DIGITAL UPHEAVAL!!
I GOT GOOSE BUMPS!
B Breathed
500 CABLE CHANNELS! IMAGINE! SO MANY SITCOMS, SO LITTLE TIME!!
COMPUTERS, TELEPHONES, TVs...MERGED IN ONE! THE WORLD'S LIBRARIES ON COMPACT DISC!
OUR LIVES AWASH IN INSTANT VISUAL INPUT!
I ASK YOU...
IS IT A WONDERFUL SHINY NEW WORLD AHEAD OR WHAT!!?!
C.D. ROM
UH... DID YOU WANT SOMETHING?
I WAS HOPING TO CURL UP WITH YOUR COPY OF "WINNIE THE POOH."

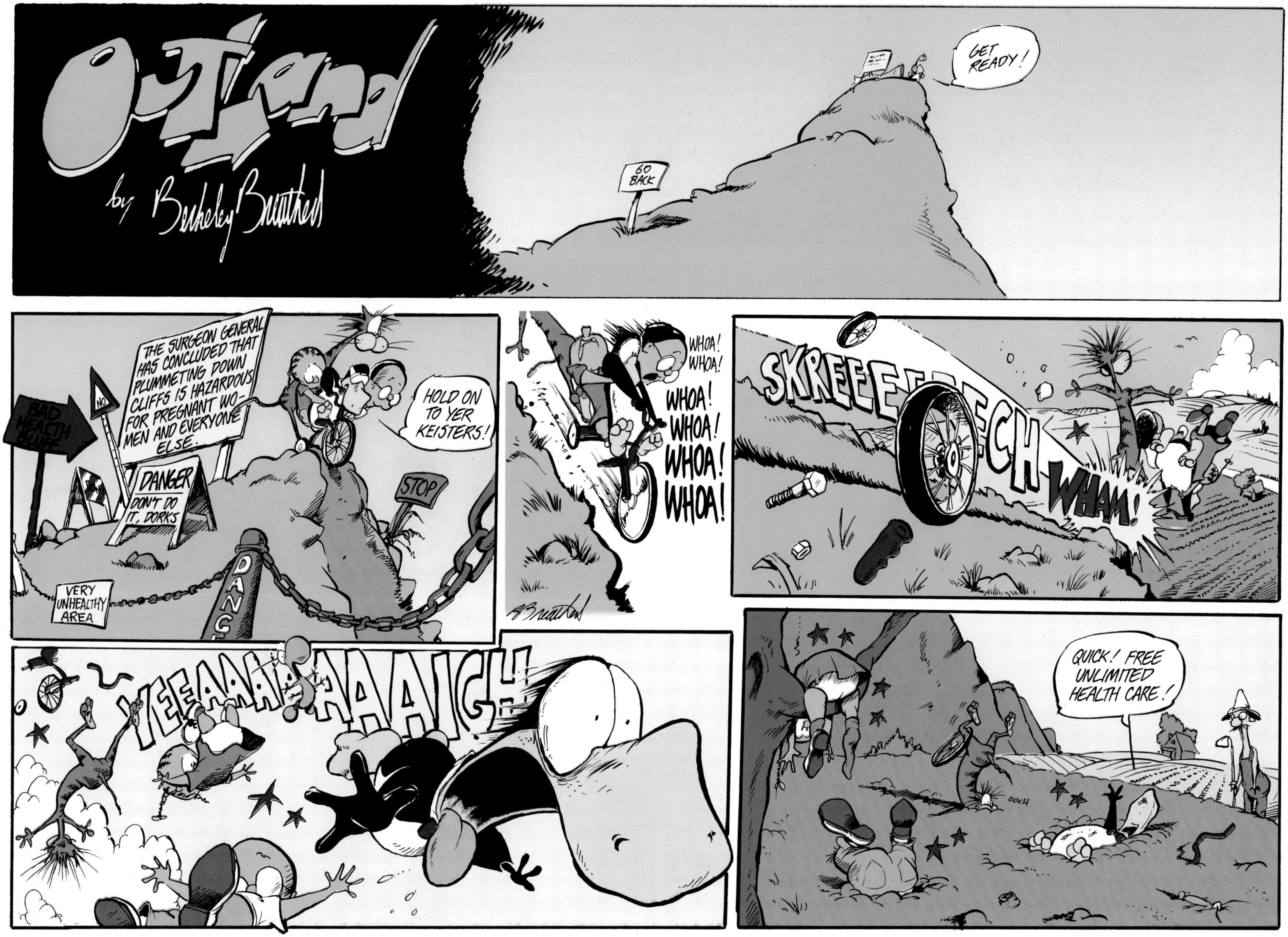
Outland
by Berkeley Breathed
GO BACK
GET READY!
BAD HEALTH OLUFF
NO
THE SURGEON GENERAL HAS CONCLUDED THAT PLUMMETING DOWN CLIFFS IS HAZARDOUS FOR PREGNANT WOMEN AND EVERYONE ELSE.
DANGER DON'T DO IT, DORKS
STOP
VERY UNHEALTHY AREA
DANGE
HOLD ON TO YER KEISTERS!
WHOA! WHOA!
WHOA! WHOA! WHOA! WHOA!
SKREEEEEEECH
WHAM!
YEEAAAHHAAAAIGH!
OOCH
QUICK! FREE UNLIMITED HEALTH CARE!

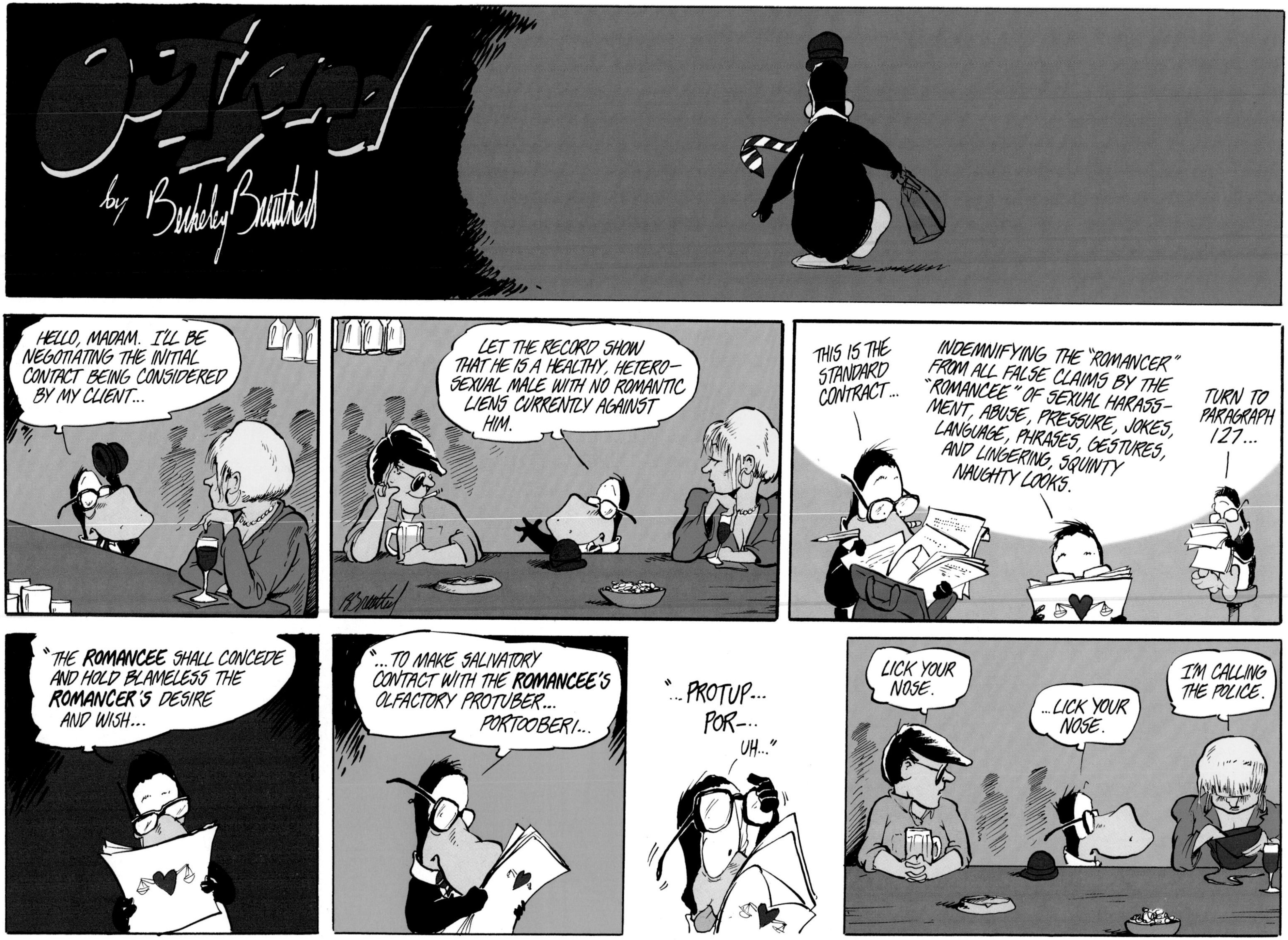
Outland
by Berkeley Breathed
HELLO, MADAM. I'LL BE NEGOTIATING THE INITIAL CONTACT BEING CONSIDERED BY MY CLIENT...
LET THE RECORD SHOW THAT HE IS A HEALTHY, HETERO-SEXUAL MALE WITH NO ROMANTIC LIENS CURRENTLY AGAINST HIM.
THIS IS THE STANDARD CONTRACT...
INDEMNIFYING THE "ROMANCER" FROM ALL FALSE CLAIMS BY THE "ROMANCEE" OF SEXUAL HARASS-MENT, ABUSE, PRESSURE, JOKES, LANGUAGE, PHRASES, GESTURES, AND LINGERING, SQUINTY NAUGHTY LOOKS.
TURN TO PARAGRAPH 127...
"THE **ROMANCEE** SHALL CONCEDE AND HOLD BLAMELESS THE **ROMANCER**'S DESIRE AND WISH...
"...TO MAKE SALIVATORY CONTACT WITH THE **ROMANCEE**'S OLFACTORY PROTUBER... PORTOOBER!...
"...PROTUP... POR-... UH..."
LICK YOUR NOSE.
...LICK YOUR NOSE.
I'M CALLING THE POLICE.

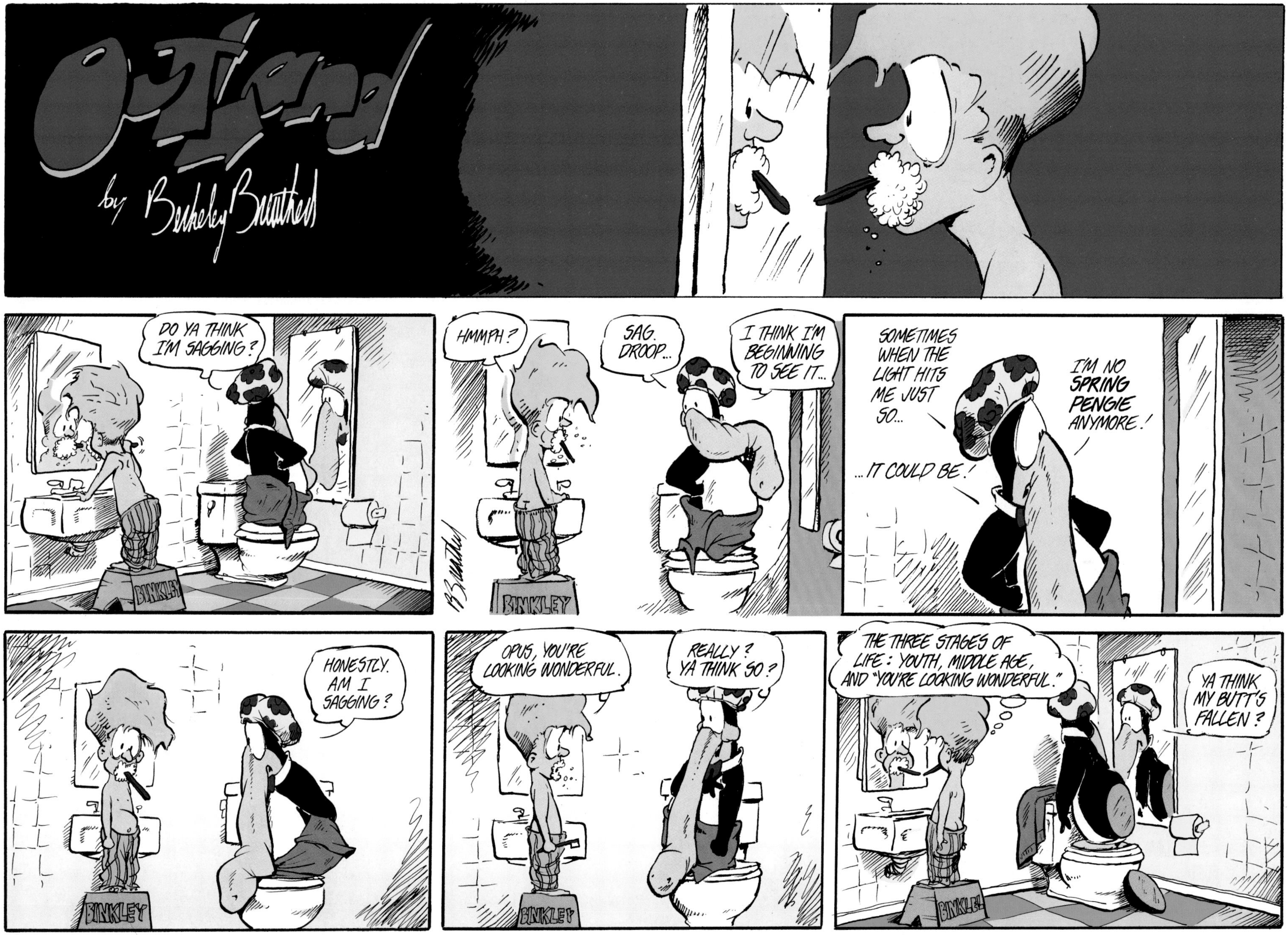
Outland
by Berkeley Breathed
DO YA THINK I'M SAGGING?
BINKLEY
HMMPH?
SAG. DROOP...
I THINK I'M BEGINNING TO SEE IT...
BINKLEY
SOMETIMES WHEN THE LIGHT HITS ME JUST SO...
...IT COULD BE!
I'M NO SPRING PENGIE ANYMORE!
HONESTLY. AM I SAGGING?
BINKLEY
OPUS, YOU'RE LOOKING WONDERFUL.
REALLY? YA THINK SO?
BINKLEY
THE THREE STAGES OF LIFE: YOUTH, MIDDLE AGE, AND "YOU'RE LOOKING WONDERFUL."
YA THINK MY BUTT'S FALLEN?
BINKLEY

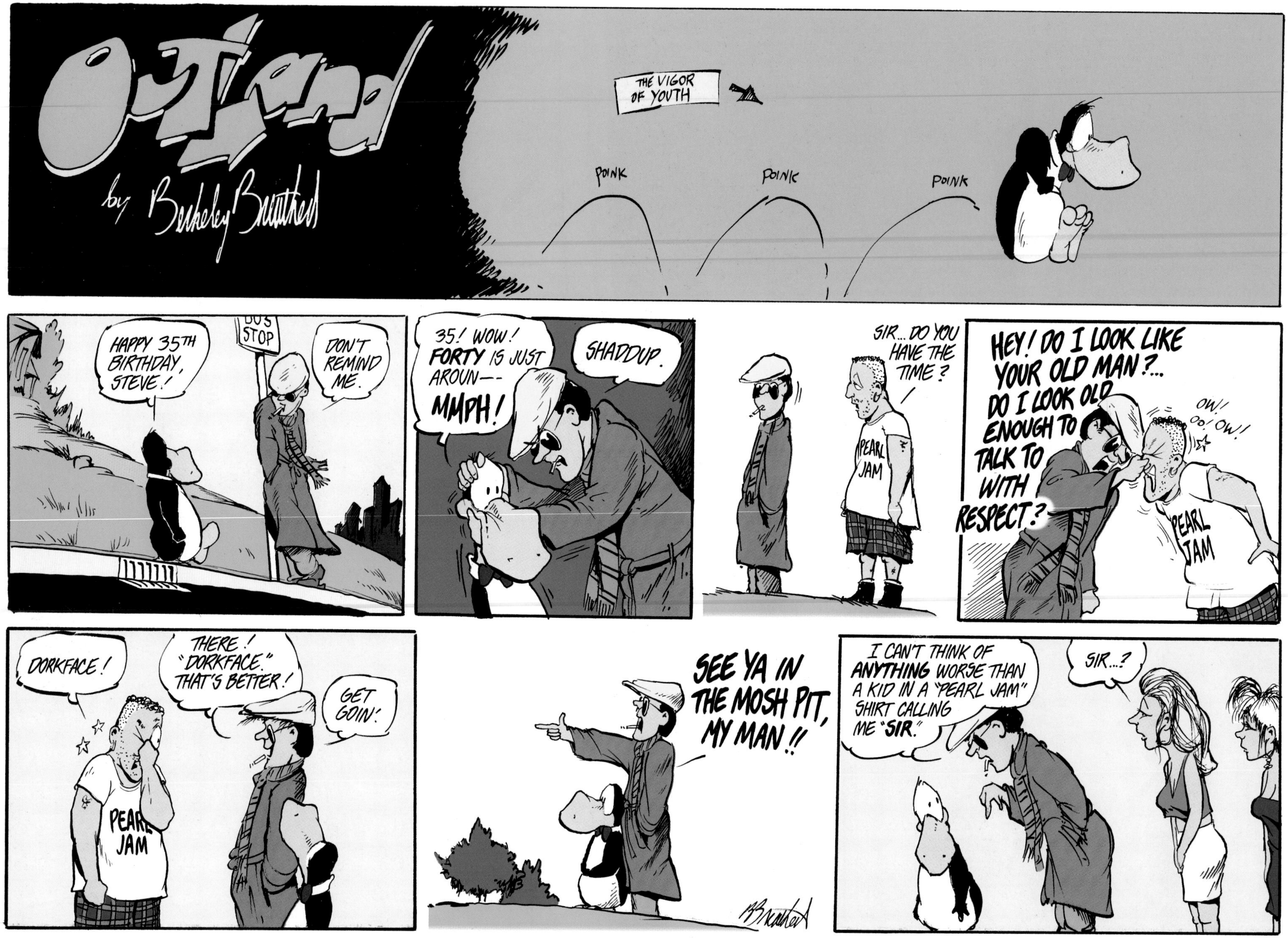
Outland
by Berkeley Breathed
THE VIGOR OF YOUTH
POINK
POINK
POINK
HAPPY 35TH BIRTHDAY, STEVE!
BUS STOP
DON'T REMIND ME.
35! WOW! FORTY IS JUST AROUN-- MMPH!
SHADDUP.
SIR... DO YOU HAVE THE TIME?
PEARL JAM
HEY! DO I LOOK LIKE YOUR OLD MAN?... DO I LOOK OLD ENOUGH TO TALK TO WITH RESPECT?
OW! OO! OW!
PEARL JAM
DORKFACE!
THERE! "DORKFACE." THAT'S BETTER!
GET GOIN'!
PEARL JAM
SEE YA IN THE MOSH PIT, MY MAN!!
I CAN'T THINK OF ANYTHING WORSE THAN A KID IN A "PEARL JAM" SHIRT CALLING ME "SIR."
SIR...?
B. Breathed

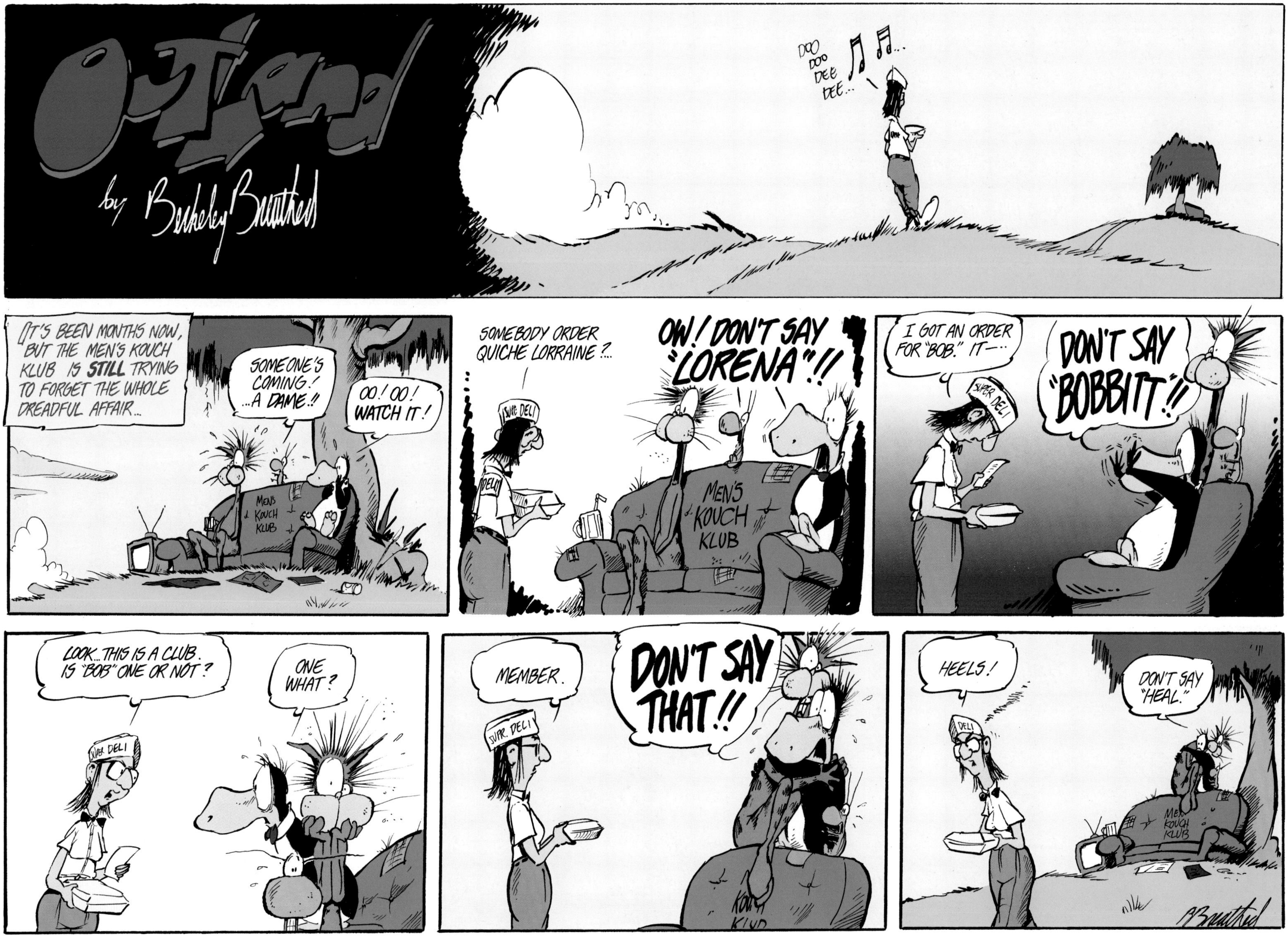

Outland
by Berkeley Breathed
DOO DOO DEE DEE...
IT'S BEEN MONTHS NOW, BUT THE MEN'S KOUCH KLUB IS STILL TRYING TO FORGET THE WHOLE DREADFUL AFFAIR...
SOMEONE'S COMING! ...A DAME!!
OO! OO! WATCH IT!
MEN'S KOUCH KLUB
SOMEBODY ORDER QUICHE LORRAINE?...
OW! DON'T SAY "LORENA"!!
SUPR. DELI
MEN'S KOUCH KLUB
I GOT AN ORDER FOR "BOB." IT—...
DON'T SAY "BOBBITT"!!
LOOK... THIS IS A CLUB. IS "BOB" ONE OR NOT?
ONE WHAT?
MEMBER.
DON'T SAY THAT!!
HEELS!
DON'T SAY "HEAL."
B. Breathed

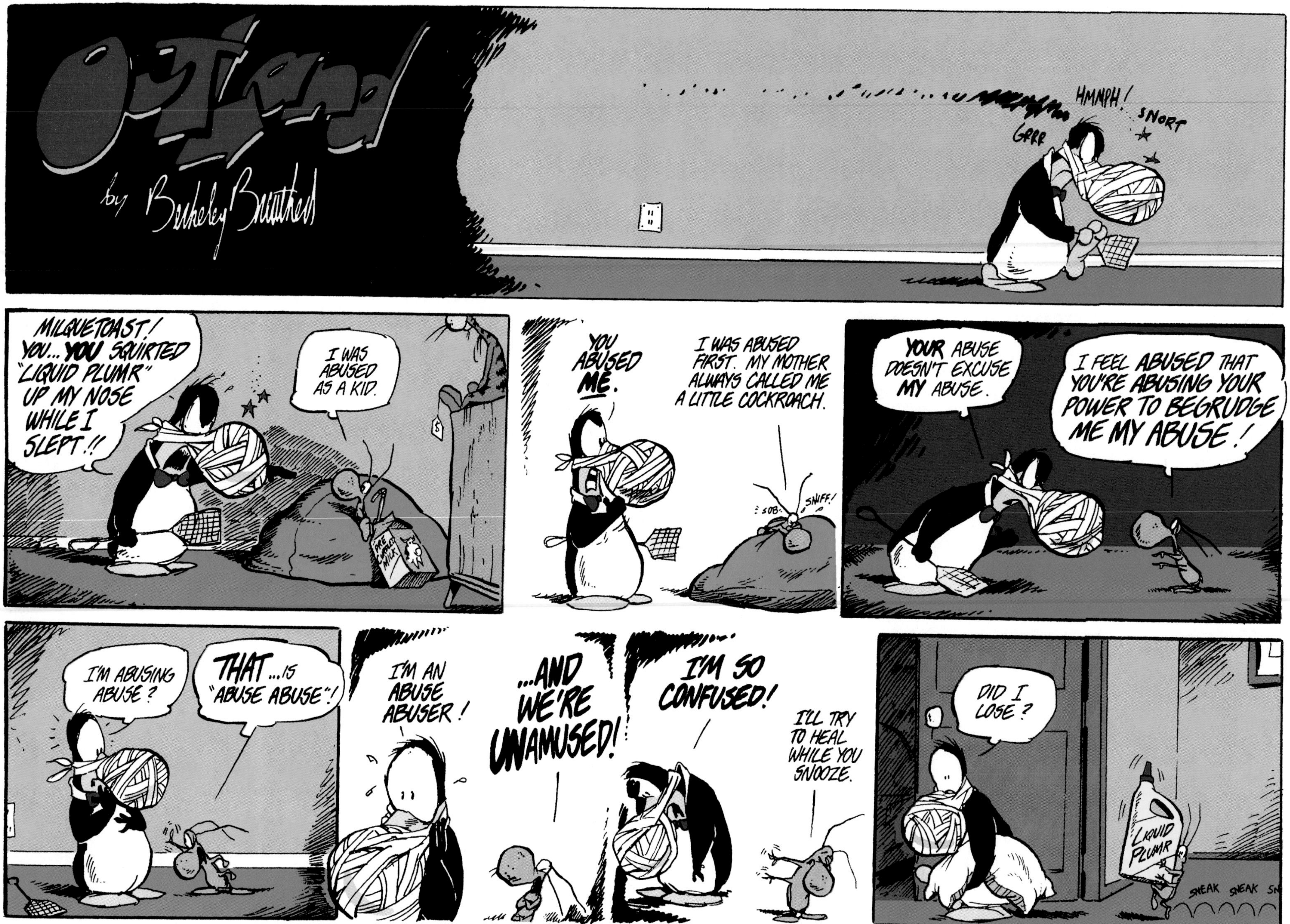

Outland
by Berkeley Breathed
HMMPH!
SNORT
GRRR
MILQUETOAST! YOU... YOU SQUIRTED "LIQUID PLUMR" UP MY NOSE WHILE I SLEPT!!
I WAS ABUSED AS A KID.
YOU ABUSED ME.
I WAS ABUSED FIRST. MY MOTHER ALWAYS CALLED ME A LITTLE COCKROACH.
SOB
SNIFF!
YOUR ABUSE DOESN'T EXCUSE MY ABUSE.
I FEEL ABUSED THAT YOU'RE ABUSING YOUR POWER TO BEGRUDGE ME MY ABUSE!
I'M ABUSING ABUSE?
THAT... IS "ABUSE ABUSE"!
I'M AN ABUSE ABUSER!
...AND WE'RE UNAMUSED!
I'M SO CONFUSED!
I'LL TRY TO HEAL WHILE YOU SNOOZE.
DID I LOSE?
LIQUID PLUMR
SNEAK SNEAK SN

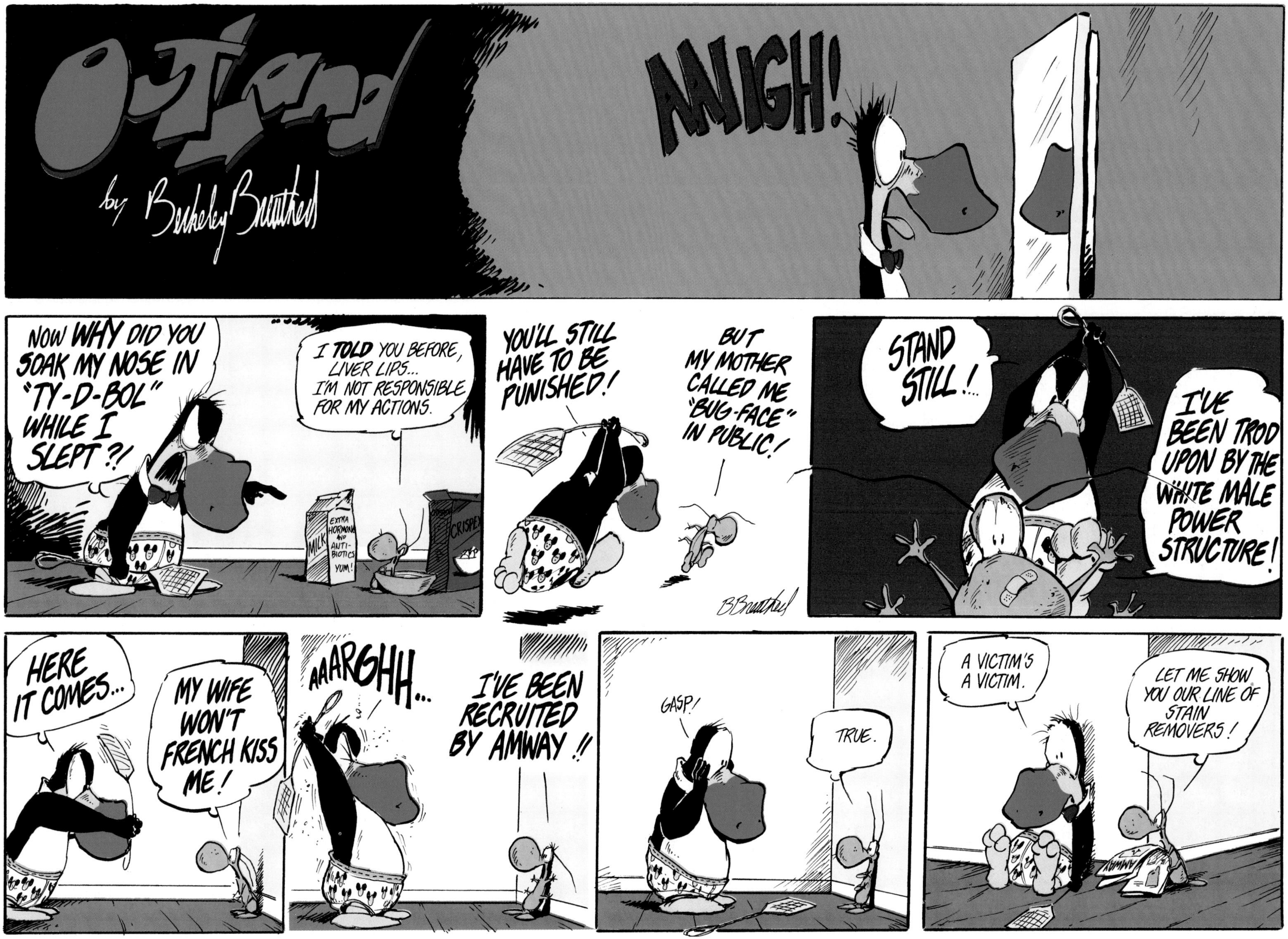
Outland
by Berkeley Breathed
AAIGH!
NOW WHY DID YOU SOAK MY NOSE IN "TY-D-BOL" WHILE I SLEPT ?!
I TOLD YOU BEFORE, LIVER LIPS... I'M NOT RESPONSIBLE FOR MY ACTIONS.
MILK
EXTRA HORMONES AND ANTI-BIOTICS YUM!
CRISPEX
YOU'LL STILL HAVE TO BE PUNISHED!
BUT MY MOTHER CALLED ME "BUG-FACE" IN PUBLIC!
B Breathed
STAND STILL!...
I'VE BEEN TROD UPON BY THE WHITE MALE POWER STRUCTURE!
HERE IT COMES...
MY WIFE WON'T FRENCH KISS ME!
AAARGHH...
I'VE BEEN RECRUITED BY AMWAY!!
GASP!
TRUE.
A VICTIM'S A VICTIM.
LET ME SHOW YOU OUR LINE OF STAIN REMOVERS!
AMWAY

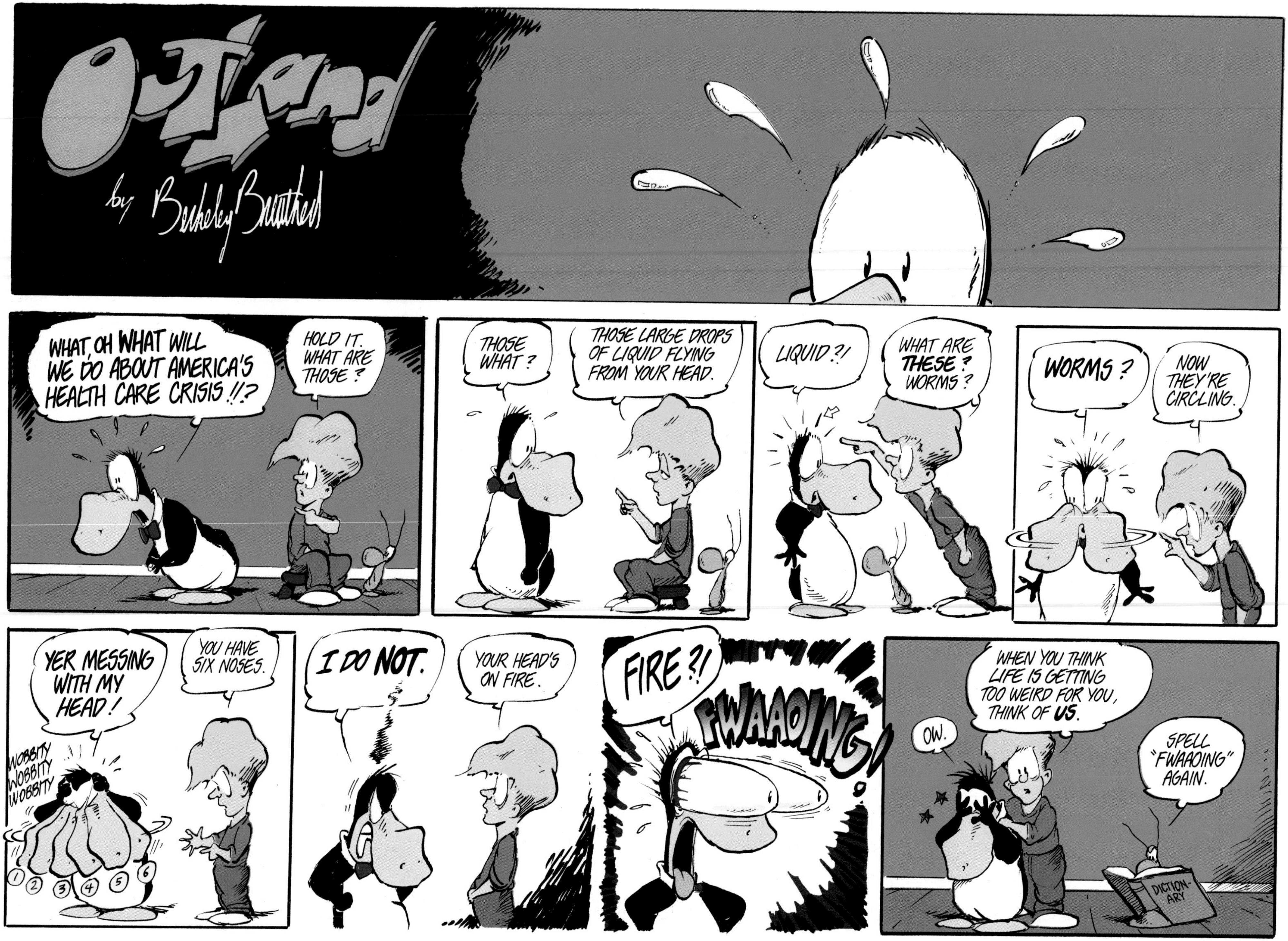
Outland
by Berkeley Breathed
WHAT, OH WHAT WILL WE DO ABOUT AMERICA'S HEALTH CARE CRISIS !!?
HOLD IT. WHAT ARE THOSE ?
THOSE WHAT ?
THOSE LARGE DROPS OF LIQUID FLYING FROM YOUR HEAD.
LIQUID ?!
WHAT ARE THESE ? WORMS ?
WORMS ?
NOW THEY'RE CIRCLING.
YER MESSING WITH MY HEAD !
WOBBITY WOBBITY WOBBITY
1 2 3 4 5 6
YOU HAVE SIX NOSES.
I DO NOT.
YOUR HEAD'S ON FIRE.
FIRE ?!
FWAAOING !
WHEN YOU THINK LIFE IS GETTING TOO WEIRD FOR YOU, THINK OF US.
OW.
SPELL "FWAAOING" AGAIN.
DICTION-ARY

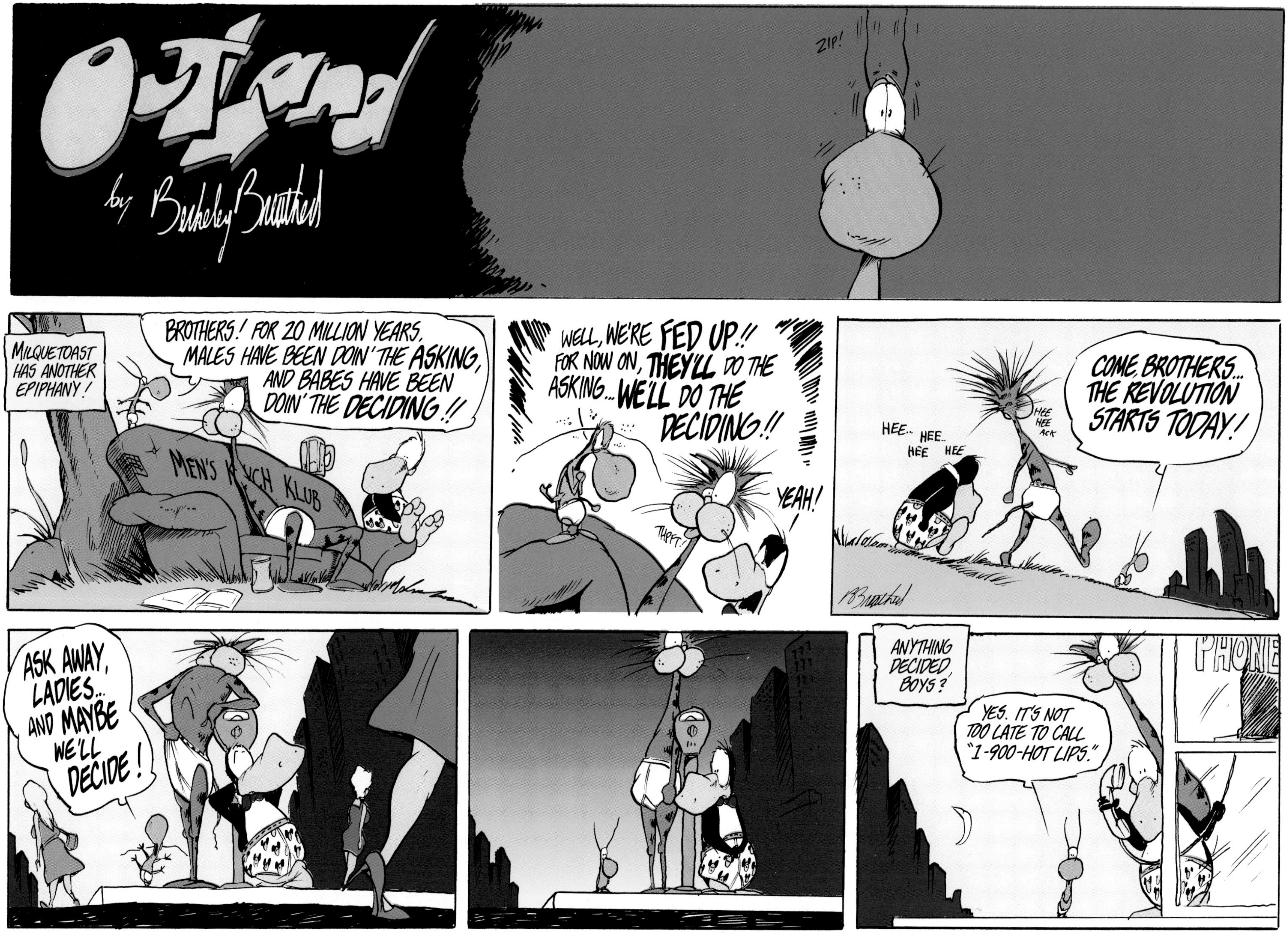

Outland
by Berkeley Breathed
ZIP!
MILQUETOAST HAS ANOTHER EPIPHANY!
BROTHERS! FOR 20 MILLION YEARS, MALES HAVE BEEN DOIN' THE ASKING, AND BABES HAVE BEEN DOIN' THE DECIDING!!
WELL, WE'RE FED UP!! FOR NOW ON, THEY'LL DO THE ASKING... WE'LL DO THE DECIDING!!
THPFT!
YEAH!
HEE.. HEE.. HEE HEE
HEE HEE ACK
COME, BROTHERS... THE REVOLUTION STARTS TODAY!
ASK AWAY, LADIES... AND MAYBE WE'LL DECIDE!
ANYTHING DECIDED, BOYS?
YES. IT'S NOT TOO LATE TO CALL "1-900-HOT LIPS."
PHONE

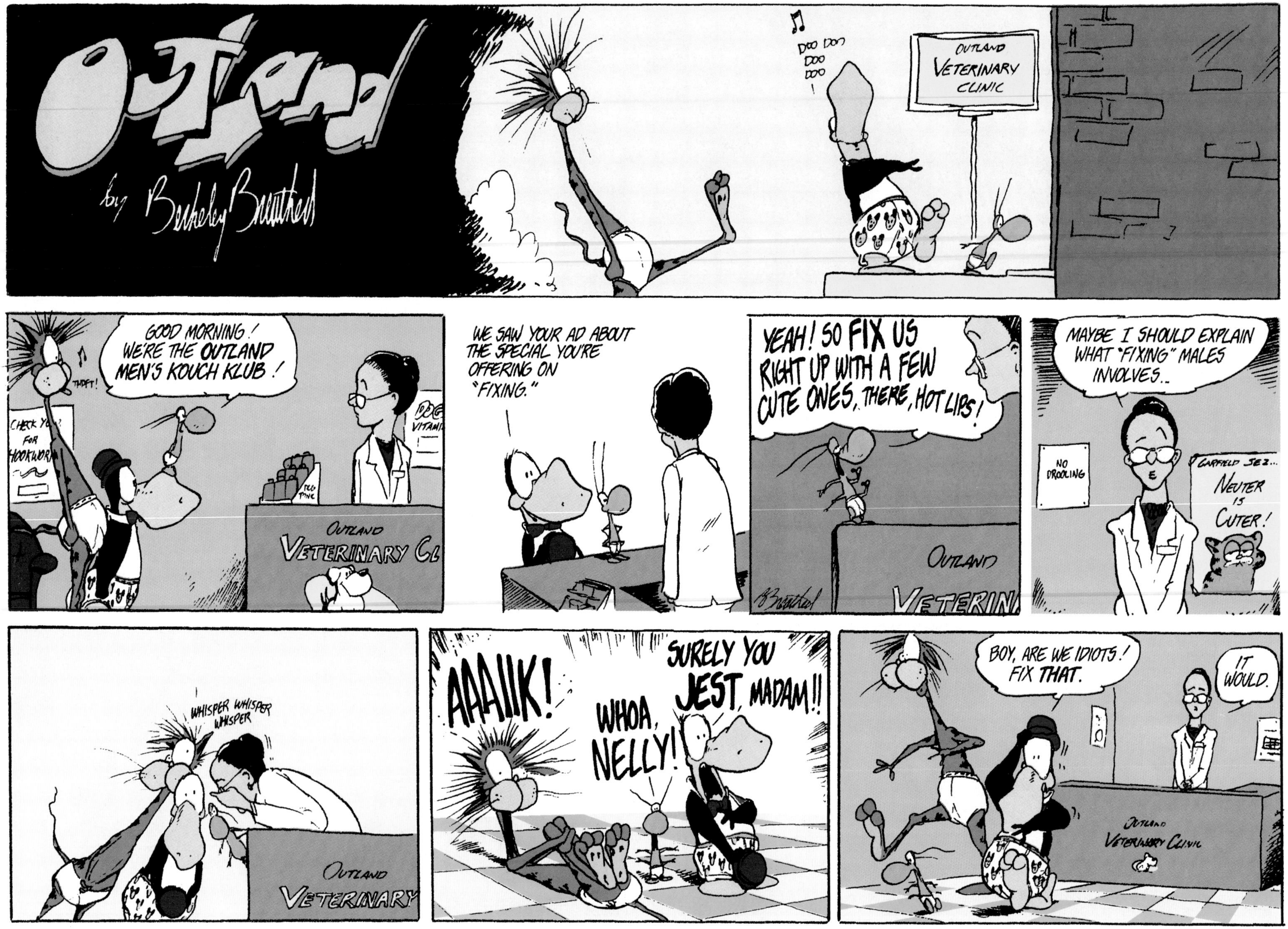
Outland
by Berkeley Breathed
DOO DOO DOO DOO
OUTLAND VETERINARY CLINIC
GOOD MORNING! WE'RE THE OUTLAND MEN'S KOUCH KLUB!
THPFT!
OUTLAND VETERINARY CL
WE SAW YOUR AD ABOUT THE SPECIAL YOU'RE OFFERING ON "FIXING."
YEAH! SO FIX US RIGHT UP WITH A FEW CUTE ONES, THERE, HOT LIPS!
OUTLAND VETERINA
MAYBE I SHOULD EXPLAIN WHAT "FIXING" MALES INVOLVES...
NO DROOLING
GARFIELD SEZ... NEUTER IS CUTER!
WHISPER WHISPER WHISPER
OUTLAND VETERINARY
AAAIIK!
WHOA, NELLY!
SURELY YOU JEST, MADAM!!
BOY, ARE WE IDIOTS! FIX THAT.
IT WOULD.
OUTLAND VETERINARY CLINIC

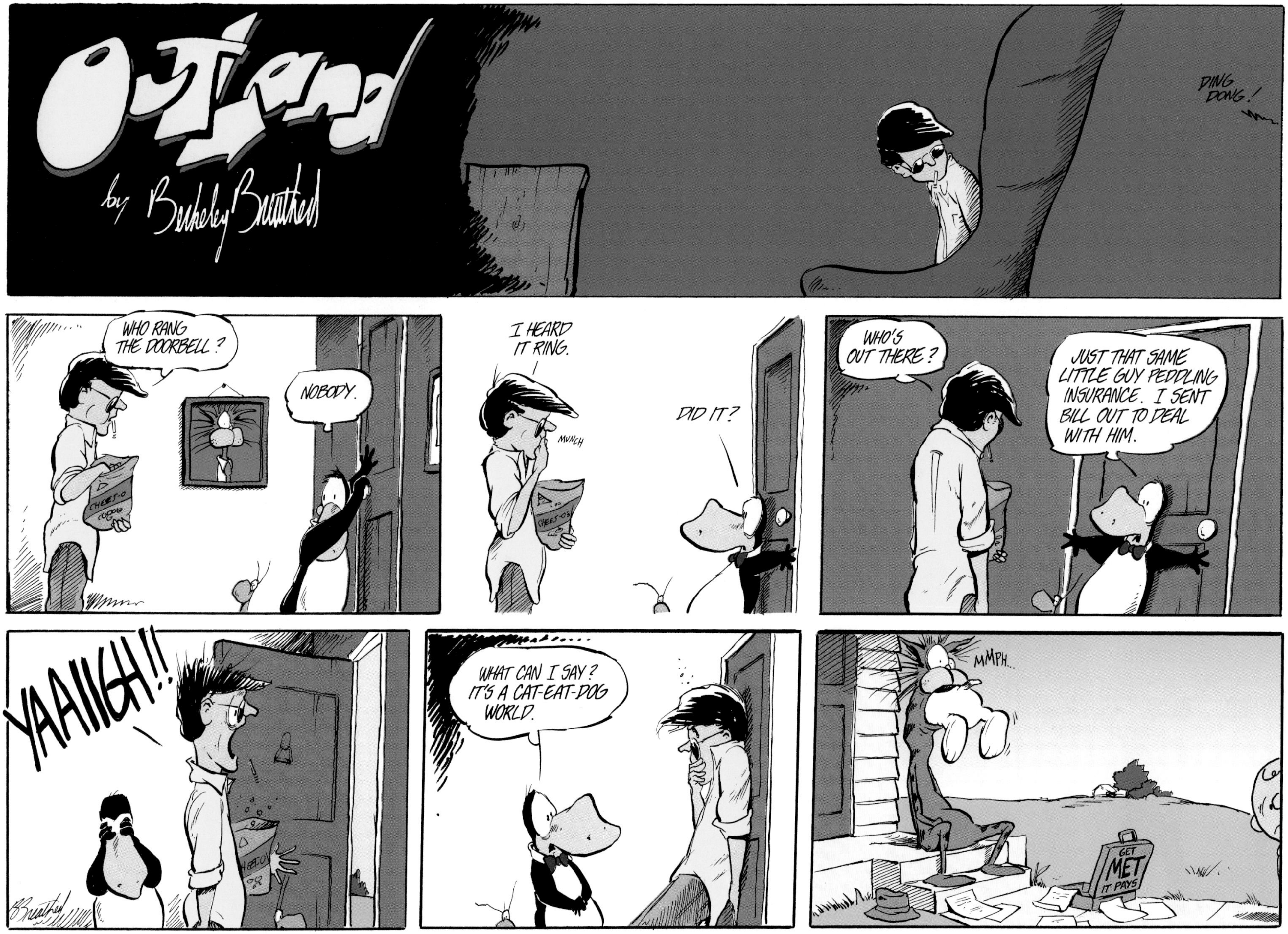
Outland
by Berkeley Breathed
DING DONG!
WHO RANG THE DOORBELL?
NOBODY.
I HEARD IT RING.
MUNCH
DID IT?
WHO'S OUT THERE?
JUST THAT SAME LITTLE GUY PEDDLING INSURANCE. I SENT BILL OUT TO DEAL WITH HIM.
YAAIIIGH!!
WHAT CAN I SAY? IT'S A CAT-EAT-DOG WORLD.
MMPH...
GET MET IT PAYS
Breathed

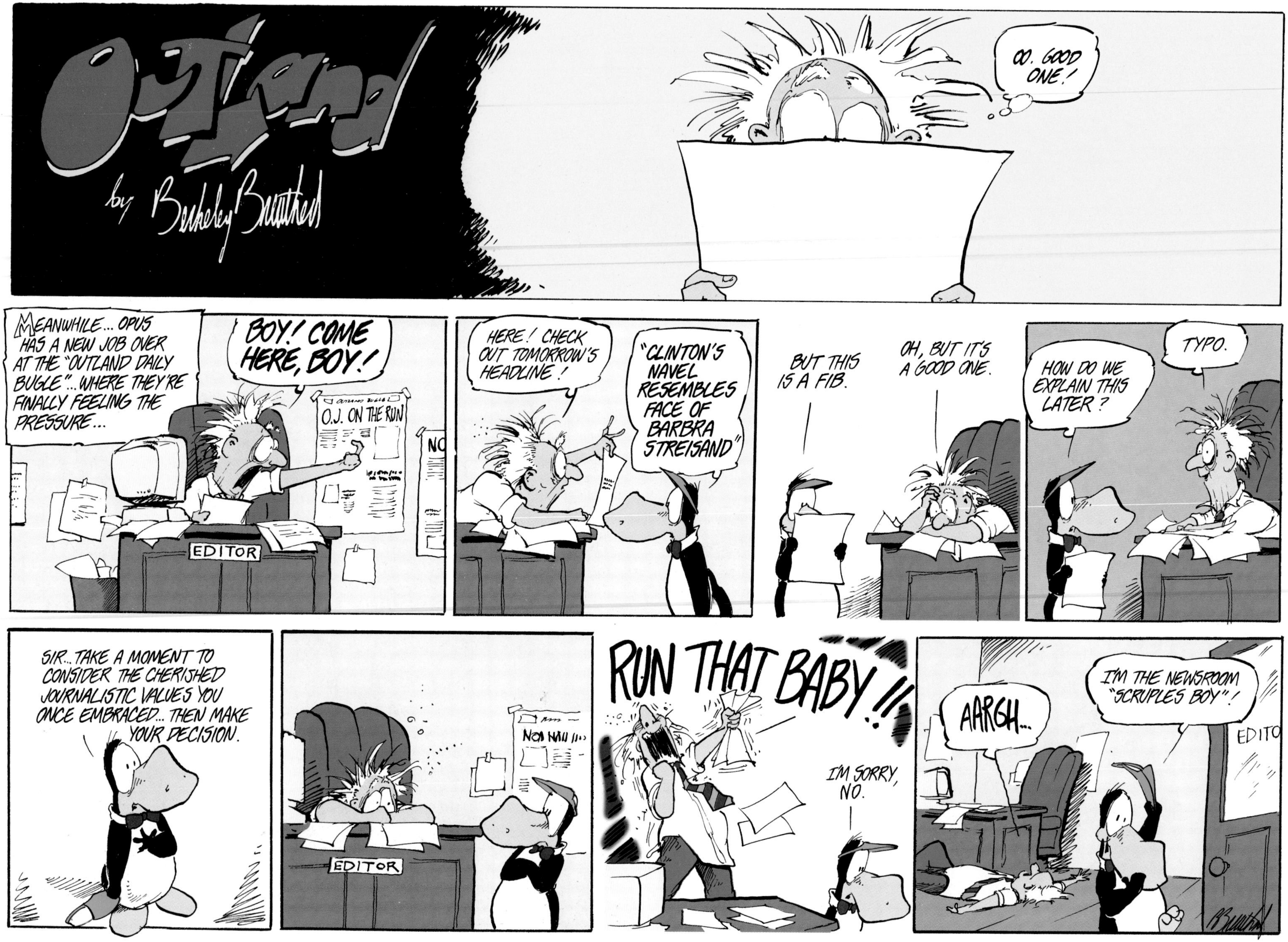
Outland
by Berkeley Breathed
OO. GOOD ONE!
MEANWHILE... OPUS HAS A NEW JOB OVER AT THE "OUTLAND DAILY BUGLE"... WHERE THEY'RE FINALLY FEELING THE PRESSURE...
BOY! COME HERE, BOY!
O.J. ON THE RUN
EDITOR
HERE! CHECK OUT TOMORROW'S HEADLINE!
"CLINTON'S NAVEL RESEMBLES FACE OF BARBRA STREISAND"
BUT THIS IS A FIB.
OH, BUT IT'S A GOOD ONE.
HOW DO WE EXPLAIN THIS LATER?
TYPO.
SIR... TAKE A MOMENT TO CONSIDER THE CHERISHED JOURNALISTIC VALUES YOU ONCE EMBRACED... THEN MAKE YOUR DECISION.
EDITOR
RUN THAT BABY!!!
I'M SORRY, NO.
AARGH...
I'M THE NEWSROOM "SCRUPLES BOY"!
EDITO

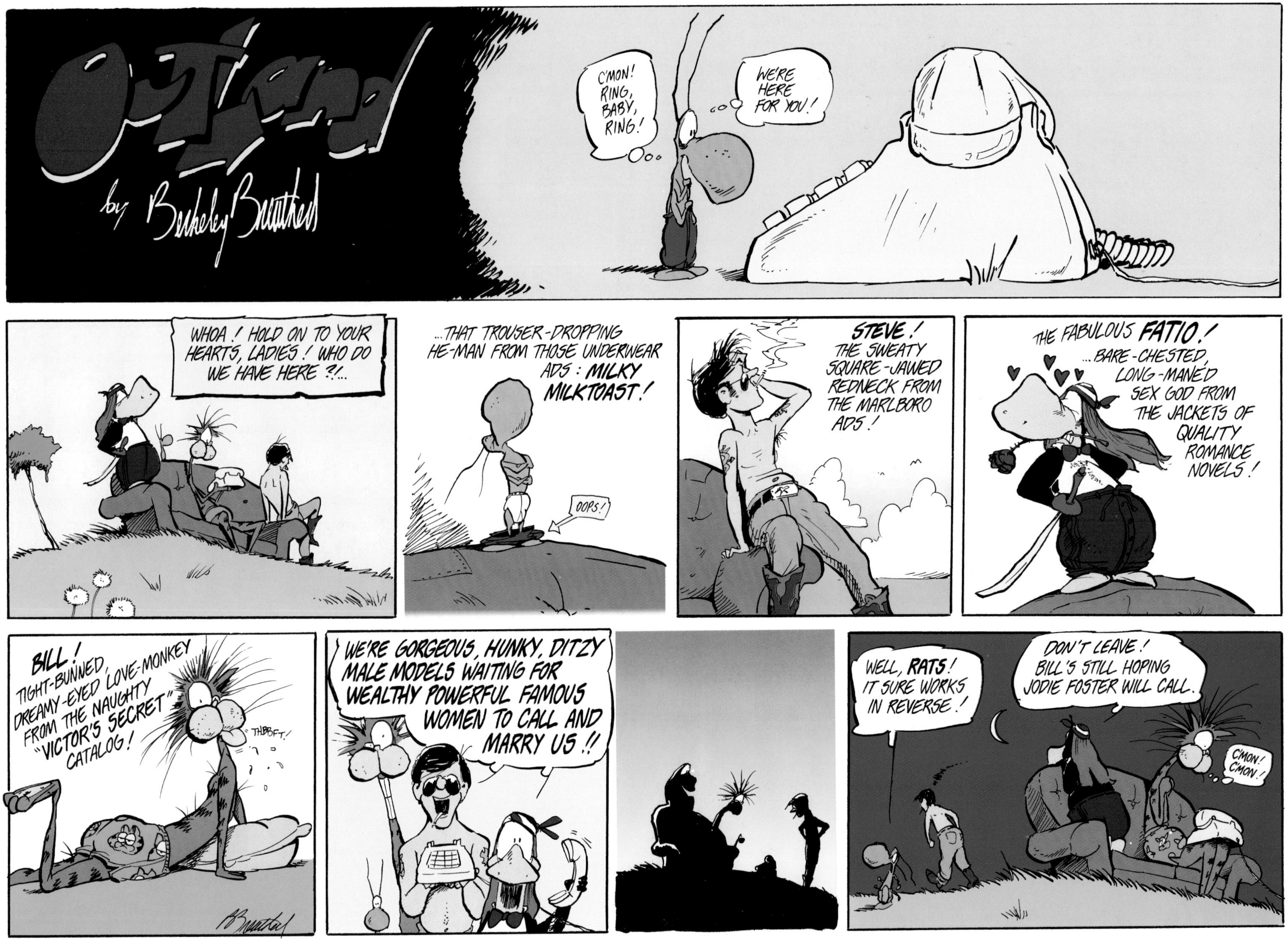

Outland
by Berkeley Breathed
C'MON! RING, BABY, RING!
WE'RE HERE FOR YOU!
WHOA! HOLD ON TO YOUR HEARTS, LADIES! WHO DO WE HAVE HERE ?!...
...THAT TROUSER-DROPPING HE-MAN FROM THOSE UNDERWEAR ADS: MILKY MILKTOAST!
OOPS!
STEVE! THE SWEATY SQUARE-JAWED REDNECK FROM THE MARLBORO ADS!
THE FABULOUS FATIO! ...BARE-CHESTED, LONG-MANED SEX GOD FROM THE JACKETS OF QUALITY ROMANCE NOVELS!
BILL! TIGHT-BUNNED, DREAMY-EYED LOVE-MONKEY FROM THE NAUGHTY "VICTOR'S SECRET" CATALOG!
THBBFT!
WE'RE GORGEOUS, HUNKY, DITZY MALE MODELS WAITING FOR WEALTHY POWERFUL FAMOUS WOMEN TO CALL AND MARRY US!!
WELL, RATS! IT SURE WORKS IN REVERSE!
DON'T LEAVE! BILL'S STILL HOPING JODIE FOSTER WILL CALL.
C'MON! C'MON!

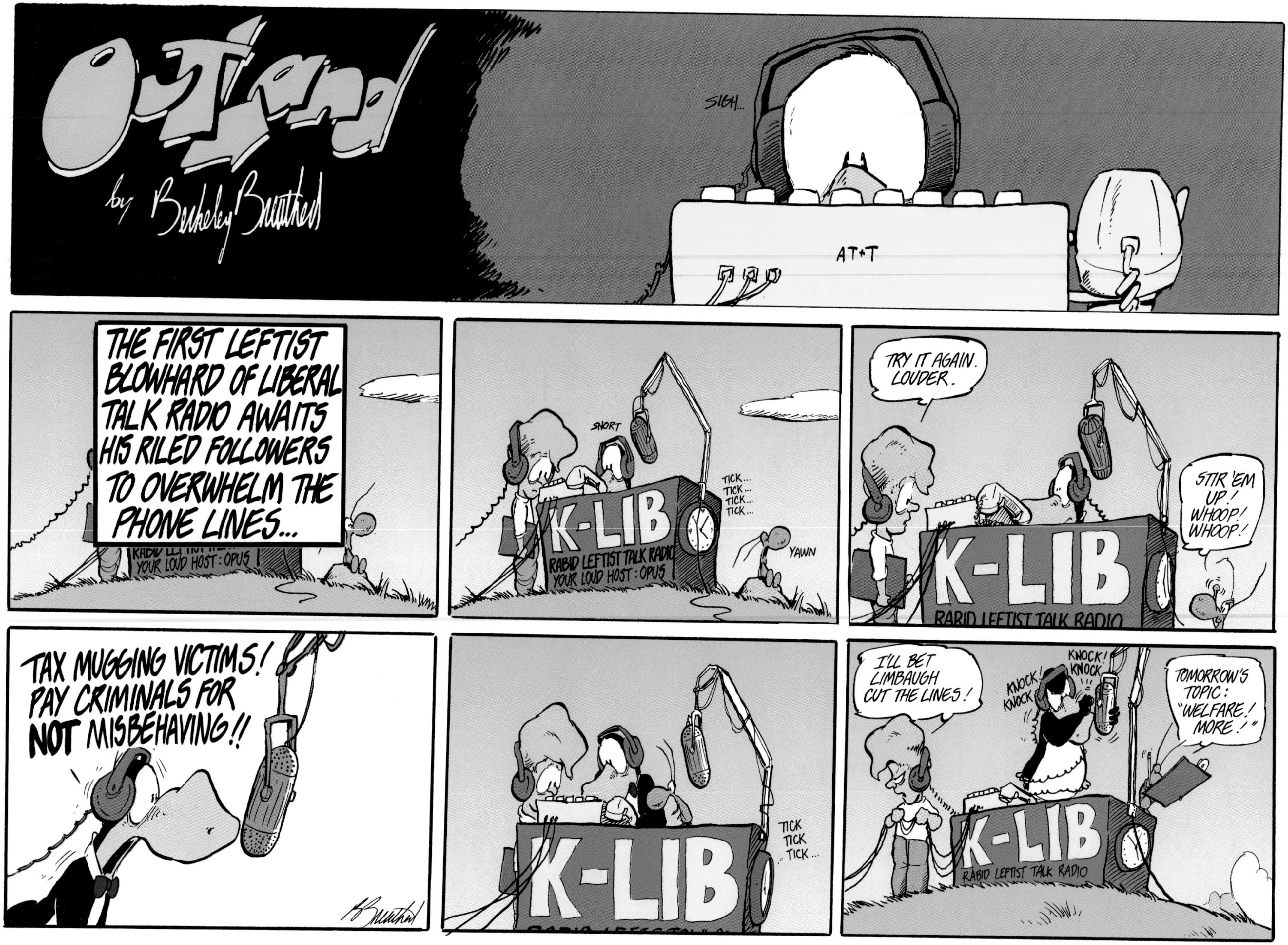
Outland
by Berkeley Breathed
SIGH...
AT&T
THE FIRST LEFTIST BLOWHARD OF LIBERAL TALK RADIO AWAITS HIS RILED FOLLOWERS TO OVERWHELM THE PHONE LINES...
YOUR LOUD HOST: OPUS
SNORT
K-LIB
RABID LEFTIST TALK RADIO
YOUR LOUD HOST: OPUS
TICK... TICK... TICK... TICK...
YAWN
TRY IT AGAIN. LOUDER.
K-LIB
RABID LEFTIST TALK RADIO
STIR 'EM UP! WHOOP! WHOOP!
TAX MUGGING VICTIMS! PAY CRIMINALS FOR NOT MISBEHAVING!!
K-LIB
TICK TICK TICK...
I'LL BET LIMBAUGH CUT THE LINES!
KNOCK! KNOCK
KNOCK! KNOCK
TOMORROW'S TOPIC: "WELFARE! MORE!"
K-LIB
RABID LEFTIST TALK RADIO

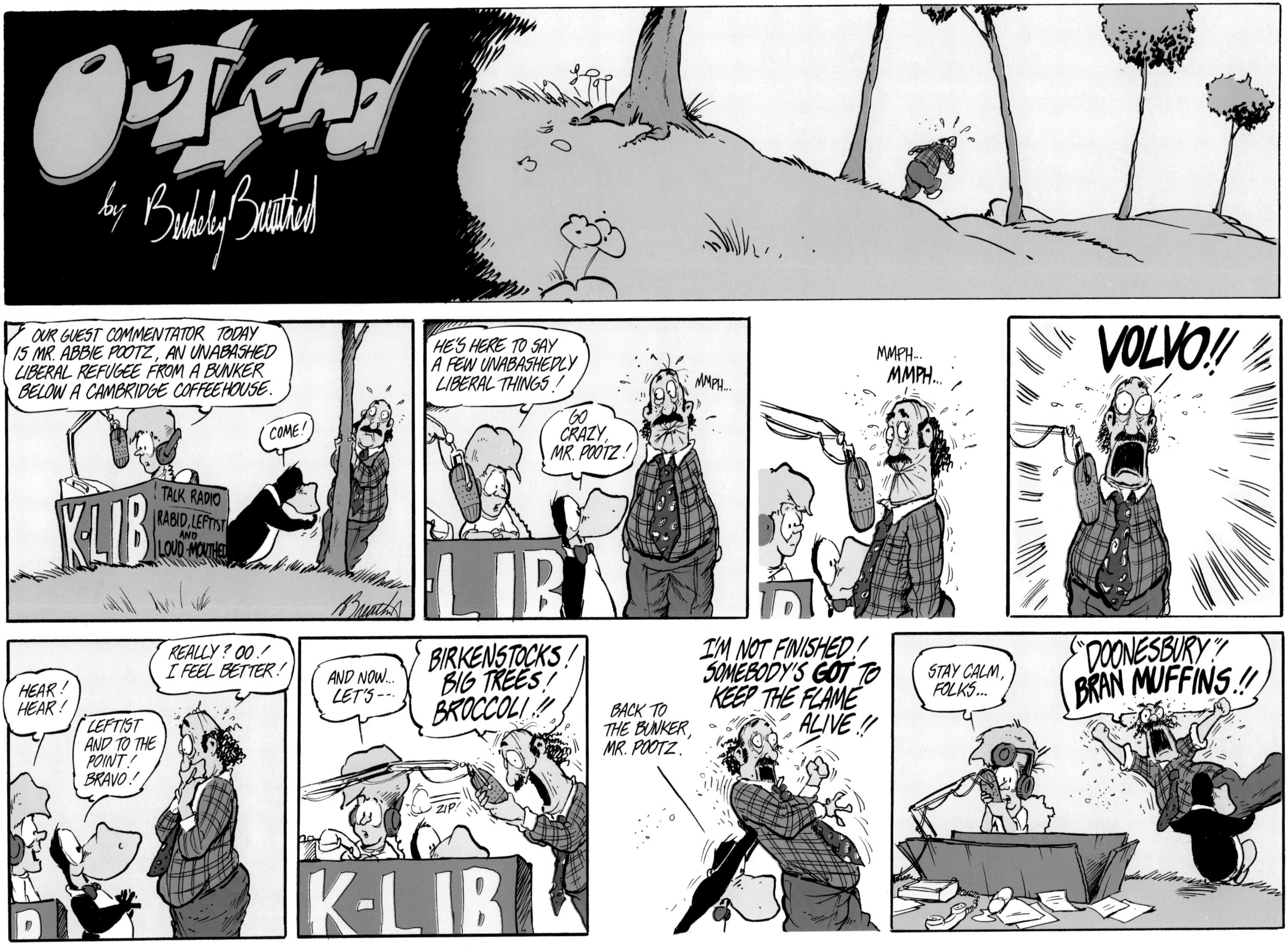

Outland
by Berkeley Breathed
OUR GUEST COMMENTATOR TODAY IS MR. ABBIE POOTZ, AN UNABASHED LIBERAL REFUGEE FROM A BUNKER BELOW A CAMBRIDGE COFFEEHOUSE.
COME!
K-LIB
TALK RADIO
RABID, LEFTIST AND LOUD-MOUTHED
HE'S HERE TO SAY A FEW UNABASHEDLY LIBERAL THINGS!
GO CRAZY, MR. POOTZ!
MMPH...
MMPH...
MMPH...
VOLVO!!
HEAR! HEAR!
LEFTIST AND TO THE POINT! BRAVO!
REALLY? OO! I FEEL BETTER!
AND NOW... LET'S--
BIRKENSTOCKS! BIG TREES! BROCCOLI!!
ZIP!
K-LIB
BACK TO THE BUNKER, MR. POOTZ.
I'M NOT FINISHED! SOMEBODY'S GOT TO KEEP THE FLAME ALIVE!!
STAY CALM, FOLKS...
"DOONESBURY"! BRAN MUFFINS!!

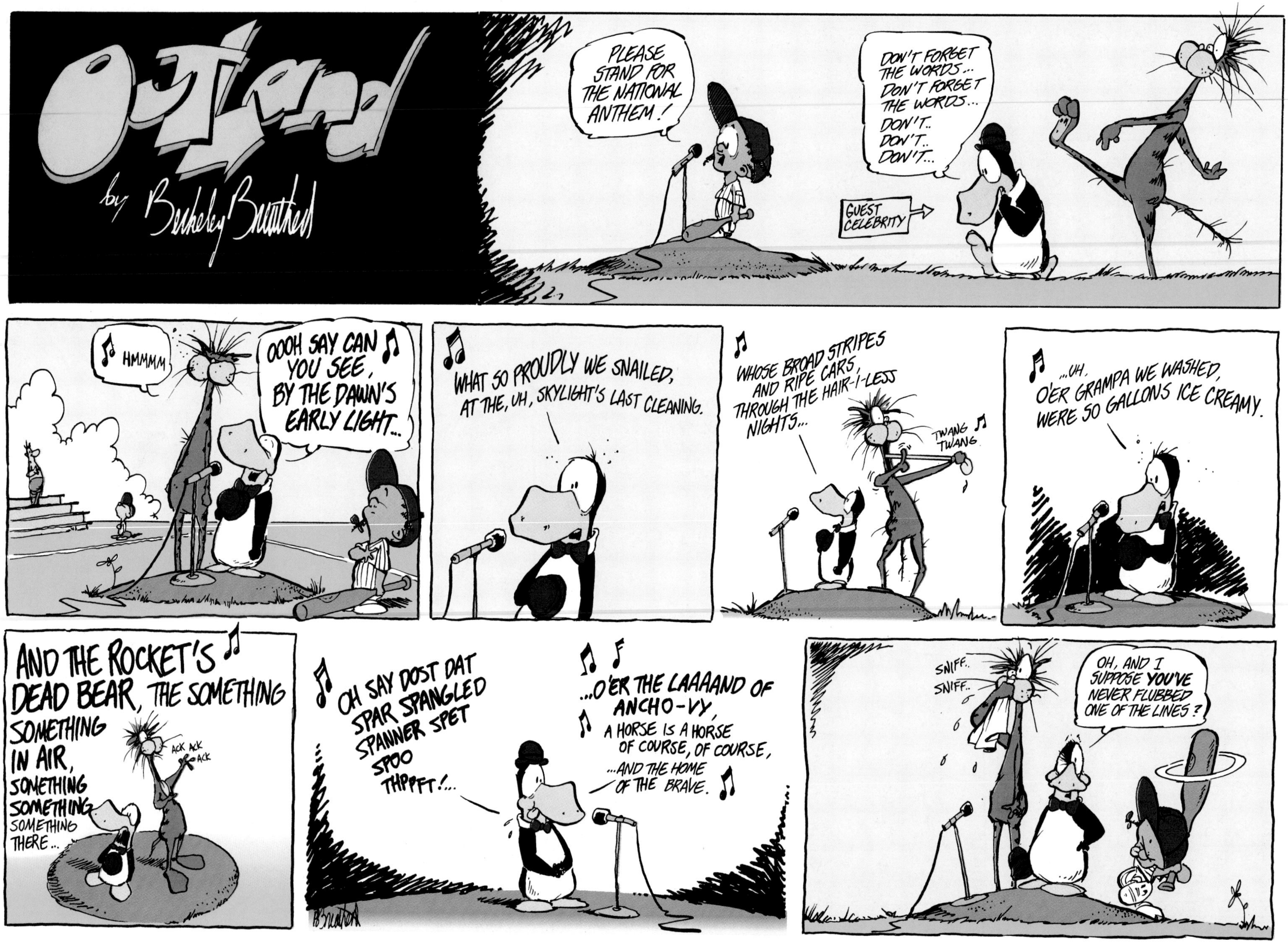
Outland
by Berkeley Breathed
PLEASE STAND FOR THE NATIONAL ANTHEM!
DON'T FORGET THE WORDS... DON'T FORGET THE WORDS... DON'T.. DON'T.. DON'T...
GUEST CELEBRITY
HMMMM
OOOH SAY CAN YOU SEE, BY THE DAWN'S EARLY LIGHT...
WHAT SO PROUDLY WE SNAILED, AT THE, UH, SKYLIGHT'S LAST CLEANING.
WHOSE BROAD STRIPES AND RIPE CARS, THROUGH THE HAIR-I-LESS NIGHTS...
TWANG TWANG
...UH, O'ER GRAMPA WE WASHED, WERE SO GALLONS ICE CREAMY.
AND THE ROCKET'S DEAD BEAR, THE SOMETHING SOMETHING IN AIR, SOMETHING SOMETHING SOMETHING THERE...
ACK ACK ACK
OH SAY DOST DAT SPAR SPANGLED SPANNER SPET SPOO THPPFT!...
...O'ER THE LAAAAND OF ANCHO-VY, A HORSE IS A HORSE OF COURSE, OF COURSE, ...AND THE HOME OF THE BRAVE.
SNIFF.. SNIFF..
OH, AND I SUPPOSE YOU'VE NEVER FLUBBED ONE OF THE LINES?

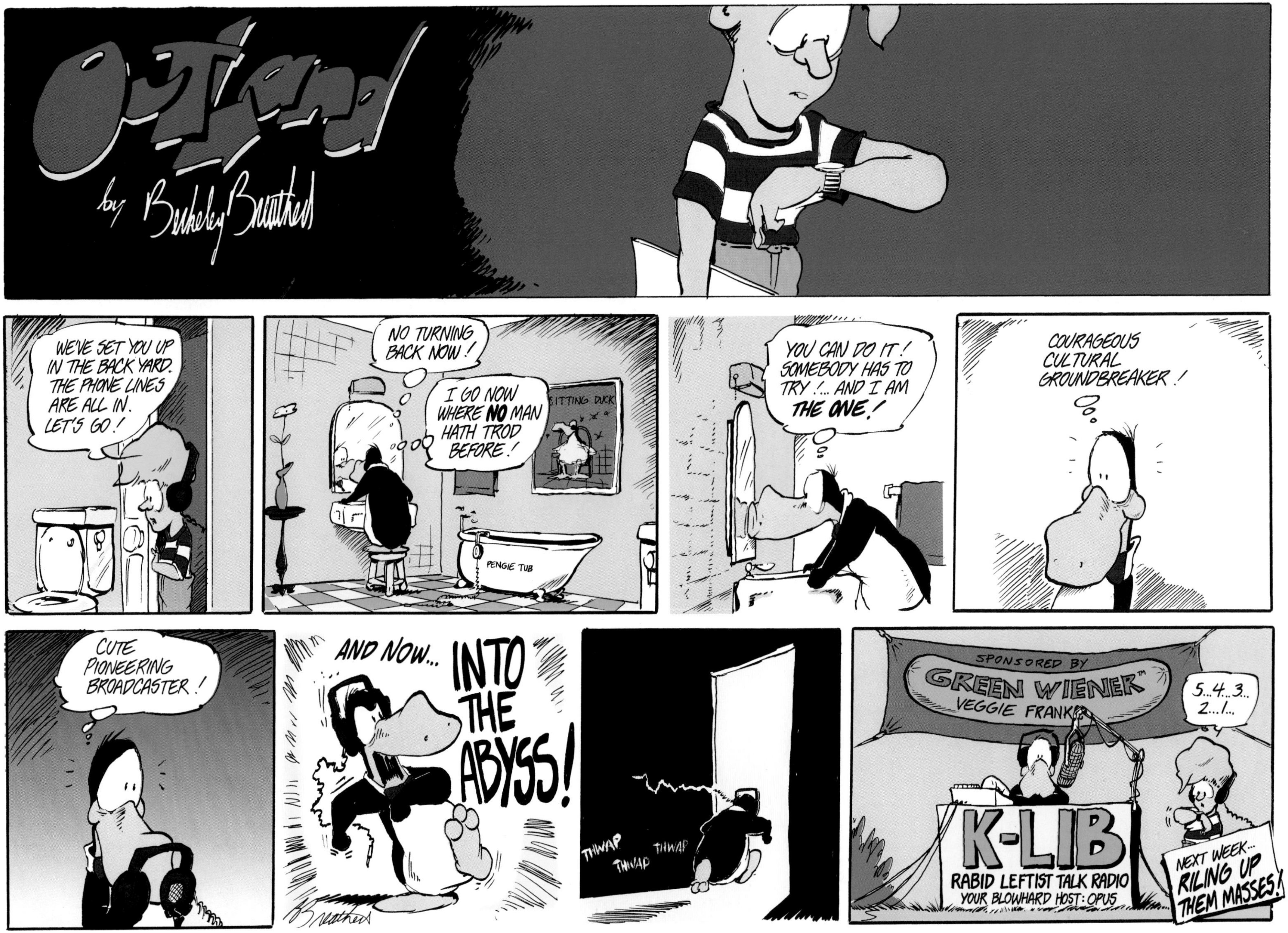

Outland
by Berkeley Breathed
WE'VE SET YOU UP IN THE BACK YARD. THE PHONE LINES ARE ALL IN. LET'S GO!
NO TURNING BACK NOW!
I GO NOW WHERE NO MAN HATH TROD BEFORE!
SITTING DUCK
PENGIE TUB
YOU CAN DO IT! SOMEBODY HAS TO TRY!... AND I AM THE ONE!
COURAGEOUS CULTURAL GROUNDBREAKER!
CUTE PIONEERING BROADCASTER!
AND NOW... INTO THE ABYSS!
THWAP THWAP THWAP
SPONSORED BY
GREEN WIENER™ VEGGIE FRANKS
5...4...3... 2...1...
K-LIB
RABID LEFTIST TALK RADIO
YOUR BLOWHARD HOST: OPUS
NEXT WEEK... RILING UP THEM MASSES!

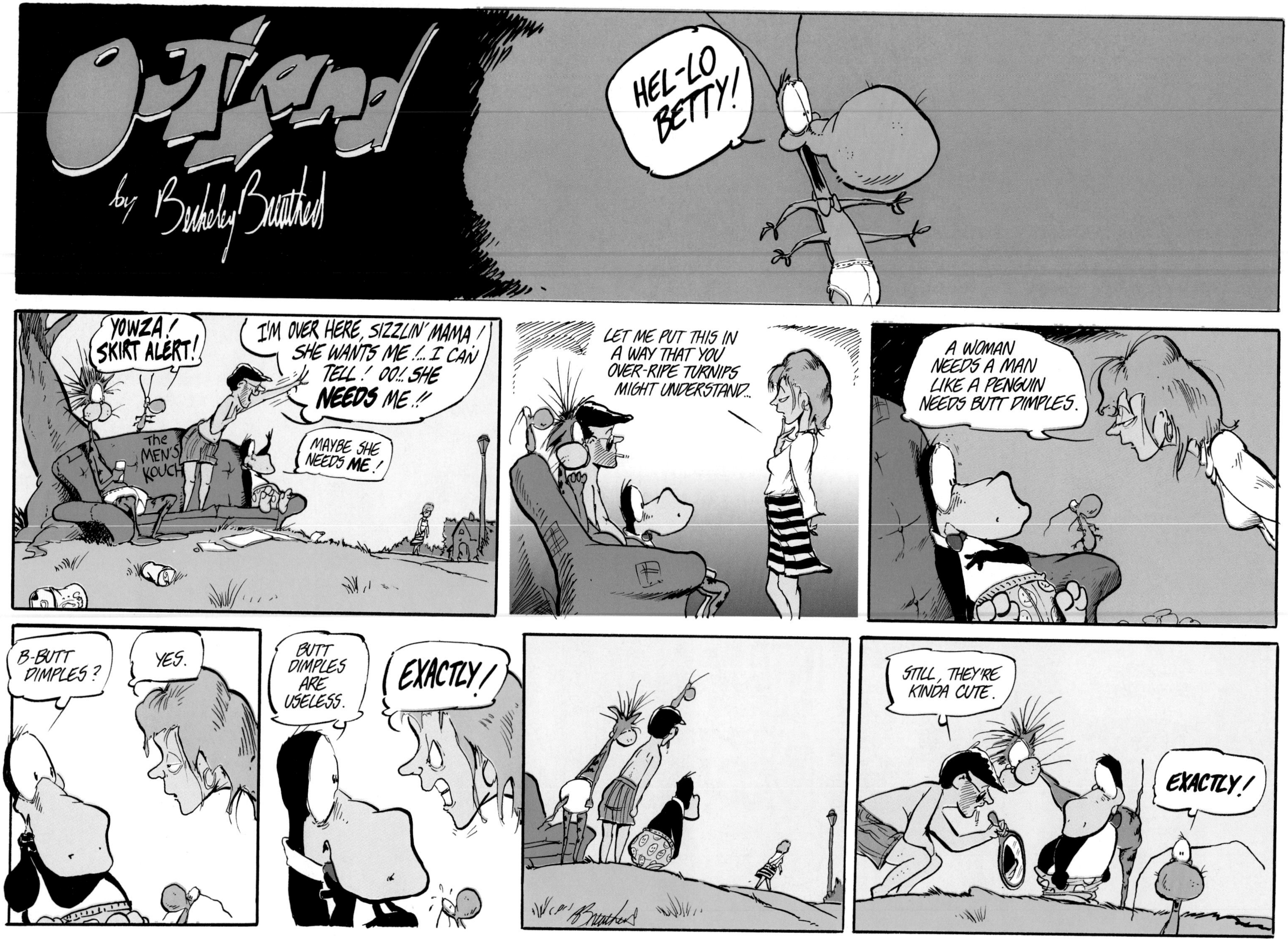
Outland
by Berkeley Breathed
HEL-LO BETTY!
YOWZA! SKIRT ALERT!
I'M OVER HERE, SIZZLIN' MAMA! SHE WANTS ME!... I CAN TELL! OO!.. SHE NEEDS ME.!!
The MEN'S KOUCH
MAYBE SHE NEEDS ME!
LET ME PUT THIS IN A WAY THAT YOU OVER-RIPE TURNIPS MIGHT UNDERSTAND...
A WOMAN NEEDS A MAN LIKE A PENGUIN NEEDS BUTT DIMPLES.
B-BUTT DIMPLES?
YES.
BUTT DIMPLES ARE USELESS.
EXACTLY!
STILL, THEY'RE KINDA CUTE.
EXACTLY!

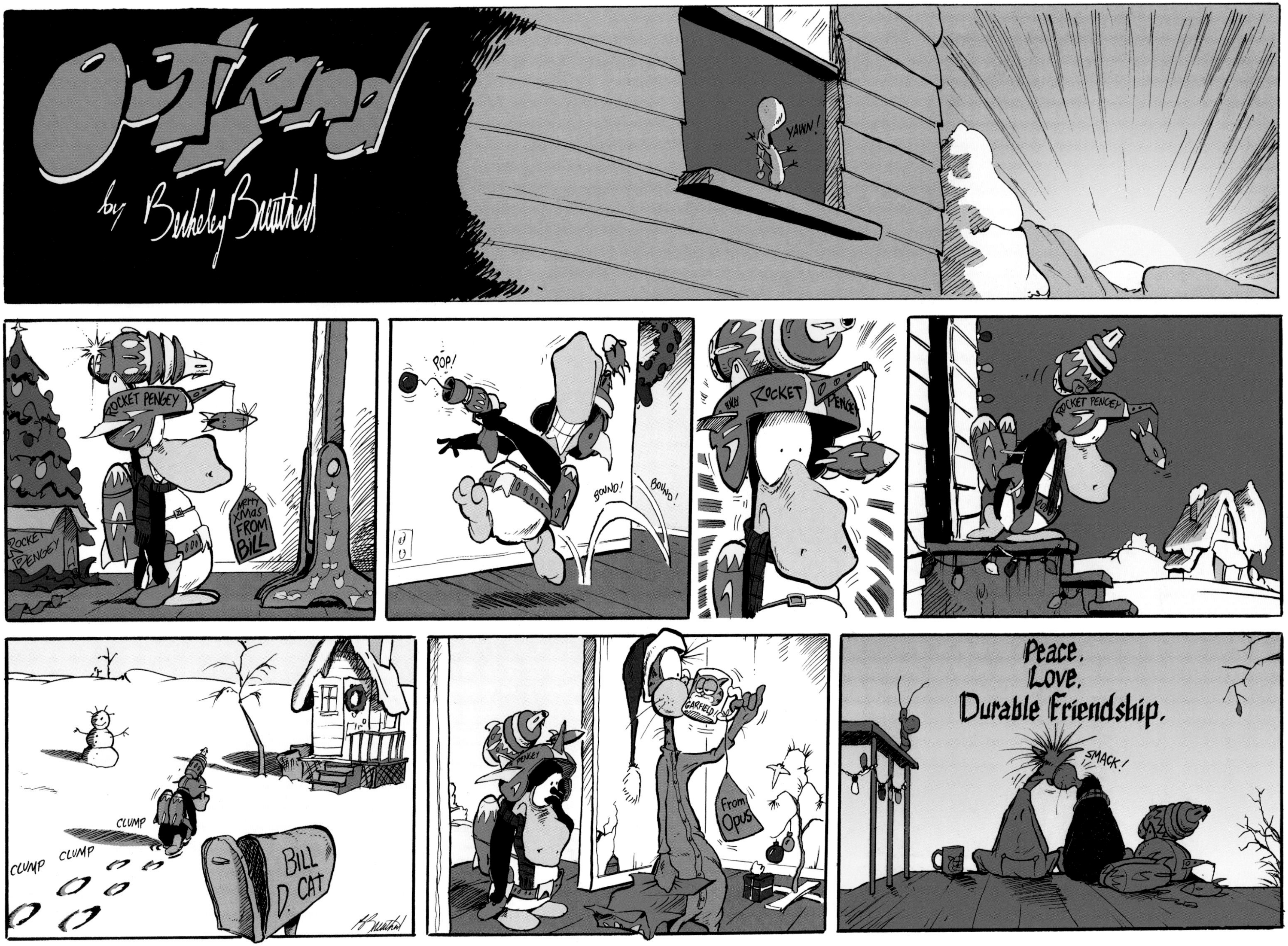
Outland
by Berkeley Breathed
YAWN!
ROCKET PENGEY
Merry Xmas FROM BILL
ROCKET PENGEY
POP!
BOUND!
BOUND!
ROCKET PENGEY
ROCKET PENGEY
CLUMP
CLUMP
CLUMP
BILL D. CAT
PENGEY
GARFIELD!
From Opus
Peace.
Love.
Durable Friendship.
SMACK!

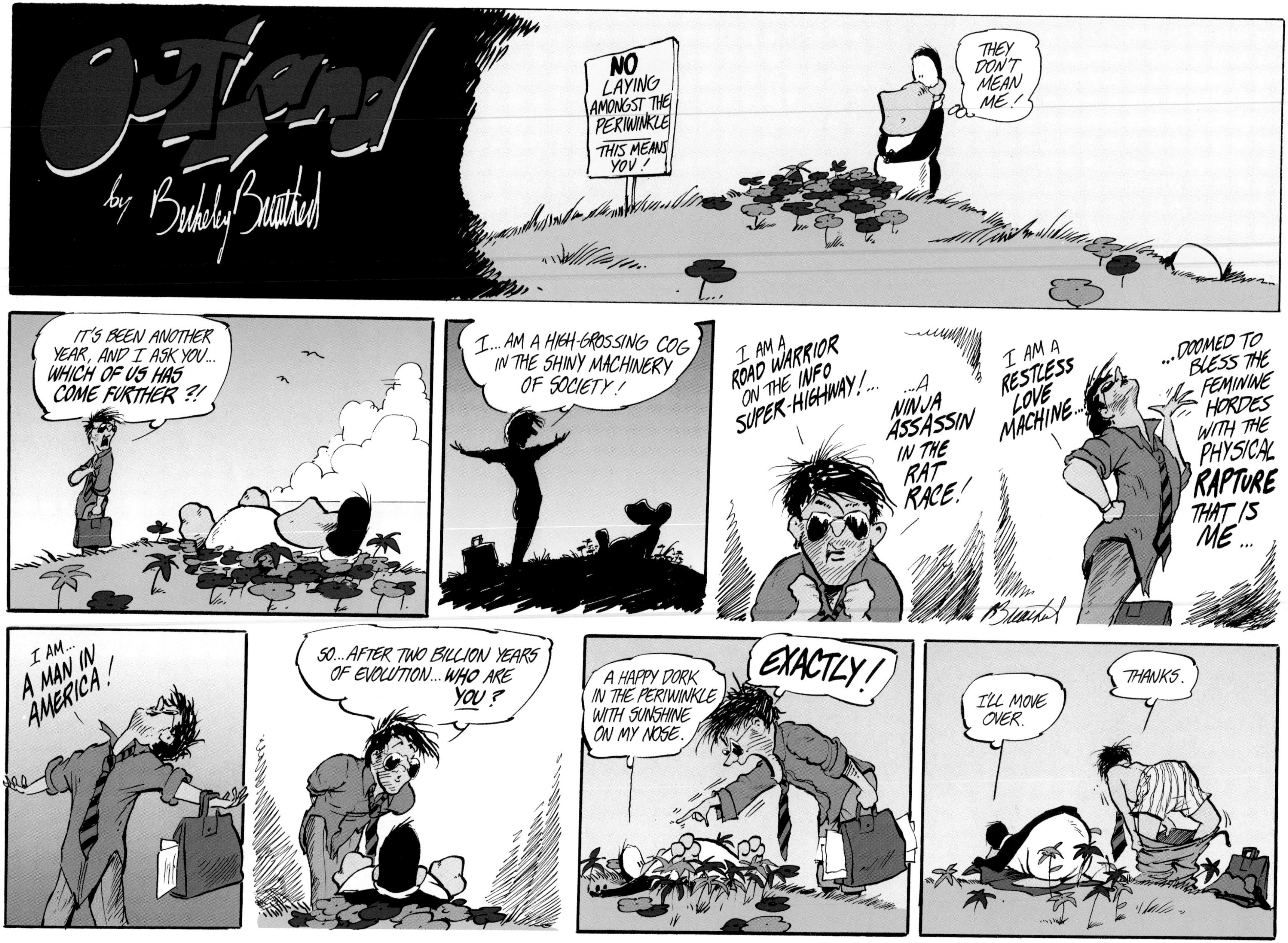
Outland
by Berkeley Breathed
NO LAYING AMONGST THE PERIWINKLE
THIS MEANS YOU!
THEY DON'T MEAN ME!
IT'S BEEN ANOTHER YEAR, AND I ASK YOU... WHICH OF US HAS COME FURTHER ?!
I... AM A HIGH-GROSSING COG IN THE SHINY MACHINERY OF SOCIETY!
I AM A ROAD WARRIOR ON THE INFO SUPER-HIGHWAY!...
...A NINJA ASSASSIN IN THE RAT RACE!
I AM A RESTLESS LOVE MACHINE...
...DOOMED TO BLESS THE FEMININE HORDES WITH THE PHYSICAL RAPTURE THAT IS ME...
Breathed
I AM... A MAN IN AMERICA!
SO... AFTER TWO BILLION YEARS OF EVOLUTION... WHO ARE YOU?
A HAPPY DORK IN THE PERIWINKLE WITH SUNSHINE ON MY NOSE.
EXACTLY!
I'LL MOVE OVER.
THANKS.

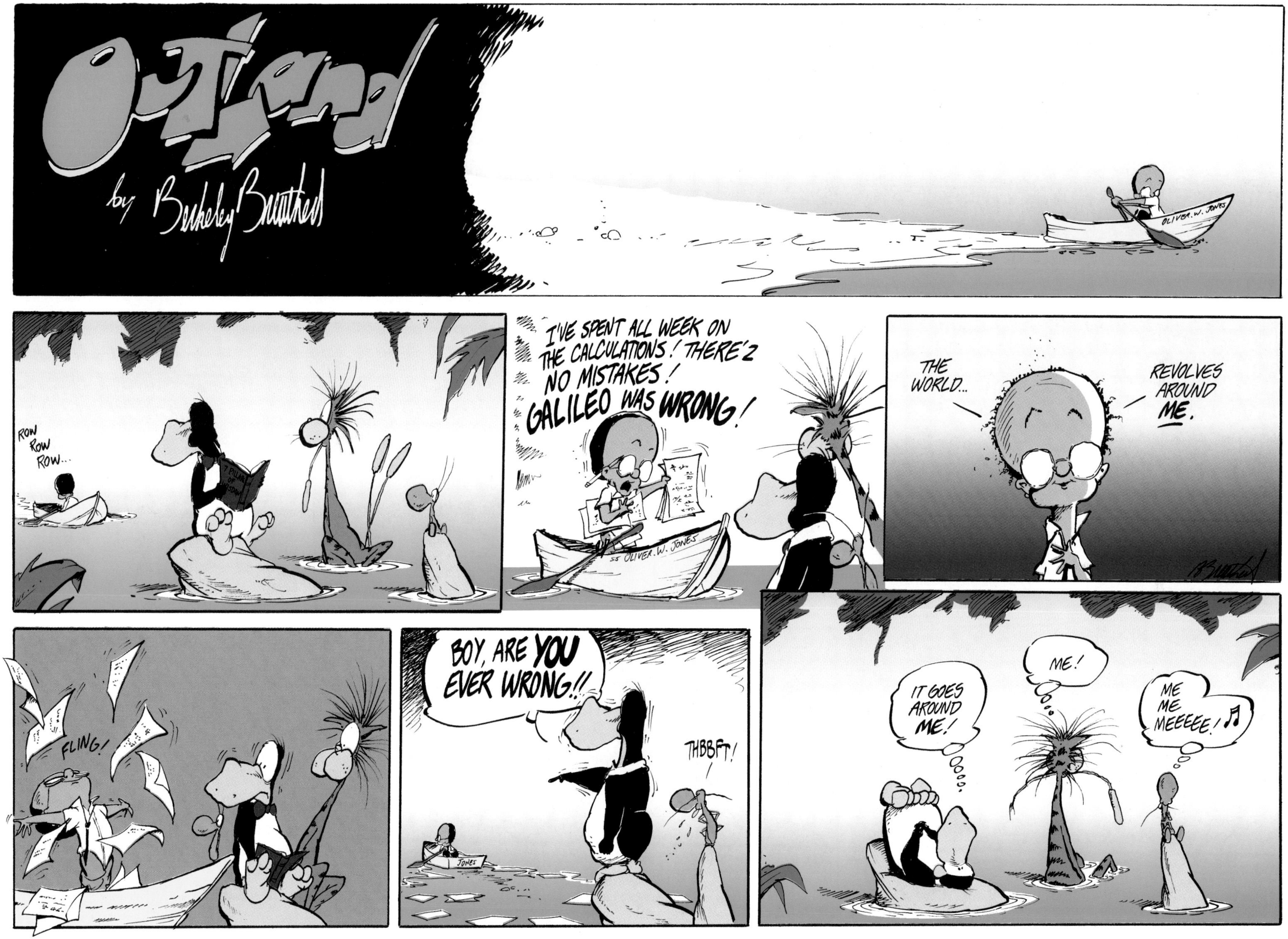

Outland
by Berkeley Breathed
OLIVER. W. JONES
ROW ROW ROW...
PILLARS OF WISDOM
I'VE SPENT ALL WEEK ON THE CALCULATIONS! THERE'Z NO MISTAKES! GALILEO WAS WRONG!
OLIVER. W. JONES
THE WORLD...
REVOLVES AROUND ME.
FLING!
BOY, ARE YOU EVER WRONG!!
THBBFT!
JONES
IT GOES AROUND ME!
ME!
ME ME MEEEEE!

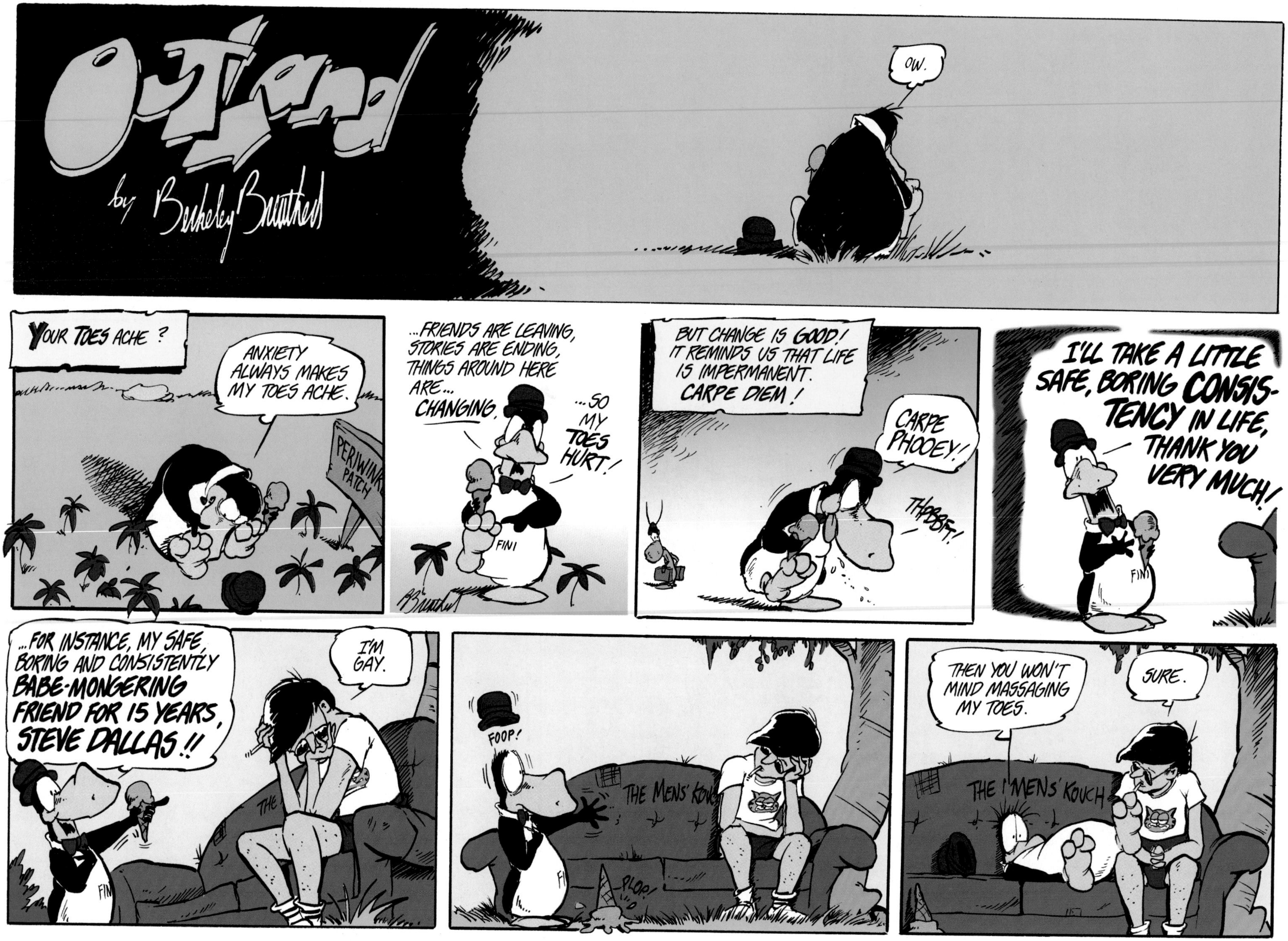

Outland
by Berkeley Breathed
OW.
YOUR TOES ACHE ?
ANXIETY ALWAYS MAKES MY TOES ACHE.
PERIWINKLE PATCH
...FRIENDS ARE LEAVING, STORIES ARE ENDING, THINGS AROUND HERE ARE... CHANGING.
...SO MY TOES HURT!
FINI
BUT CHANGE IS GOOD! IT REMINDS US THAT LIFE IS IMPERMANENT. CARPE DIEM!
CARPE PHOOEY!
THBBFT!
I'LL TAKE A LITTLE SAFE, BORING CONSISTENCY IN LIFE, THANK YOU VERY MUCH!
...FOR INSTANCE, MY SAFE, BORING AND CONSISTENTLY BABE-MONGERING FRIEND FOR 15 YEARS, STEVE DALLAS!!
I'M GAY.
FOOP!
THE MENS' KOUCH
PLOP!
THEN YOU WON'T MIND MASSAGING MY TOES.
SURE.
THE MENS' KOUCH

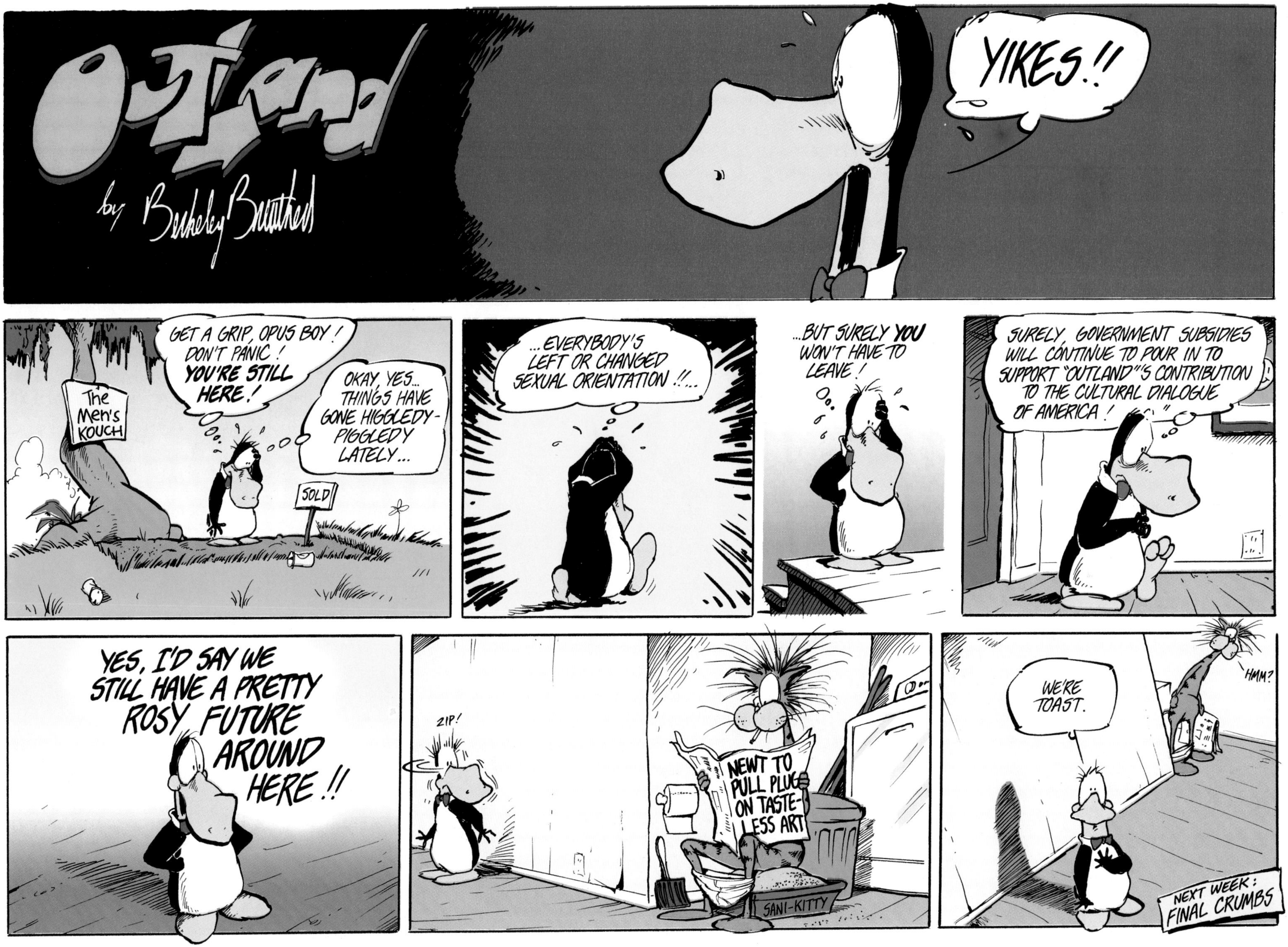
Outland
by Berkeley Breathed
YIKES.!!
GET A GRIP, OPUS BOY! DON'T PANIC! YOU'RE STILL HERE.!
The Men's KOUCH
OKAY, YES... THINGS HAVE GONE HIGGLEDY-PIGGLEDY LATELY...
SOLD
...EVERYBODY'S LEFT OR CHANGED SEXUAL ORIENTATION !!...
...BUT SURELY YOU WON'T HAVE TO LEAVE!
SURELY, GOVERNMENT SUBSIDIES WILL CONTINUE TO POUR IN TO SUPPORT "OUTLAND"'S CONTRIBUTION TO THE CULTURAL DIALOGUE OF AMERICA!
YES, I'D SAY WE STILL HAVE A PRETTY ROSY FUTURE AROUND HERE!!
ZIP!
NEWT TO PULL PLUG ON TASTE-LESS ART
SANI-KITTY
WE'RE TOAST.
HMM?
NEXT WEEK: FINAL CRUMBS

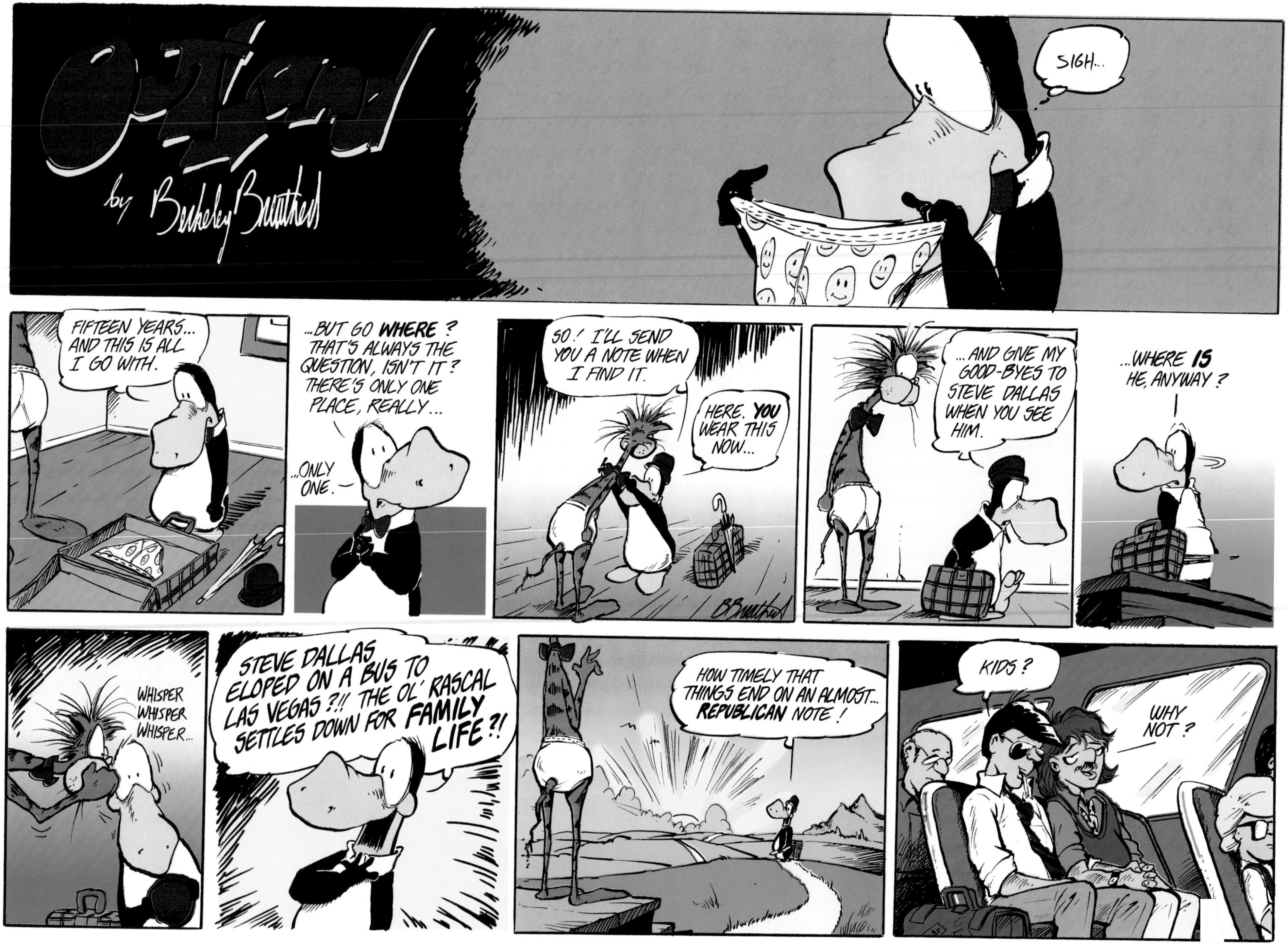
Outland
by Berkeley Breathed
SIGH...
FIFTEEN YEARS... AND THIS IS ALL I GO WITH.
...BUT GO WHERE? THAT'S ALWAYS THE QUESTION, ISN'T IT? THERE'S ONLY ONE PLACE, REALLY...
...ONLY ONE.
SO! I'LL SEND YOU A NOTE WHEN I FIND IT.
HERE. YOU WEAR THIS NOW...
B Breathed
...AND GIVE MY GOOD-BYES TO STEVE DALLAS WHEN YOU SEE HIM.
...WHERE IS HE, ANYWAY?
WHISPER WHISPER WHISPER...
STEVE DALLAS ELOPED ON A BUS TO LAS VEGAS?!! THE OL' RASCAL SETTLES DOWN FOR FAMILY LIFE?!
HOW TIMELY THAT THINGS END ON AN ALMOST... REPUBLICAN NOTE!
KIDS?
WHY NOT?

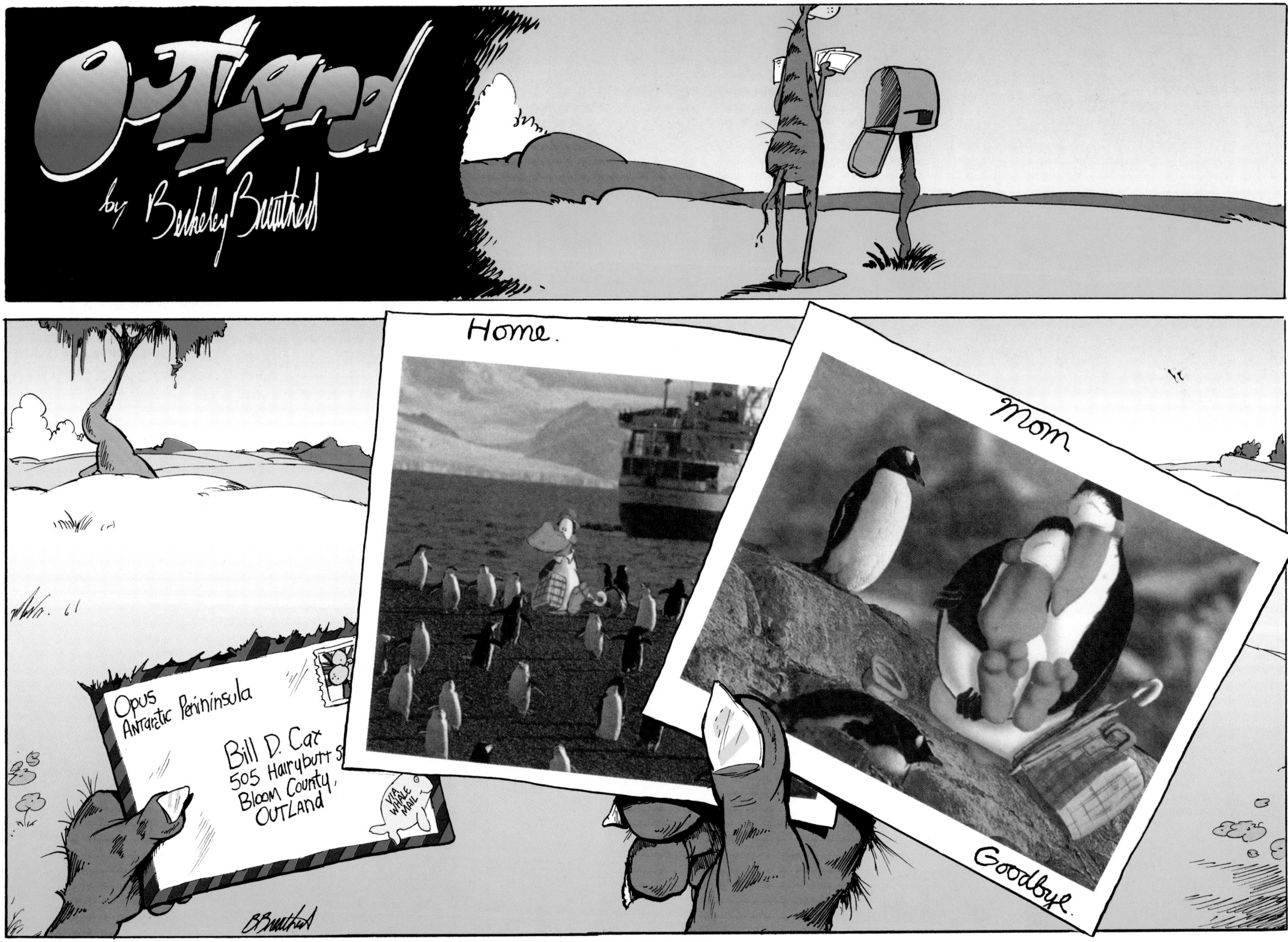
OUTLAND
by Berkeley Breathed
Home.
Mom
Goodbye.
Opus
Antarctic Penininsula
Bill D. Cat
505 Hairybutt St
Bloom County,
OUTLAND
VIA WHALE MAIL
B Breathed

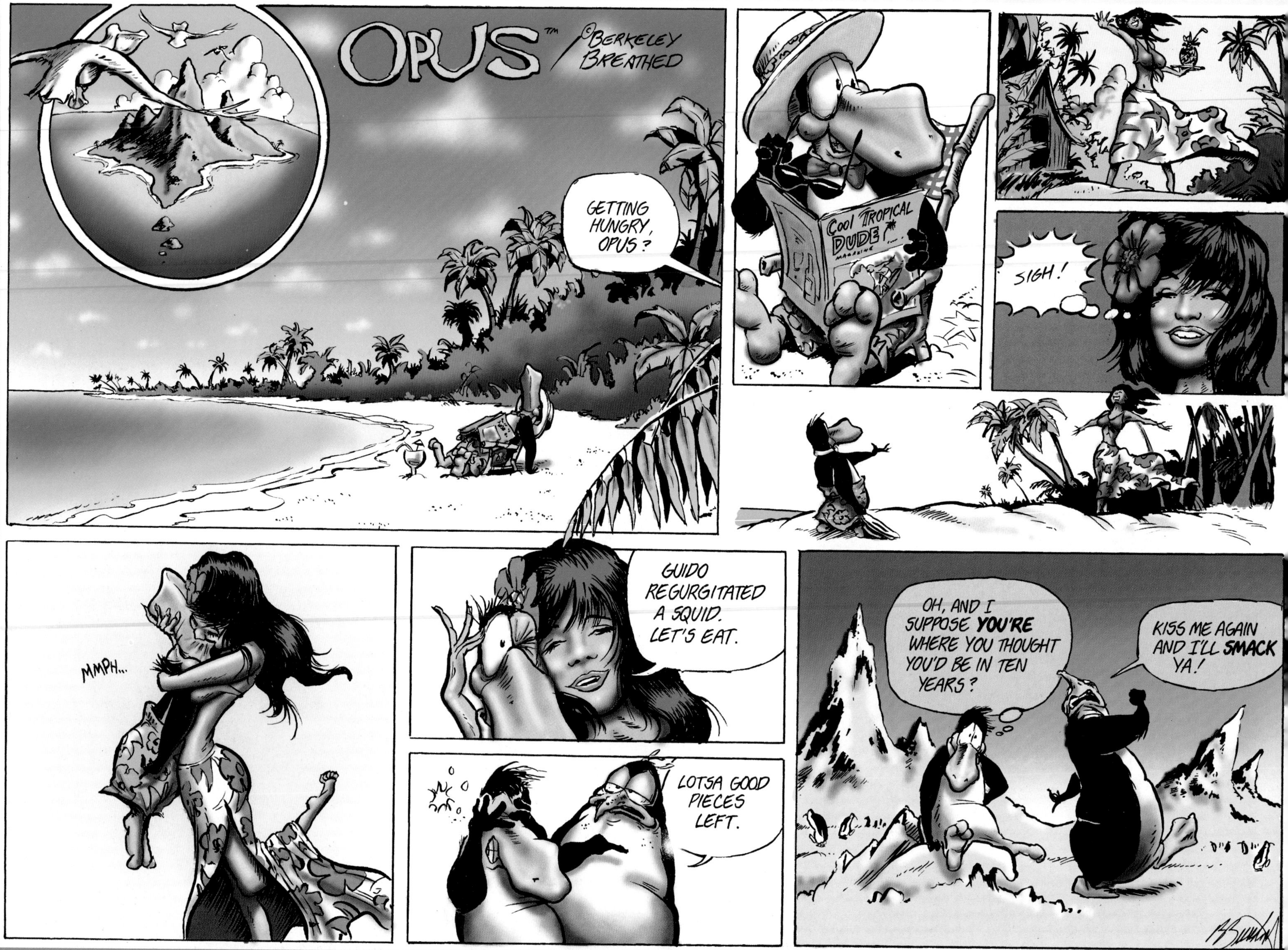
OPUS™
©BERKELEY BREATHED
GETTING HUNGRY, OPUS?
Cool TROPICAL DUDE MAGAZINE
SIGH!
MMPH...
GUIDO REGURGITATED A SQUID. LET'S EAT.
LOTSA GOOD PIECES LEFT.
OH, AND I SUPPOSE YOU'RE WHERE YOU THOUGHT YOU'D BE IN TEN YEARS?
KISS ME AGAIN AND I'LL SMACK YA!

OPUS

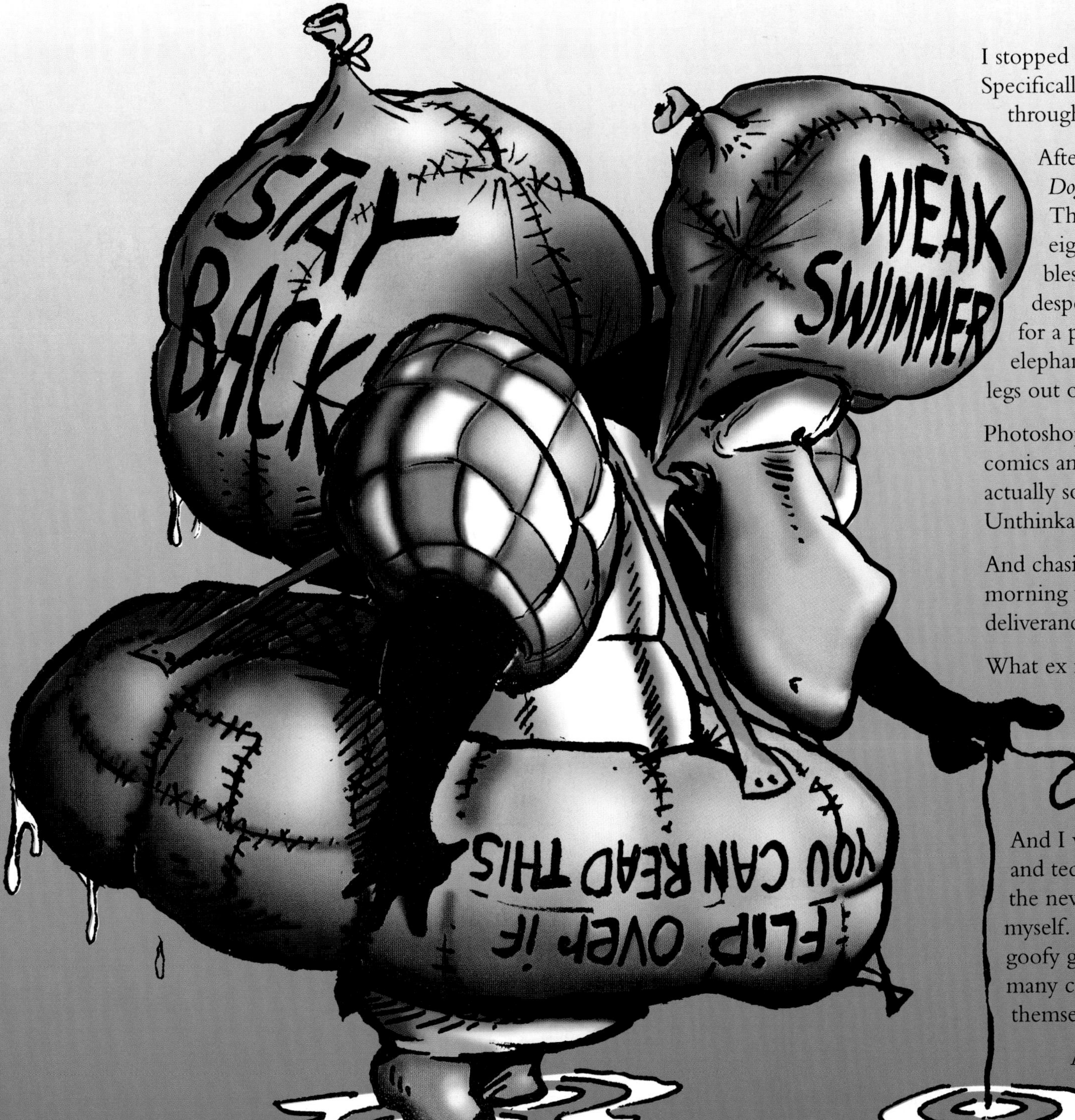
STAY BACK
WEAK SWIMMER
FLIP OVER IF YOU CAN READ THIS

I stopped *Outland* because I wanted to learn to paint. Specifically, I wanted to learn how to tell a story through paintings. I authored six picture books.

After the paint was dry on the last one — *Flawed Dogs* — I looked again at the comic strip world. There had been a technological revolution in the eight years I'd been gone: the Internet — God bless those dear Google Boys — eliminated the desperate, last-minute searches at faraway libraries for a picture of, say, a Segway scooter or what an elephant looks like from the rear when it squats — legs out or under?

Photoshop had given us the power to color our own comics and come darn close to painting them. Imagine: actually something that *looks* cool on a comic page. Unthinkable in 1990.

And chasing Fed Ex trucks in the wee hours of the morning was no more. Broadband was a permanent deliverance from that resident evil.

What ex mobster/cartoonist could resist such provocation? *"Just when I thought I was out . . . they PULL me back in!"*

And they did. I wanted to get to know Opus better and see him better defined.

And I wanted to draw. An increase in square inches and technology had allowed this. You can see that in the new strips. See something else: I'm enjoying myself. I hope that you can picture me with a stupid, goofy grin as I draw some of this stuff. Trust me: many cartoonists have long since stopped amusing themselves.

A pity.

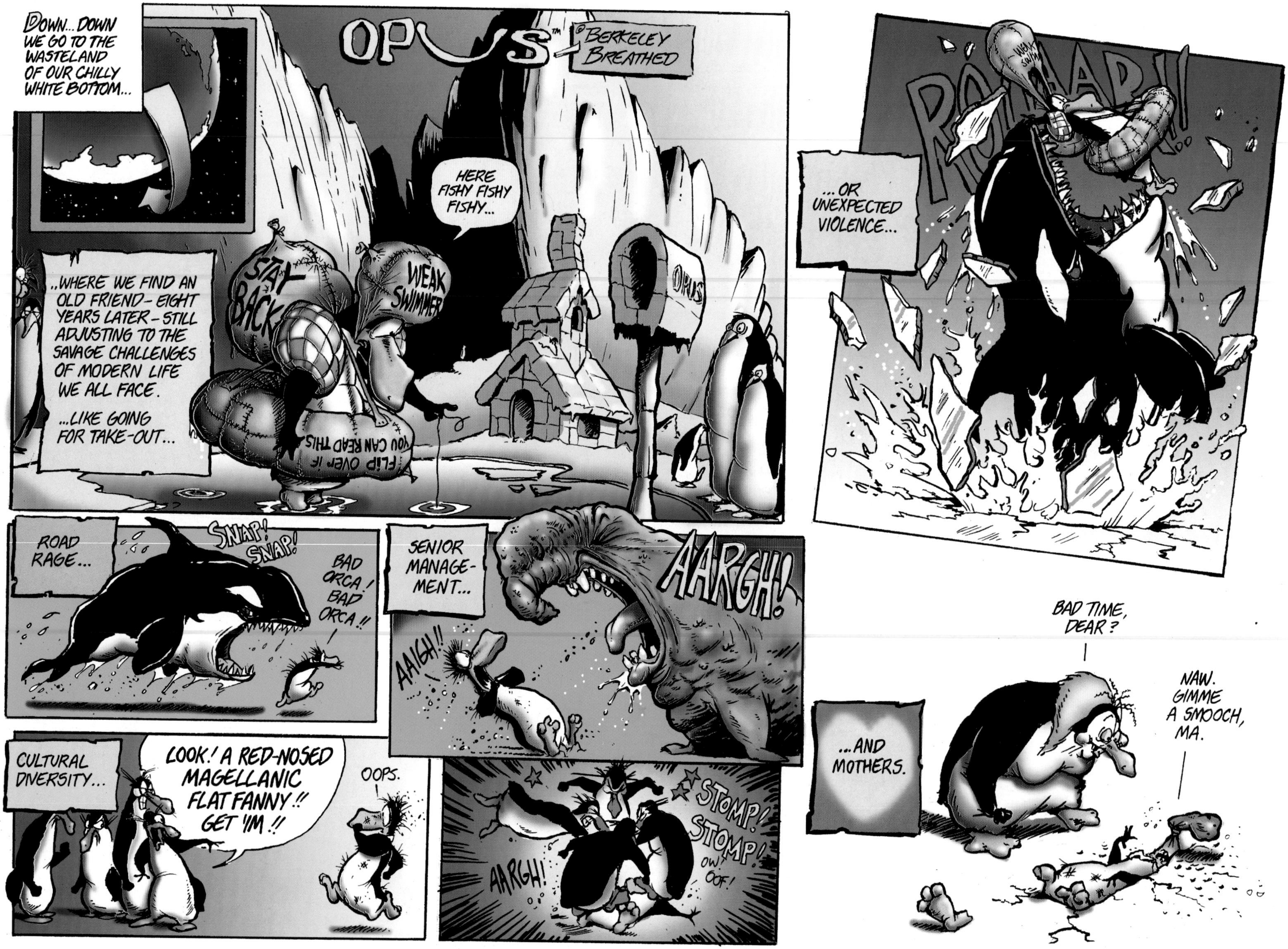
DOWN... DOWN WE GO TO THE WASTELAND OF OUR CHILLY WHITE BOTTOM...
OPUS™ ©BERKELEY BREATHED
HERE FISHY FISHY FISHY...
..WHERE WE FIND AN OLD FRIEND- EIGHT YEARS LATER- STILL ADJUSTING TO THE SAVAGE CHALLENGES OF MODERN LIFE WE ALL FACE.
...LIKE GOING FOR TAKE-OUT...
STAY BACK
WEAK SWIMMER
FLIP OVER IF YOU CAN READ THIS
OPUS
... OR UNEXPECTED VIOLENCE...
ROAD RAGE...
SNAP! SNAP!
BAD ORCA! BAD ORCA!!
SENIOR MANAGE-MENT...
AARGH!
AAIGH!!
CULTURAL DIVERSITY...
LOOK! A RED-NOSED MAGELLANIC FLAT FANNY!! GET 'IM!!
OOPS.
STOMP! STOMP!
OW! OOF!
AARGH!
...AND MOTHERS.
BAD TIME, DEAR?
NAW. GIMME A SMOOCH, MA.

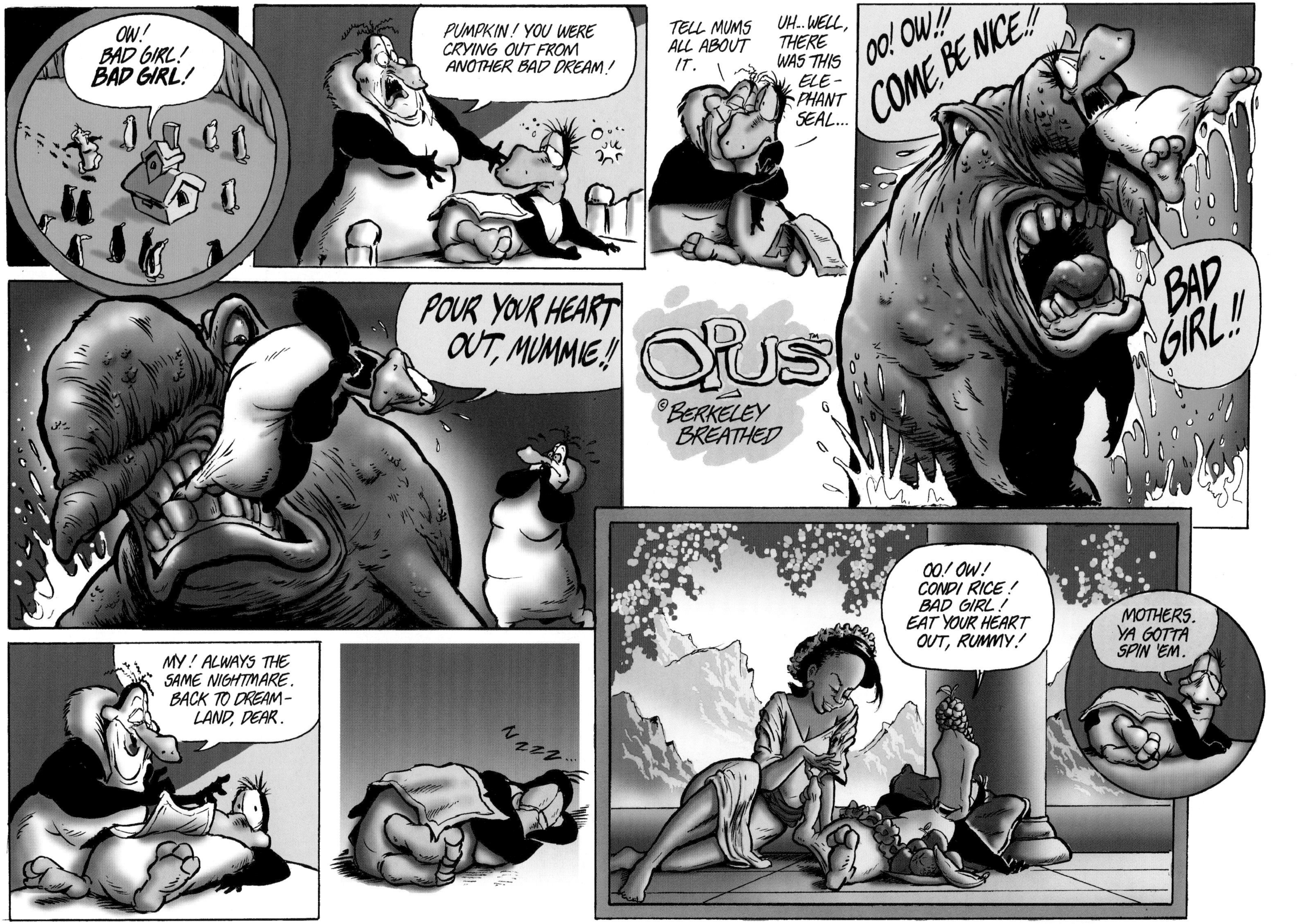
OW!
BAD GIRL!
BAD GIRL!
PUMPKIN! YOU WERE CRYING OUT FROM ANOTHER BAD DREAM!
TELL MUMS ALL ABOUT IT.
UH...WELL, THERE WAS THIS ELE-PHANT SEAL...
OO! OW!! COME, BE NICE!!
BAD GIRL!!
POUR YOUR HEART OUT, MUMMIE!!
OPUS™
© BERKELEY BREATHED
MY! ALWAYS THE SAME NIGHTMARE. BACK TO DREAM-LAND, DEAR.
ZZZZ...
OO! OW! CONDI RICE! BAD GIRL! EAT YOUR HEART OUT, RUMMY!
MOTHERS. YA GOTTA SPIN 'EM.

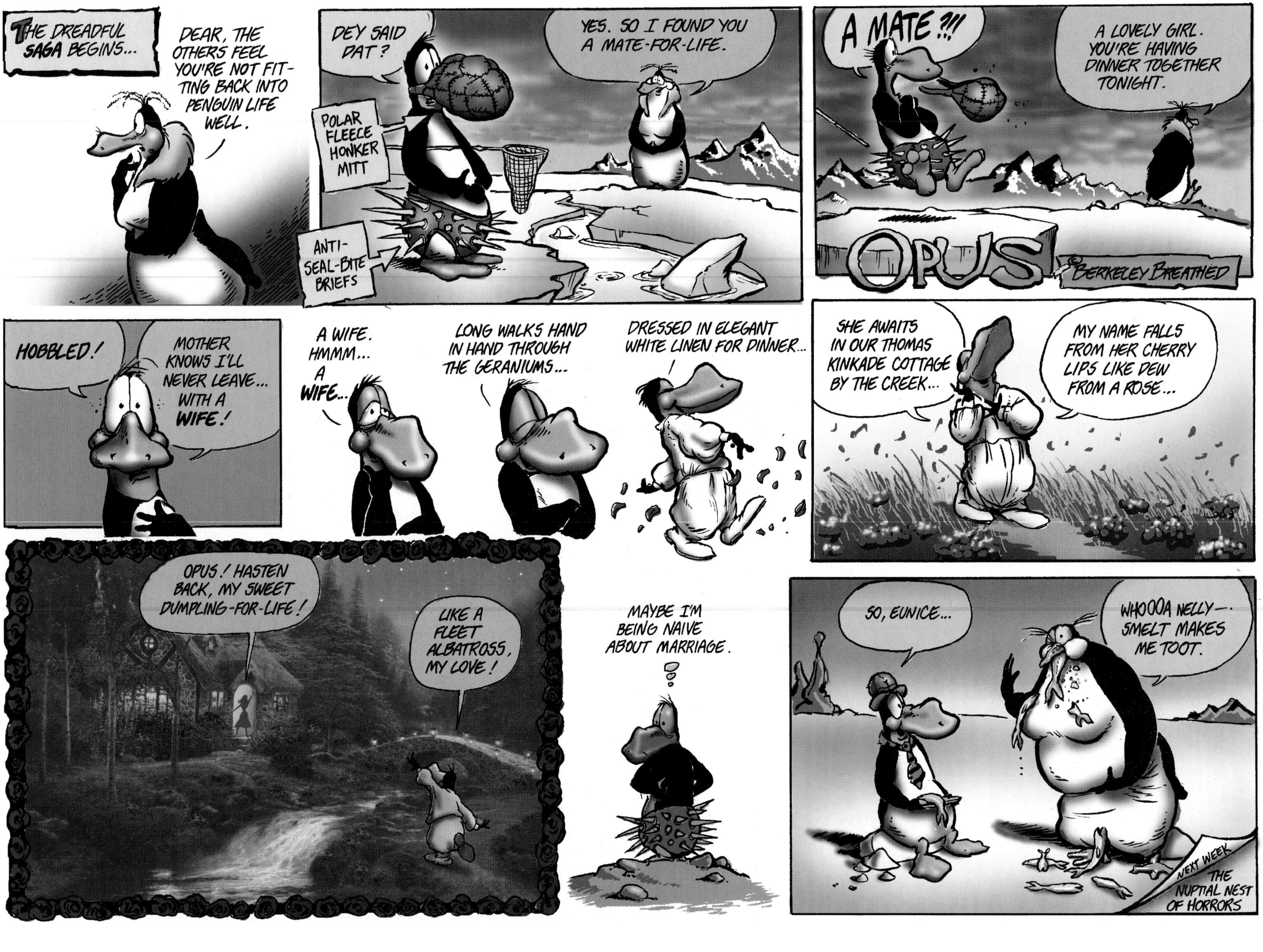
THE DREADFUL SAGA BEGINS...
DEAR, THE OTHERS FEEL YOU'RE NOT FITTING BACK INTO PENGUIN LIFE WELL.
DEY SAID DAT?
YES. SO I FOUND YOU A MATE-FOR-LIFE.
POLAR FLEECE HONKER MITT
ANTI-SEAL-BITE BRIEFS
A MATE?!!
A LOVELY GIRL. YOU'RE HAVING DINNER TOGETHER TONIGHT.
OPUS
© BERKELEY BREATHED
HOBBLED!
MOTHER KNOWS I'LL NEVER LEAVE... WITH A WIFE!
A WIFE. HMMM... A WIFE...
LONG WALKS HAND IN HAND THROUGH THE GERANIUMS...
DRESSED IN ELEGANT WHITE LINEN FOR DINNER...
SHE AWAITS IN OUR THOMAS KINKADE COTTAGE BY THE CREEK...
MY NAME FALLS FROM HER CHERRY LIPS LIKE DEW FROM A ROSE...
OPUS! HASTEN BACK, MY SWEET DUMPLING-FOR-LIFE!
LIKE A FLEET ALBATROSS, MY LOVE!
MAYBE I'M BEING NAIVE ABOUT MARRIAGE.
SO, EUNICE...
WHOOOA NELLY—. SMELT MAKES ME TOOT.
NEXT WEEK THE NUPTIAL NEST OF HORRORS

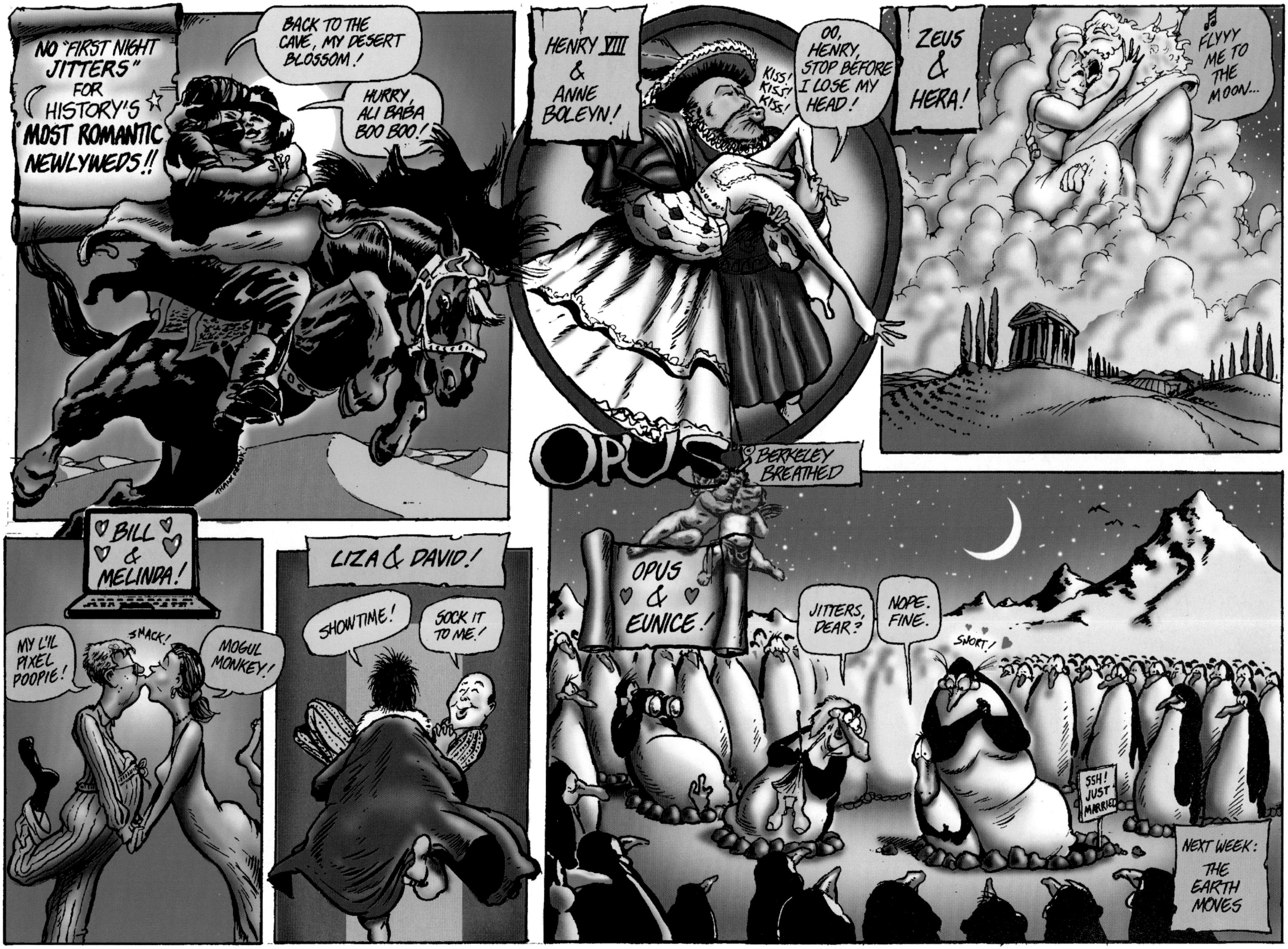
NO "FIRST NIGHT JITTERS" FOR HISTORY'S MOST ROMANTIC NEWLYWEDS!!
BACK TO THE CAVE, MY DESERT BLOSSOM!
HURRY, ALI BABA BOO BOO!
HENRY VIII & ANNE BOLEYN!
KISS! KISS! KISS!
OO, HENRY, STOP BEFORE I LOSE MY HEAD!
ZEUS & HERA!
FLYYY ME TO THE MOON...
OPUS © BERKELEY BREATHED
BILL & MELINDA!
MY L'IL PIXEL POOPIE!
SMACK!
MOGUL MONKEY!
LIZA & DAVID!
SHOWTIME!
SOCK IT TO ME!
OPUS & EUNICE!
JITTERS, DEAR?
NOPE. FINE.
SNORT!
SSH! JUST MARRIED
NEXT WEEK: THE EARTH MOVES

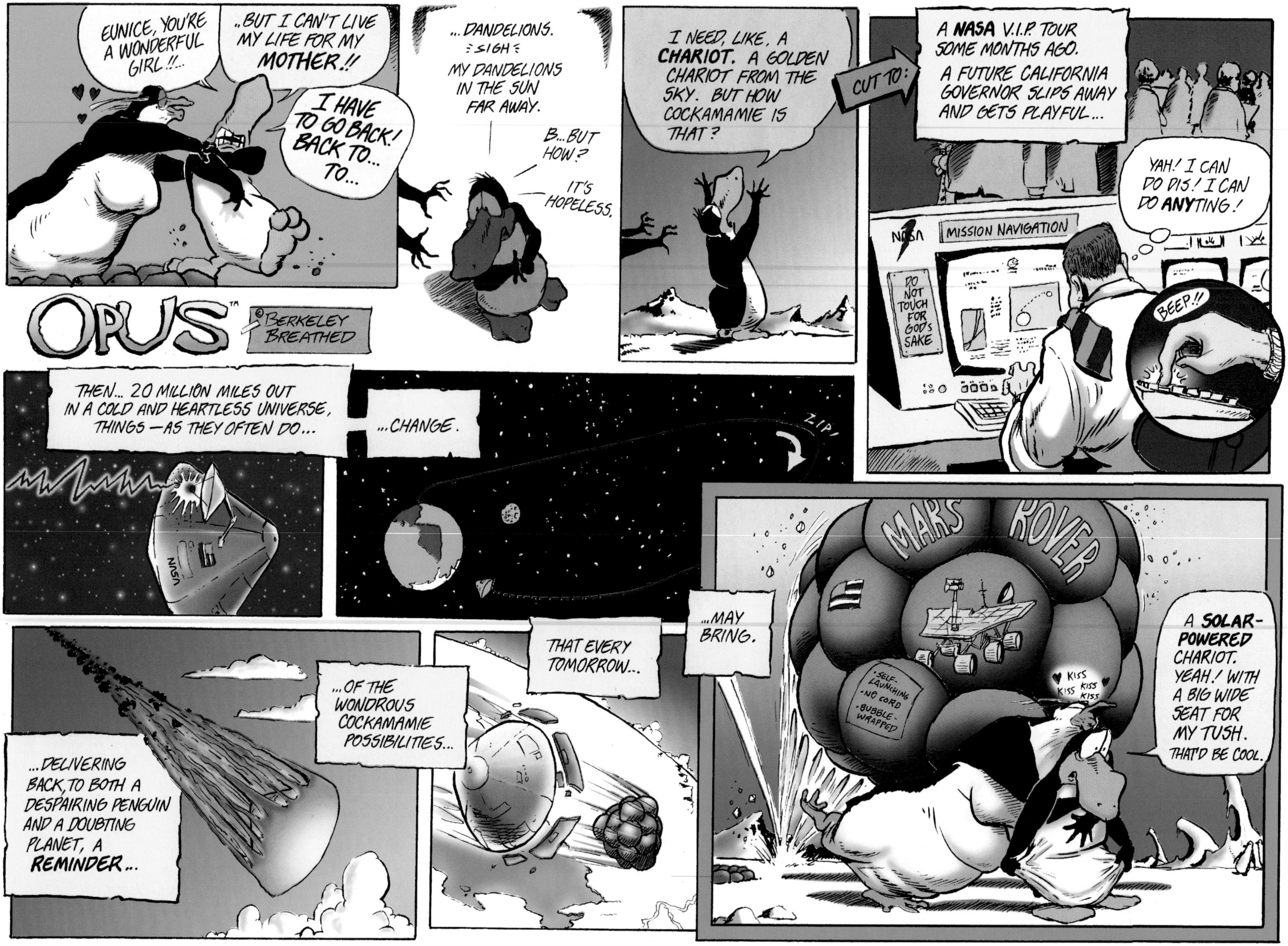
EUNICE, YOU'RE A WONDERFUL GIRL!!...
..BUT I CAN'T LIVE MY LIFE FOR MY MOTHER!!
I HAVE TO GO BACK! BACK TO... TO...
...DANDELIONS.
SIGH
MY DANDELIONS IN THE SUN FAR AWAY.
B...BUT HOW?
IT'S HOPELESS.
OPUS™
© BERKELEY BREATHED
I NEED, LIKE, A CHARIOT. A GOLDEN CHARIOT FROM THE SKY. BUT HOW COCKAMAMIE IS THAT?
CUT TO:
A NASA V.I.P. TOUR SOME MONTHS AGO.
A FUTURE CALIFORNIA GOVERNOR SLIPS AWAY AND GETS PLAYFUL...
MISSION NAVIGATION
DO NOT TOUCH FOR GOD'S SAKE
YAH! I CAN DO DIS! I CAN DO ANYTING!
BEEP!!
THEN... 20 MILLION MILES OUT IN A COLD AND HEARTLESS UNIVERSE, THINGS—AS THEY OFTEN DO...
...CHANGE.
ZIP!
NASA
MARS ROVER
•SELF-LAUNCHING •NO CORD •BUBBLE-WRAPPED
KISS KISS KISS KISS
A SOLAR-POWERED CHARIOT. YEAH! WITH A BIG WIDE SEAT FOR MY TUSH. THAT'D BE COOL.
...DELIVERING BACK, TO BOTH A DESPAIRING PENGUIN AND A DOUBTING PLANET, A REMINDER...
...OF THE WONDROUS COCKAMAMIE POSSIBILITIES...
THAT EVERY TOMORROW...
...MAY BRING.

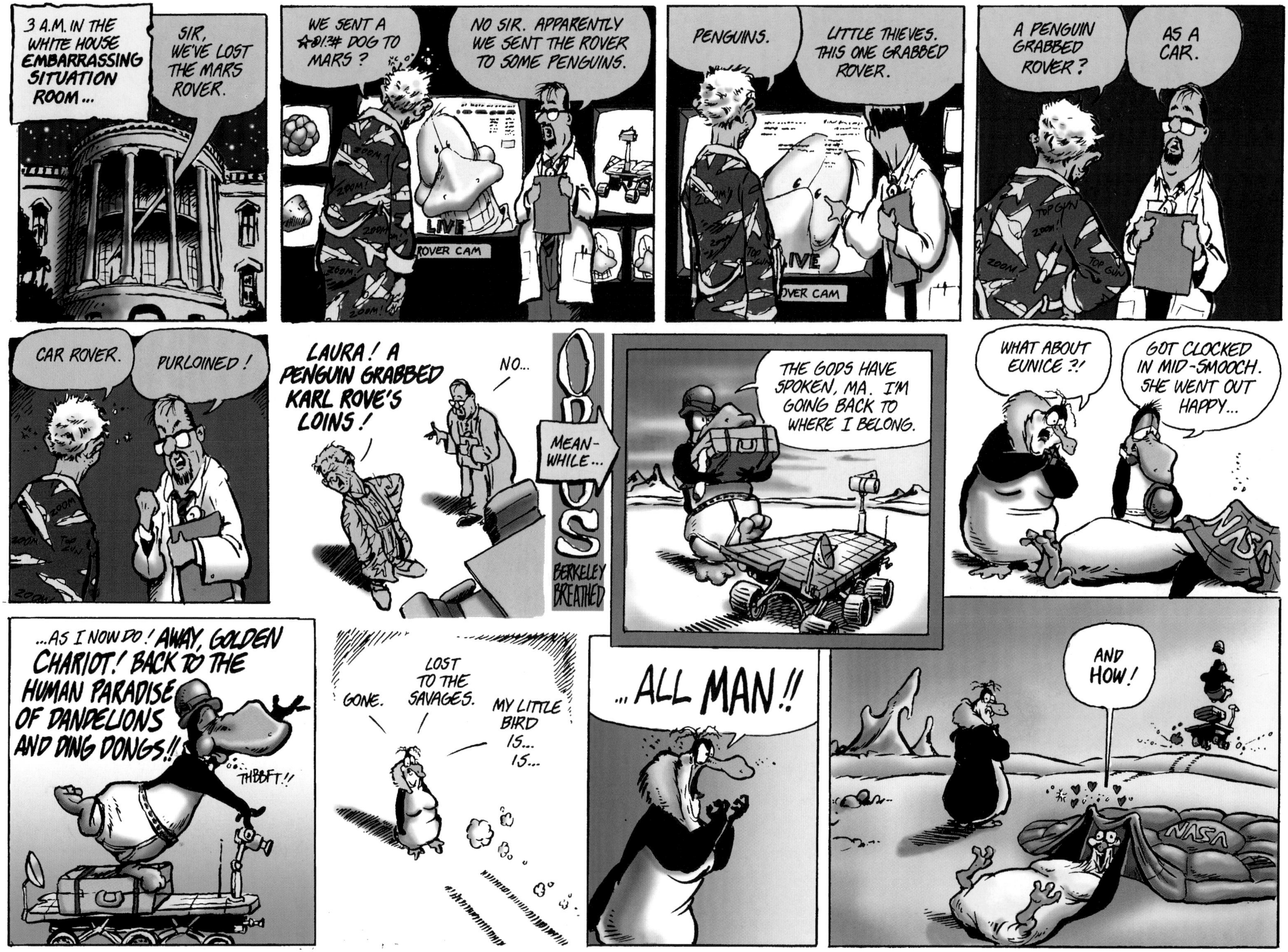

3 A.M. IN THE WHITE HOUSE EMBARRASSING SITUATION ROOM...
SIR, WE'VE LOST THE MARS ROVER.
WE SENT A ☆@!3# DOG TO MARS?
NO SIR. APPARENTLY WE SENT THE ROVER TO SOME PENGUINS.
LIVE
ROVER CAM
PENGUINS.
LITTLE THIEVES. THIS ONE GRABBED ROVER.
A PENGUIN GRABBED ROVER?
AS A CAR.
CAR ROVER.
PURLOINED!
LAURA! A PENGUIN GRABBED KARL ROVE'S LOINS!
NO...
OPUS
BERKELEY BREATHED
MEAN-WHILE...
THE GODS HAVE SPOKEN, MA. I'M GOING BACK TO WHERE I BELONG.
WHAT ABOUT EUNICE?!
GOT CLOCKED IN MID-SMOOCH. SHE WENT OUT HAPPY...
NASA
...AS I NOW DO! AWAY, GOLDEN CHARIOT! BACK TO THE HUMAN PARADISE OF DANDELIONS AND DING DONGS!!
THBBFT!!
GONE.
LOST TO THE SAVAGES.
MY LITTLE BIRD IS... IS...
...ALL MAN!!
AND HOW!
NASA

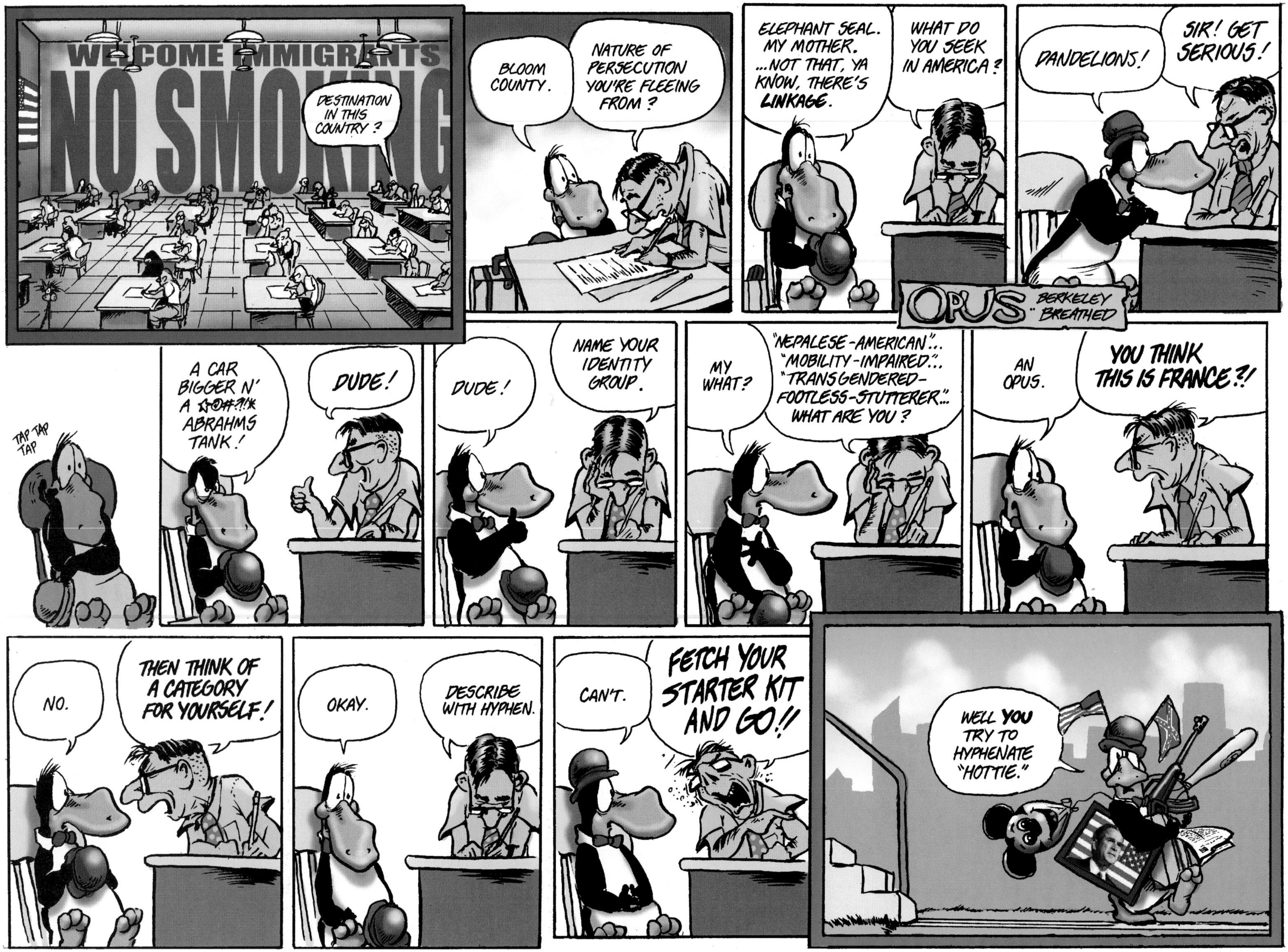
WELCOME IMMIGRANTS
NO SMOKING
DESTINATION IN THIS COUNTRY ?
BLOOM COUNTY.
NATURE OF PERSECUTION YOU'RE FLEEING FROM ?
ELEPHANT SEAL. MY MOTHER. ...NOT THAT, YA KNOW, THERE'S LINKAGE.
WHAT DO YOU SEEK IN AMERICA ?
DANDELIONS !
SIR ! GET SERIOUS !
OPUS
BERKELEY BREATHED
TAP TAP TAP
A CAR BIGGER N' A ☆@#?!* ABRAHMS TANK !
DUDE !
DUDE !
NAME YOUR IDENTITY GROUP.
MY WHAT ?
"NEPALESE-AMERICAN"... "MOBILITY-IMPAIRED"... "TRANSGENDERED-FOOTLESS-STUTTERER"... WHAT ARE YOU ?
AN OPUS.
YOU THINK THIS IS FRANCE ?!
NO.
THEN THINK OF A CATEGORY FOR YOURSELF !
OKAY.
DESCRIBE WITH HYPHEN.
CAN'T.
FETCH YOUR STARTER KIT AND GO !!
WELL YOU TRY TO HYPHENATE "HOTTIE."

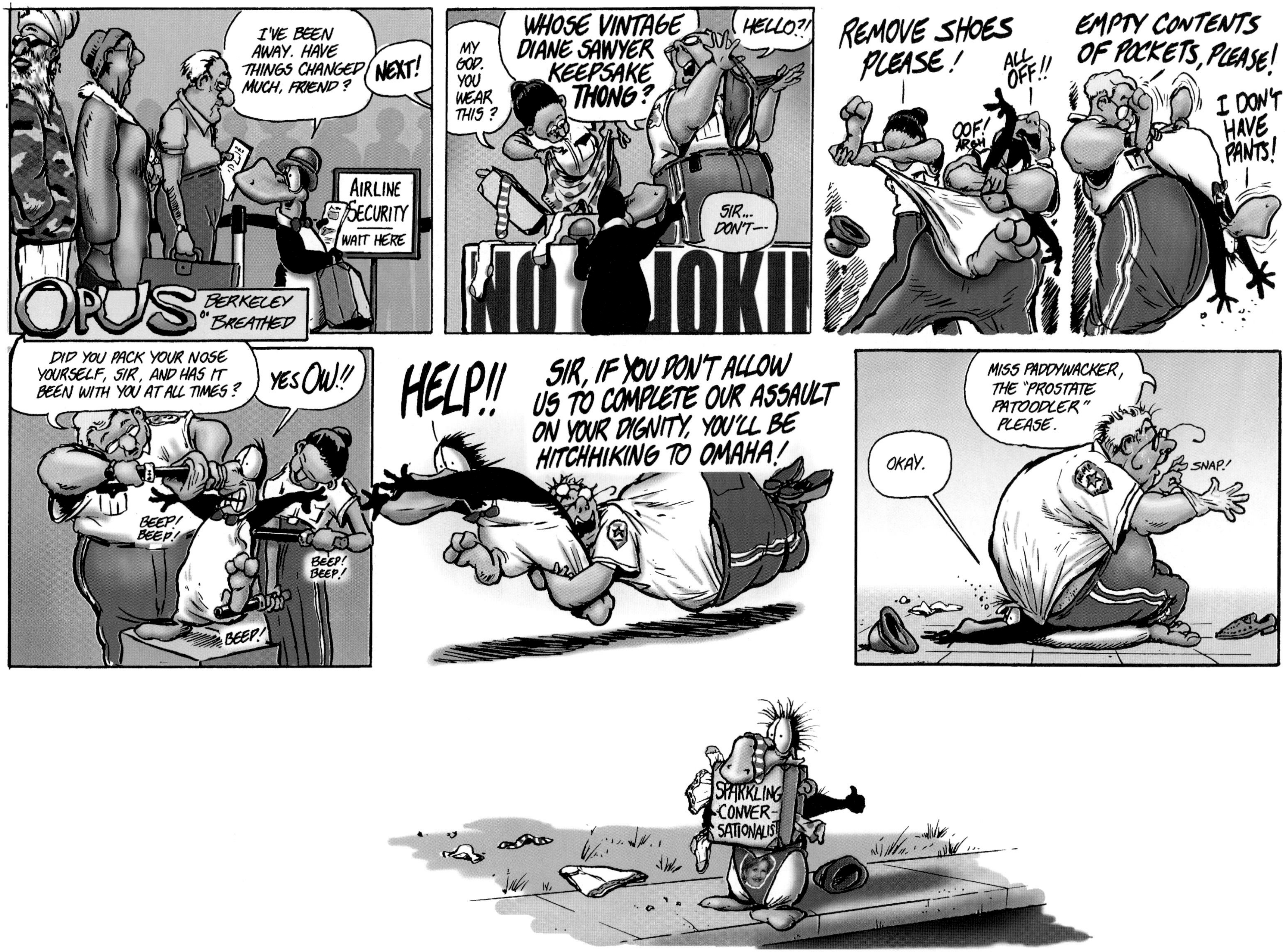
OPUS
BERKELEY BREATHED
I'VE BEEN AWAY. HAVE THINGS CHANGED MUCH, FRIEND?
NEXT!
AIRLINE SECURITY
WAIT HERE
MY GOD. YOU WEAR THIS?
WHOSE VINTAGE DIANE SAWYER KEEPSAKE THONG?
HELLO?!
SIR... DON'T--
REMOVE SHOES PLEASE!
ALL OFF!!
OOF!
ARGH
EMPTY CONTENTS OF POCKETS, PLEASE!
I DON'T HAVE PANTS!
DID YOU PACK YOUR NOSE YOURSELF, SIR, AND HAS IT BEEN WITH YOU AT ALL TIMES?
YES OW!!
BEEP! BEEP!
BEEP! BEEP!
BEEP!
HELP!!
SIR, IF YOU DON'T ALLOW US TO COMPLETE OUR ASSAULT ON YOUR DIGNITY, YOU'LL BE HITCHHIKING TO OMAHA!
MISS PADDYWACKER, THE "PROSTATE PATOODLER" PLEASE.
OKAY.
SNAP!
SPARKLING CONVER-SATIONALIST

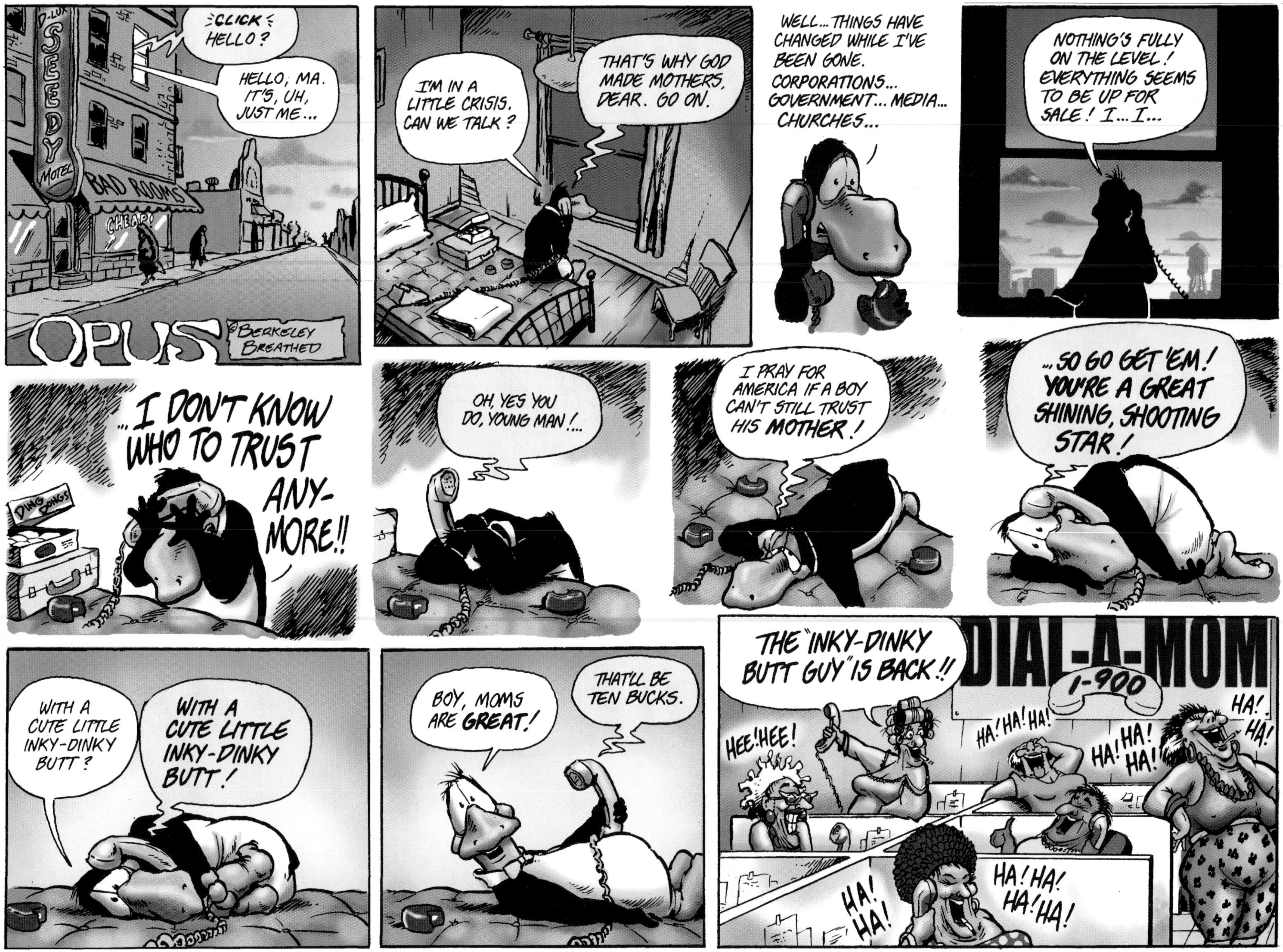
D-LUX
SEEDY
MOTEL
BAD ROOMS
CHEAP!
CLICK
HELLO?
HELLO, MA. IT'S, UH, JUST ME...
OPUS
© BERKELEY BREATHED
I'M IN A LITTLE CRISIS. CAN WE TALK?
THAT'S WHY GOD MADE MOTHERS, DEAR. GO ON.
WELL... THINGS HAVE CHANGED WHILE I'VE BEEN GONE. CORPORATIONS... GOVERNMENT... MEDIA... CHURCHES...
NOTHING'S FULLY ON THE LEVEL! EVERYTHING SEEMS TO BE UP FOR SALE! I... I...
...I DON'T KNOW WHO TO TRUST ANY-MORE!!
DING DONGS
OH, YES YOU DO, YOUNG MAN!...
I PRAY FOR AMERICA IF A BOY CAN'T STILL TRUST HIS MOTHER!
...SO GO GET 'EM! YOU'RE A GREAT SHINING, SHOOTING STAR!
WITH A CUTE LITTLE INKY-DINKY BUTT?
WITH A CUTE LITTLE INKY-DINKY BUTT!
BOY, MOMS ARE GREAT!
THAT'LL BE TEN BUCKS.
THE "INKY-DINKY BUTT GUY" IS BACK!!
DIAL-A-MOM
1-900
HEE! HEE!
HA! HA! HA!
HA! HA! HA!
HA! HA!
HA! HA!
HA! HA! HA! HA!

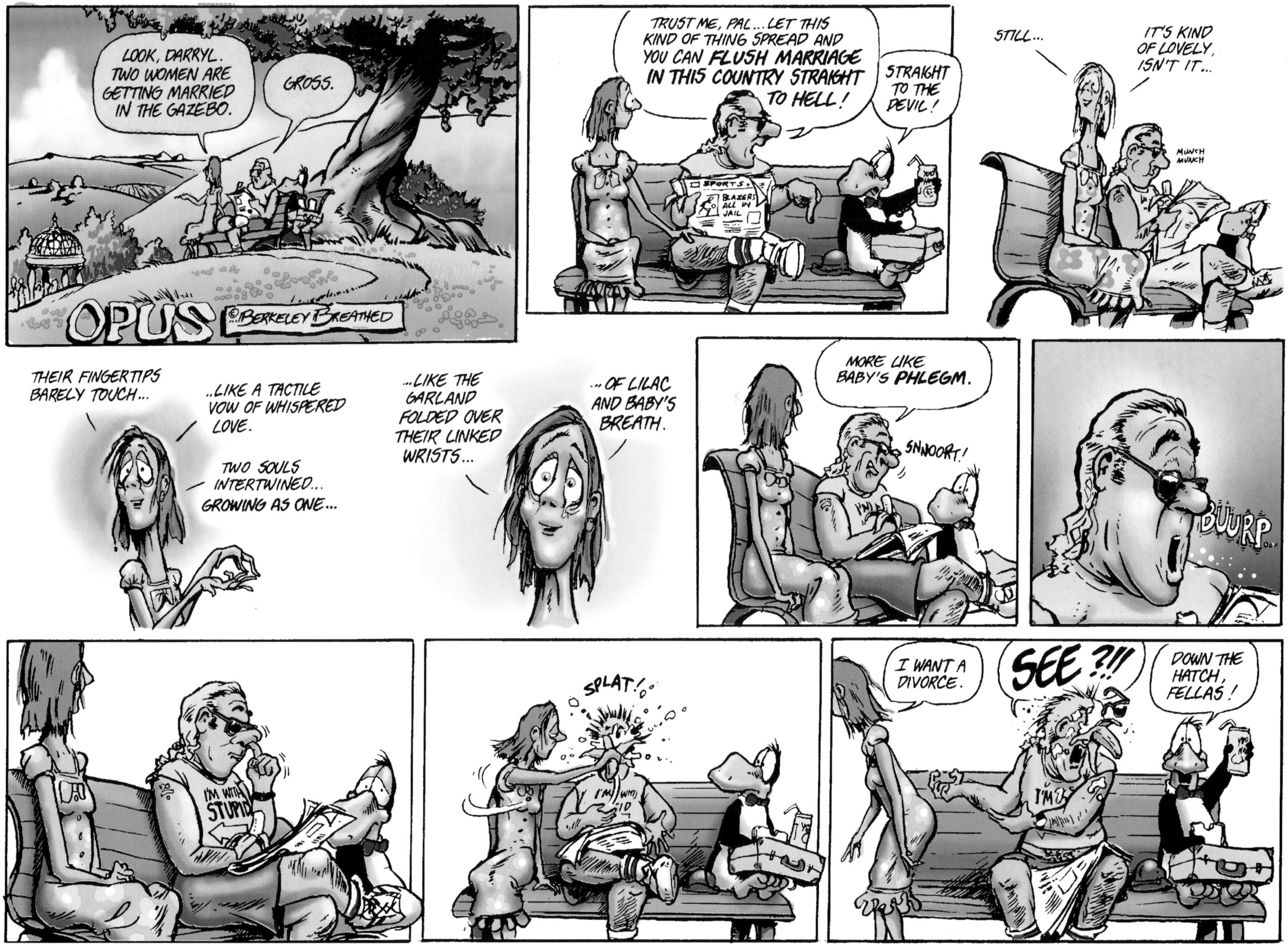

OPUS
©BERKELEY BREATHED
LOOK, DARRYL. TWO WOMEN ARE GETTING MARRIED IN THE GAZEBO.
GROSS.
TRUST ME, PAL... LET THIS KIND OF THING SPREAD AND YOU CAN FLUSH MARRIAGE IN THIS COUNTRY STRAIGHT TO HELL!
SPORTS
BLAZERS ALL IN JAIL
STRAIGHT TO THE DEVIL!
STILL...
IT'S KIND OF LOVELY, ISN'T IT...
MUNCH MUNCH
THEIR FINGERTIPS BARELY TOUCH...
..LIKE A TACTILE VOW OF WHISPERED LOVE.
TWO SOULS INTERTWINED... GROWING AS ONE...
...LIKE THE GARLAND FOLDED OVER THEIR LINKED WRISTS...
...OF LILAC AND BABY'S BREATH.
MORE LIKE BABY'S PHLEGM.
SNNOORT!
BUURP...
I'M WITH STUPID
SPLAT!
I WANT A DIVORCE.
SEE?!!
DOWN THE HATCH, FELLAS!

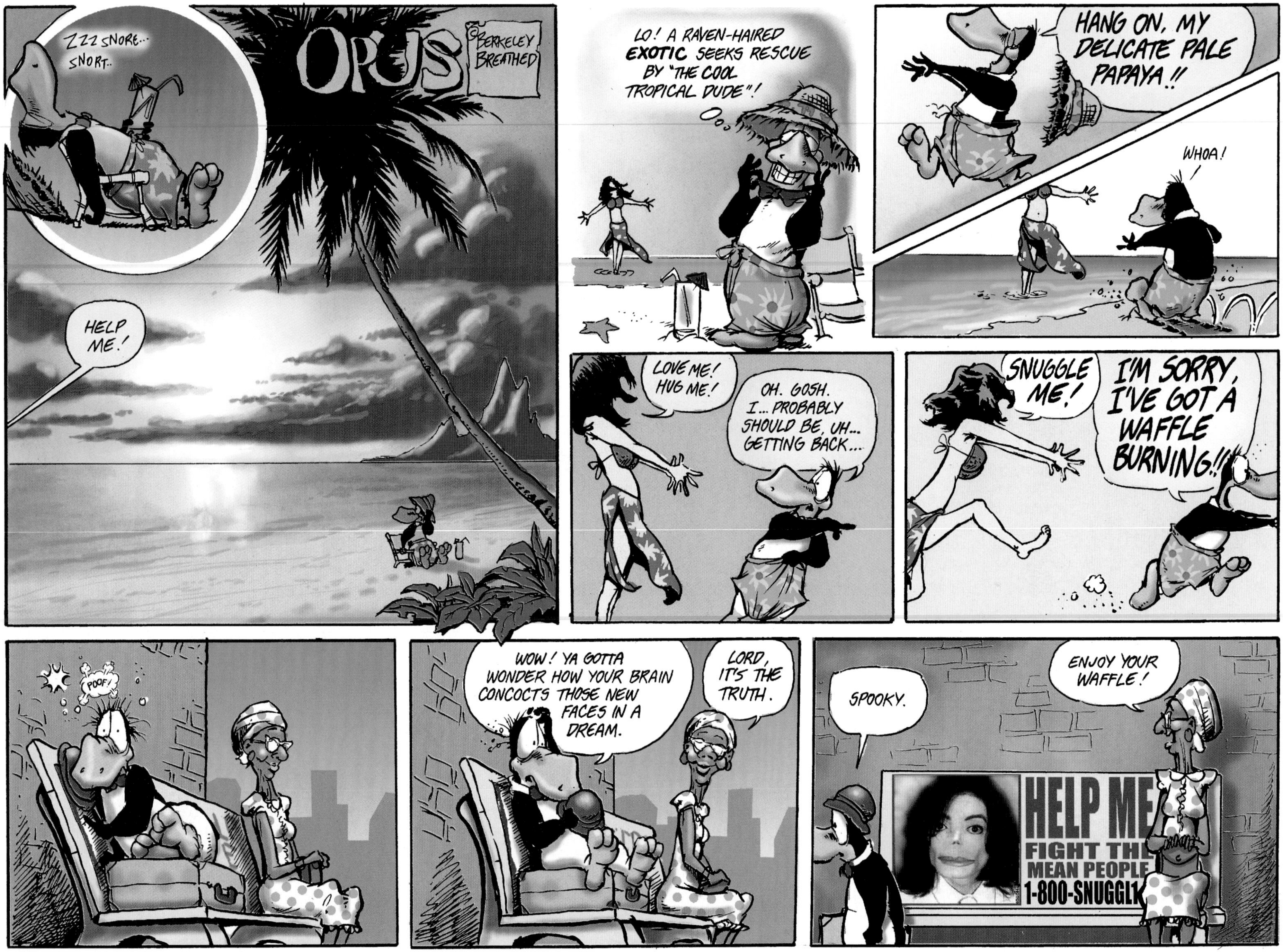
OPUS
© Berkeley Breathed
ZZZ SNORE... SNORT..
HELP ME!
LO! A RAVEN-HAIRED EXOTIC SEEKS RESCUE BY "THE COOL TROPICAL DUDE"!
HANG ON, MY DELICATE PALE PAPAYA!!
WHOA!
LOVE ME! HUG ME!
OH. GOSH. I... PROBABLY SHOULD BE, UH... GETTING BACK...
SNUGGLE ME!
I'M SORRY, I'VE GOT A WAFFLE BURNING!!
POOF!
WOW! YA GOTTA WONDER HOW YOUR BRAIN CONCOCTS THOSE NEW FACES IN A DREAM.
LORD, IT'S THE TRUTH.
SPOOKY.
ENJOY YOUR WAFFLE!
HELP ME
FIGHT THE
MEAN PEOPLE
1-800-SNUGGL1

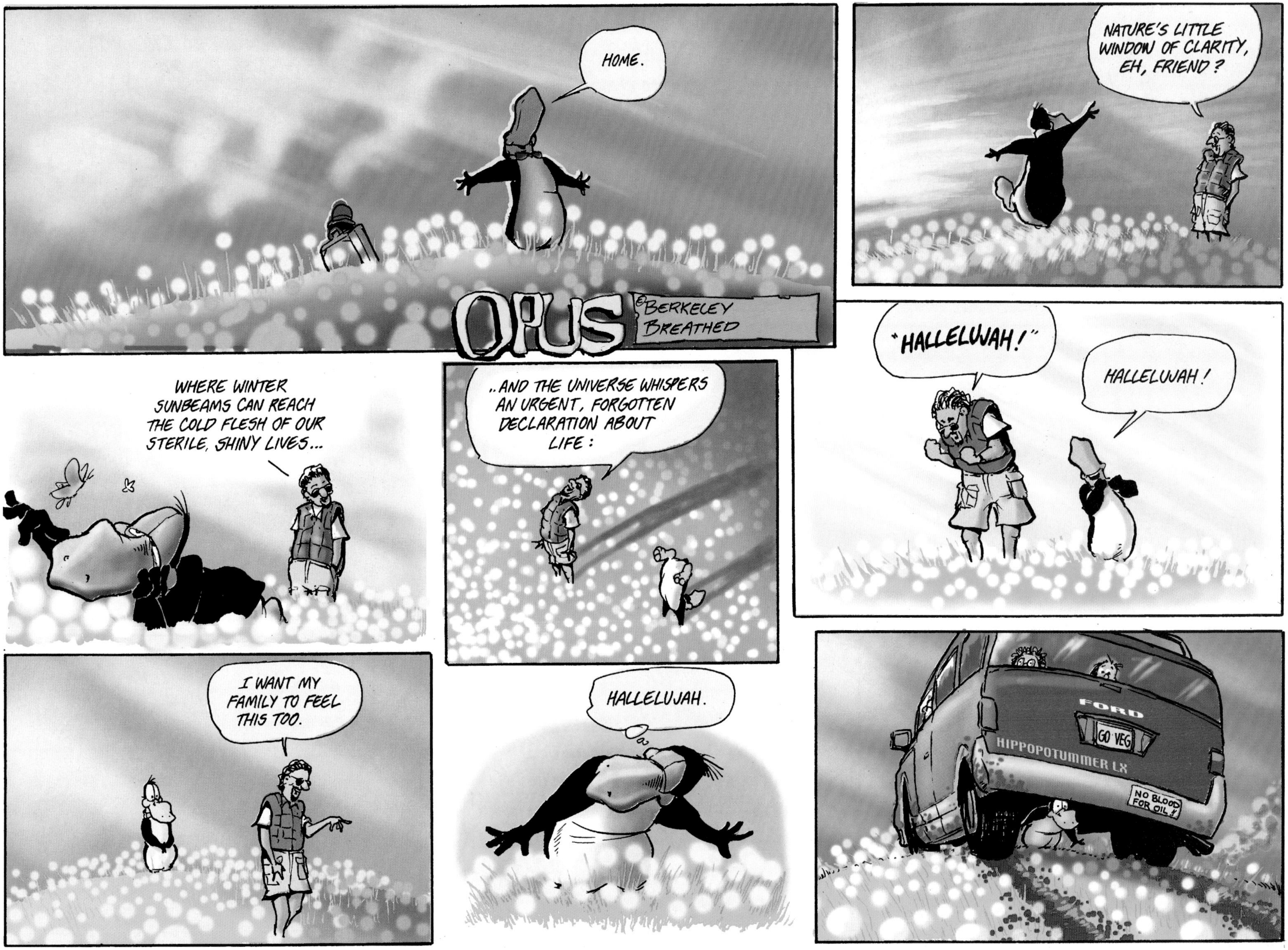
HOME.
OPUS
©BERKELEY BREATHED
NATURE'S LITTLE WINDOW OF CLARITY, EH, FRIEND?
WHERE WINTER SUNBEAMS CAN REACH THE COLD FLESH OF OUR STERILE, SHINY LIVES...
..AND THE UNIVERSE WHISPERS AN URGENT, FORGOTTEN DECLARATION ABOUT LIFE:
"HALLELUJAH!"
HALLELUJAH!
I WANT MY FAMILY TO FEEL THIS TOO.
HALLELUJAH.
FORD
GO VEG
HIPPOPOTUMMER LX
NO BLOOD FOR OIL!

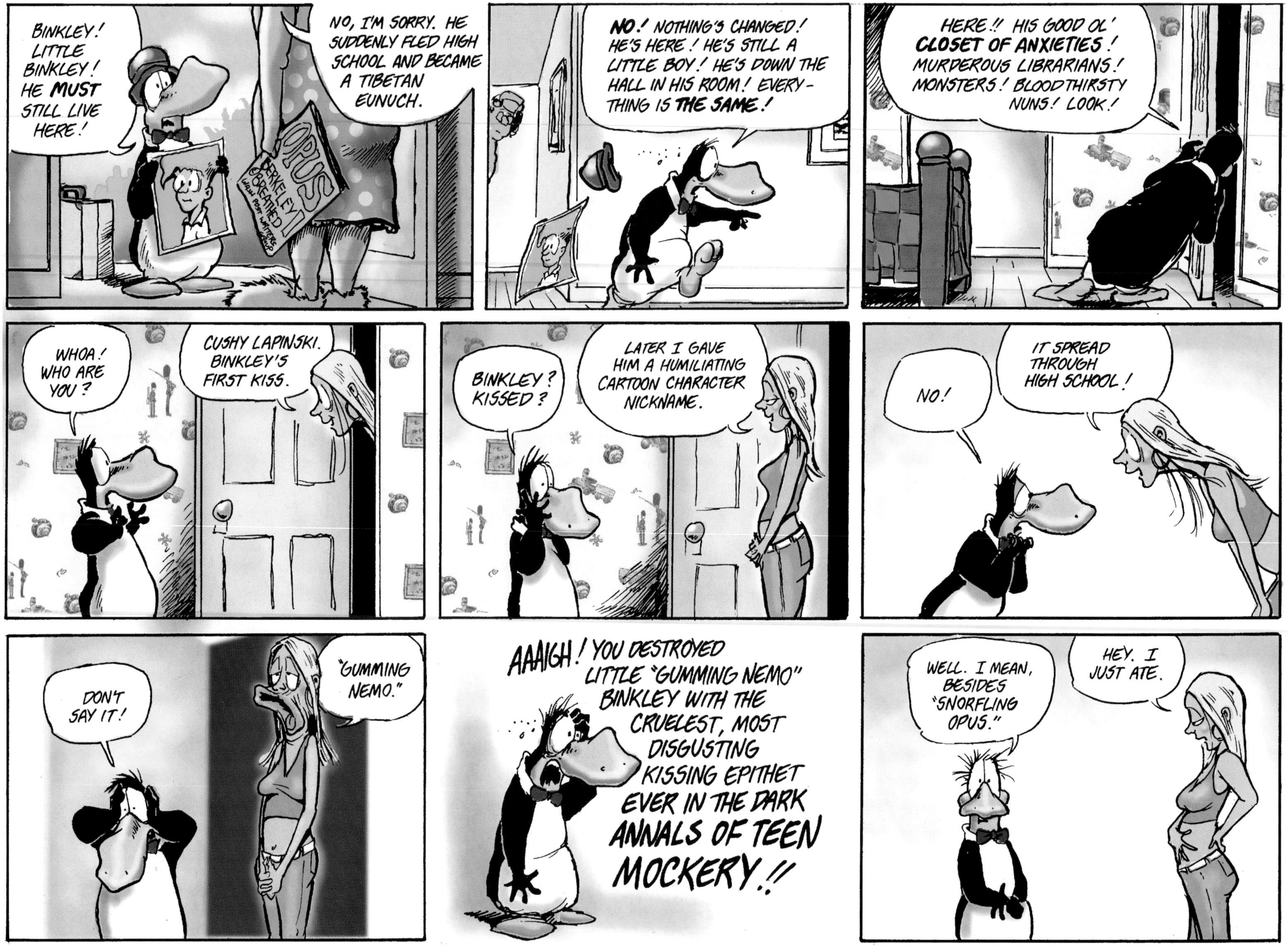

BINKLEY! LITTLE BINKLEY! HE **MUST** STILL LIVE HERE!
NO, I'M SORRY. HE SUDDENLY FLED HIGH SCHOOL AND BECAME A TIBETAN EUNUCH.
OPUS
BERKELEY BREATHED
NO! NOTHING'S CHANGED! HE'S HERE! HE'S STILL A LITTLE BOY! HE'S DOWN THE HALL IN HIS ROOM! EVERYTHING IS **THE SAME**!
HERE!! HIS GOOD OL' **CLOSET OF ANXIETIES**! MURDEROUS LIBRARIANS! MONSTERS! BLOODTHIRSTY NUNS! LOOK!
WHOA! WHO ARE YOU?
CUSHY LAPINSKI. BINKLEY'S FIRST KISS.
BINKLEY? KISSED?
LATER I GAVE HIM A HUMILIATING CARTOON CHARACTER NICKNAME.
NO!
IT SPREAD THROUGH HIGH SCHOOL!
DON'T SAY IT!
"GUMMING NEMO."
AAAIGH! YOU DESTROYED LITTLE "GUMMING NEMO" BINKLEY WITH THE CRUELEST, MOST DISGUSTING KISSING EPITHET EVER IN THE DARK ANNALS OF TEEN MOCKERY.!!
WELL. I MEAN, BESIDES "SNORFLING OPUS."
HEY. I JUST ATE.

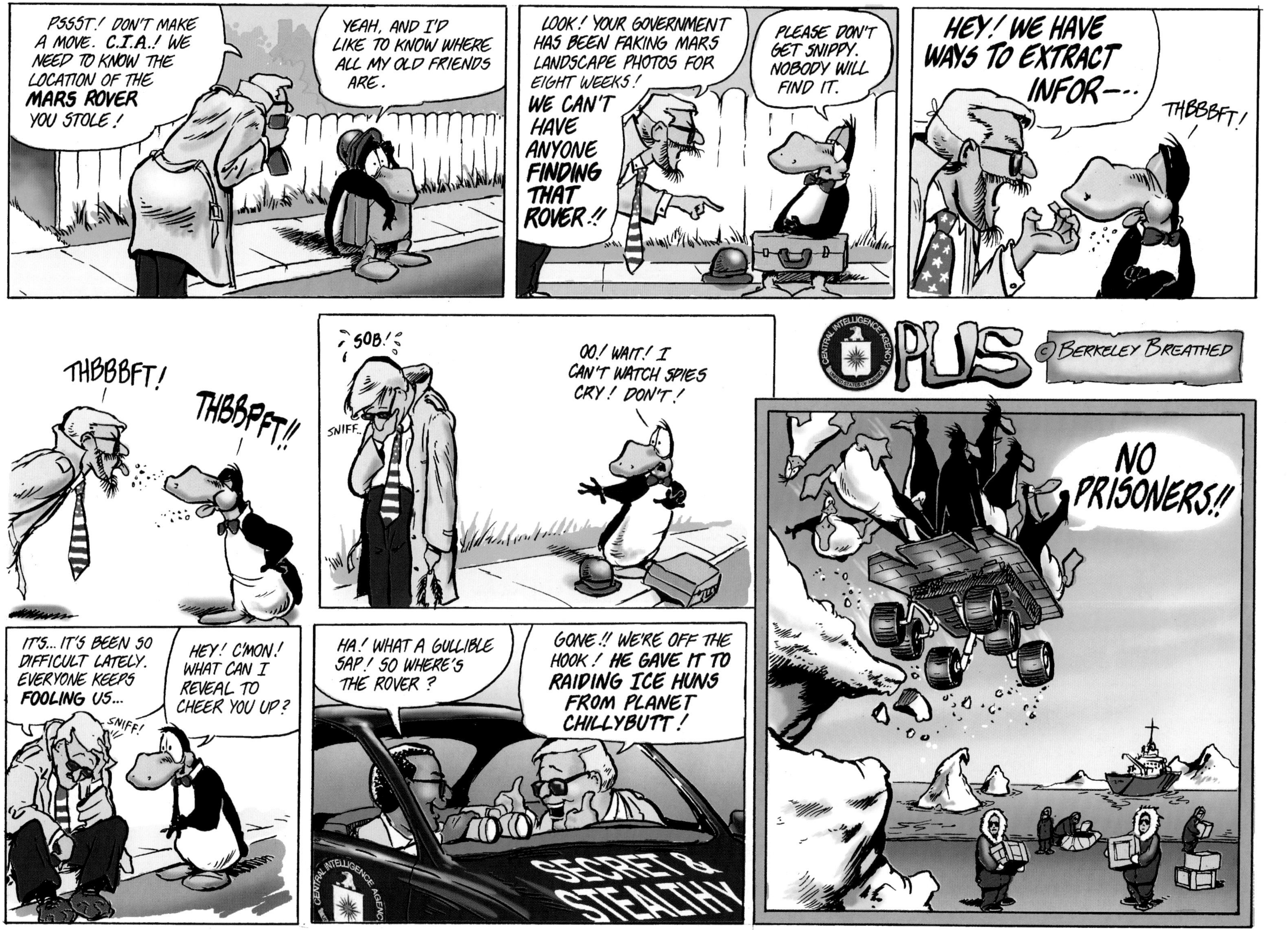
PSSST! DON'T MAKE A MOVE. C.I.A.! WE NEED TO KNOW THE LOCATION OF THE **MARS ROVER** YOU STOLE!
YEAH, AND I'D LIKE TO KNOW WHERE ALL MY OLD FRIENDS ARE.
LOOK! YOUR GOVERNMENT HAS BEEN FAKING MARS LANDSCAPE PHOTOS FOR EIGHT WEEKS! **WE CAN'T HAVE ANYONE FINDING THAT ROVER!!**
PLEASE DON'T GET SNIPPY. NOBODY WILL FIND IT.
HEY! WE HAVE WAYS TO EXTRACT INFOR—..
THBBBFT!
CENTRAL INTELLIGENCE AGENCY
UNITED STATES OF AMERICA
PUS
© BERKELEY BREATHED
THBBBFT!
THBBPFT!!
SOB!
SNIFF..
OO! WAIT! I CAN'T WATCH SPIES CRY! DON'T!
IT'S... IT'S BEEN SO DIFFICULT LATELY. EVERYONE KEEPS **FOOLING** US...
SNIFF!
HEY! C'MON! WHAT CAN I REVEAL TO CHEER YOU UP?
HA! WHAT A GULLIBLE SAP! SO WHERE'S THE ROVER?
GONE!! WE'RE OFF THE HOOK! **HE GAVE IT TO RAIDING ICE HUNS FROM PLANET CHILLYBUTT!**
CENTRAL INTELLIGENCE AGENCY
SECRET & STEALTHY
NO PRISONERS!!

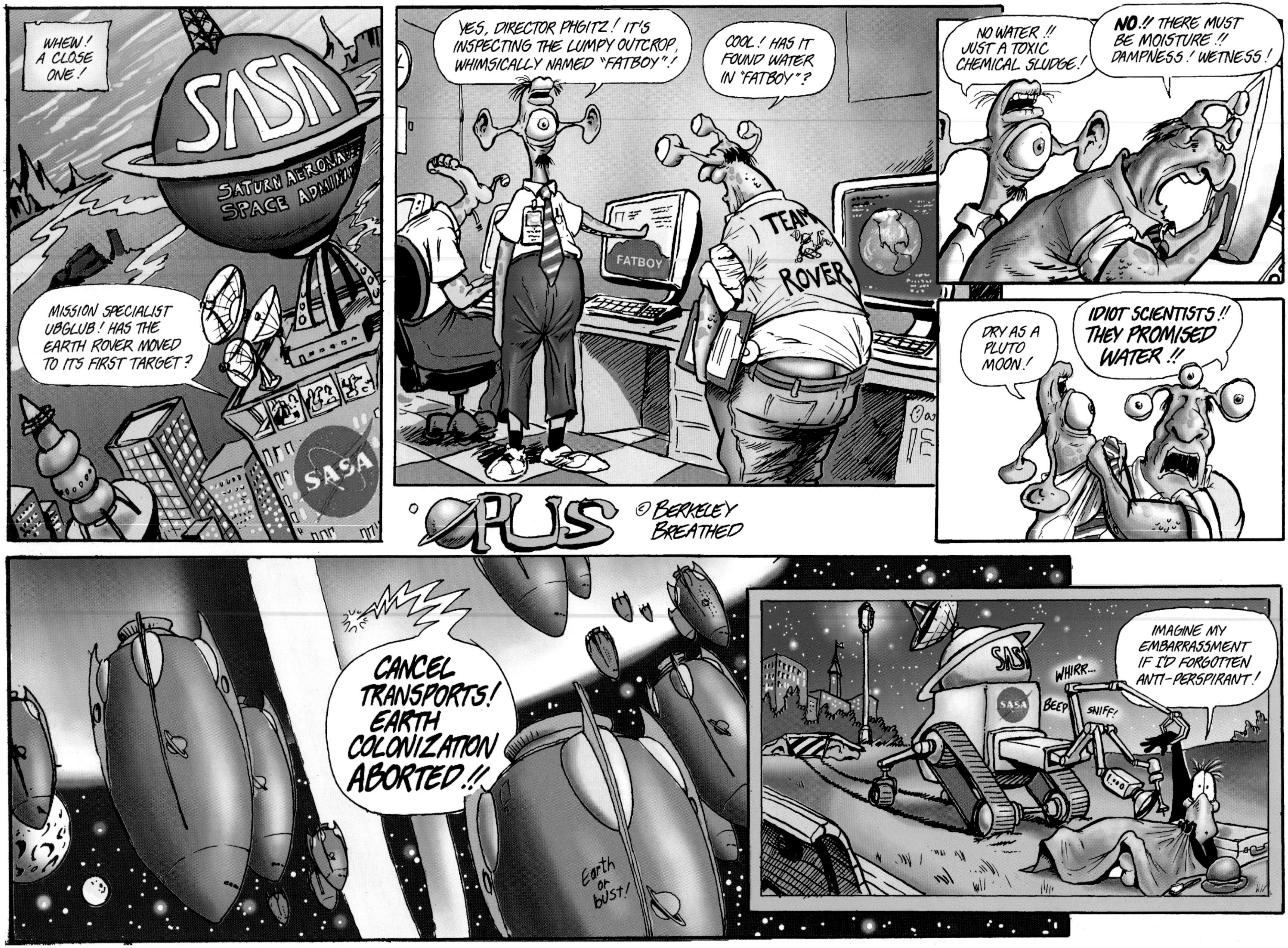
WHEW! A CLOSE ONE!
SASA
MISSION SPECIALIST UBGLUB! HAS THE EARTH ROVER MOVED TO ITS FIRST TARGET?
YES, DIRECTOR PHGITZ! IT'S INSPECTING THE LUMPY OUTCROP, WHIMSICALLY NAMED "FATBOY"!
COOL! HAS IT FOUND WATER IN "FATBOY"?
FATBOY
TEAM ROVER
NO WATER!! JUST A TOXIC CHEMICAL SLUDGE!
NO!! THERE MUST BE MOISTURE!! DAMPNESS! WETNESS!
DRY AS A PLUTO MOON!
IDIOT SCIENTISTS!! THEY PROMISED WATER!!
OPUS
© BERKELEY BREATHED
CANCEL TRANSPORTS! EARTH COLONIZATION ABORTED!!
Earth or bust!
WHIRR...
BEEP
SNIFF!
IMAGINE MY EMBARRASSMENT IF I'D FORGOTTEN ANTI-PERSPIRANT!

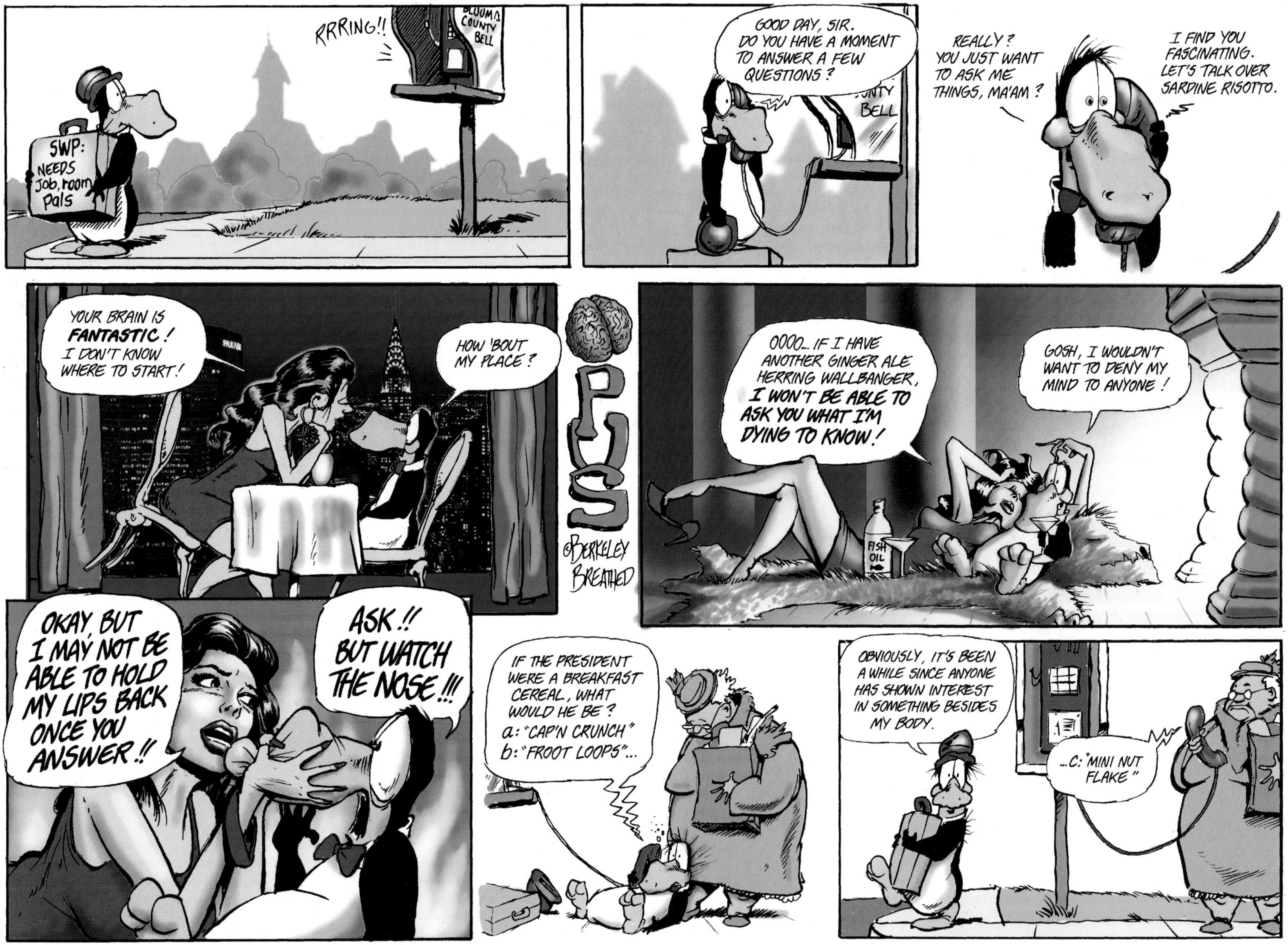
RRRING!!
BLOOM COUNTY BELL
SWP: NEEDS Job, room Pals
GOOD DAY, SIR. DO YOU HAVE A MOMENT TO ANSWER A FEW QUESTIONS?
REALLY? YOU JUST WANT TO ASK ME THINGS, MA'AM?
I FIND YOU FASCINATING. LET'S TALK OVER SARDINE RISOTTO.
YOUR BRAIN IS FANTASTIC! I DON'T KNOW WHERE TO START!
HOW 'BOUT MY PLACE?
OPUS
©BERKELEY BREATHED
OOOO... IF I HAVE ANOTHER GINGER ALE HERRING WALLBANGER, I WON'T BE ABLE TO ASK YOU WHAT I'M DYING TO KNOW!
GOSH, I WOULDN'T WANT TO DENY MY MIND TO ANYONE!
FISH OIL
OKAY, BUT I MAY NOT BE ABLE TO HOLD MY LIPS BACK ONCE YOU ANSWER!!
ASK!! BUT WATCH THE NOSE!!!
IF THE PRESIDENT WERE A BREAKFAST CEREAL, WHAT WOULD HE BE? a: "CAP'N CRUNCH" b: "FROOT LOOPS"...
OBVIOUSLY, IT'S BEEN A WHILE SINCE ANYONE HAS SHOWN INTEREST IN SOMETHING BESIDES MY BODY.
...C: "MINI NUT FLAKE"

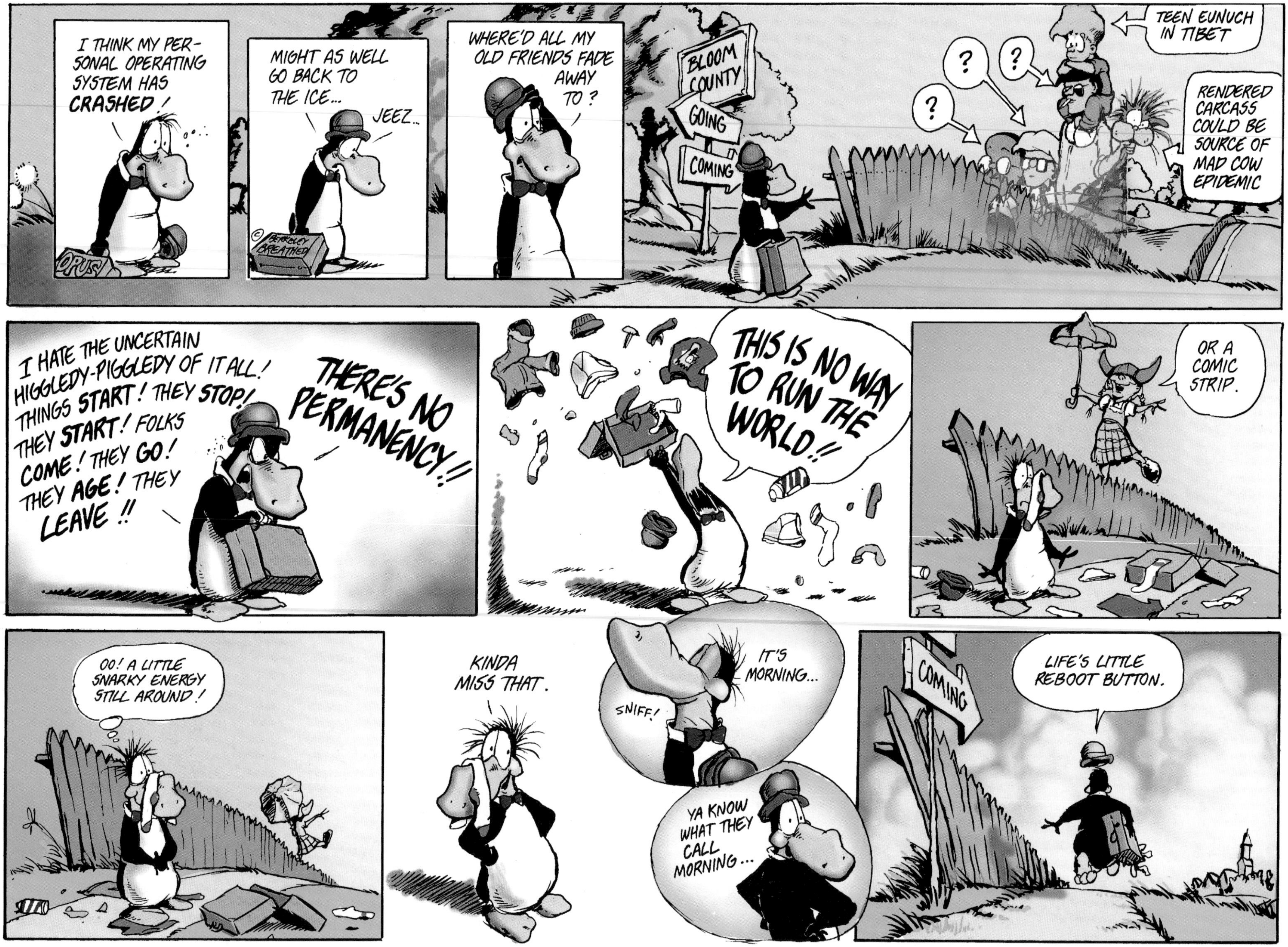
I THINK MY PERSONAL OPERATING SYSTEM HAS CRASHED!
OPUS
MIGHT AS WELL GO BACK TO THE ICE...
JEEZ...
© BERKELEY BREATHED
WHERE'D ALL MY OLD FRIENDS FADE AWAY TO?
BLOOM COUNTY
GOING
COMING
?
?
?
TEEN EUNUCH IN TIBET
RENDERED CARCASS COULD BE SOURCE OF MAD COW EPIDEMIC
I HATE THE UNCERTAIN HIGGLEDY-PIGGLEDY OF IT ALL! THINGS START! THEY STOP! THEY START! FOLKS COME! THEY GO! THEY AGE! THEY LEAVE!!
THERE'S NO PERMANENCY!!
THIS IS NO WAY TO RUN THE WORLD!!
OR A COMIC STRIP.
OO! A LITTLE SNARKY ENERGY STILL AROUND!
KINDA MISS THAT.
IT'S MORNING...
SNIFF!
YA KNOW WHAT THEY CALL MORNING...
COMING
LIFE'S LITTLE REBOOT BUTTON.